T0216606

Lecture Notes in Computer Science   1180

Edited by G. Goos, J. Hartmanis and J. van Leeuwen

Advisory Board: W. Brauer   D. Gries   J. Stoer

Springer
Berlin
Heidelberg
New York
Barcelona
Budapest
Hong Kong
London
Milan
Paris
Santa Clara
Singapore
Tokyo

V. Chandru   V. Vinay   (Eds.)

Foundations of Software Technology and Theoretical Computer Science

16th Conference
Hyderabad, India, December 18-20, 1996
Proceedings

Springer

Series Editors

Gerhard Goos, Karlsruhe University, Germany

Juris Hartmanis, Cornell University, NY, USA

Jan van Leeuwen, Utrecht University, The Netherlands

Volume Editors

Vijay Chandru
V. Vinay
Indian Institute of Science
Department of Computer Science and Automation
Bangalore - 560 012, India
E-mail: {chandru|vinay}@csa.iisc.ernet.in

Cataloging-in-Publication data applied for

Die Deutsche Bibliothek - CIP-Einheitsaufnahme

Foundations of software technology and theoretical computer science : 16th
conference, Hyderabad, India, December 18 - 20, 1996 ; proceedings / [FST and
TCS 16]. V. Chandru ; V. Vinay (ed.). - Berlin ; Heidelberg ; New York ;
Barcelona ; Budapest ; Hong Kong ; London ; Milan ; Paris ; Santa Clara ;
Singapore ; Tokyo : Springer, 1996
  (Lecture notes in computer science ; Vol. 1180)
  ISBN 3-540-62034-6

NE: Chandru, Vijay [Hrsg.]; FST and TCS <16, 1996, Hyderabad>; GT

CR Subject Classification (1991): F.1-4, G.2.2, I.3.5

ISSN 0302-9743
ISBN 3-540-62034-6 Springer-Verlag Berlin Heidelberg New York

© Springer-Verlag Berlin Heidelberg 1996
Printed in Germany

Typesetting: Camera-ready by author
SPIN 10550219   06/3142 – 5 4 3 2 1 0   Printed on acid-free paper

Preface

This volume contains the proceedings of the Sixteenth Annual Conference on Foundations of Software Technology and Theoretical Computer Science. This year the pre-conference *Workshop on Applied Formal Methods* is organized by Shankar Natarajan, Deepak Kapur, and R.K. Shyamasundar. In addition, a special programme in honour of Rohit Parikh has been arranged by R. Ramanujam and R.K. Shyamasundar. The newly formed Indian Association for Research in Computing Science (IARCS) is the umbrella organization under which all of these activities are being coordinated.

This year the call for papers attracted a total of 98 papers. Each paper was reviewed by at least three referees. Based on these reviews, the programme committee selected 28 papers at the programme committee meeting held on July 26 and 27, 1996 at the Indian Institute of Science, Bangalore. We would like to thank the programme committee members and the referees for their invaluable assistance in maintaining the quality of the programme. We are also grateful to V.S. Anil Kumar, Ramesh Hariharan, Madhavan Mukund, A. Sarala, and Ashok Subramanian for their timely assistance in the submission and review process. We would also like to thank our electronic secretaries revati and drona for their untiring efforts.

We are grateful to the invited speakers Eric Allender, Arvind, Ian Munro, and John Rushby for accepting our invitation to give talks and for providing written submissions to be included in the proceedings.

The conference is being hosted for the first time by the University of Hyderabad. The infrastructural and financial help provided by the Indian Association for Research in Computing Science, the Indian Institute of Science, the Tata Institute of Fundamental Research and the University of Hyderabad are gratefully acknowledged.

Finally, we would like to thank Alfred Hofmann and the staff at Springer-Verlag for the professional support in producing this volume.

Vijay Chandru
V Vinay

Bangalore, October 1996

PROGRAM COMMITTEE

- V. Arvind (IMSc, Madras)
- D. Bjorner (UNU/IIST, Macau)
- S. Chaudhuri (MPI, Saarbrucken)
- S-W. Cheng (HKUST, Hongkong)
- T.K. Dey (IIT, Kharagpur)
- H. Edelsbrunner (UIUC, Urbana-Champaign)
- J.J.M. Hooman (EindhovenU, Eindhoven)
- P. Jalote (IIT, Kanpur)
- S. Kannan (UPenn, Philadelphia)
- D. Kapur (SUNY, Albany)
- M. Nielsen (BRICS, Aarhus)
- S. Prasad (IIT, Delhi)
- A.K. Pujari (UHyd, Hyderabad)
- V. Raman (IMSc, Madras)
- R.K. Shyamasundar (TIFR, Bombay)
- G. Sivakumar (IIT, Bombay)
- M. Sohoni (IIT, Bombay)
- P.S. Thiagarajan (SPIC Sci. Found., Madras)
- H. Venkateswaran (GaTech, Atlanta)
- V. Vinay (IISc, Bangalore)
- V. Chandru (IISc, Bangalore)

ORGANIZING COMMITTEE

- R.K. Bagga (DRDO, Hyderabad)
- B.L. Deekshatulu (NRSA, Hyderabad)
- H. Mohanty (UHyd, Hyderabad)
- P.S. Rao (UHyd, Hyderabad)
- A. Sharma (TCS, Hyderabad)
- A.K. Shiny (UHyd, Hyderabad)
- A.K. Pujari (UHyd, Hyderabad)

List of Referees

M. Agrawal	T. K. Dey	S. A. Kumar	M.R.K.K. Rao
E. Allender	H. Edelsbrunner	V.S.A. Kumar	B. Ravikumar
N. Amato	L. Fortnow	C. Laneve	M.A. Reniers
J. H. Andersen	G. Frandsen	X. Leroy	K. H. Rose
S. R. Arikati	N. Garg	X. Liu	P. S. Sastry
V. Arvind	S. Gay	K. Lodaya	J. P. Seldin
S. R. Babu	C. George	S.V. Lokam	S. Sen
R. Balasubramanian	G. Gonthier	C. E. V. Madhavan	R. Sengupta
T. Basten	N. Gopalan	M. Mahajan	A. Seth
R. Bazzi	P. Gupta	S. Mauw	N. R. Shah
P. Beame	M. Hamdi	K. Middelburg	P. Shankar
F. Benhamou	R. Hariharan	F. Moller	R. K. Shyamasundar
A. Bernstein	M. Hennessy	P. D. Mosses	A. Singla
P. Bhaduri	J. G. Henriksen	M. Mukund	G. Sivakumar
S. Biswas	T. Hildebrandt	K. Mulmuley	Y. N. Srikant
D. Bjorner	J. J.M. Hooman	M. N. Murty	M. Sohoni
J. Blanco	J. Hsiang	Y. Narahari	I. Stark
T. Brauner	D. V. Hung	P. Narendran	K. V. Subrahmanyam
G. Calinescu	H. Huttel	V. Natarajan	A. Subramanian
S. Chandran	S. Iyer	M. Nielsen	C. R. Subramanian
V. Chandru	R. Jagadeesan	J. Peleska	K. Sunesen
G. J. Chang	P. Jalote	B. C. Pierce	R. B. Tan
R. Chang	T. Janowski	S. Prasad	P.S.Thiagarajan
S. Chaudhuri	W. Ji	J. Radhakrishnan	R. Thurimella
A. Cheng	J.-P. Jouannaud	N. Raja	D. N. Turner
S.-W. Cheng	R. Kannan	V. Raman	H. Venkateswaran
S. Dalzilio	S. Kannan	R. Ramanujam	M. Verma
O. Danvy	D. Kapur	S. Ramesh	V. Vinay
A. Dattasharma	H. Kirchner	E. Ramos	U. Waldmann
S. K. Debray	B. Knaack	A. Ranade	D. S. Warren
F. de Boer	R. Kuiper	C.P.Rangan	H. Xie
R. de Simone	K. N. Kumar	D. Ranjan	C.D. Zaroliagis
A. A. Diwan	S.Kumar	M. R. Rao	

Table of Contents

Complexity Theory

Type Theory

Circuit Complexity before the Dawn of the New Millennium

Eric Allender[*]

Department of Computer Science
Rutgers University
P.O. Box 1179
Piscataway, NJ 08855-1179
USA
allender@cs.rutgers.edu
http://www.cs.rutgers.edu/ allender

Abstract. The 1980's saw rapid and exciting development of techniques for proving lower bounds in circuit complexity. This pace has slowed recently, and there has even been work indicating that quite different proof techniques must be employed to advance beyond the current frontier of circuit lower bounds. Although this has engendered pessimism in some quarters, there have in fact been many positive developments in the past few years showing that significant progress is possible on many fronts. This paper is a (necessarily incomplete) survey of the state of circuit complexity as we await the dawn of the new millennium.

1 Superpolynomial Size Lower Bounds

Complexity theory long ago achieved its goal of presenting interesting and important computational problems that, although computable, nonetheless require such huge circuits to compute that they are computationally intractable. In fact, in Stockmeyer's thesis, the unusual step was taken of translating an *asymptotic* result into *concrete* terms:

Theorem 1. *[Sto74] Any circuit that takes as input a formula (in the language of WS1S) with up to 616 symbols and produces as output a correct answer saying whether the formula is valid or not, requires at least 10^{123} gates.*

To quote from [Sto87]:

> Even if gates were the size of a proton and were connected by infinitely thin wires, the network would densely fill the known universe.

In the intervening years complexity theory has made some progress proving that other problems A require circuits of superpolynomial size (in symbols: $A \notin$ P/poly), but no such A has been shown to exist in nondeterministic exponential

---

[*] Supported in part by NSF grant CCR-9509603.

time ($\mathrm{NTIME}(2^{n^{O(1)}})$) or even in the potentially larger class $\mathrm{DTIME}(2^{n^{O(1)}})^{\mathrm{NP}}$. Where can we find sets that are not in P/poly? A straightforward diagonalization shows that for any superpolynomial time-bound T, there is a problem in $\mathrm{DSPACE}(T(n))-$ P/poly. Recall that deterministic space complexity is roughly the same as alternating time complexity [CKS81]. It turns out that the full power of alternation is not needed to obtain sets outside of P/poly – two alternations suffice, as can be shown using techniques of [Kan82] (see also [BH92]). Combined with Toda's theorem [Tod91] we obtain the following.

Theorem 2. *[Kan82, BH92, Tod91] Let T be a time-constructible superpolynomial function. Then*

- $\mathrm{NTIME}(T(n))^{\mathrm{NP}} \not\subseteq$ P/poly.
- $\mathrm{DTIME}(T(n))^{\mathrm{PP}} \not\subseteq$ P/poly.

Is this the best that we can do? To the best of my knowledge, it is not known if the classes $\mathrm{PrTIME}(2^{n^{O(1)}})$ (unbounded error probabilistic exponential time) and $\mathrm{DTIME}(2^{n^{O(1)}})^{\mathrm{C=P}}$ are contained in P/poly (even relative to an oracle). There are oracles relative to which $\mathrm{DTIME}(2^{n^{O(1)}})^{\mathrm{NP}}$ *has* polynomial-size circuits [Hel86, Wil85], thus showing that relativizable techniques cannot be used to present superpolynomial circuit size bounds for $\mathrm{NTIME}(2^{n^{O(1)}})$. Note, however that nonrelativizing techniques have been used on closely-related problems [BFNW93]. One can hope that further insights will lead to more progress on this front.[2]

In the mean time, it has turned out to be very worthwhile to consider some important subclasses of P/poly.

2 Smaller Circuit Classes

We will focus our attention on five important circuit complexity classes:[3]

1. AC^0 is the class of problems solvable by polynomial-size, constant-depth circuits of AND, OR, and NOT gates of unbounded fan-in. AC^0 corresponds to $O(1)$-time computation on a parallel computer, and it also consists exactly of the languages that can be specified in first-order logic [Imm89, BIS90]. AC^0 circuits are powerful enough to add and subtract n-bit numbers.

2. NC^1 is the class of problems solvable by circuits of AND, OR, and NOT gates of fan-in two and depth $O(\log n)$. NC^1 circuits capture exactly the circuit complexity required to evaluate a Boolean formula [Bus93], and to recognize

---

[2] As this paper is being written I have just learned that Buhrman and Fortnow have, indeed, been able to use the techniques of [BFNW93] to show that $\mathrm{PrTIME}(2^{n^{O(1)}})$ is not contained P/poly. In fact, even the exponential-time version of the complexity class MA contains problems outside of P/poly, although this is false relative to some oracles. Thus some of the "open" questions above have just been answered [BF].

[3] Thus this survey will ignore the large body of beautiful work on the circuit complexity of larger subclasses of P and NC.

a regular set [Bar89]. There are deep connections between circuit complexity and algebra, and NC^1 corresponds to computation over any *non-solvable* algebra [Bar89].

3. ACC^0 is the class of problems solvable by polynomial-size, constant-depth circuits of unbounded fan-in AND, OR, NOT, and MODm gates. (A MODm gate takes inputs $x_1, \ldots, x_n$ and determines if the number of 1's among these inputs is a multiple of m.) To be more precise, $AC^0(m)$ is the class of problems solvable by polynomial-size, constant-depth circuits of unbounded fan-in AND, OR, NOT, and MODm gates, and $ACC^0 = \bigcup_m AC^0(m)$. In the algebraic theory mentioned above, ACC^0 corresponds to computation over any *solvable* algebra [BT88]. Thus in the algebraic theory, ACC^0 is the most natural subclass of NC^1.

4. TC^0 is the class of problems solvable by polynomial-size, constant-depth threshold circuits. TC^0 captures exactly the complexity of integer multiplication and division, and sorting [CSV84]. Also, TC^0 is a good complexity-theoretic model for "neural net" computation [PS88, PS89].

5. NC^0 is the class of problems solvable by circuits of AND, OR, and NOT gates of fan-in two and depth $O(1)$. Note that each output bit can only depend on $O(1)$ input bits in such a circuit. Thus any function in NC^0 is computed by depth two AC^0 circuits, merely using DNF or CNF expansion.

NC^0 is obviously extremely limited; such circuits cannot even compute the logical OR of n input bits. One of the surprises of circuit complexity is that, in spite of its severe limitations, NC^0 is in some sense quite "close" to AC^0 in computational power.

Quite a few powerful techniques are known for proving lower bounds for AC^0 circuits; it is known that AC^0 is properly contained in ACC^0. It is not hard to see that $ACC^0 \subseteq TC^0 \subseteq NC^1$. As we shall see below, weak lower bounds have been proven for ACC^0 and TC^0, whereas almost nothing is known for NC^1.

3 AC^0

A dramatic series of papers in the 1980's [Ajt83, FSS84, Cai89, Yao85, Hås87] gave us a proof that AC^0 circuits require exponential size even to determine if the number of 1's in the input is odd or even. (See also the excellent tutorial [BS90].) The main tool in proving this and other lower bounds for AC^0 is Håstad's Switching Lemma, one version of which states that most of the "subfunctions" of any AC^0 function f are in NC^0. (A sub-function of f is obtained by setting most of the n input bits to 0 or 1, leaving a function of the n^ϵ remaining unset bits. Such a sub-function is called a restriction of f.) An interesting new proof of the Switching Lemma was presented by [Raz95] (see also [FL95, AAR]), and further extensions were presented by [Bea], the latter motivated in particular by the usefulness of the Switching Lemma as a tool in proving bounds on the length of propositional proofs.

Although the switching lemma is the most powerful tool we have for proving lower bounds for AC^0, it is not the only one. Lower bound arguments were presented in [Rad94, HJP93] for depth three circuits, and a notion of deterministic restriction was presented in [CR96] that is useful for proving nonlinear size bounds.

It is important to note that, although the Switching Lemma tells us that any function f in AC^0 is "close to" functions computed by depth two circuits (since most restrictions of f are computed in depth two), it also provides the tools to show that for all k, there are depth $k + 1$ circuits of linear size that require exponential size to simulate with depth k circuits [Hås87]. This is in sharp contrast to the class of circuits considered in the next section, where efficient depth reduction is possible.

The Switching Lemma also provides extremely strong bounds on the difficulty of approximating the parity function (in the sense of giving the correct answer more than half of the time). This enabled Nisan and Wigderson [NW94] to construct, for any k, a pseudorandom generator that is (a) computable in AC^0, and (b) takes $\log^{O(1)} n$ bits of input and produces n bits of output, and (c) is secure against statistical tests computed by depth k AC^0 circuits. (That is, any depth k circuit has essentially the same probability of accepting when the input is the "pseudorandom" output of f, as when the input is a random string of length n.) This has many applications in derandomization. For instance, given a depth k circuit C_n, the Switching Lemma tells us that a randomly-chosen restriction ρ will simplify C_n to a depth two circuit. Can such a ρ be found quickly *deterministically*? The Nisan-Wigderson generator easily provides an algorithm running in time $2^{\log^{O(1)} n}$: Note that the set $\{(C, \rho) : C$ is a depth k circuit and C_ρ is a depth two circuit$\}$ is in AC^0. Set C to C_n and letting ρ be random; with high probability the AC^0 circuit accepts. Thus with high probability the circuit also accepts when ρ is pseudorandom. Since there are only $2^{\log^{O(1)} n}$ pseudorandom strings, this set can be searched exhaustively.

It is important to note that, although strong "non-approximability" bounds are known for some other classes of circuits (as we will see below), as of yet the AC^0 lower bounds are the only ones that are strong enough to allow use of the Nisan-Wigderson construction. Pseudorandomness for AC^0 was further studied by Sitharam [Sit95], who related pseudorandomness to polylog(n)-wise independence.

Although AC^0 circuits can produce output that looks pseudorandom to other AC^0 circuits, AC^0 *lacks* the ability to compute pseudorandom function generators for general polynomial-time computations; this was proved in [LMN93] as a corollary to their main results analyzing the Fourier spectrum of AC^0 functions. (This relates to one of the many ways of representing functions by polynomials; for a survey, see [Bei93].)

4 Toward ACC° and TC°

Algebraic considerations are what led to ACC^0 being identified as an object of study, and algebraic tools are what led to the lower bounds for the classes $AC^0(p)$ that form the basic building blocks of ACC^0. Smolensky [Smo87] (building on the work of Razborov [Raz87]) showed that if m is not a power of prime p, then the MODm function is is not in $AC^0(p)$. This can be proved by combining two arguments:

- Any depth k $AC^0(p)$ circuit is equivalent to a depth two probabilistic circuit with a single MODp output gate and $n^{\log^{O(1)} n}$ AND gates with polylogarithmic fan in on the bottom level.[4] This sort of depth-reduction stands in sharp contrast to the fact that AC^0 circuits of depth k cannot in general be simulated by depth $k - 1$ circuits without an exponential blow-up in size. This sort of depth reduction is studied in more detail in [AH94, KVVY93, Tar93, ABFR94]. Since this probabilistic depth two circuit is equivalent to the original circuit, there is some setting of the probabilistic bits that can be used to obtain a deterministic circuit (equivalently, a polynomial over GFp having degree $\log^{O(1)} n$) that agrees with the original circuit on a large number of inputs.
- The MODm function cannot agree with any low-degree polynomial over GFp^ℓ on very many inputs (for any constant ℓ).

(Also see the presentation of Smolensky's proof in [BS90]. A very different proof was later published, again by Smolensky [Smo93].)

It is encouraging that something very like the depth-reduction to depth two circuits holds also for all of ACC^0. The results of [Yao90, BT94] show that every set in ACC^0 is recognized by a depth two deterministic circuit with $n^{\log^{O(1)} n}$ AND gates at the input level, and a single symmetric gate at the root. Circuits of this sort, called SYM$^+$ circuits because they are in some sense only "a bit" more powerful than a single symmetric gate, were shown to be able to simulate an even larger class of circuits in [BTT92]. Later work by [GKR$^+$95] shows that the symmetric gate can be chosen to be the "middle bit" function (that outputs the middle bit of the number r, where r is the number of inputs to the gate that evaluate to 1).

Unfortunately, no analog to the second part of Smolensky's argument is known to hold when p is replaced by a composite number. Although initially it seems that a MOD6 gate should not be significantly more useful than a MOD7 gate for computing functions such as the MAJORITY function (or SAT), this has not been established. Indeed, as we shall see in the next section, there are certain settings where composite moduli are provably more powerful than prime moduli.

It remains unknown if there is any problem in DTIME$(2^{n^{O(1)}})^{NP}$ that is not in ACC^0. Even worse, it is not known if any problem in DTIME$(2^{n^{O(1)}})^{NP}$ requires more than polynomial size to compute on depth three circuits consisting only of MOD6 gates!

---

[4] Since so many theorems about constant-depth circuits provide simulating circuits of "quasipolynomial" size (that is, size $2^{\log^{O(1)} n}$), Barrington has given a framework where quasipolynomial circuit size is studied, instead of polynomial size [Bar92].

5 Special Cases: Depth Two and Depth Three

In this section we try to survey the recent work attacking special cases of ACC^0 and TC^0 circuits. Although there are many incomparable results (and some have probably been overlooked) there a few main streams of work that have developed.

5.1 Low-Degree Polynomials

A great deal of the work on ACC^0 and its subclasses deals with simulating circuits (in one of several ways) by polynomials of low degree. We refer the reader to the survey by Beigel [Bei93] for better coverage of this topic. Here, we will pick out only a few ideas and recent developments.

Most work on simulating circuits by polynomials concentrates on the *degree* of the polynomial as the relevant measure of complexity. It was shown in [NS94] that this measure corresponds to Boolean decision tree complexity (and remains roughly the same regardless of whether the function is being computed exactly by the polynomial or only "approximately" for one notion of "approximation"). The degree required to compute a function is fairly robust to changes in representation (for example, should {YES,NO} correspond to {1,0} or to {-1,1}, ...). Recently the size of a polynomial (i.e., the number of terms) has also been studied, and it has been shown that this is more sensitive to the choice of representation [KP96].

Low-degree polynomials over the reals can be simulated by circuits consisting of a single MAJORITY gate with small-fan-in AND gates. (These are so-called MAJ^+ circuits, also called (generalized) perceptrons.) A sequence of papers including [ABFR94, Bei94] led to the result that an AND, OR, NOT circuit with $n^{o(1)}$ MAJORITY gates can be "efficiently" simulated by depth two circuits with a single MAJORITY gate at the output, with small fan-in AND gates at the input level. This bound is shown to be optimal in [ZBT93], where a characterization of the symmetric functions computed by MAJ^+ circuits is given.

This simulation, combined with arguments about the degree required to compute the MOD2 function (even approximately), shows that any AND, OR, NOT circuit with $n^{o(1)}$ MAJORITY gates requires exponential size to compute MOD2. Barrington and Straubing [BS94] generalize this to MODm for any m.

5.2 The Surprising Power of Composite Moduli

Several papers have shown senses in which MODm gates for composite m (m not a prime power) have more computational power than MODp gates for prime p. For instance, using communication complexity, Grolmusz [Gro95a] presented a function computable by depth two MODm circuits than cannot be computed by depth two MODp circuits.

Continuing the line of work simulating circuits by polynomials, Barrington, Beigel, and Rudich defined the MODm degree of a function as the minimal degree required to represent the function over the ring of integers MODm [BBR94]. Although the OR function has degree $n/(p-1)$ for prime p, it is shown in

[BBR94] that for composite m the degree MODm is $O(\sqrt[r]{n})$, where r is the number of prime factors of m.

The definition of MODm degree is rather delicate, which led the authors of [BBR94] to define a related notion called "weak degree MODm" that is more robust to slight changes. Tardos and Barrington gave the first lower bounds for weak degree [TB95]. Later these results were extended by Grolmusz [Gro95b], who also studied the size (number of monomials) required to represent a function mod m.

[BBR94] also presents a lower bound for the MODm degree of the MODm' function. This bound is improved in [Tsa96] and again by Green in [Gre]. Green uses this bound to partially extend the lower bounds of [BS94], showing that the MODq function requires exponential size to compute on depth three circuits with an exact threshold gate at the output, MODp gates on the middle level, and small-fan-in AND gates at the inputs.

5.3 Solvability versus Nonsolvability

Another body of lower bounds comes directly from the algebraic characterization of ACC^0. (For more background about this approach to circuit complexity, see [MPT91, Lem96].) Recall that few lower bounds are known even for circuits consisting *only* of MOD6 gates. A natural conjecture is that these circuits cannot compute the AND function (just as AC^0 circuits cannot compute MOD6). The first lower bounds in this direction appear in [BST90], where the authors show that programs over a particular class of groups need exponential size in order to compute the AND function. This is translated into a lower bound for a certain kind of depth two circuits of MOD gates by Caussinus [Cau96, Cau]. A related lower bound is provided by [YP94], showing that a class of restricted depth three circuits also cannot compute the AND.

Finally, a different sort of bound on the complexity of computing the AND with MOD gates is given by [Thé], who shows that such circuits must have at least a linear number of gates on the input level.

(It is appropriate to also mention [BS95], which does not provide a circuit lower bound *per se*, but does provide a nonlinear bound on the ACC^0 *formula* size, using algebraic techniques.)

5.4 Low Levels of the TC^0 Hierarchy

The first important lower bound for threshold circuits is still one of the best. Using the techniques of communication complexity, [HMP$^+$93] shows that depth three MAJORITY circuits are exponentially more powerful than depth two circuits. (Extensions may be found in [Kra91, KW95].)

It is important to note that there are many different decompositions of TC^0 that are useful, depending on whether the basic gates are MAJORITY, exact threshold, or weighted threshold, etc., or alternatively if AC^0 circuitry is considered "cheap" and only applications of MAJORITY are considered expensive

[MT93, Mac95]. Many separations are known among the various low levels; a good survey of these separations and inclusions is found in [Raz92]. See also [GHR92, GK93, Hof96] and the articles in [RSO94].

The state of the art in this direction still only yields superpolynomial bounds for restricted classes of depth two or depth three circuits:

- Threshold-of-MODm [KP94], extending [Gol95]. An alternate proof is presented in [ES].
- Depth Three MAJORITY circuits where the middle level is AND [HG91, RW93].
- Depth Three MAJORITY circuits where the bottom level is AND [Gro94].

Sitharam presents a unified framework in which many of these bounds can be obtained [Sit]. Limitations of some of these techniques are discussed in [RSOK95]. A different technique (yielding weaker lower bounds) is presented in [Juk95].

Finally, it is appropriate to mention two other streams of work that may be viewed as initial steps for proving circuit lower bounds (although they do not explicitly yield circuit bounds in their current forms). TC^0 can be characterized in terms of first-order logic with counting quantifiers [BIS90]. Work such as that of Etessami on non-expressibility [Ete] can be viewed as providing a limited circuit lower bound. As another example, [HNW93] proves a result for read-once formulae, whose extension to general formulae would provide lower bounds for TC^0.

6   A Large Obstacle to Progress

The question of whether ACC^0 circuits can compute MAJORITY has now been considered for a decade, and has withstood all attacks so far. Similarly, the question of whether $TC^0 = NC^1$ remains open in spite of considerable attention. Although it is at least conceivable that some variation on a known proof technique will suffice to prove lower bounds for ACC^0, there is strong evidence that a radically different approach will be necessary to prove lower bounds for TC^0. This evidence comes from the work on "Natural Proofs" by Razborov and Rudich [RR94].

Razborov and Rudich formulate a notion of lower bound proof that is general enough to include all of the papers dealing with constant-depth circuits cited in the preceding sections. They show that if there is a proof of this sort (which they call a "Natural Proof") proving that NP is not contained in TC^0, then there are no cryptographically-secure functions computed in TC^0. But cryptographers believe that there are cryptographically secure functions computable in TC^0 [IN89].[5] If they are right, then [RR94] shows that any proof showing $TC^0 \neq NP$

---

[5] This is perhaps the appropriate place to mention that it has been conjectured that TC^0 is in fact equal to NC^1 [IL95]. Certainly it seems possible to do much more significant computation in TC^0 than in ACC^0, although [BC91] does present some natural computational problems that are in ACC^0. It has also been conjectured that TC^0 and NC^1 are *not* equal [BC89].

must look quite unlike any circuit lower bound proof that has been seen yet: an "unnatural" proof.

On the other hand, there is no strong evidence for the existence of cryptographically-secure functions in ACC^0. Thus the results of [RR94] do not seem to indicate any obstacles to answering whether $ACC^0 = TC^0$.

7 An Old and Unnatural Proof Technique

Razborov and Rudich were careful to argue that [RR94] should not be taken as a cause for pessimism. Rather, it should serve as a guide indicating which approaches to rule out. Certainly, many complexity theoreticians are trying to formulate arguments that avoid the problems faced by Natural Proofs.

It should be noted that one of the oldest and most powerful weapons in the arsenal of complexity theory does, in fact, yield "unnatural" proofs: Diagonalization. Unfortunately, diagonalization is not well-suited for arguments about circuit complexity, since diagonalization proceeds by satisfying a countable number of requirements (such as: Requirement i: language A is not accepted by machine i), and there are uncountably many circuit families. This problem can be sidestepped by considering only *uniform* families of circuits; circuit family $\{C_n\}$ is *uniform* if there is an efficient algorithm for the mapping $n \mapsto C_n$. We will follow the lead of [BIS90] and use "Dlogtime" uniformity. (For the purposes of this survey it will not be necessary to deal with the details of the definition of the uniformity condition.)

Since uniform TC^0 is contained in DSPACE($\log n$) $\neq$ PSPACE, it is easy to show that the standard PSPACE-complete sets require exponential-size uniform TC^0 circuits. (Similarly, although we don't know if DTIME(2^n) has polynomial-size circuits, it is easy to show that it requires exponential-size *uniform* circuits.) Can we improve on these trivial bounds?

The first paper to make explicit use of uniformity in proving a circuit lower bound was [AG94]. There, we showed that computing the permanent of a matrix requires size at least 2^{n^ϵ} on ACC^0 circuits. The proof combines the circuit simulations of [Yao90, BT94] with diagonalizations. We were able to prove lower bounds showing that complete sets for PP and $C_=P$ are hard for ACC^0 circuits to compute, too – but our size bounds are weaker there than for the permanent. If $T(T(n)) < 2^n$, then a complete set for PP requires more than size $T(n)$ to compute on uniform ACC^0 circuits. (In [AG94] this is called a *sub*-subexponential size bound. Note that this is still much larger than, say, $n^{\log n}$.)

No lower bounds for uniform TC^0 were presented in [AG94]. The first bounds of that sort were presented in [CMTV96]; there it was proved that there is a set in the counting hierarchy that requires superpolynomial size to compute on uniform TC^0 circuits. (The counting hierarchy is the union of the sequence PP, PP^{PP}, $PP^{PP^{PP}}$, ... However, the proof in [CMTV96] did not give a clue as to *which* set in the counting hierarchy would be hard, and the size bound was only superpolynomial, and not even, say, $n^{\log^* n}$. In [All] I build on [CMTV96] to show lower bounds for the permanent and for the standard complete sets for PP: these problems all require more than size $T(n)$ to compute on uniform TC^0 circuits, if $T(T(\ldots(T(n))\ldots)) = o(2^n)$ (for any constant number of compositions). Note that, although this size bound is smaller than the bound in [AG94], it is for a more powerful class of circuits.

An obvious question is whether these bounds can be improved. Can the hard sets for PP really be that much easier than the permanent? Do the hard sets for PP require exponential size on uniform TC^0 circuits? Is it possible to apply these techniques to show that smaller complexity classes require superpolynomial size TC^0 circuits? (Other applications of diagonalization in uniform circuit complexity have been presented recently by [II96].)

8 Stronger Separations from AC°

In order to define a framework where the probabilistic method might conceivably be applied to questions about countable classes in complexity theory, Lutz defined a notion of resource-bounded measure [Lut92]. With this notion it is possible to talk in a meaningful way about whether NP is a "large" or "small" subset of $DTIME(2^{n^{O(1)}})$. Several papers have been written (e.g., [LM94]) considering the hypothesis "NP is not a measure-zero subset of $DTIME(2^{n^{O(1)}})$" as a likely complexity-theoretic hypothesis, in the same way that "the polynomial hierarchy does not collapse" and "P $\neq$ NP" are used as likely complexity-theoretic hypotheses.

In order to investigate this hypothesis, one step would be to consider the analogous question "scaled down" to polynomial time. That is, is $NTIME(\log n)$ a measure zero subset of P? An initial obstacle to overcome is that the definition of measure provided by Lutz does not extend in any obvious way to classes smaller than P. Nonetheless, a notion of measure on P that generalizes Lutz's notion was defined in [AS94], thus successfully overcoming this first obstacle.

Using many techniques developed for proving lower bounds for AC^0, Cai, Sivakumar, and Strauss [CSS, Siv96] succeeded in showing that not only is $NTIME(\log n)$ a measure zero subset of P, but in fact all of AC^0 has measure zero in P (using a notion of measure that differs only slightly from that of [AS94]). This is the most exciting application of resource-bounded measure on P thus far, and it also gives cause to reconsider how likely it is that NP is a measure zero subset of $DTIME(2^{n^{O(1)}})$.

There are also results (using a slightly different notion of measure) showing that $AC^0(2)$ does *not* have P-measure zero [Siv96]. Since the Nisan-Wigderson pseudorandom generator is an important tool in proving the measure zero result of [CSS], it is tempting to speculate that there is a connection between these contrasting measure results for AC^0 and $AC^0(2)$, and our inability thus far to construct pseudorandom generators for $AC^0(2)$.

Finally, it is interesting to note that Lutz's notion of measure is actually quite closely related to notion of Natural Proof presented by [RR94]; it was shown in [RSC95] that the existence of a natural proof showing that a problem is not in some class $\mathcal{C}$ corresponds (roughly) to an argument that the class $\mathcal{C}$ is a "small" complexity class in the sense of resource-bounded measure. These connections are still not understood as well as they should be.

9 Constant-Depth Reducibility

Thus far in this survey, I have concentrated on that aspect where progress in complexity theory has been most modest: proving lower bounds. Complexity theory has been incredibly successful on another front, however. For the overwhelming majority of natural computational problems that arise in practice, there is a natural complexity class for which that problem is complete. Thus complexity theory has been very successful at classifying and characterizing the complexity of problems in terms of reducibility, completeness, and complexity classes. In this section I will discuss how to use the techniques of circuit complexity to build on this strength.

There are many important and natural problems that are in NC^1 and are in no strictly smaller complexity class; there are also many important and natural problems that are in DSPACE($\log n$) and are in no strictly smaller complexity class. These problems are "complete" for NC^1 and DSPACE($\log n$), respectively – but in order to make this precise we need a notion of completeness. Arguably the most natural notion of completeness for classes such as these is the notion given by AC^0 many-one reductions. In fact, as was pointed out by [AG91], the first time AC^0 was studied in complexity theory was precisely for this purpose [Jon75]. Also, the first-order translations of Immerman [Imm87] (which provide a notion of completeness defined entirely in terms of logic) correspond to AC^0 reductions.

Finally, it is an empirical fact that the NP-complete problems that one encounters in practice are all complete under AC^0 reductions. In fact, it is not known if there is any complexity class larger than P for which there is a set complete under polynomial-time reductions but not under AC^0 reductions. Thus we lose nothing of practical importance if we re-define all notions of NP-completeness and completeness for other classes solely in terms of AC^0 reductions.

Here are two rather startling facts about complete sets under AC^0 reducibility.

Theorem 3. *[AAR] Let C be any complexity class closed under TC^0 reductions. (Thus C can be P or NP or NC^1 or PP, etc.)*

1. *All sets complete for C under AC^0 reductions are complete under NC^0 reductions.*
2. *All sets complete for C under AC^0 reductions are isomorphic under isomorphisms computable and invertible by depth three AC^0 circuits.*

The first theorem is a sort of "Gap" theorem. It says that, although NC^0 is much weaker than AC^0, AC^0 reductions do not yield any more NP-complete sets than NC^0 reductions do. A natural and important open question asks how large this "gap" is. Are all sets complete under polynomial-time reductions also complete under NC^0 reductions? If so, then $P \neq NP$ (because this would imply that all NP-complete sets are P/poly isomorphic,[6] which implies that no finite set is NP-complete, and hence $P \neq NP$). If the "gap" is not that large, then how far does it extend?

The second theorem is an analog of the Berman-Hartmanis conjecture. It says that there are unexpected similarities among the NP-complete sets. It is particularly striking when one considers a function f computable in AC^0 that produces output that is pseudorandom to depth three AC^0 circuits. Theorem 3 says that $f(SAT)$ is isomorphic to SAT via an isomorphism that is provably too weak to distinguish meaningful inputs from noise.

10   Conclusions

The fundamental questions of complexity theory are important, and they won't go away. Let us never forget that all cryptosystems in existence today are based on conjecture and wishful thinking. Before we can have confidence that a cryptosystem is secure, it will be necessary to have non-asymptotic bounds on the average case complexity of problems. Before such bounds can be achieved, the fundamental and basic questions (such as $NP \not\subseteq TC^0$) will need to be resolved. For some of those questions, we need to have "unnatural" proof techniques.

Until these "unnatural" proofs are developed and usher in the new millennium, there are still significant and interesting advances in our understanding that are possible and amenable to the tools of circuit complexity. I have mentioned three areas that are close to my own research: (a) obtaining lower bounds for uniform circuits, (b) obtaining measure-based separation of circuit complexity classes, and (c) studying reducibilities defined in terms of circuit classes.

References

[AA96]   M. Agrawal and E. Allender. An isomorphism theorem for circuit complexity. In *IEEE Conference on Computational Complexity*, pages 2–11, 1996.

[AAR]   M. Agrawal, E. Allender, , and S. Rudich. Reductions in circuit complexity: An isomorphism theorem and a gap theorem. submitted; preliminary version appeared as [AA96].

[ABFR94] J. Aspnes, R. Beigel, M. Furst, and S. Rudich. The expressive power of voting polynomials. *Combinatorica*, 14:135–148, 1994.

[AG91]   E. Allender and V. Gore. Rudimentary reductions revisited. *Information Processing Letters*, 40:89–95, 1991.

[AG94]   E. Allender and V. Gore. A uniform circuit lower bound for the permanent. *SIAM Journal on Computing*, 23:1026–1049, 1994.

---

[6] The isomorphism is P/poly instead of P-isomorphism, because Theorem 3 actually holds only for non-uniform AC^0 and NC^0 reductions. It is natural to ask if Theorem 3 holds also for uniform circuits. [AAR] partially answers this by showing that the "gap" theorem does *not* hold for uniform circuits.

[AH94]   E. Allender and U. Hertrampf. Depth reductions for circuits of unbounded fan-in. *Information and Computation*, 112:217–238, 1994.

[Ajt83]   M. Ajtai. Σ_1^1-formulae on finite structures. *Annals of Pure and Applied Logic*, 24:1–48, 1983.

[All]   E. Allender. The permanent requires large uniform threshold circuits. Submitted. A preliminary version of this paper appeared as [All96].

[All96]   E. Allender. A note on uniform circuit lower bounds for the counting hierarchy. In *International Conference on Computing and Combinatorics Conference (COCOON)*, volume 1090 of *Lecture Notes in Computer Science*, pages 127–135. Springer-Verlag, 1996.

[AS94]   E. Allender and M. Strauss. Measure on small complexity classes, with applications for BPP. In *IEEE Symposium on Foundations of Computer Science (FOCS)*, pages 807–818, 1994.

[Bar89]   D. A. Barrington. Bounded-width polynomial-size branching programs recognize exactly those languages in NC^1. *Journal of Computer and System Sciences*, 38:150–164, 1989.

[Bar92]   D. A. Mix Barrington. Quasipolynomial size circuit classes. In *IEEE Structure in Complexity Theory Conference*, pages 86–93, 1992.

[BBR94]   D. A. Mix Barrington, R. Beigel, and S. Rudich. Representing Boolean functions as polynomials modulo composite numbers. *Computational Complexity*, 4:367–382, 1994.

[BC89]   D. A. Mix Barrington and J. Corbett. On the relative complexity of some languages in NC^1. *Information Processing Letters*, 32:251–256, 1989.

[BC91]   D. A. Mix Barrington and J. Corbett. A note on some languages in uniform ACC^0. *Theoretical Computer Science*, 78:357–362, 1991.

[Bea]   P. Beame. A switching lemma primer. manuscript, available from http://www.cs.washington.edu/homes/beame/papers.html.

[Bei93]   R. Beigel. The polynomial method in circuit complexity. In *IEEE Structure in Complexity Theory Conference*, pages 82–95, 1993.

[Bei94]   R. Beigel. When do extra majority gates help? polylog(n) majority gates are equivalent to one. *Computational Complexity*, 4:314–324, 1994.

[BF]   H. Buhrman and L. Fortnow. Personal Communication, Dagstuhl workshop on Structure and Complexity, 1996.

[BFNW93]   L. Babai, L. Fortnow, N. Nisan, and A. Wigderson. BPP has subexponential time simulations unless EXPTIME has publishable proofs. *Computational Complexity*, 3:307–318, 1993.

[BH92]   H. Buhrman and S. Homer. Superpolynomial circuits, almost sparse oracles and the exponential hierarchy. In *Foundations of Software Technology and Theoretical Computer Science (FST&TCS)*, volume 652 of *Lecture Notes in Computer Science*, pages 116–127. Springer-Verlag, 1992.

[BIS90]   D. A. Mix Barrington, N. Immerman, and H. Straubing. On uniformity within NC^1. *Journal of Computer and System Sciences*, 41:274–306, 1990.

[BS90]   R. Boppana and M. Sipser. The complexity of finite functions. In J. van Leeuwen, editor, *Handbook of Theoretical Computer Science (Vol. A: Algorithms and Complexity)*. Elsevier and MIT Press, 1990.

[BS94]   D. A. Mix Barrington and H. Straubing. Complex polynomials and circuit lower bounds for modular counting. *Computational Complexity*, 4:325–338, 1994.

[BS95]   D. A. Mix Barrington and H. Straubing. Superlinear lower bounds for bounded-width branching programs. *Journal of Computer and System Sciences*, 50:374–381, 1995.

[BST90]   D. A. Mix Barrington, H. Straubing, and D. Thérien. Non-uniform automata over groups. *Information and Computation*, 89:109–132, 1990.

[BT88]   D. A. Mix Barrington and D. Thérien. Finite monoids and the fine structure of NC^1. *Journal of the ACM*, 35:941–952, 1988.

[BT94]   R. Beigel and J. Tarui. On ACC. *Computational Complexity*, 4:350–367, 1994.

[BTT92]   R. Beigel, J. Tarui, and S. Toda. On probabilistic ACC circuits with an exact-threshold output gate. In *Proceedings of the 3rd ACM-SIGSAM International Symposium on Symbolic and Algebraic Computation (ISAAC)*, volume 650 of *Lecture Notes in Computer Science*, pages 420–429. Springer-Verlag, 1992.

[Bus93]   S. Buss. Algorithm for Boolean formula evaluation and for tree contraction. In P. Clote and J. Krajíček, editors, *Arithmetic, Proof Theory, and Computational Complexity*, volume 25 of *Oxford Logic Guides*, pages 96–115. Clarendon Press, 1993.

[Cai89]   J. Cai. With probability 1, a random oracle separates PSPACE from the polynomial-time hierarchy. *J. Computer and System Science*, 38:68–85, 1989.

[Cau]   H. Caussinus. A note on a theorem of Barrington, Straubing, and Thérien. To appear in *Information Processing Letters*.

[Cau96]   H. Caussinus. *Contributions à l'Etude du Non-déterminisme Restreint*. PhD thesis, Université de Montréal, 1996.

[CKS81]   A. Chandra, D. Kozen, and L. Stockmeyer. Alternation. *Journal of the ACM*, 28:114–133, 1981.

[CMTV96]   H. Caussinus, P. McKenzie, D. Thérien, and H. Vollmer. Nondeterministic NC^1 computation. In *Proceedings, 11th Annual IEEE Conference on Computational Complexity*, pages 12–21, 1996.

[CR96]   S. Chaudhuri and J. Radhakrishnan. Deterministic restrictions in circuit complexity. In *ACM Symposium on Theory of Computing (STOC)*, pages 30–36, 1996.

[CSS]   J.-Y. Cai, D. Sivakumar, and M. Strauss. Constant-depth circuits and the Lutz hypothesis. Manuscript.

[CSV84]   A. Chandra, L. Stockmeyer, and U. Vishkin. Constant depth reducibility. *SIAM Journal on Computing*, 13:423–439, 1984.

[ES]   P. Enflo and M. Sitharam. Stable basis families and complexity lower bounds. Submitted.

[Ete]   K. Etessami. Counting quantifiers, successor relations, and logarithmic space. To appear in Journal of Computer and System Sciences. Preliminary version appeared in IEEE Structure in Complexity Theory Conference, 1995, pp. 2-11.

[FL95]   L. Fortnow and S. Laplante. Circuit lower bounds à la Kolmogorov. *Information and Computation*, 123:121–126, 1995.

[FSS84]   M. Furst, J. Saxe, and M. Sipser. Parity, circuits, and the polynomial-time hierarchy. *Mathematical Systems Theory*, 17:13–27, 1984.

[GHR92]   M. Goldmann, J. Håstad, and A. A. Razborov. Majority gates vs. general weighted threshold gates. *Computational Complexity*, 2:277–300, 1992.

[GK93]   M. Goldmann and M. Karpinski. Simulating threshold circuits by majority circuits. In *ACM Symposium on Theory of Computing (STOC)*, pages 551–560, 1993.

[GKR+95] F. Green, J. Köbler, K. Regan, T. Schwentick, and J. Torán. The power of the middle bit of a #P function. *Journal of Computer and System Sciences*, 50:456–467, 1995.

[Gol95]   M. Goldmann. A note on the power of majority gates and modular gates. *Information Processing Letters*, 53:321–327, 1995.

[Gre]   F. Green. Complex Fourier technique for lower bounds on the Mod-m degree. Submitted. An earlier version appeared as [Gre95].

[Gre95]   F. Green. Lower bounds for depth-three circuits with equals and mod-gates. In *Annual Symposium on Theoretical Aspects of Computer Science (STACS)*, volume 900 of *Lecture Notes in Computer Science*, pages 71–82. Springer-Verlag, 1995.

[Gro94]   V. Grolmusz. A weight-size trade-off for circuits with MOD m gates. In *ACM Symposium on Theory of Computing (STOC)*, 1994.

[Gro95a]   V. Grolmusz. Separating the communication complexities of MOD m and MOD p circuits. *Journal of Computer and System Sciences*, 51:307–313, 1995.

[Gro95b]   Vince Grolmusz. On the weak mod m representation of Boolean functions. *Chicago Journal of Theoretical Computer Science*, 1995(2), July 1995.

[Hås87]   J. Håstad. *Computational Limitations for Small Depth Circuits*. MIT Press, Cambridge, MA, 1987.

[Hel86]   H. Heller. On relativized exponential and probabilistic complexity classes. *Information and Computation*, 71:231–243, 1986.

[HG91]   J. Håstad and M. Goldmann. On the power of small-depth threshold circuits. *Computational Complexity*, 1:113–129, 1991.

[HJP93]   J. Håstad, S. Jukna, and P. Pudlák. Top-down lower bounds for depth 3 circuits. In *IEEE Symposium on Foundations of Computer Science (FOCS)*, pages 124–129, 1993.

[HMP+93] A. Hajnal, W. Maass, P. Pudlák, M. Szegedy, and G. Turán. Threshold circuits of bounded depth. *Journal of Computer and System Sciences*, 46:129–154, 1993.

[HNW93]   R. Heiman, I. Newman, and A. Wigderson. On read-once threshold formulae and their randomized decision tree complexity. *Theoretical Computer Science*, 107:63–76, 1993.

[Hof96]   T. Hofmeister. A note on the simulation of exponential threshold weights. In *International Conference on Computing and Combinatorics (COCOON)*, volume 1090 of *Lecture Notes in Computer Science*, pages 136–141. Springer-Verlag, 1996.

[II96]   K. Iwama and C. Iwamoto. Parallel complexity hierarchies based on PRAMs and DLOGTIME-uniform circuits. In *IEEE Conference on Computational Complexity*, pages 24–32, 1996.

[IL95]   N. Immerman and S. Landau. The complexity of iterated multiplication. *Information and Computation*, 116:103–116, 1995.

[Imm87]   N. Immerman. Languages which capture complexity classes. *SIAM J. Comput.*, 4:760–778, 1987.

[Imm89]   N. Immerman. Expressibility and parallel complexity. *SIAM Journal on Computing*, 18:625–638, 1989.

[IN89]   R. Impagliazzo and M. Naor. Efficient cryptographic schemes provably as secure as subset sum. In *IEEE Symposium on Foundations of Computer Science (FOCS)*, pages 236–243, 1989.

[Jon75]   N. Jones. Space-bounded reducibility among combinatorial problems. *Journal of Computer and System Sciences*, 11:68–85, 1975. Corrigendum: *Journal of Computer and System Sciences* 15:241, 1977.

[Juk95]   S. Jukna. Computing threshold functions by depth-3 threshold circuits with smaller thresholds of their gates. *Information Processing Letters*, 56:147–150, 1995.

[Kan82]   R. Kannan. Circuit-size lower bounds and non-reducibility to sparse sets. *Information and Control*, 55:40–56, 1982.

[KP94]   M. Krause and P. Pudlák. On the computational power of depth 2 circuits with threshold and modulo gates. In *ACM Symposium on Theory of Computing (STOC)*, pages 48–57, 1994.

[KP95]   M. Krause and P. Pudlák. On computing Boolean functions by sparse real polynomials. In *IEEE Symposium on Foundations of Computer Science (FOCS)*, pages 682–691, 1995.

[KP96]   M. Krause and P. Pudlák. More on computing Boolean functions by sparse real polynomials and related types of threshold circuits. Technical Report 622, University of Dortmund, 1996. A preliminary version appeared as [KP95].

[Kra91]   M. Krause. Geometric arguments yield better bounds for threshold circuits and distributed computing. In *Structure in Complexity Theory Conference*, pages 314–321, 1991.

[KVVY93] R. Kannan, H. Venkateswaran, V. Vinay, and A. Yao. A circuit-based proof of Toda's theorem. *Information and Computation*, 104:271–276, 1993.

[KW95]   M. Krause and S. Waack. Variation ranks of communication matrices and lower bounds for depth two circuits having symmetric gates with unbounded fan-in. *Mathematical Systems Theory*, 28:553–564, 1995.

[Lem96]   F. Lemieux. *Finite Groupoids and their Applications to Computational Complexity*. PhD thesis, McGill University, 1996.

[LM94]   J. Lutz and E. Mayordomo. Cook versus Karp-Levin: Separating completeness notions if NP is not small. In *Annual Symposium on Theoretical Aspects of Computer Science (STACS)*, volume 775 of *Lecture Notes in Computer Science*, pages 415–426. Springer-Verlag, 1994.

[LMN93]   N. Linial, Y. Mansour, and N. Nisan. Constant depth circuits, Fourier transform, and learnability. *Journal of the ACM*, 40:607–620, 1993.

[Lut92]   J. Lutz. Almost everywhere high nonuniform complexity. *Journal of Computer and System Sciences*, 44:220–258, 1992.

[Mac95]   A. Maciel. *Threshold Circuits of Small Majority-Depth*. PhD thesis, McGill University, 1995.

[MPT91]   P. McKenzie, P. Péladeau, and D. Thérien. NC^1: The automata-theoretic viewpoint. *Computational Complexity*, 1:330–359, 1991.

[MT93]   A. Maciel and D. Thérien. Threshold circuits for iterated multiplication: Using AC^0 for free. In *Annual Symposium on Theoretical Aspects of Computer Science (STACS)*, volume 665 of *Lecture Notes in Computer Science*, pages 545–554. Springer-Verlag, 1993.

[NS94]   N. Nisan and M. Szegedy. On the degree of Boolean functions as real polynomials. *Computational Complexity*, 4:301–313, 1994.

[NW94]   N. Nisan and A. Wigderson. Hardness vs. randomness. *Journal of Computer and System Sciences*, 49:149–167, 1994.

[PS88]   I. Parberry and G. Schnitger. Parallel computation with threshold functions. *Journal of Computer and System Sciences*, 36:278–302, 1988.

[PS89]   I. Parberry and G. Schnitger. Relating Boltzmann machines to conventional models of computation. *Neural Networks*, 2:59–67, 1989.

[Rad94] J. Radhakrishnan. $\Sigma \Pi \Sigma$ threshold formulas. *Combinatorica*, 14:345–374, 1994.

[Raz87] A. A. Razborov. Lower bounds on the size of bounded depth networks over a complete basis with logical addition. *Mathematicheskie Zametki*, 41:598–607, 1987. English translation in Mathematical Notes of the Academy of Sciences of the USSR 41:333-338, 1987.

[Raz92] A. A. Razborov. On small depth threshold circuits. In *Scandinavian Workshop on Algorithm Theory (SWAT)*, volume 621 of *Lecture Notes in Computer Science*, pages 42–52. Springer-Verlag, 1992.

[Raz95] A. A. Razborov. Bounded arithmetic and lower bounds. In P. Clote and J. Remmel, editors, *Feasible Mathematics II,*, volume 13 of *Progress in Computer Science and Applied Logic*, pages 344–386. Birkhäuser, 1995.

[RR94]   A. A. Razborov and S. Rudich. Natural proofs. In *Proceedings, 26th ACM Symposium on Theory of Computing*, pages 204–213, 1994.

[RSC95] K. Regan, D. Sivakumar, and J.-Y. Cai. Pseudorandom generators, measure theory, and natural proofs. In *IEEE Symposium on Foundations of Computer Science (FOCS)*, pages 26–35, 1995.

[RSO94] V. Roychowdhury, K.-Y. Siu, and A. Orlitsky, editors. *Theoretical Advances in Neural Computation and Learning*. Kluwer, 1994.

[RSOK95] V. Roychowdhury, K.-Y. Siu, A. Orlitsky, and T. Kailath. Vector analysis of threshold functions. *Information and Computation*, 120:22–31, 1995.

[RW93]   A. A. Razborov and A. Wigderson. $n^{\Omega(\log n)}$ lower bounds on the size of depth-3 threshold circuits with AND gates at the bottom. *Information Processing Letters*, 45:303–307, 1993.

[Sit]   M. Sitharam. Approximation from linear spaces, lower bounds, pseudorandomness, and learning. Submitted.

[Sit95] M. Sitharam. Pseudorandom generators and learning algorithms for AC^0. *Computational Complexity*, 5:248–266, 1995.

[Siv96] D. Sivakumar. *Probabilistic Techniques in Structural Complexity Theory*. PhD thesis, SUNY Buffalo, 1996.

[Smo87] R. Smolensky. Algebraic methods in the theory of lower bounds for Boolean circuit complexity. In *Proceedings, 19th ACM Symposium on Theory of Computing*, pages 77–82, 1987.

[Smo93] R. Smolensky. On representations by low-degree polynomials. In *IEEE Symposium on Foundations of Computer Science (FOCS)*, 1993.

[Sto74] L. Stockmeyer. *The complexity of decision problems in automata theory and logic*. PhD thesis, Mass. Inst. of Technology, 1974.

[Sto87] L. Stockmeyer. Classifying the computational complexity of problems. *Journal of Symbolic Logic*, 52:1–43, 1987.

[Tar93] J. Tarui. Probabilistic polynomials, AC^0 functions, and the polynomial-time hierarchy. *Theoretical Computer Science*, 113:167–183, 1993.

[TB95]   G. Tardos and D. A. Mix Barrington. A lower bound on the MOD 6 degree of the OR function. In *Proc. 3rd Israel Symposium on the Theory of Computing and Systems*, pages 52–56. IEEE Press, 1995.

[Thé]   D. Thérien. Circuits constructed with MOD_q gates cannot compute AND in sublinear size. *Computational Complexity*, 4:383–388, 1994.

[Tod91]   S. Toda. PP is as hard as the polynomial-time hierarchy. *SIAM Journal on Computing*, 20:865–877, 1991.

[Tsa96]   S.-C. Tsai. Lower bounds on representing Boolean functions as polynomials in z_m. *SIAM Journal on Discrete Mathematics*, 9:55–62, 1996.

[Wil85]   C. Wilson. Relativized circuit complexity. *Journal of Computer and System Sciences*, 31:169–181, 1985.

[Yao85]   A. Yao. Separating the polynomial-time hierarchy by oracles. In *IEEE Symposium on Foundations of Computer Science (FOCS)*, pages 1–10, 1985.

[Yao90]   A. Yao. On ACC and threshold circuits. In *IEEE Symposium on Foundations of Computer Science (FOCS)*, pages 619–627, 1990.

[YP94]   P.Y. Yan and I. Parberry. Exponential size lower bounds for some depth three circuits. *Information and Computation (formerly Information and Control)*, 112:117–130, 1994.

[ZBT93]   Z.-L. Zhang, D. A. Mix Barrington, and J. Tarui. Computing symmetric functions with AND/OR circuits and a single MAJORITY gate. In *10th Annual Symposium on Theoretical Aspects of Computer Science*, volume 665 of *Lecture Notes in Computer Science*, pages 535–544. Springer-Verlag, 1993.

A Lambda Calculus with Letrecs and Barriers

Arvind[1], Jan-Willem Maessen[1], Rishiyur S. Nikhil[2], Joseph Stoy[3]

[1] MIT Laboratory for Computer Science[†]
[2] DEC Cambridge Research Laboratory[‡]
[3] Oxford University Computing Laboratory[§]

1 Introduction

It is often said that pure functional languages like Haskell[9] are merely "syntactic sugar" for a version of the lambda calculus extended with constants and data structures. In fact the semantics of these languages is more complicated than that, but an understanding of the lambda calculus is nevertheless crucial in their study. The lambda calculus also plays an important role as a vehicle for explaining the semantics of a much broader class of languages such as Lisp[13], ML[11], Scheme[8], Id[12] and pH[2] (a parallel dialect of Haskell). The importance of a small, simple, formal system cannot be overstated: at the very least it helps in teaching the language and building intuitions about it; it is also an unambiguous point of appeal for reasoning about the correctness of program equivalences.

A practically important class of program equivalences are the optimizations performed by a compiler. The lambda calculus and its variants are used as the basis for kernel languages in some compilers. The task of designing the required transformations and optimizations is eased by restricting attention to a simpler and more regular language.

In this paper we will describe some extensions which make the pure lambda calculus much more useful, both for discussing the semantic essence of "real" languages, and also as an intermediate language for a compiler.

We will begin by a quick overview of the pure lambda calculus extended with constants. This is followed by a discussion of inadequacy of this system to address some pragmatic aspects of even purely functional languages (Sect. 3). In Sect. 4 we describe λ_{let}, a lambda calculus with recursive let blocks (i.e., letrecs), and discuss why it is more appropriate as a kernel language; we also discuss the complications letrecs add. In Sect. 5, we discuss λ_B which is λ_{let} extended with sequentializing constructs called barriers. We then mention some more extensions we have studied, which continue to be the target of active research.

[†] This research was performed in part at the MIT Laboratory for Computer Science, where it was supported by ARPA contract DABT63-95-C-0150. Email: arvind@lcs.mit.edu, jmaessen@mit.edu

[‡] Email: nikhil@crl.dec.com

[§] EMail:stoy@comlab.ox.ac.uk

2   The Pure λ Calculus with Constants

We begin by looking at the pure λ calculus. The calculus itself is very small, yet it is possible to express every sequential computable function as a λ-expression. This power comes from several important notions. First, we can write anonymous (unnamed) functions. Second, the calculus is higher-order. We can thus write functions which take functions as arguments and return functions as results. Finally, λ calculus does not limit *where* we are permitted to perform evaluation. As a result, we can discuss the effects of evaluation order on the calculus.

The material in this section will be very familiar to those who have encountered the λ calculus before. This presentation highlights the aspects of λ calculus which are important to later sections and introduces some notation which will recur throughout the paper.

2.1   Syntax

The λ calculus has by far the simplest syntax of any of the calculi described here (We concern ourselves only with abstract syntax—we use parentheses freely to clarify grouping. We also freely define syntactic categories as subsets or unions of other ones, trusting that this will cause no confusion):

$$
\begin{array}{lll}
E & ::= x & \text{Identifiers} \\
& \mid \lambda x.E & \text{Abstractions} \\
& \mid E\,E & \text{Applications} \\
& \mid \mathbf{cond}(E,E,E) & \text{Conditionals} \\
& \mid \mathbf{PF}_k(E_1,\cdots,E_k) & \text{Primitive function applications, } k \geq 1 \\
& \mid \mathbf{CN}_0 & \text{Constants} \\
& \mid \mathbf{CN}_k(E_1,\cdots,E_k) & \text{Constructor applications, } k \geq 1 \\
\mathbf{PF}_1 & ::= \mathbf{not} \mid \mathbf{Proj}_1 \mid \mathbf{Proj}_2 \mid \cdots & \text{Primitive functions of arity 1} \\
\mathbf{PF}_2 & ::= + \mid - \mid \cdots & \text{Primitive functions of arity 2} \\
\vdots & & \\
\mathbf{CN}_0 & ::= \textit{Number} \mid \textit{Boolean} & \text{Constructors of arity 1} \\
\mathbf{CN}_2 & ::= \mathbf{cons} \mid \cdots & \text{Constructors of arity 2} \\
\vdots & &
\end{array}
$$

2.2   Renaming: An Equivalence Rule

In many calculi there are some choices that, though leading to syntactically different terms, do not lead to terms that differ in any *essential* way. For example, in renaming a bound variable x to avoid free-variable capture, it does not really matter whether the fresh name chosen is y or z, even though the two choices lead to terms that are not syntactically "equal". λ calculus formalizes this notion as α reduction[7]:

---

[7] As usual, the notation $e \longrightarrow e_1$ means that e reduces to e_1 by a single application of a reduction rule to e or to one of its subterms, and $e \longrightarrow\!\!\!\!\twoheadrightarrow e_1$ means that e reduces

$$\lambda x.E \longrightarrow \lambda x'.E[x/x'] \qquad\qquad x' \notin FV(E)$$

Here we read $E[x/x']$ as "substitute x' for for every free occurrence of x in E". Ordinarily, we assume that terms e_1 and e_2 interconvertible using only α renaming are *equivalent*, and write $e_1 \equiv e_2$. A reduction rule (to be introduced later) is applicable to a term if it is applicable to *any* equivalent term.

2.3 Reduction Rules for the λ Calculus

The most critical rule in λ calculus is the β rule:

$$(\lambda x.e_1)\, e_2 \longrightarrow e_1'[e_2/x]$$
where e_1' is a renaming of e_1 to avoid free variable capture

Any expression to which the β rule can be applied is referred to as a β redex. Note that redexes can occur anywhere in a λ expression; for example, in $\lambda x.((\lambda y.(\lambda z.z)\, y)\, x)\, x$ both the underlined subexpressions are β redexes.

δ rules specify the behavior of each primitive function. They are all of the form:

$$\mathrm{PF}_k(v_1, \cdots, v_k) \longrightarrow v \qquad\qquad (\delta)$$

Obviously we cannot list all the δ rules here, but an example is:

$$+(\underline{n},\ \underline{m}) \longrightarrow \underline{p} \quad\text{ where } \underline{n}, \underline{m} \text{ and } \underline{p} \text{ represent numbers and } p = n + m$$

This rule should be read as saying: the term consisting of "+" applied to two numerical constants may be rewritten as the constant that represents the sum of those two numbers.

Projection functions select fields of constructed values:

$$\mathrm{proj}_j(\mathrm{CN}_k(e_1,\ \cdots,\ e_k)) \longrightarrow e_j \qquad 1 \le j \le k \qquad (\mathrm{Proj})$$

Cond rules specify the behavior of conditional expressions:

$$\mathrm{cond}(\mathtt{True},\ e_1,\ e_2) \longrightarrow e_1 \qquad (\mathrm{CondT})$$
$$\mathrm{cond}(\mathtt{False},\ e_1,\ e_2) \longrightarrow e_2 \qquad (\mathrm{CondF})$$

2.4 Recursion

One thing λ calculus lacks is direct provision for recursion. For example, we cannot write the factorial function directly, as we might in an ordinary programming language:

$$\mathtt{fact} = \lambda n.\mathrm{cond}(n = 0,\ 1,\ n*(\mathtt{fact}\ (n-1)))$$

The problem is that $\mathtt{fact}$ isn't well defined on the right hand side of the above equation. Instead, we have to abstract away the recursive call to $\mathtt{fact}$:

---

to e_1 by a finite sequence (zero or more) of such steps. A term or subterm which is capable of reduction by one of the rules is called a *redex*.

```
fact  = fact' fact
fact' = λf.λn.cond(n = 0, 1, n*(f (n − 1)))
```

Now the `fact` function we desire is the fixed point of `fact'`, so we can write `fact` using the fixed-point combinator Y:

```
fact = Y fact'
Y    = λf.(λx.f (x x))(λx.f (x x))
```

2.5 Confluence and Equivalence

Because λ expressions can contain many redexes, the most obvious question to be asked is: Is the λ calculus confluent? That is, if we reduce different redexes, can we eventually bring the resulting terms back together? The Church-Rosser Theorem says that we can:

> The λ calculus is confluent: If $e_1 \twoheadrightarrow e_2$ and $e_1 \twoheadrightarrow e_3$, then there exists an e_4 such that $e_2 \twoheadrightarrow e_4$ and $e_3 \twoheadrightarrow e_4$.

Unfortunately, confluence does not guarantee that we *will* always reach e_4 when we reduce further; it merely states that it is possible to do so. Subterms may be infinitely reducible, distracting us from useful reduction elsewhere.

Normal Forms of λ Expressions In functional languages like the λ calculus, a program itself represents the "answer" or "output" of computation. The process of reduction gradually transforms the initial program into a form that more manifestly represents an answer (e.g., the reduction of "2+3" to "5"). Note that the answer may even be infinite, such as an infinite list of actions for the operating system to perform. At some intermediate point of computation, it is possible that the answer has thus far been only partially manifested.

There are actually many possible definitions of "answer" even for the pure λ calculus. The most obvious definition is *normal form*—no further redexes exist anywhere in the expression. Because of confluence, we know that the normal form of any expression is unique (otherwise further reductions could be performed to bring the distinct terms together!). In addition, a normal-order reduction (where the leftmost outermost redex is reduced at every step) is guaranteed to find the normal form of a term if it exists.

However, many terms do not have a normal form at all! One infamous example is the term Ω, which reduces to itself:

$$\Omega = (\lambda x.x\ x)\ (\lambda x.x\ x) \longrightarrow (\lambda x.x\ x)\ (\lambda x.x\ x) \longrightarrow \ldots$$

Thus, while normal form seems to provide a convenient notion of equality, it leaves open the question of how to treat terms which do not possess a normal form.

More commonly used is weak head normal form (WHNF), which can be defined syntactically (using the category A for "answer") as follows:

$$
\begin{aligned}
A &::= V && \text{Values} \\
&\;|\;\; P && \text{Irreducible expressions} \\
V &::= \lambda x.E && \text{Abstractions} \\
&\;|\;\; CN_0 && \text{Constants} \\
&\;|\;\; CN_k(E_1, \cdots E_k) && \text{Constructed values, } k \geq 1 \\
P &::= x && \text{Free variables} \\
&\;|\;\; P\,E && \text{Applications of irreducibles}
\end{aligned}
$$

Values, V, play a prominent role in the reduction rules of our later calculi.

Unfortunately, weak head normal forms are *not* unique. For example, the following terms have the same normal form but are both already in WHNF:

$$
\lambda x.(\lambda y.\lambda z.y)\; x\; x \qquad \text{and} \qquad \lambda x.(\lambda y.y)\; x
$$

We thus still need to define equivalence between terms.

3 Problems with the λ Calculus

There are a number of problems with the λ calculus that prevent it from closely mirroring the operation of an actual programming language implementation—even a purely functional language such as Haskell. While the existence of the Y combinator is mathematically fascinating, fixed points do not provide a simple encapsulation of recursion. For example, we would like to be able to declare mutually recursive functions and data structures in such a way that their definitions are clear and readable; the need to re-shape such definitions as fixed points plays havoc with such an endeavor.

More problematic is that the λ calculus handles sharing very poorly indeed. The problem is in β reduction itself. In the application $(\lambda x.e_1)\, e_2$ the traditional β rule makes copies of the argument expression e_2 for each occurrence of the formal parameter x.

In an effort to solve this problem, several researchers have added let blocks to the language and replaced the β rule with β_G[5, 10, 1, 3]:

$$
(\lambda x.e_1)\, e_2 \longrightarrow \{\; x' = e_2 \text{ in } e_1[x'/x]\; \} \qquad (\beta_G)
$$
where x' is a variable which does not otherwise occur.

A central feature of the β_G rule is that it performs no substitution at all; instead we add new rules for *instantiating the values of variables*. These new rules can be designed so that sharing of subexpressions is preserved. This also means that the β_G rule never *discards* the argument. This will affect the semantics of barriers and side-effects. In short, the β_G rule preserves the "graph structure" of the term, with shared subterms, instead of the "tree structure" of the traditional λ calculus, with replicated subterms. This is why we use the subscript G, for "graph." In the next section we will use the β_G rule as the core of a new calculus, λ_{let}.

The idea of sharing subexpressions to make normal-order reduction efficient was first tackled by Wadsworth in his D.Phil. Thesis as far back as 1971 [14]. In his seminal work, which came to be known as *graph reduction*, he used an explicit graph notation instead of a textual term notation. Since the source language was standard λ-calculus, there was no issue of recursive or cyclic terms—the *sharing* he obtained was just a way to avoid duplicating the function argument when the formal parameter was used multiple times in the λ body. Since then several different let-block extensions to the λ calculus have been presented in the literature to model sharing. Recently, Launchbury reformulated Wadsworth's system without using a graph notation by introducing "let" expressions into the term syntax [10]. Again, since the source language was standard λ calculus, there was no issue of recursive or cyclic terms. Launchbury did not separate *calculus* from *strategy*—he directly gave a set of rules to implement lazy evaluation.

In [3], Ariola et al. presented a calculus which did allow the definition of cyclic terms, but it was restricted to disallow substitution of a let-bound identifier in the right-hand side of its own binding, thus side-stepping a full treatment of cyclic terms. This work also did not address data structures.

In [1], Abadi et al. also presented a calculus that dealt with cyclic terms, but it deviated quite far from traditional λ-calculus in that it used de Bruijn notation, introduced *environments* and a calculus of environments, etc.

The most recent work by Ariola [6] is the first to introduce a calculus of recursive let-expressions. Our λ_{let} is essentially the same as Ariola's system, with some small differences in the details of the rules of the calculus.

4 λ_{let}: a λ Calculus with Letrec Blocks

λ_{let} extends the λ calculus with "letrec blocks", allowing us to define shared recursive bindings by binding an expression to an identifier and then using that identifier in a number of places. Our plan of action for this section is as follows. First we present the λ_{let} *calculus*, i.e., the syntax of λ_{let} terms and the reduction rules that allow us to transform terms and perform "computation". We then define a notion of printing, which captures the "important" information in a term. Finally, we discuss how we might define a standard reduction strategy which evaluates let bindings in parallel.

4.1 Syntax

λ_{let} augments the syntax of λ calculus with letrec blocks:

E	::=	$\cdots$	as before
		{ S in E }	Letrec blocks
S	::=	ϵ	Empty statements
		$x = E$	Bindings
		S ; S	Parallel

The S in a Letrec block is a composition of parallel statements, at the leaves of which are bindings and empty statements. The identifiers on the left-hand sides of all these bindings must be pair-wise distinct. The empty statement is used only as a technical convenience in λ_{let}; it will become useful in λ_B. We refer to the final expression in a block as the *return expression* of the block.

λ_{let} has *"letrec"* scope rules—any identifier on the left-hand side of any binding in a block may be referred to in any right-hand side, as well as in the return expression of the block. In other words, the collection of bindings in a block should be regarded as simultaneous, recursive bindings.

In λ_{let} we ensure that constructors are evaluated exactly once, after which they become "values" and are written using an underline. The complete syntactic category of expressions therefore contains these terms too:

$$E ::= \cdots$$
$$| \quad \underline{CN}_k(E_1, \cdots, E_k) \qquad \text{Constructor values, } k \geq 1$$

Note, however, that the underlined versions of constructors never occur in unevaluated λ_{let} terms. For the rest of this section, we will simply appeal to the reader's intuition on the distinction between constructors with and without underlines.

Values and Simple Expressions In our calculi, as in the λ calculus, we need to substitute various *uses* of an identifier with the identifier's definition. This is called *instantiation*. The way this operation is defined can have an impact on sharing. Suppose we have the following term:

```
(1)        {  x = (f a);
(2)           y = x;
           in
           w }
```

Suppose we substitute the use of x on line (2) by its definition from line (1):

```
(1)        {  x = (f a);
(2)           y = (f a);
           in
           w }
```

We now have two copies of "f a," which may be an arbitrarily complicated computation, i.e., we have replicated the computation, instead of *sharing* it. In versions of the calculus that include barriers and side-effects, this sharing is required and not merely an issue of efficiency.

Thus, our instantiation rules must be very careful about which expressions can be substituted. To maintain sharing, we identify two subsets of λ_{let} terms that are substitutable—*values* and *identifiers*, collectively known as *simple expressions*:

$$SE ::= x \qquad \text{Identifiers}$$
$$| \quad V \qquad \text{Values}$$

4.2 λ_{let} Equivalence Rules

The first two equivalence rules are analogous to α renaming; they express the idea that the particular choice of a name for a bound variable is not important:

$$\lambda x.e \qquad\qquad \equiv \lambda x'.(e[x'/x])$$
$$\{ \; SC[x = e]_S \text{ in } e_0 \; \} \equiv \{ \; SC[x' = e]_S \text{ in } e_0 \; \}[x'/x]$$
$$\text{where } x' \text{ does not otherwise occur in the program.}$$

The second set of rules states that the grouping of statements combined with semicolons is unimportant, as is the presence or absence of empty statements.

$$S_1 \; ; \; S_2 \qquad\quad \equiv S_2 \; ; \; S_1$$
$$S_1 \; ; \; (S_2 \; ; \; S_3) \equiv (S_1 \; ; \; S_2) \; ; \; S_3$$
$$\epsilon \; ; \; S \qquad\qquad \equiv S$$

Recall that we regard a reduction rule to be applicable to a term if it is applicable to any equivalent term.

4.3 λ_{let} Reduction Rules

We are now ready to look at the reduction rules themselves. They can be divided into several groups:

(1) instantiation;
(2) function application;
(3) lifting;
(4) δ rules, conditionals, and data structures.

Instantiation (Substitution) Given a statement that binds an identifier x to a simple expression a, the following rules permit a use of x to be replaced by a. Note that in all these rules a is a *simple expression*, and the x is free in $C[x]$.

$$\{ \; x = a \; ; \; S \text{ in } C[x] \; \} \qquad \longrightarrow \qquad \{ \; x = a \; ; \; S \text{ in } C[a] \; \} \qquad \text{(Inst1)}$$

$$(x = a \; ; \; SC[x]) \qquad\qquad \longrightarrow \qquad (x = a \; ; \; SC[a]) \qquad\qquad \text{(Inst2)}$$

$$x = a \qquad\qquad\qquad \longrightarrow \qquad x = C[a] \qquad\qquad\qquad \text{(Inst3)}$$
$$\text{where } a = C[x]$$

The context $C[\;]$ in which instantiation takes place is an expression with a hole (written as $[\;]$):

$$
\begin{aligned}
C[\;] \quad ::= &\; [\;] & | &\quad \lambda x.C[\;] \\
& | \;\; C[\;] \; E & | &\quad E \; C[\;] \\
& | \;\; \{ \; S \text{ in } C[\;] \; \} & | &\quad \{ \; SC[\;] \text{ in } E \; \} \\
& | \;\; PF_k(\ldots, C[\;], \ldots) \\
& | \;\; CN_k(\ldots, C[\;], \ldots) \\
& | \;\; \underline{CN}_k(\ldots, C[\;], \ldots)
\end{aligned}
$$

In this definition, $SC[\;]$ is a *statement* context for an expression; that is, a statement with a hole in place of one of the subexpressions in it. It is defined as follows:

$$SC[\;] ::= x = C[\;] \quad | \quad SC[\;] \; ; \; S$$

Function Application (β Reduction) As mentioned before, a λ expression can be applied to an argument using the β_G rule:

$$(\lambda x.e_1)\, e_2 \longrightarrow \{\ x' = e_2 \text{ in } e_1[x'/x]\ \} \qquad (\beta_G)$$
where x' is a variable which does not otherwise occur.

Expression Lifting The following rules "lift" expressions that are nested in certain ways. In all these rules "$\{S' \text{ in } e'\}$" represents an α-renaming of "$\{S \text{ in } e\}$" to avoid name conflicts with the surrounding scope, and the t's represent variables which do not otherwise occur. The side conditions $e \notin SE$ prevent infinite reduction.

$$
\begin{array}{llll}
\{\ \epsilon \text{ in } e\ \} & \longrightarrow & e & \text{(Lift0)} \\
x = \{\ S \text{ in } e\ \} & \longrightarrow & (x = e'\ ;\ S') & \text{(Lift1)} \\
\{\ S \text{ in } e\ \} & \longrightarrow & \{\ S\ ;\ t = e \text{ in } t\ \} & e \notin SE \quad \text{(Lift2)} \\
(e\ e_2) & \longrightarrow & \{\ t = e \text{ in } (t\ e_2)\ \} & e \notin SE \quad \text{(Lift3)} \\
(e_1\ e) & \longrightarrow & \{\ t = e \text{ in } (e_1\ t)\ \} & e \notin SE \quad \text{(Lift4)} \\
\mathrm{cond}(e,\ e_1,\ e_2) & \longrightarrow & \{\ t = e \text{ in } \mathrm{cond}(t,\ e_1,\ e_2)\ \} & e \notin SE \quad \text{(Lift5)} \\
PF_k(\cdots e,\ \cdots) & \longrightarrow & \{\ t = e \text{ in } PF_k(\cdots t,\ \cdots)\ \} & e \notin SE \quad \text{(Lift6)}
\end{array}
$$

The utility of these rules may be seen by considering the following example:

```
{   f = { S₁ in λx.e₁ };                              (1)
    x = f a;                                           (2)
 in
    { S₂ in λx.e₂ } e₃ }                               (3)
```

Without Lift1, we would not be able to substitute $\lambda x.e_1$ for **f** in line 2. Similarly, without Lift2, Lift3 and Lift1, we would not be able to apply $\lambda x.e_2$ to e_3.

δ Rules, Conditionals, and Data Structures A rule needs to be added to turn a nonunderlined constructor into the equivalent underlined constructor.

$$CN_k(e_1, \cdots, e_k) \longrightarrow \{\ t_1 = e_1;\ \cdots\ ;\ t_k = e_k \text{ in } \underline{CN_k}(t_1,\ \cdots,\ t_k)\ \}$$

The δ and conditional rules from the λ calculus carry over unmodified to λ_{let}.

4.4 (Non-)Confluence

The following theorem by Ariola and Klop [4] states that the introduction of let blocks has destroyed confluence:

Proposition 1 (Ariola and Klop) λ_{let} *is not confluent.*

To see this, consider the following program:

```
    Term0:
    { odd  = λn. cond(n = 0, False, even(n-1));
      even = λn. cond(n = 0, True,  odd(n-1));
    in
      .. }
```

Suppose we substitute **odd** at its use in **even**. *Term0* becomes:

> *Term1:*
> ```
> { odd  = λn. cond(n = 0, False, even(n-1));
>   even = λn. cond(n = 0, True,  cond((n-1)=0, False, even((n-1)-1)));
> in
>   .. }
> ```

Suppose, instead, we substitute **even** at its use in **odd**. *Term0* becomes:

> *Term2:*
> ```
> { odd  = λn. cond(n = 0, False, cond((n-1)=0, True, odd((n-1)-1)));
>   even = λn. cond(n = 0, True,  odd(n-1));
> in
>   .. }
> ```

At this point, we can see that it will never be possible to reduce *Term1* and *Term2* to the same term. For example, in *Term1*, if we substitute **even** into the **odd** definition, the **odd** definition will still contain a call to the **even** function; this remains true no matter how may times we repeat this substitution. In **Term2**, on the other hand, the **odd** definition has a call to the **odd** function, and if we subtitute for **odd** this remains true.

This lack of confluence is true even if we permit unrestricted instantiation, i.e., if we allowed an identifier to be substituted by the expression that it is bound to even though it may not be a simple expression. Let us call this calculus λ_0. Note that this calculus no longer preserves sharing of computations.

Proposition 2 (Ariola and Klop) λ_0 *is not confluent.*

4.5 Printable Values and the Print[] Function

We now wish to approach the question whether the calculus defined by these rules makes sense; that is to say, whether there is a consistent notion of equality which is preserved under transformation of a term according to the rules. We accordingly wish to develop a notion of the observable information contained in a term.

Trying to distinguish terms by comparing their syntax is problematic, even in the pure λ calculus. However, the problem gets harder when let blocks are an integral part of the syntax. Consider the following two terms:

$$\{\ x = 5 \text{ in } 5\ \} \qquad \text{(M1)}$$
$$\{\ x = 3; y = 2 \text{ in } 5\ \} \quad \text{(M2)}$$

M1 and M2 behave essentially the same in all contexts and thus should be equal but are syntactically very different. It is common to introduce one or more "garbage collection" rules in the calculus to attempt to remove the irrelevant clutter (see, for example,[3]. But even this is inadequate: as the (non-)confluence results of Ariola and Klop ([4]) show, there are pairs of terms which ought to be considered equal which can never reduce to compatible syntactic forms.

We therefore introduce the concept of a "printable value". This is a rudimentary notion of value—for example, in λ_{let} all λ abstractions are represented by the single symbol "λ". It is nevertheless all we need; we consider two terms as semantically distinct if they have different print-values, of course; but we also consider them to be distinct, even if they have the same print value, when there is some context that will have different print-values depending on which of these two terms is inserted.

$$
\begin{aligned}
PV \quad ::= \quad & \perp \\
\mid \quad & \lambda \\
\mid \quad & CN_0 \\
\mid \quad & CN_k(PV_1, \cdots, PV_k)
\end{aligned}
$$

We also impose an *ordering* on printable values:

$$
\begin{aligned}
& \perp && \sqsubseteq PV \\
& \lambda && \sqsubseteq \lambda \\
& CN_0 && \sqsubseteq CN_0 \\
& CN_k(v_1, \cdots, v_j \cdots, v_k) && \sqsubseteq CN_k(v_1, \cdots, v_j' \cdots, v_k) && \text{if } v_j \sqsubseteq v_j' && k \geq 1
\end{aligned}
$$

In other words, $\perp$ is strictly "less" than everything else, and the ordering on constructed terms is defined recursively based on a pair-wise ordering of corresponding arguments. There is no mutual ordering between λ-expressions, constants and constructed terms, or between constructed terms with distinct constructors.

Print$[\![\ ]\!]$ is really implemented by the Print$'[\![\ ]\!]$ function that carries along with it a second argument, the *environment*, that remembers all identifier bindings in the surrounding scope. This environment argument is a collection of bindings $x = v$.

$$
\text{Print}[\![e]\!] = \text{Print}'[\![e]\!] \text{ empty\_environment}
$$
where
$$
\begin{aligned}
\text{Print}'[\![x]\!] \text{ env} \quad &= \text{Print}'[\![v]\!] \text{ env} \qquad \text{if } [\![x = v]\!] \in \text{env} \\
\text{Print}'[\![\lambda x.e]\!] \text{ env} \quad &= \lambda \\
\text{Print}'[\![\{ \ S \text{ in } a \ \}]\!] \text{ env} \quad &= \text{Print}'[\![a]\!] \text{ env}' \\
&\quad \text{where } a \in SE \quad \text{and} \quad \text{env}' = \text{Extend}[\![S]\!] \text{ env} \\
\text{Print}'[\![CN_0]\!] \text{ env} \quad &= CN_0 \\
\text{Print}'[\![CN_k(a_1, \cdots, a_k) \ ]\!] \text{ env} &= CN_k(\text{Print}'[\![a_1]\!] \text{ env}, \ k \geq 1 \\
&\qquad\qquad\qquad\qquad \vdots \\
&\qquad\qquad\qquad \text{Print}'[\![a_k]\!] \text{ env}) \\
\textit{otherwise} \quad\qquad\qquad &= \perp
\end{aligned}
$$

Print$'[\![\ ]\!]$ uses the auxiliary Extend$[\![\ ]\!]$ function which augments an environment with all the bindings in a block's statement provided that the identifiers are bound to values (we assume that α renaming has been used to prevent name clashes among bindings in the environment).

$$
\begin{aligned}
\text{Extend} [\![\ x = v \ ]\!] \text{ env} \quad &= \text{env} + [\![x = v]\!] \\
\text{Extend} [\![\ (S_1 \ ; \ S_2) \ ]\!] \text{ env} &= \text{Extend} [\![\ S_1 \ ]\!] \ (\text{Extend} [\![\ S_2 \ ]\!] \text{ env}) \\
\text{Extend} [\![\ \cdots \ ]\!] \text{ env} \quad &= \text{env} \qquad\qquad\qquad\qquad\qquad \textit{otherwise}
\end{aligned}
$$

Note that being able to print a non-$\perp$ value from a term does not mean that the term has terminated, or even that it will ever terminate. For example, given this term:

```
{    loop = λx.loop x;
     bot  = loop (λy.y);
  in
     (λz.z)  }
```

we can print its value (λ), but the term as a whole will never terminate.

The following two properties of printing are about "monotonicity". The first captures the idea that as we continually reduce a term, its information content continually increases, i.e., printing a value following one or more reductions will only produce a "more defined" value.

Proposition 3 *If* $e \longrightarrow\!\!\!\!\rightarrow e_1$ *then* $\text{Print}[\![e]\!] \sqsubseteq \text{Print}[\![e_1]\!]$

The second expresses the notion of equality that we wanted: if one expression reduces to another then they are print-equivalent.

Proposition 4 *If* $e \longrightarrow\!\!\!\!\rightarrow e_1$ *then* $Print^*[\![e]\!] = Print^*[\![e_1]\!]$

Note, as a corollary, that if e is *convertible* to e_1 (that is, by applying rules in either direction), then $\text{Print}^*[\![e]\!] = \text{Print}^*[\![e_1]\!]$.

4.6 The Power of the λ_{let} Calculus

Our instantiation rules permit instantiation of an identifier only when it is bound to a simple expression. The following theorm by Ariola et al. [6] assures us that we have not lost any computational power due to this restriction on substitution:

Proposition 5 *(Fundamental theorem of graph reduction): If* $e \longrightarrow\!\!\!\!\rightarrow e_1$ *in* λ_0, *then* $\exists e_2$ *such that* $e \longrightarrow\!\!\!\!\rightarrow e_2$ *in* λ_{let}, *and* $Print[\![e_1]\!] \sqsubseteq Print[\![e_2]\!]$.

4.7 Reduction Strategies and Standard Reduction

When we actually sit down and perform reductions on a program, we would like to make sure we get at least as much information as one could get from *any* other choice of reductions:

> **Definition:** A *standard reduction strategy* σ ensures that, if $e \longrightarrow\!\!\!\!\rightarrow e_1$ as a result of some sequence of reduction rules, then $\exists\ e_2$ such that $e \stackrel{\sigma}{\longrightarrow}\!\!\!\!\rightarrow e_2$ according to the rules of strategy σ, and $\text{Print}[\![e_1]\!]\sqsubseteq\text{Print}[\![e_2]\!]$.

Briefly, we can devise a parallel standard reduction strategy for λ_{let} in three stages. First, we manipulate the program to put it into kernel form—a canonical form which enables us to ignore several of the lifting rules during the remainder of reduction. We then choose redexes in a fair manner, making sure that we never reduce inside the body of a λ or in the branches of a conditional. Finally, we stop when we run out of candidate redexes in permitted contexts.

5 λ_B: Adding Barriers to λ_{let}

In this section, we describe λ_B, which extends λ_{let} with a *local sequencing mechanism* called a *barrier*, which sequences statements in a let block. λ_B remains a purely functional language (i.e., it has no side-effects). The barrier's sole effect is that a program may be *less defined* than the corresponding program that has the barriers erased, i.e., the presence of barriers may prevent termination, or may even prevent printing a non-$\perp$ value. The barrier gets its practical motivation from controlling side-effects like M-structures; however, all the semantic subtlety of barriers can be studied in this simpler, purely functional setting.

In Sections 5.1, 5.2, and 5.3, we present the λ_B *calculus*, i.e., the syntax of λ_B terms and the reduction rules. In Sect. 5.4, we briefly define the notion of printing for λ_B. Finally, in Sect. 5.5 we provide some commentary on λ_B.

5.1 Syntax

λ_B extends the syntax of λ_{let} with a new type statement called a Barrier:

$$
\begin{aligned}
S ::= \;\; &\cdots && \text{as before} \\
\mid \;\; &S \text{ --- } S && \text{Barriers (sequential)}
\end{aligned}
$$

The Barrier represents sequencing: the statement before the barrier is executed to completion before the statement after the barrier; we refer to these statements as the *pre-region* and the *post-region* of the barrier, respectively. The barrier is a local sequencing construct, and only involves the two statements that are its subterms. A program can contain any number of barriers.

Our previous static recursive scoping rule for identifiers remains the same—in this respect, there is no difference between barriers and semicolons.

Values and Simple Expressions Values and Simple Expressions remain the same in λ_B as in λ_{let}.

Statements which bind names to actual values are treated specially by the barrier rules. We refer to them as "value statments", H:

$$
H ::= x = V \quad \mid \quad H \; ; \; H
$$

Contexts and Renaming Expression contexts remain the same in λ_B as in λ_{let}. Statement contexts for expresssions extend those in λ_{let} with new clauses for barriers:

$$
\begin{aligned}
SC[\,] ::= &\ldots \\
\mid \;\; &SC[\,] \text{ --- } S \quad \mid \quad S \text{ --- } SC[\,]
\end{aligned}
$$

5.2 λ_B Equivalence Rules

The α-renaming and semicolon equivalence rules remain the same in λ_B as in λ_{let}. We add a new rule for barriers:

$$(H \; ; \; S_1) \; \text{---} \; S_2 \;\; \equiv \;\; H \; ; \; (S_1 \; \text{---} \; S_2)$$

This rule allows value bindings to escape from the pre-regions of barriers. The escaped bindings may enable other instantiations in the surrounding context. When all such bindings can escape, the barrier can discharge—see Sect. 5.3 below.

5.3 λ_B Reduction Rules

The existing reduction rules remain the same. We add a new group of rules for barriers.

Barrier Rules for λ_B The following rules say that a barrier can be "discharged" (eliminated) once the pre- or post-region is empty (the first rule is the most common in practice).

$$
\begin{array}{ll}
\epsilon \; \text{---} \; S \longrightarrow S & \text{(BAR1)} \\
S \; \text{---} \; \epsilon \longrightarrow S & \text{(BAR2)}
\end{array}
$$

The following proposition regarding barriers states that once all the statements in the pre-region of a barrier have terminated, the barrier can be discharged immediately:

Proposition 6 *In any context, the following reduction is always correct:*

$$(H \; \text{---} \; S) \longrightarrow (H \; ; \; S)$$

5.4 Printable Values, and the Print[] Function

Printable values, and their ordering, remain the same in λ_B as in λ_{let}.

In the Print[] function, we add one clause to the Extend[] helper function for barrier terms:

$$\text{Extend} \; [\![\; (S_1 \; \text{---} \; S_2) \;]\!] \; \text{env} = \text{Extend} \; [\![\; S_1 \;]\!] \; \text{env}$$

Note that it omits identifiers from the post-region.

All the Print and Print* propositions of λ_{let} (in Sect. 4.5) remain unchanged.

Stable Terms and Terminated Terms As we continually reduce a term, we may reach a stage where, even though we may continue reducing it (perhaps forever), the result of applying Print[] to the term will no longer change. We say that the term has reached a stable state, and we capture this formally in the following definition:

Definition: A term e is *stable* if $\text{Print}^*[e] = \{ a \mid a \sqsubseteq \text{Print}[e] \}$

When reduction stops the term may still contain "computations" (such as applications) that are unable to make progress simply because of a deadlock condition. We would like to define the category of "terminated terms" that have not stopped for this reason, i.e., terms that have stopped cleanly and properly:

Definition: *Terminated terms* are described by the following syntax:
$$ET ::= V \quad | \quad \{ H \text{ in } SE \}$$

A terminated expression contains no applications, unless they are inside λ abstractions. Note, however, that the body of any λ expression can be an arbitrary expression. Terminated terms are stable:

Proposition 7 *If $e \in ET$, then e is stable.*

Further reductions may still be possible within λ-bodies, but this cannot affect what is printed.

Another interesting class of terms are those terms whose printed values contain no $\perp$.

Definition: A *ground-printing term* is a term e such that $\text{Print}[e]$ terminates, and the printed value does not contain $\perp$.

The printed value value may be an arbitrarily deep data structure, and this condition requires that none of the leaves are $\perp$. Note that a ground-printing term is always stable, but it may not have terminated; this is possible because Print[] does not explore "irrelevant" computations, which may not have terminated and which, indeed, may even loop forever.

5.5 Discussion of λ_B

The interaction between our β_G rule for function application and the barrier rules is subtle. Perhaps the most surprising consequence is that:

$$\lambda x.e \quad \neq \quad \{ t = e \text{ in } \lambda x.t \} \qquad \text{even if } e \text{ is only a free variable } (\neq x).$$

The inequality is not surprising in eager languages such as SML and Scheme—if e were a non-terminating computation, the left-hand side would terminate and the right-hand side would not. However, if e was merely a free variable (say, z), then the two sides *would* be equal in SML and Scheme, but they are still not equal in λ_B.

Consider the following term (where $\perp$ is any non-terminating term):

```
( K = λx.1 ;
  b = ⊥ ;
  ( x1 = K b
    ---
    S ) )
```

Even though K discards its argument, the barrier will not discharge, as demonstrated by the following sequence of reductions (for comparison, we also show what would happen with the traditional β rule):

```
( K = λx.(λy.y) ;
  b = ⊥ ;
  ( x1 = K b
    ---
    S ) )
```

$\longrightarrow$
```
( K = λx.(λy.y) ;
  b = ⊥ ;
  ( x1 = (λx.(λy.y)) b
    ---
    S ) )
```

$\longrightarrow$ *[using β_G]*   *[using traditional β]*

```
( K = λx.(λy.y) ;          ( K = λx.(λy.y) ;
  b = ⊥ ;                    b = ⊥ ;
  ( x1 = { x' = b in (λy.y) }  ( x1 = (λy.y)
    ---                        ---
    S ) )                      S ) )
```

$\longrightarrow$
```
( K = λx.(λy.y) ;          ( K = λx.(λy.y) ;
  b = ⊥ ;                    b = ⊥ ;
  ( x1 = (λy.y) ;            ( x1 = (λy.y) ;
    x' = b                    S ) )
    ---
    S ) )
```

$\longrightarrow$
```
( K = λx.(λy.y) ;          ( K = λx.(λy.y) ;
  b = ⊥ ;                    b = ⊥ ;
  x1 = (λy.y) ;              x1 = (λy.y) ;
  ( x' = b                   S )
    ---
    S ) )
```

The last term (on the left) is stuck: since b never becomes a value, the barrier never discharges. This behaviour is fundamentally related to our β_G rule which does not discard the argument b even though the function itself does not use the argument. In contrast, using the traditional β rule (on the right), the barrier does discharge.

The addition of barriers allows us to observe the *termination* of any term in the calculus. For example, the following two terms are indistinguishable in λ_{let}:

$$\{ \ x = 5 \text{ in } 5 \ \} \qquad \text{and} \qquad \{ \ x = \perp \text{ in } 5 \ \}$$

The following context will distinguish them in λ_B:

$$\{ \ (\ y = [\,] \\ \underline{\quad\quad} \\ z = 3 \ ) \\ \text{in} \\ z \ \}$$

It should be clear from this example that equality in λ_{let} does not imply equality in λ_B.

6 Conclusion

λ_B is just one example of a useful extension of pure λ_{let} which enables us to study issues of termination in the absence of other complications. pH, the parallel dialect of Haskell that we are designing, also has I-structures[7] and M-structures, which add implicitly synchronized mutable storage to the language. In Figure 1 we show various extensions we have formulated and studied, culminating in λ_S, which is intended to capture all the essential semantic properties of pH itself. λ_S is also playing the desired role in the pH compiler: each rule for code generation and optimization is written in terms of λ_S constructs.

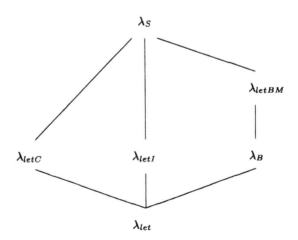

Fig. 1. A taxonomy of calculi used to study pH semantics

References

1. M. Abadi, L. Cardelli, P.-L. Curien, and J.-J. Lévy. Explicit substitutions. *Journal of Functional Programming*, 4(1):375–416, 1991.
2. Shail Aditya, Arvind, Lennart Augustsson, Jan-Willem Maessen, and Rishiyur S. Nikhil. Semantics of pH: A Parallel Dialect of Haskell. In *in Proc. Haskell Workshop (at FPCA 95), La Jolla, CA*, June 1995.
3. Z. M. Ariola, M. Felleisen, J. Maraist, M. Odersky, and P. Wadler. The call-by-need lambda calculus. In *Proc. ACM Conference on Principles of Programming Languages*, pages 233–246, 1995.
4. Z. M. Ariola and J. W. Klop. Lambda calculus with explicit recursion. Technical Report CIS-TR-96-04, Department of Computer and Information Science, University of Oregon, 1996.
5. Zena M. Ariola and Arvind. A Syntactic Approach to Program Transformations. In *Proc. Symp. on Partial Evaluation and Semantics Based Program Manipulation, Yale University, New Haven, CT*, June 1991. Also CSG Memo 322, MIT Lab for Computer Science.
6. Z.M. et al. Ariola. Cyclic lambda calculi. Technical Report CIS-TR-96-??, Department of computer and information science, University of Oregon, 1996.
7. Arvind, Rishiyur Sivaswami Nikhil, and Keshav Kumar Pingali. I-Structures: Data Structures for Parallel Computing. *ACM Transactions on Programming Languages and Systems*, 11(4):598–632, October 1989.
8. William Clinger and Jonathan Rees (eds.). Revised[4] Report on the Algorithmic Language Scheme. Technical report, MIT AI Laboratory, November 2 1991.
9. Paul Hudak, Simon Peyton Jones, Philip Wadler, Brian Boutel, Jon Fairbairn, Joseph Fasel, Maria M. Guzman, Kevin Hammond, John Hughes, Thomas Johnsson, Richard Kieburtz, Rishiyur Nikhil, Will Partain, and John Peterson. Report on the Programming Language Haskell, A Non-strict, Purely Functional Language, Version 1.2. *ACM SIGPLAN Notices*, 27(5), May 1992.
10. J. Launchbury. A natural semantics for lazy evaluation. In *Proc. ACM Conference on Principles of Programming Languages*, pages 144–154, 1993.
11. Robin Milner, Mads Tofte, and Robert Harper. *The Definition of Standard ML*. MIT Press, Cambridge, MA, 990.
12. Rishiyur Sivaswami Nikhil. Id (Version 90.1) Language Reference Manual. Technical Report CSG Memo 284-2, MIT Laboratory for Computer Science, 545 Technology Square, Cambridge, MA 02139, USA, July 15 1991.
13. Guy L. Steele Jr. *Common Lisp: The Language*. Digital Press, second edition, 1990.
14. C. P. Wadsworth. Semantics and pragmatics of the lambda-calculus. D.Phil. thesis, University of Oxford, 1971.

Tables

J. Ian Munro *
Department of Computer Science
University of Waterloo
Waterloo, ON
Canada N2L 3G1

Abstract. In representing a subset of a large finite set, or an index for text search, one is faced with the need for both time and space efficiency. In this paper, we look at some approaches that have been applied to these problems to represent objects in near minimum space and still permit queries to be performed in constant time. It is hoped that this paper will draw attention to techniques for representing large (mostly static) structures.

1 Introduction

Computer memories are growing dramatically, but problem size is growing even more quickly. As a consequence, space efficient representations of large objects are even more important than they were in the past. For example, given a large text file, we would like to preprocess the file and produce an index, so that given an arbitrary phrase one can quickly discover every occurrence of the query phrase in the text file. One natural approach is to use a search trie, say a Patricia tree [10] as a suffix trie [15, 5, 9]. The leaves of the tree are pointers to locations in the text and one descends the trie, branching according to the bit pattern of the input phrase. At a leaf one has discovered the unique location in the text in which (the prefix of) the query phrase occurs. If the phrase search stops higher in the tree, then an entire subtree indicates all occurrences of the phrase. Such a suffix trie approach permits searches in time bounded by the length of the input query, and in that sense is independent of the size of the database. However, assuming our phrase queries start at the beginning of any word and that words of text on average 5 or 6 characters in length, we have an index about 3 times the size of the text. That the index contains a reference to each word of the text accounts for less than a third of this overhead. Most of the index cost is in storing its tree structure. Indeed this is the main reason for the proposal [5, 9] of simply storing an array of references to positions in the text rather than the valuable structure of the tree.

In this paper we briefly review some techniques for representing (primarily static) information so that one can navigate through the structure efficiently. The general goal is to take as little space as possible and still perform basic operations

* imunro@uwaterloo.ca This work was supported by the Natural Science and Engineering Research Council of Canada.

in constant time. We will focus on two problems. The first is the representation of binary and ordered rooted trees. The second is the representation of moderately sparse sets. We view these relatively direct static structures as tables. While some of the higher level structures have variable sized fields, and so deviate from the most intuitive notion of a table, others are precisely simple tables of answers to all possible queries over the given domain. The goal of this paper is to point to a useful, though certainly not new, approach by way of a couple of examples. It is neither a survey of applications, nor is it a detailed treatment of the specific problems discussed.

Our model of computation is a random access machine in which each word consists of $\lg n$ bits. Here n can be the number of nodes in a tree or the size of the universe from which a set is constructed. Putting it another way, to identify an arbitrary basic object takes a word. On the other hand, we are not constrained to use representations of that sort as a word could be used as a bit vector to identify the presence or absence of $\lg n$ previously specified objects.

2 Representing Trees

In terms of clean representation of a tree, the heap of Williams[16] is the epitome of elegance. The structure is implicit [11, 12] in that only the size of the object and the records associated with particular nodes is retained. The structure represented as a heap is a balanced binary tree in which all leaves on the bottom level are shifted to the left. The nodes are numbered level by level from left to right. Hence the root is node 1, and the left and right children of node i are $2i$ and $2i + 1$ respectively. We can therefore navigate from parent to child and back through the tree by simple calculation of the index. It is also straightforward to calculate the size of a subtree rooted at node i, given only i and n. Insertion or deletion of the next/last node on the bottom now is trivial. As a consequence the structure is an absolute delight for the data type priority queue.

All this comes, in large measure, because there is only one tree on n nodes. In the case of arbitrary binary trees, we have the nth Catalan number, $C_n = \binom{2n}{n}/(n+1)$ or about 4^n, to distinguish among. In supporting a specific abstract data type, say dictionary, we can go to implicit representations of AVL trees, using the relative values of keys to encode pointer information [11]. This obviously stretches the limits of practicality in time space tradeoffs. It is also outside our realm of interest here, as we are concerned primarily with the representation of a tree without any assumption regarding the relative values in the nodes. As a consequence, just to say what tree we are dealing with requires at least $\lg C_n$ or close to $2n$ bits.

Jacobson [6, 7] proposed an encoding based on the construction of Zaks' sequences [17] and the work of others including Lee et al [8] to map the nodes of a tree onto the integers $1..n$. The idea is essentially the same as that of the heap ordering, appropriately extended to handle arbitrary binary trees. Each node is mapped to its position in the level ordering of the (basic) tree. To indicate the structure of the tree we extend the n node tree to one of $2n + 1$ nodes by appending leaves in all positions in which a child is missing in the original tree. We now consider the level ordering of the nodes in this extended tree and represent the tree by the $2n + 1$ bit pattern with a 1 for an internal (original) node and a 0 for each newly appended leaf. If we apply this procedure to a tree with the heap shape, we have the encoding $1^n 0^{n+1}$. The navigation in the general case is surprisingly like that of a standard heap, with a little help from the bit encoding. We need, however, a couple of operations on bit vectors:

- $rank(x) =$ the number of 1's up to and including position x
  and
- $select(x) =$ the position of the xth 1.

($xrank0$ and $select0$ can be defined analogously to deal with the 0's, and will be of use in encoding more general trees.)

Now we see that children and parents of node x can be found as

- $leftchild(x) = 2\, rank(x)$
- $rightchild(x) = 2\, rank(x) + 1$
- $parent(x) = select(\lfloor x/2 \rfloor)$.

2.1 Representing Ordered Rooted Trees

By an ordered rooted tree we mean a tree with a distinguished root and an ordering on the children of any node. As is well known, the added feature of a node having an arbitrary number of children precisely balances with the loss of the feature that a single child is not distinguished as left or right. These two classes of trees on n nodes are isomorphic, mapping a left child to a first child and a right child to a next sibling. Unfortunately, this mapping is not convenient for finding the ith child or its parent. The binary tree representation suggested above would infer i rank/select operations for the task. Instead Jacobson proposed an encoding due to Read [13], again based on level orderings. For convenience a super-root with one child, the root of the given tree, is added. We represent a node with k children by k 1's and a 0. Concatenating these node representations by level order of the tree, we see the ith 1 is the indication of node i's "birth" by its parent, while the ith 0 indicates its "death", having indicated all its children. Now we have

- $degree(x) = select0(rank(x) + 1) - select0(rank(x)) - 1$
- $child(x) = select0(rank(x)) + i$
- $parent(x) = select(rank0(x))$

2.2 Implementing Rank and Select

Jacobson's goal was to perform basic tree navigation by inspecting $O(\lg n)$ bits per step. As a consequence, the rank operation part of his construction translates to $O(1)$ time under a $\lg n$ bit word model. Jacobson's select, however, takes $\Theta(\lg\lg n)$ time as a consequence of a binary search over $(\lg n)^2$ bits, and so requires reworking. Clark and the author [2, 3] provide the enhancement. The implementation of both operations involve our major technical theme, the use of subtables. Jacobson's rank algorithm uses two subtables of about $n \lg \lg n / \lg n$ extra bits each. The first suffices to give the rank of each $(\lg n)^2$rd bit in the vector. The second uses $\lg \lg n$ bits to record the rank of each $(\lg n)$th bit within these subranges. This reduces to ranges of size $\lg n$, and so, we can finish off the process either by a careful coding or by using tables of size $O(n^{1/2})$ to record all possible answers on half-words. Handling the select operation in constant time is a bit more subtle, but again is based on a subtable approach. Summarizing these results:

A binary tree on n nodes, or an ordered rooted tree on n nodes, can be represented in $2n+o(n)$ bits so that each node is mapped to a distinct integer location in the range 1 to n, and that given the location associated with a node, one can determine to location of its parent, the number of children it has, and the location of any specified child in constant time.

The author's interest in compact representations of trees arose from the problem of finding compact encodings of suffix tries. The method presented here leads to a near optimal representation and constant time navigation. From an implementation point of view, it has the drawback of complication. For the particular application it has another difficulty, namely that when one does a search for a phrase, a successful search gives a subtree corresponding to all matches. If a phrase has large number of matches, one may first like to know how many there are. Hence the size of the subtree at a given node is a very useful operation. It would not appear that the representation we have outlined lends itself to this. As a consequence of both these reasons, Clark [2] chose to implement a different encoding, also explored by Jacobson, although it does not support the operation of finding a parent directly. Using this approach we store each subtree by encoding

- *small*: a flag to denote which subtree is smaller
- *subsize*: the size of the smaller subtree using some prefix encoding
- *Leftsubtree*: recursive encoding of the left subtree, of it has more than 1 node
- *Rightsubtree*: recursive encoding of the right subtree, of it has more than 1 node.

In interpreting such an encoding it is absolutely imperative that the space taken for any tree of a given size be the same, and that this size be easily determined. This is crucial, for example, in determining where the encoding of a right subtree begins. The interesting part, however, is the representation of *subsize*. First note that if we were simply to encode the size of the left subtree, then the degenerate tree that runs to the left would take $\Theta(n \lg n)$ bits. The flag *small* eliminates this problem. However, *subsize* must be represented in some manner so that small values are encoded very succinctly, and the code grows slowly with the value of *subsize*. Given that it will not be known how many bits are in this encoding, it seems well advised to use a prefix code, one in which the code for a value cannot be the prefix of the code for another. Using the simple approach of storing the subsize k with $\lg k$ zeroes followed by the number in binary (the latter must start with a 1), the entire tree can be represented in about $3n$ bits. One is tempted to try encoding $\lg k$ itself in binary and ultimately getting to the well known game of trying to guess a number, upon which we have no a priori upper bound, in the smallest number of binary questions. The optimal solution (for large k) requires $\sum \lg^{(i)} k$ guesses or bits in the problem at hand (Here $\lg^{(i)}$ denotes the lg function iterated i times, e.g. $lg^{(3)}k = \lg\lg\lg k$). Unfortunately this does not help. The problem is in encoding small values well. Suppose we do something silly, like take 3 bits to encode the value zero, then with the *small* flag we take 4 bits to say a tree of size n has a left subtree of size $n - 1$, leading to a $4n$ encoding of the tree. With care in the encoding, particularly of the small values, we can however, drop the $3n$ bit encoding to about $2.75n$ bits. Perhaps this is not enough to justify the complication, but it gives a feel for the limits to the gains. This issue of careful encoding of small numbers occurs in a number of problems. One interesting example is in trying to tighten the $O(n)$ term in the Schaffer-Sedgewick [14] average case analysis of Floyd's version [4] of heapsort.

3   Representing Subsets of a Bounded Universe

The other problem noted in the introduction is that of representing a simple subset of a finite universe, k elements from a universe of size n. As we noted, a bit vector is ideal if about half the elements are present. Fully encoding each element in $\lg n$ bits is near optimal for a sparse table and indeed perfect hashing techniques can be tuned to achieve both constant time and almost minimal space. The ground in between was explored by Brodnik and the author [1]. The approach taken is to use the two obvious methods when the set to be stored is, respectively, large or small. When k is in the range $n^{1-\epsilon}$ to $n/\lg n$ or so, elements are mapped to $k/\lg n$ buckets corresponding to $\lg n$ consecutive values in the universe. One quickly considers recursing on the universe of size $\lg n$, and one would appear to be off to a $\lg^* n$ solution by recursing until the problem size is down to a constant. However, after just two iterations the entire universe is down to $\lg n$ elements. At this point any tight encoding of the subset to be represented can be used as an index into one fixed and very small table. As a consequence we get a solution in constant time and essentially the minimal space of $\lg \binom{n}{k}$ bits.

4   Conclusion

In this brief overview we have discussed two examples of representing static structures succinctly while still permitting the basic search and navigation operations to be performed in constant time. Such problems and some of the approaches suggested for their solutions may well be of increasing importance as the size of the problems we attack continues to grow. While the focus has been on asymptotically large problems, the essence of the methods can be implemented to show real benefit on problems of even moderate size. On the other hand, problem sizes no longer seem moderate. For years I had told my students that $\lg \lg n$ was 5, as one found it hard to imagine storing a set of more than 4 billion (U.S.) elements. Well, we passed that threshold a few of years ago. $\lg \lg n$ is now 6, I don't expect to see 7.

References

1. A. Brodnik and J. I. Munro, *Membership in Constant Time and Minimum Space*, Proc. Algorithms - ESA '94, LNCS 855 (1994) 72-81.
2. D. R. Clark, Compact Pat Trees, manuscript, University of Waterloo (1996).
3. D. R. Clark and J. I. Munro, Succinct Representation of Trees, in preparation, University of Waterloo (1996).
4. R. W. Floyd, *Algorithm 245: Treesort 3*, Communications of the ACM, **7** (1964) 701.
5. G. H. Gonnet, R. A. Baeza-Yates and T. Snider, Lexicographic Indices for Text: Inverted Files vs. Pat Trees, Tech. Rpt. OED-91-01, Centre for the New OED, University of Waterloo (1991).
6. G. Jacobson, *Space Efficient Static Trees and Graphs*, Proc. 30th IEEE Symp. on Foundations of Computer Science, (1989) 549-554.
7. G. Jacobson, Succinct Data Structures, Tech. Rpt. CMU-CS-89-112, Carnegie Mellon University (1989).
8. C. C. Lee, D. T. Lee and C. K. Wong, *Generating Binary Trees of Bounded Height*, Acta Informatica, **23** (1986) 529-544.
9. U. Manber and G. Myers, *Suffix Arrays: A New Method for On-Line String Searches*, SIAM Journal on Computing, **22**(5) (1993) 935-948.
10. D. R. Morrison, *Patricia - Practical Algorithm to Retrieve Information Coded in Alphnumeric*, Journal of the ACM, **15**(4) (1968) 514-534.
11. J. I. Munro, *An Implicit Data Structure Supporting Insertion, Deletion, and Search in $O(log^2 n)$ Time*, J. Computer and System Sciences, **33**, (1986) 66-74.
12. J. I. Munro and H. Suwanda, *Implicit Data Structures for Fast Search and Update*, J. Computer and System Sciences, **21**, (1980) 236-250.
13. R. C. Read, *The Coding of Various Kinds of Unlabelled Trees*, In R. C. Read (ed.) Graph Theory and Computing, Academic Press, (1972) 153-182.
14. R. Schaffer and R. Sedgewick, *The Analysis of Heapsort*, Journal of Algorithms, **15**(1), (1993) 76-100.
15. P. Weiner, *Linear Pattern Match Algorithms*, Proc. 14th IEEE Symp. on Switching and Automata Theory, (1973) 1-11.
16. J. W. J. Williams, *Algorithm 232, Heapsort*, Communications of the ACM, **7** (1964) 347-348.
17. S. Zaks, *Lexicographic Generation of Ordered Trees*, Theoretical Computer Science, **10**(1), (1980) 63-82.

Mechanized Formal Methods: Progress and Prospects*

John Rushby

Computer Science Laboratory, SRI International,
Menlo Park, CA 94025, USA

Abstract. In the decade of the 1990s, formal methods have progressed from an academic curiosity at best, and a target of ridicule at worst, to a point where the leading manufacturer of microprocessors has indicated that its next design will be formally verified. In this short paper, I sketch a plausible history of the developments that led to this transformation, present a snapshot of the current state of the practice, and indicate some promising directions for the future. Mindful of the title of this conference, I suggest how formal methods might have an impact on software similar to that which they have had on hardware.

1 The Past

In their early days (the 1970s—though continuing to the present in some places), formal methods were associated with proofs of program correctness. This is not only a very costly and difficult exercise—it requires formalizing the semantics of real programming languages, and dealing with the scale and characteristics of real imperative programs—but it also adds very little value: traditional methods of code review and testing are highly effective and very few coding bugs of any significance escape detection. For example, of 197 critical faults detected during integration and system testing of the Voyager and Galileo spacecraft, just 3 were coding errors [17]. The large majority of faults arise in requirements, interfaces, and intrinsically difficult design problems (e.g., fault tolerance, and the coordination of concurrent activities). In the spacecraft data just cited, approximately 50% of faults were traced to requirements (mainly omissions), and 25% to each of interfaces and design.

During the 1980s, attention shifted from program correctness to the use of formalism in specifications, exemplified by approaches such as Z [32] and VDM [16]. Although these methods initially stressed the role of proof in development, they came to be used mainly as specification languages, and their advocates commended the utility of mathematical concepts such as sets, functions, and relations in constructing precise yet abstract descriptions of computational systems. The problem with this approach is that it is not necessary to be specifically *formal* to

---

* This work was supported by the Air Force Office of Scientific Research, Air Force Materiel Command, USAF, under contract F49620-95-C0044 and by the National Science Foundation under contract CCR-9509931.

make use of such mathematical modeling techniques; conversely, in the absence of formal proof, there are few tangible benefits to a strictly formal approach. By failing to exploit the singular characteristic of truly formal methods—namely, their ability to support deduction—specification-oriented formalisms missed the opportunity to combine mathematical modeling with calculation in the manner that has been so productive in other engineering disciplines.

The value of formal deduction is that it enables many questions about properties of formally specified requirements and designs to be settled by a systematic process that has the character of calculation. The reasons for favoring calculation over informal reasoning or trial and error experimentation are the same in computer science as in other engineering disciplines: calculation allows the properties of designs to be predicted and evaluated prior to construction, it allows analyses to be checked by others, enables large problems to be tackled in a systematic manner, and opens the door to mechanization. And in most engineering disciplines, it is mechanization that releases the full potential of mathematical modeling and calculation: the highly efficient wings of a modern airplane could not be designed without massive mechanization of computational fluid dynamics, finite element analysis, and several other branches of applied mathematics.

It was the arrival of efficient techniques for model checking in the early 1990s [18] (and related methods such as language inclusion) that first made large-scale mechanized calculations a practical reality for formal methods and demonstrated their utility to a wide audience. No less important than the techniques that made model checking practical was the change in approach and outlook that its use engendered. The limited expressiveness of the temporal logics employed in model checking means that it is seldom possible to use them to fully characterize the functionality required of a system; instead, attention is focussed on important properties that it should posses. Similarly, because model checking methods can only explore a limited, finite state space, the full system description must generally be considerably abstracted and simplified before subjecting it to model checking. Partly because of these limitations (and partly because it is able to provide excellent diagnostic information in the form of counterexamples), model checking has generally focused on *in*correctness—on finding bugs—rather than on trying to establish correctness. And find bugs it did: because model checking is well-suited to concurrent systems, it was immediately applied to some of the hardest problems in system design, such as multiprocessor cache-coherence protocols, where "high-value bugs" were quickly detected [7].

The changes in approach introduced by model checking opened up new opportunities for all formal methods: whereas previously the goal had been to specify the full functionality required, there was now seen to be a useful spectrum of desired properties; whereas previously the goal had been to describe the system in all its details, there was now seen to be value in isolating key problems and aggressively abstracting away as many details as possible; whereas previously the goal had been to establish unequivocal correctness, there was now seen to be a variety of other useful purposes that could be served by formal analysis; and whereas previously the applications had generally been to routine designs (see, for example, the survey [8]), there was now an enthusiasm for applying formal methods to the hardest and most difficult problems of design.

Mechanized formal methods based on theorem proving, which had become modestly effective by the mid 1980s and were continually improving, benefited from the change in attitude—and the spur of competition—that came with model checking. Decision procedures for basic theories such as linear arithmetic and equality received renewed attention and acceptance, and integrated combinations of decision procedures, rewriting, and customized tactics achieved significant automation and efficiency on interesting classes of problems [22]. Most importantly, the practitioners of these approaches to formal methods followed the lead of the model checkers in applying them to complex, real-world systems [20, 35].

2   The Present

An idea of the current capabilities and accomplishments of mechanized formal methods can be obtained by considering two examples from hardware design.

The Pentium FDIV bug, which attracted a great deal of public interest, also caught the attention of the formal verification community—not least because it caused Intel to take a $475 million charge against revenues. The bug was in the lookup table of an SRT divider [25]. Binary Decision Diagrams (BDDs) have been used successfully to verify many kinds of digital circuits—but not multipliers and dividers, where they grow exponentially large [3]. Nonetheless, Bryant was able to verify a single iteration of an SRT circuit using BDDs [4]. Explosive growth of the BDD representation has generally also precluded application of symbolic model checking to dividers; however, by using a different "word level" representation, Clarke, Khaira, and Zhao were able to apply model checking to this problem [6]. Clarke, German, and Zhao were also able to verify an SRT divider using a special-purpose theorem prover based on the Mathematica symbolic algebra system [5]. Using the PVS general-purpose verification system [21], Rueß, Shankar, and Srivas gave a formally verified treatment of the general theory of SRT division, and then verified a particular circuit and lookup table [27]. While being more general, the theorem proving treatments achieved a level of automation and efficiency comparable to the BDD and model checking approaches, and were equally adept at catching errors in the tables. However, all of these treatments dealt only with the fixed-point core of the divider, and not with the issues of IEEE-compliant floating point representation. Miner and Leathrum extended the PVS treatment to include IEEE-compliance, generalized the whole development to encompass the broader class of subtractive division algorithms that includes SRT, and presented a methodology that enabled specific algorithms to be debugged and verified quite easily—which they demonstrated on various SRT tables [19].

Cache coherence protocols for distributed shared memory multiprocessors are notoriously difficult to design. Some of the early successes with symbolic model checking were in its application to this type of problem. As interest shifted from the "snoopy" to the more scalable—and much more complicated—"directory-based" protocols, the state-explosion problem became quite severe. One response was to "downscale" (aggressively simplify) the problem, so that, for example, only two or three processors, one address, and a 1-bit data word are considered. Another was to use the various symmetries that exist in the problem to allow different, but equivalent, states to be merged. Using these and other techniques, model checkers based on both explicit state-enumeration and symbolic representations are able to tackle cache-coherence problems sufficiently well to be used in the design process for these systems [2, 10]. But although they are effective for detecting bugs, the severely downscaled models used in model checking cannot serve to verify the general case. Theorem proving techniques should be able to do this, but the difficulty of creating appropriate abstractions and sufficiently strong invariants, combined with the labor involved in guiding the theorem prover, had discouraged their application to realistic cache-coherence protocols. Recently, however, by using a method called "aggregation" to guide construction of the abstraction function, Park and Dill have been able, using PVS in a quite straightforward manner, to verify the behavior of the protocol used in the Stanford FLASH processor [24]. Furthermore, using the Murϕ explicit state-enumeration system they were able to construct an executable model for the non-sequentially-consistent memory behavior of the processor. In similar work for the Sparc V9 memory model, they were able to verify the behavior of synchronization code using Murϕ, and were able to verify the executable Murϕ model against its axiomatic specification using PVS [23].

The interesting feature of these examples is the diversity of approaches employed—and the diversity would be even greater if I had considered other examples such as pipelines, microcode, communications and switching protocols, or hybrid systems. There simply is no single best method: we are dealing with problems that are at the limit of what is computationally feasible, and different applications yield to different approaches. Thus, symbolic model checking using BDDs works well for some problems, but explicit state enumeration is better for others; some state spaces can be reduced significantly by symmetry reductions, others require partial-order reductions; some problems are best dealt with by model checking, others are better suited to theorem proving.

Just as different approaches work better for different problems, so different approaches work better for the *same* problem at different stages of its "verification lifecycle." When first encountered, a design (or its formalization) will often be full of bugs. These should be identified as quickly and as cheaply as possible. Methods that require relatively little preparation, such as typechecking, animation, or explicit state enumeration are effective here. Once the simple bugs have been eliminated, it becomes necessary to explore more and more of the state space to discover those that remain, and explicit state exploration methods that use hashing, and symbolic model checking methods, start to become more effective. Once the complete state space of downscaled instances of the problem can be explored without finding a bug, then the aggressiveness of the simplifications can be reduced, and the size of the problem instances can be increased. The "state explosion" problem is likely to hit at this point, and reduction methods based on symmetry, partial orders, or abstraction may need to be invoked. When the largest problem instances that can be examined by finite state methods no longer reveal bugs, then it is time to consider theorem proving. For concurrent systems, it is generally necessary to develop abstractions and to strengthen the desired invariant to obtain one that is inductive. Special-purpose tools can help with these activities, and finite-state methods can be invoked during the proof process to check that proposed invariants really are so, and that subgoals are true (on finite instances) [11].

Different methods come into play on a single problem as easy bugs are eliminated and those that remain become harder to find; in a related progression, different methods come into play in the treatment of *classes* of problems as our understanding and techniques improve. For example, as enumerated above, treatments of SRT division evolved from BDD-based analysis of individual iterations, to treatment of the core of a specific algorithm by special-purpose theorem proving, to general treatment of the entire class of algorithms with a general-purpose theorem prover.

3 The Future

I offer some suggestions on likely, or promising, directions for future developments in mechanized formal methods under two headings: applications to software, and tools.

3.1 Applications to Software

Compared to hardware, software is more of a challenge for successful application of mechanized formal methods. Hardware has a relatively small number of stereotypical problems (pipeline control, floating point ALUs, microcode, cache coherence), so that the cost of developing really effective solutions can be recouped over many applications, whereas software has a vastly larger supply of problems and a correspondingly smaller community of interest for any one of them. Nonetheless, we can adopt some of the strategies that seem to have been successful for hardware.

- *Go where the bugs are.* Formal methods have been effective for hardware because their use has been targeted at areas where they can offer a real payoff: areas that experience has shown to be error-prone and where other methods are ineffective. The targeted areas concern some of the *hardest* challenges in design (e.g., the stereotypical problems mentioned above). For software, correspondingly difficult and worthwhile challenges include those where local design decisions have complex global consequences, such as the fault-tolerance and real-time properties of concurrent distributed systems, and those where independently designed systems interact, such as the problems of feature interactions, protocol stacks, and component interfaces. It is generally most productive to examine these issues at the level of the algorithms concerned, rather than at the detailed design or coding level. It also helps to target applications where the costs of bugs are unacceptably high. These include applications that share with hardware the characteristic that design errors cannot be repaired in the field (e.g., embedded systems in consumer products), and those where failure is intolerable (e.g., safety and other kinds of critical systems).

- *Target the early lifecycle.* The requirements for hardware (especially processors) are quite simple (i.e., "implement a given instruction set architecture"), whereas those for software are generally complex (e.g., "control air traffic") and subject to change. The most damaging and costly errors discovered late in the software development lifecycle can usually be traced back to faulty requirements. Consequently, requirements validation consumes considerable resources (in avionics, for example, more than half the development costs can go into requirements; programming, in contrast, consumes less than 10%). Formal methods are singularly well-adapted to the specification and analysis of requirements, because they allow precision without premature detail (unlike pseudocode and prototyping), and they allow useful analyses to be performed on very abstract or incomplete descriptions [29].

- *Use powerful tools, and a spectrum of methods.* Without tools, formal methods are just documentation; it is tools that make formal methods useful, and powerful tools that make them productive. Many of the tools that have been effective in applications of formal methods to hardware can also be used for software (see, for example, [33], where the SMV model checker is applied to a software requirements specification); alternatively, *ideas* from those tools can be incorporated into new tools that are specifically tailored to the characteristics of software [15]. Even less than for hardware, no single tool or method provides universally effective support for all the diverse applications of formal methods to software, so a spectrum of tools and methods should be employed.

3.2 Tool Building

As noted several times already, most applications of mechanized formal methods require a range of capabilities and make use of a number of tools. Rather than loose integration of a number of different tools, however, what is really required is tight integration of a number of different capabilities [28, 31]. For example, loose integration of a theorem prover and a model checker might allow one to use a single specification of a problem and to examine specific instances with the model checker and to prove the general case with the theorem prover, whereas tight integration might allow the theorem prover actively to *use* the model checker—so that the theorem prover could set up the induction to prove the general case, with the base case and inductive step then being discharged by model checking [30]. Such an integration of theorem proving and model checking has been achieved [26], but it required extending the implementation of a complex verification system. Future systems should be designed in a much more "open" manner, so that components can be added, modified, interconnected, and accessed in a modular fashion. For example, an attractive application of formal reasoning to software requirements is to check consistency and completeness of the conditions that label the rows and columns of tabular specifications [14]. Depending on the logic and theories used in specifying these conditions, the deductive capabilities needed to perform the checks range from propositional tautology checking, though decision procedures for ground linear arithmetic, to full interactive theorem proving. When tautology checking proved inadequate for an example derived from the TCAS II specification [12], Czerny and Heimdahl turned to the PVS verification system in order to make use of its decision procedures. However, because those decision procedures could not be accessed separately, they had to invoke the entire PVS system, which entailed more baggage and less performance than they desired [13]. What is really needed is an open environment that provides access to components such as decision procedures and the other building blocks of theorem provers and model checkers, and in which customized combinations can be quickly constructed. The hub of such an environment must be a theorem prover, since that is what has the capability to check that problems are decomposed appropriately, that constraints on the application of certain procedures are satisfied, and that all the pieces come together to solve the whole problem in a sound manner [9]. In collaboration with David Dill of Stanford University, we are about to begin construction of such an environment.

4 Conclusion

These are exciting times for mechanized formal methods, with opportunities for rapid and significant progress in the capabilities of tools and the quality and scale of their applications. Theoretical research can assist these developments by, for example, providing better characterizations for the complexities of the various problems and algorithms encountered (almost every problem in model checking and theorem proving is NP-hard or worse), and by identifying useful special cases that admit fast solutions.

References

Papers by SRI authors are generally available from http://www.csl.sri.com/fm.html.

[1] Rajeev Alur and Thomas A. Henzinger, editors. *Computer-Aided Verification, CAV '96*, volume 1102 of *Lecture Notes in Computer Science*, New Brunswick, NJ, July/August 1996. Springer-Verlag.

[2] Ásgeir Th. Eiríksson and Ken L. McMillan. Using formal verification/analysis methods on the critical path in system design: A case study. In Pierre Wolper, editor, *Computer-Aided Verification, CAV '95*, volume 939 of *Lecture Notes in Computer Science*, pages 367–380, Liege, Belgium, June 1995. Springer-Verlag.

[3] Randal E. Bryant. Symbolic boolean manipulation with ordered binary-decision diagrams. *ACM Computing Surveys*, 24(3):293–318, September 1992.

[4] Randal E. Bryant. Bit-level analysis of an SRT divider circuit. In *Proceedings of the 33rd Design Automation Conference*, pages 661–665, Las Vegas, NV, June 1996.

[5] E. M. Clarke, S. M. German, and X. Zhao. Verifying the SRT division algorithm using theorem proving techniques. In Alur and Henzinger [1], pages 111–122.

[6] E. M. Clarke, Manpreet Khaira, and Xudong Zhao. Word level symbolic model checking—avoiding the Pentium FDIV error. In *Proceedings of the 33rd Design Automation Conference*, pages 645–648, Las Veqas, NV, June 1996.

[7] Edmund M. Clarke, Orna Grumberg, Hiromi Haraishi, Somesh Jha, David E. Long, Kenneth L. McMillan, and Linda A. Ness. Verification of the Futurebus+ cache coherence protocol. *Formal Methods in System Design*, 6(2):217–232, March 1995.

[8] Dan Craigen, Susan Gerhart, and Ted Ralston. Formal methods reality check: Industrial usage. *IEEE Transactions on Software Engineering*, 21(2):90–98, February 1995.

[9] David A. Cyrluk and Mandayam K. Srivas. Theorem proving: Not an esoteric diversion, but the unifying framework for industrial verification. In *International Conference on Computer Design: VLSI in Computers and Processors (ICCD '95)*, pages 538–544, Austin, TX, October 1995. IEEE Computer Society.

[10] David L. Dill, Andreas J. Drexler, Alan J. Hu, and C. Han Yang. Protocol verification as a hardware design aid. In *International Conference on Computer Design: VLSI in Computers and Processors*, pages 522–525. IEEE Computer Society, October 1992. Cambridge, MA.

[11] Klaus Havelund and N. Shankar. Experiments in theorem proving and model checking for protocol verification. In *Formal Methods Europe FME '96*, volume 1051 of *Lecture Notes in Computer Science*, pages 662–681, Oxford, UK, March 1996. Springer-Verlag.

[12] Mats P. E. Heimdahl. Experiences and lessons from the analysis of TCAS II. In Steven J. Zeil, editor, *International Symposium on Software Testing and Analysis (ISSTA)*, pages 79–83, San Diego, CA, January 1996. Association for Computing Machinery.

[13] Mats P. E. Heimdahl and Barbara J. Czerny. Using PVS to analyze hierarchical state-based requirements for completeness and consistency. In *IEEE High-Assurance Systems Engineering Workshop (HASE '96)*, Niagara on the Lake, Canada, October 1996. To appear.

[14] Mats P. E. Heimdahl and Nancy G. Leveson. Completeness and consistency in hierarchical state-based requirements. *IEEE Transactions on Software Engineering*, 22(6):363–377, June 1996.

[15] Daniel Jackson and Craig A. Damon. Elements of style: Analyzing a software design feature with a counterexample detector. *IEEE Transactions on Software Engineering*, 22(7):484–495, July 1996.

[16] Cliff B. Jones. *Systematic Software Development Using VDM*. Prentice Hall International Series in Computer Science. Prentice Hall, Hemel Hempstead, UK, second edition, 1990.

[17] Robyn R. Lutz. Analyzing software requirements errors in safety-critical embedded systems. In *IEEE International Symposium on Requirements Engineering*, pages 126–133, San Diego, CA, January 1993.

[18] Kenneth L. McMillan. *Symbolic Model Checking*. Kluwer Academic Publishers, Boston, MA, 1993.

[19] Paul S. Miner and James F. Leathrum, Jr. Verification of IEEE compliant subtractive division algorithms. In Srivas [34].

[20] J S. Moore. ACL2 theorems about commercial microprocessors. In Srivas [34].

[21] S. Owre, S. Rajan, J.M. Rushby, N. Shankar, and M.K. Srivas. PVS: Combining specification, proof checking, and model checking. In Alur and Henzinger [1], pages 411–414.

[22] Sam Owre, John Rushby, Natarajan Shankar, and Friedrich von Henke. Formal verification for fault-tolerant architectures: Prolegomena to the design of PVS. *IEEE Transactions on Software Engineering*, 21(2):107–125, February 1995.

[23] Seungjoon Park and David L. Dill. An executable specification, analyzer and verifier for RMO (Relaxed Memory Order). In *7th ACM Symposium on Parallel Algorithms and Architectures*, pages 34–51, July 1995.

[24] Seungjoon Park and David L. Dill. Verification of the FLASH cache coherence protocol by aggregation of distributed transactions. In *8th ACM Symposium on Parallel Algorithms and Architectures*, pages 288–296, Padua, Italy, June 1996.

[25] Vaughan Pratt. Anatomy of the Pentium bug. In *TAPSOFT '95: Theory and Practice of Software Development*, volume 915 of *Lecture Notes in Computer Science*, pages 97–107, Aarhus, Denmark, May 1995. Springer-Verlag.

[26] S. Rajan, N. Shankar, and M.K. Srivas. An integration of model-checking with automated proof checking. In Pierre Wolper, editor, *Computer-Aided Verification, CAV '95*, volume 939 of *Lecture Notes in Computer Science*, pages 84–97, Liege, Belgium, June 1995. Springer-Verlag.

[27] H. Rueß, N. Shankar, and M. K. Srivas. Modular verification of SRT division. In Alur and Henzinger [1], pages 123–134.

[28] John Rushby. Automated deduction and formal methods. In Alur and Henzinger [1], pages 169–183.

[29] John Rushby. Calculating with requirements. In *3rd IEEE International Symposium on Requirements Engineering*, Annapolis, MD, January 1997. IEEE Computer Society. To appear.

[30] N. Shankar. Computer-aided computing. In Bernhard Möller, editor, *Mathematics of Program Construction '95*, volume 947 of *Lecture Notes in Computer Science*, pages 50–66. Springer-Verlag, 1995.

[31] Natarajan Shankar. Unifying verification paradigms. In Bengt Jonsson and Joachim Parrow, editors, *Formal Techniques in Real-Time and Fault-Tolerant Systems*, volume 1135 of *Lecture Notes in Computer Science*, pages 22–39, Uppsala, Sweden, September 1996. Springer-Verlag.

[32] J. M. Spivey, editor. *The Z Notation: A Reference Manual*. Prentice Hall International Series in Computer Science. Prentice Hall, Hemel Hempstead, UK, second edition, 1993.

[33] Tirumale Sreemani and Joanne M. Atlee. Feasibility of model checking software requirements. In *COMPASS '96 (Proceedings of the Eleventh Annual Conference on Computer Assurance)*, pages 77–88, Gaithersburg, MD, June 1996. IEEE Washington Section.

[34] M. Srivas, editor. *Formal Methods in Computer-Aided Design (FMCAD '96)*, Palo Alto, CA, November 1996. To appear.

[35] Mandayam K. Srivas and Steven P. Miller. Formal verification of the AAMP5 microprocessor. In Michael G. Hinchey and Jonathan P. Bowen, editors, *Applications of Formal Methods*, Prentice Hall International Series in Computer Science, chapter 7, pages 125–180. Prentice Hall, Hemel Hempstead, UK, 1995.

The views and conclusions contained herein are those of the author and should not be interpreted as necessarily representing the official policies or endorsements, either expressed or implied, of the Air Force Office of Scientific Research or the U.S. Government.

The Parameter Space of the d-step Conjecture

J. C. Lagarias, AT&T Bell Laboratories, Murray Hill, New Jersey 07974.
E-mail: *jcl@research.att.com.*

N. Prabhu,[1] Purdue University, West Lafayette, IN 47907.
E-mail: *prabhu@ecn.purdue.edu*

J. A. Reeds, AT&T Bell Laboratories, Murray Hill, NJ 07974.
E-mail: *reeds@research.att.com*

1. Introduction

The *Hirsch conjecture* is one of the fundamental open problems in the theory of convex polytopes. If $\Delta(d, n)$ denotes the least upper bound on the diameter of the graph of a (d, n)-polytope, (*i.e.*, a d-polytope having n facets) then the *Hirsch conjecture* asserts that

$$\Delta(d, n) \leq n - d .$$

For a comprehensive review of the Hirsch conjecture and its relatives, as well as for the references to many of the results that we cite below, we direct the reader to [4]. The *d-step conjecture* is the special case $n = 2d$, and asserts that

$$\Delta(d, 2d) = d .$$

(The d-cube shows that $\Delta(d, 2d) \geq d$.) Klee and Walkup [4] showed that the truth of the d-step conjecture for all d implies the truth of the (apparently more general) Hirsch conjecture for all n and d. They also showed that $\Delta(d, n)$ is always attained by some simple (d, n)-polytope, which implies that to prove the d-step conjecture it suffices to prove it for simple polytopes. There is a further simplification due to Klee and Walkup [4]. Given a simple $(d, 2d)$-polytope P two of its vertices $\mathbf{w}_1$ and $\mathbf{w}_2$ are said to be *antipodal*, if disjoint sets of d facets are incident on them. Such a triple $(P, \mathbf{w}_1, \mathbf{w}_2)$ is called a *d-dimensional Dantzig figure*. Klee and Walkup [4] showed that $\Delta(d, 2d)$ is the length of the shortest edge path between the antipodal vertices of some d-dimensional Dantzig figure $(P, \mathbf{w}_1, \mathbf{w}_2)$. Thus if $\#(P, \mathbf{w}_1, \mathbf{w}_2)$ denotes the number of d-step paths between $\mathbf{w}_1$ and $\mathbf{w}_2$ in $G(P)$, then the *d-step conjecture* may be restated as

$$\#(P, \mathbf{w}_1, \mathbf{w}_2) \geq 1$$

for all Dantzig figures $(P, \mathbf{w}_1, \mathbf{w}_2)$ in $\mathbb{R}^d$.
While various special cases of the d-step and Hirsch conjectures have been proved, several natural generalizations of these conjectures are known to be

---

[1]Supported in part by an NSF Research Initiation Award.

false. For example the d-step conjecture fails for unbounded polyhedra in dimension 4 (Klee and Walkup [4]), and extended versions of the dual formulation of the d-step conjecture fail to hold for triangulated spheres in high dimensions (Mani and Walkup [4]). The large body of such counter-examples contributed to the consensus view that the d-step conjecture is also false for large enough d. Klee and Kleinschmidt [4] write: "We strongly suspect that the d-step conjecture fails when the dimension is as large as 12."

This paper presents a theoretical framework and experimental data suggesting that the d-step conjecture could be true in all dimensions. The theoretical framework includes a parameter space for a set of 'reduced' Dantzig figures, that covers all the combinatorial equivalence classes of Dantzig figures. We show that the d-step conjecture $\Delta(d, 2d) = d$ is equivalent to the following statement: For each "general position" $(d - 1) \times (d - 1)$ real matrix M there exist two matrices Q_τ, Q_σ drawn from a finite group $\hat{S}_d$ of $(d - 1) \times (d - 1)$ matrices isomorphic to the symmetric group $\text{Sym}(d)$ on d letters, such that $Q_\tau M Q_\sigma$ has the Gaussian elimination factorization $L^{-1}U$ in which L and U are lower triangular and upper triangular matrices, respectively, that have *positive* non-triangular elements. If $\#(M)$ is the number of pairs $(\sigma, \tau) \in \text{Sym}(d) \times \text{Sym}(d)$ giving a positive $L^{-1}U$ factorization, then $\#(M)$ equals the number of d-step paths between the antipodal vertices of an associated Dantzig figure. One consequence is that $\#(M) \leq d!$. We report on extensive numerical experiments for $3 \leq d \leq 15$. All of the numerical experiments suggested that $\#(M) \geq 2^{d-1}$, and we had initially suggested the general validity of the inequality in the *strong d-step conjecture*. Holt and Klee have shown that the strong d-step conjecture fails for $d \geq 5$. The d-step conjecture however still remains open.

The paper is organized as follows. In Section 2 we describe the parameter space $\mathcal{M}_d$ for the simplex basis exchange conjecture. In Section 3 we describe the Gaussian elimination sign conjecture and its equivalence to the d-step conjecture. In Section 4 we describe a result about sign patterns in Gaussian elimination factorizations. In Section 5 we describe computational experiments concerning the Gaussian elimination sign conjecture which computed values $\#(M)$ for various distributions of M. The proofs of the Lemmas and Theorems stated in this paper as well as a more detailed discussion can be found in [6].

2. Parameter Space for the Simplex Exchange Conjecture

First we recall a few definitions. A *simplicial basis* B of $\mathbb{R}^{d-1}$ is an ordered set of d vectors $B = \{\mathbf{b}_1, \ldots, \mathbf{b}_d\}$ that form the vertices of a $(d-1)$-simplex containing 0 in its interior. A finite set of vectors A in $\mathbb{R}^m$ is said to be a *Haar set* if every subset of size m in A is linearly independent. A pair of simplicial bases, B and B', is said to be in *general position* if $B \cup B'$ is a Haar set. It's known that for each $d \geq 2$, the d-step conjecture is equivalent to the following simplex exchange conjecture SE_d [4].

Simplex Exchange Conjecture (SE_d) *For any two simplicial bases $B, B' \subseteq \mathbb{R}^{d-1}$, in general position, there is a sequence $B_0, B_1, B_2, \ldots, B_d$ of simplicial* *bases of* $\mathbb{R}^{d-1}$, *with* $B_0 = B$ *and* $B_d = B'$, *such that each* B_{i+1} *is obtained from* B_i *by adding a vertex in* B' *and removing a vertex in* B.

Given a pair of simplicial bases, B and B' in general position, it is easy to construct a Dantzig figure from the pair. The polytope of the Dantzig figure is

$$P(B, B') := \{(\lambda_1, \dots, \lambda_{2d}) : \sum_{i=1}^{d} \lambda_i \mathbf{b}_i + \sum_{i=1}^{d} \lambda_{i+d} \mathbf{b}'_i = 0, \ \sum_{i=1}^{2d} \lambda_i = 1, \lambda_i \geq 0\} ,$$

The antipodal vertices $\mathbf{w}_1$ and $\mathbf{w}_2$ are obtained by setting $\lambda_{d+1} = \lambda_{d+2} = \dots = \lambda_{2d} = 0$ and $\lambda_1 = \dots = \lambda_d = 0$ respectively. See [4] for details.

Associated with each pair (B, B') of simplicial bases are $(d!)^2$ *exchange sequences* $B_0 = B', B_1, B_2, \dots, B_d = B'$, which are labelled by pairs of permutations $(\tau, \sigma) \in \text{Sym}(d) \times \text{Sym}(d)$ as follows: B_{i+1} is obtained from B_i by adding the vector $\mathbf{b}'_{\tau(i)} \in B'$ and removing the vector $\mathbf{b}_{\sigma(i)}$ of B. We call an exchange sequence (τ, σ) *legal* if all the resulting bases B_i are simplicial bases. Let $\#(B, B')$ denote the number of legal exchange sequences for the pair (B, B') of simplicial bases. From the construction of the Dantzig figure associated with the simplicial bases B, B' one can derive the following Lemma.

Lemma 2.1. *Let* (B, B') *be a pair of simplicial bases of* $\mathbb{R}^{d-1}$ *in general position, and let* $(P, \mathbf{w}_1, \mathbf{w}_2)$ *be the associated Dantzig figure. Then*

$$\#(B, B') = \#(P, \mathbf{w}_1, \mathbf{w}_2) . \tag{2.1}$$

In the following discussion, we'll construct a reduced set $\mathcal{M}_d$ of simplicial basis pairs that necessarily includes a counterexample to the simplex exchange conjecture SE_d if one exists. The set $\mathcal{M}_d$ is a real linear space of dimension $(d-1)^2$, and we call it a *parameter space* for the simplex basis exchange conjecture SE_d. To reduce the set of simplicial basis pairs that one needs to consider, we need the following two operations that preserve $\#(B, B')$.

Lemma 2.2. *Let* (B, B') *be a pair of simplicial bases of* $\mathbb{R}^{d-1}$.

(i). *If* $L : \mathbb{R}^{d-1} \to \mathbb{R}^{d-1}$ *is an invertible linear transformation, then*

$$\#(L(B), L(B')) = \#(B, B') . \tag{2.2}$$

(ii). *Given a strictly positive vector* $\mu = (\mu_1, \dots, \mu_d) \in \mathbb{R}^d$, *and an ordered set of vectors* $B = \{\mathbf{b}_1, \mathbf{b}_2, \dots, \mathbf{b}_d\}$ *set* $\mu \circ B := \{\mu_1 \mathbf{b}_1, \mu_2 \mathbf{b}_2, \dots, \mu_d \mathbf{b}_d\}$. *For any two such vectors* μ *and* μ',

$$\#(\mu \circ B, \ \mu' \circ B') = \#(B, B') . \tag{2.3}$$

We now construct the parameter space $\mathcal{M}_d$. Regard $\mathbb{R}^{d-1}$ as imbedded in $\mathbb{R}^d$ as the hyperplane

$$\langle e \rangle^{\perp} := \{\mathbf{x} = (x_1, \dots, x_d) : \langle e, \mathbf{x} \rangle = \sum_{i=1}^{d} x_i = 0\} , \tag{2.4}$$

where $e^T = (1, 1, \ldots, 1)$. Given an arbitrary simplicial basis pair (B, B'), we first scale the vectors of B to make 0 the centroid of B. Then we take an invertible linear transformation $L : \mathbb{R}^{d-1} \to \mathbb{R}^{d-1}$ that sends B to the *standard simplex* $\Delta_d := \{s_1, \ldots, s_d\}$, which is a regular simplex with centroid 0. Then the vertex s_i is the orthogonal projection on $\langle e \rangle^\perp$ of e_i. We rescale the image of B' under L, taking it to $Z \equiv \{z_1, z_2, \ldots, z_d\} := \mu' B' = \{\mu'_1 b'_1, \mu_2 b'_2, \ldots, \mu_d b'_d\}$ in such a way that

$$z_1 + z_2 + \ldots + z_d = 0 . \tag{2.5}$$

Lemma 2.2 implies that if (B, B') is a counterexample to the d-step conjecture, then (Δ_d, Z) is as well.

The *parameter space* $\mathcal{M}_d$ enumerates all pairs (Δ_d, Z) such that $Z = \{z_1, \ldots z_d\}$ satisfies (2.5). An element of $\mathcal{M}_d$ would then be a $d \times d$ matrix, Z whose rows are $z_1, \ldots z_d$. We observe that the rows and columns of Z add up to zero vectors. Thus $\mathcal{M}_d$ is a linear space of dimension $(d-1)^2$. Note that $\mathcal{M}_d$ contains some extra "ideal elements" not corresponding to any simplicial basis B', *i.e.* matrices Z of rank less than $d - 1$.

Inside the parameter space $\mathcal{M}_d$ there are regions $\Omega(\tau, \sigma)$ defined by the property that the permutation $(\tau, \sigma) \in \text{Sym}(d) \times \text{Sym}(d)$ gives a legal exchange sequence from the simplicial basis $\Delta_d = \{s_1, \ldots, s_d\}$ to the simplicial basis $Z = \{z_1, \ldots, z_d\}$ and $\Delta_d \cup Z$ is a Haar set. Basic properties of $\Omega(\tau, \sigma)$ are,

Lemma 2.3

(i) *Each $\Omega(\sigma, \tau)$ is an open set of $\mathcal{M}_d$.*

(ii) *For each $\tau, \sigma \in \text{Sym}(d)$,*

$$\Omega(\tau, \sigma) = P_\tau \Omega(e, e) P_\sigma^{-1} , \qquad \text{with } P_\tau, P_\sigma \in S_d . \tag{2.6}$$

(iii) *For fixed τ, all $\Omega(\tau, \sigma)$ are pairwise disjoint as σ varies. Similarly, for fixed σ, all $\Omega(\tau, \sigma)$ are pairwise disjoint as τ varies.*

The simplex exchange conjecture asserts that the $(d!)^2$ regions $\Omega(\tau, \sigma)$ must cover all of $\mathcal{M}_d$, apart from an "exceptional set" of codimension 1.

3. Gaussian Elimination and the d-Step Conjecture

The connection of triangular factorizations of a $(d-1) \times (d-1)$ matrix M with the d-step conjecture arises from study of the set $\Omega(e, e)$ in the parameter space $\mathcal{M}_d$ of the simplex exchange conjecture. A set of simplicial bases $\{\Delta_d, Z\}$ is in the set $\Omega(e, e)$ if the sequence of simplex exchanges from $B_0 = \Delta_d$ to $B_d = Z$ given by:

$$
\begin{aligned}
B_1 &= \{z_1, s_2, s_3, \ldots, s_d\} \\
B_2 &= \{z_1, z_2, s_3, \ldots, s_d\} \\
&\;\;\vdots \\
B_{d-1} &= \{z_1, z_2, \ldots, z_{d-1}, s_d\}
\end{aligned}
$$

is legal. A necessary and sufficient condition for this is that there exist strictly positive relations

$$\begin{aligned}
\lambda_{11}z_1 & \quad + \quad \lambda_{12}s_2 + \ldots + \lambda_{1d}s_d = 0 \\
\lambda_{21}z_1 & \quad + \quad \lambda_{22}z_2 + \ldots + \lambda_{2d}s_d = 0 \\
& \qquad \vdots \\
\lambda_{d-1,1,}z_1 & \quad + \quad \lambda_{d-1,2}z_2 + \ldots + \lambda_{d-1,d}s_d = 0 \; .
\end{aligned} \tag{3.1}$$

We may write this as

$$\begin{bmatrix} \lambda_{11} & 0 & \ldots & 0 \\ \lambda_{22} & \lambda_{22} & \ldots & 0 \\ & & & \\ \lambda_{d-1,1} & & \ldots & \lambda_{d-1,d-1} \end{bmatrix} \begin{bmatrix} z_1 \\ z_2 \\ \vdots \\ z_{d-1} \end{bmatrix} = - \begin{bmatrix} \lambda_{12} & \lambda_{13} & \ldots & \lambda_{1d} \\ 0 & \lambda_{23} & \ldots & \lambda_{2d} \\ & & & \\ 0 & 0 & \ldots & \lambda_{d-1,d} \end{bmatrix} \begin{bmatrix} s_2 \\ s_3 \\ \vdots \\ s_d \end{bmatrix} .$$

Since each nonnegative linear relation (3.1) is determined up to multiplication by a positive scalar, we may (uniquely) rescale these relations to require that

$$\lambda_{ii} = 1 \; , \quad 1 \leq i \leq d - 1 \; .$$

Thus, if we define the $(d-1) \times (d-1)$ matrix M by

$$\begin{bmatrix} z_1 \\ \vdots \\ z_{d-1} \end{bmatrix} = -M \begin{bmatrix} s_2 \\ \vdots \\ s_d \end{bmatrix} , \tag{3.2}$$

then M has the triangular factorization

$$M = L^{-1}U \; , \tag{3.3}$$

in which both L and U are *positive triangular matrices*, by which we mean that all entries of L and U are strictly positive except for those entries that must be zero by the triangularity condition. This construction is reversible and hence we obtain the following characterization of $\Omega(e, e)$.

Lemma 3.1. *There is an invertible linear map $\phi(Z) = M$ from $d \times d$ real matrices Z having all row and column sums zero onto the set of $(d-1) \times (d-1)$ real matrices M, such that*

$$\Omega(e, e) = \{Z \in \mathcal{M}_d : \phi(Z) \text{ has a positive triangular factorization}\} \; . \tag{3.4}$$

Now we can reformulate the d-step conjecture completely in terms of positive triangular factorizations. To do this, we observe first that the criterion for membership in $\Delta(\tau, \sigma)$ analogous to (3.2) is

$$\begin{bmatrix} z_{\tau(1)} \\ z_{\tau(2)} \\ \vdots \\ z_{\tau(d-1)} \end{bmatrix} = -M_{\tau,\sigma} \begin{bmatrix} s_{\sigma(2)} \\ s_{\sigma(3)} \\ \vdots \\ s_{\sigma(d)} \end{bmatrix} , \quad \tau, \sigma \in \text{Sym}(d) \; . \tag{3.5}$$

The $(d-1) \times (d-1)$ matrix M becomes $M_{e,e}$ in this notation. The matrices $M_{\tau,\sigma}$ are related under the action of a finite group of $\hat{S}_d$ of $(d-1) \times (d-1)$ matrices isomorphic to $\mathrm{Sym}(d)$, which we denote

$$\hat{S}_d := \{Q_\sigma : \sigma \in \mathrm{Sym}(d)\} \ .$$

The matrix Q_σ is defined by:

$$(Q_\sigma)_{i,j} = \begin{cases} 1 & \text{if } j = \sigma(i), \\ 0 & \text{if } j \neq \sigma(i) \quad \text{and} \quad 1 \leq \sigma(i) \leq d-1, \\ -1 & \text{if } \sigma(i) = d \ . \end{cases} \tag{3.6}$$

We say a $(d-1) \times (d-1)$ matrix M is in *completely general position* if for every pair $(\tau, \sigma) \in \mathrm{Sym}(d) \times \mathrm{Sym}(d)$ the matrix $Q_\tau M Q_\sigma$ has a nondegenerate triangular factorization, *i.e.* no zero elements in L and U except in the triangular parts. The set of completely general position M is an open dense subset of the space of real $(d-1) \times (d-1)$ matrices. From the above discussion, we have

Theorem 3.1. *For a $(d-1) \times (d-1)$ matrix M in completely general position the number of ordered pairs $(\tau, \sigma) \in \mathrm{Sym}(d) \times \mathrm{Sym}(d)$ for which $Q_\tau M Q_\sigma$ has a positive triangular factorization is equal to the number of d-step paths between antipodal matrices in the Dantzig figure $(P, \mathbf{w}_1, \mathbf{w}_2)$ associated to M.*

These considerations lead to a reformulation of the Simplex Exchange Conjecture.

Gaussian Elimination Sign Conjecture (GE_d). *For each $(d-1) \times (d-1)$ matrix M in completely general position there exists some pair $(\tau, \sigma) \in \mathrm{Sym}(d) \times \mathrm{Sym}(d)$ such that the matrix $Q_\tau M Q_\sigma$ has a positive triangular factorization $L^{-1}U$.*

The equivalence of the Gaussian Elimination Sign Conjecture to the d-step Conjecture is established in

Theorem 3.2. *For each $d \geq 2$, the d-step conjecture $\Delta(d, 2d) = d$ is equivalent to the Gaussian elimination sign conjecture GE_d.*

The Gaussian elimination sign conjecture is concerned with the sign patterns in the matrices in triangular factorizations of the $(d!)^2$ matrices

$$\Sigma_M := \{Q_\tau M Q_\sigma : \sigma, \tau \in \mathrm{Sym}(d)\} \ , \tag{3.7}$$

namely whether there always exists a factorization $L^{-1}U$ with L and U both positive. The number of possible sign patterns of entries in L and U together is $2^{(d-1)^2}$. This number grows much more rapidly than $(d!)^2$ as $d \to \infty$. A simple heuristic to consider is that the Gaussian elimination sign conjecture is false for large d purely from the proliferation of possible sign patterns of L and U. Call this the *sign pattern heuristic*.

The proliferation of sign patterns can easily be used to prove that the smaller set contained in Σ_M, consisting of the $(d-1)!^2$ matrices

$$\{P_\sigma M P_\tau : \sigma, \tau \in \mathrm{Sym}(d-1)\} , \tag{3.8}$$

under the action of $\mathrm{Sym}(d-1) \times \mathrm{Sym}(d-1)$ need not contain any matrix having a positive triangular factorization.

The sign pattern heuristic is nevertheless completely inaccurate in describing sign patterns of triangular factorizations of matrices in the sets Σ_M generated by the action of $\mathrm{Sym}(d) \times \mathrm{Sym}(d)$. This is shown theoretically by Theorem 4.1 of the next section, and experimentally for $d \leq 9$ by the data in §5.

4. Sign Patterns in Gaussian Elimination

In this section we make use of the *complete triangular factorization*

$$M = \tilde{L}^{-1} \tilde{D} \tilde{U} ,$$

in which $\tilde{D}$ is a diagonal matrix, and $\tilde{U}$ is an upper triangular matrix with diagonal elements $\tilde{U}_{ii} = 1$. *i.e.* $\tilde{U}$ is unipotent. This decomposition exists and is unique for any nonsingular matrix M that has an $L^{-1}U$ decomposition, with $L = \tilde{L}$ and $U = \tilde{D}\tilde{U}$. The following Theorem shows why the sign pattern heuristic fails for the action of $\mathrm{Sym}(d) \times \mathrm{Sym}(d)$ on $(d-1) \times (d-1)$ matrices.

Theorem 4.1. *There is an open dense set of $(d-1) \times (d-1)$ real matrices M having the following properties.*

(i) *For each $\tau \in \mathrm{Sym}(d)$ there exists a unique $\sigma \in \mathrm{Sym}(d)$ such that $Q_\tau M Q_\sigma$ has a triangular factorization $L^{-1}U$ in which U is positive.*

(ii) *For each $\sigma \in \mathrm{Sym}(d)$ there exists a unique $\tau \in \mathrm{Sym}(d)$ such that $Q_\tau M Q_\sigma$ has a complete triangular factorization $\tilde{L}^{-1}\tilde{D}\tilde{U}$ in which $\tilde{L}$ and $\tilde{D}$ are positive.*

(iii) *For each $\sigma \in \mathrm{Sym}(d)$ there exist exactly 2^d choices of $\tau \in \mathrm{Sym}(d)$ such that $Q_\tau M Q_\sigma$ has a triangular factorization $L^{-1}U$ in which L is positive.*

We associate to M a function $\Phi_M : \mathrm{Sym}(d) \to \mathrm{Sym}(d)$ for which $\Phi(\tau) = \sigma$ for the σ given by Theorem 4.1 (i). We also associate to M a 1 to 2^d multivalued map Ψ_M for which $\Psi_M(\sigma)$ is the set of 2^d permutations τ given by Theorem 4.1 (iii). Positive factorizations (τ, σ) correspond to "fixed points" (τ, σ) for which $\Phi_M(\tau) = \sigma$ and $\tau \in \Psi_M(\sigma)$. In looking for such "fixed points" there is one extra constraint to take into account. For any possible $Q_\sigma M Q_\tau = L^{-1}U$ in which L^{-1} and U are both positive, it is necessary that

$$det(L^{-1}U) = det(Q_\sigma)det(Q_\tau)det(M) > 0 , \tag{4.1}$$

so that we may exclude exactly half of the permutations τ above in $\Phi_M(\sigma)$. We therefore define a 1 to 2^{d-1} multivalued map Ψ_M^* that associates to each $\sigma \in$

Sym(d) the 2^{d-1} permutations τ given in Theorem 4.1 (iii) whose determinant has the correct sign. A "fixed point" (τ, σ) is one with $\Phi_M(\tau) = \sigma$ and $\sigma \in \Psi_M^*(\tau)$.

The mappings Φ_M and Ψ_M^* lead to an alternate heuristic to consider: How would "fixed points" be distributed if $\Phi_M : \text{Sym}(d) \to \text{Sym}(d)$ were a random function and $\Psi_M^* : \text{Sym}(d) \to \mathcal{P}(\text{Sym}(d))$ were a random 1 to 2^{d-1} multivalued mapping?

Lemma 4.1. Let $f : \text{Sym}(d) \to \text{Sym}(d)$ be a random mapping drawn uniformly from the set of all such functions, and let $g : \text{Sym}(d) \to \mathcal{P}(\text{Sym}(d))$ an independent multivalued random mapping drawn uniformly from the set of all 1 to 2^{d-1} multivalued maps. Then the expected number of "fixed points" (σ, τ) of the pair (f, g) is 2^{d-1}.

5. Numerical Experiments: Number of Paths

Using the multi-precision package of Bailey [1], we performed extensive computational experiments, to study the Gaussian elimination sign conjecture for dimensions $4 \leq d \leq 9$, and more limited experiments for dimensions $10 \leq d \leq 15$. Since the computations were done in floating point none of the computations we report is rigorously guaranteed to be correct. In our original tests we followed an *ad hoc* procedure of running examples over and over at higher levels of precision until the (L, U) factorizations, counts of legal exchange sequences, and entries of matrices stabilized. Based on this experience, we concluded that 250 digits of precision would be reliable on (nearly) all examples computed and we used this precision level for the computations. With these caveats we believe the computational data to be trustworthy.

The computational data describes experiments using several probability distributions. The first distribution we studied was the (essentially unique) Gaussian distribution ν_G on $(d-1) \times (d-1)$ matrices invariant under the action of $\hat{S}_d \times \hat{S}_d$ (see the appendix of [6]). To test the sign pattern heuristic the second distribution chose entries in L and U picked i.i.d. uniformly from $[-1, 1]$. The third distribution was based on permuting the entries of L and U. We picked a fixed set of $(d-1)^2$ elements, which were chosen to be a small perturbation of an arithmetic progression, then assigned them to the elements of L and U in a randomly permuted order. The fourth distribution, which we call the "twisted" distribution, depends on a positive real parameter α. Its construction was motivated by the observation that if counterexamples exist, there must be a region of $\mathcal{M}_d$ not covered by any region $\Omega(\sigma, \tau)$. Then at least one $\Omega(\sigma, \tau)$ would touch on this region, and using the symmetry under $\text{Sym}(d) \times \text{Sym}(d)$ the set $\Omega(e, e)$ also has this property. Thus to find such a region, it suffices to take a small step outside $\Omega(e, e)$ in the appropriate direction. Now $\Omega(e, e)$ has a nonlinear "twisted" shape created by L^{-1}. To obtain a large "twist," we chose a fixed

$\alpha > 0$ and considered matrices L generated by

$$
L_{ij} = \begin{cases} \alpha^{i-j} r_{ij} & \text{if} \quad i > j \\ 1 & \text{if} \quad i = j \\ 0 & \text{if} \quad i < j . \end{cases} \tag{5.1}
$$

where r_{ij} are random variables drawn i.i.d. uniform in $[0, 1]$. The matrix U was generated in a similar fashion. To step outside the region $\Omega(e, e)$, we then set

$$
L_{d-1,1} = -1 . \tag{5.2}
$$

We report on experiments using the values $\alpha = 5, 10$ and 20. We discovered empirically that stepping outside $\Omega(e, e)$ by setting the value $L_{d-1,1} = -1$ made no apparent difference in the distribution of the values of $\#(M)$, compared to remaining inside $\Omega(e, e)$ by generating $L_{d-1,1}$ using (5.1).

The data on $\#(M)$ for fifty trials each on each of these distributions, for the range $4 \leq d \leq 9$, using 250 digits precision, are given in Table 1. The major observations from Table 1 are:

(1). The values of $\#(M)$ are very large for the invariant Gaussian distribution.

(2). The i.i.d. uniform $[-1, 1]$ distribution results for L and U show that the sign pattern heuristic fails in a fairly decisive way for (L, U) taken together, for $d \leq 9$.

(3). All examples tested satisfied the bound

$$
\#(M) \geq 2^{d-1} .
$$

Equality held in many examples, for $3 \leq d \leq 9$, for the "twisted" distribution, with the frequency of such examples increasing as the parameter α is increased.

The last observation came as a surprise! We went on to check that the bound $\#(M) \geq 2^{d-1}$ held on a wide variety of other distributions. In particular, we fortuitously discovered (by a programming mistake) a modified form of the "twisted" distribution which produced a high proportion of matrices $\tilde{M}$ attaining $\#(\tilde{M}) = 2^{d-1}$. An initial matrix M was first computed using the "twisted" distribution for parameter α. This was inserted as the first $d - 1$ rows and $d - 1$ columns of a $d \times d$ matrix V whose last row and column were set to zero. The new matrix $\tilde{V} = \Delta V \Delta$ was computed, and its upper left corner is the matrix produced by the modified "twisted" distribution. Experimental data for this distribution for $7 \leq d \leq 10$ appears i n Table 2, for parameter values $\alpha = 5, 10$ and 20. We also computed a smaller number of examples in dimensions $11 \leq d \leq 15$, using the modified "twisted" distribution with parameter $\alpha = 20$. These appear in Table 3 below. None of our computations produced exceptions to $\#(M) \geq 2^{d-1}$. These computations suggested the possible truth of the d-step conjecture, in the strong form:

Conjecture 5.1 (Strong d-step Conjecture) *For all general position simplicial basis pairs (B, B') in $\mathbb{R}^d$,*

$$\#(B, B') \geq 2^{d-1} .$$

Equivalently, all d-dimensional Dantzig figures $(P, \mathbf{w}_1, \mathbf{w}_2)$ in $\mathbb{R}^d$ have

$$\#(P, \mathbf{w}_1, \mathbf{w}_2) \geq 2^{d-1} .$$

We can show that Conjecture 5.1 is true when $d = 3$ and it has been proved for dual-neighborly polytopes in [5]. However, Holt and Klee recently showed that the conjecture is true for $d = 4$ and fails for $d \geq 5$ [3]. The Holt-Klee counterexamples show a relatively small violation of the strong d-step conjecture (they construct examples in which $\#(B, B') = (\frac{3}{2})2^{d-2}$). Although there is not much theoretical evidence, both the computational data that we have presented as well as the Holt-Klee construction are consistent with an $O(2^d)$ lower bound on $\#(B, B')$. It would be interesting to determine an exact lower bound on $\#(B, B')$!

6. Acknowledgment

We thank V. Klee, G. Ziegler and an anonymous referee for helpful comments and references. Part of the work was done at the Oberwolfach meeting on Applied and Computational Convexity, January 1995.

References

[1] D. Bailey, Multiprecision translation and execution of Fortran programs, ACM Transactions on Mathematical Software **19** (1993), 288–319.

[2] J. Day and B. Peterson, Growth in Gaussian elimination, Amer. Math. Monthly, **95** (1988) 489–513.

[3] F. Holt and V. Klee, Counterexamples to the strong d-step conjecture for $d \geq 5$, manuscript, 1996.

[4] V. Klee and P. Kleinschmidt, The d-step conjecture and its relatives, Math. of Operations Research **12** (1987), 718–755.

[5] J.C. Lagarias and N. Prabhu, d-critical Dantzig figures and the strong d-step conjecture, to appear in Disc. Comp. Geom.

[6] J.C. Lagarias, N. Prabhu and J.A. Reeds, The d-step conjecture and Gaussian elimination, to appear in Disc. Comp. Geom..

[7] L. Trefethen and R. S. Schrieber, Average-case stability of Gaussian elimination, SIAM J. Matrix Anal. Appl. **11** (1990), 335–360.

Table 1. Experimental data, dimensions 4 to 9 (50 trials each distribution)

d	Distribution	Min	1-Quartile	Median	3-Quartile	Max	#
	Gaussian	8	12	14	18	24	1
4	i.i.d.	8	10	12	14	24	10
	permuted	8	8	12	12	18	16
	$\alpha = 5$	8	8	8	8	16	39
	$\alpha = 10$	8	8	8	8	12	47
	$\alpha = 20$	8	8	8	8	16	49
	Gaussian	28	40	48	60	120	0
5	i.i.d.	16	28	33	42	104	2
	permuted	16	24	28	34	50	1
	$\alpha = 5$	16	16	20	22	30	18
	$\alpha = 10$	16	16	16	16	26	37
	$\alpha = 20$	16	16	16	16	22	44
	Gaussian	72	152	183	220	454	0
6	i.i.d.	54	83	101	143	207	0
	permuted	41	81	96	112	152	0
	$\alpha = 5$	32	34	39	46	70	9
	$\alpha = 10$	32	32	32	36	44	32
	$\alpha = 20$	32	32	32	32	48	44
	Gaussian	352	572	818	1091	2242	0
7	i.i.d.	185	287	346	445	740	0
	permuted	140	198	231	293	558	0
	$\alpha = 5$	68	78	88	96	127	0
	$\alpha = 10$	64	64	68	76	128	18
	$\alpha = 20$	64	64	64	64	86	38
	Gaussian	1748	2890	3482	4489	8858	0
8	i.i.d.	521	932	1167	1589	2875	0
	permuted	355	689	854	988	1637	0
	$\alpha = 5$	129	173	202	233	566	0
	$\alpha = 10$	128	138	148	172	230	5
	$\alpha = 20$	128	128	132	138	188	21
	Gaussian	8129	12286	15269	19444	38783	0
9	i.i.d.	1367	4044	4972	5786	7596	0
	permuted	1298	2389	3084	3772	7040	0
	$\alpha = 5$	286	365	391	441	531	0
	$\alpha = 10$	256	286	323	353	447	2
	$\alpha = 20$	256	256	266	278	394	14

The last column lists the number of matrices M for which $\#(M) = 2^{d-1}$.

Table 2. Modified "twisted" distribution, dimensions 6 to 10 (50 trials each distribution)

d	Distribution	Min	1-Quartile	Median	3-Quartile	Max	#
	$\alpha = 5$	32	32	32	40	64	29
6	$\alpha = 10$	32	32	32	32	48	37
	$\alpha = 20$	32	32	32	32	36	48
	$\alpha = 5$	64	64	76	88	148	19
7	$\alpha = 10$	64	64	64	64	96	40
	$\alpha = 20$	64	64	64	64	116	42
	$\alpha = 5$	128	128	152	176	258	13
8	$\alpha = 10$	128	128	128	144	192	33
	$\alpha = 20$	128	128	128	128	192	42
	$\alpha = 5$	256	268	334	392	590	11
9	$\alpha = 10$	256	256	256	296	488	25
	$\alpha = 20$	256	256	256	256	384	42
10	$\alpha = 20$	512	512	512	512	700	39

The last column lists the number of matrices M for which $\#(M) = 2^{d-1}$.

Table 3. Modified "twisted" distribution, dimensions 11 to 15 (10 trials each distribution)

d	Distribution	Min	Median	Max	#
11	$\alpha = 20$	1024	1024	1216	8
12	$\alpha = 20$	2048	2048	2560	7
13	$\alpha = 20$	4096	4096	5184	7
14	$\alpha = 20$	8192	8280	10240	5
15	$\alpha = 20$	16384	16976	19872	4

The last column lists the number of matrices M for which $\#(M) = 2^{d-1}$.

On the Complexity of Approximating Euclidean Traveling Salesman Tours and Minimum Spanning Trees*

Gautam Das** & Sanjiv Kapoor*** & Michiel Smid[†]

Abstract. We consider the problems of computing r-approximate traveling salesman tours and r-approximate minimum spanning trees for a set of n points in $\mathbb{R}^d$, where $d \geq 1$ is a constant. In the algebraic computation tree model, the complexities of both these problems are shown to be $\Theta(n \log(n/r))$, for all n and r such that $r < n$ and r is larger than some constant. In the more powerful model of computation that additionally uses the floor function and random access, both problems can be solved in $O(n)$ time if $r = \Theta(n^{1-1/d})$.

1 Introduction

The *Traveling Salesman Problem* (*TSP*) is one of the best known combinatorial optimization problems. In the geometric version of this problem, we are given a set S of n points in $\mathbb{R}^d$, where $d \geq 1$ is a constant. A *tour* is a closed path that visits each point of S exactly once and returns to its starting point. Each edge of such a tour has a *length* that is equal to the Euclidean distance between its endpoints. The *length* of a tour is the sum of the lengths of all its edges. The *TSP* is to compute a tour along the points of S of minimal length. Since this problem is NP-complete for dimension $d \geq 2$ (see [8]), it is natural to consider the weaker problem of designing efficient algorithms that approximate the optimal tour. We call a tour having length at most r times the length of an optimal tour an *r-approximate TSP-tour*.

It is well known that for $d = 2$, a 2-approximate (resp. $(3/2)$-approximate) *TSP*-tour can be computed in $O(n \log n)$ (resp. $O(n^3)$) time. (See [6, 9].) Recently, Arora [2] gave a polynomial-time approximation scheme for the planar *TSP*. That is, there is an algorithm that for any constant $\epsilon > 0$, computes a $(1 + \epsilon)$-approximate *TSP*-tour in $n^{O(1/\epsilon)}$ time.

---

* Part of this work was done while the authors were at the Max-Planck-Institut für Informatik, Saarbrücken.

** Math Sciences Dept., The University of Memphis, Memphis, TN 38152, USA. Supported in part by NSF Grant CCR-9306822. E-mail: *dasg@next1.msci.memphis.edu.*

*** Department of Computer Science, Indian Institute of Technology, Hauz Khas, New Delhi 110016, India. E-mail: *skapoor@cse.iitd.ernet.in.*

[†] Department of Computer Science, King's College London, Strand, London WC2R 2LS, United Kingdom. E-mail: *michiel@dcs.kcl.ac.uk.*

For any dimension $d \geq 3$ and any $\epsilon > 0$, a $(2 + \epsilon)$-approximate TSP-tour can be computed in $O(n \log n + n (1/\epsilon)^d \log 1/\epsilon)$ time. (This follows from results in [5, 10, 11] and Lemma 5 below.)

On the other hand, an n-approximate TSP-tour can be computed in $O(n)$ time. This follows from the fact that *any* tour is an n-approximate TSP-tour. (See Lemma 4 below.)

This leads to the question of determining, for any dimension $d \geq 1$, the complexity of computing an r-approximate TSP-tour for sufficiently large values of n and r. In this paper, we answer this question for algorithms that belong to the algebraic computation tree model. In particular, we prove the following result.

Theorem 1. *Let $d \geq 1$ be an integer constant. In the algebraic computation tree model, any algorithm that, given a set S of n points in $\mathbb{R}^d$ and a sufficiently large real number $r < n$, computes an r-approximate TSP-tour for S, takes $\Omega(n \log(n/r))$ time in the worst case.*

Note that this lower bound even holds in dimension $d = 1$. As mentioned above, the lower bound is tight for constant values $r \geq 2$ and $d = 2$.

We prove that the lower bound is in fact tight for all values of r. That is, we give an algorithm that, given a set S of n points in $\mathbb{R}^d$ and a real number r, $8 < r < n$, computes an r-approximate TSP-tour for S in $O(n \log(n/r))$ time. This algorithm fits in the algebraic computation tree model. (The constant 8 is somewhat arbitrary here. We concentrate on "large" values of r, because it is known already how to compute an r-approximate TSP-tour in $O(n \log n)$ time for values of r that are larger than two.)

We also consider the related problem of approximating the minimum spanning tree of a set of points. Again, let S be a set of n points in $\mathbb{R}^d$. Consider a graph G having the points of S as its vertices. The *weight* of G—denoted by $wt(G)$—is defined as the sum of the lengths of all edges of G. A *minimum spanning tree* (MST) of S is a tree of minimum weight having the points of S as its vertices. We denote an MST of the point set S by $MST(S)$. Its weight is equal to $wt(MST(S))$.

For $d = 2$, an MST can be computed in $O(n \log n)$ time, which is known to be optimal. (See [9].) For dimension $d \geq 3$, the problem becomes more difficult. For example, if $d = 3$, the fastest algorithm known today constructs an MST in expected time $O(n^{4/3} \log^{O(1)} n)$. (See [1, 5].)

We call a connected graph on the points of S having weight at most r times $wt(MST(S))$ an r-approximate MST. Note that we only require the graph to be connected; it need not be a tree. It is known that for any $\epsilon > 0$, a $(1 + \epsilon)$-approximate MST can be computed in time $O(n \log n + n (1/\epsilon)^d \log 1/\epsilon)$. (See [5, 10, 11].)

We consider the problem of constructing an r-approximate MST for large values of r. Using the relation between an r-approximate MST and a $2r$-approximate TSP-tour (see Lemma 5 below) we have the following result.

Theorem 2. *Let $d \geq 1$ be an integer constant. In the algebraic computation tree model, any algorithm that, given a set S of n points in $\mathbb{R}^d$ and a sufficiently large real number $r < n$, computes an r-approximate MST for S, takes $\Omega(n\log(n/r))$ time in the worst case.*

Again, this lower bound is tight. That is, for any set S of n points in $\mathbb{R}^d$ and any real number r, $4 < r < n$, we can in $O(n\log(n/r))$ time compute a connected graph on S—in fact, a tree—having weight at most $r \cdot wt(MST(S))$. (Also here, the constant 4 is somewhat arbitrary. We concentrate on "large" values of r.)

Hence, in the algebraic computation tree model, computing an r-approximate TSP-tour, or an r-approximate MST takes $\Theta(n\log(n/r))$ time. In particular, for r a (sufficiently large) constant, the complexity is $\Theta(n\log n)$. In fact, if r is a large number like $n^{1-1/d}$, the complexity is still $\Theta(n\log n)$. To give an algorithm with running time $o(n\log n)$, we need a very large approximation factor such as $r = n/\log n$.

All results mentioned so far hold for the algebraic computation tree model. In particular, they hold for algorithms that do not use the non-algebraic floor function or random access. In the final part of the paper, we consider algorithms that do have these two operations at their disposal.

Bern et al.[4] show that for any $\epsilon > 0$ and any set of n points in the plane, a $(1+\epsilon)$-approximate MST can be computed in $O((1/\epsilon)\,n\log\log n)$ time in this more powerful model.

We give an algorithm that, given a set S of n points in $\mathbb{R}^d$, computes a $3\sqrt{d}\,n^{1-1/d}$-approximate MST for S in $O(n)$ time. This yields an algorithm that computes a $6\sqrt{d}\,n^{1-1/d}$-approximate TSP-tour for S, also in $O(n)$ time.

The rest of this paper is organized as follows. In the next section, we recall some results that will be used in the rest of the paper. In Section 3, we prove the lower bounds. Then, in Section 4, we give the algorithm that shows that the lower bounds are tight in the algebraic computation tree model. In Section 5, we give the algorithm that operates in the more powerful model of computation. Finally, in Section 6, we give some concluding remarks.

2 Some preliminary results

We assume that the reader is familiar with the algebraic computation tree model. (See Ben-Or [3], and Preparata and Shamos [9].) Our lower bound will use the following important result.

Theorem 3 Ben-Or [3]. *Let W be any set in $\mathbb{R}^n$ and let $\mathcal{A}$ be any algorithm that belongs to the algebraic computation tree model and that accepts W. Let $\#W$ denote the number of connected components of W. Then the worst-case running time of $\mathcal{A}$ is $\Omega(\log \#W - n)$.*

The following two lemmas are well known. We omit their proofs.

Lemma 4. *Let S be a set of n points in $\mathbb{R}^d$. Any tour of S is an n-approximate TSP-tour.*

Lemma 5. *Let S be a set of n points in $\mathbb{R}^d$, and let G be a connected graph on S containing m edges and having weight at most r times the weight of an MST of S. Then, in $O(m)$ time, we can compute a $2r$-approximate TSP-tour for S.*

Corollary 6. *The lower bound of Theorem 1 implies the lower bound of Theorem 2.*

3 The lower bound proof

In this section, we prove Theorem 1. By Corollary 6, this will also prove Theorem 2.

We prove Theorem 1 for algorithms that solve the r-approximate *TSP* problem for one-dimensional point sets. Clearly, this will prove the theorem for any dimension $d \geq 1$.

Throughout the rest of this section, $\mathcal{A}$ denotes any algorithm that, given a set S of n real numbers and a sufficiently large real number $r < n$, computes an r-approximate *TSP*-tour for S. We will show that the worst-case running time of $\mathcal{A}$ is $\Omega(n \log(n/r))$. In fact, we prove this lower bound for even values of n. It is easy to see that this implies the lower bound for odd values of n as well.

Hence from now on, we only consider even values of n and values of r that are larger than some appropriate constant and less than n.

Here is an outline of our proof. First, we define an algorithm $\mathcal{B}$ that, when given $n + 1$ real numbers $x_1, x_2, \ldots, x_n, r$ as input, runs algorithm $\mathcal{A}$ and constructs from $\mathcal{A}$'s output two lists SL and LL, the so-called source and length lists. $\mathcal{B}$ outputs the pair (SL, LL). Its running time is roughly the same as that of $\mathcal{A}$. Then, we consider the outputs of $\mathcal{B}$ on all inputs $\pi(1), \pi(2), \ldots, \pi(n), r$, where π ranges over all $n!$ permutations of $1, 2, \ldots, n$, and choose the one that occurs most frequent. Next, we define a set $W \subseteq \mathbb{R}^n$, consisting of all points $(x_1, x_2, \ldots, x_n) \in \mathbb{R}^n$ such that $\mathcal{B}$ computes this special output when given $x_1, x_2, \ldots, x_n, r$ as input. We show that the logarithm of the number of connected components of W is $\Omega(n \log(n/r))$. Finally, we define an algorithm $\mathcal{C}$ that accepts W and whose running time is roughly the same as that of $\mathcal{B}$ and, hence, of $\mathcal{A}$. Theorem 3 implies that algorithm $\mathcal{C}$ and, hence, also $\mathcal{A}$ have $\Omega(n \log(n/r))$ running time.

Algorithm $\mathcal{B}$ does the following when given as input $n + 1$ real numbers $x_1, x_2, \ldots, x_n, r$.

Step B1: Run algorithm $\mathcal{A}$ on the input $x_1, x_2, \ldots, x_n, r$. Let

$$(x_{i_1}, x_{i_2}, \ldots, x_{i_n}, x_{i_1})$$

be the r-approximate *TSP*-tour that is computed by $\mathcal{A}$.

Step B2: For j, $1 \leq j \leq n/2$, let $e_j := \{x_{i_{2j-1}}, x_{i_{2j}}\}$. Give each e_j a direction, from the smaller to the larger element, breaking ties arbitrarily, and denote the resulting edge by $\mathbf{e_j}$. Hence,

$$\mathbf{e_j} = (\min(x_{i_{2j-1}}, x_{i_{2j}}), \max(x_{i_{2j-1}}, x_{i_{2j}})).$$

We call the two components of e_j its *source* and *sink*, respectively. The *weight* of the edge is defined as the difference of its sink and its source.

Step B3: Compute a *source list SL* of length n. For $1 \leq j \leq n$, the j-th element of this list is equal to x_j, if x_j is the source of some edge e_ℓ, and equal to a special symbol $\star$, if x_j is the sink of some edge e_ℓ.

Step B4: Compute a *length list LL* of length n. For $1 \leq j \leq n$, the j-th element of this list is equal to the weight of the edge e_ℓ having x_j as its source, provided this edge exists. Otherwise, if x_j is the sink of some edge e_ℓ, the special symbol $\star$ occurs at position j.

Step B5: Output the pair of lists (SL, LL).

Note that the edges e_j form a perfect matching of $x_1, x_2, \ldots, x_n$. As an example, let $n = 4$, $x_3 < x_4 < x_1 < x_2$, and assume $\mathcal{A}$ computes the tour $(x_1, x_3, x_4, x_2, x_1)$. Then we have $e_1 = (x_3, x_1)$ and $e_2 = (x_4, x_2)$. The output of algorithm $\mathcal{B}$ consists of the lists $SL = (\star, \star, x_3, x_4)$ and $LL = (\star, \star, x_1 - x_3, x_2 - x_4)$.

Lemma 7. *Let $T_A(n, r)$ and $T_B(n, r)$ denote the worst-case running times of algorithms $\mathcal{A}$ and $\mathcal{B}$, respectively. Then there is a constant c independent of n and r, such that $T_B(n, r) \leq T_A(n, r) + cn$.*

Proof: We assume that the input sequence $x_1, x_2, \ldots, x_n, r$ is stored in a linked list. Moreover, we adapt algorithm $\mathcal{A}$ such that when it computes an edge (x_i, x_j) of the r-approximate *TSP*-tour, we give the occurrences of x_i and x_j in the input list pointers to this edge. Then, by walking along the input list, we can compute the lists SL and LL in $O(n)$ time, within the algebraic computation tree model. In particular, random access is not used. $\qquad\square$

We now fix an even integer n and a real number r. Let π be any permutation of $1, 2, \ldots, n$. Let (SL_π, LL_π) be the output of algorithm $\mathcal{B}$ on the input $\pi(1), \pi(2), \ldots, \pi(n), r$. Among all these $n!$ pairs (SL_π, LL_π), let $(S_{n,r}, \mathcal{L}_{n,r})$ be one that occurs most frequent.

As an example, we may have $S_{n,r} = (2, \star, \star, 1)$ and $\mathcal{L}_{n,r} = (1, \star, \star, 3)$. Then the inputs $2, 3, 4, 1, r$ and $2, 4, 3, 1, r$ *may* produce these lists.

Define W as the set of all points $(x_1, x_2, \ldots, x_n) \in \mathbb{R}^n$ such that algorithm $\mathcal{B}$, when given $x_1, x_2, \ldots, x_n, r$ as its input, outputs the pair $(S_{n,r}, \mathcal{L}_{n,r})$.

Lemma 8. *Let $\pi_1, \pi_2, \ldots, \pi_k$ be the permutations of $1, 2, \ldots, n$ such that $(SL_{\pi_i}, LL_{\pi_i}) = (S_{n,r}, \mathcal{L}_{n,r})$, $1 \leq i \leq k$. Then W has at least k connected components.*

Proof: Assume w.l.o.g. that $S_{n,r}$ has the form

$$S_{n,r} = (a_1, a_2, \ldots, a_{n/2}, \star, \star, \ldots, \star),$$

where $\{a_1, a_2, \ldots, a_{n/2}\}$ is a subset of $\{1, 2, \ldots, n\}$ of size $n/2$. Let $\mathcal{L}_{n,r}$ be given by

$$\mathcal{L}_{n,r} = (l_1, l_2, \ldots, l_{n/2}, \star, \star, \ldots, \star).$$

Note that all non-$\star$ elements of $\mathcal{S}_{n,r}$ and $\mathcal{L}_{n,r}$ are integers.

Let $1 \leq i < j \leq k$. We show that the permutations π_i and π_j belong to different connected components of W. (Note that both these permutations are elements of W.) This will prove the lemma.

Since $(SL_{\pi_i}, LL_{\pi_i}) = (SL_{\pi_j}, LL_{\pi_j}) = (\mathcal{S}_{n,r}, \mathcal{L}_{n,r})$, we can write the permutations π_i and π_j as $\pi_i = (a_1, a_2, \ldots, a_{n/2}, b_1, b_2, \ldots, b_{n/2})$ and $\pi_j = (a_1, a_2, \ldots, a_{n/2}, c_1, c_2, \ldots, c_{n/2})$, where

$$\{b_1, b_2, \ldots, b_{n/2}\} = \{c_1, c_2, \ldots, c_{n/2}\} = \{1, 2, \ldots, n\} \setminus \{a_1, a_2, \ldots, a_{n/2}\}.$$

Let ℓ be an index such that $b_\ell \neq c_\ell$.

Consider any continuous curve in $\mathbb{R}^n$ that connects π_i and π_j. Let

$$P = (p_1, p_2, \ldots, p_{n/2}, q_1, q_2, \ldots, q_{n/2})$$

be a point on this curve such that q_ℓ is not an integer. Note that point P exists, because b_ℓ and c_ℓ are distinct integers. Let us look what happens when algorithm $\mathcal{B}$ is run on input $p_1, p_2, \ldots, p_{n/2}, q_1, q_2, \ldots, q_{n/2}, r$.

In Step B1, an r-approximate TSP-tour T is computed. In the rest of algorithm $\mathcal{B}$, a source list $SL = (\alpha_1, \alpha_2, \ldots, \alpha_n)$ and a length list $LL = (\beta_1, \beta_2, \ldots, \beta_n)$ is computed. We distinguish two cases.

Case 1: $(\alpha_1, \alpha_2, \ldots, \alpha_{n/2}) \neq (a_1, a_2, \ldots, a_{n/2})$.

In this case, $SL \neq \mathcal{S}_{n,r}$. Hence, point P does not belong to our set W.

Case 2: $(\alpha_1, \alpha_2, \ldots, \alpha_{n/2}) = (a_1, a_2, \ldots, a_{n/2})$.

Since SL contains exactly $n/2$ $\star$'s, we must have $SL = \mathcal{S}_{n,r}$. Consider the perfect matching of the r-approximate TSP-tour T that is computed in Step B2. Let e be the edge that contains q_ℓ. The source of this edge is contained in the source list SL, which is equal to $\mathcal{S}_{n,r}$, and which contains only integers and $\star$'s. It follows that q_ℓ must be a sink, and the weight of e is not an integer. Since this non-integer weight occurs in the length list LL, we must have $LL \neq \mathcal{L}_{n,r}$. As a result, also in this case point P does not belong to the set W.

We have shown that any curve connecting π_i and π_j passes through a point outside W. Hence, π_i and π_j are contained in different connected components of W. $\qquad\square$

Lemma 9. *The number of permutations π of $1, 2, \ldots, n$ such that $(SL_\pi, LL_\pi) = (\mathcal{S}_{n,r}, \mathcal{L}_{n,r})$ is at least*

$$(n/2)! \left/ \left(\binom{n}{n/2} \binom{2rn + n/2}{n/2} \right) \right. .$$

Proof: Consider again the output (SL_π, LL_π) of $\mathcal{B}$ when given $\pi(1), \pi(2), \ldots, \pi(n), r$ as input. We give an upper bound on the total number of different outputs if π ranges over all permutations of $1, 2, \ldots, n$.

A source list contains $n/2$ distinct integers from $\{1, 2, \ldots, n\}$, and $n/2$ special symbols $\star$. Hence, the total number of different source lists is at most equal to

$$\binom{n}{n/2} \cdot \frac{n!}{(n/2)!}.$$

Consider one fixed source list SL. How many different length lists LL are there such that (SL, LL) is an output of algorithm $\mathcal{B}$? Such a list LL contains $n/2$ $\star$'s, and $n/2$ non-$\star$ elements. Since we have fixed SL, the positions in LL that contain these non-$\star$'s are also fixed. Every non-$\star$ is an integer. Recall that the length list represents the edge weights of a perfect matching of the r-approximate TSP-tour computed in Step B1. Since the input is a permutation of $1, 2, \ldots, n$, we know that the optimal TSP-tour has length $2(n-1) \leq 2n$. Hence, the tour computed in Step B1 has length at most $2rn$. This, in turn, implies that the sum of the non-$\star$ symbols in the length list LL is at most equal to $2rn$. It follows that for this fixed source list SL, the total number of different corresponding length lists LL is at most equal to the number of solutions of the inequality $x_1 + x_2 + \cdots + x_{n/2} \leq 2rn$ in non-negative integers x_i. It is well known (see [7, pages 103–104]) that the latter quantity is equal to

$$\binom{2rn + n/2}{n/2}.$$

We have shown that by running $\mathcal{B}$ on all $n!$ different permutations of $1, 2, \ldots, n$, we get at most

$$X := \binom{n}{n/2} \cdot \frac{n!}{(n/2)!} \cdot \binom{2rn + n/2}{n/2}$$

different outputs (SL, LL). Therefore, by the pigeon-hole principle, one of these outputs is computed on at least $n!/X$ inputs. $\qquad\square$

Now we can complete the proof of Theorem 1. First, we show that

$$Y := \ln\left(\frac{\left(\frac{n}{2}\right)!}{\binom{n}{n/2}\binom{2rn+n/2}{n/2}}\right) = \Omega(n \log(n/r)).$$

Lemma 10. *Let $0 \leq b \leq a$ be integers. Then*

$$\binom{a}{b} \leq \frac{a^a}{b^b(a-b)^{a-b}}.$$

Proof: Omitted.

Applying Lemma 10, and the inequalities $\binom{n}{n/2} \leq 2^n$ and $a! \geq (a/e)^a$ for $a = n/2$, we get

$$\frac{\left(\frac{n}{2}\right)!}{\binom{n}{n/2}\binom{2rn+n/2}{n/2}} \geq \frac{n^n (2rn)^{2rn}}{2^{2n} e^{n/2} (2rn + n/2)^{2rn+n/2}}.$$

Taking logarithms gives

$$Y \geq n \ln n + 2rn \ln(2rn) - (2rn + n/2) \ln(2rn + n/2) - 2n \ln 2 - n/2$$

$$= \frac{1}{2} n \ln \frac{n}{2r + 1/2} + n \ln \left(\frac{2r}{2r + 1/2} \right)^{2r} - 2n \ln 2 - n/2.$$

It can be shown that ,

$$\ln \left(\frac{2r}{2r + 1/2} \right)^{2r} \geq -1$$

for all sufficiently large r. Also, since $2r + 1/2 \leq 3r$, we have $\ln(n/(2r + 1/2)) \geq \ln(n/(3r)) = \ln(n/r) - \ln 3$. It follows that

$$Y \geq \frac{1}{2} n \ln \frac{n}{r} - \frac{1}{2} n \ln 3 - n - 2n \ln 2 - n/2 = \Omega(n \ln(n/r)), \qquad (1)$$

which is exactly what we wanted to prove. Note that the constant factor in the Ω-bound in (1) does not depend on n and r.

Recall that we denote the number of connected components of the set W by $\#W$. Lemmas 8 and 9, and inequality (1) imply that, for our fixed values of n and r, we have

$$\log \#W \geq c_0 \, n \log(n/r),$$

where c_0 is a constant that does not depend on n and r.

Consider the following algorithm C. It only accepts inputs of our fixed length n. On input $x_1, x_2, \ldots, x_n$, algorithm C does the following.

Step C1: Run algorithm B on the input $x_1, x_2, \ldots, x_n, r$. Let the output be the pair (SL, LL).

Step C2: Output YES if $SL = S_{n,r}$ and $LL = L_{n,r}$. Otherwise, output NO.

Since algorithm C only accepts inputs of our fixed length n, and since we also fixed r, we may assume that it "knows" the two lists $S_{n,r}$ and $L_{n,r}$. Algorithm C *exists*, although we have not explicitly computed these lists. The following lemma is clear.

Lemma 11. *Let $T_B(n, r)$ and $T_C(n, r)$ denote the worst-case running times of algorithms B and C, respectively. Then there is a constant c' independent of n and r, such that $T_C(n, r) \leq T_B(n, r) + c'n$.*

Algorithm C accepts exactly our set W. Hence, by Theorem 3, there is an input on which this algorithm takes time at least $c_1 n \log(n/r)$, for some constant c_1 that does not depend on n and r. Then, by Lemmas 7 and 11, there is an input on which algorithm A takes time at least $c_2 n \log(n/r)$, for some constant c_2. Since c_2 does not depend on n and r, this implies that the lower bound holds for all values of n and r. This completes the proof of Theorem 1.

4 Proving the matching upper bound

In this section, we show that the lower bounds of Theorems 1 and 2 are tight. By Lemma 5, it suffices to give an $O(n \log(n/r))$-time algorithm that computes an r-approximate MST for any set of n points in $\mathbb{R}^d$, and any $4 < r < n$.

Let S be a set of n points in $\mathbb{R}^d$, and let $4 < r < n$. The algorithm does the following.

Step 1: Compute the smallest axes-parallel d-dimensional cube that contains all points of S. Let ℓ be the side length of this cube. Translate the set S such that it is contained in the cube $[0, \ell]^d$.

Step 2: Let $b := (r - 2)\,\ell/(5n\sqrt{d})$. Note that

$$\frac{\ell}{b} = \frac{5n\sqrt{d}}{r - 2} \leq 10\sqrt{d}\,\frac{n}{r} \leq 3n\sqrt{d}.$$

Compute the integer $\lfloor \ell/b \rfloor$ by making a scan along the integers $1, 2, \ldots, 3n\sqrt{d}$. Build a balanced binary search tree BT, storing the integers $0, 1, 2, \ldots, \lfloor \ell/b \rfloor$ in its leaves.

For each point $p = (p_1, p_2, \ldots, p_d)$ of S, and each index i, $1 \leq i \leq d$, use this tree to find the integer $c_i^p := \lfloor p_i/b \rfloor$.

Hence, considering the grid over $[0, \ell]^d$ with mesh size b, point p is contained in the c_i^p-th slab along the i-th dimension. We call

$$C_p := (c_1^p, c_2^p, \ldots, c_d^p)$$

the *grid vector* of p.

Sort the n grid vectors lexicographically, by inserting them one after another into an initially empty balanced binary search tree BT'. With each leaf of this tree, store all points p with the same grid vector.

Step 3: For each grid vector C that occurs in BT', do the following. Let S_C be the set of points p of S for which $C_p = C$. Pick an arbitrary point q_C of S_C, and call it the *representative* of S_C. Then connect each point of $S_C \setminus \{q_C\}$ to this representative. This gives a tree T_C on S_C.

Step 4: Let R be the set of all representatives. Compute a 2-approximate MST T^R for the points of R, using any one of the (algebraic computation tree) algorithms of [5, 10, 11]. (In fact, if $d = 2$, we can even compute an exact MST for R, using the algorithm given in [9].)

Step 5: Let T be the tree obtained by taking the union of all trees T_C and the tree T^R. Output T.

Lemma 12. *The running time of this algorithm is bounded by $O(n \log(n/r))$.*

It remains to show that the tree T computed by the algorithm is an r-approximate MST. Consider the minimum spanning tree $MST(S)$ for the set S. Then we have to show that $wt(T) \leq r \cdot wt(MST(S))$.

The following argument is due to Bern et al.[4]. Imagine "moving" each point of S to the representative of the cell it is contained in. Then the tree $MST(S)$ "moves" to a graph, say T', possibly containing multiple edges and loops.

Lemma 13. $wt(T') \leq 2\sqrt{d}\,bn + wt(MST(S))$.

Proof: Consider any edge (p', q') of T'. Then there is a unique edge (p, q) in $MST(S)$ that was "moved" to (p', q'). Denoting the Euclidean distance between two points x and y by $|xy|$, and using the triangle inequality, we have

$$|p'q'| \leq |p'p| + |pq| + |qq'|.$$

Since p and p' are contained in the same grid cell, we have $|p'p| \leq \sqrt{d}\,b$. Similarly, $|qq'| \leq \sqrt{d}\,b$. Hence, $|p'q'| \leq 2\sqrt{d}\,b + |pq|$. Doing this for all $n - 1$ edges of T' proves the claim. □

Lemma 14. *The tree T is an r-approximate MST for the set S.*

Proof: Let T_{opt}^R be the exact MST for the points of R. Then the graph T^R computed in Step 4 satisfies $wt(T^R) \leq 2 \cdot wt(T_{opt}^R)$.

Since T' is a spanning graph of R, we have $wt(T_{opt}^R) \leq wt(T')$. This, together with Lemma 13, implies that $wt(T^R) \leq 4\sqrt{d}\,bn + 2 \cdot wt(MST(S))$. Now, consider the total weight of the edges in the trees T_C that are computed in Step 3. Clearly, each such edge has weight at most $\sqrt{d}\,b$. It follows that

$$wt(T) = wt(T^R) + \sum_C wt(T_C) \leq 5\sqrt{d}\,bn + 2 \cdot wt(MST(S)).$$

Our choice of ℓ in Step 1 of the algorithm guarantees that there are two points of S having distance at least ℓ. Hence,

$$wt(MST(S)) \geq \ell = \frac{5\sqrt{d}\,bn}{r - 2}.$$

This implies that $wt(T) \leq (r - 2)\,\ell + 2 \cdot wt(MST(S)) \leq r \cdot wt(MST(S))$. This completes the proof. □

We summarize our result.

Theorem 15. *Let $d \geq 1$ be an integer constant. There is an algorithm that, given a set S of n points in $\mathbb{R}^d$ and a real number $4 < r < n$, computes an r-approximate MST for S in $O(n \log(n/r))$ time. This algorithm fits in the algebraic computation tree model. Hence, the lower bound of Theorem 2 is tight.*

Corollary 16. *Let $d \geq 1$ be an integer constant. There is an algorithm that, given a set S of n points in $\mathbb{R}^d$ and a real number $8 < r < n$, computes an r-approximate TSP-tour for S in $O(n \log(n/r))$ time. This algorithm fits in the algebraic computation tree model. Hence, the lower bound of Theorem 1 is tight.*

5 A non-algebraic computation tree algorithm

The results of the previous sections imply that in the algebraic computation tree model a very large approximation factor is needed in order to get a running time of $o(n \log n)$. In this section, we consider algorithms from a more powerful model of computation. More precisely, we assume that besides the operations of the algebraic computation tree model, we have the non-algebraic floor function and random access available. We will prove the following result.

Theorem 17. *Let $d \geq 1$ be an integer constant.*

1. *There is an algorithm that, given a set S of n points in $\mathbb{R}^d$, computes an r-approximate MST for S in $O(n)$ time, where $r = 3\sqrt{d}\, n^{1-1/d}$.*
2. *There is an algorithm that, given a set S of n points in $\mathbb{R}^d$, computes an r-approximate TSP-tour for S in $O(n)$ time, where $r = 6\sqrt{d}\, n^{1-1/d}$.*

Besides the operations of the algebraic computation tree model, these algorithms use the non-algebraic floor function and random access.

Let S be a set of n points in $\mathbb{R}^d$. The following algorithm computes an approximate MST for S.

Step 1: Let $r := 3\sqrt{d}\, n^{1-1/d}$. Compute the smallest axes-parallel d-dimensional cube that contains all points of S. Let ℓ be the side length of this cube. Translate the set S such that it is contained in the cube $[0, \ell]^d$.

Step 2: Let $b := \ell/n^{1/d}$. Firstly initialize a d-dimensional array, $I[0..\lfloor \ell/b \rfloor, 0..\lfloor \ell/b \rfloor, \ldots, 0..\lfloor \ell/b \rfloor]$. Also, initialize an empty list with each array entry. Then store each point $p = (p_1, p_2, \ldots, p_d)$ of S in the list stored with $I[\lfloor p_1/b \rfloor, \lfloor p_2/b \rfloor, \ldots, \lfloor p_d/b \rfloor]$.

Step 3: For each array entry C, let S_C be the set of points of S that are stored in the list corresponding to this entry. If S_C is non-empty, pick an arbitrary point q_C in this set and call it the *representative*. Let T_C be the tree on S_C obtained by connecting each point of $S_C \setminus \{q_C\}$ to the representative.

Step 4: Walk along the $(\ell/b)^d$ entries of the array I in lexicographical order. This defines an ordering on the representatives. Connect these representatives into a tree T^R—in fact, a path—according to this ordering.

Step 5: Let T be the tree obtained by taking the union of all trees T_C and the tree T^R. Output T.

Lemma 18. *The running time of this algorithm is bounded by $O(n)$.*

Proof: It is easy to see that the running time is bounded by $O(n + (\ell/b)^d)$. By our choice of b, this is bounded by $O(n)$. □

Lemma 19. *Let $r := 3\sqrt{d}\, n^{1-1/d}$. Consider the minimum spanning tree $MST(S)$ of the set S. Then we have $wt(T) \leq r \cdot wt(MST(S))$, i.e., T is an r-approximate MST.*

Lemmas 18 and 19 prove the first claim of Theorem 17. The second claim follows from Lemma 5.

6 Concluding remarks

We have shown that in the algebraic computation tree model, the complexities of the r-approximate *TSP* and *MST* problems are $\Theta(n \log(n/r))$, for large values of r and n such that $r < n$. We have also shown that in a model that additionally uses the floor function and random access, it is possible to solve both problems in linear time for $r = c\, n^{1-1/d}$ for some constant c.

We mention the following three open problems. First, in this more powerful model, can these problems be solved in linear time for values of r that are smaller than $n^{1-1/d}$? Second, is it possible in this model to solve the planar version of the problems in $o(n \log \log n)$ time for a constant value of r (thereby improving the result of [4])? Finally, for dimension $d \geq 3$, can these problems be solved in $o(n \log n)$ time in this model for a constant value of r?

References

1. P.K. Agarwal, H. Edelsbrunner, O. Schwarzkopf, and E. Welzl. *Euclidean minimum spanning trees and bichromatic closest pairs.* Discrete & Computational Geometry 6 (1991), pp. 407-422.

2. S. Arora. *Polynomial time approximation schemes for Euclidean TSP and other geometric problems.* Proc. 37th Annual IEEE Symposium on Foundations of Computer Science, 1996, to appear.

3. M. Ben-Or. *Lower bounds for algebraic computation trees.* Proceedings 15th Annual ACM Symposium on the Theory of Computing, 1983, pp. 80-86.

4. M.W. Bern, H.J. Karloff, P. Raghavan, and B. Schieber. *Fast geometric approximation techniques and geometric embedding problems.* Proceedings 5th Annual ACM Symposium on Computational Geometry, 1989, pp. 292-301.

5. P.B. Callahan and S.R. Kosaraju. *Faster algorithms for some geometric graph problems in higher dimensions.* Proceedings 4th Annual Symposium on Discrete Algorithms, 1993, pp. 291-300.

6. N. Christofides. *Worst-case analysis of a new heuristic for the traveling salesman problem.* Report 388, Grad School of Industrial Administration, CMU, 1976.

7. J.H. van Lint and R.M. Wilson. *A Course in Combinatorics.* Cambridge University Press, 1992.

8. C.H. Papadimitriou. *The Euclidean traveling salesman problem is NP-complete.* Theoretical Computer Science 4 (1977), pp. 237-244.

9. F.P. Preparata and M.I. Shamos. *Computational Geometry, an Introduction.* Springer-Verlag, New York, 1985.

10. J.S. Salowe. *Constructing multidimensional spanner graphs.* International Journal of Computational Geometry and Applications 1 (1991), pp. 99-107.

11. P.M. Vaidya. *Minimum spanning trees in k-dimensional space.* SIAM Journal on Computing 17 (1988), pp. 572-582.

Efficient Computation of Rectilinear Geodesic Voronoi Neighbor in Presence of Obstacles

Pinaki Mitra
Dept. CSE
Jadavpur University
Calcutta 700 032, INDIA

Subhas C. Nandy
Indian Statistical Institute
Calcutta 700 035, INDIA
email : nandysc@isical.ernet.in

Abstract : In this paper, we present an algorithm to compute the rectilinear geodesic voronoi neighbor of an arbitrary query point q among a set S of m points in the presence of a set $\mathcal{O}$ of n vertical line segment obstacles inside a rectangular floor. The distance between a pair of points α and β is the shortest rectilinear distance avoiding the obstacles in $\mathcal{O}$ and is denoted by $\delta(\alpha, \beta)$. The rectilinear geodesic voronoi neighbor of an arbitrary query point q, ($RGVN(q)$) is the point $p_i \in S$ such that $\delta(q, p_i)$ is minimum. The algorithm suggests a preprocessing of the elements of the set S and $\mathcal{O}$ in $O((m + n)log(m + n))$ time such that for any arbitrary query point q, the $RGVN$ query can be answered in $O(max(logm, logn))$ time. The space required for storing the preprocessed information is $O(n + mlogm)$. If the points in S are placed on the boundary of the rectangular floor, a different technique is adopted to decrease the space complexity to $O(m + n)$. The latter algorithm works even when the obstacles are rectangles instead of line segments.

1 Introduction

Given a set S of m points, called *voronoi sites*, already placed inside a bounding rectangular region among a set $\mathcal{O}$ of n obstacles, the rectilinear geodesic voronoi/nearest neighbor of an arbitrary query point q ($RGVN(q)$) is defined to be a point $p_i \in S$ such that the shortest rectilinear distance from q to p_i avoiding the obstacles in $\mathcal{O}$, denoted by $\delta(q, p_i)$, is minimum among all points in S. In [3], an algorithm is presented where the obstacles are isothetic non-overlapping rectangles. It computes the rectilinear geodesic voronoi diagram in $O((m+n)log(m+n)logn)$ time. A more general problem of computing rectilinear geodesic voronoi diagram, where the obstacles are arbitrary polygons with a total of $O(n)$ vertices, is studied in [7]. The preprocessing time for their algorithm is $O((m + n)log^2(m + n))$. After the construction of rectilinear geodesic voronoi diagram, both the algorithms can report $RGVN(q)$ for any arbitrary query point q in $O(log(m + n))$ time. In this paper, we have shown that the preprocessing time can be reduced in the following two restricted cases of the problem :

P1 The obstacles are vertical line segments and voronoi sites are placed arbitrarily on the rectangular floor.

P2 The obstacles are non-overlapping isothetic rectangles and the voronoi sites are located on the boundary of the rectangular floor.

In both the problems, instead of computing the rectilinear geodesic voronoi diagram, we build up an appropriate data structure in the preprocessing phase for reporting efficiently the $RGVN$ queries for any arbitrary query point.

The preprocessing phase for the first problem requires $O((m + n)log(m + n))$ time, using line sweep paradigm and maintaining a layered segment tree which requires $O(n + mlogm)$ space. It allows us to solve the $RGVN$ query for any arbitrary query point q among the members in S, in $O(max(logm, logn))$ time.

The method of preprocessing for the second problem is based on the Mehlhorn's [6] algorithm for computing the voronoi neighbors of a subset of vertices on the *carrier graph* [2] for the set of rectangles in $\mathcal{O}$. This step requires $O(m+n)$ space and $O((m + n)log(m + n))$ time. Here also the $RGVN$ query for any arbitrary query point can be answered in $O(log(m + n))$ time.

2 Preliminaries

In this section, we review some existing results on the rectilinear shortest path problem in presence of a set of isothetic non-overlapping rectangular obstacles. Throughout our discussion we assume that the floor on which the obstacles and the voronoi sites are distributed, is rectangular. The query point is assumed to be inside the floor. We shall denote the x and y coordinates of a point p by p_x and p_y respectively. For a pair of points p and q on the floor, the obstacle free rectilinear shortest path is denoted by $\pi(p, q)$ and its length is denoted by $\delta(p, q)$. Surely, if the obstacles are not present, the length becomes $L_1(p, q) = (|p_x - q_x| + |p_y - q_y|)$.

Definition 1 : Given the set $\mathcal{O}$ of n rectangular obstacles, a X^+Y^+ *chain* from a point p is a path from p to the top-right corner of the floor obtained as follows:

Start from the point p and move horizontally to the right side till a rectangle in $\mathcal{O}$ or the boundary of the floor is hit; then move vertically up till the obstacle is cleared and then resume the horizontal motion. This process is repeated until the top right corner of the floor is reached.

In a similar way, we can define X^+Y^-, X^-Y^+, X^-Y^-, Y^+X^+, Y^+X^-, Y^-X^+, Y^-X^- chains (see Fig. 1). Note that, when the obstacles are vertical line segments, the Y^+X^+ and Y^+X^- chains are same as the vertical line segment from p to the top boundary of the floor. Similarly, the Y^-X^+ and Y^-X^- chains are same as the vertical line segment from p to the bottom boundary of the floor.

Definition 2 : The free space enclosed by X^+Y^+ and X^+Y^- chains is a *staircase region*, and is denoted by R_{x^+}.

Lemma 1 *[1] The shortest path from p to an arbitrary point in the R_{x^+} region is monotonic in positive direction of x-axis.*

Lemma 2 *[1] There exists a shortest path from p to an arbitrary point q in the R_{x^+} region which passes through one of the two points u_1 and u_2, where $u_1(u_2)$ is a corner point of some rectangle visible from q having $u_{1x} < q_x(u_{2x} < q_x)$ and $u_{1y} < q_y(u_{2y} > q_y)$ such that u_{1y} (u_{2y}) is greater than (less than) the y-coordinate of any other corner point r of some rectangle which is visible from q with $r_x < q_x$ and $r_y < q_y$ ($r_y > q_y$) (see Fig. 1).*

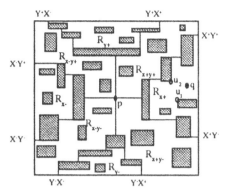

Fig. 1 : Demonstration of the properties of rectilinear geodesic shortest path among rectangular obstacles

In a similar way, we can define the other seven staircase regions, say, R_{x^-}, R_{y^+}, R_{y^-}, $R_{x^+y^+}$, $R_{x^+y^-}$, $R_{x^-y^+}$ and $R_{x^-y^-}$ respectively, as illustrated in Fig. 1. If the obstacles are vertical line segments, R_{y^+} and R_{y^-} regions will vanish.

3 $RGVN$ queries in presence of line segments

In problem P1, the set $\mathcal{O}$ of m vertical line segment obstacles and the set S of n voronoi sites are given. In the following two subsections we describe the preprocessing and query answering steps of our algorithm.

3.1 Preprocessing

The preprocessing phase of our algorithm consists of two parts : (i) computation of the geodesic voronoi neighbors of each end point of the obstacles in $\mathcal{O}$, and (ii) preprocessing of the set S of voronoi sites using layered segment tree data structure.

3.1.1 Computing voronoi neighbors of the end points of the obstacles

In this preprocessing step, a sweep line $\mathcal{L}$ is moved twice, once from the left boundary of the floor to its right boundary and then from the right boundary of the floor to its left boundary. Let C be the set of end points of all the obstacles in $\mathcal{O}$. In the left to right (right to left) sweep, the goal is to compute the left nearest neighbor (LNN) (right nearest neighbor (RNN)) of each end point $u_i \in C$ as defined below.

$$LNN(u_i) = p_j \text{ if } \delta(u_i, p_j) \le \delta(u_i, p_\ell) \forall p_\ell \in S \text{ such that } u_{i_x} > p_{\ell_x},$$
$$RNN(u_i) = p_k \text{ if } \delta(u_i, p_k) \le \delta(u_i, p_\ell) \forall p_\ell \in S \text{ such that } u_{i_x} < p_{\ell_x}.$$

Finally,

$$\begin{aligned} RGVN(u_i) &= LNN(u_i), & if\, \delta(u_i, LNN(u_i)) \le \delta(u_i, RNN(u_i)) \\ &= RNN(u_i), & otherwise \end{aligned} \tag{1}$$

In the left-to-right sweep, the points in S and the vertical line segments in $\mathcal{O}$ are processed in sorted order of their x-coordinates. The sweep line $\mathcal{L}$ halts when it encounters a member of either S or $\mathcal{O}$. Consider an instant of time when $S' \subseteq S$ and $\mathcal{O}' \subseteq \mathcal{O}$ be respectively the voronoi sites and the obstacles already encountered by $\mathcal{L}$. A disjoint set of intervals are maintained on $\mathcal{L}$ where each interval I_i corresponds to a distinct $p_i \in S'$ such that if we take an arbitrary point $\alpha \in I_i$, then α is closer to $p_i \in S'$ than any other point $p_j \in S'$, $j \neq i$. I_i is called the voronoi interval of p_i on $\mathcal{L}$. The following two lemmas suggests the course of action when (1) $\mathcal{L}$ encounters a voronoi site $p_i \in S - S'$ and (2) $\mathcal{L}$ encounters an obstacle $\ell_i \in \mathcal{O} - \mathcal{O}'$ respectively.

Lemma 3 *When the sweep line $\mathcal{L}$ encounters the voronoi site p_i, its voronoi interval on $\mathcal{L}$ is single contiguous.*

Proof : [By contradiction]
It is obvious that there is an interval $[a, b]$ around p_i on the sweep line $\mathcal{L}$ such that any point $\alpha \in [a, b]$ will be closer to p_i than any other point $p_j \in S'$. Let β be a point outside this interval whose geodesic nearest neighbor is p_i, i.e., $\delta(\beta, p_i) < \delta(\beta, p_j)$, $\forall p_j (\neq p_i) \in S'$. We have to show that no such β exists.

Without loss of generality let us assume that β is below b on $\mathcal{L}$, i.e., $\beta_y < b_y$ (see Fig. 2). Since b is a boundary point of the voronoi interval of p_i, $\delta(b, p_i) = \delta(b, p_j)$ for some $p_j \in S'$. Let us consider a point γ $(b_y > \gamma_y > \beta_y)$ in the voronoi interval of p_j. Now $\delta(\beta, p_i) = \overline{p_i \gamma} + \overline{\gamma \beta} > \delta(p_j, \gamma) + \overline{\gamma \beta}$.

Therefore β is nearer to p_j than p_i. Thus we arrive at a contradiction. $\square$

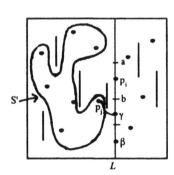

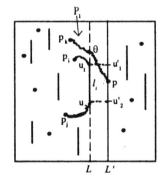

Fig. 2 : Proof of Lemma 3   **Fig. 3 :** Proof of Lemma 4

Thus Lemma 3 suggests that when a voronoi site p_i is encountered by $\mathcal{L}$, the voronoi interval of p_i is to be introduced on $\mathcal{L}$, and the neighboring voronoi intervals are to be modified. The actions to be taken here are mentioned in Step 2.1 of the algorithm **Left-to-Right-Sweep** and illustrated in Fig. 5.

Lemma 4 *If $\mathcal{L}$ is moved towards right from its current position after an encounter of a vertical line $\ell_i[u_1, u_2] \in \mathcal{O}$, $u_1 \in I_i$ and $u_2 \in I_j$, and let $u_1'(u_2')$ be the horizontal projection of $u_1(u_2)$ in the current position of $\mathcal{L}$, then*

- *before encountering any other points of S or obstacles of $\mathcal{O}$, any point $p \in [u_1', u_2']$ has its left-nearest-neighbor either p_i or p_j.*

Proof : [By contradiction]

Let $p \in [u'_1, u'_2]$ has its left-nearest-neighbor $p_k \in S'(k \neq i \ \& \ k \neq j)$ (see Fig. 3). Let P_1 be the shortest path from p_k to p. This path is monotone in the positive direction of the x-axis. Let θ be a point on the path P_1 having the same x-coordinate as that of the line ℓ_i. Without loss of generality, we assume that θ is above u_1.

$$\text{The length of } P_1 = \delta(p_k, \theta) + \delta(\theta, p) = \delta(p_k, \theta) + L_1(\theta, u_1) + L_1(u_1, p)$$
$$\text{Now, } u_1 \in I_i \implies \delta(p_k, \theta) + L_1(\theta, u_1) \geq \delta(p_i, u_1).$$
$$\implies \text{Length of } P_1 \quad \geq \delta(p_i, u_1) + L_1(u_1, p)$$

This implies that p_i is closer to p compared to p_k. If θ is below u_2, we can similarly show that p_j is closer to p compared to p_k. Thus we arrive at a contradiction. $\square$

Hence, when an obstacle $\ell_i[u_1, u_2]$ is encountered, two different situations may happen : (i) u_1 and u_2 fall in the same voronoi interval, and (ii) u_1 and u_2 fall in different voronoi intervals. The updation of voronoi intervals in both the cases are presented in Step 2.2 of algorithm **Left-to-Right-Sweep**, and explained in Fig. 6. We now state an important property of our sweep technique in Lemma 5.

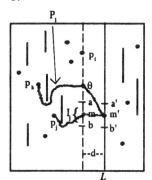

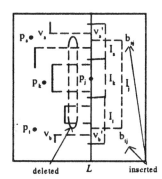

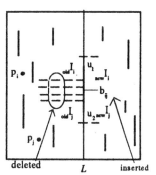

Fig. 4 : Proof of Lemma 5   Fig. 5 : Processing of a voronoi site   Fig. 6 : Processing of a line segment

Lemma 5 *When the sweep line $\mathcal{L}$ is moved towards right after encountering a point $p_i \in S$, then before encountering any other point in S or any other obstacles in $\mathcal{O}$, the status of the sweep line, i.e., the voronoi intervals I_j of each $p_j \in S$ on $\mathcal{L}$, remains unaltered.*

Proof : Refering to Fig. 4, let $[a, b]$ be the voronoi interval I_j of the point $p_j \in S'$ when the sweep line $\mathcal{L}$ encounters p_i. Let the sweep line is advanced by d units towards right so that it does not encounter any other point in S or obstacle in $\mathcal{O}$. Let $[a', b']$ be the projection of $[a, b]$ on the current position of $\mathcal{L}$. We have to prove that $[a', b']$ is also the voronoi interval of p_j at the current position of $\mathcal{L}$.

Let us take a point $m \in [a, b]$ and m' be its projection on the current position of $\mathcal{L}$. We have to show that $\delta(p_j, m') \leq \delta(p_k, m') \ \forall p_k \in S' \ (k \neq j)$.

On the contrary, let there exist a point $p_k \in S'$ $(k \neq j)$ such that $\delta(p_k, m') < \delta(p_j, m')$. The shortest path P_1 from p_k to m' is monotone in the positive direction of x-axis. Let θ be the point of intersection of the path P_1 and the sweep line $\mathcal{L}$ when it was at p_i. Thus we have $P_1 = \pi(p_k, \theta) \bigcup \pi(\theta, m')$.

As m is in the voronoi interval I_j, we have : $\delta(p_j, m) \leq \delta(p_k, \theta) + \delta(\theta, m)$. Now from Lemma 4, Length of $P_1 = \delta(p_k, \theta) + \delta(\theta, m') = \delta(p_k, \theta) + \delta(\theta, m) + \delta(m, m') \geq \delta(p_j, m) + \delta(m, m')$.

Hence, m' is nearer to p_j than p_k. Thus we arrive at a contradiction. $\qquad\square$

Let C' ($\subseteq C$) be the set of end points already encountered by $\mathcal{L}$ during its left to right sweep at the current instant of time. Let $V = C \bigcup S$ and $V' = C' \bigcup S'$. Obviously, $V' \subseteq V$. We now partition V' into subsets $V_1', V_2', \ldots, V_{|S'|}'$ such that for any element $v_k \in V_j'$, its left-nearest-neighbor is p_j.

Within each interval I_j on the sweep line $\mathcal{L}$, we maintain the shortest-path-map of p_j. In other words, within I_j we maintain those $v_k \in V_j'$ which are horizontally visible from I_j (i.e., whose horizontal projection on I_j, are not obstructed by any member in $\mathcal{O}$), in the sorted order of their y-coordinates along with $\delta(v_k, p_j)$'s.

Next, we describe our plane sweep algorithm.

Algorithm Left-to-Right-Sweep

1	sort the elements of V by their x-coordinates;
2	for each $v_i \in V$ do
2.1	if ($v_i \in S$) (* sweep line encountered a voronoi site $p_j \in S$ (see Fig. 5)*)
2.1.1	determine the voronoi interval I_k on $\mathcal{L}$ in which p_j lies;
2.1.2	sequentially search the elements of the shortest path maps attached to the voronoi intervals starting from p_j, and moving
2.1.3.1	upward till we get $v_a' \in I_s[\alpha, \beta]$ (* horizontal projection of v_a on $\mathcal{L}$ *); such that $\delta(p_s, v_a) + L_1(v_a, v_a') < L_1(p_j, v_a')$; determine a point $b_{s,j} \in I_s$ s.t. $\delta(p_s, v_a) + L_1(v_a, v_a') + L_1(v_a', b_{s,j}) = L_1(p_j, b_{s,j})$;
2.1.3.2	downward till we get $v_b' \in I_t[\gamma, \delta]$ (* horizontal projection of v_b on $\mathcal{L}$ *) such that $\delta(p_t, v_b) + L_1(v_b, v_b') < L_1(p_j, v_b')$; determine a point $b_{t,j} \in I_t$ s.t. $\delta(p_t, v_b) + L_1(v_b, v_b') + L_1(v_b', b_{t,j}) = L_1(p_j, b_{t,j})$
2.1.4	(* update voronoi intervals *)
2.1.4.1	replace $I_s = [\alpha, b_{s,j}]$ (* voronoi interval for the point p_s *) in $\mathcal{L}$;
2.1.4.2	insert $I_j = [b_{s,j}, b_{t,j}]$ (* voronoi interval of p_j *) and the point p_j in $\mathcal{L}$;
2.1.4.3	replace $I_t = [b_{t,j}, \delta]$ (* voronoi interval for the point p_t *) in $\mathcal{L}$;
2.1.4.4	delete all earlier v_j's and $b_{m,n}$'s, that fall in I_j, and insert p_j in I_j;
2.2	if ($v_i \in C$) (* $\mathcal{L}$ encountered a line segment obstacle $\ell_i[u_1, u_2] \in \mathcal{O}$ *)
2.2.1	search $\mathcal{L}$ with u_1 and u_2 to find the voronoi intervals $I_i[\alpha_i, \beta_i]$ and $I_j[\alpha_j, \beta_j]$ in which u_1 and u_2 lies respectively. (* see Fig. 6 *)
2.2.2	if ($I_i = I_j$) then
2.2.2.1	compute $\delta(u_1, p_i)$ and $\delta(u_2, p_i)$ from the shortest path map attached to I_i;
2.2.2.2	(* insertion of shortest path map of p_i (for detail see [1] *)
2.2.2.2.1	insert u_1 (with $\delta(u_1, p_i)$) and u_2 (with $\delta(u_2, p_i)$) in I_i;
2.2.2.2.2	delete all elements of I_i on $\mathcal{L}$ that lie inside the interval $[u_1, u_2]$;
2.2.3	if ($I_i \neq I_j$) then
2.2.3.1	compute $\delta(u_1, p_i)$ (* from shortest path map attached to I_i *);

	compute $\delta(u_2, p_j)$ (* from shortest path map attached to I_j *);
2.2.3.2	let the length of ℓ_i be ℓ;
2.2.3.3	insert u_1 (with $\delta(u_1, p_i)$) and u_2 (with $\delta(u_2, p_j)$) on $\mathcal{L}$;
2.2.3.4	redefine $I_i[\alpha_i, b_{i,j}]$ and $I_j[b_{i,j}, \beta_j]$ (* voronoi intervals for p_i and p_j *),

where $b_{i,j}$ is a point on $\mathcal{L}$ which is at a distance x from u_1 such that

$$\delta(u_1, p_i) + x = \delta(u_2, p_j) + \ell - x, \implies x = \frac{\delta(u_2, p_j) - \delta(u_1, p_i) + \ell}{2};$$

2.2.3.5	delete all the earlier v_j's and $b_{m,n}$'s, that lie in the interval $[u_1, u_2]$;
	endfor
	end.

Theorem 1 *The algorithm left to right sweep can be implemented in $O((n + m)log(n + m))$ preprocessing time and $O(m + n)$ space.*

In a similar way, using right-to-left sweep, we can compute $RNN(u_i)$ $(= p_j \in S)$ for each end-point $u_i \in C$. After two sweep operations for each end-point $u_i \in C$ we obtain $LNN(u_i)$ and $RNN(u_i)$, which are p_k and $p_\ell(\in S)$ respectively. Finally, for each end-point $u_i \in C$, we maintain $RGVN(u_i)$, which is $p_\alpha(\alpha = k \text{ or } \ell)$ for which $\delta(p_\alpha, u_i)$ is minimum. Thus we have the following theorem :

Theorem 2 *Given a set of m points S and a set $\mathcal{O}$ of n vertical line segments, the rectilinear geodesic voronoi neighbor for each end-point of $\ell_i \in \mathcal{O}$ can be computed in $O((m + n)log(m + n))$ time using $O(m + n)$ space.*

3.1.2   Preprocessing point sets

In this section, we will discuss the preprocessing of the point set S so that given an arbitrary isothetic query rectangle $Q[x_I, x_J][y_K, y_L]$, satisfying either $y_K = y_{min}$ or $y_L = y_{max}$, the rectilinear nearest neighbor from its four corner points can be answered efficiently. Here y_{min} and y_{max} are the coordinates of the top and bottom sides of the bounding rectangle. We shall denote the four corner points of a rectangle by NW, NE, SE and SW respectively. In this context, we note that here we will ignore all vertical line segment obstacles in $\mathcal{O}$.

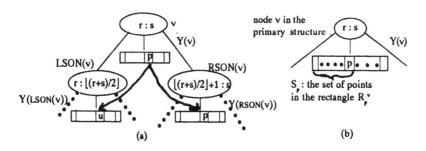

Fig. 7 : Node structure of Layered segment tree

We shall use *layered segment tree* data structure $(\mathcal{T})$ (Fig. 7) [8] for preprocessing. The points in S are placed in the leaves of $\mathcal{T}$ in sorted order with respect to their x-coordinates. A node $v[r : s]$ of the primary structure of $\mathcal{T}$

corresponds to the set of points $P(v)$ whose x-coordinates lie in the interval $[x_{(r)}, x_{(s)}]$, where $x_{(k)}$ is the k-th ranked point in the sorted order of points in S by x-coordinates. The left and right subtrees are also layered segment trees with the set of points $\{x_{(r)}, \ldots, x_{(\lfloor \frac{r+s}{2} \rfloor)}\}$ and $\{x_{(\lfloor \frac{r+s}{2} \rfloor + 1)}, \ldots, x_{(s)}\}$ respectively. The secondary structure of node v is a sorted array $Y(v)$ of the y-coordinates of the points in $P(v)$. It should be noted that a node corresponding to the point $p \in Y(v)$ of the secondary structure of the node v, represents a rectangle R_p^v with top-left (bottom-right) corner $(x_{(r)}, p_y)$ $((x_{(s)}, y_{min}))$ and it contains all the points $S_p = \{q \mid q_x \in [x_{(r)}, x_{(s)}] \ \& \ q_y \leq p_y\}$ (see Fig. 7b). We now describe the preprocessing required for answering the $RGVN$ queries for the corners of the rectangle $Q[x_I, x_J][y_K, y_L]$, where $y_L = y_{min}$. The preprocessing for the case where $y_K = y_{max}$, is similar.

For efficient searching of the secondary structure during query time, we maintain two additional links for each point p_i in the secondary structure during the preprocessing, as described below.

Note that $LSON(v)$ and $RSON(v)$ are two children of the node v of the primary structure. So, $Y(v)$ is partitioned into two lists $Y(LSON(v))$ and $Y(RSON(v))$ and any element $p \in Y(v)$ will belong to any one of them. Without loss of generality, let $p \in Y(RSON(v))$. Now, $p \in Y(v)$ has two pointers, one pointing to the point p in $Y(RSON(v))$ and the other pointing to the point u in $Y(LSON(v))$ such that $u_y = Max_{t \in Y(LSON(v))}\{t_y \mid t_y \leq p_y\}$ (see Fig. 7a).

Given the query rectangle $Q[x_I : x_J][y_K : y_L]$, with $y_L = y_{min}$, we perform a binary search at the list Y associated with the root of T to find a point p such that $p_y \leq y_K$, and its next point p' in the same Y-list with $p'_y > y_K$. In each subsequent Y-list search in the next level of the primary structure, following the pointers from p, we can determine the point t and its next point t' such that $t_y \leq y_K$ and $t'_y > y_K$, in constant time. The search in the primary structure with the interval $[x_I : x_J]$ has to consider at most $O(logm)$ nodes. Each such node v is of the form $[r : s]$, where $[x_r : x_s] \subseteq [x_I : x_J]$. Note that if a node $[r : s]$ such that $[x_r : x_s] \subseteq [x_I : x_J]$, all its successor nodes satisfy the same property and are not to be considered further. In the secondary structure (Y-list) of each of these nodes, we identify the point t and its next member t' satisfying $t_y \leq y_K$ and $t'_y > y_K$. The nearest neighbor n_v from the NW-corner of R_t^v can be found from the preprocessed data structure. From $O(logm)$ nodes of the primary structure, we get $O(logm)$ n_v's. Finally, the answer to the query will be the point among these $O(logm)$ n_v's which is at the minimum distance from the NW corner of the rectangle Q. Thus we have established the following theorem:

Theorem 3 *A set S of m points can be preprocessed in $O(mlogm)$ time and with $O(mlogm)$ storage, using layered segment tree, such that for given a query rectangle $Q[x_I : x_J][y_K : y_L]$, with either $y_K = y_{max}$ or $y_L = y_{min}$, it is possible to report the geodesic voronoi neighbor $p \in S$ from any of its four corner points in $O(logm)$ time.*

3.2 Query answering

We now discuss the method of finding the rectilinear geodesic voronoi neighbor of an arbitrary query point q among the members of the set S from the preprocessed data structure. We shall describe an algorithm for finding the right nearest neighbor for an arbitrary query point q $(RNN(q))$ in the $+X$ direction.

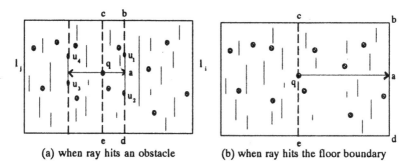

(a) when ray hits an obstacle (b) when ray hits the floor boundary

Fig 8 : Query processing

Algorithm RNN-Query
Step 1 : Shoot a ray from q towards right. The following two cases may arise :
      (i) The ray hits a vertical line obstacle $\ell_i(u_1, u_2) \in \mathcal{O}$ (see Fig. 8a).
      (ii) The ray hits right boundary of the bounding rectangle (see Fig. 8b).
Step 2 : For case (i), find $p_k = RGVN(u_1)$ and $p_\ell = RGVN(u_2)$, with
      rectilinear distances $\delta(u_1, p_k)$ and $\delta(u_2, p_\ell)$ respectively.
      Let $\delta(q, p_k) = L_1(q, u_1) + \delta(u_1, p_k)$ and $\delta(q, p_\ell) = L_1(q, u_2) + \delta(u_2, p_\ell)$.
      For case (ii), set $\delta(q, p_k) = \infty$ and $\delta(q, p_\ell) = \infty$.
Step 3 : Find the geodesic nearest neighbors of q in rectangles $\square qabc$ and $\square qade$
      from the layered segment tree $\mathcal{T}$. Let these be p_k and p_ℓ respectively.
      Compute $\delta(q, p_k) = L_1(q, p_k)$ and $\delta(q, p_\ell) = L_1(q, p_\ell)$.
Step 4 : $RNN(q) = p_\alpha$ if $\delta(q, p_\alpha) = Min(\delta(q, p_\beta), \beta = i, j, k, \ell)$.

A similar procedure LNN-**Query** determines $LNN(q)$ for the query point q. Finally, $RGVN(q)$ can be found out using (1).

Lemma 6 *Algorithm RNN-Query runs in $O(max(\log m, \log n))$ time.*

Thus Theorems 2 and Lemma 6 leads to the following theorem :

Theorem 4 *Given a set S of m points and a set $\mathcal{O}$ of n vertical line segment obstacles on a rectangular floor, the rectilinear geodesic voronoi neighbor of an arbitrary query point q can be computed in $O(max(\log m, \log n))$ time using $O((m+n)\log(m+n))$ preprocessing time. The space required to store the data structure is $O(m\log m + n)$.*

4   *RGVN* Queries Among Rectangular Obstacles

In this section, we consider the problem of computing rectilinear geodesic nearest neighbor of an arbitrary query point q, among a set S of m points located on the periphery of the rectangular floor in presence of a set $\mathcal{O}$ of n isothetic (i.e. whose sides are parallel to the enclosing box) disjoint rectangular obstacles inside the floor. Let A_1, A_2, A_3 and A_4 be the set of points on the left, top, right and bottom sides of the floor respectively. Thus $S = A_1 \bigcup A_2 \bigcup A_3 \bigcup A_4$. The rectilinear geodesic nearest neighbor of an arbitrary query point q among the set of points in A_1, A_2, A_3 and A_4 will be denoted by $p_{-x}(q)$, $p_{+y}(q)$, $p_{+x}(q)$ and $p_{-y}(q)$ respectively. Next, we explain the method of finding $p_{-x}(q)$.

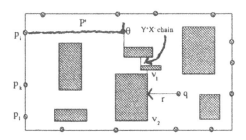

Fig 9 : Proof of Lemma 8

From the query point q, we shoot a ray towards left. It either hits the right side of an obstacle (say $R_i \in \mathcal{O}$) or the left boundary of the floor. Now let us consider the following two lemmas.

Lemma 7 *If the ray hits the left boundary of the floor at a point t, then $p_{-x}(q)$ will be the point of S placed in A_1 which is either just vertically above or is just vertically below t.*

Lemma 8 *If the ray hits right vertical edge (v_1, v_2) of a rectangular obstacle $R_i \in \mathcal{O}$, then $p_{-x}(q)$ will be the either $p_{-x}(v_1)$ or $p_{-x}(v_2)$.*

We now introduce a data structure, called *carrier graph* [2], which will be used to maintain the monotone chains from each point $p_i \in S$. There are four types of carrier graphs, G_{+X}, G_{-X}, G_{+Y} and G_{-Y}. Each graph is a directed acyclic planar graph with positive edge weights, and it contains paths that are monotonic with respect to a specified direction. These graphs exploit the knowledge that the shortest path among any two points avoiding the obstacles in $\mathcal{O}$ is monotonic in at least one of the X or Y directions [1]. Each of the four carrier graphs has $O(n)$ vertices and edges, where n is the number of rectangles in $\mathcal{O}$ and they can be computed in $O(n \log n)$ time. These graphs contain sufficient information to support shortest path queries.

For each point $p_i \in A_1$, both the $Y^+ X^+$ and $Y^- X^+$ chains and the shortest path to each corner point in C obtained from $\mathcal{O} \bigcup A_1$, are maintained in G_{+X} [2].

From the carrier graph, we shall construct four data structures Vor_{+X}, Vor_{+Y}, Vor_{-X} and Vor_{-Y}, which will be used for reporting the voronoi neighbor queries for the corner points of the obstacles in $\mathcal{O}$. We now describe the construction of Vor_{+X} based on Lemma 9 and 10. The construction of Vor_{+Y}, Vor_{-X} and Vor_{-Y} are similar.

Lemma 9 *[4] In a directed acyclic graph $G = (V, E)$, the shortest path tree from a source vertex s can be computed in $O(|V| + |E|)$ time.*

Lemma 10 *[6] Given a directed acyclic graph $G = (V, E)$ with non-negative edge weights and $\hat{V} \subset V$, where $|\hat{V}| = k$, we can partition V into subsets $V_1, V_2, \ldots, V_k$ such that $\bigcup_{i=1}^k V_i = V$ and $v_i \in \hat{V}$ is nearer to all vertices of V_i, compared to all other vertices $v_j \in \hat{V}$, $j \neq i$. This partition can be computed in $O(|V| + |E|)$ time.*

Algorithm Build_Vor$_{+X}$

Step 1 : Compute the carrier graph G_{+X} on $\mathcal{O} \bigcup A_j$ by applying plane sweep as described in [2]

Step 2 : Apply the algorithm of Mehlhorn [6] as described in Lemma 10 on G_{+X} with $\hat{V} = $ the set of vertices in A_1. Subsequently with each corner point of the rectangles in $\mathcal{O}$, we associate the point $p \in A_1$ that is found to be geodesically closest in this step, and also the shortest distance of that corner point from p.

Beside maintaining Vor$_{+X}$, Vor$_{+Y}$, Vor$_{-X}$ and Vor$_{-Y}$, we also maintain two additional structures corresponding to the horizontal and vertical trapezoidation of the free space avoiding the obstacles in $\mathcal{O}$. These will be used to answer the ray shooting queries [5]. We also maintain four sorted lists for the points in A_1, A_3 (sorted with respect to their y-coordinates), and A_2, A_4 (sorted with respect to their x-coordinates).

Theorem 5 *The time and space complexities of the preprocessing step is $O((m + n)\log(m + n))$ and $O(m + n)$ respectively.*

4.1 Answering the *RGVN* queries

Now we describe an algorithm for answering the *RGVN* queries for an arbitrary query point $q \in S$.

Algorithm Geodesic_Neighbor_A_1 (* *RGVN(q)* in A_1 is $p_{-x}(q)$ *)

Step 1 : Shoot a horizonatal ray leftward from the point q. Let it hit the vertical edge $u_i u_j$ in the horizontal trapezoidation. If $u_i u_j$ is a part of a right vertical edge of an obstacle in $\mathcal{O}$ then go to Step 2 else go to Step 3.

Step 2 : Let $v_i v_j$ be the edge of an obstacle whose part is $u_i u_j$. Let $p_k = RGVN(v_i)$ and $p_\ell = RGVN(v_j)$ respectively, obtained from Vor$_{+X}$. If $L_1(q, v_i) + \delta(v_i, p_k) < L_1(q, v_j) + \delta(v_j, p_\ell)$ then $p_{-x}(q) = p_k$ else $p_{-x}(q) = p_\ell$. Halt.

Step 3 : (* $u_i u_j$ is a part of the left side of the bounding rectangle Z *) Perform a binary search in A_1 to find p_k and p_ℓ such that $p_{ky} \leq q_y \leq p_{\ell y}$. If $L_1(p_k, q) < L_1(p_\ell, q)$ then $p_{-x} = p_k$ else $p_{-x} = p_\ell$. Halt.

In a similar way, using Vor$_{+Y}$, Vor$_{-X}$ and Vor$_{-Y}$, we determine p_{-y}, p_{+x} and p_{-y} respectively. Finally, $RGVN(q) = p_{id}(q)$, where $id \in \{+x, -x, +y, -y\}$, for which $\delta(q, p_{id}(q))$ is minimum. Thus we have the final theorem :

Theorem 6 *The RGVN query for an arbitrary query point q in S can be answered in $O(max(logm, logn))$ time using a preprocessing step which requires $O((m+n)log(m+n))$ time and $O(m+n)$ space.*

5 Conclusion and Open Problems

This paper presents two simple algorithms for finding rectilinear geodesic voronoi neighbor (site) of an arbitrary query point q, where n sites are located on a rectangular region among a set of m isothetic obstacles.

The first one works in $O(max(logm, logn))$ time, where the obstacles are vetical line segments. This requires a preprocessing step which takes $O((m+n)log(m+n))$ time using a layered segment tree data structure and stores the preprocessed information in a data structure of size $O(mlogm + n)$. This is an improvement over the previously known results [3, 7].

In the second one, the obstacles may be isothetic rectangles but the sites are located on the periphery of the bounding rectangle. This algorithm uses a planar graph, called the carrier graph, for preprocessing and solves the geodesic voronoi neighbor query in $O(max(logm, logn))$ time. The preprocessing time for this problem is $O((m+n)log(m+n))$ and it consumes $O(m+n)$ space.

The possible directions of extending the work are (i) reducing the space complexity of our first problem to $O(m+n)$, and (ii) considering the more general problem, where the obstacles are disjoint arbitrary polygons and sites are placed inside the bounding box, so that the RGVN query for any arbitrary point can be answered in $O(max(logm, logn))$ time with a preprocessing time $O((m+n)log(m+n))$ using $O(m+n)$ space.

References

[1] P. J. de Rezende, D. T. Lee and Y. F. Wu, *Rectilinear shortest paths with rectangular barrier*, Discrete Computational Geometry, vol. 4, 1989, pp. 41-53.

[2] H. Elgindy and P. Mitra, *Orthogonal shortest path queries among axes parallel rectangular obstacles*, International Journal of Computational Geometry and Applications, 1994.

[3] S. Guha and I. Suzuki, *Proximity problems for points on rectilinear plane with rectangular obstacles*, Proc. FST & TCS - 13, Lecture Notes in Computer Science, 1993, pp. 218-227.

[4] D. B. Johnson, *Efficient algorithms for shortest paths in sparse network*, Journal of the Association of Computing Machinery, 1977, pp. 1-13.

[5] D. G. Kirkpatrick, *Optimal search in planar subdivision*, SIAM Journal on Computing, vol. 12, 1983, pp. 28-35.

[6] K. Mehlhorn, *A faster approximation algorithm for the steiner problems in graphs*, Information Processing Letters, vol. 27, 1988, pp. 125-128.

[7] J. S. B. Mitchell, *L_1 shortest paths among polygonal obstacles in the plane*, Algorithmica, vol. 8, 1992, pp. 55-88.

[8] F. P. Preparata and M. I. Shamos, Computational Geometry - an Introduction, Springer-Verlag, New York, 1985.

Weak Bisimulation and Model Checking for Basic Parallel Processes

Richard Mayr

Institut für Informatik, Technische Universität München, Arcisstr. 21, D-80290 München, Germany; e-mail: mayrri@informatik.tu-muenchen.de

Abstract. Basic Parallel Processes (BPP) are a natural subclass of CCS infinite-state processes. They are also equivalent to a special class of Petri nets. We show that unlike for general Petri nets, it is decidable if a BPP and a finite-state system are weakly bisimilar. To the best of our knowledge, this is the first decidability result for weak bisimulation and a non-trivial class of infinite-state systems. We also show that the model checking problem for BPPs and the branching time logic UB$^-$ is PSPACE-complete. This settles a conjecture of [4].

Keywords: Basic Parallel Processes, bisimulation, model checking.

1 Introduction

Bisimulation equivalence [10], has become one of the most successful equivalence notions in concurrency theory, both with respect to theoretical research and to applications. In recent years, the decidability of bisimulation equivalence on several classes of infinite-state systems has been intensely studied, and a number of positive results have been obtained. Strong bisimilarity between

- two context-free processes,
- two Basic Parallel Processes (BPPs),
- a Petri net and a finite-state system

has been shown to be decidable [3, 2, 8].

A natural next step in this line of research is to extend at least some of these encouraging results to weak bisimilarity, an equivalence that allows to ignore silent internal actions. However, this task has proved to be difficult, and to the best of our knowledge only undecidability results have been obtained so far (i.e. weak bisimilarity of a Petri net and a finite-state system is undecidable [7]). In this paper we report on a first positive result: weak bisimilarity between a BPP and a finite-state system is decidable.

In the second part of the paper we shift our attention to the model checking problem for BPPs, called just the model checking problem in the sequel. This is the problem of deciding if a given BPP satisfies a property coded as a formula in a certain temporal logic. It has been shown in [4] that the model checking problem is undecidable for formulae built out of boolean operators, EX (for some successor) and EG (for some path always in the future), but decidable when the temporal operators are EX and EF (for some path eventually in the future). Therefore, the logic with the latter set of operators, called UB⁻ in [4], seems to be the largest branching time logic with a decidable model checking problem. It was shown in [4] that the model checking problem for UB⁻ is PSPACE-hard even for finite-state BPPs (notice that the size of the problem is the size of the formula plus the size of the BPP, and not the size of its associated transition system), but the exact complexity of the problem remained open. We prove that this problem is PSPACE-complete by showing that it only requires polynomial space, even for infinite-state BPPs.

2 Preliminaries

Definition 1. A binary relation R over the states of a labelled transition system (for short: LTS) is a *strong bisimulation* (often simply called bisimulation) iff

$$\forall (s_1, s_2) \in R \; \forall a \in Act. \, (s_1 \xrightarrow{a} s_1' \; \Rightarrow \exists s_2 \xrightarrow{a} s_2'. \, s_1' R s_2') \wedge$$
$$(s_2 \xrightarrow{a} s_2' \; \Rightarrow \exists s_1 \xrightarrow{a} s_1'. \, s_1' R s_2')$$

Two states s_1 and s_2 are *strongly bisimilar* iff there is a strong bisimulation R such that $s_1 R s_2$. This definition can be extended to states in different transition systems by putting them 'side by side' and considering them as a single transition system. It is easy to see that there always exists a largest strong bisimulation which is an equivalence relation called **strong bisimulation equivalence**. It is denoted by $\sim$.

Strong bisimulation equivalence is sometimes too strict. Processes can contain silent internal actions (labelled by τ) which should not be externally visible. Therefore another equivalence called weak bisimulation equivalence is defined that treats these τ-actions accordingly.

Definition 2. Let $\xrightarrow{a} := (\xrightarrow{\tau})^* \xrightarrow{a} (\xrightarrow{\tau})^*$ for $a \in Act$ and $\xrightarrow{\hat{a}} := \begin{cases} \xrightarrow{a}, & \text{if } a \neq \tau \\ (\xrightarrow{\tau})^*, & \text{if } a = \tau \end{cases}$
A binary relation R over the states of an LTS is a *weak bisimulation* if

$$\forall (s_1, s_2) \in R \; \forall a \in Act. \, (s_1 \xrightarrow{a} s_1' \; \Rightarrow \exists s_2 \xrightarrow{\hat{a}} s_2'. \, s_1' R s_2') \wedge$$
$$(s_2 \xrightarrow{a} s_2' \; \Rightarrow \exists s_1 \xrightarrow{\hat{a}} s_1'. \, s_1' R s_2')$$

Two states s_1 and s_2 are *weakly bisimilar* iff there is a weak bisimulation R such that $s_1 R s_2$. Again this can be extended to states in different transition systems. There always exists a largest weak bisimulation which is an equivalence relation called **weak bisimulation equivalence**. It is denoted by $\approx$. It is clear that $\sim \subseteq \approx$ for every LTS.

A process that is weakly bisimilar to a finite-state LTS is called *weakly finite*.

Another approach to bisimulation is via bisimulation games. A game consists of a triple $(\mathcal{T}, s_1, s_2)$, where $\mathcal{T}$ is an LTS and s_1, s_2 are states, and two players A (Attacker) and D (Defender). It is the aim of player A to prove that s_1 and s_2 are not bisimilar, while player D attempts to frustrate this. A round in the game goes like this:

1. Player A chooses an $i \in \{1, 2\}$, an action a and a move $s_i \xrightarrow{a} s'_i$. If it is impossible to make any move in s_1 or s_2 then player D wins.
2. Then player D takes the $j \in \{1, 2\}$ s.t. $i \neq j$ and tries to imitate the move, i.e. find a s'_j s.t. $s_j \xrightarrow{a} s'_j$. If this is impossible then player A wins.

After this round the resulting state is $(\mathcal{T}, s'_1, s'_2)$ and the play repeats. Player D wins every infinite game.

s_1 and s_2 are *strongly bisimilar up to n* if there is a strategy for player D to defend (prevent player A from winning) for at least n rounds. This is denoted as $s_1 \sim_n s_2$. It is easy to see that $\sim_n$ is an equivalence relation for every $n \in \mathbb{N}$. If the graph of $\mathcal{T}$ is finitely branching, then $\sim = \bigcap_{n=1}^{\infty} \sim_n$.

Weak bisimulation up to n (denoted by $\approx_n$) is defined in the same way, except that player D makes moves $s_j \xRightarrow{\hat{a}} s'_j$ instead of $s_j \xrightarrow{a} s'_j$. It follows immediately that $\sim_n \subseteq \approx_n$. Unlike for strong bisimulation the relation $\approx_n$ is not an equivalence relation in general. Also $\approx \neq \bigcap_{n=1}^{\infty} \approx_n$, because $\bigcap_{n=1}^{\infty} \approx_n \not\subseteq \approx$. The other inclusion $\approx \subseteq \bigcap_{n=1}^{\infty} \approx_n$ holds.

The Basic Parallel Processes (BPP) were introduced by Christensen in his Ph.D. dissertation [1] as a very natural subclass of the class of CCS processes [10]. They are a simple model of infinite-state concurrent systems. Assume a countably infinite set of atomic actions $Act = \{a, b, c, \ldots\}$ and a countably infinite set of process variables $Var = \{X, Y, Z, \ldots\}$. The class of BPP expressions is defined by the following abstract syntax [1, 2]:

$$E \stackrel{\text{def.}}{=} 0 \mid X \mid aE \mid E + E \mid E \| E$$

$\alpha, \beta, \gamma, \ldots$ denote merges of process variables. A BPP is defined by a family of recursive equations $\{X_i := E_i \mid 1 \leq i \leq n\}$ where the X_i are distinct and the E_i are BPP expressions at most containing the variables $\{X_1, \ldots, X_n\}$. It will be assumed that every variable occurrence in the E_i is *guarded*, i.e. appears within the scope of an action prefix. The variable X_1 is singled out as the *leading variable* and $X_1 := E_1$ is called the *leading equation*. Any finite family of BPP equations determines a labelled transition system. For every $a \in Act$ the transition relation $\xrightarrow{a}$ is the least relation satisfying the following inference rules:

$$aE \xrightarrow{a} E \quad \frac{E \xrightarrow{a} E'}{E+F \xrightarrow{a} E'} \quad \frac{F \xrightarrow{a} F'}{E+F \xrightarrow{a} F'} \quad \frac{E \xrightarrow{a} E'}{E\|F \xrightarrow{a} E'\|F} \quad \frac{F \xrightarrow{a} F'}{E\|F \xrightarrow{a} E\|F'} \quad \frac{E \xrightarrow{a} E'}{X \xrightarrow{a} E'}(X := E)$$

BPP processes generate finitely branching transition graphs, i.e. $\{F \mid E \xrightarrow{a} F\}$ is finite for each E and a. This would not be true if unguarded expressions were allowed. For example, the process $X := a + a\|X$ generates an infinitely branching transition graph. A BPP is in *normal form*, if every expression E_i at the right hand side of an equation is of the form $a_1\alpha_1 + \ldots + a_n\alpha_n$. It is shown in [1] that every BPP is strongly bisimilar to a BPP in normal form.

A BPP in normal form can be translated into a labelled Petri net s.t. their transition graphs are isomorphic. Introduce a place for each process variable and a transition for each transition rule. For a rule $X \xrightarrow{a} Y_1^{m_1} \cdots Y_n^{m_n}$ introduce a transition t labelled by a, an arc labelled by 1 leading from place X to t and arcs labelled by m_i leading from t to places Y_i. It is important to note that in these nets every transition has exactly one input place with an arc labelled by 1. Such Petri nets will be called *communication-free nets*. Communication-free nets will be denoted by N and their markings by Σ. Translating a communication-free net N back into a BPP-algebra is analogous. Any marking Σ of N can then be translated into a BPP in this algebra. So there is a one-to-one correspondence between BPP-algebras and communication-free nets, as well as between elements of the algebra and markings of the net.

Definition 3. For labelled Petri nets there is a labeling function $L : T \to Act$ that assigns actions to the transitions. The labeling function L is extended to sequences of transitions in the standard way. If a sequence of transitions σ is fireable at a marking Σ and leads to a new marking Σ' this is denoted by $\Sigma \xrightarrow{\sigma} \Sigma'$.

A sequence σ' is called a **smaller sequence** than σ if its Parikh-vector is smaller (componentwise) than the one of σ. In this case σ is called a **greater sequence** than σ'. σ' is called a **subsequence** of σ if it is a smaller sequence and the transitions occur in the same order.

Definition 4. The *size* of a communication-free net $N = (S, T, W)$ is the space needed to describe it. This implies that if n is the size of N then $|S| \leq n$, $|T| \leq n$ and $\forall t \in T \, \forall s \in S. W(t, s) \leq 2^n$, where W is the weight function that assigns weights to the arcs in the net. The size of a BPP-algebra is the size of the corresponding communication-free net. The size of a marking Σ of N is defined as the number of tokens in it. So the space needed to describe Σ is $O(log(size(\Sigma)))$.

3 Deciding Weak Bisimilarity of a BPP and a Finite State Labelled Transition System

Strong bisimilarity is undecidable for general Petri nets [7] and CCS [10]. However, it is decidable, if a Petri net and a finite-state LTS are strongly bisimilar [8].

On the other hand it is undecidable if a general Petri net and a finite-state LTS are weakly bisimilar [7]. In this section we show that it is decidable if a BPP and a finite-state LTS are weakly bisimilar.

The basic idea is to show that if a weakly finite BPP can reach a state (via a sequence of τ-transitions) that is weakly bisimilar to a finite-state LTS, then it can reach such a state via a sequence of bounded length.

Lemma 5 Dickson's lemma. *For every infinite sequence of vectors $M_1, M_2, \ldots$ in $\mathbb{N}^k$ there are $i < j$ s.t. $M_i \leq M_j$ ($\leq$ taken componentwise).*

Lemma 6. *Weak bisimilarity is a congruence for BPP. Let $\alpha, \beta, \gamma, \delta$ be BPP-processes. $\alpha \approx \beta \land \gamma \approx \delta \Rightarrow \alpha\gamma \approx \beta\delta$.*

Proof The relation $\{(xz, yw) \mid x \approx y, z \approx w\}$ is a weak bisimulation containing $(\alpha\gamma, \beta\delta)$. This is because BPPs are equivalent to communication-free nets, where every transition has only one place in its preset with an arc labelled by 1. $\square$

Lemma 7. *Let R be an LTS with m states. Let $r_1, r_2 \in R$ be states of R. Then $r_1 \approx r_2 \Leftrightarrow r_1 \approx_{(m^2-m)/2} r_2$.*

Proof As R has a finite number of states the relation $\overset{\hat{a}}{\Rightarrow}$ is finitely branching for any $a \in Act$. Therefore $r_1 \approx r_2 \Leftrightarrow \forall n \in \mathbb{N}.r_1 \approx_n r_2$. So if $r_1 \not\approx r_2$, then there must be an $i \in \mathbb{N}$ and a strategy for player A, s.t. he can win every bisimulation game in $\leq i$ rounds. A bisimulation game is described by a sequence of pairs $(r, r') \in R \times R$. There are at most $(m^2 - m)/2$ different such pairs (r, r') (modulo symmetry) with $r \neq r'$. So there must be such an i with $i \leq (m^2 - m)/2$, and therefore $r_1 \not\approx r_2 \Rightarrow r_1 \not\approx_{(m^2-m)/2} r_2$. The other direction is trivial. $\square$

Definition 8. In a communication-free net tokens can move freely through the net, because every transition has only one place in its preset and the arc leading from this place to the transition is labelled by 1. When a transition fires it takes a token from the place in its preset and puts some tokens on the places in its postset. If there are places in the postset of the transition one can freely choose any one of these tokens and call it the *continuation* of the original token. All the others will be called *spin-offs*. Assume a firing sequence σ. A subsequence σ' of σ that does nothing but move a token back to its original place, generating some spin-offs on the way is called a *cycle*. When a cycle is possible it can be repeated an arbitrary number of times, because the resulting marking is bigger than the original one. A cycle does not change a marking, except that it generates some new tokens (the spin-offs).

Sequences not containing any cycles have bounded length.

Lemma 9. *Let (N, Σ) be a communication-free net with marking Σ. Let n be the size of N and x the number of tokens in Σ. Let σ be a firing sequence starting in Σ and not containing any cycle σ' as subsequence. Then $length(\sigma) \leq x\frac{2^{n^2-n}-1}{2^n-1}$.*

Proof Any non-cyclic path in N has a length of at most $n - 1$. As there are no cycles a token can move at most $n - 1$ steps. The firing of a transition increases the number of tokens in the net by at most $2^n - 1$. So the sequence σ has a maximal length of $\sum_{i=0}^{n-2} x * (2^n)^i = x\frac{1-(2^n)^{n-1}}{1-2^n} = x\frac{2^{n^2-n}-1}{2^n-1}$ $\square$

Definition 10. Let N be a Petri net and S the set of its places. For every $x \in \mathbb{N}$ the relation $\leq_x$ on the set of markings of N is defined by

$$\Sigma \leq_x \Sigma' :\Leftrightarrow \Sigma \leq \Sigma' \qquad \land$$
$$\forall s \in S. \, \Sigma(s) < \Sigma'(s) \Rightarrow \Sigma(s) \geq x$$

For every x the relation $\leq_x$ is a partial order.

The following lemmas are used to show that two weakly finite markings Σ, Σ' of a communication-free net with $\Sigma \leq_k \Sigma'$ are weakly bisimilar if k is sufficiently large.

Lemma 11. *Let N be a communication-free net with n places and two markings Σ_1 and Σ_2 s.t. $\Sigma_1 \leq_x \Sigma_2$ for an $x \geq n$. Then for any sequence $\Sigma_2 \xrightarrow{\sigma} \Sigma_2'$ s.t. $L(\sigma) \in \tau^* a \tau^*$ there is a subsequence σ' s.t. $L(\sigma') \in \tau^* a \tau^*$, $\Sigma_1 \xrightarrow{\sigma'} \Sigma_1'$ and $\Sigma_1' \leq_{[x/n]} \Sigma_2'$.*

Proof The only difference between σ and the subsequence σ' are the moves of tokens starting in places s s.t. $\Sigma_1(s) < \Sigma_2(s)$. For such places $\Sigma_1(s) \geq x$. By a sequence of τ-moves in σ a token starting in s is either moved to a place s' (possibly doing cycles on the way, and generating spin-offs) or finally vanishes (by a transition that has no places in its postset). In σ' some, but not necessarily all (at most $[x/n]$) of these moves are imitated. As $\Sigma_1(s) \geq x$ there are enough tokens to move up to $[x/n]$ tokens to any place s' reachable from s, if necessary. If $\Sigma_2'(s) \geq [x/n]$ then keep $[x/n]$ tokens on s, otherwise move further tokens away, s.t. $\Sigma_2'(s) = \Sigma_1'(s)$. All the cycles in σ are imitated in σ'. This is no problem, since cycles just generate new tokens. The single a-move is also imitated. So one gets a Σ_1' that on any place either has the same number of tokens as Σ_2', or at least $[x/n]$. Thus $\Sigma_1' \leq_{[x/n]} \Sigma_2'$. $\qquad\square$

Lemma 12. *Let N be a communication-free net with n places and two markings Σ_1 and Σ_2 s.t. $\Sigma_1 \leq_x \Sigma_2$ for an $x \geq n$. Then for any sequence $\Sigma_1 \xrightarrow{\sigma} \Sigma_1'$ s.t. $L(\sigma) \in \tau^* a \tau^*$ there is a greater sequence σ' s.t. $L(\sigma') \in \tau^* a \tau^*$, $\Sigma_2 \xrightarrow{\sigma'} \Sigma_2'$ and $\Sigma_1' \leq_{[x/n]} \Sigma_2'$.*

Proof Again the only difference between σ and σ' are the moves of tokens starting in places s s.t. $\Sigma_1(s) < \Sigma_2(s)$. For such places $\Sigma_1(s) \geq x$. By a sequence of τ-moves in σ a token starting in s is either moved to a place s' (possibly doing cycles on the way, and generating spin-offs) or finally vanishes (by a transition which has no places in its postset). As $\Sigma_1(s) \geq x$ at least one of the following conditions must be satisfied:

1. There is a path in the net going only through τ-transitions that leads from s to some place s' such that in σ tokens are moved from s to s' s.t. $\Sigma_1'(s') \geq [x/n]$. (Note that it is possible that $s = s'$).
2. There is a path in the net going only through τ-transitions that have only one place in their postset leading from s to a τ-transition t with $t\cdot = \{\}$. (Tokens on s can vanish by a sequence of τ-moves).

In σ' first imitate all the moves of σ. If $\Sigma_1'(s) < [x/n]$ then do the following, depending on which of the conditions is satisfied.

1. If the first condition is satisfied then track the moves of a token that moves from s to s' in σ. Imitate these moves in σ' for all the extra tokens on place s in Σ_2 until the same number of tokens on s is reached as in Σ_1'. The result may be that $\Sigma_2'(s') \gg \Sigma_1'(s')$, but still $\Sigma_1'(s') \geq [x/n]$.

2. In this case let the extra tokens on s in the marking Σ_2 vanish by sequences of τ-moves as described in the second condition, and get $\Sigma_2'(s) = \Sigma_1'(s)$.

Adding these extra τ-moves to σ yields a σ' s.t. σ' is a greater sequence than σ, $\Sigma_2 \xrightarrow{\sigma'} \Sigma_2'$ and $\Sigma_2' \geq_{[x/n]} \Sigma_1'$. □

Lemma 13. *Let Σ_1, Σ_2 be markings of a communication-free net of size n, and r_1, r_2 states in a finite-state LTS. If $r_1 \approx \Sigma_1 \geq_{nk} \Sigma_2 \approx r_2$ then $r_1 \approx_k r_2$.*

Proof by induction on k. If player A makes a move $r_1 \xrightarrow{a} r_1'$, then there exists $\Sigma_1 \xrightarrow{\sigma} \Sigma_1'$ s.t. $L(\sigma) \in \tau^* a \tau^*$ and $r_1' \approx \Sigma_1'$. By Lemma 11 there is a subsequence σ' s.t. $\Sigma_2 \xrightarrow{\sigma'} \Sigma_2'$, $L(\sigma') \in \tau^* a \tau^*$ and $\Sigma_1' \geq_{nk-1} \Sigma_2'$. As $r_2 \approx \Sigma_2$ there is a sequence σ'' s.t. $r_2 \xrightarrow{\sigma''} r_2'$, $L(\sigma'') \in \tau^* a \tau^*$ and $\Sigma_2' \approx r_2'$. By induction hypothesis the result follows. For an attack $r_2 \xrightarrow{a} r_2'$ the strategy is analogous, except that Lemma 12 is used and σ' is a greater sequence than σ (see Figure 1). □

Fig. 1. Strategy for player D to defend for at least k rounds

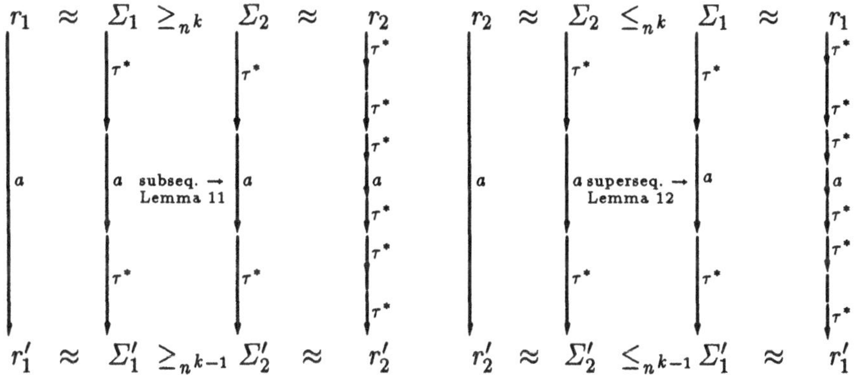

The relation $\bigcup_{i=0}^{n}(\xrightarrow{\tau})^i$ is also denoted by $\xrightarrow{\tau \leq n}$. Let

$$\Lambda(\Sigma, a, l) := \begin{cases} \{\tilde{\Sigma} \mid \Sigma \xrightarrow{\tau \leq l} \xrightarrow{a} \xrightarrow{\tau \leq l} \tilde{\Sigma}\}, & \text{if } a \neq \tau \\ \{\tilde{\Sigma} \mid \Sigma \xrightarrow{\tau \leq 2l+1} \tilde{\Sigma}\}, & \text{if } a = \tau \end{cases}$$

Now we show a bound for the length of a sequence needed to reach a marking that is weakly bisimilar to a finite-state LTS.

Lemma 14. *Let N be a communication-free net of size n and Σ a marking of N containing x tokens. If $\Sigma \xrightarrow{\sigma} \Sigma'$ then for every $k \in \mathbb{N}$ there is a subsequence $\tilde{\sigma}$ of σ s.t. $\Sigma \xrightarrow{\tilde{\sigma}} \tilde{\Sigma}$ and $\tilde{\Sigma} \leq_k \Sigma'$ and*

$$length(\tilde{\sigma}) \leq n^2 k + (x + (2^n - 1)n^2 k) * \frac{2^{n^2-n} - 1}{2^n - 1}$$

Proof $\tilde{\sigma}$ is the same as σ, except that it possibly contains fewer cycles. What is the maximal number of cycles in $\tilde{\sigma}$ that are needed to reach such a $\tilde{\Sigma}$ with $\tilde{\Sigma} \leq_k \Sigma'$? Cycles just generate new tokens, and at most k new tokens need to be produced per place in N. So at most $n * k$ cycles are needed in $\tilde{\sigma}$. In every cycle $\leq n$ transitions are fired, so $\leq (2^n - 1)n^2 k$ new tokens are produced. So at most $x + (2^n - 1)n^2 k$ tokens are in the net for moves without cycles. By Lemma 9 at most $(x + (2^n - 1)n^2 k) * \frac{2^{n^2-n}-1}{2^n-1}$ non-cyclic moves can be made [1]. By adding the numbers of moves belonging to cycles and the non-cyclic moves we get $length(\tilde{\sigma}) \leq n^2 k + (x + (2^n - 1)n^2 k) * \frac{2^{n^2-n}-1}{2^n-1}$. $\qquad\square$

Lemma 15. *Let N be a communication-free net and Σ a marking of N. Let R be a finite-state system and $r \in R$ a state of R. Let n be the size of the net N, x the number of tokens in Σ and m the number of states in R. There is a function $l : \mathbb{N}^3 \to \mathbb{N}$ s.t. $(\Sigma \approx r \ \wedge \ r \overset{a}{\to} r') \ \Rightarrow \ \exists \tilde{\Sigma} \in \Lambda(\Sigma, a, l(n, m, x)). \ \tilde{\Sigma} \approx r'$*

Proof From $r \overset{a}{\to} r'$ and $\Sigma \approx r$ it follows that there exists a Σ' s.t. $\Sigma \overset{\hat{a}}{\Rightarrow} \Sigma'$ and $\Sigma' \approx r'$. Let σ be the sequence leading from Σ to Σ'. By Lemma 14 there is a subsequence $\tilde{\sigma}$ s.t. $\Sigma \overset{\tilde{\sigma}}{\to} \tilde{\Sigma}$, $\tilde{\Sigma} \leq_{n(m^2-m)/2} \Sigma'$ and

$$length(\tilde{\sigma}) \leq n^2 * n^{(m^2-m)/2)} + (x + (2^n - 1)n^2 * n^{(m^2-m)/2)}) \frac{2^{n^2-n} - 1}{2^n - 1} =: l(n, m, x)$$

Therefore $\tilde{\Sigma} \in \Lambda(\Sigma, a, l(n, m, x))$.

It remains to prove that $\tilde{\Sigma} \approx r'$. As $\Sigma \approx r$ and $\Sigma \overset{\tilde{\sigma}}{\to} \tilde{\Sigma}$ there must be a $\tilde{r} \in R$ s.t. $\tilde{\Sigma} \approx \tilde{r}$. Because of Lemma 7 it now suffices to prove that $r' \approx_{(m^2-m)/2} \tilde{r}$. As $\tilde{r} \approx \tilde{\Sigma} \leq_{n(m^2-m)/2} \Sigma' \approx r'$ the result follows from Lemma 13. $\qquad\square$

Definition 16. Let A be a finite set of pairs of the form (r, Σ), where r is a state in a finite-state system R with m states and Σ a marking of a communication-free net of size n. Let $l : \mathbb{N}^3 \to \mathbb{N}$ be the function from Lemma 15. A' is a *bounded weak expansion* of A iff:

- For every pair $(r, \Sigma) \in A$ and every step $r \overset{a}{\to} r'$ there exists a $\Sigma' \in \Lambda(\Sigma, a, l(n, m, x))$ with $(r', \Sigma') \in A'$, where x is the size of Σ.
- For every pair $(r, \Sigma) \in A$ and every step $\Sigma \overset{a}{\to} \Sigma'$ there exists an $r' \in \Lambda(r, a, m - 1)$ with $(r', \Sigma') \in A'$. Note that unlike in the previous case this is no restriction, because R has only m states.
- A' is minimal; no proper subset of A' satisfies these two properties.

Let $bwexp(A)$ be the bounded weak expansions of A. Note that $bwexp(A)$ is finite if A is finite.

---

[1] This does not necessarily mean that the cycles are done first, and the non-cyclic moves afterwards. Moves belonging to cycles and non-cyclic moves can occur in any order.

Lemma 17. *Let A be a finite set of pairs of the form (r, Σ), where r is a state in a finite-state system, Σ a marking of a communication-free net and $r \approx \Sigma$. Then there is a bounded weak expansion $A' \in bwexp(A)$ s.t. $\forall (r', \Sigma') \in A'.r' \approx \Sigma'$.*

Proof directly from Definition 16 and Lemma 15. □

Theorem 18. *It is decidable if a BPP and a finite-state transition system are weakly bisimilar.*

Proof The general structure of the proof is similar to the proof of the decidability of strong bisimulation equivalence for BPP [2]. Basically the decision algorithm builds a finite tableau. Lemma 6 and Dickson's lemma (5) are used to achieve finite depth and Lemma 17 is used to make sure that the proof tree is finitely branching. Details can be found in [9]. □

4 Model Checking Communication-free Nets

Model checking algorithms fall into two classes: iterative algorithms and tableau-based algorithms. While iterative algorithms compute all the states of the system which have the desired property, tableau-based algorithms are designed to check whether a particular expression has a temporal property. This is called local model checking which avoids the investigation of irrelevant parts of the process being verified. Thus they are applicable to the verification of systems with infinite-state spaces. The algorithm here is tableau-based and decides the truth of a formula for an infinite-state concurrent system by examining only finitely many states.

The branching time temporal logic UB^- of [4] is used to describe properties of Petri-nets N. The syntax of the calculus is as follows:

$$\Phi \stackrel{\text{def}}{=} s \geq k \mid s \leq k \mid \neg \Phi \mid \Phi_1 \wedge \Phi_2 \mid \Diamond \Phi$$

where s ranges over the places of N and $k \in \mathbb{N}$. Disjunction and another modal operator $\Box$ can be added by defining $\Box := \neg \Diamond \neg$.

Let $\mathcal{F}$ be the set of all formulae. Let Ω be the set of all markings of N. The denotation $\|\Phi\|$ of a formula Φ is the set of markings of N inductively defined by the following rules:

$$
\begin{aligned}
\|s \geq k\| &= \{\Sigma \mid \Sigma(s) \geq k\} \\
\|s \leq k\| &= \{\Sigma \mid \Sigma(s) \leq k\} \\
\|\neg \Phi\| &= \Omega - \|\Phi\| \\
\|\Phi_1 \wedge \Phi_2\| &= \|\Phi_1\| \cap \|\Phi_2\| \\
\|\Diamond \Phi\| &= \{\Sigma \mid \exists \Sigma \xrightarrow{\sigma} \Sigma'.\Sigma' \in \|\Phi\|\}
\end{aligned}
$$

$\Sigma \in \|\Phi\|$ is also denoted by $\Sigma \models \Phi$. An instance of the model checking problem is a net N with a marking Σ and a formula Φ. The question is if $\Sigma \models \Phi$.

It is possible to add the usual one-step nexttime-operator EX to this logic. For labelled nets it is often denoted as $[a]$, with $a \in Act$ and defined by

$$\|[a]\Phi\| = \{\Sigma \mid \exists \Sigma \xrightarrow{a} \Sigma' \in \|\Phi\|\}$$

The complexity results of this section carry over to this extended logic.

While model checking with UB^- is undecidable for general Petri nets [4] it is still decidable for communication-free nets [4]. The exact complexity of the problem was unknown so far. We show that this model checking problem for communication-free nets is PSPACE-complete.

Definition 19. $\mathcal{F}_d \subset \mathcal{F}$ is defined as the set of all formulae with a nesting depth of modal operators $\Diamond$ of at most d. (It follows that formulae in $\mathcal{F}_0$ contain no modal operators.)

We show that in order to decide $\Sigma \models \Diamond \Phi$ it suffices to check $\Sigma' \models \Phi$ for those Σ' that can be reached from Σ by a sequence of bounded length.

Lemma 20. *Let N be a communication-free net of size n and Σ_1 and Σ_2 two markings of N. Let $\Phi \in \mathcal{F}_d$ and $\hat{k}$ be the maximal k occurring in a subterm of Φ of the form $s \geq k/s \leq k$. If $\Sigma_1 \leq_{(\hat{k}+1)n^d} \Sigma_2$ then $\Sigma_1 \models \Phi \Leftrightarrow \Sigma_2 \models \Phi$.*

Proof by induction on d.

1. If $d = 0$ then Φ doesn't contain any modal operators and $\Sigma_1 \leq_{(\hat{k}+1)} \Sigma_2$. Thus for all places s and any $k \leq \hat{k}$ $\Sigma_1(s) \geq k \Leftrightarrow \Sigma_2(s) \geq k$ and $\Sigma_1(s) \leq k \Leftrightarrow \Sigma_2(s) \leq k$. By induction on the structure of Φ the result follows.
2. Now $d > 0$. For any subterm ψ of Φ s.t. $\psi \in \mathcal{F}_{d-1}$ the induction hypothesis yields $\Sigma_1 \models \psi \Leftrightarrow \Sigma_2 \models \psi$. It only remains to prove that $\Sigma_1 \models \psi \Leftrightarrow \Sigma_2 \models \psi$ for the minimal subterms ψ of Φ s.t. $\psi \in \mathcal{F}_d - \mathcal{F}_{d-1}$. These subterms are of the form $\psi = \Diamond \varphi$ for a $\varphi \in \mathcal{F}_{d-1}$.
   $\Rightarrow$ If $\Sigma_1 \models \Diamond \varphi$ then there is a sequence σ s.t. $\Sigma_1 \xrightarrow{\sigma} \Sigma_1'$ and $\Sigma_1' \models \varphi$. By Lemma 12 there is a greater sequence σ' s.t. $\Sigma_2 \xrightarrow{\sigma'} \Sigma_2'$ and $\Sigma_1' \leq_{(\hat{k}+1)n^{(d-1)}} \Sigma_2'$. By induction hypothesis $\Sigma_2' \models \varphi$ and therefore $\Sigma_2 \models \Diamond \varphi$.
   $\Leftarrow$ If $\Sigma_2 \models \Diamond \varphi$ then there is a sequence σ s.t. $\Sigma_2 \xrightarrow{\sigma} \Sigma_2'$ and $\Sigma_2' \models \varphi$. By Lemma 11 there is a subsequence σ' s.t. $\Sigma_1 \xrightarrow{\sigma'} \Sigma_1'$ and $\Sigma_1' \leq_{(\hat{k}+1)n^{(d-1)}} \Sigma_2'$. By induction hypothesis $\Sigma_1' \models \varphi$ and therefore $\Sigma_1 \models \Diamond \varphi$.

$\square$

Lemma 21. *Let N be a communication-free net of size n, Σ a marking with x tokens, $\Phi \in \mathcal{F}_d$ and $\hat{k}$ be the maximal k in a subterm of Φ of the form $s \geq k/s \leq k$. Then $\Sigma \models \Diamond \Phi \Leftrightarrow \exists \Sigma \xrightarrow{\tilde{\sigma}} \tilde{\Sigma}. \tilde{\Sigma} \models \Phi \wedge length(\tilde{\sigma}) \leq O((x + \hat{k}) * 2^{n^2} * n^d)$*

Proof There must be a sequence σ s.t. $\Sigma \xrightarrow{\sigma} \Sigma'$ and $\Sigma' \models \Phi$. By Lemma 14 there is a subsequence $\tilde{\sigma}$ s.t. $\Sigma \xrightarrow{\tilde{\sigma}} \tilde{\Sigma}$, $\tilde{\Sigma} \leq_{(\hat{k}+1)n^d} \Sigma'$ and

$$length(\tilde{\sigma}) \leq n^2 * ((\hat{k} + 1)n^d) + (x + (2^n - 1) * n^2 * (\hat{k} + 1)n^d) * \frac{2^{n^2-n} - 1}{2^n - 1}$$

So $\Sigma \xrightarrow{\tilde{\sigma}} \tilde{\Sigma}$, $length(\tilde{\sigma}) \leq O((x + \hat{k}) * 2^{n^2} * n^d)$ and by Lemma 20 $\tilde{\Sigma} \models \Phi$. $\square$

Lemma 22. *Let N be a communication-free net, Σ a marking of N and $\Phi \in \mathcal{F}_d$. The problem $\Sigma \models \Diamond\Phi$ can be solved in Σ^p_{d+1}.*

Proof by induction on d. Let n be the size of the whole problem. It follows that N has $\leq n$ places and if $\hat{k}$ is the maximal k occurring in a subterm of Φ of the form $s \leq k/s \geq k$ then $\hat{k} \leq O(2^n)$. Also $x := size(\Sigma) \leq O(2^n)$ and $d \leq O(n)$.

1. If $d = 0$ then Φ doesn't contain any modal operators. By Lemma 21 it suffices to look for a $\Sigma \xrightarrow{\tilde{\sigma}} \tilde{\Sigma}$ s.t. $length(\tilde{\sigma}) \leq O((x + \hat{k})2^{n^2} * n^d)$ and $\tilde{\Sigma} \models \Phi$. As $\hat{k} \leq O(2^n)$ and $x \leq O(2^n)$ and $d \leq O(n)$ the Parikh-vector of $\tilde{\sigma}$ can be written in polynomial space. Esparza [5] showed that for communication-free nets it is decidable in polynomial time if there is a fireable sequence of transitions with a given Parikh-vector. (Let P be the Parikh-vector and M the matrix describing the net. There is a fireable sequence σ with vector P iff $\Sigma + M \cdot P \geq 0$ and every nonempty siphon of the subnet generated by the transitions occurring in P is marked by Σ.) Now guess a Parikh-vector and check in polynomial time if there is a $\tilde{\sigma}$ with this Parikh-vector s.t. $\Sigma \xrightarrow{\tilde{\sigma}} \tilde{\Sigma}$ and $\tilde{\Sigma} \models \Phi$. It only takes polynomial time to compute the resulting marking $\tilde{\Sigma}$ and to check if $\tilde{\Sigma} \models \Phi$. So the problem can be solved in $NP = \Sigma^p_1$.

2. Now $d > 0$. Again by Lemma 21 it suffices to guess a Parikh-vector of polynomial size. Now check in polynomial time if there is a fireable sequence $\tilde{\sigma}$ with this Parikh-vector s.t. $\Sigma \xrightarrow{\tilde{\sigma}} \tilde{\Sigma}$ and compute $\tilde{\Sigma}$ in polynomial time. As $size(\Sigma) = x$ and $length(\tilde{\sigma}) \leq O((x + \hat{k})2^{n^2} * n^d)$ one can assume that $size(\tilde{\Sigma}) \leq O(x + 2^n((x + \hat{k})2^{n^2} * n^d))$. It follows that $size(\tilde{\Sigma}) \leq O(2^{n^2})$. It is possible to apply the induction hypothesis and check if $\tilde{\Sigma} \models \Phi$ in polynomial time with the help of a Σ^p_d-oracle. Therefore the problem can be solved in $NP^{\Sigma^p_d} = \Sigma^p_{d+1}$.

$\square$

Lemma 23. *Let N be a communication-free net, Σ a marking of N and $\Phi \in \mathcal{F}_d$. The problem $\Sigma \models \Diamond\Phi$ is Σ^p_{d+1}-hard.*

Proof by Esparza in [4]. $\square$

This hardness result even holds for communication-free nets with a finite state space. It remains true if the logic is restricted to statements of the form $s > 0$ instead of $s \geq k/s \leq k$.

Theorem 24. *Let N be a communication-free net, Σ a marking of N and $\Phi \in \mathcal{F}_d$. The problem $\Sigma \models \Diamond\Phi$ is Σ^p_{d+1}-complete.*

Proof directly from Lemma 22 and Lemma 23. $\square$

Theorem 25. *Let N be a communication-free net, Σ a marking of N and $\Phi \in \mathcal{F}$. The problem $\Sigma \models \Phi$ is PSPACE-complete.*

Proof By analyzing the proof of Lemma 22 we show a bound for the size of the subsequently computed markings. $size(\tilde{\Sigma}) \leq O(size(\Sigma) * (2^{n^2} * n^d))$. As only d such markings are computed the maximal size is $O(2^{(n^2+log(n)*d)*d})$. As $d \leq O(n)$ the algorithm is in $NSPACE(O(n^3)) \subseteq PSPACE$. PSPACE-hardness follows from the proof of Lemma 23 as the influence of parameter d is linear. $\square$

5 Conclusion

Basic Parallel Processes are a weak model of concurrent computation. It can be argued that any decent model of concurrent computation should be at least as powerful as BPP. What makes them interesting is that they are a model for infinite state concurrent systems that seems to lie just on the "border of decidability". Some properties that are undecidable for more powerful models of concurrent systems are still decidable for BPP. These include strong bisimulation equivalence [2], weak bisimulation equivalence to a finite-state LTS (see section 3) and model checking with the weak branching time temporal logic UB$^-$ of section 4. On the other hand BPP are powerful enough to make some properties undecidable, like model checking with the modal μ-calculus [4] and language equivalence [6].

Acknowledgement

Many thanks to Javier Esparza for helpful discussions.

References

1. S. Christensen. *Decidability and Decomposition in Process Algebras.* PhD thesis, Edinburgh University, 1993.
2. S. Christensen, Y. Hirshfeld, and F. Moller. Bisimulation equivalence is decidable for basic parallel processes. In E. Best, editor, *Proceedings of CONCUR 93*, number 715 in LNCS. Springer Verlag, 1993.
3. S. Christensen, H. Hüttel, and C. Stirling. Bisimulation equivelence is decidable for all context-free processes. In W.R. Cleaveland, editor, *Proceedings of CONCUR 92*, number 630 in LNCS. Springer Verlag, 1992.
4. Javier Esparza. Decidability of model checking for infinite-state concurrent systems. *Acta Informatica*, 1995.
5. Javier Esparza. Petri nets, commutative context-free grammars and basic parallel processes. In Horst Reichel, editor, *Fundamentals of Computation Theory*, number 965 in LNCS. Springer Verlag, 1995.
6. Y. Hirshfeld. Petri nets and the equivalence problem. In *Proceedings of CSL'93*, number 832 in LNCS, pages 165–174. Springer Verlag, 1993.
7. P. Jančar. Undecidability of bisimilarity for petri nets and some related problems. *Theoretical Computer Science*, 1995.
8. P. Jančar and F. Moller. Checking regular properties of petri nets. In Insup Lee and Scott A. Smolka, editors, *Proceedings of CONCUR'95*, number 962 in LNCS. Springer Verlag, 1995.
9. Richard Mayr. Some results on basic parallel processes. Technical Report TUM-I9616, TU-München, March 1996.
10. R. Milner. *Communication and Concurrency.* Prentice Hall, 1989.

Testing Processes for Efficiency

Kamal Jain and S. Arun-Kumar*

Department of Computer Science and Engineering, Indian Institute of Technology,
Hauz Khas, New Delhi 110 016 India.
E-mail: kjain@cc.gatech.edu and sak@cse.iitd.ernet.in

Abstract. *Two notions for comparing the efficiencies of equivalent concurrent systems have been developed and axiomatized in [1] and [2]. Recently Natarajan and Cleaveland have defined a notion of testing [6] which incorporates these ideas as an extension of the testing methodology ([3], [4]). Their extension bounds the run of a test in an effort to compare processes for their relative efficiencies, measured in terms of the amount of internal activity in a process.*

In this paper we explore the feasibility of obtaining other efficiency based preorders in the setting of the testing methodology. We generalize the testing methodology and cast [3] and [6] in the new framework. Further, we provide a variation that is equivalent to that of [6].

Another alternative that we explore is what we call "testing for efficiency". Rather than bound the test runs externally, testing for internal activity in a process is woven into the test itself. This turns out to be a more powerful and flexible method of testing processes for a variety of properties.

The main result of this paper is that the testing-efficiency preorders obtained from all the variations previously considered are coarser than that obtained by "testing for efficiency". We prove appropriate alternate characterizations that are independent of any testing formalism. We also show that the existing methodologies (including [3]) or their equivalent variations can be simulated in the "testing for efficiency" framework.

1 Introduction

The theory of *bisimulation*, originally due to David Park and subsequently adopted by Milner [5] in the study of CCS is one of the simplest and most widely studied among theories for describing and reasoning about concurrent systems. Within this framework two notions for comparing the efficiencies of equivalent concurrent systems have been developed and axiomatized in [1] and [2]. Both these notions integrate a crude notion of efficiency (based on the number of synchronizations a system needs to perform in order to achieve a desired functionality) to compare the efficiencies of extensionally equivalent concurrent systems.

* Supported by project grant SR/OY/M-08/92 of the Department of Science and Technology, Govt. of India.

These notions have the advantages that they are useful for comparing nonterminating interactive systems and they can be smoothly integrated into the existing theory of bisimulation equivalence for concurrent processes.

Among the most important rival theories for reasoning about concurrency is the theory of *testing equivalences* ([3], [4]). It has the advantage over bisimulations that it possesses a good denotational model and is coarser than bisimulation. Intuitively, two *processes* may be considered equal if by interacting with them no observer can distinguish between them. In general, an *observer* (or *test*) is an abstraction of an interacting environment in which a *process* may be placed. In the sequel we formalize these notions in some detail and summarize the most important results obtained in this framework.

This paper is an attempt at developing a theory of testing by which processes may be distinguished not just on their functionalities but that functionally equivalent processes may be compared for their relative efficiencies within a single unified concept of "testing for efficiency". In other words we aim at a generalization of the theory of testing developed in [3] to include efficiency considerations as well.

Our notion of efficiency is, broadly speaking, a relative measure of the amount of internal computation, (which is a measure of the amount of synchronizations required between subprocesses) a process engages in, between interactions with the environment. The testing relation should refine the nondeterminism preorders (defined in [3]) which, for functionally related processes, places a determinate process higher in the hierarchy of well-definedness than an indeterminate one.

Recently Natarajan and Cleaveland [6] have extended the testing methodology of [3] in this direction. The modification they propose is to bound the number of computation steps in any run of the process in a test environment. They obtain preorders which are strictly finer than the testing preorders of [3]. However, the methodology in [6] uses an external (or "meta-testing") constraint, viz. a bound on how long one may conduct a test on a process. Further their preorders suggest that by postponing internal activity more efficient processes are obtained ($a\tau bc$ is considered less efficient than $ab\tau c$). One could explore other ways of constraining the test environment, or even propose alternate ways of tabulating and collating information relating to the results of a test, while retaining the basic testing methodology of [3].

But it would be more satisfactory if, without resorting to such external constraints or to tricky and complicated book-keeping/ mechanisms, one could retain the simplicity of the de Nicola-Hennessy methodology, by ensuring that the activity of testing itself also tests for efficiency and behaviour at one go. In other words, the test must have, woven within itself, the ability to detect and measure the amount of internal activity (signifying the number of synchronizations required between sub-processes) a process engages in during the run of the test. We call this the "testing for efficiency" paradigm. In this paper we generalize and explore various testing methodologies, including "testing for efficiency", and compare them.

The paper is organized as follows. Section 2 defines a generalized framework for testing methodologies; section 3 gives a brief summary of the de Nicola-Hennessy testing methodology in the new framework; section 4 recasts the work of [6], and also treats a modification of the methodology. In section 5 "testing for efficiency" is formalized and behavioural characterizations of the preorders are given. The relationships between the various methodologies for testing processes for efficiency are discussed and proved in section 6. In this section we also suggest a different view of testing methodologies and show why "testing for efficiency" is in some sense more general than the others.

Throughout the paper we use the language of CCS (parameterized on the set of permitted actions) as a vehicle for representing processes and tests. The reader may refer to [3] to gather an understanding of this language. However, the thrust of this paper is to explore testing methodologies in a generalized system setting with an interleaving semantics, in which behaviours may be finite or infinite and system behaviour is characterized by synchronization, causality, nondeterminism and independence of actions.

2 The Testing Methodology

An *Experimental System* ($\mathcal{ES}$) is a structure of the form $\langle Conf, \mapsto, Success, \downarrow \rangle$, where $Conf$ is a set of *configurations* of the form $p\|t$, where p is a *process*, t is a *test* and $\|$ is the *interconnection* (or *interface*) between them. *Success* is a subset of $Conf$, representing *successful* configurations; $\downarrow$ is a postfix unary predicate over the set $Conf$, such that for any $\gamma \in Conf$, $\gamma \downarrow$ means γ is *immediately convergent*; $\mapsto$ is an infix binary relation over $Conf$. $\gamma_1 \mapsto \gamma_2$ means that γ_1 can move via $\mapsto$ to γ_2. $\mapsto^+$ is the transitive closure of $\mapsto$.

A *test run* is represented by a nonempty sequence

$$\gamma_0 \mapsto \gamma_1 \mapsto \gamma_2 \mapsto \cdots \mapsto \gamma_k \mapsto \cdots \qquad (1)$$

of configurations. Such a sequence is a *computation* if it is maximal, i.e. it is infinite or it is finite with a *terminal configuration* which cannot move. Assume the test run 1 is a computation. The *success* of a computation depends on whether it reaches a *successful* configuration. The computation (1) is *successful* if some γ_k is in *Success*. A computation *converges*, denoted by the postfix predicate $\Downarrow$, if it contains a *successful* configuration preceded by immediately convergent configurations only. So (1) *converges* if some γ_k is in *Success* and for all $i < k$, $\gamma_i \downarrow$.

$Comp(\gamma)$ represents the set of all computations with starting configuration γ. We say that γ **may** lead to *success* if $Comp(\gamma)$ contains a *successful* computation, and γ **must** lead to *success* if all the computations in $Comp(\gamma)$ *converge*. Notice that $Comp(\gamma)$ will never be empty, hence γ **must** lead to *success* implies that γ **may** lead to *success*.

In this paper we assume $Conf = (\mathbf{P} \times \mathbf{I} \times \mathbf{T})$, where $\mathbf{P}$ is a set of *processes*, $\mathbf{T}$ is a set of *tests*, both defined as sets of CCS processes and $\mathbf{I}$ is the set of possible *interconnections* between them. The interactions that processes and tests can engage in is synchronization on actions. We therefore assume the existence of two sets Act_P and Act_T denoting the *actions* from which processes and tests are built up respectively. Sometimes however processes and tests make moves independently. Throughout this paper we assume that there exists a distinguished *silent action* τ in Act_P. $V_P = Act_P - \{\tau\}$ is the set of *visible* actions. Typically α, β, ... range over actions and a, b, ... range over the visible actions. Further we always assume $Act_P \subseteq Act_T$ and Act_T contains another distinguished visible action ω signifying *success*. For any set Act of actions, $CCS(Act)$ denotes the set of all CCS processes, where each process is built up using only a finite number of actions in Act. The operational semantics is defined by the *labelled transition system (lts)* $\langle CCS(Act), Act, \longrightarrow \rangle$ where $\longrightarrow \subseteq CCS(Act) \times Act \times CCS(Act)$ is the *transition relation* and $\downarrow$ is as defined in [3]. The set *Success* of successful configurations is defined as $(\mathbf{P} \times \mathbf{I} \times \{t \in \mathbf{T} : t \xrightarrow{\omega}\})$ and $(p\|t) \downarrow$ if $p \downarrow$ and $t \downarrow$.

Definition 1. Let $s \in Act^*$ be a sequence of actions.

1. $s \geq s'$ (or $s' \leq s$) if s can be obtained by removing *some* τ actions from s'.
2. $|s|$ is the length of s.
3. $\|s\|$ is the number of τ actions in s.
4. $\hat{s}$ is the visible content of s (obtained by removing *all* τ actions from s).

Definition 2. Let $s \in Act^*$ be a sequence of actions.

1. $p \xrightarrow{s} p'$ is defined inductively as: $p \xrightarrow{\varepsilon} p$ and $p \xrightarrow{\alpha s'} p'$ if $\exists p'' : p \xrightarrow{\alpha} p'' \xrightarrow{s'} p'$.
2. $p \xRightarrow{s} p'$ is defined inductively as: $p \xRightarrow{\varepsilon} p'$ if $p(\xrightarrow{\tau})^* p'$ and $p \xRightarrow{as'} p'$ if $p \xRightarrow{\varepsilon} \xrightarrow{a} \xRightarrow{s'} p'$.
3. $p \xrightarrow{s}$ (resp. $p \xRightarrow{s}$) if for some p', $p \xrightarrow{s} p'$ (resp. $p \xRightarrow{s} p'$).
4. $p \Downarrow$ iff $p \downarrow$ and $(\forall p' : p \xrightarrow{\tau} p' \Rightarrow p' \Downarrow)$.
5. $p \Downarrow s$ is defined inductively as: $p \Downarrow \varepsilon$ if $p \Downarrow$, and $p \Downarrow \alpha s'$ if $p \Downarrow$ and for all p' such that $p \xRightarrow{\alpha} p'$, $p' \Downarrow s'$.

Definition 3. Let $p \in \mathbf{P}$ and $v \in V_P^*$.

1. $L(p) = \{u \in V_P^* : p \xRightarrow{u}\}$.
2. $S(p) = \{a \in V_P : p \xRightarrow{a}\}$.
3. $L_e(p) = \{r \in Act_P^* : \exists s \geq r : p \xrightarrow{s}\}$
4. $l_{min}(p, v) = inf\{|s| : p \xrightarrow{s} \wedge \hat{s} = v\}$
5. $l_{max}(p, v) = sup\{|s| : p \xrightarrow{s} \wedge \hat{s} = v \wedge p \Downarrow v\}$
6. $l'_{min}(p, v) = inf\{\|s\| : p \xrightarrow{s} \wedge \hat{s} = v\}$
7. $l'_{max}(p, v) = sup\{\|s\| : p \xrightarrow{s} \wedge \hat{s} = v \wedge p \Downarrow v\}$

3 The NH Methodology

The testing methodology (NH) of [3] uses a single interconnection between processes and tests (denoted by $\|$). It defines preorders that relate processes depending on their responses to tests.

Definition 4. Given $Act_T = Act_P \cup \{\omega\}$.

1. The configuration transition relation, $\mapsto$, is defined by the following rules.
   (a) $p \xrightarrow{a} p', t \xrightarrow{a} t' \Rightarrow p\|t \mapsto p'\|t'$
   (b) $p \xrightarrow{\tau} p' \Rightarrow p\|t \mapsto p'\|t$
   (c) $t \xrightarrow{\tau} t' \Rightarrow p\|t \mapsto p\|t'$
2. p **may** t if some computation of $p\|t$ is successful. p **must** t if every computation of $p\|t$ is convergent.
3. $p \sqsubseteq_{may} q$ if for every test t, p **may** $t \Rightarrow q$ **may** t. $p \sqsubseteq_{must} q$ if for every test t, p **must** $t \Rightarrow q$ **must** t.

In general, proofs of $p \sqsubseteq_{may} q$ and $p \sqsubseteq_{must} q$ are non-trivial. In [3] the authors give alternate characterizations of relations $\sqsubseteq_{may}$ and $\sqsubseteq_{must}$ which are reproduced below.

Theorem 5. *Alternate Characterization of NH Preorders.*

1. $p \sqsubseteq_{may} q$ *iff* $L(p) \subseteq L(q)$
2. $p \sqsubseteq_{must} q$ *iff for every* $v \in V_P^*$ *the following holds.*

$$p \Downarrow v \Rightarrow \begin{cases} q \Downarrow v \text{ and} \\ q \xRightarrow{v} q' \Rightarrow \exists p' : p \xRightarrow{v} p' \land S(p') \subseteq S(q') \end{cases}$$

Proof. Refer to [3]. □

4 The NC Methodology

The testing framework of [6] distinguishes processes on the basis of their ability to satisfy a test, given a *bound* on the number of computational steps. The set $\mathbf{I} = \{\|_k : k \geq 0\}$ of interconnections between processes and tests is no longer a singleton but incorporates the bound on the number of computational steps permitted.

Definition 6. Given $Act_T = Act_P \cup \{\omega\}$,

1. The configuration transition relation, $\mapsto$, is defined by the following rules.
   (a) $p \xrightarrow{a} p', t \xrightarrow{a} t', k > 0 \Rightarrow p\|_k t \mapsto p'\|_{k-1} t'$
   (b) $p \xrightarrow{\tau} p', k > 0 \Rightarrow p\|_k t \mapsto p'\|_{k-1} t$
   (c) $t \xrightarrow{\tau} t', k > 0 \Rightarrow p\|_k t \mapsto p\|_{k-1} t'$
2. p **Nmay**$_k$ t if some computation of $p\|_k t$ is successful[2]. p **Nmust**$_k$ t if every computation of $p\|_k t$ is convergent.

---

[2] In [6] **Nmay**$_k$ has been mistakenly defined to hold for convergent computations, as a result of which the processes Ω and $\Omega + a$ are identified in the may case. This then invalidates their Proposition 3.2(1) which attempts to characterize the may-preorder of the NH methodology in terms of NC, and Theorem 3.6(1) which gives an alternate characterization of $\sqsubseteq_{emay}$.

3. $p \sqsubseteq_{Nmay} q$ if for every test t and every natural number k, p **Nmay**$_k$ $t \Rightarrow$ q **Nmay**$_k$ t. $p \sqsubseteq_{Nmust} q$ if for every test t and every natural number k, p **Nmust**$_k$ $t \Rightarrow q$ **Nmust**$_k$ t.

Their motive for defining the new preorders is to obtain comparisons between processes which firstly preserve the nondeterminism preorders of the NH methodology and secondly capture a notion of efficiency in terms of the numbers of computation steps taken by related processes when placed under identical test conditions. Intuitively, for processes p and q, $p \sqsubseteq_{Nmay} q$ if for every successful computation of p under a test t, there exists a successful computation of q (under t) that is at most as long. Similarly, $p \sqsubseteq_{Nmust} q$ if for any test t such that if p **must** t then q **must** t and the longest computation of q (under t) is no longer than the longest computation of p (under t).

Theorem 7. *Alternate Characterization of NC Preorders.*

1. $p \sqsubseteq_{Nmay} q$ *iff* $\forall v \in V_P^* : l_{min}(q, v) \leq l_{min}(p, v)$
2. $p \sqsubseteq_{Nmust} q$ *iff for every* $v \in V_P^*$ *the following holds.*

$$p \Downarrow v \Rightarrow \begin{cases} q \Downarrow v \text{ and} \\ q \xrightarrow{v} q' \Rightarrow \exists p' : p \xrightarrow{v} p' \wedge S(p') \subseteq S(q') \text{ and} \\ l_{max}(q, v) \leq l_{max}(p, v) \end{cases}$$

Proof. Refer to [6]. □

We now define a slight modification of the NC methodology and call it the mNC methodology ('m' for "modified"). Since all comparative relations presume satisfaction of tests under the NH methodology, it only remains to compare the numbers of silent moves that processes make in order to compare them for efficiency. Hence we may completely disregard the synchronizations between process and test and the independent moves performed by a test and impose a bound only on the independent (silent) moves performed by the process. We therefore define a new set $\{\|^k : k \geq 0\}$ of interconnections between processes and tests which incorporates the bound on the number of silent moves a process may perform.

Definition 8. Given $Act_T = Act_P \cup \{\omega\}$,

1. The configuration transition relation, $\mapsto$, is defined by the following rules.
   (a) $p \xrightarrow{a} p', t \xrightarrow{a} t' \Rightarrow p\|^k t \mapsto p'\|^k t'$
   (b) $p \xrightarrow{\tau} p', k > 0 \Rightarrow p\|^k t \mapsto p'\|^{k-1} t$
   (c) $t \xrightarrow{\tau} t' \Rightarrow p\|^k t \mapsto p\|^k t'$
2. p **N'may**$_k$ t if some computation of $p\|^k t$ is successful. p **N'must**$_k$ t if every computation of $p\|^k t$ is convergent.
3. $p \sqsubseteq_{N'may} q$ if for every test t and every natural number k, p **N'may**$_k$ $t \Rightarrow$ q **N'may**$_k$ t. $p \sqsubseteq_{N'must} q$ if for every test t and every natural number k, p **N'must**$_k$ $t \Rightarrow q$ **N'must**$_k$ t.

Theorem 9. *Alternate Characterization of mNC Preorders.*

1. $p \sqsubseteq_{N'may} q$ iff $\forall v \in V_P^* : l'_{min}(q, v) \le l'_{min}(p, v)$
2. $p \sqsubseteq_{N'must} q$ iff for every $v \in V_P^*$ the following holds.

$$p \Downarrow v \Rightarrow \begin{cases} q \Downarrow v \text{ and} \\ q \overset{v}{\Longrightarrow} q' \Rightarrow \exists p' : p \overset{v}{\Longrightarrow} p' \wedge S(p') \subseteq S(q') \text{ and} \\ l'_{max}(q, v) \le l'_{max}(p, v) \end{cases}$$

Proof. The proof of the above theorem is similar to that of Theorem 7. □

Theorem 10. *The equivalence of NC and mNC preorders.*

1. $p \sqsubseteq_{N'may} q$ iff $p \sqsubseteq_{Nmay} q$.
2. $p \sqsubseteq_{N'must} q$ iff $p \sqsubseteq_{Nmust} q$.

Proof. Notice that for any process p and sequence v, $l_{min}(p, v) \le l_{min}(q, v)$ (resp. $l_{max}(p, v) \le l_{max}(q, v)$) if and only if $l'_{min}(p, v) \le l'_{min}(q, v)$ (resp. $l'_{max}(p, v) \le l'_{max}(q, v)$). The claims then follow immediately. □

There are other variations equivalent to NC, but our particular reason for choosing this form of mNC will be made clear in section 6.

5 Testing for Efficiency

In this section we define a new methodology called TFE (an abbreviation of "testing for efficiency"). We introduce a new distinguished invisible action ι in the language of tests. This action is meant to provide a measure of the amount of internal activity in a process. The externally imposed bounds on the lengths of computations in NC and mNC are removed by the introduction of this action into the test; since tests may be nondeterministic, different choices within a test may possess different bounds on the internal activity. Further, the set **I** of interconnections is a two-element set $\{\|_?, \|_!\}$.

Definition 11. Given $Act_T = Act_P \cup \{\omega, \iota\}$.

1. The configuration transition relation, $\mapsto$, is defined by the following rules (with $\| \in \mathbf{I}$).
   1.1 $p \overset{a}{\longrightarrow} p', t \overset{a}{\longrightarrow} t' \Rightarrow p \parallel t \mapsto p' \parallel t'$
   1.2 $p \overset{\tau}{\longrightarrow} p', t \overset{\iota}{\longrightarrow} t' \Rightarrow p \parallel t \mapsto p' \parallel t'$
   1.3 $t \overset{\tau}{\longrightarrow} t' \Rightarrow p \parallel t \mapsto p \parallel t'$.
   2.emay $t \overset{\iota}{\longrightarrow} t' \Rightarrow p \parallel_? t \mapsto p \parallel_? t'$
   2.emust $p \overset{\tau}{\longrightarrow} p' \Rightarrow p \parallel_! t \mapsto p' \parallel_! t$
2. p **emay** t if for some $c \in Comp(p \parallel_? t)$, c is successful. p **emust** t if for every $c \in Comp(p \parallel_! t)$, c is convergent.
3. $p \sqsubseteq_{emay} q$ if for every test t, p **emay** $t \Rightarrow q$ **emay** t. $p \sqsubseteq_{emust} q$ if for every test t, p **emust** $t \Rightarrow q$ **emust** t.

The configuration transition rules **1.1** to **1.3** capture the correctness criteria of the NH methodology. The rules **1.2**, **2.emay** and **2.emust** show how the ι action in our methodology is used to measure the amount of internal activity in a process. As far as **emay**-testing is concerned the rules **1.2** and **2.emay** indicate that every internal move of the process must synchronize with an ι move of the test. However, the test may perform ι moves independently. Hence the number of ι moves in the test represents the *maximum* allowable internal activity which a process may possess in order to pass the test. Consider two processes p and q which are equivalent under the NH methodology ([3]) such that $p \sqsubseteq_{emay} q$ and for some t, **not**$(p \textbf{ emay } t)$ but $q \textbf{ emay } t$. p does not pass the test t because every run of p requires more internal activity than permitted by t, whereas there does exist a run of q which respects the bound on internal activity imposed by t.

The **emust** testing rules are designed to distinguish semantically equivalent processes by their "worst-case" behaviours. How the transition rules work in the case of the the **emust** preorder is best explained by the following example. Note that in the **emust** case a test is not allowed to move independently on ι, though the process is allowed to move independently on τ.

Example 1. Consider the processes $p \equiv \tau\tau a$ and $q \equiv \tau a$ and the test $t \equiv \iota(\iota + a\omega) + a\omega$. It is easy to see that $q \textbf{ emust } t$, whereas **not**$(p \textbf{ emust } t)$ because of the unsuccessful computation

$$p \|_\iota t \mapsto \tau a \|_\iota \iota + a\omega \mapsto a \|_\iota nil$$

The above is the only computation in which all the internal actions of p always synchronize with the ι actions of the test. Every other computation of $p\|_\iota t$ is successful. In fact, any computation in which p performs one or more internal moves independently of t is successful for the same reasons that the computations of $q\|_\iota t$ are all successful.

Theorem 12. *Alternate Characterization of TFE Preorders.*

1. $p \sqsubseteq_{emay} q$ *iff* $L_e(p) \subseteq L_e(q)$
2. $p \sqsubseteq_{emust} q$ *if for every* $s \in Act_P^*$ *the following holds.*

$$p \Downarrow s \Rightarrow \begin{cases} q \Downarrow s \text{ and} \\ q \overset{s}{\Longrightarrow} q' \Rightarrow \exists p' : p \overset{s}{\Longrightarrow} p' \wedge S(p') \subseteq S(q') \end{cases}$$

Proof. 1. ($\Longleftarrow$): Let $p \textbf{ emay } t$ for some test t. Now consider any successful computation of $p\|_? t$

$$p\|_? t \equiv p_0\|_? t_0 \mapsto p_1\|_? t_1 \mapsto p_2\|_? t_2 \mapsto \ldots \mapsto p_n\|_? t_n$$

which implies for some s_p and s_t, $p \overset{s_p}{\longrightarrow} p_n$, $t \overset{s_t}{\longrightarrow} t_n$ and $s_p \geq s_t[\varepsilon/\tau][\tau/\iota]$, where $[r/\alpha]$ denotes the replacement of the action α by the sequence r. Therefore $s_p \in L_e(p)$ and $s_p \in L_e(q)$. Hence for some $s_q \geq s_p$, $q \overset{s_q}{\longrightarrow} q_{n'}$, $t \overset{s_t}{\longrightarrow} t_n$ and $q \textbf{ emay } t$.
($\Longrightarrow$):Define $t_?(s)$ for $s \in Act_P^*$ as

- $t_?(\varepsilon) = \omega$
- $t_?(as) = at_?(s)$
- $t_?(\tau s) = \iota t_?(s)$

For any $s \in L_e(p)$, $p \xrightarrow{s'}$, for some $s' \geq s$. Therefore p **emay** $t_?(s)$ from which we get q **emay** $t_?(s)$ and $s \in L_e(q)$. Hence $L_e(p) \subseteq L_e(q)$.

2. ($\Longleftarrow$): Consider any test, t, such that **not**(q **emust** t). Consider any prefix of an unsuccessful computation of $q\|_!t$.

$$q\|_!t \equiv q_0\|_!t_0 \mapsto q_1\|_!t_1 \mapsto q_2\|_!t_2 \mapsto \ldots \mapsto q_n\|_!t_n \qquad (2)$$

Then there exist s_q and s_t such that $s_q \leq s_t[\varepsilon/\tau][\tau/\iota]$, $q \xrightarrow{s_q} q_n$ and $t \xrightarrow{s_t} t_n$. Now **not**($q \Downarrow s_q$) implies **not**($p \Downarrow s_q$). So assume $q \Downarrow s_q$ and $p \Downarrow s_q$. $q \xrightarrow{s_q} q_n$ implies $\exists p_n : p \xRightarrow{s_q} p_n \wedge S(p_n) \subseteq S(q_n)$. Hence a computation of $p\|_!t$ which mimics (2) with the following prefix exists,

$$p\|_!t \equiv p_0\|_!t_0 \mapsto^+ p_1\|_!t_1 \mapsto^+ p_2\|_!t_2 \mapsto^+ \cdots p_n\|_!t_n \qquad (3)$$

where $p \xrightarrow{s_p} p_n$, and $s_p \leq s_q$. From $S(p_n) \subseteq S(q_n)$ it follows that if $q_n\|_!t_n$ is a terminal configuration then so is $p_n\|_!t_n$. Hence every unsuccessful computation of $q\|_!t$ can be mimicked by an unsuccessful computation of $p\|_!t$. Therefore **not**(p **emust** t) and hence $p \sqsubseteq_{emust} q$.

($\Longrightarrow$): Define $t_!(s, A)$ for any $s \in Act_P^*$ and any finite subset A of Act_P as

- $t_!(\varepsilon, A) = \sum_{a \in A} a\omega$, where $\sum$ is defined in the usual fashion.
- $t_!(as, A) = \tau\omega + at_!(s, A)$
- $t_!(\tau s, A) = \tau\omega + \iota t_!(s, A)$

Notice that

- $p \Downarrow s$ iff p **emust** $t_!(s, \{\tau\})$.
- $p \Downarrow s$ implies that $p \xRightarrow{s}$ iff **not**(p **emust** $t_!(s, \emptyset)$)

Now for any $s \in Act_P^*$ such that $p \Downarrow s$, we have p **emust** $t_!(s, \{\tau\})$ which implies q **emust** $t_!(s, \{\tau\})$ and hence $q \Downarrow s$. If $q \xRightarrow{s} q'$ then **not**(q **emust** $t_!(s, \emptyset)$) which implies **not**(p **emust** $t_!(s, \emptyset)$). Since $p \Downarrow s$ we have $p \xRightarrow{s}$. Hence the set $\{S(p') \subseteq V_P : p \xRightarrow{s} p'\}$ is nonempty and finite (since p is built up from a finite set of actions); let it be the set $\{S_1, \ldots, S_k\}$. If for some $i \leq k$, $S_i \subseteq S(q')$ then the claim follows. Otherwise choose for each $i \leq k$, an action $a_i \in S_i - S(q')$ and consider the set $S = \{a_1, \ldots, a_k\}$. Now we have p **emust** $t_!(s, S)$ and **not**(q **emust** $t_!(s, S)$), which is a contradiction. $\square$

Remark. The tests of the form $t_?(s)$ (resp. $t_!(s, A)$) are sufficient for $\sqsubseteq_{emay}$ (resp. $\sqsubseteq_{emust}$) in the sense that if two processes can be distinguished in the **emay** (resp. **emust**) case by some test, then they can be distinguished by a test of the form $t_?(s)$ (resp. $t_!(s, A)$).

6 Discussion

We have so far considered various testing methodologies and now we prove certain relationships among the preorders defined by the various methodologies considered so far.

Proposition 13. *Relationships among the preorders*

1. $\sqsubseteq_{emay} \subset \sqsubseteq_{N'may} = \sqsubseteq_{Nmay} \subset \sqsubseteq_{may}$
2. $\sqsubseteq_{emust} \subset \sqsubseteq_{N'must} = \sqsubseteq_{Nmust} \subset \sqsubseteq_{must}$

Proof. The equivalence between the preorders of NC and mNC has been established in Theorem 10 and the relationship between the preorders of NC and NH has been established in [6].

1. $\sqsubseteq_{emay} \subset \sqsubseteq_{N'may}$ follows by simply restricting the set of tests to $\{t|\iota^k : t \in CCS(Act_P \cup \{\omega\}), k \geq 0\}$. The strict containment follows from the fact that $\tau ab \sqsubseteq_{N'may} a\tau b$ but not $\tau ab \sqsubseteq_{emay} a\tau b$.
2. $\sqsubseteq_{emust} \subset \sqsubseteq_{N'must}$ follows by restricting the set of tests to $\{t|\iota^{k+1}\Omega : t \in CCS(Act_P \cup \{\omega\}), k \geq 0\}$. The example processes of the last part prove the strictness of the containment.

$\square$

Remark. The proposition above may be easily proven from the alternate characterizations of the relevant preorders. However, we have given proofs that illustrate the relationships between the methodologies themselves rather than merely the preorders induced by them.

Since TFE defines finer preorders than NC (or mNC), one may debate the relative merits of the two methodologies. Our contention is that a process can be made more efficient only by eliminating redundant or wasteful internal activity, and mere postponement (as in the case of $\tau ab \sqsubseteq_{N'may} a\tau b$) does not necessarily constitute greater efficiency. However, consider the processes $p \equiv a + a\tau b$ and $q \equiv a\tau + ab$ which are equivalent in NH. It may be easily shown by the tests $a(\tau\omega + \iota b\omega)$ (which p passes under **emust**, but q does not) and $a(\iota\omega + b\omega)$ (which q passes under **emust**, but p does not) that the two processes are incomparable under **emust**. There may be good reasons to believe that q is a more efficient process than p. Nevertheless, there is a far more important reason for favouring the TFE methodology over the others. We can show that TFE is more general than the other methodologies, because they (or equivalent variations of them) may all be simulated in TFE by simply restricting the set of tests allowed, or by translating the tests in those methodologies to tests in TFE. Let $|$ denote the parallel composition operator in CCS.

1. The NH methodology is simulated in TFE by restricting the set of tests to $\{t|\text{rec } x. \iota x : t \in CCS(Act_P \cup \{\omega\})\}$
2. The mNC methodology is simulated in TFE by restricting the set of tests to $\{t|\iota^k\omega : t \in CCS(Act_P \cup \{\omega\}), k \geq 0\}$

In this sense TFE is the most general methodology studied in this paper. It is also for this reason that we have defined mNC since a direct translation from NC to TFE is more complicated.

In general we may view a testing methodology as a collection **P** of *processes* and a collection Π of *properties*. For any choice $\Gamma \subseteq \Pi$ of properties of interest it is possible to define a preorder $\sqsubseteq_\Gamma$ such that for all processes p and q, $p \sqsubseteq_\Gamma q$ iff for every property π in Γ, p satisfies π implies q also satisfies π. In TFE the set of properties Π may be defined as the set $EMUST \cup EMAY$ where $EMUST = \{\_\mathbf{emust}\ t : t \in CCS(Act_P \cup \{\omega, \iota\})\}$ and $EMAY = \{\_\mathbf{emay}\ t : t \in CCS(Act_P \cup \{\omega, \iota\})\}$. We say p *satisfies* $\_\mathbf{emust}\ t$ (resp. p *satisfies* $\_\mathbf{emay}\ t$) if p **emust** t (resp. p **emay** t). The set of properties of interest for $\sqsubseteq_{emay}$ is $EMAY$ and similarly for $\sqsubseteq_{emust}$ it is $EMUST$. The other methodologies can also be represented in this framework.

We say that a methodology $\mathcal{A}$ with property set Π_A is more *general* than methodology $\mathcal{B}$ with property set Π_B, if they are defined over the same set of *processes* and there exists an algorithmic translation of every property, π_B in Π_B to a property π_A in Π_A, such that for any process p, p *satisfies* π_A iff p *satisfies* π_B. The significance of such a definition is that the methodology $\mathcal{B}$ can be entirely simulated in $\mathcal{A}$. Having defined the sets $MUST$ and MAY in the methodology NH in a manner similar to $EMUST$ and $EMAY$ above, it is easy to see that TFE is more general than NH. Similarly TFE is also more general than mNC as the following shows. Assuming that the sets $N'MAY$ and $N'MUST$ have been constructed, we have that

1. $\_\mathbf{N'may}_k\ t$ may be translated to $\_\mathbf{emay}t|\iota^k\Omega$
2. $\_\mathbf{N'must}_k\ t$ may be translated to $\_\mathbf{emust}t|\iota^{k+1}\Omega$

It is not clear whether it is possible to give an algorithmic translation from NC to TFE.

References

1. S. Arun-Kumar and M. Hennessy. An efficiency preorder for processes. *Acta Informatica*, 29:737–760, 1992.
2. S. Arun-Kumar and V. Natarajan. Conformance: A precongruence close to bisimilarity. In *STRICT, Berlin 1995*, number 526 in Workshops in Computing Series, pages 55–68. Springer-Verlag, 1995.
3. R. de Nicola and M. Hennessy. Testing equivalence for processes. *Theoretical Computer Science*, 34:83–133, 1983.
4. M. Hennessy. *Algebraic Theory of Processes*. MIT Press, 1988.
5. R. Milner. *Communication and Concurrency*. Prentice-Hall International, 1989.
6. V. Natarajan and R. Cleaveland. An algebraic theory of process efficiency. In *Logic in Computer Science '96*. IEEE Computer Society Press, 1996.

Regularity is Decidable for Normed PA Processes in Polynomial Time

Antonín Kučera
e-mail: tony@fi.muni.cz

Faculty of Informatics, Masaryk University
Botanická 68a, 60200 Brno
Czech Republic

Abstract. A process Δ is regular if it is bisimilar to a process Δ' with finitely many states. We prove that regularity of normed PA processes is decidable and we present a practically usable polynomial-time algorithm. Moreover, if the tested normed PA process Δ is regular then the process Δ' can be effectively constructed. It implies decidability of bisimulation equivalence for any pair of processes such that one process of this pair is a normed PA process and the other process has finitely many states.

1 Introduction

We consider the problem of deciding regularity of normed PA processes. A process Δ is regular if there is a process Δ' with finitely many states such that $\Delta \sim \Delta'$. Finite-state processes have been intensively studied in the last decades (see e.g. [16]). Almost all interesting properties are decidable for finite-state processes. Moreover, designed algorithms are practically usable.

This is no more true if one moves to process classes which contain also processes with infinitely many states (up to bisimilarity). Some problems can remain decidable—for example, bisimilarity is known to be decidable for BPA (see [1, 5, 9, 10, 7]) and BPP (see [6]) processes. The same problem becomes undecidable for labelled Petri nets (see [11]). But even if a given property is decidable, the algorithm is usually not interesting from the practical point of view due to its complexity. Before running a complex algorithm, it is a good idea to ask whether the process we are dealing with can be replaced with some equivalent (bisimilar) process with finitely many states. If so, we can usually run a much more efficient algorithm. Natural questions are, whether the regularity is decidable for a given class of processes and whether the equivalent finite-state process can be effectively constructed.

Mauw and Mulder showed in [15] that "regularity" of BPA processes is decidable. The quotes are important here because Mauw and Mulder used the word regularity in a different sense—a BPA process is "regular" if each of its variables denotes a regular process. This notion is thus strongly dependent on BPA syntax. It is not clear how to define "regularity" e.g. for Petri nets. However, with a help of this result one can easily conclude that regularity is decidable for normed BPA processes (see [13]). A similar result holds for normed BPP processes (see [13]). Both algorithms are polynomial and easy to implement.

A recent result of Esparza and Jančar [8] says that regularity is decidable for labelled Petri nets. The algorithm is obtained by a combination of two semi-decidability results and hence there are no complexity estimations. Furthermore, Burkart, Caucal and Steffen showed in [4] that regularity is decidable for all BPA processes.

An interesting related problem is decidability of various behavioural equivalences and preorders for pairs of processes such that one process of this pair is regular. For example, Jančar and Moller proved in [12] that bisimilarity is decidable for a pair of labelled Petri nets provided one net of this pair is bounded (regular). The same result holds for trace equivalence and simulation equivalence.

In this paper we prove that regularity is decidable for normed PA processes. PA processes appeared as a natural subclass of ACP processes (see [2]). It is strictly greater than the union of normed BPP and normed BPA processes and it is incomparable with the class of labelled Petri nets. Our regularity test for normed PA processes is of polynomial time complexity. Moreover, if the tested normed PA process is regular then we can also construct a bisimilar finite-state process—and therefore we can also decide bisimilarity for pairs of processes such that one process of this pair is a normed PA process and the other has finitely many states. The problem of decidability of bisimulation equivalence for (normed) PA processes is open, hence this result can be seen as the first small step towards the solution.

2 Basic definitions

2.1 PA processes

Let $Act = \{a, b, c, \ldots\}$ be a countably infinite set of *atomic actions*. Let $Var = \{X, Y, Z, \ldots\}$ be a countably infinite set of *variables* such that $Var \cap Act = \emptyset$. The class of recursive PA expressions is defined by the following abstract syntax equations:

$$E_{PA} ::= a \mid X \mid E_{PA}.E_{PA} \mid E_{PA}\|E_{PA} \mid E_{PA}\|E_{PA} \mid E_{PA} + E_{PA}$$

Here a ranges over Act and X ranges over Var. The symbol Act^* denotes the set of all finite strings over Act.

As usual, we restrict our attention to guarded expressions. A PA expression E is *guarded* if every variable occurence in E is within the scope of an atomic action.

A *guarded PA process* is defined by a finite family Δ of recursive process equations

$$\Delta = \{X_i \stackrel{def}{=} E_i \mid 1 \leq i \leq n\}$$

where X_i are distinct elements of Var and E_i are guarded PA expressions, containing variables from $\{X_1, \ldots, X_n\}$. The set of variables which appear in Δ is denoted by $Var(\Delta)$.

The variable X_1 plays a special role (X_1 is sometimes called "the leading variable")—it is a root of a labelled transition system, defined by the process Δ and following rules:

$$\frac{}{a \stackrel{a}{\to} \epsilon} \qquad \frac{E \stackrel{a}{\to} E'}{E.F \stackrel{a}{\to} E'.F} \qquad \frac{E \stackrel{a}{\to} E'}{E + F \stackrel{a}{\to} E'} \qquad \frac{F \stackrel{a}{\to} F'}{E + F \stackrel{a}{\to} F'}$$

$$\frac{E \stackrel{a}{\to} E'}{E \| F \stackrel{a}{\to} E' \| F} \qquad \frac{F \stackrel{a}{\to} F'}{E \| F \stackrel{a}{\to} E \| F'} \qquad \frac{E \stackrel{a}{\to} E'}{E \| F \stackrel{a}{\to} E' \| F} \qquad \frac{E \stackrel{a}{\to} E'}{X \stackrel{a}{\to} E'} \; (X \stackrel{def}{=} E \in \Delta)$$

The symbol ϵ denotes the empty expression with usual conventions: $\epsilon \| E = E$, $E \| \epsilon = E$, $\epsilon.E = E$, $\epsilon \| E = E$ and $E \| \epsilon = E$. Nodes of the transition system generated by Δ are PA expressions, which are often called *states of Δ*, or just "states" when Δ is understood from the context. We also define the relation $\stackrel{w}{\to}^*$ where $w \in Act^*$ as the reflexive and transitive closure of $\stackrel{a}{\to}$ (we often write $E \to^* F$ instead of $E \stackrel{w}{\to}^* F$ if w is irrelevant). Given two states E, F, we say that F is *reachable from* E, if $E \to^* F$. States of Δ which are reachable from X_1 are said to be *reachable*.

Bisimulation The equivalence between process expressions (states) we are interested in here is *bisimilarity* [17], defined as follows:

Definition 1. A binary relation R over process expressions is a *bisimulation* if whenever $(E, F) \in R$ then for each $a \in Act$

- if $E \stackrel{a}{\to} E'$, then $F \stackrel{a}{\to} F'$ for some F' such that $(E', F') \in R$
- if $F \stackrel{a}{\to} F'$, then $E \stackrel{a}{\to} E'$ for some E' such that $(E', F') \in R$

Processes Δ and Δ' are *bisimilar*, written $\Delta \sim \Delta'$, if their leading variables are related by some bisimulation.

Normed processes An important subclass of PA processes can be obtained by an extra restriction of *normedness*. A variable $X \in Var(\Delta)$ is *normed* if there is $w \in Act^*$ such that $X \stackrel{w}{\to}^* \epsilon$. In that case we define the *norm* of X, written $[X]$, to be the length of the shortest such w. Thus $[X] = \min\{length(w) \mid X \stackrel{w}{\to}^* \epsilon\}$. A process Δ is *normed*, if all variables of $Var(\Delta)$ are normed. The norm of Δ is then defined to be the norm of X_1.

A normal form for PA processes Before we present a normal form for PA processes, we need to introduce the set of *VPA expressions* defined inductively as follows:

1. The empty expression ϵ is a *VPA* expression.
2. Each variable $X \in Var$ is a *VPA* expression.
3. If α, β are nonempty *VPA* expressions, then $\alpha.\beta$, $\alpha \| \beta$ and $\alpha \| \beta$ are *VPA* expressions.
4. Each *VPA* expression can be constructed using the rules 1, 2 and 3 in a finite number of steps.

We use Greek letters $\alpha, \beta, \dots$ to range over *VPA* expressions. The set of *VPA* expressions which contain only variables from $Var(\Delta)$, where Δ is a PA process, is denoted $VPA(\Delta)$. Finally, the set of variables which appear in a *VPA* expression α is denoted $Var(\alpha)$.

Definition 2. A PA process Δ is said to be in *normal form* if all its equations are of the form

$$X_i \stackrel{def}{=} \sum_{j=1}^{n_i} a_{ij} \alpha_{ij}$$

where $1 \leq i \leq n$, $n_i \in N$, $a_{ij} \in Act$ and $\alpha_{ij} \in VPA(\Delta)$. Moreover, we also require that for each X_i, $1 \leq i \leq n$ there is a reachable state $\alpha \in VPA(\Delta)$ such that $X_i \in Var(\alpha)$.

Any PA process can be effectively presented in normal form (see [3]). From now on we assume that all PA processes we are working with are presented in normal form. This justifies also the assumption that all reachable states of a PA process Δ are elements of $VPA(\Delta)$.

2.2 Regular processes

The main question considered in this paper is whether regularity of normed PA processes is decidable. The next definition explains what is meant by the notion of regularity.

Definition 3. A process Δ is *regular* if there is a process Δ' with finitely many states such that $\Delta \sim \Delta'$.

It is easy to see that a process is regular iff it can reach only finitely many states up to bisimilarity. In [16] it is shown that regular processes can be represented in the following normal form:

Definition 4. A regular process Δ is said to be in normal form if all its equations are of the form

$$X_i \stackrel{def}{=} \sum_{j=1}^{n_i} a_{ij} X_{ij}$$

where $1 \leq i \leq n$, $n_i \in N$, $a_{ij} \in Act$ and $X_{ij} \in Var(\Delta)$.

Thus a process Δ is regular iff there is a regular process Δ' in normal form such that $\Delta \sim \Delta'$. In the next section we show that regularity of normed PA processes is decidable. Moreover, if a given normed PA process Δ is regular then the process Δ' can be effectively constructed.

Lemma 5. A process Δ is not regular iff there is an infinite path $X_1 = \alpha_0 \stackrel{a_0}{\rightarrow} \alpha_1 \stackrel{a_1}{\rightarrow} \alpha_2 \stackrel{a_2}{\rightarrow} \cdots$ such that $\alpha_i \not\sim \alpha_j$ for $i \neq j$.

Proof. It can be found e.g. in [13].

3 Decidability of regularity for normed PA processes

3.1 The inheritance tree

Let Δ be a normed PA process. The aim of the following definition is to describe all variables in a state $\alpha \in VPA(\Delta)$ which can potentially emit an action:

Definition 6. Let Δ be a normed PA process. For each $\alpha \in VPA(\Delta)$ we define the set $FIRE(\alpha)$ in the following way:

$$FIRE(\alpha) = \begin{cases} \emptyset & \text{if } \alpha = \epsilon \\ \{X\} & \text{if } \alpha = X \\ FIRE(\beta_1) & \text{if } \alpha = \beta_1.\beta_2 \text{ or } \alpha = \beta_1 \| \beta_2 \\ FIRE(\beta_1) \cup FIRE(\beta_2) & \text{if } \alpha = \beta_1 \| \beta_2 \end{cases}$$

The following function is needed in some proofs of this section:

Definition 7. The function $Length : VPA \to N \cup \{0\}$ returns for each $\alpha \in VPA$ the number of variables contained in α, distinguishing multiple occurence of the same variable.

Lemma 8. Let Δ be a normed PA process, $\alpha \in VPA(\Delta)$. Then for each $X \in Var(\alpha)$ there is $\beta \in VPA(\Delta)$ such that $\alpha \to^* \beta$ and $X \in FIRE(\beta)$.

The following concept stands behind many constructions of this paper:

Definition 9. For each $\alpha \in VPA$ we define the set $Tail(\alpha) \subseteq Var$ in the following way:

$$Tail(\alpha) = \begin{cases} \{X\} & \text{if } \alpha = X \\ \emptyset & \text{if } \alpha = \epsilon \text{ or } \alpha = \beta \| \gamma \text{ where } \beta \neq \epsilon \neq \gamma \\ Tail(\gamma) - Var(\beta) & \text{if } \alpha = \beta.\gamma \text{ or } \alpha = \beta \| \gamma \text{ where } \beta \neq \epsilon \neq \gamma \end{cases}$$

Remark 10. The set $Tail(\alpha)$ provides two important pieces of information:

1. If $X \in Var(\alpha)$ such that $X \notin Tail(\alpha)$, then there is α' such that $\alpha \to^* \alpha'$, $X \in FIRE(\alpha')$ and $Length(\alpha') \geq 2$.
2. If $X \in Tail(\alpha)$, then the only occurence of X in α can become active (i.e. X can emit an action) after all other variables disappear.

Definition 11. Let Δ be a normed PA process. A variable $X \in Var(\Delta)$ is *growing* if there is $\alpha \in VPA(\Delta)$ such that $X \to^* \alpha$, $X \in FIRE(\alpha)$ and $Length(\alpha) \geq 2$.

Lemma 12. Let Δ be a normed PA process. The problem whether $Var(\Delta)$ contains a growing variable is decidable in polynomial time.

Proof. We define the binary relation $GROW$ on $Var(\Delta)$ in the following way:

$$(X, Y) \in GROW \overset{\text{def}}{\Longleftrightarrow} \exists \beta \in VPA(\Delta) \text{ such that } X \to^* \beta \text{ where}$$
$$Length(\beta) \geq 2 \text{ and } Y \in FIRE(\beta).$$

Clearly $Var(\Delta)$ contains a growing variable iff there is $X \in Var(\Delta)$ such that $(X, X) \in GROW$. We show that the relation $GROW$ can be effectively constructed in polynomial time. We need two auxiliary binary relations on $Var(\Delta)$:

$X \rightsquigarrow Y \quad \overset{\text{def}}{\Longleftrightarrow} \quad$ there is a summand $a\alpha$ in the defining equation for X in Δ such that $Length(\alpha) \geq 2$, $Y \in Var(\Delta)$ and $Y \notin Tail(\alpha)$

$X \hookrightarrow Y \quad \overset{\text{def}}{\Longleftrightarrow} \quad$ there is a summand $a\alpha$ in the defining equation for X in Δ such that $Y \in Var(\alpha)$.

It is easy to prove that $GROW = \hookrightarrow^* . \rightsquigarrow . \hookrightarrow^*$ where $\hookrightarrow^*$ denotes the reflexive and transitive closure of $\hookrightarrow$. Moreover, the composition $\hookrightarrow^* . \rightsquigarrow . \hookrightarrow^*$ can be constructed in polynomial time.

Let Δ be a normed PA process. If Δ is not regular then there is (due to Lemma 5) an infinite path $\mathcal{P}$ of the form $X_1 = \alpha_0 \overset{a_0}{\to} \alpha_1 \overset{a_1}{\to} \alpha_2 \overset{a_2}{\to} \cdots$ such that $\alpha_i \not\sim \alpha_j$ for $i \neq j$. To be able to examine properties of $\mathcal{P}$ in a detail, we define for $\mathcal{P}$ the corresponding *inheritance tree*, denoted $IT_\mathcal{P}$. The aim of this construction is to describe the relationship between variables which are located in successive states of $\mathcal{P}$. The way how $IT_\mathcal{P}$ is constructed is similar to the construction of a derivation tree for a word $w \in L(G)$ where $L(G)$ is a language generated by a context-free grammar G. We start with an example which shows how $IT_\mathcal{P}$ looks for a given prefix of $\mathcal{P}$.

Example 1. Let Δ be a normed PA process given by the following set of equations:

$$\{ X \overset{\text{def}}{=} b + a(Y.(Z\|Y)), \ Y \overset{\text{def}}{=} c + b(Y.Z.X), \ Z \overset{\text{def}}{=} a + a((Z\|Y).X) \}$$

Let $\mathcal{P} = X \overset{a}{\to} Y.(Z\|Y) \overset{c}{\to} Z\|Y \overset{a}{\to} ((Z\|Y).X)\|Y \overset{b}{\to} ((Z\|Y).X)\|(Y.Z.X) \cdots$. If we draw a fragment of $IT_\mathcal{P}$, we get the following picture:

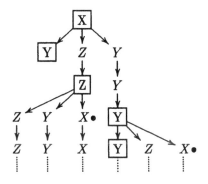

Nodes of $IT_{\mathcal{P}}$ are labelled with variables of $Var(\Delta)$. The state $\alpha_i, i \in N \cup \{0\}$ of $\mathcal{P}$ corresponds to the set of nodes in $IT_{\mathcal{P}}$ which have the distance i from the root of $IT_{\mathcal{P}}$ (the root itself has the distance 0). This set of nodes is called the ith *Level* of $IT_{\mathcal{P}}$. Each transition $\alpha_i \overset{a_i}{\to} \alpha_{i+1}$ is due to a single variable $A \in Var(\alpha_i)$ and a transition $A \overset{a_i}{\to} \gamma$ where the expression $a_i\gamma$ is a summand in the defining equation for A in Δ (see Definition 2). Moreover, α_{i+1} can be obtained from α_i by replacing one occurence of A with γ (here we must distinguish between multiple occurence of the variable A within the state α_i). We call the variable A the *active variable* of α_i and the transition $A \overset{a_i}{\to} \gamma$ the *step* of α_i. The nodes of $IT_{\mathcal{P}}$ which correspond to active variables are called *active*. Each active node is placed within a box in the previous example.

Nodes and edges of $IT_{\mathcal{P}}$ are defined inductively—we define all nodes in the *Level* $i+1$ together with their labels, using the nodes from the *Level* i. Moreover, we also define all edges between nodes in these two levels.

1. **i=0:** There is just one node N in the *Level* 0 — the root, labelled X_1.
2. **induction step:** Let us suppose that nodes of *Level* i have been already defined. For each node U from *Level* i we define its immediate successors. There are two possibilities:
   - **U is not active:** Then U has just one immediate successor whose label is the same as the label of U.
   - **U is active:** Let $A \overset{a_i}{\to} \gamma$ be the step of α_i and let $n = Length(\gamma)$. The node U (whose label is A) has n immediate successors (if $n = 0$ then U is a leaf). The label of the lth immediate successor of U is the lth variable from γ, reading γ from left to right. Here l ranges from 1 to n. As we cannot afford to lose the information about the structure of γ completely, we distinguish the case when $Tail(\gamma) = \{B\}$ where $B \in Var(\Delta)$. Then we say, that the last successor of U is a *tail* of U. In the example above, tails are marked with a black dot.

A node of $IT_{\mathcal{P}}$ which has at least two immediate successors is called a *branching node*. Branching nodes are especially important because their labels are potential candidates to be growing. This is the basic idea which stands behind the notion of the *Allow set*.

Definition 13. For each node U of $IT_{\mathcal{P}}$ we define the set $Allow(U) \subseteq Var(\Delta)$ in the following way:

- If U is the root of $IT_{\mathcal{P}}$, then $Allow(U) = Var(\Delta)$.
- If U is an immediate successor of a node V, then
  - If V is not branching, then $Allow(U) = Allow(V)$.
  - If V is branching and U is not a tail of V, then $Allow(U) = Allow(V) - \{Label(V)\}$.
  - If V is branching and U is a tail of V, then $Allow(U) = Allow(V)$.

The next lemma explains what is the relationship between a node U and the set $Allow(U)$:

Lemma 14. *Let U be a node of $IT_\mathcal{P}$. If $Label(U) \notin Allow(U)$ then $Label(U)$ is a growing variable.*

Now we prove the first main theorem of this paper:

Theorem 15. *A normed PA process Δ is regular iff $Var(\Delta)$ does not contain any growing variable.*

Proof.
($\Rightarrow$) : Let $X \in Var(\Delta)$ be a growing variable. We show that Δ can reach infinitely many pairwise non-bisimilar states. To do this, it suffices to show that for any $k \in N$ there is a reachable state $\alpha \in VPA(\Delta)$ such that $[\alpha] \geq k$ (bisimilar processes must have the same norm). As X is growing, there is $\gamma \in VPA(\Delta)$ such that $X \to^* \gamma$, $X \in FIRE(\gamma)$ and $Length(\gamma) \geq 2$. Moreover, there is a reachable state $\beta_1 \in VPA(\Delta)$ such that $X \in FIRE(\beta_1)$ (it follows from the Definition 2 and Lemma 8). Thus $\beta_1 \to^* \beta_2$ where β_2 is obtained from β_1 by replacing one occurence of X with γ. As $X \in FIRE(\beta_1)$, each variable from $FIRE(\gamma)$ belongs to $FIRE(\beta_2)$—hence $X \in FIRE(\beta_2)$. Moreover, $Length(\beta_2) > Length(\beta_1)$ because $Length(\gamma) \geq 2$. As $X \in FIRE(\beta_2)$, we can repeat this construction producing β_3 and so on. As $Length(\beta_i) > Length(\beta_j)$ for each $i > j$, the state β_k has the property $Length(\beta_k) \geq k$, thus $[\beta_k] \geq k$.

($\Leftarrow$) : This part of the proof is more complicated. The basic scheme is similar to the method which was used by Mauw and Mulder in [15] and can be described in the following way: We need to show that if Δ is not regular then there is a growing variable $X \in Var(\Delta)$. As Δ is not regular, there is (due to Lemma 5) an infinite path $\mathcal{P}$ of the form $X_1 = \alpha_0 \overset{a_0}{\to} \alpha_1 \overset{a_1}{\to} \alpha_2 \overset{a_2}{\to} \cdots$ such that $\alpha_i \not\sim \alpha_j$ for $i \neq j$. We show that if $Var(\Delta)$ does not contain any growing variable, then there are $i \neq j$ such that $\alpha_i \sim \alpha_j$. It contradicts the assumption above—hence $Var(\Delta)$ contains at least one growing variable.

Let $IT_\mathcal{P}$ be the inheritance tree for the path $\mathcal{P}$. To complete the proof we need to divide $IT_\mathcal{P}$ into more manageable units called *blocks*.

Levels of $IT_\mathcal{P}$ which contain just one node are called *delimiters* of $IT_\mathcal{P}$. A *block* of $IT_\mathcal{P}$ is a subgraph S of $IT_\mathcal{P}$ composed of:

1. all nodes and edges between two successive delimiters i and j where $i < j$. The only node of *Level i* is called the *opening* node of S and the only node of *Level j* is called the *closing* node of S. Out-going edges of the closing node and in-going edges of the opening node are not a part of S.
2. all nodes below the delimiter i (including *Level i*), if there is no delimiter j with $j > i$. The only node of *Level i* is called the *opening* node of S. In-going edges of the opening node are not a part of S.

As *Level* 0 is a delimiter of $IT_\mathcal{P}$, we can view $IT_\mathcal{P}$ as a vertical sequence of blocks.

The *width* of $IT_\mathcal{P}$ is defined to be the least $n \in N$ such that the cardinality of ith *Level* of $IT_\mathcal{P}$ is less or equal n for each $i \in N \cup \{0\}$. If there is no such n, we define the width of $IT_\mathcal{P}$ to be ∞.

Similarly, if S is a block of $IT_{\mathcal{P}}$, the *width* of S is the least $n \in N$ such that the cardinality of each *Level* which is a part of S is less or equal n. If there is no such n, we define the width of S to be ∞.

Furthermore, we define the *branching degree* of $IT_{\mathcal{P}}$ to be the least $n \in N$ such that each node U of $IT_{\mathcal{P}}$ has at most n immediate successors. The branching degree of $IT_{\mathcal{P}}$ is always finite (it actually depends only on Δ—let $\mathcal{M}$ be the set of all *VPA* expressions, which appear in defining equations of Δ (see Definition 2). The branching degree of $IT_{\mathcal{P}}$ is then at most $\max\{Length(\beta) \mid \beta \in \mathcal{M}\}$). We denote the branching degree of $IT_{\mathcal{P}}$ by $\mathcal{D}$ in the rest of this proof.

Each node U of $IT_{\mathcal{P}}$ defines its associated subtree, rooted by U. This subtree is denoted $Subtree(U)$. Although the notions of block, width, branching node, tail, etc. were originally defined for $IT_{\mathcal{P}}$, they can be used also for any $Subtree(U)$ of $IT_{\mathcal{P}}$ in an obvious way.

We prove that if $Var(\Delta)$ does not contain any growing variable, then for each node U of $IT_{\mathcal{P}}$ the $Subtree(U)$ has the width at most $\mathcal{D}^{n-1}$, where $n = card(Allow(U))$.

We proceed by induction on $n = card(Allow(U))$: First, if $Var(\Delta)$ does not contain any growing variable, then $Subtree(U)$ does not contain any node U with $Allow(U) = \emptyset$. This is due to Lemma 14—clearly $Label(U) \notin \emptyset$, thus $Label(U)$ would be a growing variable. Hence n is at least 1.

1. **n=1:** Let $Allow(U) = \{X\}$. We show that $Subtree(U)$ does not contain any branching node. Let us assume the opposite. Then there is a branching node V in $Subtree(U)$ with $Allow(V) = \{X\}$, thus $Label(V) = X$. As V is branching, at least one immediate successor V' of V has the property $Allow(V') = Allow(V) - \{Label(V)\} = \emptyset$. Hence $Label(V')$ is a growing variable and we have a contradiction. As $Subtree(U)$ does not contain any branching node, the width of $Subtree(U)$ is $1 = \mathcal{D}^{n-1}$.

2. **induction step:** Let $card(Allow(U)) = n$. We prove that each block of $Subtree(U)$ has the width at most $\mathcal{D}^{n-1}$. Let S be a block of $Subtree(U)$ and let V be its opening node. Clearly $card(Allow(V)) \leq n$. If V has no successors then the width of S is 1. If V is not branching then the only immediate succesor of V is a closing node of S, thus the width of S equals 1. If V is branching, there are two possibilities:

   - V does not have a tail. Then each immediate successor V' of V has the property $card(Allow(V')) \leq n - 1$. By induction hypothesis, the width of $Subtree(V')$ is at most $\mathcal{D}^{n-2}$. As V can have at most $\mathcal{D}$ immediate successors, the width of $Subtree(V)$ is at most $\mathcal{D}.\mathcal{D}^{n-2} = \mathcal{D}^{n-1}$. Thus the width of S is also at most $\mathcal{D}^{n-1}$.

   - V has a tail T. Each immediate successor V' of V which is different from T has the property $card(Allow(V')) \leq n - 1$. Hence we can use the induction hypothesis for each such V'. The only problem is the node T. We show, that if T has a branching successor T' then the node T' is either the closing node of the block S or it is a successor of the closing node of the block S—hence the block S can have the width at most $(\mathcal{D} - 1).\mathcal{D}^{n-2} + 1$.

Suppose that T has a branching successor T'. Branching nodes are always active—thus T has at least one active successor. Let W be the active successor of T which has the least distance from T. The node T' is clearly either the node W (if W is branching), or a successor of W. We show, that the node W is the closing node of the block S. But it follows directly from the definition of the tail (see Remark 10)—as W is active, there are no successors of V in the level of W except the node W itself.

We have just proved that if $Var(\Delta)$ does not contain any growing variable then the width of $IT_{\mathcal{P}}$ is at most $\mathcal{D}^{card(Var(\Delta))-1}$. Hence each element α_i of $\mathcal{P}$ has the property $Length(\alpha_i) \leq \mathcal{D}^{card(Var(\Delta))-1}$. As $Var(\Delta)$ is finite, there are only finitely many $VPA(\Delta)$ expressions whose $Length$ is at most $\mathcal{D}^{card(Var(\Delta))-1}$. Therefore there are $i, j \in N \cup \{0\}$, $i \neq j$, such that $\alpha_i = \alpha_j$ and thus $\alpha_i \sim \alpha_j$.

3.2 A construction of the process Δ' in normal form

In this section we show that if a given normed PA process Δ is regular, then Δ can be effectively transformed into a regular process Δ' in normal form such that $\Delta \sim \Delta'$. Due to the lack of space we describe the algorithm just informally—but we provide a concrete example which should explain how it works. All details can be found in [14]. In order to simplify the construction, we identify several VPA expressions by the *structural congruence*:

Definition 16. Let $\equiv$ be the smallest congruence relation over VPA expressions such that the following laws hold: associativity for sequential composition and associativity and commutativity for parallel composition.

The algorithm is based on the following fact:

Lemma 17. *A normed PA process Δ is regular iff Δ can reach only finitely many states up to $\equiv$.*

The algorithm finds all reachable states $\alpha \in VPA(\Delta)$ of Δ up to $\equiv$. For each such α a new variable and a new defining equation is added to Δ'. The defining equation is obtained by *unfolding* α — we apply the CCS expansion law (see [16]) and the right distribution law (see [2]) in a suitable order. Resulting expression is of the form $\sum_{i=1}^{n} a_i \alpha_i$ where $n \in N$, $a_i \in Act$ and $\alpha_i \in VPA(\Delta)$. Each α_i is now replaced with a single variable—either with an old one (if some VPA expression which is structurally congruent to α_i was already unfolded) or with a fresh variable. We repeat the whole construction for each newly added variable and the corresponding VPA expression. As each VPA expression which is unfolded is a reachable state of Δ, the algorithm has to terminate (due to Lemma 17).

Example 2. Let Δ be a normed PA process defined as follows:

$$\{ X \stackrel{def}{=} b + a(Y\|Z).X, \; Y \stackrel{def}{=} c + a(Z\|(Z.Z)), \; Z \stackrel{def}{=} c \}$$

The process Δ' is constructed in the following way:

$$
\begin{aligned}
A &= X & &= b + a(Y\|Z).X & &= b + aB \\
B &= (Y\|Z).X & &= a(Z\|(Z.Z)\|Z).X + c(Z.X) + c(Y.X) & &= aC + cD + cE \\
C &= (Z\|(Z.Z)\|Z).X & &= c((Z\|Z\|Z).X) + c((Z\|(Z.Z)).X) & &= cF + cG \\
D &= Z.X & &= cX & &= cA \\
E &= Y.X & &= cX + a((Z\|(Z.Z)).X) & &= cA + aG \\
F &= (Z\|Z\|Z).X & &= c((Z\|Z).X) & &= cH \\
G &= (Z\|(Z.Z)).X & &= c(Z.Z.X) + c((Z\|Z).X) & &= cI + cH \\
H &= (Z\|Z).X & &= c(Z.X) & &= cD \\
I &= (Z.Z.X) & &= c(Z.X) & &= cD
\end{aligned}
$$

Using this algorithm it is possible to decide bisimilarity for any pair of processes (Δ_1, Δ_2), where Δ_1 is a normed PA process and Δ_2 is a regular process in normal form. First, we check whether Δ_1 is regular. If not, then $\Delta_1 \not\sim \Delta_2$. Otherwise, we construct a bisimilar regular process Δ_1' in normal form and check whether $\Delta_1' \sim \Delta_2$.

Theorem 18. *Bisimilarity is decidable for any pair of processes such that one process of this pair is a normed PA process and the other process is a regular process in normal form.*

4 Conclusions

We proved that regularity of normed PA processes is decidable in polynomial time. As our result is constructive, we obtained also decidability of bisimulation equivalence for any pair of processes such that one process of this pair is a normed PA process and the other process is regular.

A natural question is whether it is possible to replace the pure merge operator ('$\|$') with another form of parallel composition without the loss of decidability of regularity. It can be easily shown that presented results are still valid if we replace the merge operator with the full parallel operator of CCS (which allows synchronisations on complementary actions). However, if we use e.g. the operator '$\|_A$' of CSP (which can *force* synchronisations), regularity becomes undecidable—see [13] for details.

An interesting open problem is whether our result can be extended to the class of all (not necessarily normed) PA processes. Another related open problem is the decidability of bisimulation equivalence in the class of (normed) PA processes.

5 Acknowledgement

I would like to thank Ivana Černá and Mojmír Křetínský for reading the first draft of this paper. Their comments made this article much more readable.

References

1. J. C. M. Baeten, J. A. Bergstra, and J. W. Klop. Decidability of bisimulation equivalence for processes generating context-free languages. In *Proceedings of PARLE 87*, volume 259 of *LNCS*, pages 93–114. Springer-Verlag, 1987.
2. J. C. M. Baeten and W. P. Weijland. *Process Algebra*. Number 18 in Cambridge Tracts in Theoretical Computer Science. Cambridge University Press, 1990.
3. A. Bouajjani, R. Echahed, and P. Habermehl. Verifying infinite state processes with sequential and parallel composition. In *Proceedings of POPL 95*, pages 95–106. ACM Press, 1995.
4. O. Burkart, D. Caucal, and B. Steffen. Bisimulation collapse and the process taxonomy. In *Proceedings of CONCUR 96*, volume 1119 of *LNCS*, pages 247–262. Springer-Verlag, 1996.
5. D. Caucal. Graphes canoniques de graphes algebriques. Rapport de Recherche 872, INRIA, 1988.
6. S. Christensen, Y. Hirshfeld, and F. Moller. Bisimulation is decidable for all basic parallel processes. In *Proceedings of CONCUR 93*, volume 715 of *LNCS*, pages 143–157. Springer-Verlag, 1993.
7. S. Christensen, H. Hüttel, and C. Stirling. Bisimulation equivalence is decidable for all context-free processes. In *Proceedings of CONCUR 92*, volume 630 of *LNCS*, pages 138–147. Springer-Verlag, 1992.
8. J. Esparza and P. Jančar. Deciding finiteness of Petri nets up to bisimilarity. In *Proceedings of ICALP 96*, volume 1099 of *LNCS*, pages 478–489. Springer-Verlag, 1996.
9. J. F. Groote. A short proof of the decidability of bisimulation for normed BPA processes. *Information Processing Letters*, 42:167–171, 1991.
10. H. Hüttel and C. Stirling. Actions speak louder than words: Proving bisimilarity for context-free processes. In *Proceedings of LICS 91*, pages 376–386. IEEE Computer Society Press, 1991.
11. P. Jančar. Decidability questions for bisimilarity of Petri nets and some related problems. In *Proceedings of STACS 94*, volume 775 of *LNCS*, pages 581–592. Springer-Verlag, 1994.
12. P. Jančar and F. Moller. Checking regular properties of Petri nets. In *Proceedings of CONCUR 95*, volume 962 of *LNCS*, pages 348–362. Springer-Verlag, 1995.
13. A. Kučera. Deciding regularity in process algebras. BRICS Report Series RS-95-52, Department of Computer Science, University of Aarhus, October 1995.
14. A. Kučera. Regularity is decidable for normed PA processes in polynomial time. Technical report, Faculty of Informatics, Masaryk University, 1996.
15. S. Mauw and H. Mulder. Regularity of BPA-systems is decidable. In *Proceedings of CONCUR 94*, volume 836 of *LNCS*, pages 34–47. Springer-Verlag, 1994.
16. R. Milner. *Communication and Concurrency*. Prentice-Hall International, 1989.
17. D.M.R. Park. Concurrency and automata on infinite sequences. In *Proceedings 5th GI Conference*, volume 104 of *LNCS*, pages 167–183. Springer-Verlag, 1981.

Dynamic Maintenance of Shortest Path Trees in Simple Polygons

Sanjiv Kapoor and Tripurari Singh [*]
Dept. of Computer Science and Engineering
Indian Institute of Technology, Hauz Khas, New Delhi.

Abstract

We present a scheme to dynamically maintain a rooted shortest path tree in a simple polygon. Both insertion and deletion of vertices of the simple polygon are supported. Both operations require $O(k \log(n/k))$ time where k is the number of changes in the shortest path tree. Only simple balanced binary trees are used in the data structure. $O(n)$ space is required.

1 Introduction

We consider the problem of dynamically maintaining shortest paths in simple polygons. Dynamic maintenance of geometric structures is an important area of research. Several algorithms have been devised to solve a variety of dynamic mainenance problems in computational geometry [CT].

Consider a simple polygon, P with source vertex s. The shortest paths from s to other vertices of P form a rooted tree denoted by $SPT(P, s)$. The shortest path from vertex q to s can be obtained as the unique path from q to s in $SPT(P, s)$. In the static case several optimal techniques for computing the shortest path tree exist [GHLST],[GH] [LP]. The query versions of the shortest path problem has been solved in [GH]. In the dynamic case Goodrich and Tamassia [GT] have devised a scheme for maintaining shortest path queries that uses $O(n)$ space and requires $O(\log^2 n)$ steps for updates in general. The operations include insertions and deletion of vertices and edges. Their data structure requires $O(\log^2 n)$ query time and $O(\log n)$ update time for these specific operations. Reporting the shortest path requires $O(\log^2 n + s)$ steps where s is the size of the shortest path.

Here we show how to maintain the shortest path tree, rooted at a fixed node s such that the tree can be updated in $O(k \log(n/k))$ steps when there are k changes in the shortest path tree. We allow for insertions and deletions of points. The operation of moving a point can also be handled similarly. The algorithm uses very simple data structures. By using a data structure for Dynamic Trees [ST], the shortest distance query problem for points on the simple polygon to s can be solved in $O(\log n)$ steps. The maintenance time is $O(k \log n)$ when there are $O(k)$ changes in the Shortest Path Tree. The shortest path itself can be reported in linear time. We thus exhibit a trade-off. We can achieve optimal query and report time, at the expense of maintainence time. Since the number of changes to the shortest path tree is expected to be small when there is a single polygon change, this scheme is advantageous when a large number of queries are required to be performed. In fact for uniformly distributed edge

---
[*]This work was supported by grant No. SR/OY/E13/92 from Dept. of Sc. & Techn., Govt. of India.

sets the degree of a node in the shortest path tree appears to be a constant with high probability though we do not consider a detailed probabilistic analysis here.

Related work to this may be found in Vegter[V] where the visibility graph of a set of line segments in the plane is maintained in $O(\log^2 n + k \log n)$ steps where k is the total number of changes in the visibility graph upon insertion and deletion of a line segment.

The paper is organized as follows: Section 2 gives definitions and preliminaries. Section 3 describes the procedure to maintain the Shortest Path Tree when a vertex is inserted. Secion 4 describes the deletion procedure.

2 Definitions and Preliminaries

A *polygonal chain* is denoted by $CH(a, b)$, where a, b are its end points. It may also be denoted by $(a \ldots b)$ or by $(a \ldots c \ldots b)$ where a, b are the end points and c is some point on the chain. The three point notation is used for clarity.

A *Convex chain* $CH(a, b)$ is a polygonal chain which is convex.

A *Funnel* $\mathcal{F}(a, b, c)$ is composed of two convex chains $CH(a, b), CH(a, c)$ s.t. b is visible from c and $CH(a, b), CH(a, c)$ are inward convex, i.e. the boundary of the region enclosed by the funnel and (b, c) is composed of two concave chains and the edge (b, c). The point a is known as the cusp of the funnel and the (imaginary) edge (b, c) is known as its mouth. The points b, c are known as the mouth points of the funnel.

A *Partial funnel* $\mathcal{PF}(a, b, c, b', c')$ is a funnel obtained from the funnel $\mathcal{F}(a, b, c)$ such that $b' \in CH(a, b)$, $c' \in CH(a, c)$ and b' is visible from c'. Note that b', c' could be vertices of $CH(a, b), CH(a, c)$ as well as points on their edges.

The path $SP(P, s, x)$ is the *shortest path* from the point s to the point x which is constrained to lie in the interior of the polygon P. $SP(P, s, x)$ will also be used to denote the length of the path itself.

The *Shortest Path Tree*, $SPT(P, s)$ ($SPT(P)$), in a simple polygon P is a directed tree formed by the union of shortest paths $SP(P, s, x)$ from the source vertex s to all other vertices $x \in P$.

The shortest path tree, $SPT(P)$ partitions the simple polygon into regions where each region is a funnel. An edge e in $SPT(P)$ occurs in at most two funnels. The following property *Adjacency* is true of funnels in $SPT(P)$.

Property Adjacency: Let $e = (u, v) \in \mathcal{F}_i \& \mathcal{F}_j$. Let u be closer to the cusp of $\mathcal{F}_i$ and $\mathcal{F}_j$ than v. Then u is the cusp of at least one of $\mathcal{F}_i$ and $\mathcal{F}_j$.

The above property follows from the fact that adjacent funnels cannot share a boundary having more than one edge since this boundary cannot be simultaneously inward convex for the two adjacent funnels.

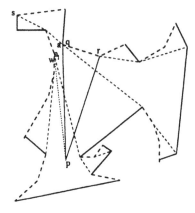

Figure 1: p lies inside P

3 Insert

3.1 Outline of the Insertion algorithm

In this section, we will characterize the shortest path changes first. Consider the insertion of a point p between the adjacent pair of points q, r in the polygon P with $SP(P, s, q) < SP(P, s, r)$. Insertion of the point involves removing the edge (q, r) and adding edges (q, p) and (p, r) so that the resultant polygon, Q is a simple polygon. Two cases arise.

(i) p lies outside P.

(ii) p lies inside P.

In the first case the update to the Shortest Path Tree, $SPT(P)$, requires only finding the shortest path from s to p, $SP(P, s, p)$. No modifications of the shortest paths to other vertices are required. We have the following lemma.

Lemma 3.1 *Insertion of a point p outside a polygon P does not change the shortest path to vertices other than p, i.e. $SP(P, s, x) = SP(Q, s, x), \forall x \in P, x \neq p$. Furthermore, if $(q, r) \notin SPT(P)$ then the $SPT(Q)$ edge incident into p is a tangent to the funnel $\mathcal{G}$ in $SPT(P)$ whose mouth is (q, r); otherwise the $SPT(Q)$ edge incident into p is (q, p).*

When p lies inside P, we have to do the following.

• Find the shortest path tree edge incident into p.

• Carry out the changes required in the existing shortest path tree.

We will now show that these changes will be restricted to points x such that $SP(P, s, x)$ crosses triangle (p, q, r).

Lemma 3.2 *Let $x \in P$. The insertion of p will modify the shortest path to point x if $SP(P, s, x)$ intersects the triangle (p, q, r). For all points x in P, if no edge of $SP(P, s, x)$ crosses (p, r), then $SP(P, s, x) = SP(Q, s, x)$*

Let $\mathcal{K}_0$ be the funnel containing p in $SPT(P)$. $SP(P, s, p)$ can be computed by constructing a tangent from p to $\mathcal{K}_0$. Let w be the point in $\mathcal{K}_0$ s.t. (p, w) is a tangent to $\mathcal{K}_0$. The next lemma states that this is also the shortest path from s to p in Q.

Lemma 3.3 $SP(P, s, p)$ *is the same as* $SP(Q, s, p)$

If the triangle (p, q, r) does not intersect any edge of $SPT(P)$ then, by lemma 3.2, addition of (w, p) to $SPT(P)$ yields $SPT(Q)$, otherwise further modifications are required. We partition the set of points whose shortest paths is intersected by the triangle (p, q, r), onto the set C of points into which the intersected edges are incident, and the set D of the remaining points.

Our algorithm computes $SPT(Q)$ from $SPT(P)$ in 3 phases. In the first Phase the edges in $SPT(P)$ intersected by the triangle (p, q, r) are determined and removed and $SP(Q, s, p)$ is computed. In Phase 2, the shortest paths to the points in C are computed. The partially constructed funnels thus formed are then 'grown' in Phase 3 till all the changes required are complete.

The Data Structure: Our data structure will represent the simple polygon and its shortest path tree.

The shortest path tree will be represented as a collection of funnels and their adjacency information. Each funnel will be represented by its two boundaries stored in separate red-black search trees with their roots linked to each other. In this scheme, an edge separating two adjacent funnels will be represented twice — once in each funnel. The adjacency of these two funnels will be captured by linking the two instances of the common edge. The simple polygon will be represented as a list of edges, each with a pointer into the shortest path tree. An edge is either in the boundary of a funnel or is the mouth of one. If it is in the boundary, its polygon representation will contain a pointer to its shortest path tree representation, otherwise this pointer will be to the shortest path tree representation of an edge incident *into* one of the mouth points of the funnel. The data structure requires $O(n)$ space.

3.2 The Insertion Algorithm

We will only consider the case where p lies inside P.

3.3 Phase 1 : Remove intersected edges, find $SP(Q, s, p)$.

Phase 1 has 3 steps. In the first step, the tree edges intersected by the triangle (p, q, r) are determined. In the second step the shortest path to p is computed, and in the third step the intersected edges are removed and the data structure is updated.

Step 1 : Consider the edges of $SPT(P)$ intersected by the triangle (p, q, r). Let the number of intersected edges be l. Order the edges in the sequence of their intersection points with the edge (p, r), from p to r. Denote the ith edge by (a_i, c_i), and its point of intersection with (r, p) by b_i. Note that $c_l = r$. Also denote the funnel in $SPT(P)$ containing the edges $(a_i, c_i), (a_{i+1}, c_{i+1})$ by $\mathcal{K}_i$ and the number of vertices in $\mathcal{K}_i$ by n_i

Phase 1 takes as input a pointer to the polygon representation of the edge (q, r) and follows the pointer stored there to the shortest path tree, and then iteratively determines the intersected edges $(a_i, c_i), 1 \leq i \leq l - 1$ in descending order of i.

The iterative determination of (a_i, c_i) in $\mathcal{K}_i$ given (a_{i+1}, c_{i+1}) in $\mathcal{K}_{i+1}$ is done by the following scheme: First traverse up the search tree of the boundary of $\mathcal{K}_{i+1}$ containing c_{i+1} and obtain the pointer to the root of the search tree of the other boundary of $\mathcal{K}_{i+1}$ (containing c_i). Next search in this tree for (a_i, c_i), and finally, enter $\mathcal{K}_i$ by following the pointer stored with (a_i, c_i) to its instance in $\mathcal{K}_i$.

Each iteration of this procedure involves two tree searches, and each tree is searched at most once. Thus the total time required is $O(\sum_{i=1}^{l} \log n_i)$.

Step 2 : By lemma 3.3, the shortest path edge incident into p is the tangent from p to the funnel $\mathcal{K}_0$. A pointer to (a_1, c_1) in $\mathcal{K}_0$ is available from the last iteration of step 1, and tangent from p is computed using the search tree in $O(\log n_1)$ time. In what follows the 'incomplete funnel' consisting of $\mathcal{K}_0$'s cusp, the path from the cusp to p, and $\mathcal{K}_0$'s non intersected boundary will be referred to as $\mathcal{K}_0'$.

Step 3: The removal of edges of C partitions each funnel $\mathcal{K}_i, 1 \leq i \leq l$. We denote the section of $\mathcal{K}_i$ containing its cusp by $\mathcal{K}_i^1$. The set $\{\mathcal{K}_i^1, 1 \leq i \leq l\}$ has the following property : At most one $\mathcal{K}_j^1$ is composed of two non-null convex chains and is a funnel, all the others being composed of only one convex chain.

$\mathcal{K}_i^1, 1 \leq i \leq l$ together with the tangent (w, p) forms the funnel $\mathcal{F}(x, q, p)$ in $SPT(Q)$. The cusp x is either the cusp of the funnel $\mathcal{K}_j^1$, or it is the point w if no such funnel exists. To see this observe that all edges of funnels $\mathcal{K}_i^1$ are present in $SPT(Q)$ by lemma 3.2. Moreover (q, p) forms the mouth of the new funnel. In this step we carry out the data structure updates required to effect these changes.

We first partition the intersected funnels by splitting the search trees representing their boundaries at $a_i, 1 \leq i \leq l$. These splits take a total of $O(\sum_{i=1}^{l} \log n_i)$, $\sum_{i=1}^{l} n_i \leq n$ time which evaluates to $O(l \log(\frac{n}{l}) + l)$

Next we merge the trees generated by the splits by recursively merging them in pairs. This takes $O(l \log(\frac{n}{l}) + l)$ time. Thus the total time required for Phase 1 is $O(l \log(\frac{n}{l}) + l)$. We formally state these results in the following lemma.

Lemma 3.4 *Phase 1 correctly determines the intersected edges* $(a_i, c_i), 1 \leq i \leq l$, *and constructs the funnel* $\mathcal{F}(x, q, p)$ *of* $SPT(Q)$ *in* $O(l \log(\frac{n}{l}) + l)$ *time.*

3.4   Phase 2 : Construct the shortest paths to C

We present an algorithm *Join*, which constructs the shortest paths to points in C. It first adds edges from p to c_1 and c_l, both of which are visible from p. It then iteratively constructs the shortest paths to the remaining points $c_i, 2 \leq i \leq l - 1$ in ascending order of i by constructing tangents to the shortest path from p to c_{i-1}. *Join* adds an incoming edge into each $c_i \in C$, and each edge added by *Join* is in $SPT(Q)$.

Each vertex $c_i, 1 \leq i \leq l$ is visited once with failure, i.e. no tangent is constructed with that vertex as an endpoint, and whenever it is an endpoint of a tangent, $(h_j, c_j), i \leq j \leq l$. Since l tangents are constructed the total time required for tangent constructions is $O(l)$. The construction of the list search structures also takes linear time as the insertions take place at the ends of the search trees. Hence *Join* takes $O(l)$ time.

3.5   Phase 3 : Compute shortest paths to D

In this phase the shortest paths to points in D will be recomputed. We first characterize T_{Join} and the changes required to it.

By definition, the shortest paths in the polygon P to points in D pass through the points in C, and as such only the subtrees rooted at C need to be considered. The pair of successive points $c_i, c_{i+1}, 1 \leq i \leq (l - 1)$, of C defines the mouth of a funnel $\mathcal{H}_i$ of T_{Join}. Note that in the degenerate case c_i, c_{i+1} may be connected by a T_{Join} edge, in which case $\mathcal{H}_i$ is composed solely of (c_i, c_{i+1}). This edge forms one of the boundaries of $\mathcal{H}_i$ and its mouth; the other boundary being null.

In $SPT(P)$, $c_i, c_{i+1}, 1 \leq i \leq l - 1$ are vertices on the opposite boundaries of $\mathcal{K}_i$. The concatenation of the new funnel $\mathcal{H}_i$, and the section of $\mathcal{K}_i$ emanating from c_i, c_{i+1}

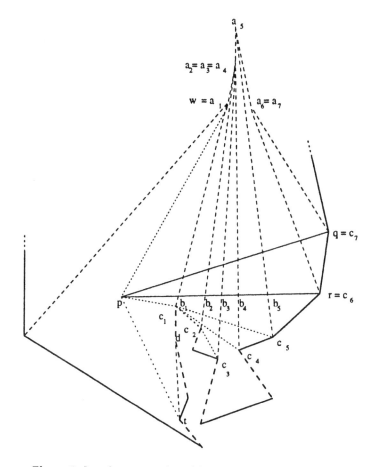

Figure 2: Iterative construction of shortest paths to points C by Join

forms a funnel like structure which will be referred to as a *Bi-Convex* funnel and denoted by $\mathcal{B}_i, 1 \leq i \leq l-1$. The boundary of $\mathcal{B}_i$ containing c_i is convex at c_i as the boundary of $\mathcal{H}_i$ containing c_i lies outside $\mathcal{K}_i$. The boundary of $\mathcal{B}_i$ containing c_{i+1} may not, in general, be convex at c_{i+1}. We now formally define a *Bi-Convex Funnel.*

Definition A *Bi-Convex Funnel* $\mathcal{B}(a, b, c, d)$ is composed of a point a called its *cusp*, and two boundaries, one of which is the convex chain $CH(a, b)$, the other one being composed of the convex chains $CH(a, c)$, $CH(c, d)$. The boundary $CH(a, b)$ of the Bi-Convex funnel is referred to as its *Single boundary*. The boundary composed of $CH(a, c)$, $CH(c, d)$ is referred to as its *Double boundary* and $CH(a, c)$ $CH(c, d)$ are referred to as the first chain and second chain respectively of the double boundary.

In addition to $\mathcal{B}_i, 1 \leq i \leq l-1$, T_{Join} also contains the bi-convex funnel $\mathcal{B}_0$ composed of $\mathcal{K}'_0$, the edge (p, c_1), and the section of $\mathcal{K}_0$ emanating from c_1.

$SPT(Q)$ is next computed from T_{join} by recomputing the shortest paths to the trees emanating from the bi-convex funnels $\mathcal{B}_i, 0 \leq i \leq l-1$, since all points in $C \cup D$ are contained in these trees. Furthermore, only the second convex chain of the double

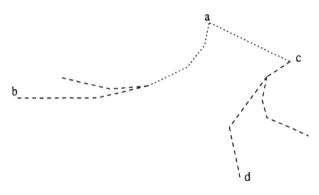

Figure 3: A biconvex funnel

boundary of $\mathcal{B}_i$ needs to have its shortest path recomputed. We will recompute the shortest path to trees emanating from each bi-convex funnel individually using the *Modify* procedure outlined in the next sub-section.

Before applying *Modify*, we will preprocess the bi-convex funnels, $\mathcal{B}_i$, of T_{join} to obtain a new set of biconvex funnels $\mathcal{B}'_i, 0 \leq i \leq l-1$ whose single boundaries are newly constructed chains. This is done for biconvex funnels $\mathcal{B}_i$, except for $\mathcal{B}_0$, by simply removing the section of $\mathcal{K}_i$ emanating from c_i and redefining the point c_i as the end point of its single boundary. To justify the removal of the section of $\mathcal{K}_i$ emanating from c_i, we have to show that this chain is in $SPT(Q)$ and that all $SPT(Q)$ edges incident on it are already present. The first condition is met since only the second chain of the double boundary of a bi-convex chain is not in $SPT(Q)$. The second condition follows from the fact that any tangent from a point on $\mathcal{K}_i$ which is a descendant of c_i will not have its end point affected.

We now consider the special case of the bi-convex funnel $\mathcal{B}_0$. We construct a bi-convex funnel containing the subset of vertices of $\mathcal{B}_0$ whose shortest path edges have to be changed. We do this by adding the tangent (p, t) from p to the second convex chain of the double boundary of $\mathcal{B}_0$ and removing the edge (d, t), where d is the predecessor of t. If (d, t) is not a polygon edge, its removal will lead into a region of the simple polygon bounded by a convex chain $CH(d, u)$ (by the *Adjacency* property, section 2). $\mathcal{B}'_0 = \mathcal{B}(p, t, c_1, u)$, thus obtained, has the point p as its cusp, the tangent (p, t) as its single boundary, the edge (p, c_1) as the first convex chain of its double boundary, and the chain $CH(c_1, u)$, containing the chain $CH(d, u)$ as the second convex chain on its double boundary.

The correctness of this construction follows readily from the fact that the subtree of $SPT(P)$ emanating from t does not lie in $\mathcal{B}'_0$, and that the second chain $CH(c_1, u)$ of the double boundary is not concave at d, since it existed in $SPT(P)$. All points in $\mathcal{B}_0$ whose shortest path edge may have to be recomputed also lie in $\mathcal{B}'_0$ since the section of $\mathcal{B}_0$ not in $\mathcal{B}'_0$ forms a funnel and hence is in $SPT(Q)$.

The time required to construct $\mathcal{B}'_0$ is bounded by k if a linear scan, from c_1 towards the mouth of $\mathcal{K}_0$, is used to determine the tangent (p, t).

Modify the Tree emanating from a Bi-Convex Funnel: Suppose we are given a Bi-Convex Funnel $\mathcal{B}(a, b, c, d)$ with cusp a and composed of three convex chains $CH(a, b)$ and $CH(a, c)$ and $CH(c, d)$. We assume, without loss of generality, that $CH(a, c)$ occurs in the counter-clockwise direction after $CH(a, b)$. In this section we will show how to reconstruct the shortest paths for nodes in $\mathcal{B}$ as well as descendant nodes in the shortest path tree $SPT(P)$.

The algorithm, *Modify*, first considers nodes in the Bi-Convex Funnel $\mathcal{B}$. Points on $CH(a, b)$ have their shortest paths already determined. Also, the shortest paths to points on $CH(a, c)$ is already determined. Thus the algorithm first determines the set $\{x | x \in CH(c, d)\}$ that the shortest path subtree in $SPT(P)$ tree, rooted at p, needs to be changed to obtain $SPT(Q)$.

To determine this set of points the algorithm first finds a point called the *terminus*.

Definition The terminus point t of $CH(c, d)$ is the last point, x, on the convex chain $CH(c, d)$, starting from c, such that a valid tangent from x to the funnel $\mathcal{F}(a, b, c)$ can be constructed.

The terminus point is essentially the point on $CH(c, d)$ which is one end point of the common tangent between $CH(c, d)$ and the partial funnel obtained from the convex chains $CH(a, b)$ and $CH(a, c)$. All points on $CH(c, d)$ starting from c and going up to t have their shortest path edge modified. The terminus is found by traversing $CH(c, d)$ linearly to determine the common tangent.

After finding the terminus t on $(a \ldots c \ldots d)$ we find the tangent from t to $CH(a, b)$, say h. Let d' be the predecessor of t on $CH(c, d)$. We remove the edge (d', t), and add the edge (h, t). If (d', t) is not a polygon edge, its removal will lead into a region of the simple polygon bounded by a convex chain $CH(d', u)$. Now $(c \ldots d' \ldots u)$ is a convex chain. Hence we obtain a new Bi-Convex Funnel with $(a \ldots c)$, $(c \ldots u)$ as the two convex chains of its double boundary and the convex chain $(a \ldots h, t)$ as its right boundary. We recur on this BCF. After we finish processing the subtree rooted at d' we construct the tangent from d'. We then process the predecessor of d' in a similar fashion. This sequence of tangent finding is the postorder traversal of a *dfs* which traverses the outgoing edges incident on a vertex in the counterclockwise order starting from the incoming edge. The adjacency list of a point p is denoted by $\text{ADJ}(p)$. $\text{Next}(\text{ADJ}(p))$ refers to the next item in the adjacency list of p when the adjacency list is arranged in counter-clockwise order. We assume that $\text{Next}(\text{ADJ}(p))$ is the first edge in the adjacency list at the beginning of the *dfs* processing of p.

We next describe the terminus finding procedure, $FindTerminus(\mathcal{B}, d,' t, h)$, which takes as input the Bi-Convex Funnel $\mathcal{B}(a, b, c, d)$ and returns the terminus t and the tangent (h, t). d' is a point on $CH(c, d)$ such that $t \in CH(d', d)$. The tangent h can lie either on $CH(a, b)$ or on $CH(a, c)$. *FindTerminus* first assumes that h lies on $CH(a, b)$. The problem, then, is to find the common tangent to $CH(a, b)$, $CH(c, d)$. *FindTerminus* does this by a linear scan starting simultaneously at d' and b. If h indeed lies on $(a \ldots b)$, then this takes $O(|(h \ldots b)| + |(d' \ldots t)|)$ time. If it doesn't, then this condition is detected in $O(|(a \ldots b)| + |(d' \ldots r)|)$ time, where r is a point on $(d' \ldots t)$. The problem now is to find the common tangent to $(a \ldots c)$ and $(d' \ldots d)$. This is again done by a linear scan starting simultaneously at a and d'. This takes $O(|(a \ldots h)| + |(d' : \ldots t)|)$ time. The total time, then, is $O(|(h \ldots b)| + |(d' \ldots t)|)$, both when h lies on $CH(a, b)$ and when it lies on $CH(a, c)$.

Correctness and time complexity of Modify: We will let $OLDT(a)$ denote the shortest path tree rooted at a point p before the invocation of *Modify*. Let k' be the number of edges added by *Modify*. Let m' be the number of vertices (and edges) in the section $(b \ldots a \ldots c)$ of the original Bi-Convex Funnel $\mathcal{B}$. Let n' be the number of vertices in $OLDT(a)$.

Lemma 3.5 *Given a Bi-Convex Funnel $\mathcal{B}(a, b, c, d)$ Modify correctly computes the shortest path sub-tree rooted at a in $O(k' + m' + k' \log(n'/k'))$ steps.*

Time Complexity of Phase 3: In Phase 3 *Modify* is applied on each biconvex funnel $\mathcal{B}_i, 0 \leq i \leq l - 1$. Hence the total time required is $\sum_{i=0}^{l-1} O(k_i' + m_i' + k_i' \log(n_i'/k_i'))$ which evaluates to $O(k + k \log(n/k))$.

3.6 Correctness and Time Complexity of Insert

The correctness of the insert algorithm follows from the correctness of the three phases. We next consider the time complexity. Phase 1 requires $O(l \log(n/l) + l)$ steps. Phase 2 requires $O(l)$ steps and Phase 3 requires $O(k \log(n/k) + k)$ steps when there are $O(k)$ changes in total. This gives us the following result:

Lemma 3.6 *On insertion of a point p the Shortest Path Tree, SPT(P,s), can be updated in $O(k \log(n/k))$ steps when the insertion results in k changes.*

It is interesting to note that all the shortest paths which needed to be recomputed as consequence of the insertion of p pass through p. This follows from the fact that the shortest paths to all the biconvex funnels constructed by *Join* traverses p and that all other shortest paths pass through the cusp of one of these bi-convex funnels.

4 Delete

Deletion of a point, in some respects, is the reverse of insertion. Let the original polygon be Q and its shortest path tree be $SPT(Q)$. Let p be the deleted vertex, and q, r be the vertices adjacent to it, such that $SP(Q, s, q) < SP(Q, s, r)$. Let P be the polygon obtained after deleting p and inserting the edge (q, r). For the update operation to be defined, $p \neq s$.

Two cases arise, the first when p lies outside P and the second when it lies inside P. In the first case, $SPT(P)$ can be obtained from $SPT(Q)$ by deleting the edge (w, p) incident into p. As the following lemma states, no other changes are required.

Lemma 4.1 *Deletion of a point p outside the polygon P does not change $SP(Q, s, x), \forall x \in P, x \neq p$.*

Suppose p lies inside P. As noted in insert, all the shortest paths affected by the insertion of a point pass through it, and since deletion is the inverse process of insertion, it follows that the deletion of p will only affect the shortest paths passing through it.

In a manner analogous to insert, we partition the set of points whose shortest paths to s is affected by the deletion into the sets C and D with C containing the points into which the edges emanating from p are incident, and D containing the remaining points. Further, we order the points in C in decreasing order of the angle made by the edge connecting the point to p with the edge (p, r) and refer to the ith point as $c_i, 1 \leq i \leq l$. Note that $c_l = r$. Also we assume that q is termed c_{l+1}.

The updation of the shortest path tree, after a delete, is in two phases. The first phase constructs the shortest paths to $c_i \in C$, and the second phase 'grows' the biconvex funnels formed in the first phase, using a slight variant of *Modify*, till $SPT(P)$ is obtained.

Phase 1: Compute the shortest paths to C: Let $\mathcal{G}_{l+1}$ be the funnel in $SPT(P)$ with (q, p) as its mouth and let (w, p) be the $SPT(Q)$ edge incident into p. On deletion of p, this edge ceases to exist. We will imagine its existence for the time being to simplify our explanation, and then show that the point p is not used.

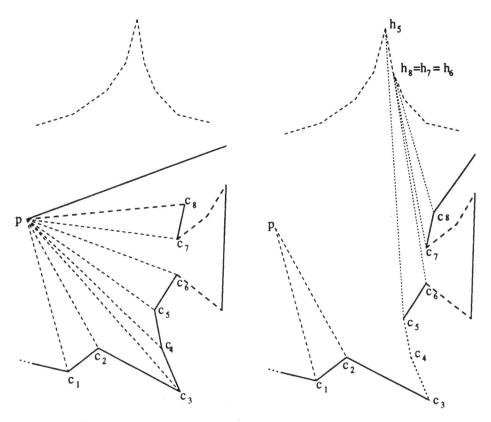

Figure 4: Iterative construction of shortest paths to points C by *Connect*

The shortest paths to the points $c_i \in C$ pass through the funnel $\mathcal{G}_{l+1}$, and our procedure *Connect* computes the shortest path edges incident into c_i in decreasing order of i. The $SPT(P)$ edge incident into $r = c_l$ is computed by constructing a tangent (h_l, c_l) to $\mathcal{G}_{l+1}$ and the $SPT(P)$ edges incident into $c_i, i \leq l - 1$, are then iteratively computed by constructing a tangent (h_i, c_i) to the funnel $\mathcal{G}_{i+1}$ (which has (c_{i+1}, p) as its mouth) formed in the previous iteration.

A funnel $\mathcal{G}_{i+1}$ formed by the above scheme is composed of two types of convex chains — the old chains which were present prior to the invocation of *Connect* and new chains constructed by *Connect*. The latter are composed wholly of points in C. The boundary of $\mathcal{G}_{i+1}$ containing p is an old chain while the boundary containing c_{i+1} contains a new chain and may also contain an old chain. If it contains an old chain then this old chain starts at the cusp. The new chain always ends at c_{i+1}.

Connect deals with old and new chains differently. New chains are maintained simply as linked lists, and tangent searches on them are done by means of linear scans. Old chains, on the other hand, are maintained as search trees. Tangent searching is done by means of tree searches and splits are effected at the tangent points h_i by keeping fingers. After tangents to all points in C have been found, the data structure is cleaned up by splitting search trees on old chains at the fingers, constructing search trees on the new chains, and merging the appropriate old and new trees.

Lemma 4.2 Connect *adds an incoming edge into each* $c_i \in C, 1 \le i \le l$, *and each edge added by* Connect *is in* $SPT(P)$.

The time required by *Connect* is divided into time spent on new chains and time spent on old chains.

The time spent on new chains comprises time spent on tangent construction and time spent on search tree construction. Tangent construction takes linear time as each vertex $c_i, 1 \le i \le l$ is visited at most twice — once when the tangent (h_i, c_i) is constructed and once when it is examined as a candidate for h_j, for some $j < i$. The search trees can be constructed in linear time and hence the time spent on new chains is $O(k)$.

The time spent on old chains consists of the time spent on tree searches, tree splits and tree merges. As the time required for splitting red-black trees is of the same order as the time required for searching for the split points, we will not consider the splits.

We first calculate the time required to search the tangent points. Consider the jth search tree T_j. Let n_j be the number of vertices in T_j and let k_j be the number of searches performed in it.

Partition the tree T_j into (i) the forest F_j containing trees with more than $\frac{n_i}{k_j}$ vertices s.t. its subtrees have fewer than $\frac{n_i}{k_j}$ vertices, and (ii) the root tree T_j^R rooted at the root of T_j and containing the remaining vertices. The children of the leaves of T_j^R, thus, are the roots of the trees of F_j, and $|T_j^R| \le k_j$.

Consider the search procedure. It visits a node at most twice, and hence it can spend at most $2k_j$ time in T_j^R and at most $O(k_j \log \frac{n_i}{k_j})$ time in the forest F_j. Thus the total search time is $O(\sum_j (k_j + k_j \log \frac{n_i}{k_j}))$. This evaluates to $O(k + k \log \frac{n}{k})$ since $\sum_j k_j \le k$, $\sum_j k_j(n_j/k_j) \le n$.

The final step is the merger of the old and new search trees. The merge time can also be computed to be $O(k \log \frac{n}{k} + k)$ since there are at most k merges and no tree undergoes more than one merge. Hence the total time taken by *Connect* is $O(k + k \log \frac{n}{k} + k)$.

Phase 2 : Compute the shortest paths to D: The tree output by *Connect* is similar to the tree output by the *Join* phase of insert in that both trees contain Bi-Convex funnels, and *all* further changes can be effected by modifying these bi-convex funnels. We first describe the bi-convex funnels in $T_{Connect}$, the tree output by *Connect*.

The bi-convex funnels in $T_{Connect}$ are composed of the newly constructed funnels $\mathcal{H}_i, 1 \le i \le (l+1)$ and the fragments of the funnels $\mathcal{K}_i$ emanating from c_i, c_{i+1}, where $\mathcal{K}_i$ is the funnel in $SPT(Q)$ containing the points c_i, c_{i+1}.

The bi-convex funnels generated by *Connect* are different from those generated by *Join* in that some of the edges of the funnels $\mathcal{H}_i$ created by *Connect* are old edges, i.e. edges in $SPT(Q)$. The number of such old edges is independent of k, and their presence prevents us from using a linear scan for terminus finding. We, instead, use the search trees on these chains for this purpose.

Phase 2 requires the computation of the trees emanating from the bi-convex funnels $\mathcal{B}_i, 1 \le i \le l$ by *Modify*. The substitution of the linear scan for tangent finding by binary tree searches means that the time taken by *Modify* on $\mathcal{B}_i$ is $O(k_i \log(\frac{n_i}{k_i}) + k_i)$ where n_i is the number of vertices in the $SPT(Q)$ tree emanating from $\mathcal{B}_i$ and k_i is the number of changes in this tree (the analysis is similar to that of the algorithm *Connect*). This evaluates to $O(k \log(\frac{n}{k}) + k)$.

Correctness of delete follows from the fact that *Connect* and Phase 2 correctly compute the shortest path from all points x s.t. $SP(Q, s, x)$ uses p. Combining the time complexity of the phases, we get

Lemma 4.3 *Delete computes $STP(P)$ in $O(k \log(\frac{n}{k}))$ time.*

5 Conclusion

Combining the results of insertion and deletion, we get:

Theorem 5.1 *The shortest path tree in a simple polygon with n vertices can be maintained in $O(k \log(\frac{n}{k}))$ time on an insertion or a deletion of a vertex. k is the number of changes in the shortest path tree as a result of the insertion or deletion.*

Consider shortest distance queries next. For these queries, we need to maintain a data structure which supports this operation under changes to the shortest path tree. This is done using the data structure for dynamic trees by Sleator and Tarjan [ST]. This allows us to answer queries in $O(\log n)$ steps . The maintenance cost of the Shortest Path Tree is $O(k \log n)$ where k changes occur in the Shortest Path Tree.

Move a Point: In this operation, one of the points of the polygon is moved with the restriction that the polygon remains a simple polygon. There are two cases: Either the new polygon $Q \subset P$, in which case a solution similar to that developed for the case of insertions can be applied. Or the new polygon $Q \supset P$, in which case a solution similar to that for the case of deletion applies.

References

[1] [CT] "Dynamic algorithms in computational geometry" by Y.J. Chiang and R. Tamassia, Proc. IEEE, 80(9):1412-1434

[2] [GH] "Optimal Shortest Path Queries in a Simple Polygon", L.J. Guibas and J.Hershberger. Proceedings of the 3rd ACM Symposium on computational Geometry, Waterloo, Canada (1987), pp 50-63.

[3] [GHLST] "Linear time algorithms for visibility and shortest path problems inside simple polygons" by L.Guibas, J.Hershberger, D.Leven, M.Sharir and R.Tarjan, Proc. of the 3rd ACM Symposium on Computational Geometry, June 1987.

[4] [GT] "Dynamic trees and dynamic point location", by M. Goodrich and R. Tamassia,Proceedings of the 23rd Annu. ACM Sympos. Theory Comput., pp 523-533, 1991.

[5] [LP] "Euclidean Shortest Paths in the Presence of Rectilinear Barriers", D.T. Lee and F.P. Preparata., Networks, vol.14 (1984), pp.393-410.

[6] [ST] "A Data Structure for Dynamic Trees", D.D.Sleator and R.E. Tarjan, Jour. of Computer and System Sciences ,26, 362-391 (1983).

[7] [V] "Dynamically maintaining the visibility graph", G. Vegter, WADS, 1991, pp 425-436.

Close Approximations of Minimum Rectangular Coverings

(Extended Abstract)

Christos Levcopoulos   Joachim Gudmundsson

Department of Computer Science
Lund University, Box 118, S-221 00 Lund, Sweden

Abstract. We consider the problem of covering arbitrary polygons with rectangles. The rectangles must lie entirely within the polygon. (This requires that the interior angles of the polygon are all greater than or equal to 90 degrees.) We want to cover the polygon with as few rectangles as possible. This problem has an application in fabricating masks for integrated circuits.

In this paper we will describe the first polynomial algorithm, guaranteeing an $O(\log n)$ approximation factor, provided that the n vertices of the input polygon are given as polynomially bounded integer coordinates. By the same technique we also obtain the first algorithm producing a covering which is within a constant factor of the optimal in exponential time (compared to the doubly-exponential known before).

1   Introduction

The problem of covering polygons with various types of simpler polygons has a number of important practical applications [7,8] and has received considerable attention from a theoretical perspective. One application for this problem is the fabrication of VLSI chips. According to [7], a common method for fabricating VLSI chips is the optical method of the automatic blockflasher, which exposes rectangles of, in practice, almost any size and any orientation. In order to minimize the cost of the fabrication it is desirable to cover the polygonal area of each layer of the circuit with as few rectangles as possible. For more information about the VLSI fabrication process see [7].

O'Rourke and Supowit [13] showed that the problems of covering polygons with a minimum number of convex polygons, star-shaped polygons or spiral polygons are all NP-hard, if the polygon contains holes. The rectilinear case, i.e. when the polygons, as well as the rectangles, have sides that are vertical or horizontal, has been treated in several papers [8,5,15]. Culberson and Reckhow [4] showed this case to be NP-hard even when the given polygon was hole-free. Berman and DasGupta [1] showed that if the rectilinear polygon has holes, the problem is also MAXSNP-hard. In the more general, non-rectilinear, case it is not known whether the optimal solution can be computed even in exponential time. Using the proof technique in [12] (see also [2] and [11]), Tarski's decidability results can be applied to prove that the decision version of the problem is computable, but no upper bounds better than $2^{2^{O(n)}}$ was known for its execution time. Hegedüs [7] implemented a program (the so-called GENCOV-algorithm) which covers general polygons with rectangles and presented some empirical results concerning its performance. The results show that the algorithm is rather good in practice, but no theoretical analysis is presented in [7]. Another approximation algorithm was presented in [9], and with refined analysis in [10], which produces $O(n \log n + \mu(P))$ rectangles to cover an arbitrary coverable polygon P in time $O(n \log n + \mu(P))$, where n is the number of vertices of P and $\mu(P)$ is the minimum number of rectangles required to cover P. (A polygon can be covered by rectangles iff it has no acute interior angles.)

A problem with the above algorithm is that, even when $\mu(P) = O(n^{0.5 + \epsilon})$, where ϵ is any fixed constant greater than zero, the algorithm may produce a covering with $\Omega(n \log n)$ rectangles, as is very far from being optimal, as is shown in [10]. To get a reasonable approximation in the case when $\mu(P) \ll n$ we need a different approach. In order to find a better covering in the rectilinear case one has used the approach of finding a superset of rectangles which includes the rectangles in an optimal covering. If we could find such a set for the general case we could easily translate the polygon-covering problem into the set-covering problem. The main difference between the rectilinear case and the general case is that there are only $O(n^2)$ possible maximal rectangles in the rectilinear case versus infinite many possible maximal rectangles in the general case. Instead we will in this paper construct a set of rectangles, denoted C_R, and prove that C_R includes a covering which is within a constant factor of the optimal. In fact we show that C_R possesses an even stronger property, namely that every possible rectangle within a polygon P can be covered by a constant number of rectangles in C_R (Lemmas 4-6).

By reducing the original problem into the set-covering problem, by rectangles from C_R, we can find a covering which is within a constant factor of the optimal in exponential time (details in subsection 4.1). We also present the first polynomial algorithm, guaranteeing an $O(\log n)$ approximation factor, provided that the n vertices of the polygon are given as polynomially bounded integer coordinates.

2 Defining the pool of rectangles

Let P be an arbitrary polygon, possibly with polygonal holes. The shortest distance, within P, between two non-incident edges in P is denoted $s(P)$ and the largest distance between two points in P is denoted $d(P)$. When it is clear from the context which polygon we refer to, we shall simply write d and s instead of $s(P)$ and $d(P)$. Construct a $(6d/s \times 6d/s)$ grid such that every square in the grid has length and height $s/6$, and P lies entirely within the grid, Fig. 1.

Lemma 1. *Let P be a polygon of n vertices, without any acute interior angles. Then it holds that $n = O((\frac{d}{s})^2)$.*

Proof. Omitted in this version, see [6].

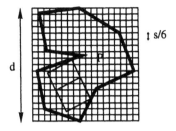

Fig. 1. The polygon P within the grid and two of the rectangles in C_R.

Let C_P be a set of points, such that:

1. every vertex of P is a point in C_P,
2. every crossing between P's perimeter and the grid is a point in C_P, and
3. every crossing in the grid is a point in C_P.

The number of points in C_P is $O((d/s)^3)$, according to Lemma 1. We construct a set of rectangles, C_R, by first inserting into C_R each maximal rectangle which lies within P and which has a side with endpoints in C_P, Fig. 1. Thus the number of rectangles in C_R is now $O((d/s)^6)$.

We will need to extend the number of rectangles in C_R, with two sets of rectangles. First we add the following set.

For every pair of vertices v_i, v_j of P, where v_i is visible from v_j, let s_{ij} be the maximal segment, within P, that passes through or ends at v_i and v_j. For every segment s_{ij} denote every crossing between s_{ij} and a segment of the grid plus v_i and v_j by $p_1, \ldots, p_q$, (thus $q = O(d/s)$). For every possible pair of points (p_l, p_k), $1 \leq l, k \leq q$, on a segment s_{ij}, we insert into C_R all maximal rectangles within P (there are 0,1 or 2 such rectangles) which have a side with endpoints in p_l and p_k. The total number of rectangles inserted in this step is at most $n^2 \cdot (d/s)^2 = O((d/s)^6)$.

The second set of rectangles added to C_R is needed to cover the rectangles in Lemma 5, *Case d*. The rest of this section is devoted to the construction of these special rectangles. We will need the following definitions:

Definition 2. The shortest distance between a rectangle T, within P, and a point p, with a perpendicular projection on one of T's long sides (or any side if T is a square), is denoted the *v-distance* between T and p. If p doesn't have a perpendicular projection on T's long sides then the v-distance is infinite.

The v-distance between a rectangle T, within a polygon P, and P's perimeter is the shortest v-distance between T and a point on P's perimeter.

In order to facilitate an easier description, we assume w.l.o.g. that the two longer sides of a rectangle T, within P, lie horizontally, that is, we rotate T, P and the grid until T's long sides lie horizontally. Let A, B, C and D be the corners of T in a counter-clockwise order, where A and B are the endpoints of

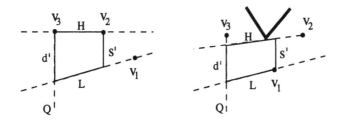

Fig. 2. Two 3v-trapezoids.

T's lowest long-side, Fig. 6. Thus the segments AB and CD are at least as long as AD and BC.

Definition 3. Let T be any rectangle within P with short sides of length at most $5s/6$ and long sides of length at least $4s$, whose opposite long sides touch two vertices v_1 respectively v_2, where v_1 touches AB and v_2 touches CD.

If there exist some other vertices of P, to the left or right of v_1 and v_2, closer than the v-distance $s/6$ from T, then let v_3 be the left- or rightmost vertex of P such that the v-distance between T and v_3 is less than $s/6$. We may assume, according to symmetry, that v_3 lies to the left of v_1 and v_2, and that v_3 lies closer to CD than to AB. Rotate P, T and the grid such that v_3 and v_2 have the same y-coordinate, Fig. 2.

Let Q be the vertical segment of length s with upper endpoint at v_3. Let H be a segment within P between v_2 and Q, such that the crossing between Q and H is as close as possible to v_3, and let, if possible, L be a segment within P between v_1 and Q such that L's and H's extensions cross to the right of v_1 and v_2 and the crossing between Q and L has the smallest possible y-coordinate. Let s' be the longest of the two vertical segments between v_2 and L (or its extension), respectively v_1 and H (or its extension), and let d' be the segment on Q between H and L. If there exists a trapezoid whose boundaries, the two vertical segments s' and d', and the segments of H and L between s' and d', is well-defined, as described above, then the trapezoid is denoted a *3v-trapezoid*. A 3v-trapezoid is hole-free since the shortest diagonal of a hole in P is at least s and $|d'| \leq s$. $\quad \Box$

For every 3v-trapezoid t in P, construct at most $\lceil |d'|/|s'| \rceil$ rectangles with short-sides of length $|s'|$ where every rectangle has one endpoint on s''s lower endpoint and one on d'. We place the rectangles in such a way that a rectangle's short side, closest to d', touches both d' and the upper long-side of the rectangle below, Fig. 3b. The rectangles will at least cover the part of t at distance more than $s/2$ from s' and d', Fig. 3b. Add these rectangles to C_R. These rectangles can always be constructed since a 3v-trapezoid is hole-free. Rotate the 3v-trapezoid in such a way that s' and d' are vertical. Let l_1 be the horizontal distance between d' and the crossing of H's and L's extensions, and let l_2 be the horizontal distance between s' and the crossing of H's and L's extensions, Fig. 3a. Note that $l_2 > s/2$ since the shortest distance between v_1 and v_2 is s

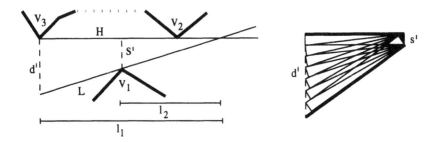

Fig. 3. (a) Finding a $3v$-trapezoid.   (b) A $3v$-trapezoid covered by rectangles.

and the vertical distance is at most $5s/6$. So for every $3v$-trapezoid in P we will construct at most $|d'|/|s'|$ rectangles, and by simple trigonometry we have: $|d'|/|s'|=(l_1/l_2)<(d/l_2)<2\cdot d/s$. Since P consists of n vertices there can be at most $O(n^3)$ $3v$-trapezoids in P, and since $n=O((d/s)^2)$, according to Lemma 1, we will add at most $n^3\cdot 2\cdot(d/s)=O((d/s)^7)$ rectangles to C_R. So the total number of rectangles in C_R will be $O((d/s)^7)$. It is easily seen that C_R can be constructed in time linear with respect to the number of rectangles in C_R.

3   Covering Rectangles

In Lemmas 4-6 we will show that every rectangle T within an arbitrary polygon P can be covered by a constant number of rectangles in C_R. For convenience we divide the rectangles into three cases according to their shape.

Lemma 4. *Every rectangle T, within P, whose longest side is shorter than $s/2$ can be covered by a constant number of rectangles in C_R.*

Proof. We have two cases:

Case a: *The shortest distance between T and P's perimeter is at least $s/\sqrt{18}$.*

The distance between T and P's perimeter is at least as long as the diagonal of a square in the grid, so T will never lie within the same square as P's perimeter. Since the diagonal of T is at most $1/\sqrt{2}s$, T can at most overlap six rows or columns of squares in the grid. And since every side of a square is the base of a rectangle in C_R, the rectangle T can be covered by at most six rectangles in C_R.

Case b: *The rectangle T lies closer than $s/\sqrt{18}$ from P's perimeter.*

Let e_1 be an edge closest to T. Let r_1 be the rectangle in C_R with base e_1. If r_1 covers T then we are finished, otherwise let e_2 be the edge incident to e_1 that lies on the same side of e_1 as the part of T that isn't covered by r_1, Fig. 4a. The vertex connecting e_1 and e_2 is denoted v. Now, two cases can occur:

  (i) The angle (e_1,e_2) is less than or equal to 180 degrees. Since T lies closer than $s/\sqrt{18}$ from e_1, the largest distance between a point in T and e_1 is $\frac{s}{\sqrt{18}}+\frac{s}{\sqrt{2}}=\frac{\sqrt{8}}{3}s<s$. The height of r_1 is at least s. That is, the part of T with

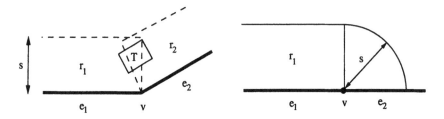

Fig. 4. (a) T is covered by r_1 and r_2. (b) The quadrant bounds the area which T may overlap.

a perpendicular projection on e_1 is covered by r_1. It remains to show that there exists a rectangle r_2 in C_R that covers the rest of T. Since every point in T lies within distance less than s from e_1, the upper right quadrant of a circle with its center in v and radius s bounds the area outside r_1 where T partly can overlap, Fig. 4b. The rectangle r_2 covers the entire area described by the quadrant, so the remaining part of T that isn't covered by r_1 is covered by r_2.

(ii) If the interior angle (e_1, e_2) is greater than 180 degrees then partition T into nine rectangles, $T_1, \ldots, T_9$ of equal size, such that the longest side of each sub-rectangle T_i, $1 \le i \le 9$, is at most of length $s/6$. Now we can cover every sub-rectangle T_i separately. Every sub-rectangle that lies at least $s/\sqrt{18}$ from P's perimeter is covered according to *Case a*. Let T' be any of the sub-rectangles, T_i, that lies closer than $s/\sqrt{18}$ from P's perimeter. Let v_1 (v_2) and v be the vertices of e_1 (e_2). Recall that on every edge and its extensions there exist $O((d/s)^2)$ rectangles in C_R. Let r_1 (r_2) be the maximal rectangle in C_R with base on e_1 (e_2) and its extension, such that one corner lies in v_1 (v_2) and one corner on the extension of e_1 (e_2) between $s/2$ and $(s/2+s/\sqrt{18})$ from v, Fig. 5. Since the shortest distance from v to a non-incident edge is s, it follows that the height of r_1 and r_2 is at least $s/2$. Also, since the length of T's diagonal is at most $s/\sqrt{18}$, we have that a point in T' lies within distance not greater than $(s/\sqrt{18}+s/\sqrt{18}) < s/2$ from e_1. Thus r_1 and r_2 covers T', and T can be covered by a constant number of rectangles in C_R.

When the rectangles are thin we need to cover the rectangles in different ways depending on the v-distance between the rectangle and P's perimeter.

Lemma 5. *Every rectangle T, within P, whose shortest side is at most of length $s/2$, can be covered by a constant number of rectangles in C_R.*

Proof. If $|AB| \le 4s$ then partition T into eight equal rectangles, whose long sides are of length at most $s/2$, which are then covered according to Lemma 4. Otherwise insert four points A', B', C' and D' on T's perimeter, where A' and B' are points on AB at a distance s from A, respectively B, and C' and D' are points on CD at a distance s from C, respectively D. Partition T into three rectangles

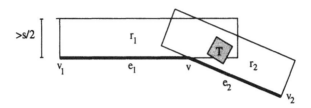

Fig. 5. r_1 and r_2 cover every small rectangle that lies closer than $s/\sqrt{18}$ from P's perimeter.

by inserting two segments $A'D'$ and $B'C'$ in T. We denote these partitions, from left to right, T_l, T_m and T_r, Fig. 6. Partition T_l, respectively T_r, into two equal rectangles with long sides of length $s/2$ and cover these according to Lemma 4. We distinguish four cases:

Case a: The v-distance between T and P's perimeter is at least $s/6$.

We claim that there exists a rectangle r in C_R that covers T_m. To prove this claim, let p_1 be the point in C_P with largest y-coordinate below or on AA', such that the horizontal distance from p_1 to the extension of DA is between $s/6$ and $5s/6$, and symmetrically, let p_2 be the point in C_P with largest y-coordinate below or on BB', such that the horizontal distance from p_2 to the extension of CB is between $s/6$ and $5s/6$, Fig. 6.

Let r be the rectangle in C_R with base $p_1 p_2$. Since the vertical differenc between p_1 and p_2 is less than $s/6$ and since $|p_1 p_2| > s$, it follows that the slope of r's left and right side is greater than six and, hence r covers T_m.

Case b: The v-distance between one of T's long sides and P's perimeter is less than $s/6$, and the v-distance between the opposite long side and P's perimeter is at least $s/6$.

We can w.l.o.g. assume that AB is the long side of T with shortest v-distance to P's perimeter. Let p_1 be the point in C_P with largest y-coordinate below or on AA', such that the horizontal distance from p_1 to the extension of DA is between $s/6$ and $5s/6$. Symmetrically, let p_2 be the point in C_P with largest

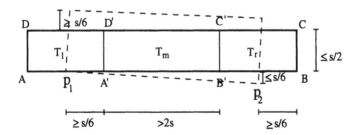

Fig. 6. T partitioned into sub-rectangles and, the rectangle with base p_1, p_2 covers T_m.

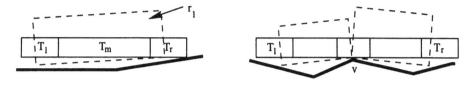

Fig. 7. Covering T according to Lemma 5, Case b.

y-coordinate below or on BB', such that the horizontal distance from p_2 to the extension of CB is between $s/6$ and $5s/6$, Fig. 6.

If p_1 and p_2 can be connected by a straight line segment within P, then let r be the rectangle in C_R with base p_1p_2. Since the vertical differenc between p_1 and p_2 is less than $s/6$ and since $|p_1p_2|>s$, the slope of r's left and right side is greater than six, hence r covers T_m, Fig. 7(left).

Otherwise, if p_1 and p_2 can't be connected by a straight line segment within P, then there exists a vertex v, the closest to AB and lying between AB and p_1p_2. If $|p_1v|<s$ or $|p_2v|<s$ then we partition the area in T with x-coordinates between p_1 and v (or p_2 and v), into two rectangles which are then covered according to Lemma 4. We may assume w.l.o.g. that $|p_1v|$ is longer than s. We will now show that the uncovered area of T_m can be covered by a rectangle in C_R. If $|p_2v|$ is also longer than s we do the corresponding procedure to the right of v. The region of T at most $s/4$ to the left and right of v is covered according to Lemma 4, Fig. 7(right). Recall that there exist rectangles in C_R that lie on the visibility lines and their extensions for every two vertices of T. Thus, there exists a rectangle r in C_R with lower right corner in v and with lower left corner, denoted p', between 0 and $s/6$ below AA' and with horizontal distance between $s/6$ and $5s/6$ from AD. Note that p' and p_1 don't necessarily coincide. Since the vertical differenc between p' and v is less than $s/6$, and since $|p'v|>s$, the slope of r's left and right side is greater than six, thus r covers the uncovered area of T_m to the left of v, Fig. 7(right).

Before we show the case when the v-distance between both T's long sides and P's perimeter is less than $s/6$, we need to prove the following special case.

Case c: Two diagonally opposite corners of T touch a vertex in P.

We can assume w.l.o.g. that the vertex v_1 coincides with A, and the vertex v_2 coincides with C, Fig. 8. Let p_1 be the point in C_P with largest y-coordinate below or on BB', such that the horizontal distance from p_1 to the extension of BC is between $s/4$ and s. Let r_1 be the rectangle in C_R with base v_1p_1 and let α be the angle (v_1p_1, AB). If r_1 covers T_m then we are finished, otherwise there exists a vertex v_3 above CD that prevented r_1 from covering T_m. Recall that there exist rectangles in C_R that lie on the visibility lines and their extensions for every two vertices of T. Thus there exists a rectangle r_2 in C_R with upper right corner at v_2 and upper left corner, denoted p_2, between 0 and $s/6$ above DD' and at horizontal distance between 0 and $s/4$ from AD, Fig. 8(right). Let β be the angle (v_2p_2, CD). We know that $\beta<\alpha$, since β is at most equal to the

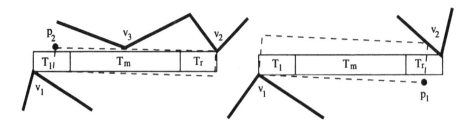

Fig. 8. T_m is covered by a rectangle in C_R.

angle (v_2v_3, CD), (i.e. v_3, v_2, D). Thus r_2 can't be stopped by any part of the perimeter above r_1's base, and it follows that r_2 covers T_m.

Case d: The v-distance between both T's long sides and P's perimeter is less than $s/6$.

Let v_2 be the vertex in P, above or on $C'D'$, with smallest v-distance to $C'D'$, and let v_1 be the vertex in P, below or on $A'B'$, with smallest v-distance to $A'B'$. We may assume w.l.o.g. that v_1 lies to the right of v_2 . The region of T between v_1 and v_2 is covered according to *Case c*, since the part of T between v_1 and v_2 can be expanded in such a way that v_1 and v_2 touch T's opposite long sides. Let T_l' be the uncovered region of T to the left of v_2 and to the right of T_l and let T_r' be the uncovered region of T to the right of v_1 and to the left of T_r. Assume that T_l''s both long sides lie closer to P's perimeter than $s/6$. We will now prove that it is possible to cover T_l' with a constant number of rectangles in C_R. If T_r''s both long sides lie closer to P's perimeter than $s/6$ then we do the corresponding procedure on T_r', otherwise we cover T_r' according to *Case a* or *b*.

Let v_3 be the leftmost vertex in P, such that the v-distance from v_3 to T_l' is less than $s/6$. Let Q be the vertical segment of length s with one endpoint in v_3, Fig. 9. The part of T_l' to the left of Q can be covered according to *Case a* or *b*, since the shortest v-distance from P's perimeter to one of T_l''s long sides to the left of Q is greater than $s/6$. Let L be the lowest segment between v_1 and Q and let H be the highest segment between v_2 and Q, such that H's and L's extensions cross to the right of v_1. The segment on Q between H and L is denoted d'.

The shortest vertical segment from v_2 to L is denoted s'. The length of s' is the largest possible thickness of T. The two areas between s' and d' of T closer than $s/2$ from s' or d' are covered according to Lemma 4. Let t be the trapezoid bounded by the two parallel segments s' and d', and the part of the segments H and L between s' and d'. This trapezoid is a 3v-trapezoid, according to Definition 3, and according to the definition of C_R, the uncovered area of t is entirely covered by rectangles in C_R. Therefore, since the thickness of these rectangles is s', the part of T in t can be covered by two of these rectangles in C_R. Thus the original rectangle T can be covered by a constant number of rectangles in C_R.

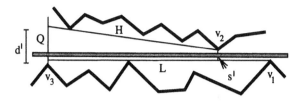

Fig. 9. A $3v$-trapezoid within P.

Lemma 6. *Every rectangle T, within a polygon P, whose shortest side is longer than $s/2$, can be covered by a constant number of rectangles in C_P.*

Proof. If $|AB| \leq 3s$ we partition T into six equal rectangles which are then covered according to Lemma 5. Otherwise partition T in such a way that we can cover the border of T, that is the region in T that lies at most s from T's perimeter, according to Lemma 5. Let T_m be the uncovered region of T. Let p_1 be the point in C_P with largest y-coordinate below or on the extension of T_m's base, such that p_1 lies between $s/4$ and $3s/4$ from AD, and let p_2 be the point in C_P with largest y-coordinate below or on the extension of T_m's base, such that p_2 lies between $s/4$ and $3s/4$ from BC. Let r be the rectangle in C_R with base p_1p_2. Since the vertical distance between p_1 and p_2 is less than $s/6$, according to the definition of C_P, and since $|p_1p_2|$ is greater than T_m's height, the rectangle r will cover T_m.

4 Two algorithms and their complexity

In Lemmas 4-6, we have shown that C_R includes a covering which is within a constant factor of the optimal. Thus it is possible to translate the original geometrical covering problem into the **set-covering problem**, as follows.

An instance (X, F) of the **set-covering problem** consists of a finite set X and a family F of subsets of X, such that every element of X belongs to at least one subset in F. We want to cover the polygon P with a minimum number of rectangles in C_R. Define X to be the set of all cells in the partition induced by the perimeters of all the rectangles in C_R, (thus $|X| = O(|C_R|^2)$), and we define F, such that every element $f \in F$ corresponds to a rectangle r in C_R, where f is the subset of X that is included in r. In the following two sections we will show how one can use this translation to find two algorithms for the polygon-covering problem by using two known set-covering algorithms. Before we show the algorithms we note the following observation:

Observation 7. *If the input polygon is given as integer coordinates in the universe $[0..u]$ then $s \geq \frac{1}{\sqrt{2} \cdot u}$.*

Proof. The proof of Observation 7 is given in the full version [6].

4.1 An exponential algorithm

This is a simple straight-forward algorithm which checks if there is any subset of k rectangles in C_R that cover P. If such a subset is found then we are finished, otherwise increment k and continue as described above. The initial value of k is 1 and from Lemmas 4-6 we know that C_R includes a covering which is within a constant factor of the optimal, thus $k=1, \ldots, O(\mu(P))$. Since there are no more than $((d/s)^7)^{O(\mu(P))}$ subsets of C_R with $O(\mu(P))$ rectangles, we can find a covering with $O(\mu(P))$ rectangles in time:

$$\sum_{k=1}^{O(\mu(P))} ((d/s)^7)^k = (d/s)^{O(\mu(P))} = 2^{O(\mu(P) \cdot \log d/s)}.$$

According to Theorem 1 in [9] it holds that $\mu(P) = O(n \cdot \log d/s)$, thus we get the time complexity $2^{O(n \cdot (\log d/s)^2)}$. Hence by Observation 7 we obtain the following theorem:

Theorem 8. *When the vertices of the input polygon are given as integer coordinates in the range $[0..u]$, the algorithm described above will produce a covering within a constant factor of the optimal in $2^{O(n \cdot (\log u)^2)}$ time.*

4.2 A polynomial algorithm

A natural approach to find an approximation algorithm would be to use a known set-covering algorithm, for example a greedy algorithm. A Greedy-Set-Cover algorithm [3] can easily be implemented to run in time $O(|X||F|min(|X|, |F|))$, with a ratio bound of $(\ln |X| + 1)$. Recall that $|X| = |C_R|^2$ and $F = C_R$.

If the input polygon P is given in integer coordinates, where the coordinates are in the universe $[0..u]$, the above greedy algorithm produces a covering which is within a logarithmic factor of the optimal, $(\ln |C_R|^2 + 1)$, in pseudo-polynomial time $O(((d/s)^7)^4) = O((d/s)^{28})$. Since $s \geq \frac{1}{\sqrt{2} \cdot u}$ and $d \leq \sqrt{2} \cdot u$ we have that the time-complexity for the greedy algorithm is $O(u^{56})$. So we obtain the following:

Theorem 9. *When the n vertices of the input polygon are given as polynomially bounded integer coordinates, the algorithm described above will produce a covering with a $O(\log n)$ approximation factor in polynomial time.*

5 Lower Bounds

From Lemmas 4-6 we derived the following proposition:

Proposition 10. *There exists some constant, say c, such that for any polygon P there exists a finite set, C, of rectangles, lying within P, where every other rectangle in P can be covered by c rectangles from C.*

Two questions arise naturally in connection with these proofs:

a) What is the minimum constant c, for which the above proposition holds? That is, if we don't have any restrictions on C except that it should be finite?

b) How large does C have to be in the worst case, in terms of n, d and s, in order for the proposition to hold?

Therefore, in this section we give lower bounds for (a) and (b).

Theorem 11. *For all integers $n \geq 8$, there exists a polygon P_n with n vertices, such that for any finite set of rectangles, C lying inside P_n, there exists a rectangle T within P that can't be covered by less than six rectangles in C.*

Proof. Omitted in this version, see [6].

Theorem 12. *For every $n \geq 5$, and $d > s > 0$ there exists a polygon P, such that for any set of rectangles, C, for which it holds that every possible rectangle within P can be covered by at most c rectangles of C, it holds that $|C| = (\frac{d}{s})^{\Omega(1/c)}$.*

Proof. Omitted in this version, see [6].

References

1. P. Berman and B. DasGupta, *Approximating the Rectilinear Polygon Cover Problems*, Proc. 4th Canadian Conf. Computational Geometry, pp.229-235, 1992.
2. B.M. Chazelle, *Computational Geometry and Convexity*, Ph.D. Thesis, Carnegie-Mellon Univ., Dept. Comput. Sci., 1980.
3. Carmen, T.H., Leiserson, C.E. and Rivest, R.L., *Introduction to Algorithms*, MIT Press, 1990.
4. J.C. Culberson and R.A. Reckhow, *Covering Polygon is Hard*, Journal of Algorithms, 17:2-44, 1994.
5. D. Franzblau and D. Kleitman, *An Algorithm for Constructing Regions with Rectangles*, In Proc. 16th Ann. ACM Symp. Theory of Comp., pp. 167-174, 1984.
6. C. Levcopoulos and J. Gudmundsson, *Close Approximation of Minimum Rectangular Coverings*, LU-CS-TR 96-164, Dept. of Comp. Sci., Lund University, 1996.
7. A. Hegedüs, *Algorithms for covering polygons by rectangles*, Computer Aided Design, vol. 14, no 5, 1982.
8. J.M. Keil, *Minimally Covering a Horizontally Convex Orthogonal Polygon*, Proceedings 2nd Annual Symposium on Computational Geometry, pp.43-51, 1986.
9. C. Levcopoulos, *A Fast Heuristic for Covering Polygons by Rectangles*, Proceedings FCT'85, Cottbus, GDR, 1985 (LNCS 199, Springer-Verlag).
10. C. Levcopoulos, *Improved Bounds for Covering General Polygons with Rectangles*, Proc. 7th Conf. on FST&TCS, Pune, India, 1987 (LNCS 287, Springer-Verlag).
11. L. Monk, *Elementary-recursive Decision Procedures*, PhD thesis, University of California, Berkeley, 1975.
12. J. O'Rourke, *The decidability of Covering by Convex Polygons*, Report JHU-EE 82-1, Dept. Elect. Engrg. Comp. Sci., Johns Hopkins Univ., Baltimore, MD,1982.
13. J. O'Rourke and K.J. Supowit, *Some NP-hard Polygon Decomposition Problems*, IEEE Transactions on Information Theory, vol. IT-29, pp.181-190, 1983.
14. F.P. Preparata and M.I. Shamos, *Computational Geometry*, New York, Springer-Verlag, 1985.
15. M. Yamashita, T. Ibaraki and N. Honda, *The minimum number cover problem of a rectilinear region by rectangles*, EATCS'84.

A New Competitive Algorithm for Agent Searching in Unknown Streets

Pallab Dasgupta, P.P.Chakrabarti and S.C.DeSarkar

Dept. of Computer Sc. & Engg.,
Indian Institute of Technology, Kharagpur,
INDIA 721302.
{pallab,ppchak,scd}@cse.iitkgp.ernet.in

Abstract. In this paper we present a simple on-line strategy based on a continuous angle bisector approach for searching an unknown *street* polygon. The proposed strategy achieves a competitive ratio of $1 + \log_e(1 + \cos\frac{\alpha}{2}) + \delta$, where $0 \le \alpha \le \pi$, and δ is a given constant greater than zero. By choosing an arbitrarily small value for δ, the value of this ratio is 1.7, which is significantly better than the previous upperbound of 2.83 (derived by Kleinberg [6]), considering that the lowerbound for this problem is $\sqrt{2}(> 1.41)$ (derived by Klein [5]).

1 Introduction

In recent times, problems related to path planning with incomplete information have motivated the development of competitive on-line strategies for searching in various structures, such as lines, rays, and grids [1], layered graphs [7], polygons [2, 5, 6], and *b-ary* trees [3]. In such problems, the search model considers a robot in a terrain whose geometry is unknown and the robot has to take decisions based on the information gathered through (say visual or tactile) sensors. Typically, the objective is to develop a search strategy for the robot such that the ratio of the distance traversed by the robot (before finding the goal) to the shortest path to the goal is minimum. If a constant ratio can be achieved for the worst case situation then the problem is said to admit competitive searching and the ratio is called the *competitive factor*.

It has been shown [5] that while general polygons do not admit competitive searching, there is an important special class of polygons called *streets* for which competitive strategies exist. A street is defined as follows [5]:

Street: A simple polygon P with two distinguished vertices s and t is called a street if the clockwise polygonal chain L from s to t and the anticlockwise polygonal chain R from s to t are mutually weakly visible, that is, each point of L can be seen from at least one point of R, and vice versa.

The only known lowerbound for the task of searching in an unknown street is $\sqrt{2}(> 1.41)$, which was established by Klein in [5]. He also presented a strategy which achieves a competitive factor of $1 + \frac{3}{2}\pi(< 5.72)$. Recently, Kleinberg [6] has improved this ratio to $2\sqrt{2}(< 2.83)$. In this paper, we present a strategy whose

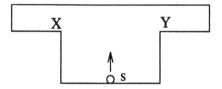

Fig. 1. Figure illustrating the lower bound case

competitive ratio is bounded by $1+\log_e(1+\cos\frac{\alpha}{2})+\delta$, where α, $(0 \leq \alpha \leq \pi)$, is a constant whose value is determined by the geometry of the polygon, and δ is any given constant greater than zero. By choosing an infinitesimally small value for δ we show that this ratio has the value 1.7, which is interesting for the following reasons:

- The new ratio is significantly better than the previous upperbound of 2.83 (established by Kleinberg [6]).
- The new ratio is fairly close to the lowerbound of 1.41. Since this lowerbound is derived from a rather trivial situation, it was generally believed [5, 6] that there is a good scope of improving the lowerbound. The new upperbound of 1.7 leads us to believe that the lowerbound of 1.41 is in fact much tighter than was thought before.

In the algorithm presented in this paper, the robot is required to move along the curve defined by the *continuous* bisector of the angle extended by the extreme *cavemouths* of the robot's *extended* view on its present position. The curve has the interesting property that the distance of the robot from the goal decreases monotonically. Recently Icking and Klein have also applied a similar idea to a different problem [4].

2 Preliminaries

The lowerbound of $\sqrt{2}$ on the competitive ratio for searching an unknown street was derived by Klein [5] from the very simple situation shown in Fig 1. Since the goal t could be either at X or Y, it would be best for the robot to walk straight upto the segment $\overline{XY}$ from where it can see t, and then to move directly to t.

We borrow a few definitions from Kleinberg's paper [6] to describe the robot's view of the problem:

Extended view of the robot: Let P be the given street within which the robot is located at present. The *extended view* of the robot is the set of all points on the boundary of P that the robot has seen so far (See Fig 2).

Cave: A *cave* is a portion of the boundary of P which is hidden from the robot's view, except for the endpoints of that portion, which is visible.

Cavemouth: At some point p' on the robots path, the two endpoints of the cave were on the same line of sight from p'. The one closer to p' is called the *mouth* of the cave. Each cavemouth v is a reflex vertex of P (See Fig 2). In

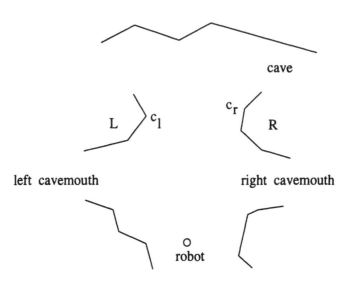

Fig. 2. The extended view of the robot

the neighborhood of v, P lies either to the left or right of the ray $p'v$. We accordingly refer to v as being either a right or left cavemouth.

In the extended view, let c_l denote the rightmost among all left cavemouths and c_r denote the leftmost among all right cavemouths. We state a result established by Kleinberg [6] which we shall use in our analysis.

Lemma 1. *If the goal t has not yet been seen, and if the robot has moved in way such that the points in its extended view immediately to its left and right belong to L and R respectively, then we may conclude that the goal t lies in the cave of either c_l or c_r. Consequently, the shortest path from x to t touches either c_l or c_r.* □

3 The search algorithm

In this section, we present the proposed algorithm for searching unknown streets. The competitive ratio of this algorithm has been determined in the next section. Let Γ denote the shortest path from s to t. Based on the robot's extended view the following cases are to be considered.

Case 1: If t is visible, the robot moves directly to t.
Case 2: If c_r (c_l) is not defined (See Fig 3), then from lemma 1, it follows that the shortest path Γ passes directly through c_l. The robot therefore moves directly to c_l.
Case 3: If c_r and c_l are both visible, but they lie on the same line of sight (see Fig 3), then clearly the shortest path passes through the closer of the two, and so the robot moves towards that vertex.

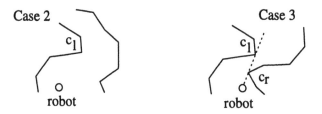

Fig. 3. Figures illustrating case 2 and case 3 situations

Case 4: Otherwise, both c_l and c_r are visible and are on different lines of sight. The robot does not know which of these vertices belong to the shortest path Γ. It is precisely under this situation that the strategies presented for searching streets differ. For example, Klein suggests [5] that the robot should start moving towards a point on the line segment $\overline{c_l c_r}$ which is determined by a strategy that tries to minimize the *local absolute detour*. In Kleinberg's strategy [6], the robot may choose any direction of motion such that c_l lies to the left and c_r lies to the right. Choosing the proper direction is of utmost importance for the overall performance of the strategy. We propose the following course of motion for the robot.

- The robot follows a curve, such that at any point p on the curve the direction of motion of the robot (which is a tangent to the curve at that point) is along the bisector of the angle $\angle c_l p c_r$ formed between the rays pc_l and pc_r. In other words, the robot always moves along the angle bisector of the angle extended by the vertices c_l and c_r on its present position.

The robot will move along the above curve until either of the cases 1,2 or 3 applies, or c_l (and/or c_r) is redefined (that is a new left (right) cavemouth is seen which is to the right (left) of the present c_l (c_r)) (Fig 4 shows a sample situation). In such a case the robot continues following the above course of motion using the new pair of cavemouths. It should be noted that when a new left (right) cavemouth is sighted, then it is in the same line of sight as c_l (c_r). Thus the robot does not have to take any sharp turn; it follows a smooth curve.

4 Analysis of the algorithm

In this section we analyze the competitive ratio of the proposed strategy. We shall use the following terminology throughout this section.

$D_{min}(x, y)$: Length of the shortest path from x to y.
$D(x, y)$: Length of the path traversed by the robot to move from x to y.
$Det(x, y)$: Detour of the robot to move from x to y, that is,

$$Det(x, y) = D(x, y) - D_{min}(x, y)$$

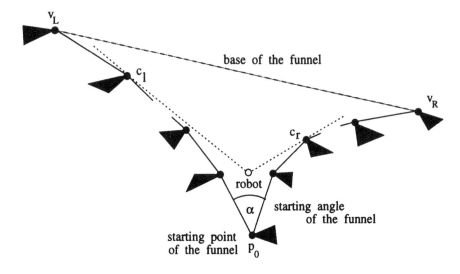

Fig. 4. The case 4 situation: A funnel

Let Γ denote the shortest path from s to t. Let $v_1 = s, v_2, \ldots, v_k = t$ be the vertices of the polygon P belonging to Γ that are visited by the robot (in that order). It follows from the definition that an upperbound on the competitive ratio r of the strategy is as follows:

$$r \leq \max\left\{ \frac{Det(v_i, v_{i+1}) + D_{min}(v_i, v_{i+1})}{D_{min}(v_i, v_{i+1})}, \quad 1 \leq i < k \right\} \tag{1}$$

We shall first compute an upperbound on the maximum detour of the robot for moving from v_i to v_{i+1} $(1 \leq i < k)$ and then compute the competitive ratio using the above formula.

Let us consider the situation when the robot has visited the vertex v_i $(1 \leq i < k)$, but is yet to visit the vertex v_{i+1}. Let x denote the present position of the robot. Then the detour from the shortest path from v_i to v_{i+1} is at least:

$$D(v_i, x) + D_{min}(x, v_{i+1}) - D_{min}(v_i, v_{i+1})$$

If at this point either of the cases 1,2 or 3 of section 3 applies then the detour does not increase any more. Clearly, the detour may increase only as long as case 4 applies. This leads us to the task of efficiently searching a *funnel* which has been defined by Klein [5] as follows:

Funnel: A funnel (F_L, F_R) consists of a left convex chain, F_L, and a right convex chain, F_R, leading from a common startpoint, p_0, to endpoints v_L and v_R that are mutually visible. We call the point p_0 the *startpoint* of the funnel and the line segment $\overline{v_L v_R}$ the *base* of the funnel. The *start-angle* α of the funnel is the angle extended at p_0 by the first edge of the left chain and the first edge of the right chain (see Fig 4).

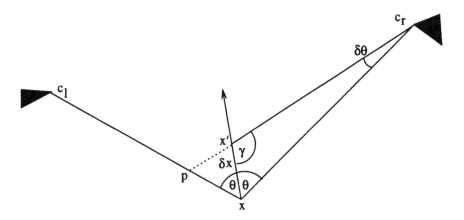

Fig. 5. A small section of the robots path

As long as case 4 applies, the robot is able to see a rightmost left cavemouth c_l and a leftmost right cavemouth c_r along distinct lines of sight. It is easy to see that as long as case 4 applies repeatedly, the sequence of such c_ls define a convex chain (that is, the left convex chain) and the sequence of c_rs define the right convex chain (Fig 4 shows a sample). Either the left chain of the funnel or the right chain belongs to the shortest path.

Case 4 may continue to apply until the robot reaches the *base* of the funnel. Since the detour can increase only as long as case 4 applies, the core of the problem of searching an unknown street is to efficiently navigate the robot out of a funnel. This result has been formally established by Klein [5]. We therefore skip the formal proof of this result and proceed to compute an upperbound on the maximum detour in navigating a funnel using the proposed strategy.

Without loss of generality we assume that the right chain of the funnel belongs to the shortest path. Let x denote the position of the robot at an arbitrary point on its path. We consider an infinitesimally small segment xx' of the robot's path starting from x (see Fig 5). Since xx' is arbitrarily small, it can be approximated by the line segment $\overline{xx'}$. Let Δx denote the length of this segment. Let θ denote the angle between the line segments $\overline{xx'}$ and $\overline{xc_r}$. Likewise $\Delta\theta$ denotes the angle between the line segments $\overline{c_r x}$ and $\overline{c_r x'}$. We choose the size Δx of the segment $\overline{xx'}$ such that the angle $\Delta\theta$ is also infinitesimally small.

Lemma 2. *The distance of the robot from the goal decreases monotonically.*
Proof: Let us extend the line segment $\overline{c_r x'}$ to meet the line segment $\overline{xc_l}$ at the point p (see Fig 5). We prove the result assuming that c_r is on the shortest path. The result holds symmetrically when c_l is on the shortest path. Since γ is an exterior angle to the triangle $\Delta pxx'$, we have:

$$\gamma = \angle x'px + \theta \geq \theta$$

Therefore, in the triangle $\Delta xc_r x'$, the side opposite to θ (that is, $\overline{x'c_r}$) is less than the side opposite to γ (that is, $\overline{xc_r}$). Since the shortest path from x to the goal t passes through c_r, and x' is closer to c_r than x, it follows that by moving from x to x', the robot has moved closer to the goal. $\square$

It should be noted that either the left chain or the right chain of a funnel belongs to the shortest path. Let v_L and v_R denote the last vertices of the left and the right chains of the funnel respectively. The following lemma establishes that the robot touches the one which belongs to the shortest path.

Lemma 3. *The robot always touches that vertex at the base of the funnel which belongs to the shortest path.*
Proof: Without loss of generality we assume that v_R belongs to the shortest path. The robot leaves the funnel when either of the cases 1, 2 or 3 applies. In each of these cases the target vertex will either be v_R or some vertex on the line of sight of v_R. The result follows. $\square$

Let v_i denote the *starting point* of a funnel. Without loss of generality let us assume that the right chain of the funnel is the one that belongs to the shortest path. Then, by lemma 3 there exists v_j $(j > i)$, such that $v_j = v_R$ (where v_R is the last vertex of the right chain). Let x denote the current position of the robot (see Fig 5). The shortest path from x to v_R is through c_r. If it follows this path, then the total detour while moving from v_i to v_j is as follows:

$$Det_x(v_i, v_j) = D(v_i, x) + \overline{xc_r} - D_{min}(v_i c_r)$$

On the other hand, if the robot moves to x', and then follows the shortest path to v_R (again through c_r), then the total detour is as follows:

$$Det_{x'}(v_i, v_j) = D(v_i, x) + \Delta x + \overline{x'c_r} - D_{min}(v_i c_r)$$
$$= \Delta x + \overline{x'c_r} - \overline{xc_r} + Det_x(v_i, v_j)$$

Thus the movement from x to x' causes an additional detour of $\Delta x + \overline{x'c_r} - \overline{xc_r}$. At the starting point of the funnel, the detour is zero. The total detour is the sum of the detours caused by the segments such as $\overline{xx'}$. We now compute the detour $Det_{xx'}$ caused by the segment $\overline{xx'}$ (see Fig 5) as follows:

$$Det_{xx'} = \Delta x + \overline{x'c_r} - \overline{xc_r} = \overline{xc_r}\left(\frac{\sin(\Delta\theta) + \sin(\theta)}{\sin(\gamma)} - 1\right)$$

Since $\gamma = \pi - \theta - \Delta\theta$, $\sin(\gamma) = \sin(\theta + \Delta\theta)$. Thus:

$$Det_{xx'} = \overline{xc_r}\left(\frac{\sin(\Delta\theta) + \sin(\theta) - \sin(\theta + \Delta\theta)}{\sin(\theta + \Delta\theta)}\right)$$
$$= \overline{xc_r}\left(\frac{\sin(\Delta\theta) + \sin(\theta) - \sin(\theta)\cos(\Delta\theta) - \cos(\theta)\sin(\Delta\theta)}{\sin(\theta + \Delta\theta)}\right)$$
$$= \overline{xc_r}\left(\frac{1 - \cos(\theta)}{sin(\theta + \Delta\theta)}\sin(\Delta\theta) + \frac{2\sin^2(\Delta\theta/2)}{sin(\theta + \Delta\theta)}\sin(\theta)\right)$$

Since $\sin(\Delta\theta) \leq \Delta\theta$ and $\sin(\theta + \Delta\theta) \geq \sin(\theta)$ for $\theta < \pi/2$, we have:

$$Det_{xx'} \leq \overline{xc_r}\left(\tan(\theta/2)\Delta\theta + (\Delta\theta)^2/2\right) \tag{2}$$

The following lemma now establishes a bound on the maximum detour for navigating out of a funnel.

Lemma 4. *Given any constant δ greater than zero, the maximum detour for moving from the starting point v_i of a funnel to the last vertex v_j is upperbounded as follows:*

$$Det_{max}(v_i, v_j) \leq D_{min}(v_i, v_j)\left(\log_e(1 + \cos(\alpha/2)) + \delta\right)$$

where α is the starting angle of the funnel.
Proof: Given the constant δ, we choose an infinitesimally small constant ϵ such that $c > \epsilon\pi/2$. We also choose $\Delta\theta$ in expression 2, such that $\Delta\theta < 2\epsilon$. Therefore,

$$Det_{xx'} \leq \overline{xc_r}\left(\tan(\theta/2)\Delta\theta + \epsilon\Delta\theta\right)$$

Further, by lemma 2 we have $\overline{xc_r} \leq D_{min}(v_i, v_j)$, where v_i is the starting point of the funnel and $v_j = v_R$ is the last vertex on the right chain of the funnel. Therefore:

$$Det_{xx'} \leq D_{min}(v_i, v_j)\left(\tan(\theta/2)\Delta\theta + \epsilon\Delta\theta\right) \tag{3}$$

Summing up the detours corresponding to every segment $\overline{xx'}$ in the path of the robot gives the total detour for moving from the starting point v_i of the funnel to the last vertex $v_j(= v_R)$. Let α denote the starting angle of the funnel. Then the minimum value of θ (in Fig 5) is $\alpha/2$. In the worst case the robot may reach the base of the funnel before either of the cases 1, 2 or 3 apply. Therefore the maximum value of θ is $\pi/2$.

Using equation 3 with infintesimally small $\Delta\theta$ and the fact that the robot moves along a smooth curve within the funnel (even when new cavemouths are seen), we obtain the maximum detour as follows:

$$\begin{aligned}
Det_{max}(v_i, v_j) &\leq D_{min}(v_i, v_j)\int_{\alpha/2}^{\pi/2}\left[\tan(\theta/2) + \epsilon\right]d\theta \\
&\leq D_{min}(v_i, v_j)\left[\log_e(1 + \cos(\alpha/2)) + \epsilon\pi/2\right] \\
&\leq D_{min}(v_i, v_j)\left[\log_e(1 + \cos(\alpha/2)) + \delta\right]
\end{aligned}$$

□

The constant term δ can be neglected for all practical purposes since we are free to choose an arbitrarily small value of δ when the robot moves in infitesimally small steps. However, we retain the term for the sake of formal correctness. The competitive ratio of the proposed strategy can now be computed from equation 1 using lemma 4.

Theorem 5. *The competitive ratio r of the proposed strategy is as follows:*

$$r \leq 1 + \log_e(1 + \cos(\alpha/2)) + \delta$$

where α is the minimum among the starting angles of the funnels encountered by the robot, and δ is any given constant.
Proof: The result follows from equation 1 and lemma 4. $\square$

Since $\alpha \geq 0$, by choosing an infinitesimally small value of δ we have $r \leq 1 + \log_e(2)$ which has the value 1.7.

5 Conclusion

The analysis in this paper uses only two properties of the strategy of following the locus of the angle bisector. Firstly, it guarantees that the distance of the robot from the goal decreases monotonically. Secondly it ensures that the robot follows a smooth curve while navigating a funnel. Clearly there are other curves as well which satisfy both these properties, and therefore it is likely that other strategies exist whose competitive ratio is bounded by 1.7. It also appears very likely that the empirical bound of 1.8 obtained by Klein [5] for searching in streets is actually the real bound of his strategy (and not 5.72, which he had proved). The new upperbound of 1.7 also indicates that the lowerbound of 1.41 may be tighter than was thought before.

Acknowledgements
The authors would like to thank Dr. T.K.Dey for helpful discussions.

References

1. BAEZA-YATES, R. A., J.C.CULBERSON, AND G.J.E.RAWLINS. Searching in the plane. *Information and Computation 106* (1993), 234–252.
2. BLUM, A., P.RAGHAVAN, AND B.SCHIEBER. Navigating in unfamiliar geometric terrains. In *STOC* (1991), pp. 494–504.
3. DASGUPTA, P., P.P.CHAKRABARTI, AND S.C.DESARKAR. Agent searching in a tree and the optimality of iterative deepening. *Artificial Intelligence 71* (1994), 195–208.
4. ICKING, C., AND R.KLEIN. Searching for the kernel of a polygon: A competitive strategy. In *Proc. of the 11th Computational Geometry Conference* (1995), pp. 258–266.
5. KLEIN, R. Walking an unknown street with bounded detour. *Computational Geometry: Theory and Applications 1* (1992), 325–351.
6. KLEINBERG, J. M. On-line search in a simple polygon. In *Proc. of SODA '94* (1994), pp. 8–15.
7. PAPADIMITRIOU, C. H., AND M.YANNAKAKIS. Shortest paths without a map. *Theoretical Computer Science 84* (1991), 127–150.

On the Design of Hybrid Control Systems Using Automata Models

Dang Van Hung * and Wang Ji**

International Institute for Software Technology
The United Nations University, P.O.Box 3058, Macau
email: {dvh, wj}@iist.unu.edu

Abstract. The paper gives a systematic way for the development of hybrid control systems, i.e. to refine specifications written in DC (Duration Calculus) into automata models. Firstly, DC formulas are extended with iteration form and a technique for deriving plant automata from DC formulas is presented. Then, a specification of control automata can be synthesized from plant automata with respect to requirements , based on a necessary and sufficient condition for a plant automaton and a requirement to have a control automaton. Water tank and Gas burner examples are demonstrated to illustrate our method.

1 Introduction

In this paper, we shall deal with hybrid control systems which consist of continuous plants controlled by decision makers via controllers. Typical hybrid systems can be found widely in the areas of robots, process control, aviation and so on. Because of safety critical properties of these systems, many efforts have been involved from computing science and control theory to get a well founded methodology for specification, design and analysis of hybrid control systems [1, 5]. Our aim is to provide a systematic way associated with formal techniques to support the refinement of hybrid systems from specifications written in DC (Duration Calculus) into automata models.

The model of hybrid systems used in this paper is taken from [3, 4, 9]. It consists of three distinct levels: Decision Maker, Controllers and Plant. The decision maker and controllers communicate via the interface that translates signals into symbols for the decision maker to use, and symbols into command signals for the controller input. A decision maker (control program) reads data of the plant provided by a controller (or sensor), computes the next control law, and imposes it on the controllers to control the plant. The plant will continue to use this control law until the next such intervention. The plant, the controllers

---

* On leave from the Institute of Information Technology, Nghia Do, Tu Liem, Hanoi, Vietnam.

** On leave from Department of Computer Science, Changsha Institute of Technology, Changsha 410073, P.R. China. email: wj@dns.cit.whnet.edu.cn. Partly supported by National NSF and National Hi-tech Programme of China.

and the interface are taken together to result in a so-called discrete state system *DES plant*.

The challenge is to develop methodologies which, given a performance specification and system description, extract control programs which will force the plants to meet their performance specifications. The key point is to link the different abstraction levels. We use the stepwise refinement approach to develop a systematic way for dealing with the problem. Starting with a top level specification and a description of the components of a system, we refine specifications of the system in more detail according to the physical laws and control laws in the problem domain. Iterate this step until it determines a plant automaton, of which each state consists of plant states controlled by the same controllers such that the necessary data of the plant given to the decision maker can be decided on entering the states. After obtaining the plant automaton, it is time to determine which control laws are needed to force the plant in which situations to ensure that the plant automaton has the allowable behaviors. It can be determined also whether a transition is caused by one of: time elapsing, disturbance or the control program. From this observation, a specification of the decision maker can be derived and the control program is designed from the specification.

Water Tank Example [7]. The aim is to design a decision maker to open and to close the valve such that the water level is maintained between 68 and 76. Let $w(t)$ be the water level at time t. One description of the system can be depicted as the automaton in Fig. 1.

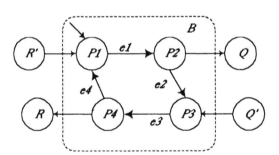

$$D1: \text{ the valve is closed} \qquad\qquad D2: \text{ the valve is open}$$
$$P1: 68 \leq w \leq 76 - \delta \wedge D1 \qquad\qquad P2: 76 - \delta < w \leq 76 \wedge D1$$
$$P3: 68 + \delta \leq w \leq 76 \wedge D2 \qquad\qquad P4: 68 \leq w < 68 + \delta \wedge D2$$
$$Q: w > 76 \wedge D1, \ Q': w > 76 \wedge D2 \quad R: w < 68 \wedge D2, \ R': \ w < 68 \wedge D1$$
$$e1, e3: \text{ time elapsing} \qquad\qquad e2: \text{ open the valve}, \ e4: \text{ close the valve}$$

Fig. 1. Automaton of Water Tank

The behaviors that satisfy the requirement $\forall t.68 \leq w(t) \leq 76$ are represented by the graph B (indicated by the box B in Fig.1). In order to achieve these behaviors, started from $P1$, the automaton needs to receive from the decision maker the command 'open the valve' when it is in $P2$ and the command 'close the valve' when it is in $P4$. On the other hand, on entering the states $P2$ and $P4$, the plant needs to send a signal to the decision maker (say, e.g. the name of the states $P2$ and $P4$ resp.). The decision maker, on receiving the signals, issues the commands 'open the valve' with the delay time less than $t1$ time units or 'close the valve' with the delay time less than $t2$ time units depending on the signals which are $P2$ and $P4$ respectively. The automaton achieving this behavior is depicted in Fig. 2a. The plant controlled by the decision maker (which is the parallel composition of the plant and the decision maker) is represented by the automaton depicted in Fig. 2b, which is the same as the graph B. In the figure, the transition named by the pair (f, e) indicates that the transition f of the decision maker occurs in parallel with the transition e of the plant. ϵ is the idle action. Here, for simplicity, we have assumed that the communication takes no time, and that on receiving a command the controllers can change the state of the plant automaton immediately. One thing should be noticed here is that it takes some time for the decision maker to give the commands. Thus, the roles of the automaton of the decision maker and of the DES plant automaton are not symmetrical.

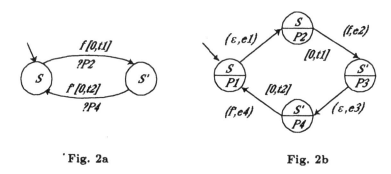

'Fig. 2a   Fig. 2b

From the example we note the following: (1) From a description of the plant behaviors in the form of plant automaton, and from the set of the behaviors of the plant automaton that satisfy the requirement, a specification of the decision maker can be derived such that if its behaviors satisfy the specification, then the controlled plant will satisfy the requirement; (2) The DES plant may give no outputs, and transitions in the DES plant may have no inputs. However, it needs to be such that the pair of the sequence of inputs (commands) and the sequence of outputs of its behaviors that satisfy the requirement is distinguishable from that of the behaviors that do not satisfy the requirement. Hence, a possible approach to the design of hybrid control systems is to derive the DES plant automata from the requirement, and the description of the system such that input and output functions can be added to make the automata satisfy item (2) above. Then a decision maker can be derived directly. In this way, we can reduce the complexity of the proof of the correctness of the design.

In the following sections, we shall elaborate this approach in a formal model of hybrid control systems. In the next section, we present an automata model of hybrid control systems and show how to represent the behaviors of the DES plant automaton by using the duration calculus (DC). Then in Section 3, we present a necessary and sufficient condition for a plant automaton and a requirement to have a decision maker and therefore give an algorithm for deriving a desired decision maker if it exists. Section 4 concludes with some comparison to the related work.

2 From DC^* to Real-time Communicating Automata

2.1 Real-time Communicating Automata

We add the input and output functions to real-time automata (see, e.g.[2]) to obtain real-time communicating automata.

Definition 1. A *Real-time Communicating Automata* A is a tuple

$$(S,\ I,\ O,\ E,\ d,\ s_0,\ \phi)$$

where:

1. S is a set of states, $s_0 \in S$ is the initial state,
2. I is an input alphabet, O is an output alphabet
3. $E \subseteq S \times (I \cup \{\epsilon\}) \times S$ is a set of transitions, $d : E \rightarrow \{[a,b] : a,b \in \mathbf{R}^+ \cup \{\infty\}, a \leq b\}$ is the delay-time function of transitions.
4. $\phi : S \rightarrow O \cup \{\epsilon\}$ is an output function.

A real-time communicating automaton A is *deterministic* iff it is not the case that $(s,a,s') \in E \wedge (s,a,s'') \in E \wedge s' \neq s''$ and neither the case that $(s,\epsilon,s') \in E \wedge (s,a,s') \in E \wedge s \neq s'$ for some a. The transitions of the form (s,ϵ,s') represent internal transitions. In this paper, the symbol ϵ is treated as the empty word, and a singleton will be identified with its element.

Let $w = b_0 b_1 \ldots \in I^\alpha$. A *behavior* σ_w of A *corresponding to* w is $\sigma_w = (e_0, t_0)(e_1, t_1) \ldots$, where $e_i = (s_i, b_i, s_{i+1}) \in E$, $t_i \in d(e_i)$, $b_i \in I \cup \{\epsilon\}$ such that $b_0 b_1 \ldots = w$. t_i is the time that A stays in s_i (delay time of e_i) from when it is enabled (the automaton is in the state s_i and the input b_i is available). σ is a behavior if it is a behavior corresponding to w for some w. Notice that for a behavior σ, there exists only one w such that $\sigma = \sigma_w$, which is denoted by $in(\sigma)$. Output $out(\sigma)$ of the behavior σ is defined by $out(\sigma) = \phi(s_1)\phi(s_2)\ldots$. Therefore, A can be considered as a mapping

$$A(w) = \{out(\sigma_w) | \sigma_w \text{ is a behavior corresponding to } w\}.$$

Signal $signal(\sigma)$ of a behavior σ is defined by $(\phi(s_0), t_0)(\phi(s_1), t_1)\ldots$. By convention, $(\epsilon, t) = \epsilon$. An input with real-time constraints is $w_t = (a_0, t_0)(a_1, t_1)\ldots$, where $a_0 a_1 \ldots \in I^\alpha$. Informally, t_i is the time constraint on the processing of the input a_i. A behavior σ_{w_t} of A that has no internal transitions, corresponding to w_t is $\sigma_{w_t} = (e_0, t'_0)(e_1, t'_1)\ldots$, where $(e_0, t'_0)(e_1, t'_1)\ldots$ is a behavior corresponding to $a_0 a_1 \ldots$, and $t'_i = t_i$. A is considered as a mapping $A_t(w_t) = \{out(\sigma_{w_t}) | \sigma_{w_t} \text{ is a behavior corresponding to } w_t\}$. Notice that by our assumption on A, e_i is a transition with the input a_i. *Trace $tr(\sigma)$* of the behavior σ is defined by $tr(\sigma) = e_0 e_1 \ldots$.

Let $Behaviors(A)$ be the set of all behaviors of A. For a $\sigma \in Behaviors(A)$, $\sigma = (e_0, t_0)(e_1, t_1) \ldots$ is an infinite behavior iff $\sum_{i=0}^{|\sigma|-1} t_i = \infty$. By adding some special transitions with delay-time ∞ into the definition of the real-time communicating automata, we can assume that every behavior of A can be extended to an infinite behavior. Our intention is to use real-time communicating automata to represent both the decision makers and the DES plants. However, the interaction between the two is not symmetrical as mentioned in the introduction. Furthermore, the plant automata may give no output on entering a new state, while the decision makers need to give a new command on entering a new state.

Definition 2. Let $A = (S, I, O, E, d, s_0, \phi)$, and $A' = (S', O, I, E', d', s'_0, \phi')$ be real-time communicating automata. Assume that there is no internal transition in E. *Parallel composition $A \times A'$* of A and A' is the *real-time* automaton defined by $A \times A' \mathrel{\hat{=}} (S \times S', E'', D, (s_0, s'_0))$, where

1. $S \times S'$ is the set of states of $A \times A'$, and (s_0, s'_0) is the initial state $A \times A'$,
2. The set of transitions $E'' \subseteq (S \times S')^2$ and the delay-time function D are defined as follows: $e'' = ((s_1, s'_1), (s_2, s'_2)) \in E''$ iff
   - either $e = (s_1, \phi'(s'_1), s_2) \in E$, $e' = (s'_1, \phi(s_2), s'_2) \in E'$, and e, e' are not internal transitions; in this case, $D(e'') = d(e) \cap d'(e)$, or
   - $s_1 = s_2$, $e' = (s'_1, \epsilon, s'_2) \in E'$ and $\phi'(s'_1) = \epsilon$; $D(e'') = d'(e')$.
   In both cases, we write $e'' = (e, e')$, where $e \in E \cup \{\epsilon\}$, $e' \in E'$.

Notice that the parallel composition operation of two real-time communicating automata is not symmetrical, and by our definition, the automaton A', when it sends a signal to the automaton A, must wait for a command from A, which means that in a state with a nonempty output, only transitions with a nonempty input can occur.

For a behavior $\sigma = ((e_1, e'_1), t_1)((e_2, e'_2), t_2) \ldots$ of $A \times A'$ (defined in usual way), the projection of σ on A and A' are defined respectively by

$$\sigma_A = (e_1, t_1)(e_2, t_2) \ldots, \qquad \sigma_{A'} = (e'_1, t_1)(e'_2, t_2) \ldots.$$

The following proposition follows directly from the definition.

Proposition 3. *1. For any behavior σ of $A \times A'$, σ_A is a behavior of A corresponding to $signal(\sigma_{A'})$, and $\sigma_{A'}$ is a behavior of A' corresponding to $out(\sigma_A)$.*

2. *If σ_2 is a behavior of A' corresponding to w for some $w \in O^*$, and if σ_1 is a behavior of A corresponding to $signal(\sigma_2)$ such that $w = out(\sigma_1)$, then there exists a behavior σ of $A \times A'$ satisfying $\sigma_A = \sigma_1$ and $\sigma_{A'} = \sigma_2$.*

2.2 Duration Calculus with Star

We present an extension of duration calculus (DC^*) that can represent the behaviors of real-time automata. Our extension is to add the closure of the modality ';' to DC: if D is a formula, then so is D^+. The semantic structure of DC^* shares the same with that of DC. An interpretation $\mathcal{I}$ is a function $\mathcal{I} \in (V \rightarrow (time \rightarrow \{0,1\}))$, for which each $\mathcal{I}(X)$, $X \in V$ has at most finitely many discontinuity points in any interval $[a,b]$. The semantics of D^+ is defined as

$$\mathcal{I}, [a,b] \models D^+ \text{ iff } \mathcal{I}, [m_i, m_{i+1}] \models D, \ i = 0, 1, \ldots, n$$
$$\text{for some } a = m_0 < m_1 < \ldots < m_{n+1} = b, \ n \geq 0$$

For a DC^* formula D, we define $D^* \hat{=} D^+ \vee \lceil\ \rceil$.

The readers are referred to [12, 13] for the set of axioms and rules of DC which are the same as in DC^*. We just list some of the additional axioms and rules in the calculus. Let D and A be DC^* formulas.

1. (Monotonicity for star) If $D \Rightarrow A$ then $D^* \Rightarrow A^*$
2. D^+ holds iff there is $n > 0$ such that D^n holds, where D^n is defined by $D^1 \hat{=} D$, $D^{m+1} \hat{=} D; D^m$ for all natural $m > 1$
3. $D^*; D^+ \Rightarrow D^+$, and $D^+ \Rightarrow D^*$.

Theorem 4. *Let* P_i, $i = 1, 2, \ldots, n$ *be state expressions. Let* $D \hat{=} \lceil \bigvee_{i=1}^{n} P_i \rceil$. *Then*

$$D \Leftrightarrow (\bigvee_{i=1}^{n} \lceil P_i \rceil)^+$$

2.3 Representing the Behavior of Real-time Automata

DC^* formulas can be used to describe the behavior of finite real-time automata (considered as a real-time communicating automaton with $I = O = \{\epsilon\}$) in the same way that the regular expressions represent the behavior of finite automata. For example, the real-time automaton in Fig. 3 is represented by the formula $(\lceil N \rceil \wedge \ell \geq 30; \lceil Leak \rceil \wedge \ell \leq 1)^*; (\lceil N \rceil \vee \lceil\ \rceil)$.

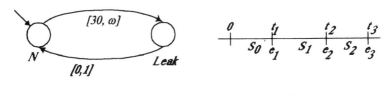

Fig. 3   **Fig. 4**

Definition 5. Let A be a real-time automaton with a set S of states which satisfies the condition that its every behavior can be extended to an infinite behavior. Each infinitely timed sequence of consecutive transitions $\sigma = (e_1, t_1)(e_2, t_2) \ldots$ of A defines an interpretation $\mathcal{I}^\sigma$ of state functions in S in the natural way (see Fig. 4). Namely, for a state $s \in S$,

$$s_{\mathcal{I}^\sigma}(t) \hat{=} 1 \Leftrightarrow \exists i > 0, s' \in S \bullet e_i = (s, s') \wedge \sum_{j=1}^{i-1} t_j \leq t < \sum_{j=1}^{i} t_j.$$

A *DC* formula *D* is said to represent the behavior of *A* iff for all *infinite* $\sigma \in Behaviors(A) \Leftrightarrow \forall t \bullet \mathcal{I}^\sigma, [0, t] \models D$.

Definition 6. Simple DC^* formulas are the DC^* formulas generated by the syntax: $D ::= \lceil\ \rceil \mid \lceil P \rceil \mid \lceil P \rceil \wedge a \leq \ell \leq b \mid D_1; D_2 \mid D^* \mid D^+ \mid D_1 \vee D_2$, where *P* stands for any state expression.

For a real-time automaton *A*, let us denote by $(\lceil s \rceil \wedge a \leq \ell \leq b)$ the transition $e = (s, s')$ with $d(e) = [a, b]$. Then, in the same way as in the theory of formal languages (see, e.g. [8]) we have the following theorem:

Theorem 7. *For any real-time automaton A with a finite set of states and a finite set of transitions, there exists a simple DC^* formula D such that D represents the behaviors of A. Conversely, for any simple DC^* formula D such that $D \Rightarrow D; \ell = r$ (i.e. prefix-closed) and such that the time constraint of D (the replacements of $\lceil P \rceil$ by $\ell > 0$, $\lceil\ \rceil$ by $\ell = 0$ in D) is a valid DC^* formula, there exists a real-time automaton A with a finite set of states and a finite set of transitions such that the behaviors of A are represented by D.*

2.4 Refinement of *DC* Formulas into Automata

Now we present a systematic method for refining *DC* formulas into automata models. Our purpose is to derive from the physical descriptions of a system and the requirement written as a DC^* formula *D* a DES plant automaton *A'*. Starting from $D_1 = D$, by stepwise refinements, we find DC^* formulas $D_2, D_3, \ldots, D_n$ such that $D_i \Rightarrow D_{i-1}$, $i = 2, \ldots, n$, and D_n is a simple DC^* formula. By Theorem 7, *A'* is derived directly from D_n.

Gas Burner Example[12]. A physical description of the system (the plant automata) may be as follows.

1. States:
   Non-leak (*N*): *OnReq, OffReq, Burn, Idle, Rec* (*N* is an abstract state);
   Leak (*Leak*).
2. Events:

   $On \mathrel{\widehat=} (Idle, OnReq)$ (heat request) $Off \mathrel{\widehat=} (Burn, OffReq)$ (off request)
   $R \mathrel{\widehat=} (Leak, Rec)$ (recover) $IgOK \mathrel{\widehat=} (OnReq, Burn)$ (ignition OK)
   $Igfl \mathrel{\widehat=} (OnReq, Leak)$ (ignition failure) $Ffl \mathrel{\widehat=} (Burn, Leak)$ (flame failure)

3. Control laws: $C1$: to recover from *Leak*, $C2$: to become ready.

In [12], the requirement has been formalized as $D_1 \mathrel{\widehat=} \ell \geq 60 \Rightarrow \int Leak \leq 0.05 * \ell$ and the design decision is

$$D_2 \mathrel{\widehat=} (\Box(\lceil Leak \rceil \Rightarrow \ell \leq 1)) \wedge (\Box(\lceil Leak \rceil; \lceil N \rceil; \lceil Leak \rceil \Rightarrow \ell \geq 30))$$

It has been proved that $D_2 \Rightarrow D_1$ (see [12]). We wish to derive a plant automaton that has duration formulas built from physical states of the system and has behaviors satisfying the requirement. An abstract description of the system is

$\lceil N \vee Leak \rceil$, which is $(\lceil N \rceil \vee \lceil \ \rceil); (\lceil Leak \rceil; \lceil N \rceil)^*; (\lceil Leak \rceil \vee \lceil \ \rceil)$ by Theorem 4. Those behaviors of the system that satisfy D_2 are represented by $(\lceil N \rceil \vee \lceil \ \rceil); ((\lceil Leak \rceil \wedge \ell \leq 1); (\lceil N \rceil \wedge \ell \geq 30))^*; ((\lceil Leak \rceil \wedge \ell \leq 1) \vee (\lceil Leak \rceil \wedge \ell \leq 1); \lceil N \rceil \vee \lceil \ \rceil)$. A real-time automaton derived from this formula is depicted in Fig. 3. Since $\lceil N \rceil \wedge \ell \geq 30$ is not a state of the plant automaton, we need to refine the formula. By the description of the system and by Theorem 4,

$$\lceil N \rceil \wedge \ell \geq 30 \Leftrightarrow \lceil OnReq \vee OffReq \vee Burn \vee Idle \vee Rec \rceil \wedge \ell \geq 30$$
$$\Leftrightarrow (\lceil Idle \rceil \vee \lceil OnReq \rceil \vee \lceil OffReq \rceil \vee \lceil Rec \rceil \vee \lceil Burn \rceil)^+ \wedge \ell \geq 30.$$

From the description of events and noticing that for $s \neq s'$, $true; \lceil s \rceil; \lceil s' \rceil; true$ iff (s, s') is an event, it follows:

$$\lceil N \rceil \wedge \ell \geq 30 \Leftrightarrow (\lceil Rec \rceil; (\lceil Idle \rceil; \lceil OnReq \rceil; \lceil Burn \rceil; \lceil OffReq \rceil)^*;$$
$$(\lceil Idle \rceil; \lceil OnReq \rceil; \lceil Burn \rceil \vee \lceil Idle \rceil; \lceil OnReq \rceil \vee \lceil Idle \rceil \vee \lceil \ \rceil))$$
$$\wedge \ell \geq 30.$$

Let

$$D_3 \mathrel{\hat{=}} \lceil Rec \rceil \wedge \ell = 30; (\lceil Idle \rceil; \lceil OnReq \rceil; \lceil Burn \rceil; \lceil OffReq \rceil)^*;$$
$$(\lceil Idle \rceil; \lceil OnReq \rceil; \lceil Burn \rceil \vee \lceil Idle \rceil; \lceil OnReq \rceil \vee \lceil Idle \rceil \vee \lceil \ \rceil).$$

We have $D_3 \Rightarrow \lceil N \rceil \wedge \ell \geq 30$. D_3 is a simple DC^* formula. An automaton having the behavior represented by this formula has the state diagram illustrated as Fig. 5. Therefore, we get an automaton with the state diagram in Fig. 6.

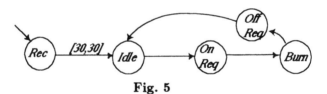

Fig. 5

3 Deriving Decision Maker from Plant Automata

In this section, we present a method to derive a decision maker from the plant automata w.r.t. the requirements. In our approach, a hybrid system is modeled as a parallel composition of 2 real-time communicating automata, decision maker and DES plant automaton. The DES plant automaton describes the possible behavior of the plant under effects of physical laws, and decision maker is to make the plant behave as we desire. In our context, a decision maker is a real-time communicating automaton $A = (S, I, O, E, d, s_0, \phi)$, in which there are no internal transitions and $\forall s \in S \bullet \phi(s) \neq \epsilon$. O is the alphabet of control law names; A DES plant automaton is a real-time communicating automaton $A' = (S', O, I, E', d', s'_0, \phi')$. A hybrid system is in fact the parallel composition of its decision maker and plant automaton, $A \times A'$. Therefore, the development of hybrid systems can be specified as follows. *Given a DES plant automaton A' that represents the physical descriptions and control laws of the system and a set of behaviors B of A', where B is the set of the desired behaviors containing only infinite behaviors, find a decision maker A such that the projection of the set of infinite behaviors of $A \times A'$ on A' is a nonempty subset of B, and such that every behavior of $A \times A'$ can be extended to an infinite behavior.* Such a real-time communicating automaton A is called a decision maker of A' w.r.t. B.

From Proposition 3 we can derive directly a functional specification of a decision maker from a DES plant automaton and requirement. That is, every behavior of the decision maker corresponds only to the signal of a behavior of the DES plant that satisfies the requirement which in turn corresponds to its output. However, the decision maker needs to satisfy some additional conditions, such as deadlock-freedom, etc.. This is formulated in the following theorem.

Theorem 8. *A real-time communicating automaton A with no internal transitions is a solution of the problem of designing a decision maker if and only if for all $\sigma \in Behaviors(A)$, the following holds: for any behavior $\sigma' \in Behaviors(A')$ such that σ corresponds to $signal(\sigma')$ and σ' corresponds to $out(\sigma)$, σ' can be extended to a behavior σ'' in B such that σ can be extended to a behavior σ_1 corresponding to $signal(\sigma'')$ and σ'' is a behavior corresponding to $out(\sigma_1)$.* $\square$

Next, we consider a necessary condition on A' and B for the existence of an automaton A satisfying the conditions of the theorem, which says that the $signal(\sigma)$ of behavior σ of A' needs to carry enough information for designing decision makers.

Theorem 9. *A necessary condition for a DES plant automaton A' and a set B of the infinite behaviors of A' to have a decision maker is that there exists a nonempty subset B' of B such that for all $\sigma, \sigma' \in Behaviors(A')$, if $(in(\sigma), signal(\sigma)) = (in(\sigma'), signal(\sigma'))$ (component-wise) then σ can be extended to a behavior in B' iff σ' can.* $\square$

When we have a subset of the behaviors of the plant automaton satisfying the requirement which is represented by a finite subgraph of the plant automaton, the condition in Theorem 9 becomes a sufficient condition as well, and there is an algorithm for deriving a decision maker.

Theorem 10. *Let A' be a plant automaton, and B be a set of its infinite behaviors. Assume that there is a sub-automaton A'' of A' (its graph representation is a subgraph in the graph representation of A') such that*

1. *A'' has a finite set of states,*
2. *All infinite behaviors of A'' are in B, and*
3. *For all $\sigma, \sigma' \in Behaviors(A')$, if $(in(\sigma), signal(\sigma)) = (in(\sigma'), signal(\sigma'))$ then σ can be extended to an infinite behavior in $Behaviors(A'')$ iff σ' can.*

Then, there is a decision maker A of A'' w.r.t. B. $\square$

From Theorem 10, we can extract an algorithm to construct a decision maker from a plant automaton that satisfies the assumptions of the theorem.

Algorithm.

1. Let $\varphi : E \to O' \times I' \times d(E)$ be a letter substitution homomorphism defined as follows. For $e = (s, a, s') \in E$, where E is the transition set of A'',

$$\varphi(e) \;\hat{=}\; \begin{cases} (\phi'(s), a, d(e)) & \text{if } \phi'(s) \neq \epsilon \\ \epsilon & \text{otherwise} \end{cases}$$

2. Let R be a regular expression over a finite set of the transitions E of A'' which represents the set of all the traces of the behavior of A'' (prefix-closed set). Constructing a deterministic automaton A_1 in a standard way, such that its behaviors are presented by the regular expression $\varphi(R)$. Let G be a graph representation of A_1.

3. Modifying G such that for any vertex s of G, the incoming edges are labeled by triples having the same middle component. For any vertex s of G, let $difference(s)$ be the number of incoming edges labeled by triples having different middle components. If $difference(s) \neq 0$, let $E_s(a)$ be the set of the incoming edges of s labeled by triples having a as the middle component. For $a \neq b$ such that $E_s(a) \neq \emptyset$ and $E_s(b) \neq \emptyset$, add a new vertex s' and change the edges in $E_s(b)$ to point to s'. For an incoming edge f of s that is neither in $E_s(b)$ nor $E_s(a)$, add a new edge f' pointing to s' with the same label and the same beginning vertex as f. For an outgoing edge f of s, add a new edge f' leaving s' with the same label and the same ending vertex as f.

4. Deriving the decision maker A from the modified G:
   (a) Each state of A is a vertex s of G, with output a, where a is the middle component of any incoming edge of s.
   (b) Each transition of A from s to s' is an edge of G from s to s' labeled by a triple $(m, a, d(e))$, which has delay time $d(e)$ and input m.

Gas Burner Example (Continued). The behavior of a gas burner can be represented by the real-time communicating automaton A'' in Fig. 6, with the states *Rec, Idle, OnReq, Burn, OffReq, Leak* and with inputs $C1$, $C2$, *ig*, *off*, with the following meaning. (1) $C1$: Close the gas valve for recovering from *Leak*; (2) $C2$: Give the green light (to show ready state); (3) *off*: Turn off the system (Close the gas valve); (4) *ig*: Ignite the burner. The output function is defined as follows.

$$\phi(s) = \begin{cases} s, & s \in \{Rec, OnReq, OffReq, Leak\} \\ \epsilon & otherwise \end{cases}$$

Here, we have reduced the diagram so that all its infinite behaviors are desired behaviors, and every behavior can be extended to an infinite behavior. The traces of the system are represented by the prefix-closure of the language generated by the regular expression $R = (e1(e2e3e4e5)^*e2(e7 + e3e6)e8)^*$.

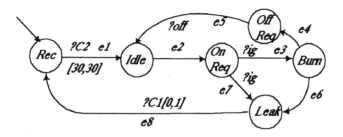

Fig. 6. Gas Burner Example: Plant Automaton

By induction on the length of the behaviors, it can be shown that A'' satisfies the condition in Theorem 10. The homomorphism φ is defined by:

$$\varphi(e1) \mathrel{\hat{=}} f1 \mathrel{\hat{=}} (Rec, C2, [30, 30]) \quad \varphi(e5) \mathrel{\hat{=}} f5 \mathrel{\hat{=}} (OffReq, off, \epsilon)$$
$$\varphi(e3) \mathrel{\hat{=}} f3 \mathrel{\hat{=}} (OnReq, ig, \epsilon) \quad \varphi(e7) \mathrel{\hat{=}} f7 \mathrel{\hat{=}} (OnReq, ig, \epsilon)$$
$$\varphi(e8) \mathrel{\hat{=}} f8 \mathrel{\hat{=}} (Leak, C1, [0, 1]) \quad \varphi(e2) \mathrel{\hat{=}} \varphi(e4) \mathrel{\hat{=}} \varphi(e6) \mathrel{\hat{=}} \epsilon$$

Hence, since $f_3 = f_7$, $\varphi(R) = (f_1(f_3 f_5)^*(f_7 + f_3)f_8)^* = (f_1(f_7 f_5)^* f_7 f_8)^*$. From this expression, we can construct an automaton as shown in Fig. 7a to recognize the prefix-closure of $\varphi(R)$. Here, the label of each incoming edge of a state has the same middle component. Thus, we do not need to modify the graph. The real-time communicating automaton representing the decision maker constructed according to the algorithm is shown in Fig. 7b.

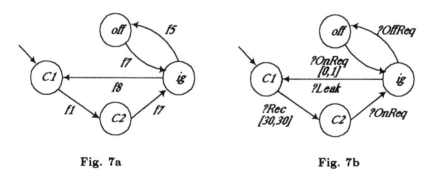

Fig. 7a   **Fig. 7b**

4   Conclusion

We have given a template of the refinement of hybrid system specifications written in DC into automata models: By using real-time communicating automata and their parallel composition, we formalize the conceptual model for hybrid control systems; DC formulas are extended with iteration form and a technique is presented for deriving plant automata from DC formulas; An algorithm is presented to synthesize a specification of control automata from plant automata with respect to requirements.

ProCoS presents the significant results on how to develop an embedded system from a *DC* specification [6, 10, 11]. Requirements captured in Duration Calculus can be systematically refined into CSP like implementations. Here, we confine ourselves to a more restricted class of hybrid systems and pursue more automatic techniques. We share the dual language framework with Hybrid Temporal Logic and Phase Transition System [7], but we pay emphasis on design rather than verification. The backbone of our approach presented in this paper is to accommodate design calculation to a set of pragmatic techniques for the development of hybrid systems.

Acknowledgment: The authors thank Prof. Zhou Chaochen, Chris George and Dr. Xu Qiwen for their comments and criticism.

References

1. R.Alur, T. Henzinger and E. Sontag (Eds.), Hybrid Systems, Lecture Notes in Computer Science 1066, Springer Verlag, 1996.
2. R. Alur and D. L. Dill, A Theory of Timed Automata, *Theoretical Computer Science*, 126, 183-235, 1994.
3. P. J. Antsaklis, J. A. Stiver, M. Lemmon, Hybrid System Modeling and Autonomous Control Systems, LNCS 736, Springer Verlag, 366-392, 1993.
4. Chen Zongji, Wang Ji, Yu Xinyao and Zhou Chaochen, An Abstraction of Hybrid Control Systems, *IEEE Intelligent Control and Instrumentation*, Singapore, 1995.
5. R.L. Grossman, A. Nerode, A.P. Ravn and H. Rischel (Eds.), Hybrid Systems, Lecture Notes in Computer Science 736, Springer Verlag, 1993.
6. J. He, C. A. R. Hoare, M. Franzle, M. Muller- Olm, E.- R. Olderog, M. Schenke, M. R. Hansen, A. P. Ravn, and H. Rischel, Provably Correct Systems. In Formal Techniques in Real-Time and Fault-Tolerant Systems, LNCS 863, pages 288-335, Springer Verlag, 1994.
7. T. A. Henzinger, Z. Manna, A. Pnueli, Towards Refining Temporal Specifications into Hybrid Systems, LNCS 736, Springer Verlag, 60-76, 1993.
8. J.E. Hopcroft, J.D. Ullman, *Introduction to Automata Theory, Languages and Computation*, Reading, MA, Addison-Wesley, 1979.
9. X. Nicollin, A. Olivero, J. Sifakis, S. Yovine, An Approach to the Description and Analysis of Hybrid Systems, LNCS 736, Springer Verlag, 149-178, 1993.
10. A. Ravn, Design of Embedded Real-Time Computing Systems. Department of Computer Science, Technical University of Denmark, 1994.
11. A. Ravn, H. Rischel and K.M. Hansen, Specifying and Verifying Requirements of Real-time Systems, IEEE Trans. on Software Engineering, 1993.
12. Zhou Chaochen, C. A. R. Hoare, A. P. Ravn, A Calculus of Durations, *Information Processing Letters*, 40, 269-276, 1991.
13. Zhou Chaochen, A. P. Ravn, M. R. Hansen, Extended Duration Calculus for Hybrid Real-time Systems, LNCS 736, Springer Verlag, 36-59, 1993.

Constraint Retraction in FD

Philippe Codognet[1] Daniel Diaz[1] Francesca Rossi[2]

[1] INRIA - Rocquencourt, B.P. 105, 78153 Le Chesnay Cedex, France.
E-mail: {Philippe.Codognet,Daniel.Diaz}@inria.fr
[2] Università di Pisa, Dipartimento di Informatica, Corso Italia 40, 56100 Pisa, Italy.
E-mail: rossi@di.unipi.it

Abstract. The possibility of deleting a piece of information is very convenient in many programming frameworks. However, this feature is not available in constraint languages such as Constraint Logic Programming or Concurrent Constraint Programming, which allow only for a monotonic accumulation of constraints. This is mainly due to its high complexity and also to its non-monotonic nature, which would make such a system much more complex to reason with. In this paper we consider the CLP framework over FD (finite domain) constraints, and we propose an incremental algorithm which deletes a constraint from a set of FD constraints, while maintaining partial arc-consistency. The algorithm follows the chain of dependencies among variables which are set by the nature of the FD constraints, and by doing so it updates only the part of the constraint set which is affected by the deletion. This makes constraint deletion in FD a feasible task that can be efficiently implemented.

1 Introduction

Constraint Logic Programming (CLP) [9, 15] and Concurrent Constraint Programming (CC) [13] are both based on the notion of monotonic refinement of domains of variables. In fact, the computation consists of a monotonic accumulation of constraints. However, it is clear that the possibility of removing constraints could be very useful in many applications, especially those requiring some level of interaction between the system and the user. Nevertheless, extending constraint solvers to non-monotonic behaviors selectively raises a number of difficulties, much similar in nature to those appearing in non-monotonic reasoning. Observe however that we have in CLP a distinction between the logical predicates (or the agents in the CC framework) and the constraints and that we will only consider non-monotonicity in the constraint part, making things somewhat easier.

The main point of this paper is the problem of the incrementality of the operations to be done on constraint deletion, because one cannot be satisfied with an algorithm that recomputes the whole status of the computation from scratch or from the point where the constraint that one wants to delete was introduced (as a traditional CLP system would do, relying on chronological backtracking). Instead, the hope is to get an incremental algorithm which is able to keep as much as possible of the computation already done, redoing only the subcomputations directly depending on the deleted constraint.

In domains where the solver has a global view over the store, i.e. all constraints are always present and accessible, it is possible to delete a constraint and all its effects on variables domains in a single step close to a normal constraint solving step. Instances of global solvers traditionally used in CLP are simplex methods for linear arithmetic constraints over reals or rationals, and boolean solvers based on Binary Decision Diagrams. Incremental deletion of linear arithmetic constraint has recently been studied in [8]. However in domains where the constraint solver has only a local view over the store, i.e. constraints are only accessible through variables on which they depend, constraint deletion is more complex. Propagation techniques like AC [10], AC-4 [11] and AC-5 [17] for finite domains, or unification over first-order terms are instances of such local solvers. Up to now, the deletion of unification constraints in Prolog-like systems has been tackled by so-called selective reset in extended intelligent backtracking methods [3, 7]. However, even if such methods can be extended to finite domain constraints [5, 14], they rely on complex dependency-recording mechanisms that amount to runtime overhead, even if no deletion is later used. Instead, we would like to take advantage of the dependency information already present in the constraint network (and use only this information) for avoiding such forward overhead and rather (re)compute constraint dependencies explicitly in an efficient way whenever a constraint deletion occurs.

This paper presents an algorithm for the incremental deletion of constraints over finite domains in the FD constraint system [16]. More precisely, we extend and adapt traditional propagation techniques to selectively delete, from the current constraint set, a constraint and all its consequences on affected variables, while maintaining the rest of the problem untouched.

The algorithm presented here is close in spirit to the one described in [12]. However, due to the different constraint system considered (in [12] they delete constraints from a set of constraints explicitly represented as sets of allowed tuples, as in classical constraint solving [10]) and to the fact the FD constraints are always kept in a partially arc-consistent state, we have to address different problems in order to obtain an algorithm which achieves the desired deletion.

2   The FD Constraint System

The FD constraint system has been extensively used in many CLP and CC programming systems (like cc(FD) [16], clp(FD) [6, 4], or AKL(FD) [2]), the main reason being that it provides the user with the full range of arithmetic and symbolic constraints while being very simple and efficient to handle at the implementation level. For instance, the clp(FD) system, a constraint logic programming language based on FD constraints, shows that flexibility and efficiency can indeed be combined, as it is on average several times faster than the CHIP system [1].

A *domain* in FD is a (non empty) finite set of natural numbers (i.e. a *range*). More precisely a range is a subset of $\{0, 1, ..., infinity\}$ where $infinity$ is a particular integer denoting the greatest value that a variable can take. We use the interval notation $k_1..k_2$ as a shorthand for the set $\{k_1, k_1 + 1, ..., k_2\}$. From a range r we define $min(r)$ (resp., $max(r)$) as the lower (resp., upper) bound of r. In addition to standard operations on sets (e.g. union, intersection, complementation) we define *pointwise operations* $(+, -, *, /)$ between a range r and an integer i as the set obtained by applying the corresponding operation on each element of d. Finally, $\mathcal{V}_d$ is the set of FD variables, i.e. variables constrained to take a value in a given domain.

Constraints in FD are all of the form X in r. Intuitively, a constraint X in r enforces X to belong to the range denoted by r that can be not only a *constant range* (e.g. 1..10) but also an *indexical range* using $\mathrm{dom}(Y)$ that represents the whole current domain of Y, or $\min(Y)$ that represents the minimal value of the current domain of Y, or $\max(Y)$ that represents the maximal value of the current domain of Y. When an X in r constraint uses an indexical on another variable Y it becomes *store-sensitive* and must be checked each time the domain of Y is updated. A *store* is a finite set of constraints. See [4] for the complete syntax of FD constraints.

Complex constraints such as linear equations and inequations can be defined in terms of the FD constraints. For instance the constraint $X = Y + C$, where C is a constant, is translated (via a clausal notation) into two FD constraints as follows :

```
X=Y+C :- X in min(Y)+C..max(Y)+C,
         Y in min(X)-C..max(X)-C.
```

Observe that this translation has also an operational flavour. In fact, it specifies the type of propagation chosen to solve the constraint: in the above example partial lookahead is used, but full lookahead could have been specified as well by using the $\mathrm{dom}(Y)$ indexical term (see algorithm *Add* in the next section). The X in r constraint can thus be seen as embedding the *core* propagation mechanism for constraint solving over FD.

Let c be a constraint of the form X in r. X is called the *constrained variable* of c, denoted by $cv(c)$. We write $V(c)$ for the set of variables on which c depends (i.e. appearing in the indexical range r). Consider a store (set of constraints) S containing c, we note $C(X)$ the set of all constraints depending on X (i.e. $C(X) = \{c' \in S/X \in V(c')\}$). A constraint c is said *static* if $V(c) = \emptyset$. A store S on a set of variables Var is *well-formed* if $\forall X, Y \in Var, ((\exists c \in C(X)$ s. t. $Y = cv(c)) \Rightarrow (\exists c' \in C(Y)$ s. t. $X = cv(c')))$. We will consider a graph-like description of the store, where variables are nodes and FD constraints are hyperarcs, say c, whose sources are the variable involved in the range (that is, $V(c)$) and whose target is the constrained variable $cv(c)$.

Given a set of FD constraint C, a constraint c *entailed* by C is just a piece of information which is already contained in C. More formally, consider a set of FD constraints C, involving the set of variables V. Let us call $Sol(C)$ the set of all instantiations of variables in V to elements of their domains such that all constraints in C are satisfied. Then, two sets of FD constraints C and C' are said *equivalent* if $Sol(C) = Sol(C')$. Consider now a set of FD constraints C over V and a constraint c over $V' \subseteq V$. Then we say that C entails c, written $C \vdash c$, if $Sol(C)$ projected over V' is a subset of $Sol(c)$.

As said above, FD constraints are always kept in a stable state, which can be called *partially arc-consistent* for its resemblance to arc-consistency [10]. More precisely, given a set of FD constraints C, we say that C is partially arc-consistent if, for each constraint X in r in C, the domain of X is smaller than or equal to the value of r. For example, the set of FD constraints {X in 2..10, X in dom(Y)+1, Y in 9..10} is not partially arc-consistent, since the domain of X contains all values between 2 and 10, whereas the range of the second constraint evaluates to $\{10, 11\}$. Instead, the set of FD constraints {X in {10}, X in dom(Y)+1, Y in 9..10} is partially arc-consistent. Observe that we talk about *partial* arc-consistency firstly because of the use of directional constraints (such as X in dom(Y)+1 in the previous example, which has no Y in dom(X)-1 counterpart for ensuring full arc-consistency) and, secondly, because of the possible use of the *min* and *max* indexicals. Also, arc-consistency assumes binary constraints while we may have constraints with arity greater than 2.

Observe that both classical arc-consistency [10] and partial arc-consistency for FD constraints do not ensure global consistency (i.e., satisfiability). This makes it possible to have polynomial algorithms, whereas checking satisfiability is NP-complete.

3   Constraint Addition

Whenever a new constraint is added to the current set, the corresponding FD constraints are added to the current set of FD constraints. This makes some variable domain to be restricted (the domain of the constrained variable), and such a restriction propagates to other variable domains through the FD constraints, until stability (that is, partial arc-consistency). Formally, for any variable X, let us call D_X the current value of the domain of X. Then the algorithm which achieves stability over a set C of FD constraints, called $Add(C)$ in the following, can be described as follows.

1. **forall** $c \in C$ **do** push(c)
2. **while stack not empty do**
3. c := pop
4.   let $c = X$ in r
5.   compute r in the current store
6. D_X-old := D_X
7. D_X := $D_X \cap r$
8.   if D_X-old $\neq D_X$
9.   **then forall** $c' \in C(X)$ **do** push(c')

In words, this algorithm considers each constraint, say X in r, to see whether it can be used to reduce the domain of X. If so, then such a domain is reduced (line 7) and all constraints depending on X are put into the stack to be considered (line 9). For example, assume we have the following constraints: $c_1 = $ X in dom(Y)-1, $c_2 = $ X in 1..10, $c_3 = $ Y in dom(Z)-1, $c_4 = $ Y in 1..10 and $c_5 = $ Z in 10..20. Then, by considering c_3, the domain of Y is restricted to contain only 9 and 10, thus: Y in 9..10. Then, by considering c_1 (and the newly induced domain of Y), we get X in 8..9. Thus the stable situation is the one in which c_2 is replaced by X in 8..9 and c_4 by Y in 9..10. Note that c_5 remains the same, although it is clear that there could be no solution if Z is different from 10 or 11, because there is no indexical constraint which constraints Z.

Theorem 1 (termination). *Given a set of FD constraints C, algorithm $Add(C)$ terminates in a finite number of steps.*

Proof. The statement of the theorem follows from the fact that all domains are finite and can only decrease in size, and that thus the condition in line 8 can be satisfied only a finite number of times.□

Theorem 2 (equivalence). *Given a set of FD constraints C, consider the store $C' = Add(C)$. Take now any constraint c. Then, $C \vdash c$ if and only if $C' \vdash c$.*

Proof. The only changes performed by algorithm Add to the given store C are effect of the execution of line 7, which possibly reduces the domain of a variable, say X, to the elements which are in the current range of a constraint c constraining X. Thus, the elements which are removed from D_X are values that, if given to X, would violate some of the constraints (at least c). This means that the set of variable instantiations which satisfy all the constraints in C remains the same after the application of the algorithm. Since a constraint entailed by a store S is just a subset of the instantiations allowed by all the constraints in S, also such subsets will be the same.□

Theorem 3 (order independence). *Given a set of FD constraints C, consider the application of algorithm Add to C via a certain strategy S_1 to push constraints into the stack, resulting in a store C_1. Consider also the application of the same algorithm to C via a different strategy S_2, resulting in a store C_2. Then we have that $C_1 = C_2$.*

Proof. It is easy to see that the operation of domain reduction is a closure operator. That is, it is idempotent (that is, by performing the same reduction on the same domain twice nothing changes), extensive (that is, by reducing a domain we always get a smaller domain), and monotone (that is, if we start from a smaller domain, then we get a smaller result). Classical results on closure operators state that they are characterized by their fixed points and not by the way such points are reached. Thus the statements of the theorem.□

Theorem 4 (partial arc-consistency). *Given a set of FD constraints C and the set $C' = Add(C)$, C' is partially arc-consistent.*

Proof. This follows immediately from the fact that line 7 of the algorithm continues to restrict the domain of a variable constrained by a constraint c to the values that are in the range of c until no more restrictions can be done. Thus, when the algorithm terminates, for any constraint c, we have that its range cannot be smaller than the domain of the variable constrained by c.□

The algorithm above is not incremental, that is, it achieves stability over a set of constraints without considering which constraint has been added more recently and whether the set of constraints was in a stable state before its addition. An incremental version which assumes to start from a stable set of FD constraints C and a new constraint to be added, say $c = $ X in r, can be obtained by the algorithm above by replacing line 1 with the following: push(c). The new algorithm is thus a function with two arguments, and thus will be referred to in the following by $Add(C, c)$. In this way the domain reduction is initiated by constraint c and is propagated through the graph via adjacent constraints, and constraints which have nothing to do with X are never considered. For this incremental algorithm, all properties proved above still hold, except for the one proved by Theorem 4, which now holds only if we start from a partially arc-consistent store. In more general terms, one could consider the addition of more than one constraint at a time. In this case the algorithm $Add(C, S)$, where C and S are sets of constraints, starts by pushing all the constraints in S in the queue, that is, line 1 of $Add(C)$ becomes: forall $c \in S$ do push(c).

Time Complexity. Assume that m is the number of constraints in C, d the maximal cardinality of a variable domain, a the maximal number of variables a constraint might depend on (that is, its arity minus one), and k the maximal cardinality of $C(X)$ for any X. The **while** loop can be executed as many times as constraints can be pushed in the stack. A constraint c will be pushed only if the domain of one of the variables it depends on (i.e. X such that $c \in C(X)$) has been modified. This can happen only d times at most for each variable. As a constraint can only depend on a variables at most, it can be pushed into the stack only $a \times d$ times. Therefore the **while** loop can be executed at most $m \times a \times d$ times. Within each execution of the loop, the only operations that can require more than a constant time are the computation of the range and the pushing of new constraints in the stack. At most k constraints can be pushed. The complexity of the range computation depends on the syntax of the range: if only **min** and **max** indexicals are used, then the operation is constant, if instead one **dom** indexical range is used, then it may require d steps[3]. Considering a and k as constants, the complexity of algorithm $Add(C)$ is therefore either $O(md)$ if only min/max indexicals are used or $O(md^2)$ in the general case. As predictable, the worst-case complexity of our algorithm is the same as that of algorithm AC-5 [17] on comparable constraints. For the more general $Add(C, S)$ algorithm, the complexity is the same, considering m as $|C| + |S|$. Although in the average case the work to be done by this incremental algorithm will be less (because C is already stable), in the worst case the addition of a single constraint can trigger recomputations in the whole graph.

---

[3] If one considers an extended syntax where two **dom** indexical ranges are allowed within a range, then the range computation becomes quadratic in d. It can be shown that using more than two **dom** indexicals does not bring extra expressive power.

4 Constraint Deletion

Consider a constraint c of the form X in r to be removed in a store S. If $V(c) \neq \emptyset$ (that is, some variables are involved in its range), c may have been activated several times during the computation, e.g. each time the domain of any variable in $V(c)$ is updated (via algorithm *Add* of the previous section), leading to several reduction of D_X, the domain of X. Also, each reduction of D_X may have (re)activated all the constraints in $C(X)$, leading to further domain reductions for other variables. All these reductions – consequences of c –, and only these ones, have to be undone when c is deleted.

To achieve this goal, first we recompute the domain of X in the store which is the current one minus c. This could lead to a larger domain for X, if the restriction imposed by c over X is not imposed by any other constraint. Then we propagate this new domain for X through all constraints in $C(X)$. This leads to recompute new domains for all variables Y such that $Y = cv(c')$ for some $c' \in C(X)$. Thus now we have to deal with this variables as we do with X, that is, we enlarge their domain and we propagate such enlargement through $C(Y)$. This phase ends when a stable state (w.r.t. domain enlargement) is reached. The previous steps could have enlarged the domains too much if we desire a partially arc-consistent state. Thus a subsequent phase where domains are reduced due to the restrictions imposed by the currently present constraints is needed. This computation again ends when a stable state (w.r.t. domain modification) is reached. Note that this second phase can be implemented via algorithm *Add*. Since the domain enlargement phase is performed through the constraint network as long as domains should be enlarged, while it stops when reaching variables whose domain is not affected by the deletion, we thus achieve our objective of minimal recomputation of the store, as parts of the network independent of the deletion are not reconsidered.

Our algorithm, called $Del(C, c)$, deletes a constraint c of the form X in r from a set of FD constraints C. The algorithm works on the set of constraints $C - \{c\}$, and C is assumed to be partially arc-consistent. Two stacks S and S' are used: S to push constraints in the enlarging phase, and S' to push constraints pointing to an enlarged variable and will be used in the later restricting phase. Enlarged variables are recognized via a marking.

```
1.  D_new := D_X^s - (r - D_X)
2.  if D_X ≠ D_new
3.      then D_X := D_new
4.          forall c' ∈ C(X) do push(c') in S
5.          while S not empty do
6.              c := pop from S
7.              let c = Y in r
8.              compute r in the current store
9.              D_Y-old := D_Y
10.             D_Y := r ∩ D_Y^s
11.             if D_Y-old ≠ D_Y
```

```
12.                    then mark Y
13.                        forall c′ ∈ C(Y) do push(c′) in S
14.                    forall c′ ∉ C(Y) s.t. cv(c′) is marked do push(c′) in S′
15.              Add′(C − {c}, S′)
```

Line 1 of the algorithm computes the domain of X in the store $C − \{c\}$. This is done by taking the initial value of such domain (D_X^s) and eliminating from it those elements that are not in D_X because of constraints other than c. In fact, consider a partially arc-consistent set of FD constraints and a constraint X in r in such a set. If $D_X \neq r$, then it has to be properly smaller by definition of partial arc-consistency. Let us then take the non-empty set $S = (r − D_X)$. The elements in S are elements which are not present in D_X but which would be allowed by constraint c. Thus their absence from D_X is caused by some other constraint $c′ \neq c$. One could just write $D_X := D_X^s$ and the algorithm would produce the same result, but less efficiently. In fact, in that case, the values in $(r - D_X)$ would for sure be deleted later by the algorithm, since some of the other constraints (and not the removed one) are responsible for their deletion from D_X. If the domain of X is not changed, then we have nothing to do, otherwise (line 2) we set the new domain of X (line 3) and start the enlarging phase. Line 4 pushes into the stack all those constraints which depend on X (that is, which have X in their range expression). Line 5 is the starting point of a while statement which will end only when the stack S is empty, that is, there are no more constraints to reconsider for the enlarging phase. Line 6 and 7 extract one constraint from the stack S and give a shape to the popped constraint. Say it is Y in r. Line 8 recomputes r in the current store. Due to the enlarged domain of X, r may now have a different value than before. Line 9 records the current domain of Y (D_Y) in the variable D_Y-old. Line 10 enlarges the domain of Y to the newly computed value of r, being careful however to not enlarge D_Y more than its initial value. If the domain of Y has been actually enlarged (line 11), we also have to propagate the effect of this enlargement to other variables. More precisely, we have to mark Y (line 12) to record that it has been enlarged and push into the stack S all those constraints which depend on Y (line 13). If instead the domain has not changed (line 14), then we have to add to the stack $S′$ all constraints $c′$ which depend on Y and constrain enlarged variables. Line 15 takes this stack $S′$ and use it to achieve partial arc-consistency and reach a stable state. In fact the enlarged domains might have been enlarged too much and this phase is indeed required if we desire a partially arc-consistent state. This is achieved via the application of algorithm $Add′$, which is identical to Add, except that it only pushes into the stack constraints pointing to marked variables. In fact the other variables in the graph have not been enlarged and this part of the graph is therefore still partially arc-consistent.

Theorem 5 (termination). *Given any set of FD constraints C, and any constraint $c \in C$, algorithm $Del(C, c)$ terminates after a finite number of steps.*

Proof. Since the initial domains of all the variables are finite, each variable can be enlarged only a finite number of times. Each enlarging of a variable domain pushes a finite number of constraints into the stack S. Thus, after a finite number of steps S will be empty, and therefore the **while** loop will be over. Also from Theorem 1 we know that line 15 takes a finite amount of time. Thus, $Del(C, c)$ terminates in finite time. □

Theorem 6 (equivalence). *Given a set of FD constraints C and a constraint $c \in C$, consider $C' = Del(C, c)$. Then $Sol(C - \{c\}) = Sol(C')$, where by $C - \{c\}$ we mean the set of FD constraints C where c has been deleted and all variables have been restored to their initial domain.*

Proof. We already know, by Theorem 2, that algorithm *Add* does not change the set of solutions. Therefore neither will line 15 of algorithm *Del*. The only other changes that are made during algorithm *Del* are in lines 1 and 10, when domains are enlarged. The domains are not restored to their initial value but set to the intersection of their initial (static) value and a range (see line 10). Values that are hence excluded are not allowed by that range and therefore cannot participate to any solution. Let us now consider the variables whose domain is not changed by *Del*. The first case is a variable that is considered in the **while** loop, but its domain is not enlarged by line 10. Then the same reasoning as above ensures that the excluded values cannot participate to any solution. The last case concerns a variable that is not even considered for enlarging. This implies that all the variables adjacent to it have not been enlarged. Therefore all current ranges of constraints pointing to such a variable are the same as those that have lead to the domain of that variable (since we assume that we start from a partially arc-consistent state). Hence all the values that are not present in this domain are not allowed by the current ranges and thus cannot participate to any solution. □

Theorem 7 (partial arc-consistency). *Given a set of FD constraints C and a constraint $c \in C$, consider $C' = Del(C, c)$. If C is partially arc-consistent, then C' is so.*

Proof. This follows from the fact that line 15 of algorithm *Del* is an application of *Add*, restricted to the part of the graph which has been changed (enlarged variables). As the rest of the graph has not been changed by lines 1 to 14, it is still partially arc-consistent, as assumed. □

Theorem 8 (order independence). *Given a set of FD constraints C and a constraint $c \in C$, consider the application of algorithm $Del(C, c)$ via a certain strategy S_1 to push constraints into S, resulting in a store C_1. Consider also the application of the same algorithm to C via a different strategy S_2, resulting in a store C_2. Then we have that $C_1 = C_2$.*

Proof. Stack S' is only used in line 14, which behaves like *Add*. Thus by Theorem 3 we know that the order in which constraints are pushed into or popped from such stack is not important. Consider now stack S. It is easy to see that the operation of domain enlargement is a closure operator. That is, it is idempotent (that is, by performing the same enlargement on the same domain twice nothing changes), extensive (that is, by enlarging a domain we always get a bigger domain), and monotone (that is, if we start from a bigger domain, we get a bigger result). Classical results on closure operators state that they are characterized by their fixed points and not by the way such points are reached. Thus the statements of the theorem holds.□

Since algorithm Del implements the deletion of a constraint c from a set of FD constraints C, and produces the new set of FD constraints C' (we recall that a domain is again an FD constraint), it would be nice if one could prove that the information given by c is not present in C' any longer. That is, that $C' \not\vdash c$. However, this is unfortunately not true. In fact, consider the store containing the constraints $X = Y + 1$, $Y = Z + 1$ and $X = Z + 2$ (actually, the store contains their FD counterparts), and assume we delete $X = Z + 2$ via algorithm Del. Then it is possible to see that the resulting store still entails the information that X is equal to Z plus 2. This behaviour however is not due to the fact that Del does not work well, but that the deleted constraint was indeed redundant, that is, it was entailed by the other constraints. Thus it is reasonable that its deletion does not change the set of constraints entailed by the store. Note that this behavior occurs also in other constraint deletion algorithms, like the one for classical constraint solving described in [12]. More precisely, the formal general statement of the behaviour of Del w.r.t. entailment is as follows: given a set of FD constraints C and two constraints $c, c' \in C$ (possibly $c = c'$), consider the set $C' = Del(C, c)$. Then $C' \vdash c'$ if and only if $(C - \{c\}) \vdash c'$. The proof of this statement follows from the definition of entailment and from Theorem 6.

Time Complexity. It is easy to see that lines 1 to 13 have the same structure as algorithm Add and therefore a similar complexity formula. However, let us call m' the number of constraints considered in this part of Del. It is easy to see that this number is bounded by the number of constraints in the subgraph EG involving the enlarged variables and their immediate neighbors. Thus the complexity of lines 1 to 14 is either $O(m'd)$ if only min/max indexicals are used or $O(m'd^2)$ in the general case. Note that line 14 only adds $O(k)$ to each execution of the **while** loop and thus does not change the complexity. The last line of algorithm Del is $Add'(C - \{c\}, S')$, that is, an application of algorithm Add to graph EG (observe that constraints in S' are in EG and that the definition in Add' forbid to go out from EG). Thus its complexity is again either $O(m'd)$ if only min/max indexicals are used or $O(m'd^2)$ in the general case. Therefore the complexity of the overall Del algorithm is $O(m'd)$ in the restricted case and $O(m'd^2)$ in the general case. Note however that, even if in the worst-case m' is equal to m, most of the time it will be much smaller. The complexity of a batch algorithm, which will rebuilt $C - \{c\}$ from scratch and apply partial arc-consistency (with the Add algorithm) is always $O(md)$ in the restricted case and $O(md^2)$ in the general case.

Example: Consider the following set of constraints :

{ X in 1..10, Y in 1..20, Z in 1..10, U in 1..10, V in 1..10,

$$X \geq Y \ , \ X=Z+1 \ , \ X \neq 5 \ , \ Y=Z+U \ , \ Y \geq V \ \}$$

This translates in terms of FD constraints as follows :

X in 1..10, Y in 1..20, Z in 1..10, U in 1..10, V in 1..10,

X in min(Y)..infinity,	(1)
Y in 0..max(X).	(1')
X in dom(Z)+1,	(2)
Z in dom(X)-1.	(2')
X in -{5}	(3)
Z in min(Y)-max(U)..max(Y)-min(U),	(4)
U in min(Y)-max(Z)..max(Y)-min(Z),	(4')
Y in min(Z)+min(U)..max(Z)+max(U).	(4")
Y in min(V)..infinity,	(5)
V in 0..max(Y).	(5')

Let us first apply the *Add* algorithm for achieving partial arc-consistency. This reduces the domain of X, Y, Z, U and V as follows :

{ X in 2..4:6..10, Y in 2..10, Z in 1..3:5..9, U in 1..9, V in 1..10 }

Assume now that constraint $X \neq 5$ is deleted. As the domain of X is enlarged to 2..10 (cf. beginning of algorithm *Del*), X is marked and all constraints depending on X (that is, 1' and 2') have to be reconsider and pushed to S. Let us consider that 1' is popped first and recomputed. It does not change the value of Y, therefore only constraint 1 (because it constrains X) is reconsidered among those depending on Y (that is, 1, 4' and 5'), and therefore pushed into S'. Let us now turn to 2'. This leads to the enlarging of Z, which is restored to 1..9; this variable is marked. Therefore all constraints depending on Z (that is, 2, 4' and 4") have to be reconsidered and pushed in S. Also 2 is pushed into S' because X is marked. Recomputing constraint 2 does not change the domain of X (but 2' is pushed in S' because Z is marked), neither does recomputing 4' for U (but 4 is pushed in S' because Z is marked) nor does recomputing 4" for Y (pushing nothing more in S', because 4 is already present). However reconsidering 4 does not change Z and no more constraints are pushed in S, that is then empty. Hence the first phase of $Del(X \neq 5)$ terminates. The second phase will recompute constraints in S' (i.e. 1, 2, 2' and 4), and restore consistency for marked variables, i.e. the domain of X will be reduced to 2..10 (by 2) and that of Z to 1..9 (by 2') Those changes will not be propagated to variables outside the marked subgraph because the rest of the graph is already stable. The second phase of $Del(X \neq 5)$ therefore terminates and the final constraint store is :

{ X in 2..10, Y in 2..10, Z in 1..9, U in 1..9, V in 1..10 }

It is worth noticing that it has not recomputed 5 nor 5', because Y and U have not been affected by the deletion of $X \neq 5$. If there have been a larger part of the constraint network linked to Y and U, it would have been kept untouched as well. This means that the recomputations involved by the constraint deletion are kept small, localized to the affected part of the network.

References

1. A. Aggoun and N. Beldiceanu. Overview of the CHIP Compiler System. In *Constraint Logic Programming: Selected Research*, A. Colmerauer and F. Benhamou (Eds.). MIT Press, 1993.

2. B. Carlson, M. Carlsson and S. Janson. Finite Domain Constraints in AKL(FD). In *Proceedings of ILPS 94*, MIT Press, 1994.

3. C. Codognet and P. Codognet. Non-deterministic Stream AND-Parallelism based on Intelligent Backtracking. In *Proceedings of 6th ICLP*, Lisbon, 1989. The MIT Press.

4. P. Codognet and D. Diaz. Compiling Constraints in clp(FD). *Journal of Logic Programming*, vol. 27(3), 1996.

5. P. Codognet, F. Fages and T. Sola. A meta-level compiler for CLP(FD) and its combination with intelligent backtracking. In *Constraint Logic Programming : Selected Research*, A. Colmerauer, F. Benhamou (Eds.), MIT Press, 1993.

6. D. Diaz and P. Codognet. A minimal extension of the WAM for CLP(FD). In *proceedings of the 10th International Conference on Logic Programming*, D. S. Warren (Ed.), Budapest, Hungary, MIT Press 1993.

7. W. S. Havens. Intelligent Backtracking in the Echidna Constraint Logic Programming System. Research Rep. CSS-IS TR 92-12, Simon Fraser University, Vancouver, Canada, 1992.

8. T. Huynh and K. Marriott. Incremental Constraint Deletion in Systems of Linear Constraints. Draft Report, IBM T. J. Watson Research Center, 1992.

9. J. Jaffar and J.L. Lassez. Constraint Logic Programming. In *Proceedings of POPL'87*, ACM Press, 1987.

10. A.K. Mackworth. Consistency in networks of relations. *Artificial Intelligence*, vol.8, n.1, 1977.

11. B. A. Nadel. Constraint Satisfaction Algorithms. *Computational Intelligence 5 (1989)*.

12. B. Neveu and P. Berlandier. Maintaining Arc Consistency through Constraint Retraction. *Proc. TAI94*, IEEE Press.

13. V.A. Saraswat. *Concurrent Constraint Programming*. MIT Press, 1993.

14. T. Sola. Deduction Maintenance in Constraint Logic Programs. Ph.D. thesis, University of Paris XI, December 1995.

15. P. Van Hentenryck. *Constraint Satisfaction in Logic Programming*. Logic Programming Series, The MIT Press, Cambridge, MA, 1989.

16. P. Van Hentenryck, V. Saraswat and Y. Deville. Constraint processing in cc(FD). In *Constraint Programming : Basics and Trends*, A. Podelski (Ed.), LNCS 910, Springer Verlag 1995. First version: Research Report, Brown University, Jan. 1992.

17. P. Van Hentenryck, Y. Deville and C-M. Teng. A generic arc-consistency algorithm and its specializations. *Artificial Intelligence 57 (1992)*, pp 291-321.

Winskel is (Almost) Right
Towards a Mechanized Semantics Textbook

Tobias Nipkow *

Abstract. We present a formalization of the first 100 pages of Winskel's *The Formal Semantics of Programming Languages* in the theorem prover Isabelle/HOL: 2 operational, 2 denotational, 1 axiomatic semantics, a verification condition generator, and the necessary soundness, completeness and equivalence proofs, all for a simple imperative language.

Are theorem provers capable of formalizing significant portions of mathematics or computer science? If we talk about leading edge research, the answer is at best "with difficulty". However, if we talk about foundations and textbooks, the answer must be a guarded "yes". The first and best known example is the translation of Landau's "Grundlagen" into Automath [12]. Our paper summarizes the formalization of the first 100 pages of a textbook on programming language semantics [13]. It deals with various semantics for a simple imperative language and proves their equivalence. The main purpose of the whole development is

- To lay the foundation for a unified treatment of the many facets of a programming language ranging from its denotational semantics to the soundness and completeness of a verification condition generator. This formalization allows performing proofs both about the language, e.g. compiler verification, and about programs in the language in the same system.
- To demonstrate not just the mere possibility of such an undertaking, but to show that the result is both readable and fairly close to the original text.

It is a tribute to Winskel's thoroughness that we only found one serious mistake in his proofs, which is the source of the "almost" in the title. The mistake occurs in the completeness proof for Hoare logic (Section 5.2) and is easily fixed.

The idea of embedding the semantics of a programming language in a theorem prover goes back at least to Gordon [3]. His paper has spawned many further language embeddings, ours included. However, we are not aware of any previous unified treatment of all the different semantic formalisms covered by our paper.

After a short introduction to HOL, the rest of the paper is structured like Winskel's book: operational, denotational and axiomatic semantics are presented together with their equivalence proofs. In addition we prove the soundness and completeness of a verification condition generator (Section 5.3) and treat the thorny issue of partial functions in a logic of total functions (Section 6).

The complete formalization (including proofs) is available on the web via `http://www4.informatik.tu-muenchen.de/~nipkow/isabelle/HOL/IMP/`.

---
* Institut für Informatik, TU München, 80290 München, Germany.
  `http://www4.informatik.tu-muenchen.de/~nipkow/`
  Research supported by DFG Schwerpunktprogramm *Deduktion*.

1   Isabelle/HOL

Isabelle/HOL is the instantiation of the generic interactive theorem prover Isabelle [8] with Church's formulation of Higher Order Logic and is very close to Gordon's HOL system [4]. In this paper HOL is short for Isabelle/HOL.

Below you find a short introduction to HOL's surface syntax (as rendered by Regensburger's LaTeX-converter):

Formulae The syntax is standard, except that there are two implications ($\longrightarrow$ and $\Longrightarrow$) and two equalities (= and $\equiv$) which stem from the object and meta-logic, respectively. The distinction can be ignored while reading this paper. The notation $[A_1; \ldots; A_n] \Longrightarrow A$ is short for the nested implication $A_1 \Longrightarrow \ldots \Longrightarrow A_n \Longrightarrow A$.

Types follow the syntax for ML-types, except that the function arrow is $\Rightarrow$.

Theories introduce constants with the keyword **consts**, non-recursive definitions with **defs**, and primitive recursive definitions with **primrec**. Further constructs are explained as we encounter them.

Although we do not present any of the proofs, we usually indicate their complexity. If we state that some proof is automatic, it means that it was either solved by rewriting or by the "classical reasoner", `fast_tac` in Isabelle parlance [9]. The latter provides a reasonable degree of automation for predicate calculus proofs. Note, however, that its success depends on the right selection of lemmas supplied as parameters.

2   IMP

IMP is a simple imperative programming language with WHILE-loops. The syntax for **commands** (aka statements) is

$$c ::= \text{SKIP} \mid X := a \mid c;c \mid \text{IF } b \text{ THEN } c \text{ ELSE } c \mid \text{WHILE } b \text{ DO } c$$

where X is a **location** (aka variable), a an **arithmetic expression** and b a **boolean expression**.

Datatypes in HOL resemble those in functional programming languages and allow a direct representation of the abstract syntax of commands:

datatype com = SKIP
```
      | ":="  loc aexp        (infixl 90)
      | ";"   com com         (infixl 90)
      | Cond  bexp com com    ("IF _ THEN _ ELSE _" 100)
      | While bexp com        ("WHILE _ DO _" 100)
```

The annotations define the concrete syntax.

Winskel also treats syntax and semantics of arithmetic and boolean expressions, which we followed in an earlier formalization of IMP [6]. Because expressions add nothing new, we have taken a semantic view, i.e. we have identified expressions with their semantics. The central semantic concept is that of a **state**, i.e. a mapping from locations to **values**. We formalize both locations loc and values val as unspecified types and define state, aexp and bexp as function spaces:

types state = loc $\Rightarrow$ val
        aexp = state $\Rightarrow$ val
        bexp = state $\Rightarrow$ bool

Alternatively, we could have made loc and val explicit parameters of all types, which would have cluttered up the types considerably.

Bypassing the syntax of expressions in favour of semantics means that concrete expressions look a bit unusual. For example, $X := X + 1$ becomes $X := (\lambda s.s(X) + 1)$. It is routine to modify the parser and pretty printer to translate between the two forms automatically [3]. We ignore these syntactic issues and focus on the semantic side of things.

3 Operational Semantics

There are two standard forms of operational semantics which are often called "natural" and "transition" semantics. Winskel concentrates on natural semantics but connects it to transition semantics in an exercise.

3.1 Natural Semantics

Natural semantics expresses the evaluation of commands as a relation between a command, an initial state and a final state. In HOL we declare a constant evalc as a set of such triples

consts evalc :: (com * state * state)set

and add some syntactic sugar for better readability:

translations $<c,s> \overset{c}{\rightarrow} t \equiv (c,s,t) \in$ evalc

This means we read and write $<c,s> \overset{c}{\rightarrow} t$ instead of $(c,s,t) \in$ evalc. The relation evalc is defined inductively by a set of inference rules, i.e. implications:

inductive evalc
    $<$SKIP,s$> \overset{c}{\rightarrow} s$

    $<x := a,s> \overset{c}{\rightarrow} s[a(s)/x]$

    $[\ <c1,s> \overset{c}{\rightarrow} s1;\ <c2,s1> \overset{c}{\rightarrow} s2\ ] \implies <c1;c2,\ s> \overset{c}{\rightarrow} s2$

    $[\quad b\ s;\ <c1,s> \overset{c}{\rightarrow} t\ ] \implies <$IF b THEN c1 ELSE c2, s$> \overset{c}{\rightarrow} t$
    $[\ \neg b\ s;\ <c2,s> \overset{c}{\rightarrow} t\ ] \implies <$IF b THEN c1 ELSE c2, s$> \overset{c}{\rightarrow} t$

    $\neg b\ s \implies <$WHILE b DO c, s$> \overset{c}{\rightarrow} s$
    $[\ b\ s;\ <c,s> \overset{c}{\rightarrow} s1;\ <$WHILE b DO c, s1$> \overset{c}{\rightarrow} s2\ ] \implies <$WHILE b DO c, s$> \overset{c}{\rightarrow} s2$

The assignment command is defined in terms of an auxiliary function on states:

consts assign :: state $\Rightarrow$ val $\Rightarrow$ loc $\Rightarrow$ state ("_[_/_]")
defs   s[m/x] $\equiv$ (λy. if y=x then m else s y)

The keyword **inductive** means that evalc is defined as the least relation closed under the given rules. HOL automatically derives a corresponding induction principle, called **rule induction** in [13], which will be our major weapon in the proofs to come.

3.2 Transition Semantics

An alternative semantics is the **transition semantics** which is a relation between **configurations**, i.e. pairs of commands and states. A configuration (c, s) represents a computation in state s which is about to execute c. Each transition is regarded as one step in the computation. This semantics is particularly appropriate for concurrent languages where different executions have to be interleaved.

Winskel outlines the transition semantics for IMP and leaves the details, in particular the equivalence proof of natural and transition semantics, as exercises. This section provides the details, uncovers a minor slip in one of Winskel's hints, and presents an alternative equivalence proof.

Winskel distinguishes two kinds of transitions: $(c, s) \rightarrow_1 (c', s')$ and $(c, s) \rightarrow_1 s'$, where the latter indicates the termination of the computation. To simplify matters we have abolished the second kind of transition and consider $(\mathsf{SKIP}, \mathsf{s})$ a terminal configuration. Hence we need only a single relation:

consts evalc1 :: ((com∗state) ∗ (com∗state))set

Syntactic sugar is introduced in the customary manner:

translations $\mathsf{cs} \xrightarrow{1} \mathsf{cs'} \equiv (\mathsf{cs},\mathsf{cs'}) \in \mathsf{evalc1}$

The inductive definition of evalc1 is straightforward:

inductive evalc1
$(\mathsf{x} := \mathsf{a},\mathsf{s}) \xrightarrow{1} (\mathsf{SKIP},\mathsf{s[a(s)/x]})$

$(\mathsf{SKIP};\mathsf{c},\mathsf{s}) \xrightarrow{1} (\mathsf{c},\mathsf{s})$
$(\mathsf{c0},\mathsf{s}) \xrightarrow{1} (\mathsf{c1},\mathsf{t}) \implies (\mathsf{c0};\mathsf{c2},\mathsf{s}) \xrightarrow{1} (\mathsf{c1};\mathsf{c2},\mathsf{t})$

$\mathsf{b\ s} \implies (\mathsf{IF\ b\ THEN\ c1\ ELSE\ c2},\mathsf{s}) \xrightarrow{1} (\mathsf{c1},\mathsf{s})$
$\neg\ \mathsf{b\ s} \implies (\mathsf{IF\ b\ THEN\ c1\ ELSE\ c2},\mathsf{s}) \xrightarrow{1} (\mathsf{c2},\mathsf{s})$

$\mathsf{b\ s} \implies (\mathsf{WHILE\ b\ DO\ c},\mathsf{s}) \xrightarrow{1} (\mathsf{c};\mathsf{WHILE\ b\ DO\ c},\mathsf{s})$
$\neg\ \mathsf{b\ s} \implies (\mathsf{WHILE\ b\ DO\ c},\mathsf{s}) \xrightarrow{1} (\mathsf{SKIP},\mathsf{s})$

The desired equivalence theorem is

$$(<\mathsf{c}, \mathsf{s}> \xrightarrow{c} \mathsf{t}) = ((\mathsf{c}, \mathsf{s}) \xrightarrow{*} (\mathsf{SKIP}, \mathsf{t})) \tag{1}$$

where $\xrightarrow{*}$ is the transitive and reflexive closure of $\xrightarrow{1}$. The proof also employs $\xrightarrow{n}$, the n-fold iteration of $\xrightarrow{1}$. Both arrows are syntactic sugar for the postfix operators ^{n} and * which are part of HOL's theory of relations:

translations $cs \xrightarrow{n} cs' \equiv (cs,cs') \in \text{evalc1}^n$

$\qquad\qquad cs \xrightarrow{*} cs' \equiv (cs,cs') \in \text{evalc1}^*$

The $\Longrightarrow$-direction of (1) is proved by rule induction on $<c,s> \xrightarrow{c} t$ and uses the following lemma

$[\ (c1,s1) \xrightarrow{n} (\text{SKIP},s2);\ (c2,s2) \xrightarrow{*} (\text{SKIP},s3)\ ] \Longrightarrow (c1;c2,s1) \xrightarrow{*} (\text{SKIP},s3)$

which is proved by induction on n.

The $\Longleftarrow$-direction of (1) is proved by induction on c and a nested induction on the length of $(c,s) \xrightarrow{*} (\text{SKIP},t)$ in the WHILE-case. The nested induction requires the following lemma:

$(c1;c2,s1) \xrightarrow{n} (\text{SKIP},s3) \Longrightarrow \exists s2\ m.\ (c1,s1) \xrightarrow{*} (\text{SKIP},s2) \wedge (c2,s2) \xrightarrow{m} (\text{SKIP},s3) \wedge m \leq n$

This lemma is stronger than the one suggested by Winskel, where $\xrightarrow{n}$ and $\xrightarrow{m}$ are replaced by $\xrightarrow{*}$ and $m \leq n$ disappears. The reason for the stronger lemma is the induction on the length in the WHILE-case: unless we have $m \leq n$, the induction hypothesis is not applicable.

There is an alternative proof of (1) which does not drag in natural numbers via $\xrightarrow{n}$ at all. For a start, we can prove the generalized lemma

$[\ (c1,s1) \xrightarrow{*} (\text{SKIP},s2);\ (c2,s2) \xrightarrow{*} cs3\ ] \Longrightarrow (c1;c2,s1) \xrightarrow{*} cs3$

directly by induction on the structure (as opposed to the length) of $(c1,s1) \xrightarrow{*}$ $(\text{SKIP},s2)$. As above, this yields the $\Longrightarrow$-direction of (1). Note that the generalization of $(\text{SKIP},s3)$ to $cs3$ is not really essential in this context but improves our understanding of what is going on. The proof of the opposite direction was suggested by Ranan Fraer (personal communication) and is based on similar proofs of his in the Coq system (see [1] for related material). The key lemma

$[\ (c,s) \xrightarrow{1} (c',s');\ <c',s'> \xrightarrow{c} t\ ] \Longrightarrow <c,s> \xrightarrow{c} t$

is proved by rule induction on $(c,s) \xrightarrow{1} (c',s')$. An induction on the structure of $(c,s) \xrightarrow{*} (c',s')$ now yields

$[\ (c, s) \xrightarrow{*} (c', s');\ <c',s'> \xrightarrow{c} t\ ] \Longrightarrow <c,s> \xrightarrow{c} t$

which directly implies the $\Longleftarrow$-direction of (1).

4 Denotational Semantics

Winskel starts with a low cost version of denotational semantics which is entirely based on sets. It is sometimes called "relational semantics" because the denotation of a command is a relation between initial and final states:

types $\text{com\_den} = (\text{state} * \text{state})\text{set}$

This approach suits us fine because it avoids partial functions, a sticky issue in HOL. In Section 6 we come back to this point. For the time being, we work with relations. The semantic function C is defined by primitive recursion on commands:

consts C :: com ⇒ com_den
primrec
  C(SKIP) = id
  C(x := a) = {(s,t). t = s[a(s)/x]}
  C(c1;c2) = C(c2) O C(c1)
  C(IF b THEN c1 ELSE c2) = {(s,t). (s,t) ∈ C(c1) ∧ b(s)} ∪
                                        {(s,t). (s,t) ∈ C(c2) ∧ ¬ b(s)}
  C(WHILE b DO c) = lfp(Γ b (C c))

where Γ is an auxiliary function:

consts Γ :: bexp ⇒ com_den ⇒ (com_den ⇒ com_den)
defs   Γ b cd ≡ (λR.{(s,t). (s,t) ∈ (R O cd) ∧ b(s)} ∪
                      {(s,t). s=t ∧ ¬ b(s)})

This definition relies heavily on HOL's theory of sets and relations: O and id are identity and composition of relations, and lfp :: (α set ⇒ α set) ⇒ α set computes the least fixpoint of a monotone function on sets. The two key theorems about lfp express that the result of lfp is indeed a fixpoint and satisfies an induction principle (⋀ is the universal quantifier of Isabelle's meta-logic):

$$\mathsf{mono}(f) \Longrightarrow \mathsf{lfp}(f) = f(\mathsf{lfp}(f)) \tag{2}$$

$$[\![\ a \in \mathsf{lfp}(f);\ \mathsf{mono}(f);\ \bigwedge x.\ x \in f(\mathsf{lfp}(f) \cap \{x.\ P(x)\}) \Longrightarrow P(x)\ ]\!] \Longrightarrow P(a) \tag{3}$$

Monotonicity of Γ, i.e. mono(Γ b cd), is proved automatically. A simple consequence is the following recursion equation:

$$\mathsf{C}(\mathsf{WHILE}\ b\ \mathsf{DO}\ c) = \mathsf{C}(\mathsf{IF}\ b\ \mathsf{THEN}\ c; \mathsf{WHILE}\ b\ \mathsf{DO}\ c\ \mathsf{ELSE}\ \mathsf{SKIP}) \tag{4}$$

4.1 Denotational is Natural

The equivalence proof between the natural and the denotational semantics follows Winskel closely and is pretty much automatic:

$$<c,s> \overset{c}{\to} t \Longrightarrow (s,t) \in C(c)$$

is proved by rule induction. The opposite direction

$$(s,t) \in C(c) \Longrightarrow <c,s> \overset{c}{\to} t$$

is proved by induction on c and an application of the lfp induction principle (3) in the WHILE-case. This is slightly different from Winskel's proof, which uses induction on ℕ in the WHILE-case because Γ is continuous.

Apart from the application of the induction rules and a few explicit unfoldings of lfp — equation (2) is not a terminating rewrite rule and has to be applied "by hand" — the proofs are automatic. The final equivalence is now trivial:

$$(s,t) \in C(c) = (<c,s> \overset{c}{\to} t) \tag{5}$$

5 Axiomatic Semantics

In this section we diverge most significantly from Winskel's treatment: on the one hand we take a short cut by not formalizing the syntax of the assertion language, on the other hand we provide a more satisfactory treatment of verification conditions.

A complete formalization of syntax and semantics of assertions, i.e. first order arithmetic, is a project in its own right. Therefore we have taken the semantic way out:

types assn = state $\Rightarrow$ bool

This is the same trick we used for arithmetic and boolean expressions.

Validity of Hoare triples is now straightforward:

consts hoare_valid :: assn $\Rightarrow$ com $\Rightarrow$ assn $\Rightarrow$ bool ("$\models$ {_} _ {_}")
defs $\models$ {P} c {Q} $\equiv$ $\forall$s t. (s,t) $\in$ C(c) $\longrightarrow$ P(s) $\longrightarrow$ Q(t)

Hoare logic is formalized just like operational semantics, i.e. as a relation:

consts hoare :: (assn $*$ com $*$ assn) set
translations $\vdash$ {P} c {Q} $\equiv$ (P,c,Q) $\in$ hoare

The inference rules of the logic constitute an inductive definition:

inductive hoare
  $\vdash$ {P} SKIP {P}

  $\vdash$ {λs.P(s[a(s)/x])} x := a {P}

  [$\vdash$ {P} c1 {Q}; $\vdash$ {Q} c2 {R}] $\implies$ $\vdash$ {P} c1;c2 {R}

  [$\vdash$ {λs. P(s) $\wedge$ b(s)} c1 {Q}; $\vdash$ {λs. P(s) $\wedge$ $\neg$ b(s)} c2 {Q}]
  $\implies$ $\vdash$ {P} IF b THEN c1 ELSE c2 {Q}

  $\vdash$ {λs. P(s) $\wedge$ b(s)} c {P} $\implies$ $\vdash$ {P} WHILE b DO c {λs. P(s) $\wedge$ $\neg$ b(s)}

  [$\forall$s. P'(s) $\longrightarrow$ P(s); $\vdash$ {P} c {Q}; $\forall$s. Q(s) $\longrightarrow$ Q'(s)] $\implies$ $\vdash$ {P'} c {Q'}

The last rule is called the **rule of consequence**.

Having identified assertions with their semantics we have to write λs. P(s) $\wedge$ b(s) instead of the usual P $\wedge$ b, which is not well typed. This effect was already discussed in the context of expressions (see the end of Section 2).

5.1 Soundness

The proof of

$\vdash$ {P} c {Q} $\implies$ $\models$ {P} c {Q}

is by rule induction on the derivation of $\vdash$ {P} c {Q}. All cases are automatic except for the WHILE-rule which requires an explicit lfp induction step (3).

5.2 Relative Completeness

The adjective "relative" refers to the fact that it is relative to the completeness of the proof system for the assertion language. In our setting this is already built in, because we do not have a proof system but merely the semantics of the assertion language. Hence we drop "relative" in the sequel.

Although we can prove completeness of our formalization of Hoare logic

$$\models \{P\} \ c \ \{Q\} \implies \vdash \{P\} \ c \ \{Q\} \tag{6}$$

it falls short of the corresponding completeness statement in the literature. The reason is our semantic view of assertions. Although (6) shows that all valid triples can be derived, this does not preclude that the derivation makes use of semantic assertions which cannot be expressed syntactically. Such non-expressible assertions can enter a derivation even if the derived triple itself only contains expressible assertions: in the rule of consequence P and Q occur in the premises but not the conclusion. In fact, our proof follows Winskel's up to the point where he uses the rule of consequence but shows that the chosen P and Q are expressible.

Winskel's proof hinges on the fact that the weakest liberal precondition is expressible. We follow Winskel and drop the adjective "liberal" in the sequel. Semantically, the weakest precondition is trivial:

consts swp :: com $\Rightarrow$ assn $\Rightarrow$ assn
defs   swp c Q $\equiv$ (λs. $\forall$t. (s,t) $\in$ C(c) $\longrightarrow$ Q(t))

The assertion swp c Q characterizes all initial states which lead to Q, provided c terminates. The name swp was chosen to distinguish it from a second wp-like operator further down.

Winskel calls an assertion language **expressive** if for every command c and assertion Q, there is an assertion P with semantics swp c Q. He shows that a) first order arithmetic is expressive and b) expressiveness implies completeness. In our setting expressiveness is not an issue because we can use swp. It remains to be shown that it leads to completeness.

The key lemma looks trivial

$$\forall Q. \vdash \{swp \ c \ Q\} \ c \ \{Q\} \tag{7}$$

but is a bit tricky. The proof is by induction on c. All cases except IF and WHILE are proved automatically. The IF-case needs the rule of consequence, which has to be applied "by hand". Fortunately, Isabelle's logical variables save us from having to supply instantiations as well. The really interesting case is WHILE, because this is the only major slip in any of Winskel's proofs. Let us look at it in some detail. The subgoal is

$\forall Q. \vdash \{swp \ c \ Q\} \ c \ \{Q\} \implies$
$\vdash \{swp \ (WHILE \ b \ DO \ c) \ Q\} \ WHILE \ b \ DO \ c \ \{Q\}$

Winskel claims (in our notation) that from $\models \{\lambda s. \ P(s) \wedge b(s)\} \ c \ \{P\}$, where $P \equiv swp \ (WHILE \ b \ DO \ c) \ Q$, it follows by induction hypothesis that $\vdash \{\lambda s. \ P(s)$

∧ b(s)} c {P}. At this point he is jumping the gun, as a look at the induction hypothesis shows. It appears that his mind is already fixed on completeness.

Fortunately the proof can be repaired quite easily. Let us first show

$$P(s) \wedge b(s) \longrightarrow swp \ c \ P \ s \tag{8}$$
$$P(s) \wedge \neg b(s) \longrightarrow Q \tag{9}$$

$$\{swp \ c \ P\} \ c \ \{P\} \tag{10}$$

where again $P \equiv swp$ (WHILE b DO c) Q. The first two follow essentially from (4) via the lemmas

$b(s) \Longrightarrow swp$ (WHILE b DO c) Q s = swp (c;WHILE b DO c) Q s
$\neg b(s) \Longrightarrow swp$ (WHILE b DO c) Q s = Q s

The third one is an instance of the induction hypothesis.

From (8) and (10) we obtain {λs. P(s) ∧ b(s)} c {P} by the rule of consequence. The WHILE-rule turns this into {P} WHILE b DO c {λs. P(s) ∧ ¬ b(s)}. Using (9) and the rule of consequence this yields the desired {P} WHILE b DO c {Q}. The Isabelle proof requires some guidance but no instantiations.

Having proved (7), completeness (6) follows easily by the rule of consequence.

5.3 Verification Conditions

Using Hoare logic directly is tedious, and some of that tedium can be automated. The idea is to extract a set of assertions, the **verification conditions**, from the program such that the program is correct if the assertions are, thus bypassing Hoare logic and reducing the verification problem to the assertion language. The automatic extraction of verification conditions requires a program where all loops are annotated with their invariants.

Winskel follows Gordon [2] in his treatment of verification conditions, who inserts rather more annotations than strictly speaking necessary. This complicates the syntax of annotated commands. We go for the minimal amount of annotation, namely loop invariants. Since there is no such thing as inheritance in HOL, we have to define a new type of **annotated commands**

```
datatype acom = Askip
              | Aass  loc aexp
              | Asemi  acom acom
              | Aif    bexp acom acom
              | Awhile bexp assn acom
```

and a function for stripping an annotated command of its annotations:

```
consts astrip :: acom ⇒ com
primrec
  astrip Askip = SKIP
  astrip (Aass x a) = (x:=a)
  astrip (Asemi c d) = (astrip c ; astrip d)
  astrip (Aif b c d) = (IF b THEN astrip c ELSE astrip d)
  astrip (Awhile b I c) = (WHILE b DO astrip c)
```

The computation of the verification conditions needs two functions

consts vc,wp :: acom $\Rightarrow$ assn $\Rightarrow$ assn

where vc returns the verification condition and wp the weakest (liberal) precondition. The soundness property we are aiming for is

$$(\forall s.\ vc\ c\ Q\ s) \Longrightarrow \vdash \{wp\ c\ Q\}\ astrip\ c\ \{Q\} \tag{11}$$

The reason for dragging in wp is twofold: vc only takes the postcondition (hence we need to know w.r.t. which precondition vc guarantees correctness) and there are no annotations between sequential commands (hence we need wp c2 in order to compute vc (Asemi c1 c2)). This time we cannot take the semantic way out (see swp) because we are really meant to compute an assertion, i.e. some syntactic entity. The following definition of wp is classical, except for the final clause:

primrec
wp Askip Q = Q
wp (Aass x a) Q = (λs.Q(s[a(s)/x]))
wp (Asemi c1 c2) Q = wp c1 (wp c2 Q)
wp (Aif b c1 c2) Q = (λs. (b(s) $\longrightarrow$ wp c1 Q s) $\wedge$ ($\neg$ b(s) $\longrightarrow$ wp c2 Q s))
wp (Awhile b I c) Q = I

In the final clause we use the the invariant I as the weakest precondition. What if the programmer has supplied an invariant which is too strong or not invariant? If I is too strong, wp computes too strong a precondition and the conclusion of (11) is weaker than it could be. If I is not even invariant, the verification conditions computed by vc are not valid either, thus rendering (11) trivial because its premise cannot be discharged.

The verification condition generator vc is defined by primitive recursion:

primrec
vc Askip Q = (λs.True)
vc (Aass x a) Q = (λs.True)
vc (Asemi c d) Q = (λs. vc c (wp d Q) s $\wedge$ vc d Q s)
vc (Aif b c d) Q = (λs. vc c Q s $\wedge$ vc d Q s)
vc (Awhile b I c) Q = (λs. (I(s) $\wedge$ b(s) $\longrightarrow$ wp c I s) $\wedge$ (I(s) $\wedge$ $\neg$ b(s) $\longrightarrow$ Q(s)) $\wedge$
            vc c I s)

The final clause again deserves some comments: I(s) $\wedge$ b(s) $\longrightarrow$ wp c I s guarantees that I is an invariant, I(s) $\wedge$ $\neg$ b(s) $\longrightarrow$ Q(s) guarantees that upon exit the postcondition Q holds, and vc c I takes care of the verification conditions in the loop body.

The proof of soundness (11) is by induction on c. It needs a little guidance in the Aif and Awhile cases but is automatic otherwise.

Completeness requires two monotonicity properties:

$\forall$P Q. ($\forall$s. P s $\longrightarrow$ Q s) $\longrightarrow$ ($\forall$s. wp c P s $\longrightarrow$ wp c Q s)
$\forall$P Q. ($\forall$s. P s $\longrightarrow$ Q s) $\longrightarrow$ ($\forall$s. vc c P s $\longrightarrow$ vc c Q s)

Both proofs are by induction on c and automatic except for the Awhile case. The proof of the completeness theorem

$\vdash \{P\}\ c\ \{Q\} \implies (\exists ac.\ astrip\ ac = c \wedge (\forall s.\ vc\ ac\ Q\ s) \wedge (\forall s.\ P\ s \longrightarrow wp\ ac\ Q\ s))$

is a straightforward rule induction on $\vdash \{P\}\ c\ \{Q\}$. This time we have to provide the witness ac by hand in each case.

If one is interested in a more efficient computation of verification conditions, vc and wp can be combined into a single function returning a pair of the weakest precondition and the verification condition. This function only traverses the command once, in contrast to the above solution. For lack of space we do not present the details. The structure of the combined function can also be found in the work of Homeier and Martin [5], who prove soundness but not completeness of their verification condition generator.

6 Denotational Semantics in HOLCF

Although Winskel introduces partial functions as relations and uses the complete powerset lattice to introduce the basics of fixpoint theory (see Section 4 above), he goes on to develop domain theory based on complete partial orders (cpos). This section recasts IMP's denotational semantics in a cpo framework. Winskel just sketches the necessary steps because on the surface not much changes. Logically, however, it implies leaving the safe haven of HOL's total functions and venturing into the sea of continuity and undefinedness. The purpose of this section is to demonstrate that, given the right infrastructure (HOLCF!), this step need not be painful.

HOLCF [10, 11] is a conservative extension of HOL with the notions of domain theory [7]. In particular it provides

- a class pcpo (pointed cpo) of types which come equipped with a complete partial order $\sqsubseteq$ and a least element $\bot$.
- a space $\rightarrow$ of continuous functions between pcpos, together with its own abstraction Λ, infix application ', composition oo, and fixpoint operator fix.

We only want to move into HOLCF for those aspects which require domain theory. To embed HOL types into pcpos we use the concept of **lifting**:

datatype (α)lift $=$ Def α | Undef

We turn (α)lift into a pcpo by defining $\bot \equiv$ Undef and $x \sqsubseteq y \equiv x=$Undef $\vee$ x=y. The type (τ)lift is usually written $\tau_\bot$. The functional

consts lift1 :: $(\alpha \Rightarrow (\beta::pcpo)) \Rightarrow ((\alpha)$lift $\rightarrow \beta)$
defs   lift1 f $\equiv (\Lambda al.\ case\ al\ of\ Def(a) \Rightarrow f(a)\ |\ Undef \Rightarrow \bot)$

lifts HOL functions into HOLCF by lifting their domain, thus turning it into a pcpo. The type β is constrained to be a pcpo already. Winskel's notation $f_\bot$ is close to but not identical with lift1 f because he lifts both domain and range.

Now we can define D, the HOLCF version of C:

consts D :: com ⇒ (state)lift → (state)lift
primrec
  D(SKIP) = (Λs.s)
  D(x := a) = lift1(λs. Def(s[a(s)/x]))
  D(c1;c2) = (D c2) oo (D c1)
  D(IF b THEN c1 ELSE c2) = lift1(λs. if b(s) then D c1'(Def s) else D c2'(Def s))
  D(WHILE b DO c) = fix'(Λw. lift1(λs. if b(s) then w'(D c'(Def s)) else Def s))

Winskel suggests (in our notation) D :: com ⇒ state → (state)lift, but we cannot follow him: state → (state)lift is not a legal type in HOLCF because **state** is not a **pcpo** and is thus not a valid argument type for →. Winskel gets away with it because instead of **pcpos** he works with cpos which do not require ⊥ elements. Using the discrete ordering, any type, in particular **state**, can be turned into a cpo, and the continuous functions between cpos again form a cpo.

To show the equivalence of C and D it seems natural to prove

$$(D\ c'Def(s) = Def(t))\ =\ ((s,t) \in C(c))$$

by induction on c. This should work fine, except that it requires a good deal of machinery to relate the two fixpoint operators lfp on sets and fix on cpos. This is beyond the scope of this paper and we turn to proof reuse: the equivalence

$$(D\ c'Def(s) = Def(t))\ =\ (<c,s> \overset{c}{\to} t)$$

is proved like its relative (5): the ⟹-direction by induction on c with nested fixpoint induction in the WHILE-case, the ⟸-direction by rule induction. However, this time things are not quite as straightforward. Without going into details, let us just say that an unexpected amount of HOLCF specific reasoning is necessary. For example, we needed to show that D is strict: D c'⊥ = ⊥. None of these proofs are very hard, but they do require familiarity with domain theory.

7 The Future

We have only presented part of our actual formalization. There is also a simple compiler to a stack machine and its correctness proof. But this is still only a beginning. We expect to extend our formalization in two directions: the language will become richer (e.g. procedures) and the semantics finer (e.g. time and space complexity). Ideally, all formal reasoning about programs should be based upon a unified semantic framework like the one presented in this paper.

Acknowledgements. I wish to thank Glynn Winskel for his excellent book, Heiko Lötzbeyer and Robert Sandner for their initial formalization, Robert Sandner for his HOLCF proofs, Franz Regensburger and Birgit Schieder for (amongst other things) their debugging of my initial vc, Olaf Müller for HOLCF expertise, and Larry Paulson for the subtitle.

References

1. Y. Bertot and R. Fraer. Reasoning with executable specifications. In *TAPSOFT '95: Theory and Practice of Software Development*, volume 915 of *Lect. Notes in Comp. Sci.*, pages 531–545. Springer-Verlag, 1995.
2. M. Gordon. *Programming Language Theory and its Implementation*. Prentice-Hall, 1988.
3. M. Gordon. Mechanizing programming logics in higher order logic. In G. Birtwistle and P. Subrahmanyam, editors, *Current Trends in Hardware Verification and Automated Theorem Proving*. Springer-Verlag, 1989.
4. M. Gordon and T. Melham. *Introduction to HOL: a theorem-proving environment for higher-order logic*. Cambridge University Press, 1993.
5. P. V. Homeier and D. F. Martin. Trustworthy tools for trustworthy programs: A verified verification condition generator. In T. Melham and J. Camilleri, editors, *Higher Order Logic Theorem Proving and its Applications*, volume 859 of *Lect. Notes in Comp. Sci.*, pages 269–284. Springer-Verlag, 1994.
6. H. Lötzbeyer and R. Sandner. Proof of the equivalence of the operational and denotational semantics of IMP in Isabelle/ZF. Project report, Institut für Informatik, TU München, 1994.
7. L. C. Paulson. *Logic and Computation*. Cambridge University Press, 1987.
8. L. C. Paulson. *Isabelle: A Generic Theorem Prover*, volume 828 of *Lect. Notes in Comp. Sci.* Springer-Verlag, 1994.
9. L. C. Paulson. Generic automatic proof tools. Technical Report 396, University of Cambridge, Computer Laboratory, 1996.
10. F. Regensburger. *HOLCF: Eine konservative Erweiterung von HOL um LCF*. PhD thesis, Technische Universität München, 1994.
11. F. Regensburger. HOLCF: Higher Order Logic of Computable Functions. In E. Schubert, P. Windley, and J. Alves-Foss, editors, *Higher Order Logic Theorem Proving and its Applications*, volume 971 of *Lect. Notes in Comp. Sci.*, pages 293–307. Springer-Verlag, 1995.
12. L. van Benthem Jutting. *Checking Landau's "Grundlagen" in the AUTOMATH System*. PhD thesis, Eindhoven University of Technology, 1977.
13. G. Winskel. *The Formal Semantics of Programming Languages*. MIT Press, 1993.

An Optimal Deterministic Algorithm for Online b-Matching

Bala Kalyanasundaram and Kirk Pruhs

Computer Science Dept., University of Pittsburgh, Pittsburgh, PA 15260, USA.
{kalyan,kirk}@cs.pitt.edu, http://www.cs.pitt.edu/{~kalyan,~kirk}

Abstract. We study the online unweighted b-matching problem where at most $b \geq 1$ requests can be matched to any server site. We present a deterministic algorithm BALANCE whose competitive ratio is $1 - \frac{1}{(1+\frac{1}{b})^b}$. We show that the competitive ratio of every deterministic online algorithm is at least $1 - \frac{1}{(1+\frac{1}{b})^b}$. Hence, BALANCE is optimally competitive, including low order terms. For large b, the competitive ratio of BALANCE approaches $1 - \frac{1}{e} \approx .63$.

1 Introduction

We consider the natural online version of the well-known b-matching problem on an unweighted bipartite graph $G = (S, R, E)$, where S and R are the vertex partitions and E is the edge set. At the ith unit of time, $1 \leq i \leq n$, the vertex $r_i \in R$ and all the edges incident to r_i are revealed to the online algorithm $\mathcal{A}$. $\mathcal{A}$ then must either decline to ever service r_i, or irrevocably select a site s_k adjacent to r_i in G to service r_i. No server site may be used more than b times. Hence, it may well not be possible to service every request. The goal of the online algorithm is to maximize the number of requests that it services. We analyze this problem using the standard competitive ratio. For this problem, the competitive ratio of an online algorithm $\mathcal{A}$ is the supremum over all possible instances I, of the cardinality of the matching constructed by $\mathcal{A}$ on I divided by the maximum cardinality matching in I. Note that the instance I specifies G as well as the order in which the r_i's appear.

As one example application, consider the problem of assigning client computers to support stations studied by Grove, Kao, Krishnan and Vitter [1]. In this problem each support station has a maximum range of service and a limit on the number of clients that it can support. Clients arrive over time and must each be assigned to a support station that is not too distant and that is not fully utilized. So the competitive ratio will be the fraction (relative to the maximum matching) of the clients that can be guaranteed support without reassignment.

1.1 Related Results

Karp, Vazirani, and Vazirani [5] give the following results for online bipartite matching, the special case of b-matching where $b = 1$. It is not hard to observe that any deterministic algorithm that never refuses to match a request, if it is possible to do so, is $\frac{1}{2}$-competitive, and that no deterministic algorithm can be better than $\frac{1}{2}$-competitive. [5] give a randomized algorithm RANKING whose competitive ratio is $1 - \frac{1}{e} + o(1)$ against an oblivious adversary that must specify the input a priori. RANKING initially selects uniformly at random a linear order of the server sites, and then matches each request with the the first available server. [5] show that the competitive ratio of every randomized algorithm is at least $1 - \frac{1}{e} + o(1)$. Hence, RANKING is optimally competitive, up to low order terms.

Kao and Tate [4] extended the results of [5] by considering the case where requests appear in batches. They showed that the results of [5] cannot be improved even if request appear in batches of size $o(n)$ each.

Grove, Kao, Krishnan and Vitter [1] consider the problem of maintaining a maximum cardinality matching with a minimal number of reassignments of servers in the special case that the maximum degree of each $r_i = 2$. [1] show that the greedy algorithm, that switches assignments along the shortest augmenting path, is $O(\log n)$-competitive, i.e. the greedy algorithm makes at most $O(\log n)$ times as many reassignments as the optimal number of reassignments required to maintain a maximum cardinality matching. [1] show the competitive ratio of every deterministic algorithm for this problem is $\Omega(\log n)$. [1] also give some results for case that requests may depart.

Results for online weighted matching problems, on graphs where the edge weights satisfy the triangle inequality, can be found in [2, 3, 6]. In particular, an optimally competitive deterministic algorithm for the case $b = 1$ can be found in [2, 6]. In [3], the case of arbitrary b is studied under the assumption that the online algorithm has more servers per site than the adversary. Note that the triangle inequality is not generally satisfied by non-edges in unweighted matching.

1.2 Summary of Results

In this paper, we give the following results for online b-matching. In section 2, we show that the competitive ratio of any deterministic online algorithm for this problem is at least $1 - \frac{1}{(1+\frac{1}{b})^b}$. This lower bound holds even if each request has degree at least at least $\frac{m}{3b}$. In section 3, we give a simple deterministic algorithm BALANCE with competitive ratio $1 - \frac{1}{(1+\frac{1}{b})^b}$. Hence, BALANCE is optimally competitive, including low order terms. As b grows, $1 - \frac{1}{(1+\frac{1}{b})^b}$ approaches $1 - \frac{1}{e} \approx .63$. In response to a request r_i, BALANCE selects an arbitrary server site among all server sites adjacent to r_i in G that have used a minimum number of servers to date. The idea of trying to balance the number of servers used per site can also be found in an online matching algorithm given in [3].

As in [3, 7], we also compare the performance of the online algorithm against the performance of an offline algorithm with fewer servers. This will give us an idea on how well BALANCE peforms against a less malicious input given by the adversary. We show that BALANCE, with αb servers, is $1 - \frac{1}{(1+\frac{1}{b})^{\alpha b}}$ competitive against an offline adversary with b servers per site. We also show that this ratio is optimal for deterministic algorithms. Here α must be an integer.

2 The Lower Bound

In order to prove the desired lower bound, we first present an adversary. Throughout our arguments we think of the server site s_i as containing b different servers that handle the requests.

Adversary : Let $\mathcal{A}$ be the given deterministic online algorithm.

There are $(b+1)^b$ server sites with exactly b servers per site, and there will be $b \cdot (b+1)^b$ requests. The requests are partitioned into groups. The first group R_1 consists of the first $b(1+b)^{b-1}$ requests, the second group R_2 consists of the next $b^2(1+b)^{b-2}$ requests, and in general, R_i, i, $1 \leq i \leq b$, contains the $b^i(1+b)^{b-i}$ requests from request numbered $1 + \sum_{j=1}^{i-1} b^j(1+b)^{b-j}$ to the request numbered $\sum_{j=1}^{i} b^j(1+b)^{b-j}$, inclusive. R_{b+1} contains the last b^{b+1} requests.

The adversary maintains $b+1$ sets $S_1, S_2, \ldots S_{b+1}$ of server sites such that $S_i \supset S_{i+i}$. Initially, S_1 is the set S of all server sites. The first b groups are handled in the following manner. The adversary makes a request $r_j \in R_i$ adjacent to those vertices in S_i that have not yet answered a request in R_i. If $\mathcal{A}$ uses s_k to service r_j then s_k is added to S_{i+1}. In R_{b+1}, each request can be matched to any server site in S_{b+1}. So the following is the adversary's algorithm for requests in R_i, $i \leq b$. Note that for every server site s_j, the set M_j is initialized to the empty set. Assuming that the first $i-1$ phase has been completed, consider the ith phase where $i \leq b$.

> $S_{i+1} = \emptyset$
> for each request $r_j \in R_i$ in chronological order
> reveal r_j and edges from r_j to sites in $S_i - S_{i+1}$.
> if $\mathcal{A}$ matches r_j to a server at site $s_k \in S_i - S_{i+1}$.
>   Add s_k to S_{i+1}.
> else { $\mathcal{A}$ opts not to match r_j }
>   choose some arbitrary site $s_k \in S_i - S_{i+1}$.
>   Add s_k to S_{i+1} and r_j to M_k.
> endfor

Lemma 1. For each i $(1 \leq i \leq b)$,
(a) $S_i \supset S_{i+1}$,
(b) $|S_{i+1}| = |R_i| = b^i(1+b)^{b-i}$, and
(c) $|S_i| - |S_{i+1}| = b^{i-1}(1+b)^{b-i}$,

For ease of notation, let us assume that the set S_{b+2} is empty.

Lemma 2. There exists an offline perfect matching that, for each i satisfying $1 \leq i \leq b+1$, matches every request in R_i to a server site in $S_i - S_{i+1}$.

Proof. Notice that every request in R_i can be matched to any server in sites from $S_i - S_{i+1}$. It suffices to show that $b \cdot |S_i - S_{i+1}| \geq |R_i|$ since each site has b servers. For $1 \leq i \leq b$ this follows from lemma 1. For $i = b + 1$ it follows since $|S_{b+1}| = b^b$, $|S_{b+2}| = 0$, and $|R_{b+1}| = b^{b+1}$

Lemma 3. *The number of requests matched by $\mathcal{A}$ does not exceed $\sum_{i=1}^{b} |R_i|$.*

Proof. Consider the sites in S_{b+1}. Since each site in S_{b+1} went through b phases starting from the set S_1, the maximum number of requests from R_{b+1} that the servers from sites in S_{b+1} can match is $\sum_{s_k \in S_{b+1}} |M_k|$. The number of requests in $\cup_{i=1}^{b} R_i$ matched by $\mathcal{A}$ to servers in $S - S_{b+1}$ is $\sum_{i=1}^{b} |R_i| - \sum_{s_k \in S} |M_k|$. The result follows since $S \supseteq S_{b+1}$.

Theorem 4. *The competitive ratio of any deterministic online algorithm for the b-matching problem is at most $1 - \frac{1}{(1+\frac{1}{b})^b}$.*

Proof. Let $\mathcal{A}$ be the given online algorithm, and apply the adversary described in this section. Combining lemma 3 and lemma 2 we get that the competitive ratio is

$$\frac{\sum_{i=1}^{b} |R_i|}{\sum_{i=1}^{b+1} |R_i|} = \frac{\sum_{i=1}^{b} |R_i|}{|R_{b+1}| + \sum_{i=1}^{b} |R_i|}$$

Substituting $\sum_{i=1}^{b+1} |R_i| = b(b+1)^b$, $|R_{b+1}| = b^{b+1}$, and $\sum_{i=1}^{b} |R_i| = b(b+1)^b - b^{b+1}$ yields the claimed bound.

Note that in this lower bound each request has degree at least $\frac{|S|}{3b}$.

Theorem 5. *Assume that the adversary has b servers per site while the online algorithm has αb servers per site, where α is some positive integer. In this model, the competitive ratio of any deterministic online algorithm for the b-matching problem is $1 - \frac{1}{(1+\frac{1}{b})^{\alpha b}}$.*

Proof. We modify the adversary in the following way. Let the number of server sites be $(b+1)^{\alpha b}$ and for all $1 \leq i \leq \alpha b$, R_i consists of $b^i (1+b)^{\alpha b - i}$ requests. $R_{\alpha b+1}$ consists of $b^{\alpha b+1}$ requests. The rest of the argument go through as before.

3 The Algorithm Balance

In this section we present the algorithm BALANCE, and show that the competitive ratio of BALANCE **exactly** matches the deterministic lower bound from the previous section.

Algorithm BALANCE: Each request r_j is served by an arbitrary adjacent server site that has a maximum number of servers remaining.

Definition 6.
(a) Let OPT be an arbitrary maximum cardinality matching.
(b) Let B be the set of request vertices matched in OPT.
(c) Let X be the set of requests in B not matched by BALANCE.
(d) If the request r_j is matched by BALANCE to a server site that has already used $i-1$ servers, then we say that the *rank* of r_j is i.
(e) For $1 \leq i \leq b$, let R_i be the set of all requests with rank i.
(f) For $1 \leq i \leq b$, let $M_i \subseteq R_i$ be the set of all requests with rank i that are not in B.
(g) For $1 \leq i \leq b+1$, let S_i be the set of server sites in the maximum matching that service requests in $X \cup (\cup_{j=i}^{b}(R_j - M_j))$.

Lemma 7. *The competitive ratio of* BALANCE *is*

$$\frac{\sum_{i=1}^{b}|R_i|}{|X| + \sum_{i=1}^{b}|R_i - M_i|} = \frac{\sum_{i=1}^{b}|R_i|}{(|X| - \sum_{i=1}^{b}|M_i|) + \sum_{i=1}^{b}|R_i|}$$

Lemma 8. *For any i satisfying $2 \leq i \leq b+1$, each $s_k \in S_i$ is matched by* BALANCE *to at least $i-1$ requests. Hence, $|R_{i-1}| \geq |S_i|$.*

Proof. First consider the case that s_k is matched in OPT with an $r_j \in X$. Then since BALANCE didn't match r_j, it must be the case that BALANCE has used all the servers from s_k. Hence, s_k is adjacent to a rank $i-1$ request.

Now suppose that in OPT the site s_k matches a request $r_a \in R_j$, $j \geq i$. Notice that r_a is also matched by BALANCE to some server at site s_b. Note that it may be the case $s_k = s_b$. Since r_a can be matched to either s_k or s_b, it must be the case that BALANCE has already matched a $j-1$st rank request to s_k. The result then follows since $j \geq i$.

Lemma 9. *For any $1 \leq i \leq b+1$,*

$$|S_i| \geq \frac{1}{b}(|X| - \sum_{j=i}^{b}|M_j| + \sum_{j=i}^{b}|R_j|)$$

Proof. This follows from the definition of S_i, the fact that each site has at most b servers, the fact that $M_i \subseteq R_i$, and the fact that the R_i's are disjoint.

Lemma 10. *For $0 \leq i \leq b$,*

$$b \cdot |S_{b-i+1}| \geq (1 + \frac{1}{b})^i \cdot (|X| - \sum_{j=b-i+1}^{b}|M_j|)$$

Proof. We prove this by induction on i. First consider the case $i = 0$. Since at most b requests can be matched to servers at any site, we have $b \cdot |S_{b+1}| \geq |X|$.

Assume that the induction hypothesis holds for $i \leq k$. We now want to show that it also holds for $i = k + 1$. Applying lemma 9 we have

$$b \cdot |S_{b-(k+1)+1}| = |S_{b-k}| = |X| - \sum_{j=b-k}^{b} |M_j| + \sum_{j=b-k}^{b} |R_j|$$

Applying lemma 8, that is $|R_j| \geq |S_{j+1}|$, we get,

$$\sum_{j=b-k}^{b} |R_j| \geq \sum_{j=b-k}^{b} |S_{j+1}| = \sum_{i=0}^{k} |S_{b-i+1}|$$

Applying the induction hypothesis we get,

$$b \cdot \sum_{i=0}^{k} |S_{b-i+1}| \geq \sum_{i=0}^{k} (1 + \tfrac{1}{b})^i \cdot (|X| - \sum_{j=b-i+1}^{b} |M_j|)$$
$$\geq \sum_{i=0}^{k} (1 + \tfrac{1}{b})^i \cdot (|X| - \sum_{j=b-k+1}^{b} |M_j|)$$
$$= (|X| - \sum_{j=b-k+1}^{b} |M_j|) \cdot \sum_{i=0}^{k} (1 + \tfrac{1}{b})^i$$
$$\geq (|X| - \sum_{j=b-k}^{b} |M_j|) \cdot \sum_{i=0}^{k} (1 + \tfrac{1}{b})^i$$
$$= (|X| - \sum_{j=b-k}^{b} |M_j|) \cdot b \cdot ((1 + \tfrac{1}{b})^{k+1} - 1)$$

Therefore, we get

$$b \cdot |S_{b-(k+1)+1}| \geq (|X| - \sum_{j=b-k}^{b} |M_j|) + (|X| - \sum_{j=b-k}^{b} |M_j|) \cdot [(1 + \tfrac{1}{b})^{k+1} - 1]$$
$$= (1 + \tfrac{1}{b})^{k+1} \cdot (|X| - \sum_{j=b-k}^{b} |M_j|)$$

Theorem 11. *The competitive ratio of* BALANCE *is* $1 - \frac{1}{(1+\frac{1}{b})^b}$.

Proof. Applying lemma 8 and lemma 10, we get

$$\sum_{i=1}^{b} |R_i| \geq \sum_{i=2}^{b+1} |S_i|$$
$$= \sum_{i=0}^{b-1} |S_{b-i+1}|$$
$$\geq \tfrac{1}{b} \sum_{i=0}^{b-1} (1 + \tfrac{1}{b})^i (|X| - \sum_{j=b-i+1}^{b} |M_j|)$$
$$\geq \tfrac{1}{b} \cdot (|X| - \sum_{j=1}^{b} |M_j|) \cdot \sum_{i=0}^{b-1} (1 + \tfrac{1}{b})^i$$
$$\geq (|X| - \sum_{j=1}^{b} |M_j|) \cdot ((1 + \tfrac{1}{b})^b - 1)$$

Applying the bound to the competitive ratio computed in lemma 7, yields the desired bound.

We now claim that BALANCE is optimally competitive against an adversary with fewer servers.

Theorem 12. *The competitive ratio of* BALANCE, *with* αb *servers per site, against an adversary, with only* b *servers per site, is* $1 - \frac{1}{(1+\frac{1}{b})^{\alpha b}}$.

Proof. The above arguments need to be modified by allowing the rank of a request to range from 1 to αb. By appropriately extending the definitions, the same argument will go through.

4 Conclusion

We show that the algorithm BALANCE is optimal optimally competitive among deterministic algorithms for the online b-matching problem. The obvious open question is to find an optimally competitive randomize algorithm. We are currently analyzing the following algorithm that is a mix of RANKING and BALANCE. Initially, uniformly at random linearly order the server sites. Then run BALANCE. If there is more than one site with a minimum number of servers that can handle a request, break the tie by selecting the highest ranked site.

In the case where the number servers per site vary from site to site, the competitive factor of BALANCE does not exactly match with that of the lower bound. Is there a deterministic algorithm with competitive factor $1 - \frac{1}{(1+\frac{1}{b_a})^{b_a}}$ where b_a is the average number of servers per site used by OPT?

References

1. E. Grove, M. Kao, P. Krishnan, and J. Vitter, "Online Perfect Matching and Mobile Computing", *Proceedings of the Workshop on Algorithms and Data Structures*, 1995.
2. B. Kalyanasundaram, and K. Pruhs, "Online weighted matching", *Journal of Algorithms*, **14**, 478–488, 1993.
3. B. Kalyanasundaram, and K. Pruhs, "The Online Transportation Problem", *Proc. of European Symposium on Algorithms*, Vol. 979 (*LNCS*), 484–493, 1995.
4. M. Kao, and S. Tate, "Online Matching with Blocked Input", *Information Processing Letters*, 38, 113–116, 1991.
5. R. Karp, U. Vazirani, and V. Vazirani, "An Optimal Algorithm for Online Bipartite Matching", *STOC*, 352–358, 1990.
6. S. Khuller, S. Mitchell, and V. Vazirani, "On-line algorithms for weighted matchings and stable marriages", *Theoretical Computer Science*, **127**(2), 255–267, 1994.
7. D. Sleator and R. Tarjan, "Amortized efficiency of list update and paging rules", *Communications of the ACM*, **28**, 202–208, 1985.

Tight Bounds for Prefetching and Buffer Management Algorithms for Parallel I/O Systems

Peter J. Varman[1] * and Rakesh M. Verma[2] **

[1] ECE Department, Rice University, Houston TX 77251, USA
E-mail: pjv@rice.edu
[2] Department of Computer Science, University of Houston, Houston TX 77204, USA
E-mail: rmverma@cs.uh.edu

Abstract. The growing importance of multiple-disk parallel I/O systems requires the development of appropriate prefetching and buffer management algorithms. We answer several fundamental questions on prefetching and buffer management for such parallel I/O systems. Specifically, we find and prove the optimality of an algorithm, P-MIN, that minimizes the number of parallel I/Os. Secondly, we analyze P-CON, an algorithm which always matches its replacement decisions with those of the well-known demand-paged MIN algorithm. We show that P-CON can become fully sequential in the worst case. Finally, we define and analyze P-LRU, a semi-on-line version of the traditional LRU buffer-management algorithm. Unexpectedly, we find that the performance of P-LRU is independent of the number of disks.

1 Introduction

The increasing imbalance between the speeds of processors and I/O devices has resulted in the I/O subsystem becoming a bottleneck in many applications. The use of multiple disks to build a parallel I/O subsystem has been advocated to increase I/O performance and system availability [5], and most high-performance systems incorporate some form of I/O parallelism. Performance is improved by overlapping accesses at several disks using judicious prefetching and buffer management algorithms that ensure that the most useful blocks are accessed and retained in the buffer.

A parallel I/O system consists of D independent disks, each with its own disk buffer, that can be accessed in parallel. The data for the computation is spread out among the disks in units of *blocks*. A block is the unit of retrieval from a disk. The computation is characterized by a computation sequence, which is the ordered sequence of blocks that it references. In our model all accesses are read-only. Prefetching (reading a data block before it is needed by the computation)

---

* Research partially supported by a grant from the Schlumberger Foundation
** Research partially supported by NSF grant CCR-9303011

is a natural mechanism to increase I/O parallelism. When the computation demands a disk-resident block of data, concurrently a data block can be prefetched from each of the other disks in parallel, and held in buffer until needed. This requires discarding a block in the buffer to make space for the prefetched block. Some natural questions that arise are: under what conditions is it worthwhile to discard a buffer-resident block to make room for a prefetch block which will be used only some time later in the future? And, if we do decide to discard a block, what replacement policy should be used in choosing the block to be replaced.

In this paper we answer several fundamental questions on prefetching and buffer management for such parallel I/O systems. The questions we address are: what is an optimal prefetch and buffer management algorithm, and how good are the algorithms proposed earlier for sequential (single) disk systems in this context. We obtain several interesting results, which are informally stated below and more precisely stated in Section 2. We find and prove the optimality of an algorithm, P-MIN, that minimizes the number of parallel I/Os. This contrasts with the recent results on prefetching to obtain CPU-disk overlap [4], where no efficient algorithm to find the optimal policy is known. Secondly, we show that P-CON, an algorithm that attempts to optimize the number of I/Os on each disk, can have very poor parallel performance. Finally we investigate the behavior of semi-on-line algorithms using parallel I/O. The concept of semi-on-line algorithms that we consider in this paper captures the dual requirements of prefetching (which needs some future knowledge) and on-line behavior (no future knowledge). We define and analyze P-LRU, a semi-on-line version of the traditional Least Recently Used (LRU) buffer-management algorithm. We find the performance of P-LRU is independent of the number of disks, in contrast to P-CON where the performance can degrade in proportion to the number of disks.

In contrast to single-disk systems (sequential I/O) for which these issues have been studied extensively (e.g. [2, 6]), there has been no formal study of these issues in the parallel I/O context. In the sequential setting the number of block accesses (or I/Os) is a useful performance metric; scaling by the average block access time provides an estimate of the I/O time. In contrast, in the multiple-disk case there is no direct relationship between the number of I/Os and the I/O time, since this depends on the I/O parallelism that is attained. The goals of minimizing the number of I/Os done by each disk and minimizing the parallel I/O time can conflict. Traditional buffer management algorithms for single-disk systems have generally focused on minimizing the number of I/Os. In the parallel context it may be useful to perform a greater than the absolute minimal (if the disk were operated in isolation) number of I/Os from each disk, if this allows a large number of them to be overlapped.

The rest of the paper is organized as follows. Section 1.1 summarizes related work. Section 2 develops the formal model and summarizes the main results. In Section 3.1 we derive a tight upper bound for P-CON algorithm. In Section 3.2 we prove the optimality of P-MIN. Section 3.3 analyzes the performance of the semi-on-line algorithm P-LRU.

1.1 Related Work

In single-disk systems, buffer management (or paging problem) algorithms were studied [2, 6, 11], and several policies (LRU, FIFO, Longest Forward Distance, etc.) were proposed and analyzed. The Longest Forward Distance [2] policy minimizes the number of page faults, and is therefore called the MIN algorithm. All these policies use demand I/O and deterministic replacement, i.e. they fetch only when the block being referenced is not in the buffer, and the choice of the replaced block is deterministic. (Randomized replacement algorithms, e.g. see [8], are beyond the the scope of this paper.) In the sequential case, it is well known [11] that prefetching does not reduce the number of I/Os required.

Sleator and Tarjan [11] analyzed the competitive ratio of on-line paging algorithms relative to the off-line optimal algorithm MIN. They showed that LRU's performance penalty can be proportional to the size of fast memory, but no other on-line algorithm can, in the worst case, do much better. These fundamental results have been extended in several ways, most often to include models that allow different forms of lookahead [3, 1, 9, 7]. All these works deal with the question of which buffer block to evict. In contrast, in our situation the additional question that arises is *when* to fetch a block and evict some other.

Cao et al. [4] examined prefetching from a single disk to overlap CPU and I/O operations. They defined two off-line policies called *aggressive* and *conservative*, and obtained bounds on the elapsed time relative to the optimal algorithm. We use prefetching to obtain I/O parallelism with multiple disks, and use the number of parallel I/Os (elapsed I/O time) as the cost function. The P-MIN and P-CON algorithms analyzed here generalize the aggressive and conservative policies respectively. However, while aggressive is suboptimal in the model of [4], P-MIN is proved to be the optimal algorithm in our model. The prefetching algorithm for multiple disks analyzed in [10] assumed a global buffer and read-once random data.

We also investigate semi-on-line algorithms using parallel I/O. Since prefetching involves reading blocks that are required in the future (relative to where the computation has progressed), this presents a natural situation where lookahead is necessary. This inspires us to define a lookahead version of LRU, P-LRU, in which the minimum possible lookahead of one block beyond those currently in the buffer is known for each disk.[3] We find the performance of P-LRU is independent of the number of disks, in contrast to P-CON whose performance can degrade in proportional to the number of disks.

2 Preliminaries

The computation references the blocks on the disks in an order specified by the *consumption sequence*, Σ. When a block is referenced the buffer for that disk is checked; if the block is present in the buffer it is consumed by the computation,

---

[3] Recently, Breslauer [7] arrived at this lookahead definition independently in a sequential demand context.

which then proceeds to reference the next block in Σ. If the referenced block is not present in the disk buffer, then an I/O (known as a *demand I/O*) for the missing block is initiated from that disk. If only demand I/Os were initiated, then the other disks in the system would idle while this block was being fetched. However, every demand I/O at a disk provides a *prefetch* opportunity at the other disks, which may be used to read blocks that will be referenced in the near future. For example, consider a 2-disk system holding blocks (a_1, a_2) and (b_1, b_2) on disks 1 and 2 respectively. If $\Sigma = a_1, b_1, b_2, a_2$, then strictly demand I/O would require four non-overlapped I/Os to fetch the blocks. A better strategy is to overlap reads using prefetching. During the demand I/O of block a_1, the second disk could concurrently prefetch b_1; after a_1 and b_1 have been consumed, a demand I/O for block b_2 will be made concurrently with a prefetch of block a_2. The number of parallel I/Os in this case is now two.

While prefetching can increase the I/O parallelism, the problem is complicated by the finite buffer sizes. For every block read from a disk some previously fetched block in the corresponding buffer must be replaced. For prefetch blocks the replacement decision is being made earlier than is absolutely necessary, since the computation can continue without the prefetched block. These early replacement choices can be much poorer than replacement choices made later, since as the computation proceeds, other, more useful replacement candidates may become available. Of course, once a block becomes a demand block then the replacement cannot be deferred. A poor replacement results in a greater number of I/Os as these prematurely discarded discarded blocks may have to be fetched repeatedly into the buffer. Thus there is a tradeoff between the I/O parallelism that can be achieved (by using prefetching), and the increase in the number of I/Os required (due to poorer replacement choices).

2.1 Definitions

The consumption sequence Σ is the order in which blocks are requested by the computation. The subsequence of Σ consisting of blocks from *disk i* will be denoted by Σ^i. Computation occurs in *rounds* with each round consisting of an *I/O phase* followed by a *computation phase*. In the I/O phase a parallel I/O is initiated and some number of blocks, at most one from any disk, are selected to be read. For each selected disk, a block in the corresponding disk buffer is chosen for replacement. When all new blocks have been read from the disks, the computation phase begins. The CPU consumes zero or more blocks that are present in the buffer in the order specified by Σ. If at any point the next block of Σ is not present in a buffer, then the round ends and the next round begins. The block whose absence forced the I/O is known as a *demand block*; blocks that are fetched together with the demand block are known as *prefetch blocks*. An I/O phase may also be initiated before the computation requires a demand block. In this case all the blocks fetched in are prefetch blocks. We will often refer to the I/O phase of a round as an I/O time step.

Definition 1. An *I/O schedule* with *makespan T*, is a sequence $\langle \mathcal{F}_1, \cdots \mathcal{F}_T \rangle$, where $\mathcal{F}_k$ is the set of blocks (at most one from each disk) fetched by the parallel

I/O at time step k. The makespan of a schedule is the number of I/O time steps required to complete the computation.

Definition 2. A *valid schedule* is one in which axioms A1 and A2 are satisfied.
- A1: A block must be present in the buffer before it can be consumed.
- A2: There are at most M, where M is the buffer size, blocks in any disk buffer at any time.

Definition 3.
- An *optimal schedule* is a valid schedule with minimal makespan among all valid schedules.
- A *normal schedule* is a valid schedule in which each $\mathcal{F}_k$, $1 \le k \le T$, contains a demand block.
- A *sequential schedule* is a valid schedule in which the blocks from each disk i are fetched in the order of Σ^i.

At the start of a round, let U_i denote the next referenced block of Σ^i that is not currently in the buffer of disk i. Define a *min-block* of disk i, to be the block in disk i's buffer with the longest forward distance to the next reference.

Definition 4. A P-MIN schedule $\mathcal{S} = \langle \mathcal{F}_k, k = 1, \cdots, T \rangle$, is a normal, sequential schedule in which at I/O step k, $U_i \in \mathcal{F}_k$ unless all blocks in disk i's buffer are referenced before U_i. If $U_i \in \mathcal{F}_k$, then replace the min-block of disk i with U_i.

Definition 5. A P-CON schedule $\mathcal{S} = \langle \mathcal{F}_k, k = 1, \cdots, T \rangle$, is a normal, sequential schedule in which at every I/O step k, $U_i \in \mathcal{F}_k$ provided the min-block of disk i now is the same as the min-block if U_i were fetched on demand. If $U_i \in \mathcal{F}_k$ then replace the min-block of disk i with U_i.

Definition 6. A P-LRU schedule $\mathcal{S} = \langle \mathcal{F}_k, k = 1, \cdots, T \rangle$, is a normal, sequential schedule in which at every I/O step k, $U_i \in \mathcal{F}_k$ unless all blocks in disk i's buffer are referenced before U_i. If $U_i \in \mathcal{F}_k$ then from among the blocks in the buffer whose next reference is not before that of U_i choose the least recently used block and replace it with U_i.

Notice that all three schedules defined above are normal. That is in every I/O step, one disk is performing a demand fetch and the rest are either performing a prefetch or are idle. Of these P-MIN and P-LRU are greedy strategies, and will almost always attempt to prefetch the next unread block from a disk. The only situation under which a disk will idle is if every block in the buffer will be referenced before the block to be fetched. Note that this greedy prefetching may require making "suboptimal" replacement choices, that can result in an increase the number of I/Os done by that disk. We show, however, that P-MIN policy has the minimal I/O time, and is therefore optimal.

An example with $D = 2$ and $M = 3$ is presented below. Let the blocks on disk 1 (2) be $a_i, i = 1, \cdots 4$ (respectively $b_i, i = 1, \cdots 4$). Assume that:

$$\Sigma = a_1 a_2 a_3 b_1 a_4 a_1 a_2 b_2 b_3 b_4 a_3 b_1 b_2 b_3 a_1 a_2 a_3 b_1 a_4 a_1 a_2$$

Round	Disk 1	Disk 2	CPU
1	$a_1/-$	$b_1/-$	a_1
2	$a_2/-$	$b_2/-$	a_2
3	$a_3/-$	$b_3/-$	a_3, b_1
4	a_4/a_3	b_4/b_1	$a_4, a_1, a_2, b_2, b_3, b_4$
5	a_3/a_1	b_1/b_4	$a_3, b_1, b_2, b_3, a_1, a_2, a_3, b_1$
6	a_4/a_3	$-/-$	a_4, a_1, a_2

P-MIN Schedule

Round	Disk 1	Disk 2	CPU
1	$a_1/-$	$b_1/-$	a_1
2	$a_2/-$	$b_2/-$	a_2
3	$a_3/-$	$b_3/-$	a_3, b_1
4	a_4/a_3	$-/-$	a_4, a_1, a_2, b_2, b_3
5	a_3/a_1	b_4/b_3	b_4, a_3, b_1, b_2
6	$-/-$	b_3/b_1	b_3, a_1, a_2, a_3, b_1
7	a_4/a_3	$-/-$	a_4, a_1, a_2

P-CON Schedule

Round	Disk 1	Disk 2	CPU
1	$a_1/-$	$b_1/-$	a_1
2	$a_2/-$	$b_2/-$	a_2
3	$a_3/-$	$b_3/-$	a_3, b_1
4	a_4/a_1	b_4/b_1	a_4
5	a_1/a_2	$-/-$	a_1
6	a_2/a_3	$-/-$	a_2, b_2, b_3, b_4
7	a_3/a_4	b_1/b_2	a_3, b_1
8	$-/-$	b_2/b_3	b_2
9	$-/-$	b_3/b_4	b_3, a_1, a_2, a_3, b_1
10	a_4/a_1	$-/-$	a_4
11	a_1/a_2	$-/-$	a_1
12	a_2/a_3	$-/-$	a_2

P-LRU Schedule

Fig. 1. Examples of I/O Schedules

Figure 1 shows the I/O schedule using different policies for the example sequence. The entries in the second and third columns indicate the blocks that are fetched and replaced from that disk at that round. Bold and italic faced blocks indicate a demand block, and a prefetch block respectively.

In contrast to P-MIN, the conservative strategy [4] P-CON, is pessimistic. It does not perform a prefetch unless it can replace the "best" block, so that the number of I/Os done by any disk is the smallest possible. However, while minimizing the number of I/Os done by a disk, it may result in serialization of these accesses, and perform significantly worse than the optimal algorithm. Note that in Figure 1 at step 4, no block is fetched from disk 2 by P-CON. This is because the only candidate for replacement at this time (the current min-block) is block b_1; however, if b_4 were a demand block, the min-block would be b_3.

To take advantage of a prefetch opportunity, any algorithm must know which is the next unread block in Σ^i. That is, it requires to have a lookahead upto at least one block beyond those currently in its buffer. The replacement decision made by P-LRU is based solely by examining the current blocks in the buffer, and tracking which of them will be referenced before the next unread block. From those whose next reference is not before that of the next unread block, the least recently consumed block is chosen as the replacement candidate. If P-LRU is applied to the sequence Σ used for P-MIN and P-CON, a schedule of 12 I/O steps will be obtained (see Fig. 1). In the next section, we quantify precisely the performance of these three algorithms.

2.2 Summary of Results

Let $T_{\text{P-MIN}}$, $T_{\text{P-CON}}$ and $T_{\text{P-LRU}}$ be the number of I/O time steps required by P-MIN, P-CON and P-LRU respectively. Let T_{opt} be the number of I/O steps required by an optimal schedule. Let N denote the length of Σ; also recall that

D is the number of disks and M the size of each disk buffer in blocks. The technical results of the paper are as follows.

1. The worst-case ratio between the makespan of a P-CON schedule and the corresponding optimal schedule is bounded by D. That is, at worst P-CON can serialize all disk accesses without increasing the number of I/Os performed by any disk (see Theorem 7).
2. The worst-case bound of P-CON stated above is tight. That is, there are consumption sequences, for which P-CON completely serializes its accesses (see Theorem 8).
3. P-MIN is an optimal schedule. That is it minimizes the number of parallel I/O time steps over all other valid schedules (see Theorem 11.)
4. The worst-case ratio between the makespan of a P-LRU schedule and the corresponding optimal schedule is bounded by M. That is, at worst P-LRU can inflate the number of I/Os performed by any disk to that done by a serial LRU algorithm (see Theorem 13).
5. The worst-case bound of P-LRU stated above is tight. That is, there are consumption sequences, for which P-LRU does inflate the accesses for each disk by a factor of M (see Theorem 14).

3 Detailed Results

3.1 Bounds for P-CON

We begin with a simple upper bound for $T_{\text{P-CON}}$. Let T_{MIN} denote the maximum number of I/Os done by the sequential MIN algorithm to a single disk.

Theorem 7. *For any consumption sequence,* $T_{\text{P-CON}} \leq D\,T_{\text{opt}}$.

Proof. We show that $T_{\text{P-CON}} \leq DT_{\text{MIN}} \leq DT_{\text{opt}}$. The I/Os made by P-CON to disk i for consumption sequence Σ, are exactly the I/Os done by the sequential MIN algorithm to disk i for sequence Σ^i. Hence the number of I/Os performed by any disk in P-CON is bounded by T_{MIN}. At worst, none of the accesses of any of the disks can be overlapped whence the first inequality follows. Finally, the second inequality follows since the optimal parallel time for D disks cannot be smaller than the minimal number of I/Os for a single disk. □

Theorem 8. *The bound of Theorem 7 is tight.*

Proof (sketch). Construct the following four length-M sequences, where $B_i(j)$ is the jth block on disk i. Aslo define Σ as follows, where $(u)^N$ means N repetitions of the parenthesized sequence.

$$
\begin{aligned}
\alpha_i &= B_i(2M)B_i(1)B_i(2)\cdots B_i(M-1)\\
\beta_i &= B_i(M), B_i(1)B_i(2)\cdots B_i(M-1)\\
\gamma_i &= B_i(M)B_i(M+1)B_i(M+2)\cdots B_i(2M-1)\\
\delta_i &= B_i(2M)B_i(M+1)B_i(M+2)\cdots B_i(2M-1)\\
\Sigma &= (\alpha_1\beta_1\alpha_2\beta_2\cdots\alpha_D\beta_D\gamma_1\delta_1\gamma_2\delta_2\cdots\gamma_D\delta_D)^N
\end{aligned}
$$

It can be argued that for Σ, $T_{\text{P-CON}} = M + D + (2N - 1)MD = 2NMD - (M-1)(D-1)+1$, and that the P-MIN schedule has length $2NM + D - 1$, for $M \geq D$; hence $T_{\text{opt}} \leq 2NM + D - 1$. Thus, $T_{\text{P-CON}}/T_{\text{opt}}$ is lower bounded by $\frac{2NMD-(M-1)(D-1)+1}{2NM+D-1} \geq D(1 - 1/2N)$. □

3.2 Optimality of P-MIN

In this section we show that P-MIN requires the minimal number of parallel I/O steps among all valid schedules. For the proof, we show how to transform an optimal schedule OPT with makespan L, into a P-MIN schedule with the same makespan.

Definition 9. Schedules α and β are said to *match* for time steps $[T]$, if for every t, $t \in \langle 1 \cdots T \rangle$, the blocks fetched and replaced from each disk in the two sequences are the same.

Lemma 10. *Assume that α is a valid schedule of length W. Let γ be another schedule which matches α for $[T-1]$. After the I/O at time step T, the buffers of α and γ for some disk i differ in one block: specifically α has block V but not block U, and γ has block U but not block V. Assume that V is referenced after U in the consumption sequence following the references at time $T-1$. We can construct a valid schedule β of length W, such that β and α match for $[T-1]$ and β and γ match at time step T.*

Proof. Let $T + \delta, \delta > 0$, be the first time step after T that α fetches or discards either block V or U. It can either discard block V, or fetch block U, or do both, at $T + \delta$. Construct schedule β as follows: β matches α for time steps $[W]$ *except* at time steps T and $T + \delta$.

At T, β fetches and replaces the same blocks as γ. At $T + \delta$, one of the following must occur:

- α fetches a block $Z \neq U$ and discards block V: then in the construction β will also fetch block Z, but will discard block U.
- α fetches block U and discards block Z, $Z \neq V$: then β will fetch block V and will also discard block Z.
- α fetches block U and discards block V: then β does not fetch or discard any block.

In all three cases above, following the I/O at $T + \delta$ both β and α will have the same blocks in the buffer. Since β fetches and replaces the same blocks as α for all time steps $t \geq T + \delta + 1$, the buffers of α and β will be the same for all time steps after the I/O at $T + \delta$.

At each time step t, $1 \leq t \leq W$, β will consume the same blocks as done by α at t. Clearly, β satisfies axiom A2. We show that β is a valid schedule by showing that axiom A1 is satisfied for all blocks consumed by β.

Since α and β have the same buffer before the I/O at T and after the I/O at $T + \delta$, the blocks consumed by α at any time step t, $t \leq T - 1$ or $t \geq T + \delta$ can also be consumed by β at the same time step.

Let $T', T' \geq T$ be the first time step after the I/O at T that either block U or V is consumed by α. Since α does not have U in buffer till at least after the I/O at $T + \delta$, and by the hypothesis, V is consumed *after U*, $T' \geq T + \delta$. Hence only blocks, $X \neq U, V$ can be consumed by α at time steps t, $T \leq t \leq T + \delta - 1$. Since the buffers of α and β agree except on $\{U, V\}$, X can also be consumed by β at the same time step. Since α is a valid schedule, all consumptions of β also satisfy axiom A1. Hence, β is a valid schedule. $\qquad\square$

Theorem 11. *P-MIN is an optimal schedule.*

Proof. Let Δ and Ω denote the schedules created by P-MIN and OPT algorithms respectively. We successively transform Ω into another valid schedule that matches Δ and has the same length as Ω. This will show that the P-MIN schedule is optimal.

The proof is by induction. For the Induction Hypothesis assume that at time step t, Ω has been transformed to a valid schedule Ω_t which matches Δ at time steps $[t]$. We show how to transform Ω_t to Ω_{t+1} below.

We discuss the transformation for an arbitrary disk at time step $t + 1$. The same construction is applied to each disk independently. If Δ and Ω_t match at $t + 1$, then let Ω_{t+1} be the same as Ω_t. Suppose Δ and Ω_t differ at time step $t + 1$. Then one of the following three cases must occur at $t + 1$: We consider each case separately.

- **Case 1** - Δ fetches a block but Ω_t does not fetch any block: Let Δ fetch block P and discard block Q at $t + 1$. Since Δ always fetches blocks in the order in which they are referenced, P will be referenced before Q. From the Induction Hypothesis, Δ and Ω_t have the same buffer at the start of time step $t + 1$. Hence after the I/O at $t + 1$, Δ and Ω_t differ in one block: Δ has block P but not block Q, while Ω_t has Q but not P.
  Using Lemma 10 with $\alpha = \Omega_t, \beta = \Omega_{t+1}, \gamma = \Delta, U = P, V = Q, T = t + 1$, we can construct valid schedule Ω_{t+1} that matches Ω_t at time steps $[t]$ and Δ at time $t + 1$. Hence, the Induction Hypothesis is satisfied for $t + 1$.

- **Case 2** - Ω_t fetches a block but Δ does not fetch any block: Since Δ does not fetch any block at time step $t + 1$, every block in the buffer at the start of time step $t + 1$, will be consumed before any block not currently in the buffer is referenced.
  Since Δ and Ω_t have the same buffer at the start of time step $t + 1$, if Ω_t brings in a fresh block (P) at $t + 1$, it must discard some block (Q). Since Δ chose to retain block Q in preference to fetching block P, then either Q must be referenced before P, or neither P nor Q will be referenced again.
  In the first case, using Lemma 10 with $\alpha = \Omega_t, \beta = \Omega_{t+1}, \gamma = \Delta, U = Q, V = P, T = t + 1$, we can construct Ω_{t+1}, a schedule that satisfies the Induction Hypothesis for $t + 1$.
  In the second case, Ω_{t+1} is the same as Ω_t, except that at time step $t + 1$, Ω_{t+1} does not fetch any block. Since, the buffers of Ω_t and Ω_{t+1} agree on all blocks except P and Q, and these two blocks are never referenced again,

all blocks consumed by Ω_t at a time step can also be consumed by Ω_{t+1} at that time.

- **Case 3** - Δ and Ω_t fetch different blocks: Suppose that Δ fetches block P and discards block Q at $t+1$, and Ω_t fetches block Y and discards block Z at $t+1$. Assume that $Q \neq Z$, since otherwise the buffers of Ω_t and Δ differ in just the pair of blocks $\{P, Y\}$, and we can easily construct Ω_{t+1} as before by using Lemma 10 with $\alpha = \Omega_t, \gamma = \Delta, \beta = \Omega_{t+1}, U = P, V = Y, T = t+1$. By the Induction Hypothesis, Δ and Ω_t have the same buffer at the start of time step $t+1$. Hence after the I/O at $t+1$, Δ and Ω_t differ in two blocks; specifically, $buffer(\Delta) = (buffer(\Omega_t) - \{Y, Q\}) \cup \{P, Z\}$, where $buffer(\Theta)$ is the set of blocks in the buffer of schedule Θ.

  Let $t + \delta, \delta > 1$, be the first time after $t+1$ that Ω_t fetches or replaces a block $W \in \{P, Q, Y, Z\}$. It can either discard block Q or Y, or fetch block P or Z, or some appropriate combination of these (see cases below), at $t + \delta$. Construct schedule Ω'_{t+1} as follows: Ω'_{t+1} matches Ω_t at all time steps except $t + 1$ and $t + \delta$. At $t + 1$, Ω'_{t+1} fetches P and discards Q, following the actions of Δ at this time step. Hence after the I/O at $t + 1$, $buffer(\Omega'_{t+1}) = (buffer(\Omega_t) - \{Y, Q\}) \cup \{P, Z\}$.

  At $t + \delta$, one of the following will occur:

  - Ω_t fetches block $S \notin \{P, Z\}$ and discards Q: then Ω'_{t+1} also fetches S, but discards Z. After the I/O at $t + \delta$, $buffer(\Omega'_{t+1}) = (buffer(\Omega_t) - \{Y\}) \cup \{P\}$.
  - Ω_t fetches P and discards Q: then Ω'_{t+1} fetches Y and discards Z. After the I/O at $t + \delta$, $buffer(\Omega'_{t+1}) = buffer(\Omega_t)$.
  - Ω_t fetches Z and discards Q: then Ω'_{t+1} does nothing at this step. After the I/O at $t + \delta$, $buffer(\Omega'_{t+1}) = (buffer(\Omega_t) - \{Y\}) \cup \{P\}$.
  - Ω_t fetches $S \notin \{P, Z\}$ and discards Y: then Ω'_{t+1} also fetches S, but discards P. After the I/O at $t+\delta$, $buffer(\Omega'_{t+1}) = (buffer(\Omega_t) - \{Q\}) \cup \{Z\}$.
  - Ω_t fetches P and discards Y: then Ω'_{t+1} does not fetch any block at this time step. After the I/O at $t + \delta$, $buffer(\Omega'_{t+1}) = (buffer(\Omega_t) - \{Q\} \cup \{Z\}$.
  - Ω_t fetches Z and discards Y: then Ω'_{t+1} fetches Q and discards P. After the I/O at $t + \delta$, $buffer(\Omega'_{t+1}) = buffer(\Omega_t)$.
  - Ω_t fetches P and discards block $S \notin \{Q, Y\}$: then Ω'_{t+1} fetches Y and discards block S. After the I/O at $t + \delta$, $buffer(\Omega'_{t+1}) = (buffer(\Omega_t) - \{Q\}) \cup \{Z\}$.
  - Ω_t fetches Z and discards block $S \notin \{Q, Y\}$: then Ω'_{t+1} fetches Q and discards block S. After the I/O at $t + \delta$, $buffer(\Omega'_{t+1}) = (buffer(\Omega_t) - \{Y\}) \cup \{P\}$.

Consider the consumptions made by Ω_t at time steps $T, t+1 \leq T \leq t+\delta-1$. Notice that in the consumption sequence P must precede both Q and Y, and Z must precede Q. The constraints on P follow since Δ fetches P and discards Q, and fetches P in preference to Y. The constraint on Z follows since Δ discards Q rather than Z.

We now show how to transform Ω'_{t+1} to Ω_{t+1}. If the buffers of Ω'_{t+1} and Ω_t are the same after the I/O at $t + \delta$, then let $\Omega_{t+1} = \Omega'_{t+1}$. Otherwise, the buffers must differ in either the pair of blocks $\{Q, Z\}$ or $\{Y, P\}$.

We will construct Ω_{t+1} by concatenating the prefix of Ω'_{t+1} between time steps 1 and $t + \delta - 1$ with a schedule β that will be constructed using Lemma 10, as described below.

Let α and γ be, respectively, the schedules consisting of the suffixes of Ω_t and Ω'_{t+1} for time steps greater than or equal to $t + \delta$. If at the end of the I/O at $t + \delta$, the buffers of Ω_t and Ω'_{t+1} differ in $\{Y, P\}$, then let $U = P$ and $V = Y$; otherwise, if they differ in $\{Q, Z\}$, then let $U = Z$ and $V = Q$. Applying Lemma 10 with $T = 1$, we can construct the desired sequence β. Ω_{t+1} is obtained by concatenating the prefix of Ω'_{t+1} between 1 and $t + \delta - 1$ with β.

The consumptions of blocks in Ω_{t+1} are as follows: for time steps T, $1 \leq T \leq t + \delta - 1$, the consumptions are those of Ω_t, and for $T \geq t + \delta$ the consumptions are determined by β. All consumptions from 1 till t are valid since Ω_t is a valid schedule, and Ω_{t+1} and Ω_t match for $[t]$. By construction blocks consumed after $t + \delta$ onwards are valid. We need to show that Ω_{t+1} can consume the same blocks as Ω_t at time steps T, $t + 1 \leq T \leq t + \delta - 1$. Since Ω_t does not have P or Z in buffer at the end of the I/O at $t + 1$, it can consume P or Z only after the I/O at time $t + \delta$, or later. Also, since Q and Y must be consumed *after* P, none of the blocks P, Q, Y, Z can be consumed by Ω_t before the I/O at $t + \delta$. Since after the I/O at $t + 1$, the buffers of Ω_t and Ω_{t+1} agree except on $\{P, Q, Y, Z\}$, all blocks consumed by Ω_t between $t + 1$ and $t + \delta - 1$ can also be consumed by Ω_{t+1} at that time step.

This concludes the proof. □

3.3 Bounds for P-LRU

We now obtain an upper bound on the worst-case performance of P-LRU, and show that this bound is tight. We use the following lemma whose proof is omitted for brevity.

Lemma 12. *Let S be a contiguous subsequence of Σ which references M or less distinct blocks from some disk i. Then in consuming S, none of these blocks will be fetched more than once by P-LRU.*

Theorem 13. *For all consumption sequences, $T_{\text{P-LRU}} \leq M T_{\text{opt}}$.*

Proof. Inductively assume that consumptions made in the first t steps by P-MIN can be done in Mt or less steps by P-LRU. (This holds for $t = 1$.) Let U_i be the set of references made by P-MIN at $t + 1$ from disk i. $|U_i| \leq M$, since at most M distinct blocks can be consumed from any disk at a time step of P-MIN. Since P-LRU will fetch a block of U_i at most once (Lemma 12), all P-MIN's consumptions at $t + 1$ can be done in at most an additional M steps. □

Theorem 14. *The worst-case bound of Theorem 13 is tight.*

Proof (sketch). We show the construction of Σ for two disks; a_i and b_i are blocks from disks 1 and 2 respectively. Note that after the first M accesses of Σ (common to both P-LRU and P-MIN), P-LRU makes M accesses for every access of P-MIN.
$$\Sigma = (a_1, \ldots, a_M, b_1, a_{M+1}, a_1, \ldots, a_{M-1}, b_2, \ldots, b_{M+1}, a_M, b_1, \ldots, b_M)^N \qquad \square$$

4 Discussion

In this paper we defined a model for parallel I/O systems, and answered several fundamental questions on prefetching and buffer management for such systems. We found and proved the optimality of an algorithm, P-MIN, that minimizes the number of parallel I/Os (while possibly increasing the number of I/OS done by a single disk). In contrast, P-CON, an algorithm which always matches its replacement decisions with with those of the well-known single-disk optimal algorithm, MIN, can become fully serialized in the worst case. The behavior of an on-line algorithm with lookahead, P-LRU was analyzed. The performance of P-LRU is independent of the number of disks. Similar results can be shown to hold for P-FIFO, a parallel version of FIFO with lookahead.

References

1. S. Albers. The influence of lookahead in competitive paging algorithms. In *Proc. 1st European Symposium on Algorithms LNCS, Springer Verlag, Berlin, Germany 1993*, pages 1–12, 1993.
2. L. A. Belady. A Study of Replacement Algorithms for Virtual Storage. *IBM Systems Journal*, 5:78–101, 1966.
3. S. Ben-David and A. Borodin. A New Measure for the Study of On-Line Algorithms. *Algorithmica*, 11:73–91, 1994.
4. P. Cao, E. Felten, A. Karlin, and K. Li. A Study of Integrated Prefetching and Caching Strategies. In *Proc. ACM SIGMETRICS Conference*, 1995.
5. P. M. Chen, E. K. Lee, G. A. Gibson, R. H. Katz, and D. A. Patterson. RAID: High-Performance Reliable Secondary Storage. *ACM Computing Surveys*, 26(2):145–185, 1994.
6. E. G. Coffman and P. J Denning. *Operating Systems Theory.* Addison-Wesley, Englewood Cliffs, N.J., 1973.
7. D.Breslauer. On competitive on-line paging with lookahead. In *Proc. Symposium Theor. Aspects of Computer Science*, pages 593–603, 1996.
8. A. Fiat, R. Karp, M.Luby, L. McGeoch, D. D. Sleator, and N. E. Young. Competitive Paging Algorithms. *J. Algorithms*, 12:685–699, 1991.
9. E. Koutsoupias and C. H. Papadimitriou. Beyond competitive analysis. In *Proc. 35th IEEE Symposium on Foundations of Computer Science*, pages 394–400, 1994.
10. V. Pai, A. Schäffer, and P.Varman. Markov Analysis of Multiple-Disk Prefetching Strategies for External Merging. *Theo. Comp. Sci.*, 12:211–239, 1994.
11. D. Sleator and R. E. Tarzan. Amortized Efficiency of List Update and Paging Rules. *Comm. ACM*, 28(2):202–208, 1985.

Complexity of the Gravitational Method for Linear Programming

T.L. Morin, N. Prabhu[1] and Z. Zhang.

Purdue University, West Lafayette, IN 47907.

1 Introduction

In contrast to its excellent practical performance the worst case time complexity of every Simplex algorithm that has been analyzed is known to grow exponentially with the size of the input Linear Program (LP).

Since Dantzig's Simplex method moves from vertex to adjacent vertex along edges on the polyhedron, the length of the shortest edge-path on the polyhedron between the initial and the final vertices provides a lower bound on the number of iterations made by the best Simplex algorithm. Since a given $n \times d$ LP (an LP in the form: $Max\{c^T x \mid Ax \leq b\}$ where A is an $n \times d$ matrix) could represent an arbitrary rational polyhedron of dimension at most d and with at most n facets, and since any pair of vertices of a given polyhedron could be the initial and the final vertices of Simplex computation, previous research has sought to determine $\Delta(d, n)$, the *least upper bound* on the length of the shortest edge-path between an arbitrary pair of vertices of an arbitrary rational polyhedron of dimension at most d and with at most n facets. Clearly, in order for polynomial-time Simplex algorithm to exist, $\Delta(d, n)$, must be bounded from above by a polynomial of n and d. However, the best known upper bound on $\Delta(d, n)$, due to Kalai and Kleitman is $\Delta(d, n) \leq d^{2 \log n} + 3$, which is superpolynomial in d. Hence, it is still unclear if a polynomial-time Simplex algorithm exists at all.

In the light of the as yet unsuccessful attempts to prove a polynomial upper bound on $\Delta(d, n)$, the *Gravitational Method for LP* assumes added significance. In the gravitational method, a *point particle* is dropped from an interior point of the polyhedron and allowed to move under the influence of a gravitational field parallel to the direction of the objective function in the LP. Once the particle falls onto the boundary of the polyhedron its subsequent motion is confined to be on the surface of the polyhedron and the particle always moves along the *feasible gradient* direction which is defined as follows.

Definition 1 *Given a polyhedron P, an objective function direction C, and a point $x \in P$, let $q \in P$ be the point of P such that*

$$\frac{C^T(q - x)}{\|q - x\|} \geq \frac{C^T(y - x)}{\|y - x\|}$$

for any point $y \in P$. Then the projection of C onto the direction $\frac{q-x}{\|q-x\|}$ will be called the feasible gradient *(of C) at x.*

---

[1]Supported in part by an NSF Research Initiation Award.

In each iteration, the particle moves as far along the feasible gradient of the current point as possible while remaining within the polytope.

Thus, in each iteration, particle moves from one point on the boundary to another through a k-dimensional face of the polytope, $1 \leq k \leq d - 1$. Consequently, it was believed that even if the as yet undetermined diameter function $\Delta(d, n)$ had a superpolynomial lower bound, thereby precluding the existence of a polynomial-time Simplex algorithm, the Gravitational method would still continue to be a candidate for a polynomial-time Simplex-like surface algorithm for LP since it is not constrained to move along the edges of the polyhedron. Murty and Chang report extensive computational experiments with their version of the gravitational method on problems with 10 to 400 constraints and 5 to 200 variables [1, pages 23-237]. The performance of their code was consistently superior to that of the MINOS 5.0 LP code on an average, ranging from nearly five-fold speed-up on small problems to more than two-fold speed-up on larger problems. The theoretical reasons outlined above as well as the rather impressive practical performance of the method, seemed to suggest that the gravitational method had the promise of yielding a theoretically efficient LP algorithm. In this paper however, we'll show that the Gravitational method performs exponentially many iterations in the worst-case.

The paper is organized as follows. In Section 2, we construct a class of LPs and show that Simplex algorithm using the steepest edge pivot rule performs exponentially many iterations in the worst case on our LPs. In Section 3, we show that the gravitational method has exponential time complexity in the worst case.

2 Another Bad LP for Steepest Edge Pivot Rule

In this section, we'll construct an LP for which the Simplex algorithm with steepest-edge pivot rule requires exponentially many iterations. Our construction draws from Goldfarb and Sit's construction in [3]. Due to space constraints we have omitted the proofs of all the claims in this section. The proofs closely parallel Goldfarb and Sit's arguments; hence after reading [3], the reader can verify the claims in this section quite easily. Alternatively, the unabridged version of this paper may be obtained from the second author.

Let $B = \{0, 1\}$ and $\beta \geq 3$. For $k = 1, 2, \cdots, n$, let $\pi_k : R^k \to R$ be the projection function mapping a k-dimensional vector to its kth coordinate; i.e., $\pi_k((\alpha_1, \ldots, \alpha_k)) = \alpha_k$. Further, define a function $v_k : B^k \to R^k$ inductively as follows.

1. $k = 1$:

$$v_1(0) = 0, v_1(1) = 1. \tag{1}$$

2. $k \geq 2$: For $k = 2, \cdots, n$ and $a \in B^{k-1}$, define

$$v_k(a, 0) = (v_{k-1}(a), \beta \pi_{k-1} v_{k-1}(a)), \tag{2}$$

$$v_k(a, 1) = (v_{k-1}(a), \beta^{2(k-1)} - \beta \pi_{k-1} v_{k-1}(a)). \tag{3}$$

Also, it is trivially verified (inductively) that $v_k(0,\ldots,0) = (0,\ldots,0)\ \forall k$. Hence, v_n maps $(0,\ldots,0) \in B^n$ to the origin of R^n.
Define

$$P_n = \text{conv}\{v_n(a) \mid a \in B^n\}.$$

Following Goldfarb and Sit [3, Proposition 2, (a)–(c), page 279] one can show

Lemma 1   1. $P_n \subseteq R^n$ is the solution set of the following system of linear inequalities:

$$0 \leq x_1 \leq 1,$$
$$\beta x_{j-1} \leq x_j \leq \beta^{2(j-1)} - \beta x_{j-1}, \ (j = 2, \cdots, n), \quad \beta \geq 3. \qquad (4)$$

2. At any extreme point, say $p = (x_1, x_2, \cdots, x_n)$, of P_n only one of the following equations hold $\forall i \geq 2$.

   (a) $\beta x_{j-1} = x_j$ or

   (b) $x_j = \beta^{2(j-1)} - \beta x_{j-1}$

   where $\beta \geq 3$.

3. $v_n(B^n)$ is the vertex set of P_n.

4. P_n is combinatorially equivalent to the n-cube, $0 \leq x_1, \ldots, x_n \leq 1$.

Let $a = (a_1, a_2, \cdots, a_n) \in B^n$ where a_i is the ith coordinate of a. For each vertex $v_n(a) \in P_n$, the n adjacent vertices are $v_n(a^k)$, $k = 1, 2, \cdots, n$, where

$$a^k = (a_1, \cdots, \overline{a_k}, \cdots, a_n)$$

and $\overline{a_k}$ is the binary complement of a_k.

Lemma 2

$$v_n(a^k) - v_n(a) = \mu(0, 0, \cdots, 0, \beta^{k-1}\sigma_{k,k}, \beta^k\sigma_{k,k+1}, \cdots, \beta^{n-1}\sigma_{k,n}),$$

where $\sigma_{r,s} = \sigma_{r,s}(a) = \prod_{i=r}^{s}(\overline{a_i} - a_i)$, for $1 \leq r \leq s \leq n$ and μ is a positive number that depends only on k and β.

The LP we need is,

$$\left.\begin{array}{l} \text{Maximize } \sum_{i=1}^{n} \alpha^{i-1} x_i \\ \text{S.T.} \\ \qquad 0 \leq x_1 \leq 1, \\ \qquad \beta x_{j-1} \leq x_j \leq \beta^{2(j-1)} - \beta x_{j-1}, \ (j = 2, \cdots, n). \end{array}\right\} \quad L_n(\alpha, \beta)$$

where $\alpha \geq 2, \beta \geq 3, \beta \geq \alpha$.

From Lemma 2 it follows that the directional derivative $\nabla^k(a)$ of the objective function $\sum_{i=1}^n \alpha^{i-1} x_i$, at vertex $v_n(a)$ in the direction of $v_n(a^k) - v_n(a)$ is

$$\nabla^k(a) = \frac{\sum\limits_{j=k}^n \sigma_{k,j}(\alpha\beta)^{j-1}}{\sqrt{\sum\limits_{j=k}^n \beta^{2(j-1)}}}.$$

Lemma 3 *Assume* $\alpha \geq 2$, $\beta \geq 3$ *and* $n \geq 2$. *Let* $a = (a_1, a_2, \cdots, a_n) \in B^n$ *and* $\sigma_{r,s}$ *be defined as above. Then, for any* k, $(1 \leq k \leq n)$, $\nabla^k(a) > 0$, *if and only if* $\sigma_{k,n}(a) = 1$.

Lemma 4 *Assume* $\beta \geq 3$, $\alpha \geq 2$, $\beta \geq \alpha$ *and* $n \geq 2$. *Let* $a = a_1 a_2 \cdots a_n \in B^n$ *and* $\sigma_{r,s}$ *be defined as above. Let* $m = m(a)$ *be the smallest index such that* $\sigma_{m,n}(a) = 1$. *Then, for any* $k > m$, *such that* $\sigma_{k,n}(a) = 1$, *we have* $\nabla^m(a) > \nabla^k(a)$.

Corollary 1 *Consider LP* $L_n(\alpha, \beta)$ *with* $\beta \geq 3, \alpha \geq 2$ *and* $\beta \geq \alpha$. *At any nonoptimal vertex* $v_n(a)$ *of* P_n *(the polyhedron underlying the LP) the Steepest-edge Simplex algorithm proceeds along the edge from* $v_n(a)$ *to* $v_n(a^m)$ *where* m *is the smallest index for which* $\sigma_{m,n}(a) = 1$.

Given $a = (a_1, a_2, \cdots a_n) \in B^n$, define $d_1, d_2, \cdots, d_n \in B^1$ by

$$d_j = \begin{cases} 0, & \sigma_{j,n}(a) = 1 \\ 1, & \sigma_{j,n}(a) = -1 \end{cases}$$

and

$$p(a) = \sum_{j=1}^n d_j 2^{j-1}.$$

The following Lemma is a straightforward consequence of the definitions of $\sigma_{r,s}$, $p(a)$ and a^m.

Lemma 5 *Let* $a = (a_1, a_2, \cdots, a_n) \in B^n$. *If* m *is the smallest index for which* $d_m = 0$, *then* $p(a^m) = p(a) + 1$.

From Lemma 5 and Corollary 1 of Lemma 4, we conclude that if Simplex algorithm with steepest edge pivot rule starts at the vertex $v_n(0)$ at which $p(0) = 0$, then it continues until there is no k for which $d_k = 0$, that is until $p(a) = 2^n - 1$. Therefore, from Lemma 5, the path has length $2^n - 1$ and we obtain

Theorem 1 *Simplex algorithm with steepest-edge pivot rule, if started at the vertex* $v_n(0)$ *of the LP* $L_n(\alpha, \beta)$ *with* $\beta \geq 3, \alpha \geq 2, \beta \geq \alpha$, *performs* $2^n - 1$ *iterations before reaching the optimal vertex.*

3 Main Result

The following Lemmas are needed in the proof of the main result.

Lemma 6 *Let $A_k = (a_{i,j})_{k \times k}$ be a $k \times k$ matrix, where $A_k^T = A_k$ and*

$$a_{i,j} = \begin{cases} \beta^2 + 1, & i = j, \ i = 1, 2, \cdots, k, \\ \theta_j \beta, & j = i+1, i = 1, 2, \cdots, k-1, \\ 0, & |\, i - j\, | \geq 2, \end{cases}$$

where $\theta_j = \pm 1, j = 2, \cdots, k$ and $\beta \geq 2$. Then

$$\det(A_k) = \frac{\beta^{2(k+1)} - 1}{\beta^2 - 1}.$$

Proof: The matrix A_k is in the form:

$$A_k = \begin{pmatrix} \beta^2 + 1 & \theta_2 \beta & 0 & \cdots & 0 & 0 \\ \theta_2 \beta & \beta^2 + 1 & \theta_3 \beta & \cdots & 0 & 0 \\ 0 & \theta_3 \beta & \beta^2 + 1 & \cdots & 0 & 0 \\ & \cdots & & \cdots & & \cdots \\ 0 & 0 & 0 & \cdots & \beta^2 + 1 & \theta_k \beta \\ 0 & 0 & 0 & \cdots & \theta_k \beta & \beta^2 + 1 \end{pmatrix}$$

For $k = 1$,

$$\det(A_1) = \beta^2 + 1 = \frac{\beta^{2(1+1)} - 1}{\beta^2 - 1}.$$

For $k = 2$,

$$\begin{aligned} \det(A_2) &= (\beta^2 + 1)^2 - \beta^2 = \beta^4 + \beta^2 + 1 \\ &= \frac{\beta^{2(2+1)} - 1}{\beta^2 - 1}. \end{aligned}$$

So the Lemma is true for $k \leq 2$.
Assume that the Lemma is true for all $k \leq w$, where $w \geq 2$. For $k = w + 1$

$$\begin{aligned} \det(A_{w+1}) &= (\beta^2 + 1)\det(A_w) - \beta^2 \det(A_{w-1}) \\ &= (\beta^2 + 1)\frac{\beta^{2(w+1)} - 1}{\beta^2 - 1} - \beta^2 \frac{\beta^{2w} - 1}{\beta^2 - 1} \\ &= \frac{\beta^{2(w+2)} - 1}{\beta^2 - 1}. \end{aligned}$$

By induction, the Lemma is proved. □

Lemma 7 *Given a matrix $A = (a_{i,j})_{m \times m}$, $A^T = A$,*

$$a_{i,j} = \begin{cases} \beta^2 + 1, & i = j, \ i = 1, 2, \cdots, m, \\ \theta_j \beta, & j = i+1, i = 1, 2, \cdots, m-1, \\ 0, & |\, i - j\, | \geq 2, \end{cases}$$

where $\theta_i = \pm 1$, $i = 2, \cdots, m$ and $\beta \geq 2$. Then A^{-1} exists, and if $A^{-1} = (b_{i,j})_{m \times m}$, then

$$\mid b_{i,j} \mid \leq \frac{6^m}{\beta^2}.$$

Proof: From Lemma 6 we know A^{-1} exists. One may express A^{-1} using the adjoint matrix of A, say $\overline{A}$, as $A^{-1} = \frac{1}{det(A)} \overline{A}$.

Since $\beta \geq 2$, $\mid a_{i,j} \mid \leq \beta^2 + 1$. Each entry of $\overline{A}$ is the determinant of an $(m - 1) \times (m - 1)$ matrix obtained by deleting a row and a column from A. The determinant of any matrix is the sum of terms, where each term in the sum is a product containing exactly one element from each row and column.

Since each column of A has at most *three* nonzero entries (the form of the matrix is shown in the proof of Lemma 6) the determinant of any $(m - 1) \times (m - 1)$ submatrix M of A has at most 3^{m-1} nonzero terms in the sum yielding $det(M)$. Further, since $\mid a_{i,j} \mid \leq \beta^2 + 1$, for any $(m - 1) \times (m - 1)$ submatrix M of A

$$det(M) \leq 3^{m-1}(\beta^2 + 1)^{m-1}$$

Therefore any element of A^{-1}

$$\mid b_{i,j} \mid \leq \frac{3^{m-1}(\beta^2 + 1)^{m-1}}{\frac{\beta^{2(m+1)} - 1}{\beta^2 - 1}} \leq 3^{m-1} \frac{(2\beta^2)^{m-1} \beta^2}{\beta^{2(m+1)} - 1} = 6^{m-1} \frac{(\beta^2)^m}{\beta^{2(m+1)} - 1} \leq \frac{6^m}{\beta^2}. \quad (5)$$

The last inequality follows by recalling that $\beta \geq 2$ and $m \geq 1$. $\square$

In the following discussion, we set $\alpha = 2$ and choose a $\beta \geq n^3 12^n$ in LP $L_n(\alpha, \beta)$ to get $L_n(\alpha = 2, \beta \geq n^3 12^n)$ which can be written in matrix notation as

$$\left. \begin{array}{l} Maximize \quad c^T x \\ S.T. \\ \qquad\qquad A_1 x \leq b_1 \\ \qquad\qquad A_2 x \leq b_2 \end{array} \right\} \qquad L_n(\alpha = 2, \beta \geq n^3 12^n)$$

where

$$A_1 = \begin{pmatrix} -1 & \cdots & 0 & 0 \\ \beta & \cdots & 0 & 0 \\ 0 & \cdots & 0 & 0 \\ \cdots & \cdots & \cdots \\ 0 & \cdots & -1 & 0 \\ 0 & \cdots & \beta & -1 \end{pmatrix}, \quad A_2 = \begin{pmatrix} 1 & \cdots & 0 & 0 \\ \beta & \cdots & 0 & 0 \\ 0 & \cdots & 0 & 0 \\ \cdots & \cdots & \cdots \\ 0 & \cdots & 1 & 0 \\ 0 & \cdots & \beta & 1 \end{pmatrix},$$

$$b_1 = \begin{pmatrix} 0 \\ 0 \\ \vdots \\ 0 \end{pmatrix}, b_2 = \begin{pmatrix} \delta_1 \\ \delta_2 \\ \vdots \\ \delta_n \end{pmatrix}, C = \begin{pmatrix} 1 \\ 2 \\ \vdots \\ 2^{n-1} \end{pmatrix}, \quad \text{and } \delta_i = \beta^{2(i-1)}, \ 1 \leq i \leq n$$

$$\beta \geq n^3 12^n. \quad (6)$$

Lemma 8 *The objective function direction C of LP $L_n(\alpha = 2, \beta \geq n^3 12^n)$ is not a feasible direction at any extreme point of P_n.*

Proof: From Part 2 of Lemma 1, we know that at any extreme point, say $p = (x_1, x_2, \cdots, x_n)$, exactly one of the following equations $\beta x_{i-1} = x_i$ or $x_i = \beta^{2(i-1)} - \beta x_{i-1}$ hold $\forall i \geq 2$.

The $(i-1)^{th}$ and the ith coordicates of $p + \epsilon C$ are $(p + \epsilon C)_{i-1} = x_{i-1} + \epsilon \alpha^{i-2}$ and $(p + \epsilon C)_i = x_i + \epsilon \alpha^{i-1}$, respectively, for any ϵ, $(0 < \epsilon < 1)$.

Then, if $\beta x_{i-1} = x_i$ for some $i \geq 2$,

$$\beta(p + \epsilon C)_{i-1} = \beta x_{i-1} + \epsilon \beta \alpha^{i-2} = x_i + \epsilon \beta \alpha^{i-2} > x_i + \epsilon \alpha^{i-1} = (p + \epsilon C)_i$$

for any $\epsilon > 0$. So $p + \epsilon C$ violates $\beta x_{i-1} \leq x_i$.

If $x_i = \delta_i - \beta x_{i-1}$, then

$$\delta_i - \beta(p + \epsilon C)_{i-1} = \delta_i - \beta x_{i-1} - \epsilon \beta \alpha^{i-2} < x_i < x_i + \epsilon \alpha^{i-1} = (p + \epsilon C)_i$$

for such C and any $\epsilon > 0$. So, $x_i \leq \delta_i - \beta x_{i-1}$ is violated for such direction C.

Hence, C is not a feasible direction at any extreme point of P_n. $\qquad\square$

From Lemma 8 it follows that at any extreme point of P_n, the feasible gradient direction must be along the boundary of P_n. We will now prove the main result. Theorems 1 and 2 imply that the gravitational method requires exponential time in the worst case.

Theorem 2 *At every nonoptimal vertex v of LP $L_n(\alpha = 2, \beta \geq n^3 12^n)$, the feasible gradient direction coincides with the direction of the steepest edge incident at v.*

Proof: Let v be a nonoptimal vertex of LP $L_n(\alpha = 2, \beta \geq n^3 12^n)$ and S the set of normals of the n facet-defining hyperplanes incident at v. From Part 2 of Lemma 1, it follows that the normals can be labelled $\Lambda_1, \ldots, \Lambda_n$, where Λ_i^T is either the ith row of A_1 or the ith row of A_2 (A_1 and A_2 are defined in equation (6)). Therefore, for $i, j \in \{1, \ldots, n\}$,

$$\Lambda_i^T \Lambda_j = \begin{cases} 1, & i = j = 1; \\ \beta^2 + 1, & i = j, i \neq 1; \\ \beta \text{ or } -\beta, & |i - j| = 1; \\ 0, & \text{otherwise.} \end{cases} \tag{7}$$

The hyperplane with normal Λ_i will be denoted H_i, $1 \leq i \leq n$.

Let G_v be the feasible gradient at v. Also, given any point $p \in R^n$ and a direction $q \in R^n$, let $\text{Ray}(p, q)$ be the ray from p along q. Then, we'll show that $\text{Ray}(v, G_v)$ cannot lie on the intersection of $n - 2$ or fewer of the facet-defining supporting hyperplanes incident at v. The proof is by contradiction.

If possible, let $H_{j_1}, \ldots, H_{j_r}$, be the set of all the hyperplanes containing $\text{Ray}(v, G_v)$, $1 \leq r \leq n - 2$. Set $I_1 = \{j_1, \ldots, j_r\}$ and $I_2 = \{1, \ldots, n\} \setminus I_1$.

Clearly G_v is the projection of C onto the $(n - r)$-dimensional affine subspace $H_{j_1} \cap \ldots \cap H_{j_r}$. We observe that the $(n - r)$-dimensional space $H_{j_1} \cap \ldots \cap H_{j_r}$

is orthogonal to the vectors $\Lambda_{j_1}, \ldots, \Lambda_{j_r}$. Thus if

$$M_1 = [\Lambda_{j_1} \quad \cdots \quad \Lambda_{j_r}] \quad W = \begin{bmatrix} w_1 \\ \vdots \\ w_r \end{bmatrix}$$

then

$$G_v = C - M_1 W \text{ and } G_v^T M_1 = 0. \tag{8}$$

Further for G_v to be a feasible gradient (at v), $G_v^T \Lambda_j \leq 0$, $\forall j \in I_2$. Hence if

$$M_2 = \begin{bmatrix} \Lambda_{i_1} & \cdots & \Lambda_{i_{n-r}} \end{bmatrix}, \quad i_1, \ldots, i_{n-r} \in I_2$$

then $G_v^T M_2 \leq 0$. To summarize, if $\text{Ray}(v, G_v) \subset H_{j_1} \cap \ldots \cap H_{j_r}$, $r \leq n - 2$ then

$$G_v^T M_1 = 0 \tag{9}$$
$$G_v^T M_2 \leq 0 \tag{10}$$

Noting that $G_v = C - M_1 W$, we conclude

$$(C^T - W^T M_1^T) M_1 = 0 \quad \equiv \quad W^T M_1^T M_1 = C^T M_1 \tag{11}$$
$$(C^T - W^T M_1^T) M_2 \leq 0 \quad \equiv \quad W^T M_1^T M_2 \geq C^T M_2 \tag{12}$$

Since $rank(M_1) = r$, $M_1^T M_1$ is invertible and hence

$$W^T = (C^T M_1)(M_1^T M_1)^{-1} \text{ or } W = (M_1^T M_1)^{-1} M_1^T C \tag{13}$$

Therefore equation (12)

$$W^T M_1^T M_2 \geq C^T M_2 \equiv \underbrace{M_2^T M_1}_{T} \underbrace{(M_1^T M_1)^{-1}}_{U^{-1}} \underbrace{M_1^T C}_{V} \geq M_2^T C. \tag{14}$$

We'll show that the systems (11) and (12) cannot be simultaneously satisfied (for $r \leq n - 2$) by showing that the system (14) is infeasible. Recall that if systems (11) and (12) cannot be simultaneously satisfied, then G_v cannot be the feasible gradient at v which in turn shows that the feasible gradient at v cannot be contained in $n - 2$ or fewer hyperplanes incident at v. In order to prove the infeasibility of the system (14) we first look at the structure of the matrix $M_1^T M_1$.

Structure of $M_1^T M_1$: From equation (7) $\Lambda_i^T \Lambda_j = 0$ if $| i - j | > 1$ and hence $M_1^T M_1$ is a block-diagonal matrix

$$M_1^T M_1 = \begin{pmatrix} D_1 & & & \\ & D_2 & & \\ & & \ddots & \\ & & & D_s \end{pmatrix} \quad 1 \leq s \leq r. \tag{15}$$

Each diagonal block D_i corresponds to a maximal subsequence of consecutive integers occuring in $\{j_1, \ldots, j_r\}$. For example, if

$$j_2 = j_1 + 1, \; j_3 = j_1 + 2, \; \ldots j_p = j_1 + (p-1) \text{ and } j_{p+1} > j_1 + p$$

then D_1 is a $p \times p$ matrix.
Further from equation (7)

$$D_1 = \begin{pmatrix} 1 & \theta_{1,2}\beta & 0 & \cdots & 0 & 0 \\ \theta_{1,2}\beta & \beta^2+1 & \theta_{1,3}\beta & \cdots & 0 & 0 \\ 0 & \theta_{1,3}\beta & \beta^2+1 & \cdots & 0 & 0 \\ \cdots & & & \cdots & & \\ 0 & 0 & 0 & \cdots & \beta^2+1 & \theta_{1,t_1}\beta \\ 0 & 0 & 0 & \cdots & \theta_{1,t_1}\beta & \beta^2+1 \end{pmatrix} \quad \text{if } j_1 = 1 \quad (16)$$

$$D_1 = \begin{pmatrix} \beta^2+1 & \theta_{1,2}\beta & 0 & \cdots & 0 & 0 \\ \theta_{1,2}\beta & \beta^2+1 & \theta_{1,3}\beta & \cdots & 0 & 0 \\ 0 & \theta_{1,3}\beta & \beta^2+1 & \cdots & 0 & 0 \\ \cdots & & & \cdots & & \\ 0 & 0 & 0 & \cdots & \beta^2+1 & \theta_{1,t_1}\beta \\ 0 & 0 & 0 & \cdots & \theta_{1,t_1}\beta & \beta^2+1) \end{pmatrix} \quad \text{if } j_1 \neq 1 \quad (17)$$

and for $2 \leq j \leq s$,

$$D_j = \begin{pmatrix} \beta^2+1 & \theta_{j,2}\beta & 0 & \cdots & 0 & 0 \\ \theta_{j,2}\beta & \beta^2+1 & \theta_{j,3}\beta & \cdots & 0 & 0 \\ 0 & \theta_{j,3}\beta & \beta^2+1 & \cdots & 0 & 0 \\ \cdots & & & \cdots & & \\ 0 & 0 & 0 & \cdots & \beta^2+1 & \theta_{j,t_j}\beta \\ 0 & 0 & 0 & \cdots & \theta_{j,t_j}\beta & \beta^2+1 \end{pmatrix} \quad \text{for } 2 \leq j \leq s \quad (18)$$

where all $\theta_{i,j} = \pm 1$.

Proof that system (14) is infeasible: Recall that the feasible gradient at v, G_v was assumed to lie in the intersection $H_{j_1} \cap \ldots \cap H_{j_r}$. Consider two cases: $j_1 = 1$ and $j_1 \neq 1$.

1. $\mathbf{j_1 \neq 1}$: Then the diagonal blocks $D_1, \ldots, D_s$ of U are of the form (see equations (16), (17) and (18))

$$\begin{pmatrix} \beta^2+1 & \theta_2\beta & 0 & \cdots & 0 & 0 \\ \theta_2\beta & \beta^2+1 & \theta_3\beta & \cdots & 0 & 0 \\ 0 & \theta_3\beta & \beta^2+1 & \cdots & 0 & 0 \\ \cdots & & & \cdots & & \\ 0 & 0 & 0 & \cdots & \beta^2+1 & \theta_l\beta \\ 0 & 0 & 0 & \cdots & \theta_l\beta & \beta^2+1 \end{pmatrix} \quad (19)$$

where all $\theta_l = \pm 1$. Therefore if

$$U^{-1} = \begin{pmatrix} D_1^{-1} & & & \\ & D_2^{-1} & & \\ & & \ddots & \\ & & & D_s^{-1} \end{pmatrix} = (b_{i,j})_{r \times r}$$

then from Lemma (7) $|b_{i,j}| \leq \frac{6^r}{\beta^2} \leq \frac{6^n}{\beta^2}$.

Since $T = M_2^T M_1$ (see equation (14)), every element of T is of the form $\Lambda_i^T \Lambda_j$ where $i \in I_2$ and $j \in I_1$. Hence $i \neq j$ and from equation (7) we conclude that every element of the matrix is at most β.

Finally we see that the columns of matrix M_1 being just the rows of the matrices A_1 or A_2 in LP $L_n(\alpha = 2, \beta \geq n^3 12^n)$ (see equation (6)), every element of $M_1^T = V$, is at most β.

From the three previous paragraphs we conclude that every element of the matrix $TU^{-1}V$ is at most $n^2 6^n$. Therefore every element of the vector $TU^{-1}VC$ is at most $n^3 6^n \alpha^{n-1}$. However the right hand side of the last inequality of system (14) ($TU^{-1}VC \geq M_2^T C$) is $(\beta \pm \alpha)\alpha^{i_{n-r}-2}$ (recall that $I_2 = \{i_1, \ldots, i_{n-r}\}$). Further, I_2 has at least two elements since $r \leq n-2$. Thus for the system (14) to be feasible

$$n^3 6^n \alpha^{n-1} \geq (\beta \pm \alpha)\alpha^{i_{n-r}-2} \tag{20}$$

where $\alpha = 2$ and $i_{n-r} \leq n$. If $\beta \geq n^3 12^n$ then, as we verify below, $(\alpha = 2)$

$$n^3 6^n 2^{n-1} < (\beta - 2)2^{i_{n-r}-2} \tag{21}$$

and hence for $\beta \geq n^3 12^n$, inequality (20) cannot be valid.

$$n^3 6^n 2^{n-1} \quad < \quad (\beta - 2)2^{i_{n-r}-2} \equiv \frac{n^3 6^n 2^{n-1} + 2^{i_{n-r}-1}}{2^{i_{n-r}-2}} < \beta \tag{22}$$

But since $2 \leq i_{n-r} \leq n$, setting $i_{n-r} = n$ in the numerator and $i_{n-r} = 2$ in the denominator we get

$$\frac{n^3 6^n 2^{n-1} + 2^{i_{n-r}-1}}{2^{i_{n-r}-2}} \leq (n^3 6^n + 1)2^{n-1} < (2n^3 6^n)2^{n-1} = n^3 12^n \tag{23}$$

Hence if $\beta \geq n^3 12^n$, then $n^3 6^n 2^{n-1} < (\beta - 2)2^{i_{n-r}-2}$.

2. $j_1 = 1$: Either the matrix U (see equation (15)) has only one diagonal block or more than one diagonal block. We consider the two possibilities separately.

U HAS ONLY ONE DIAGONAL BLOCK:

Then since $j_1 = 1, j_2 = 2, \ldots, j_r = r$. $I_1 = \{1, \ldots, r\}$ and $I_2 = \{r + 1, \ldots, n\}$. Hence the last row of the matrix T with elements $\Lambda_n^T \Lambda_j$, $j =$

$1, \ldots, r$ is zero since $r \le n - 2$. Therefore the last inequality of the system $TU^{-1}VC \ge M_2^T C$ (equation (14)) becomes

$$0 \ge \Lambda_n^T C \equiv 0 \ge (\beta \pm \alpha) \alpha^{n-2}$$

which is obviously impossible since $\beta > \alpha = 2$.

U HAS MORE THAN ONE DIAGONAL BLOCK:

Let D_1 in U (see equation (15)) be a $p \times p$ matrix, $1 \le p < r$. Hence we write

$$U^{-1} = \left(\begin{array}{c|c} (D_1^{-1})_{p \times p} & 0_{p \times (r-p)} \\ \hline 0_{(r-p) \times p} & D_{(r-p) \times (r-p)} \end{array} \right) \tag{24}$$

where D is itself a block diagonal matrix comprising all the diagonal blocks of U^{-1} except D_1^{-1}. The dimensions of the matrices are indicated as subscripts.

Recall that $I_1 = \{j_1, \ldots, j_r\}$ (the index set of hyperplanes incident at v) and $I_2 = \{1, \ldots, n\} \setminus I_1 = \{i_1, \ldots, i_{n-r}\}$. Since $j_1 = 1, j_2 = 2, \ldots, j_p = p$ we conclude $j_{p+1} > p + 1$. Hence, $i_1 = p + 1$. And since $r \le n - 2$ by assumption, I_2 must have at least two elements. Therefore $i_{n-r} \ge p + 2$. From equation (7) we then conclude that

$$\Lambda_{i_{n-r}}^T \Lambda_{j_1} = \Lambda_{i_{n-r}}^T \Lambda_{j_2} = \ldots = \Lambda_{i_{n-r}}^T \Lambda_{j_p} = 0.$$

Hence, the first p entries in the last row of the matrix $T = M_2^T M_1$ are zeroes. We write

$$T = \left(\begin{array}{c|c} E_{(n-r-1) \times p} & F_{(n-r-1) \times (r-p)} \\ \hline 0_{1 \times p} & H_{1 \times (r-p)} \end{array} \right) \tag{25}$$

Finally, let

$$M_1^T = V = \left(\begin{array}{c} X_{p \times n} \\ \hline Y_{(r-p) \times n} \end{array} \right) \tag{26}$$

Then

$$TU^{-1}V = \left(\begin{array}{c} ED_1^{-1}X + FDY \\ \hline HDY \end{array} \right) \tag{27}$$

Every element of Y (coming from the matrices A_1 or A_2) is at most β. From Lemma (7) every element of D is at most $\frac{6^n}{\beta^2}$. Finally, since every element of H is of the form $\Lambda_{i_{n-r}}^T \Lambda_j$, where $j \ne i_{n-r}$, every element of H is at most β (see equation (7)). Therefore every element of HDY is at most $n^2 6^n$. Hence in the last equation of the system $TU^{-1}VC \ge M_2^T C$, i.e.,

$(HDY)C \geq \Lambda_{i_{n-r}}^T C$ the left hand side is at most $n^3 6^n 2^{n-1}$ while the right hand side is $(\beta \pm 2)2^{i_{n-r}-2}$. But from equation (21),

$$n^3 6^n 2^{n-1} < (\beta - 2)2^{i_{n-r}-2} \tag{28}$$

if $\beta \geq n^3 12^n$. (As before, $2 \leq i_{n-r} \leq n$.) Hence for $\beta \geq n^3 12^n$

$$n^3 6^n 2^{n-1} \not\geq (\beta + 2)2^{i_{n-r}-2} \tag{29}$$

and the system (14) is inconsistent.

We have proved that at any nonoptimal vertex v of P_n, the projection of the objective function direction onto the intersection of $n - 2$ or fewer facet-defining supporting hyperplanes incident at v, is an infeasible direction. Therefore, the direction of the feasible gradient at any nonoptimal vertex v coincides with the direction of the steepest edge incident at v. $\qquad \square$

4 Acknowledgment

We thank Katta Murty for drawing our attention to the problem of determining the upper bound on β.

References

[1] Chang S Y and Murty K G, *The Steepest Descent Gravitational Method for LP*, Discrete Applied Mathematics, Vol. 25, 211-240, 1989.

[2] Dantzig G B, *Linear Programming and Extensions,* Princeton University Press, Princeton, NJ, 1963.

[3] Goldfarb D and Sit W, *Worst Case Behavior of the Steepest Edge Simplex Method,* Discrete Applied Mathematics 4, 367-377, 1973.

[4] Klee V and Kleinschmidt P, *The d-step Conjecture and its Relatives,* Mathematics of Operations Research 12, 718-755, 1987.

[5] Klee V and Minty G J, *How Good is the Simplex Algorithm?*, in: Inequalities III (O. Shisha, ed), Academic Press, New York, 159-175, 1972.

[6] Murty K G, *The Gravitational Method for LP*, OPSEARCH, Vol. 23, No. 4, 206-214, 1986.

Optimal and Information Theoretic Syntactic Pattern Recognition Involving Traditional and Transposition Errors[+]

B. J. OOMMEN[1] AND R. K. S. LOKE
School of Computer Science
Carleton University
Ottawa ; CANADA : K1S 5B6

ABSTRACT

In this paper we present a foundational basis for optimal and information theoretic, syntactic Pattern Recognition (PR) for syntactic patterns which can be "linearly" represented as strings. In an earlier paper Oommen and Kashyap [25] we had presented a formal basis for designing such systems when the errors involved were arbitrarily distributed Substitution, Insertion and Deletion (SID) syntactic errors. In this paper we generalize the framework and permit these traditional errors and Generalized Transposition (GT) errors. We do this by developing a rigorous model, M^{G*}, for channels which permit all these errors in an arbitrarily distributed manner. The scheme is *Functionally Complete* and *stochastically consistent*. Besides the synthesis aspects, we also deal with the analysis of such a model and derive a technique by which $\Pr[Y|U]$, the probability of receiving Y given that U was transmitted, can be computed in quartic time using dynamic programming. Experimental results which involve dictionaries with strings of lengths between 7 and 14 with an overall average noise of 70.5% demonstrate the superiority of our system over existing methods.

I. INTRODUCTION

In the field of statistical Pattern Recognition (PR), the patterns are represented using numerical features. As opposed to this, in syntactic and structural PR the classifiers are designed to be trained and tested by representing the patterns symbolically using primitive (elementary) symbols. Essentially, the system models the noisy variations of typical samples of the patterns symbolically, and these models are utilized in the training and testing phases. In statistical PR, the noisy samples from a class are modeled (either parametrically or non-parametrically) using the class conditional probability distributions. If these distributions are known we can get *information theoretic, minimum probability of error* classification [5,7].

In this paper we shall attempt to lay the foundation for information theoretic, minimum probability of error *syntactic* PR systems which permit arbitrarily distributed noise[2]. In an earlier paper, Oommen and Kashyap [25] had presented a

---

[+] Partially supported by the Natural Sciences and Engineering Research Council of Canada.

[1] Senior Member IEEE. E-mail addresses of the authors are :
    oommen@scs.carleton.ca, loke@turing.scs.carleton.ca.

[2] In this paper we shall only deal with syntactic PR of patterns which are represented "linearly" as strings. The problem of developing information theoretic classifiers for PR systems using two-dimensional structures such as trees and webs remains open. We currently have some initial results for the case of ordered tree representations.

formal basis for designing information theoretic syntactic PR systems when the errors involved were arbitrarily distributed *traditional* SID syntactic errors. In this paper we generalize the framework and permit these traditional errors and Generalized Transposition (GT) errors. To achieve this we have, as in [25], "decoupled" the occurrence of noisy observations into two distinct modules. The first of these formally describes the module which accounts for the "dictionary" of ungarbled observations and the second describes the channel which syntactically corrupts error-free signals. This approach differs significantly from the original traditional way by which the problem was approached by the pioneer Fu[3][24] and his co-authors. The latter represented the set of garbled occurrences of possible patterns using stochastic string grammars from the well-known Chomsky hierarchy, or by web or tree grammars.

The alternate strategy for designing syntactic PR recognition systems works as follows. The system has a dictionary[4] which is a collection of all the ideal representations of the objects in question. When a noisy sample has to be processed, the system compares it with every element in the dictionary. This comparison is done sequentially or using a grammatical parsing mechanism. The question of comparing patterns reduces to one of comparing their string representations, and this is typically achieved using three standard operations - Substitutions, Insertions and Deletions (SIDs). To achieve this, one usually assigns a distance for the elementary *symbol* operations, and the inter-pattern distance is computed using these.

If GTs are also considered as edit operations, the elementary distances can be assigned in a variety of ways. If $\mathbf{R}^+$ is the set of nonnegative real numbers, we define four functions $d_s(.,.)$, $d_i(.)$, $d_e(.,.)$, $d_t(.,.)$ as : (i) $d_s(.,.)$ is a map from $\mathbf{A} \times \mathbf{A} \rightarrow \mathbf{R}^+$ and is called the Substitution Map. In particular, $d_s(a,b)$ is the distance associated with substituting b for a, $a,b \in \mathbf{A}$. For all $a \in \mathbf{A}$, $d_s(a,a)$ is generally assigned the value zero, although this is not mandatory, (ii) $d_i(.)$ is a map from $\mathbf{A} \rightarrow \mathbf{R}^+$ and is called the Insertion Map. The quantity $d_i(a)$ is the distance associated with inserting the symbol $a \in \mathbf{A}$, (iii) $d_e(.)$ is a map from $\mathbf{A} \rightarrow \mathbf{R}^+$ and is called the Deletion or Erasure Map. The quantity $d_e(a)$ is the distance associated with deleting (or erasing) the symbol $a \in \mathbf{A}$, and, (iv) $d_t(.,.)$ is a map from $\mathbf{A}^2 \times \mathbf{A}^2 \rightarrow \mathbf{R}^+$ called the Transposition Map. The quantity $d_t(ab,cd)$ is the distance associated with transposing the string "ab" into "cd". This can be thought of as a "serial" operation: "ab" is first transposed to "ba" and subsequently the individual characters are substituted, and hence the name, "Generalized Transpositions".

For the case of the *SID operations*, the distance is called the Levenshtein distance if for all a, $b \in \mathbf{A}$ $d_s(a, b)$ is unity if $a \neq b$, and is zero if a =b. Furthermore, for all $a \in \mathbf{A}$, $d_i(a) = d_e(a) = 1$.

In this setting a more interesting and novel assignment of the distances is the parametric distances recently introduced by Bunke *et al* [2]. In this case, for all a, $b \in \mathbf{A}$ the *substitution* distances are :

---

[3]Prof. Fu has authored or co-authored dozens of papers and books in this area. We recommend [24] as an ideal reference for the entire field as it was studied in its infancy.

[4]A discussion of the various dictionary models encountered in syntactic PR is given in [25] and the unabridged paper [18].

$$d_S(a, b) \quad = r \quad \text{if } a \neq b$$
$$= 0 \quad \text{if } a = b.$$

The parametric string distance has some amazingly interesting properties derived in [2]. The assignment of 'r' and the application of the inter-string distance in PR has also been alluded to in [2][5].

If, however, the elementary symbol edit distances are *symbol* dependent, the distance is called the Generalized Levenshtein Distance. The question of how the elementary symbol edit distances can be assigned is relatively open; indeed, they can be parametrically assigned as in [2] or can be related to the inter-symbol confusion probabilities via their negative logarithms as recommended in [10,17,19].

Recently, the way by which the elementary distances can be assigned using the confusion probabilities has been specified for SID and GTs. The details of this are omitted now but will be briefly explained later.

The fundamental problem that arises from all the above three assignment strategies is that the final classified string obtained using such edit distances has *no probabilistic significance* except in some rather simple cases. Furthermore, if $D(X, Y)$ is the edit distance associated with editing X to Y, the latter has no explicit relationship to $\Pr(X \rightarrow Y)$ except in a few rather trivial cases.

A little insight into the problem would reveal that the fundamental question which traditional strategies avoid is one of stochastically modeling the structural behaviour of the patterns. This is the central problem studied in this paper, and as mentioned earlier, it is a generalization of Oommen and Kashyap's results for information theoretic syntactic PR models for the traditional SID errors [25]. This is done by explicitly modelling the channel as a generator whose input is a string U and whose output is the *random* string Y. The model for the channel is that Y is obtained by mutating the input string with an arbitrary sequence of string deforming operations. The operations considered in [25] were the traditional substitution, deletion and insertion errors. No such predecessor has been reported for the case of SID and GT errors and so, in one sense, the results presented here can be considered to be of a pioneering sort. The proofs of all the results claimed here are omitted in the interest of brevity. They are proved in the unabridged paper [18].

I.1 Generalized Transposition Errors

Historically, the first breakthrough in comparing strings using the three (SID) elementary edit transformations was the concept of the Levenshtein metric introduced in coding theory [13,14,19], and its computation. Although some work has been done to extend the traditional set of SID operations to include the transposition of adjacent characters [12,19] the problem of editing is relatively open for "Generalized" Transposition (GT) errors. The difference between the latter operations and those traditionally considered as "transpositions" is the following. Currently, transpositions merely imply errors caused when the order of adjacent symbols is reversed. Such an error could cause the string "develop" to be mutated into "dveelop". As opposed to this, *Generalized* Transpositions (GTs) permit these transposed symbols to be subsequently substituted. Thus, if one was working on a typewriter keyboard, this could cause the string "develop" to be mutated into "dbrelop" -- which would arise

---

[5]Incidentally, the problem of designing parametric distances for SID *and* GT errors remains open.

when the typist inherently "reversed" the two characters ("ev") due to the sequence in which the fingers touched the keyboard, but also accidentally shifted his/her hands to the right of the keyboard one key too far -- which happens all too often. Clearly, GT errors can be represented as a sequence of two substitutions ('e' $\rightarrow$ 'b', and 'v' $\rightarrow$ 'r').

This "new" GT operation is not only applicable in the recognition of typewritten and cursive script, but also has vast potential application in processing of chain-coded images and biological macromolecules [18,19].

From a systems point of view, our paper is a generalization of the classic paper of Bahl *et. al.* [1] for SID and GTs. In addition to the channel properties described in [1], ours is functionally complete even though the distribution for the number of insertions is not necessarily a mixture of geometric distributions. Finally, and most importantly, if the input is itself an element of a dictionary, the technique for computing the probability Pr[Y|U] can be utilized in a Bayesian way to compute the *a posteriori* probabilities. Thus we can obtain optimal and information theoretic, minimum probability of error pattern classification.

II. NOTATION

Let A be a finite alphabet, and A^* be the set of strings over A. $\lambda \notin A$ is the null symbol. A string $X \in A^*$ of the form $X = x_1 x_2 ... x_N$ is said to be of length $|X| = N$. Its prefix of length i will be written as X_i, where $i < N$. Upper case symbols represent strings, and lower case symbols, elements of the alphabet under consideration. The symbol $\cup$ represents the set union operator.

Let Y' be any string in $(A \cup \{\lambda\})^*$, the set of strings over $(A \cup \{\lambda\})$. The string Y' is called an output edit sequence. The operation of transforming a symbol a $\in A$ to λ will be used to represent the deletion of the symbol a. To differentiate between the deletion and insertion operation, the symbol ξ is introduced. Let X' be any string in $(A \cup \{\xi\})^*$, the set of strings over $(A \cup \{\xi\})$. The string X' is called an input edit sequence. Observe that ξ is distinct from λ, the null symbol, but is used in an analogous way to denote the insertion of a symbol. Transforming ξ to b $\in A$ will be used to represent the insertion of b.

The Output Compression Operator, C_O is a mathematical function which maps from $(A \cup \{\lambda\})^*$ to A^*. $C_O(Y')$ is Y' with all the occurrences of the symbol λ removed. Note that C_O preserves the order of the non-λ symbols in Y'. Thus, for example, if $Y' = f\lambda o\lambda r$, $C_O(Y') = $ for. Analogously, the Input Compression Operator, C_I is a mathematical function which maps from $(A \cup \{\xi\})^*$ to A^*. $C_I(X')$ is X' with all the occurrences of the symbol ξ removed. Again, note that C_I preserves the order of the non-ξ symbols in X'.

For every pair (U,Y), U,Y$\in A^*$, the finite set $\Gamma(U,Y)$ is defined by means of the compression operators C_I and C_O, as a subset of $(A \cup \{\xi\})^* \times (A \cup \{\lambda\})^*$ as:

$\Gamma(U,Y) = \{(U', Y') \mid (U', Y') \in (A \cup \{\xi\})^* \times (A \cup \{\lambda\})^*$, each (U',Y') obeys (i)-(iii)$\}$

    (i) $C_I(U') = U$; $C_O(Y') = Y$

    (ii) $|U'| = |Y'|$

    (iii)   For all $1 \leq i \leq |U'|$, it is not the case that $u'_i = \xi$ and $y'_i = \lambda$.

By definition, if (U', Y') $\in \Gamma(U,Y)$, then, Max[|U|, |Y|] $\leq$ |U'| = |Y'| $\leq$ |U| + |Y|.

The meaning of *any* pair (U', Y') ∈ Γ(U,Y) is that it can be seen to represent one way of editing U into Y, using the edit operations of substitution, deletion, insertion and transposition. The details of this are given in [18]. Certain fundamental results about the edit sets can now be derived.

Lemma O.
The number of elements in the set Γ(U,Y) is given by :

$$|\Gamma(U,Y)| = \sum_{k=\text{Max}(0,|Y|-|U|)}^{|Y|} \frac{(|U|+k)!}{(k!\,(|Y|-k)!\,(|U|-|Y|+k)\,!)} \tag{1}$$

Proof : The theorem is proved in the unabridged paper [18]. ◆◆◆

Lemma I.
The number of possible strings U', given that k insertions and h transpositions are permitted, is #(Possible U'), where,

$$\#(\text{Possible U'}) = \binom{|U|+k-h}{k}. \tag{2}$$

Proof : The proof of the result is found in [18]. ◆◆◆

Lemma II.
The number of ways h transpositions can occur in a string is $\binom{|U|-h}{h}$.

Proof : The result is proved in the unabridged paper. [18] ◆◆◆

The size of Γ(U,Y) increases combinatorially with the lengths of U and Y. Observe that we have chosen to use Γ(U,Y) to represent the set of all ways by which U can be transformed to Y, and this set represents many duplicate entries in terms of the edit operations themselves. The difference between the duplicate entries is the **sequence** in which the operations are accomplished.

III. MODELING -- THE STRING GENERATION PROCESS

We now describe the model, M^{G*}, by which a string Y is generated from an input U ∈ A*. First of all we assume that the model M^{G*} utilizes a probability distribution G over the set of positive integers. The random variable in this case is referred to as Z and is the number of insertions that are performed in the mutating process. G is called the **Quantified** Insertion Distribution, and in the most general case, can be conditioned on the input string U. The quantity G(z|U) is the probability that Z =z given that U is the input word. The sum of G(z|U) over all z must be unit. Examples of the distribution G are the Poisson and the Geometric Distributions.

The second distribution that M^{G*} utilizes is the probability distribution Q over the alphabet under consideration. Q is called the **Qualified** Insertion Distribution. The quantity Q(a) is the probability that a ∈ A will be the inserted symbol conditioned on the fact that an insertion operation is to be performed. Note that the sum of Q(a) over all a ∈ A has to be unity.

Apart from G and Q, the distribution which the model M^{G*} utilizes is a probability distribution S over A x (A∪{λ}) called the Substitution and Deletion

Distribution. S(b|a) is the conditional probability that the symbol a ∈ A in the input string is mutated by a stochastic substitution or deletion - i.e., it will be transformed into a symbol b ∈ (A ∪ {λ}). S(c|a) is the conditional probability of a ∈ A being substituted for by c ∈ A, and S(λ|a) is the conditional probability of a ∈ A being deleted. Observe that the sum of S(b|a) over all b ∈ (A ∪ {λ}) must be unity.

The final distribution which characterizes M^{G^*} is the distribution, T. The random variable in this case is referred to as H and is the number of transpositions performed in the mutation. T is called the *Quantified* Transposition Distribution, and can be conditioned on the input string U. The quantity T(h|U) is the probability that H =h given that U is the input word. The sum of T(h|U) over all h must be unity.

The distribution T also has to be conditioned on the maximum number of permissible transpositions possible, and this is dictated by the length of the input string. Clearly, T will have to satisfy a *normalizing* condition to bound h.

Using the above distributions we now informally describe the model for the garbling mechanism (or equivalently, the string generation process). Let |U| = N. Using the distribution T, the generator randomly determines the number of symbols to be transposed. Let H be the random variable denoting the number of transpositions that are to be performed in the mutation process. Based on the random choice of H let us assume that H takes the value h. The algorithm then randomly determines the positions of the transpositions among the individual symbols of U and replaces the two transposed symbols with a special character, ψ, with each ψ being associated with its respective transposed symbols. We assume that each of the possible strings are equally likely.

With the distribution G, the generator now randomly determines the number of symbols to be inserted. Let Z be random variable denoting the number of insertions that are to be inserted in the mutation. Based on the random choice of Z let us assume that Z takes the value z. The algorithm determines the position of the insertions among the individual symbols of U. This is done by randomly generating an input edit sequence U'∈ $(A ∪ \{ξ\})^*$. Note that now the input edit sequence also has the ψ symbols. Again, we assume that all the possible strings are equally likely.

Note that $C_I(U')$ is U with occurrences of ψ and that while the positions of the symbol ξ in U' represents the positions where symbols will be inserted into U, a ψ symbol represents a pair of transposed symbols which will subsequently be substituted for. First, the occurrences of ξ are transformed independently into the individual symbols of the alphabet using the distribution Q. The non-inserted and non-ψ symbols in U' are now substituted for or deleted using the distribution S. Finally, the ψ symbols are substituted for using the distribution S. Note that the ψ symbols cannot be deleted because transposed symbols can only be substituted for, as it is "meaningless" for a pair of transposed symbols to be deleted. This defines the model M^{G^*} completely. A graphical display of the model M^{G^*} is shown in Figure I. We now derive its analytic properties using the notation that |U| = N and |Y| = M.

Theorem I

Let $r = \lfloor \frac{|U|}{2} \rfloor$ and $q = \lfloor \frac{|Y|}{2} \rfloor$. Then lf the edit operations occur independently Pr[Y|U], the probability of receiving Y from M^{G^*} given that U is transmitted is :

$$\Pr[Y|U] = \sum_{z=Max(0,M-N)} \frac{G(z).(N!z!)}{((N+z)!)} \sum_{h=0}^{Max(r,q)} \frac{T(h).((N-2h)! \; h!)}{(N-h)!} \sum_{U'} \sum_{Y'} \Theta(U',Y') \qquad (3)$$

where, $\Theta(U',Y')$ is the product of the probabilities of the edit operations represented

by (U', Y'), of the form $\prod p(y'_i|u'_i)$ in which :

(a) y'_i and u'_i are the individual symbols of Y' and U' respectively,

(b) $p(y'_i|u'_i)$ is interpreted as $Q(y'_i)$ if u'_i is ξ, and ,

(c) $p(y'_i|u'_i)$ is interpreted as $S(y'_i|u'_i)$ if u'_i is not ξ.

(d) $p(y'_{i-1}y'_i|u'_{i-1}u'_i)$ represents the probability of the GT $\{(u'_{i-1} \rightarrow y'_i),$

$(u'_i \rightarrow y'_{i-1})\}$ if $u'_{i-1}, u'_i, y'_{i-1}, y'_i$ are all in A. $\qquad$ (4)

Furthermore, the probability framework is both functionally complete and consistent.

Proof : The theorem is quite intricate and is included in [18]. $\qquad \blacklozenge\blacklozenge\blacklozenge$

We now demonstrate the efficient computation of the probability $\Pr[Y|U]$.

IV. ANALYSIS : COMPUTING P[Y|U] EFFICIENTLY

Now that the "synthesis" aspect of M^{G^*} has been considered we shall show how the relatively cumbersome expression given by (3) (i.e., by Theorem I) can be computed efficiently.

Consider the problem of M^{G^*} transforming U to YConsider the problem of editing U to Y, where $|U|=N$ and $|Y|=M$. Suppose we edit a prefix of U into a prefix of Y, using exactly i insertions, e deletions, s substitutions and t transpositions. Since the number of edit operations are specified, this corresponds to editing U_{e+s+2t} $= u_1 \cdots u_{e+s+2t}$, the prefix of U of length e+s+2t, into $Y_{i+s+2t} = y_1 \cdots y_{i+s+2t}$, the prefix of Y of length i+s+2t. Let $\Pr[Y_{i+s+2t}|U_{e+s+2t} \; ; Z=i, H=t]$ be the probability of obtaining Y_{i+s+2t} given that U_{e+s+2t} was the original string, and that exactly i insertions and t transpositions took place in garbling. Then, by definition,

$$\Pr[Y_{i+s+2t}|U_{e+s+2t} \; ; Z=i, H=t] = 1 \quad \text{if } i=e=s=t=0 \qquad (5)$$

To obtain an explicit expression for the above quantity for values of i, e, s and t which are nonzero, we have to consider all the possible ways by which Y_{i+s+2t} could have been obtained from U_{e+s+2t} using exactly i insertions and t transpositions. Let r=e+s+2t and q=i+s+2t. Let $\Gamma_{i,e,s,t}(U,Y)$ be the subset of the pairs in $\Gamma(U_r,Y_q)$ in which every pair corresponds to i insertions, e deletions, s substitutions and t transpositions. Since we shall consistently be using the strings U and Y, $\Gamma_{i,e,s,t}(U,Y)$ will be referred to as $\Gamma_{i,e,s,t}$. Using (3) and (4),

$$\Pr[Y_{i+s+2t}|U_{e+s+2t} \; ; \; Z=i, \; H=t] = \frac{(s+e-2t)! \; t!}{(s+e-t)!} \; \frac{(s+e)! \; i!}{(s+e+i)!} \sum_{U'} \sum_{Y'} \Theta(U',Y'),$$

if i, e, s or t > 0

where, (U'_r, Y'_q) is the arbitrary element of the set $\Gamma_{i,e,s,t}$, with u'_{rj} and y'_{qj} as the jth symbols of U'_r and Y'_q respectively, and $\Theta(U',Y')$ is interpreted as in (4).

Let W(.,.,.,.) be the array whose general element W(i,e,s,t) is the sum of the product of the probabilities associated with the general element of $\Gamma_{i,e,s,t}$ defined as :

$$W(i,e,s,t) = 0, \qquad\qquad \text{if i,e, s or t} < 0$$

$$= \frac{(s+e-t)!}{(s+e-2t)! \; t!} \; \frac{(s+e+i)!}{i! \; (s+e)!} \Pr[Y_{i+s+2t}|U_{e+s+2t} \; ; \; Z=i, \; H=t] \text{ otherwise. } (7)$$

Using the expression for $\Pr[Y_{i+s+2t}|U_{e+s+2t} \; ; \; Z=i, \; H=t]$ we obtain the explicit form of W(i,e,s,t) for all nonnegative values of i, e, s and t as in (12).

$$W(i,e,s,t) \qquad = 1, \qquad\qquad\qquad\qquad\qquad \text{if i = e = s = t = 0}$$

$$= \sum_{U'} \sum_{Y'} \Theta(U',Y'), \qquad\qquad \text{if i, e, s or t} > 0 \quad (8)$$

where $\Theta(U',Y')$ is interpreted as in (4)

To obtain bounds on the magnitudes of the variables i, e, s and t we observe that they are constrained by the lengths of the strings U and Y. Thus, if r=e+s+2t, q=i+s+2t and R=Min [M, N], these variables will have to obey the following obvious constraints :

$$0 \le t \le \min\left[\left\lfloor\frac{N}{2}\right\rfloor, \left\lfloor\frac{M}{2}\right\rfloor\right]; \; \text{Max}[0,M-N] \le i \le q \le M; \; 0 \le e \le r \le N; \; 0 \le s \le \text{Min}[M,N].$$

Values of quadruples (i,e,s,t) which satisfy these constraints are termed as the feasible values of the variables. Let,

$$H_t = \{ j \mid 0 \le j \le \min\left[\left\lfloor\frac{N}{2}\right\rfloor, \left\lfloor\frac{M}{2}\right\rfloor\right] \}, \quad H_i = \{ j \mid \text{Max}[0,M-N] \le j \le M \},$$

$$H_e = \{ j \mid 0 \le j \le N \}, \text{ and } H_s = \{ j \mid 0 \le j \le \text{Min } [M, N] \}. \qquad (13)$$

H_i, H_e, H_s and H_t are called the set of permissible values of i, e, s and t. Observe that a quadruple (i,e,s,t) is feasible if apart from $i \in H_i$, $e \in H_e$, $s \in H_s$ and $i \in H_i$, $i + s + 2t \le M$, and $e + s + 2t \le N$. (14)

The following specifies the permitted forms of the feasible quadruples seen when transforming U_r, the prefix of U of length r, to Y_q, the prefix of Y of length q.

Theorem II.

To edit U_r, the prefix of U of length r, to Y_q, the prefix of Y of length q, the set of feasible triples is given by

{ (i, r-q+i, q-i-2t, t) | Max[0, q-r] $\le$ i $\le$ q-2t }.

Proof : The proof is included in [18]. ◆◆◆

Theorem III states the recursively computable property for the array W(.,.,.,.).

Theorem III.

Let W(i, e, s, t) be the quantity defined as in (8) for any two strings U and Y. Then, for all nonnegative i, e, s and t,

$$W(i, e, s, t) = W(i-1, e, s, t) \cdot p(y_{i+s+2t}|\xi) + W(i, e-1, s, t) \cdot p(\lambda|u_{e+s+2t})$$
$$+ W(i,e,s-1,t) \cdot p(y_{i+s+2t}|u_{e+s+2t})$$
$$+ W(i,e,s,t-1) \cdot p(y_{i+s+2t-1}|u_{e+s+2t}) \cdot p(y_{i+s+2t}|u_{e+s+2t-1}) \quad (15)$$

where $p(b|a)$ is interpreted as in (4).

Proof : The proof is quite involved and found in [18]. ◆◆◆

The computation of the probability $Pr[Y|U]$ from the array $W(.,.,.,.)$ merely involves weighting the appropriate terms by factors that are dependent only on the number of insertions and transpositions.

Theorem IV

If $h(t) = T(t) \cdot \dfrac{(N-2t)! \; t!}{(N-t)!}$, $z(i) = G(i) \dfrac{N! \; i!}{(N+i)!}$ and let $r = \left\lfloor \dfrac{|U|}{2} \right\rfloor$ and $q = \left\lfloor \dfrac{|Y|}{2} \right\rfloor$,

the quantity $Pr[Y|U]$ can be evaluated from the array $W(i, e, s, t)$ as :

$$Pr[Y|U] = \sum_{t=0}^{Max(r,q)} \sum_{i=Max(0,M-N)}^{M} h(t) \cdot z(i) \cdot W(i, N-M+i, M-i-2t, t) \quad (16)$$

Proof : The proof is included in [18]. ◆◆◆

To evaluate $Pr[Y|U]$ we make use of the fact that although the latter index itself does not seem to have any recursive properties, the index $W(.,.,.,.)$, which is closely related to it has the interesting properties proved in Theorem III. The Algorithm EvaluateProbabilities which we now present, evaluates the array $W(.,.,.,.)$ for all permissible values of the variables i, e, s and t subject to the constraints given in (14). Using the array $W(i, e, s, t)$, it then evaluates $Pr[Y|U]$ by adding the weighted contributions of the pertinent elements in $W(.,.,.,.)$ as specified above.

The evaluation of the array $W(.,.,.,.)$ has to be done in a systematic manner, so that any quantity $W(i, e, s, t)$ must be evaluated before its value is required in any further evaluation. This is easily done by considering a four-dimensional coordinate system whose axes are i, e, s and t respectively using dynamic programming as explained in [18]. Finally, the quantity $Pr[Y|U]$ is evaluated by adding the weighted contributions of $W(.,.,.,.)$ associated with the points that lie on the four-dimensional line given by the parametric equation : $i = i$; $e = N - M + i$; $s = M - i - 2t$; $t = t$

In this paper we use only two three-dimensional arrays instead of a four-dimensional array; one to keep track of the array for the current value of t and the other keep track of it for the previous one as follows. Consider the four-dimensional trellis described above. We shall successively evaluate the array Wc (for current W-array) in cubes *hyper-parallel* to the cube t = 0. Two arrays are maintained, namely,

(i) Wp: the cube *hyper-parallel* to t = 0, maintained for the previous value of t, and,

(ii) Wc: the cube *hyper-parallel* to t = 1 maintained for the current value of t.

The algorithm, given formally below, merely evaluates these two arrays in a systematic manner. Also, prior to updating Wp, its pertinent component required in the computation of $Pr[Y|U]$ is used to update the latter.

Algorithm EvaluateProbabilities

Input: The strings $U = u_1 u_2 \ldots u_N$, $Y = y_1 y_2 \ldots y_M$, and the distributions G, Q, S and a *normalized* distribution T conditioned on U.

Notation: $R = \text{Min}\left[\left\lfloor \frac{|U|}{2} \right\rfloor, \left\lfloor \frac{|Y|}{2} \right\rfloor\right]$. Also, for every symbol u_k we define d_k to be $1.0 - S(\lambda | u_k)$. The probability of substituting symbols mustbe *normalized* for transpositions.

Output: The array Wc(i, e, s, t) for all permissible values of i, e, s and t and the probability Pr[Y|U] as defined by (7).

Method:

Pr[Y|U] = 0.0

For t = 1 to R **Do**

For i =1 to M-2t **Do**

For e =1 to N-2t **Do**

For s =1 to Min[(M-i-2t) , (N-e-2t)] **Do**

$Wc(i, e, s, t) = Wc(i-1, e, s).Q(y_{i+s+2t}) + Wc(i, e-1, s).S(\lambda | u_{e+s+2t})$

$+ Wc(i, e, s-1).S(y_{i+s+2t} | u_{e+s+2t})$

$+ Wp(i,e,s). \dfrac{S(y_{i+s+2t} | u_{e+s+2t-1})}{d_{e+s+2t-1}} . \dfrac{S(y_{i+s+2t-1} | u_{e+s+2t})}{d_{e+s+2t}}$

If i=e=s=t=0 **Then** W(i, e, s) = 1.0

EndFor

EndFor

EndFor

For i =1 to M-2t **Do**

For e =1 to N-2t **Do**

For s =1 to Min[(M-i-2t) , (N-e-2t)] **Do**

Wp(i, e, s) = Wc(i, e, s)

EndFor

EndFor

EndFor

For i = Min[0 , M-N] to M **Do**

$Pr[Y|U] = Pr[Y|U] + T(t). \dfrac{(N-2t)! \, t!}{(N-t)!} . G(i). \dfrac{N! \, i!}{(N+i)!} . Wc(i, N-M+i, M-i-2t)$

EndFor

EndFor

END Algorithm EvaluateProbabilities

IV.1 An Information Theoretic Bound

Using the model M^{G*} proposed in the previous sections, it is easy to see how optimal syntactic pattern recognition can be obtained. Indeed, if the distributions G, Q, S and T are known (the inference (estimation) problem of these distributions from the set of transmitted words and their corresponding noisy versions remains open) PR can be achieved by evaluating the string U^* which maximizes the probability Pr[Y|U] over all U in the dictionary. Viewed from a Bayesian perspective this would be equivalent to computing the *a posteriori* probabilities if all the strings are equally likely *a priori*, and thus yield optimal, minimum probability of error pattern classification. In a non-Bayesian approach this represents a maximum likelihood pattern classification scheme.

We shall now conclude this section by stating the result that the PR obtained by utilizing M^{G*} is not only optimal; it also attains the information theoretic upper bound. To show this, we have used arguments analogous to those used in developing bounds for sorting and other computer science operations and compared M^{G*} with all other models which have the same common underlying garbling philosophy.

Theorem V

If transmitted symbols can only be substituted for or deleted and received symbols are obtained as either a result of transmitted symbols being substituted for or as inserted symbols, then, for specific distributions G, Q, S and T the garbling model M^{G*} attains the information theoretic bound for accuracies.

Proof : The theorem is proved in the unabridged paper [18].   ♦♦♦

V. EXPERIMENTAL RESULTS

To investigate the power of our new model (and its computation) and to demonstrate the accuracy of our new scheme in the original PR problem, various experiments were conducted. The details of the experiments are omitted here in the interest of brevity - they are found in [18]. The results obtained were remarkable. The algorithm was compared with PR results obtained with (i) Algorithm_GLD : A PR scheme which used any traditional editing [9,10,13,16,19,21,23] algorithm using symbol-dependent costs, (ii) Algorithm_LW : A PR scheme which used the acclaimed editing [12,16,19] algorithm for traditional operations and the straightforward transposition of adjacent elements, and (iii) Algorithm_OL : A PR scheme which used the recent editing algorithm published by us [17] for traditional operations and the GT operation. The dictionary consisted of 342 words obtained as a subset of the 1023 most common English words [4] augmented with words used in computer literature. The length of the words was greater than or equal to 7 and the average length of a word was approximately 8.3 characters.

From these, a set of 1026 noisy strings were generated using the method described in Section III. The conditional probability of inserting any character a $\in$ A given that an insertion occurred was assigned the value 1/26; and the probability of deletion was set to be 1/20. The table of probabilities for substitution (typically called the confusion matrix) was based on the proximity of the character keys on a standard QWERTY keyboard and is given in [18]. The percentage error was intentionally made large (70.5%) to test the algorithms for non-trivial error conditions. A subset of some of the words in S is given in [18]. Some of the words used are very similar even before garbling such as "official" and "officials"; "attention", "station" and "situation". These are words whose noisy versions can themselves easily be mis-recognized.

The four algorithms, Generalized Levenshtein Distance (Algorithm_GLD), Lowrance & Wagner's (Algorthm_LW), our recent algorithm (Algorithm_OL) and this algorithm (Algorithm_OPT_GT_PR), were tested with the set of 1026 noisy words, S. A subset of these words, their noisy versions and noise characteristics is given in Table I. The results obtained in terms of the recognition accuracy for the set are 40.94%, 81.77%, 92.40% and 98.25% respectively. Note that our scheme far outperforms the traditional algorithms - the power of our strategy is obvious !!

VI. CONCLUSIONS

In this paper we have shown that we can obtain optimal and information theoretic syntactic Pattern Recognition for syntactic patterns which can be "linearly" represented as strings. In an earlier paper [1] Oommen and Kashyap had presented a formal basis for designing such systems when the errors involved were arbitrarily distributed substitution, deletion and insertion syntactic errors. In this paper we have shown experimentally that we can generalize the framework and permit these traditional errors and Generalized Transposition (GT) errors. Experimental results which involve dictionaries with strings of lengths between 7 and 14 with an overall average noise of 70.5% demonstrate the power of our system over existing methods.

ABRIDGED LIST OF REFERENCES

1. R. L. Bahl and F. Jelinek, Decoding with channels with insertions, deletions and substitutions with applications to speech recognition, *IEEE T Inf. Th.*, IT-21:404-411 (1975).
2. Bunke, H. and Csirik, J, Parametric string edit distance and its application to pattern Recognition, *IEEE T. Syst, Man and Cybern.*, SMC-25:202-206 (1993).
3. L. Devroye, *Non-Uniform Random Variate Generation*, Springer-Verlag, (1986).
4. G. Dewey, *Relative Frequency of English Speech Sounds*, Harvard Univ. Press, (1923).
5. R. O. Duda, P.E. Hart. *Pattern Classification and Scene Analysis*. Wiley & Sons, 1973.
6. G.D. Forney, The Viterbi Algorithm, *Proceedings of the IEEE*, Vol. 61. (1973).
7. K. Fukunaga. *Introduction to Statistical Pattern Recognition*. Academic Press, 1972.
8. P. A. V. Hall and G.R. Dowling, Approximate string matching, *Comp. Sur.*, 12:381-402 (1980).
9. R. L. Kashyap and B. J. Oommen, A common basis for similarity and dissimilarity measures involving two strings, *Internat. J. Comput. Math.*, 13:17-40 (1983).
10. R. L. Kashyap and B. J. Oommen, An effective algorithm for string correction using generalized edit distances -I. Description of the algorithm and its optimality, *Inf. Sci.*, 23(2):123-142 (1981).
11. R. L. Kashyap, and B. J. Oommen, String correction using probabilistic methods, *Pattern Recognition Letters*, 147-154 (1984).
12. R. Lowrance and R. A. Wagner, An extension of the string to string correction problem, *J. Assoc. Comput. Mach.*, 22:177-183 (1975).
13. A. Levenshtein, Binary codes capable of correcting deletions, insertions and reversals, *Soviet Phys. Dokl.*, 10:707-710 (1966).
14. W. J. Masek and M. S. Paterson, A faster algorithm computing string edit distances, *J. Comput. System Sci.*, 20:18-31 (1980).
15. D. L. Neuhoff, The Viterbi algorithm as an aid in text recognition, *IEEE T. Inf. Th.*, 222-226 (1975).
16. T. Okuda, E. Tanaka, and T. Kasai, A method of correction of garbled words based on the Levenshtein metric, *IEEE T. Comput.*, C-25:172-177 (1976).

17. Oommen, B.J. and Loke, R. K. S., "Pattern Recognition of Strings Containing Traditional and Generalized Transposition Errors", *Proceedings of the 1995 IEEE International Conference on Systems, Man and Cybernetics*, Vancouver, October 1995, pp. 1154-1159.

18. B. J. Oommen and R. Loke, Information Theoretic Syntactic Pattern Recognition Involving Traditional and Transposition Errors. Unabridged version of the present paper.

19. D. Sankoff and J. B. Kruskal, *Time Warps,String Edits and Macromolecules: The Theory and practice of Sequence Comparison*, Addison-Wesley (1983).

20. R. Shinghal, and G. T. Toussaint, Experiments in text recognition with the modified Viterbi algorithm, *IEEE T. on Pat. An. and M. Intel.*, 184-192 (1979).

21. S. Srihari, *Computer Text Recognition and Error Correction*, IEEE Computer Press, (1984).

22. A. J. Viterbi, Error bounds for convolutional codes and an asymptotically optimal decoding algorithm, *IEEE T. on Information Theory*, 260-26 (1967).

23. R. A. Wagner and M. J. Fisher, The string to string correction problem, *J. Assoc. Comput. Mach.*, 21:168-173 (1974).

24. K. S. Fu, *Syntactic Methods in Pattern Recognition*, Academic Press, New York, 1974.

25. Oommen, B.J. and Kashyap, R. L., "Optimal and Information Theoretic Syntactic Pattern Recognition for Traditional Errors". To appear in the *Proceedings of SSPR-96, the 1996 International Symposium on Syntactic and Structural Pattern Recognition*, Leipzig, Germany, August 1996.

Original word (dictionary)	Noisy word	Total number of errors
administration	sdmlnistratib	5
advance	ewafawdvxsance	7
advantage	taodbivawafxe	8
affairs	kafruvkfnixsrs	9
artillery	vuaegrdtuilllordiery	11
beginning	ssbehsimgjninmmg	10
community	cmmunrieztd	6
control	fodvntopl	5
cooperation	coeopewryaueipxn	8
developed	cdexsvfesulohned	9
employed	frmmpwuoycemac	10
executive	yslxvkrcutivoe	7
facilities	fbacmwlifipeab	8
followed	zdslfdxllwkedekuid	14
sitting	psxruttoing	6
strength	mzeckieeotrenxsbth	13
striking	yvysatqrickinwet	10
victory	vbtctlavrdy	7
without	xvwigobuhnout	8

Table I : A subset of the dictionary, some noisy strings and their error characteristics.

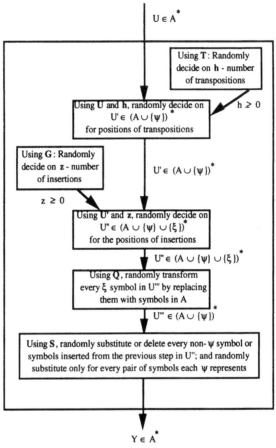

Figure I : A pictorial representation for the model for the channel. The input to the channel is the string U, and the output is the random string Y.

Minimal Relative Normalization in Orthogonal Expression Reduction Systems

John Glauert and Zurab Khasidashvili

School of Information Systems, UEA
Norwich NR4 7TJ England
jrwg@sys.uea.ac.uk, zurab@sys.uea.ac.uk *

Abstract. In previous papers, the authors studied normalization relative to desirable sets S of 'partial results', where it is shown that such sets must be *stable*. For example, the sets of normal forms, head-normal-forms, and weak head-normal-forms in the λ-calculus, are all stable. They showed that, for any stable S, S-*needed* reductions are S-normalizing. This paper continues the investigation into the theory of relative normalization. In particular, we prove existence of *minimal* normalizing reductions for *regular* stable sets of results. All the above mentioned sets are regular. We give a sufficient and necessary criterion for a normalizing reduction (w.r.t. a regular stable S) to be minimal. Finally, we establish a relationship between relative minimal and optimal reductions, revealing a conflict between minimality and optimality: for regular stable sets of results, a term need not possess a reduction that is minimal and optimal at the same time.

1 Introduction

The *Normalization Theorem* in the λ-calculus, due to Curry and Feys [CuFe58], states that contraction of leftmost-outermost redexes in a term t yields a normal form whenever t is normalizable, even if t has infinite reduction sequences.

Generalizing this fundamental theorem to a large class of Orthogonal Term Rewriting Systems (OTRSs), Huet and Lévy laid the foundations of a regular theory of 'normalization by neededness' in [HuLé91]. They proved that any term t not in normal form, in an OTRS, has a *needed* redex, and that contraction of needed redexes in a normalizable term results in a normal form. Here a redex u in t is needed if some residual of it is contracted in every normalizing reduction starting from t.

Barendregt et al. [BKKS87] applied the neededness notion to the λ-calculus, and studied neededness not only w.r.t. normal forms, but also w.r.t. head-normal forms. The authors proved correctness of the two needed strategies for computing corresponding normal forms. In [Mar92], Maranget also studied a strategy that computes a weak head-normal form of a term in an OTRS. Normalization w.r.t. another interesting set of 'normal forms', that of constructor head-normal forms in constructor OTRSs, is studied by Nöcker [Nök94].

In [GlKh94], the present authors studied normalization with respect to any desired set of final terms, and found the sufficient and necessary properties, called

---

* This work was supported by the Engineering and Physical Sciences Research Council of Great Britain under grant GR/H41300

stability, that a set S of terms must possess in order for the neededness theory of Huet and Lévy still to make sense. That is, they showed that, for any stable S, each S-normalizable term not yet in S (not in S-normal form) has at least one S-needed redex, and that repeated contraction of S-needed redexes in a term t will lead to an S-normal form of t whenever there is one. It is shown also that if a stable S is *regular*, i.e., if S-unneeded redexes cannot duplicate S-needed ones, then the S-needed strategy is hypernormalizing as well. This work was performed in the context of Orthogonal *Expression Reduction Systems* (OERSs) [Kha92], a form of higher-order rewriting which subsumes TRSs and the λ-calculus and is similar to Klop's *Combinatory Reduction systems* (CRSs) [Klo80]. Most of these results were later generalized to an abstract framework of Deterministic Residual Structures [GlKh96].

Normalization theory has developed in other directions as well, of which we mention only a few. Boudol extended neededness theory to non-orthogonal TRSs [Bou85]. Khasidashvili defined a similar normalizing strategy, the *essential* strategy, in the λ-calculus, OTRSs and OERSs [Kha88, Kha93, Kha94]. Kennaway and Sleep [KeSl89] generalized the needed strategy to Klop's orthogonal CRSs [Klo80]. Sekar and Ramakrishnan [SeRa93] study a normalizing strategy which in each multi-step contracts a *necessary* set of redexes – a set at least one member of which is contracted in every normalizing reduction. A different approach to normalization in not-necessarily orthogonal rewrite systems is developed in Kennaway [Ken89] and Antoy&Middeldorp [AnMi94]. Antoy et al. [AEH94] designed a needed narrowing strategy. Gardner [Gar94] described a *complete* way of encoding neededness information using a type assignment system. Kennaway et al. [KKSV95] studied a needed strategy for infinitary OTRSs.

The contribution of this paper is to develop a theory of *minimal* reduction in the framework of relative normalization, and to establish a relationship between minimal and *optimal* [Lév78] reductions. While normal forms are unique in an OERS, a term may have many S-normal forms. A reduction $P : t \twoheadrightarrow s$ with $t \notin S$ and $s \in S$ is said to be *S-minimal* if it does no more work than any other S-normalizing reduction $Q : t \twoheadrightarrow e$, i.e., the *residual* [Lév78] P/Q of P under Q is empty. The final term in the S-minimal reduction is said to be an *S-minimal S-normal form*.

S-minimal S-normal forms are useful to compute since any other S-normal form is accessible from the S-minimal one. Further, strategies computing partial results, such as head-normal-forms (hnfs) and weak hnfs, in the λ-calculus, usually compute minimal reductions, and it is natural to ask whether optimality can be achieved while retaining minimality. The prime example is the leftmost outermost strategy computing the so called 'principal' hnf and whnf of a λ-term, and used in constructions of Böhm [Bar84] and Lévy-Longo [Lév76, Lon83] (also called *lazy* [AbOn93]) trees, respectively. These trees represent the values of the term according to different semantics – Böhm semantics and Lévy- or lazy semantics, respectively. Clearly this property of minimality is not useful for full normal forms, but full normal forms are rarely used in the practice of functional programming.

Our research on minimal S-normalizing reductions was inspired by a result of Maranget [Mar92], stating that *standard* reductions are minimal among reductions computing a 'stable prefix' of a given term. However, we will show that standard reductions are not always minimal in the relative case, and a different concept of standard reduction is required.

The earliest minimality result was obtained by Berry and Lévy in [BeLé79], where existence of minimal reductions was shown for any (finite or infinite) approximation of a possibly infinite value of a term, for Recursive Program Schemes. Minimal reductions were used to design optimal reductions, both finite and infinite, and minimality and optimality of *outermost complete family-reductions* were shown.

In this paper, we restrict ourselves to finite reductions only. We show that, for any stable and regular S, any S-normalizable term not yet in S possesses an S-needed S-*unabsorbed* redex, and repeated contraction of such redexes gives S-minimal S-normalizing reductions. We further give a sufficient and necessary criterion for an S-normalizing reduction to be S-minimal. We show also that S-minimal reductions need not exist if S is stable but is irregular.

It has been shown in [GlKh96] that complete S-needed family-reductions, which contract all members of a *redex-family* containing an S-needed redex in a multi-step, are *optimal* in the sense that they reach S in the least number of family-reduction steps. S-needed complete family reductions, though optimal, need not be S-minimal, because they may contract S-unneeded redexes that are S-essential. It is tempting to think that contracting only the S-needed redexes of S-needed families would yield S-optimal reductions that are S-minimal at the same time. We show however that this is not the case either in the λ-calculus or in OTRSs. As a consequence, a term need not have a reduction that is both minimal and optimal at the same time.

The paper is organized as follows. In section 2, we introduce higher order rewriting through *Expression Reduction Systems*. In section 3, we review the theory of relative normalization. In section 4, we study S-minimal reductions for regular stable sets S, and in section 5, we relate relative optimal and minimal reductions. Conclusions appear in section 6. More details can be found in [GlKh94a].

2   Orthogonal Expression Reduction Systems

Klop introduced *Combinatory Reduction Systems* (CRSs) in [Klo80] to provide a uniform framework for reductions with substitutions (also referred to as higher order rewriting) as in the λ-calculus [Bar84]. Several interesting formalisms have been introduced later [Kha92, Nip93, OR94]. We refer to van Raamsdonk [Raa96] for a survey. Here we use a system of higher order rewriting, *Expression Reduction Systems* (ERSs), defined in [Kha92] (under the name of CRSs); the present formulation follows [GlKh94] and is simpler.

Definition 2.1 Let Σ be an *alphabet*, comprising *variables*, denoted by $x, y, z, \ldots$; *function symbols*, also called *simple operators*; and *operator signs* or *quantifier signs*. Each function symbol has an *arity* $k \in N$, and each operator sign σ has an *arity* (m, n) with $m, n \neq 0$ such that, for any sequence $x_1, \ldots, x_m$ of pairwise distinct variables, $\sigma x_1 \ldots x_m$ is a *compound operator* or a *quantifier* with arity n. Occurrences of $x_1, \ldots, x_m$ in $\sigma x_1 \ldots x_m$ are called *binding variables*. Each quantifier sign σ, as well as any corresponding quantifier $\sigma x_1 \ldots x_m$ and binding variables $x_1 \ldots x_m$, has a *scope indicator* $(k_1, \ldots, k_l)$ to specify the arguments in which $\sigma x_1 \ldots x_m$ binds all free occurrences of $x_1, \ldots, x_m$. *Terms* are constructed from variables using functions and quantifiers in the usual way.

Metaterms are constructed similarly from *terms* and *metavariables* $A, B, \ldots$, which range over terms. In addition, *metasubstitutions*, expressions of the form $(t_1/x_1, \ldots, t_n/x_n)t_0$, with t_j as arbitrary metaterms, are allowed, where the *scope* of each x_i is t_0. Metaterms without metasubstitutions are *simple metaterms*. An *assignment* maps each metavariable to a term over Σ. If t is a metaterm and θ is an assignment, then the θ-*instance* $t\theta$ of t is the term obtained from t by replacing metavariables with their values under θ, and by replacing metasubstitutions $(t_1/x_1, \ldots, t_n/x_n)t_0$, in the left to right order, with the result of substitution of terms $t_1, \ldots, t_n$ for free occurrences of $x_1, \ldots, x_n$ in t_0.

For example, a β-redex in the λ-calculus appears as $Ap(\lambda x\, t, s)$ in our notation, where Ap is a function symbol of arity 2, and λ is an operator sign of arity (1,1) and scope indicator (1). Integrals such as $\int_s^t f(x)\, dx$ can be represented as $\int x\, s\, t\, f(x)$ using an operator sign $\int$ of arity (1,3) and scope indicator (3).

Definition 2.2 An *Expression Reduction System* (ERS) is a pair (Σ, R), where Σ is an *alphabet*, described in Definition 2.1, and R is a set of *rewrite rules* $r : t \to s$, where t and s are closed metaterms (i.e., no free variables) such that t is a simple metaterm and is not a metavariable, and each metavariable that occurs in s occurs also in t.

Further, each rule r has a set of *admissible assignments* $AA(r)$ which, in order to prevent undesirable confusion of variable bindings, must satisfy the condition that:

(a) for any assignment $\theta \in AA(r)$, any metavariable A occurring in t or s, and any variable $x \in FV(A\theta)$, either every occurrence of A in r is in the scope of some binding occurrence of x in r, or no occurrence is.

For any $\theta \in AA(r)$, $t\theta$ is an r-*redex* or an R-*redex*, and $s\theta$ is the *contractum* of $t\theta$. We call R *simple* if right-hand sides of R-rules are simple metaterms.

Our syntax is similar to that of Klop's CRSs [Klo80], but is simpler and is closer to the syntax of the λ-calculus and of First Order Logic. For example, the β-rule is written as $\beta : Ap(\lambda x A, B) \to (B/x)A$, where A and B can be instantiated by any terms; the η-rule is written as $\lambda x(Ax) \to A$ which requires that an assignment θ is admissible iff $x \notin (A\theta)$, otherwise an x occurring in $A\theta$ and therefore bound in $\lambda x(A\theta x)$ would become free. A rule like $f(A) \to \exists x(A)$ is also allowed, but an assignment θ with $x \in A\theta$ is not. The recursor rule is written as $\mu(\lambda x A) \to (\mu(\lambda x A)/x)A$.

Below we restrict ourselves to the case of non-conditional ERSs, i.e., ERSs where an assignment is admissible iff the condition (a) of Definition 2.2 is satisfied. We ignore questions relating to renaming of bound variables. As usual, a rewrite step consists of replacement of a redex by its contractum. Subterms of a redex corresponding to metavariables are *arguments* of the redex, and the rest is its *pattern*. Note that the use of metavariables in rewrite rules of ERSs is not really necessary – free variables can be used instead, as in TRSs. We will indeed do so at least when giving TRS examples.

Notation 2.1 We use a, b, c, d for constants, t, s, e, o for terms, u, v, w for redexes, and N, P, Q for reductions. We write $s \subseteq t$ if s is a subterm of t. A one-step reduction contracting a redex $u \subseteq t$ is written as $t \xrightarrow{u} s$ or $t \to s$ or just u. We write $P : t \twoheadrightarrow s$ if P denotes a reduction of t to s. $P + Q$ denotes the concatenation of P and Q.

The definition of *orthogonality* in ERSs is similar to the case of CRSs: all the rules are left-linear and in no term redex-patterns can overlap [Klo80]. As in the case of the λ-calculus [Bar84], for any co-initial reductions P and Q, one can define in OERSs the notion of *residual of P under Q*, written P/Q, due to Lévy [Lév78]. We write $P \trianglelefteq Q$ if $P/Q = \emptyset$ ($\trianglelefteq$ is the *Lévy-embedding* relation); P and Q are called *Lévy-equivalent, strongly-equivalent,* or *permutation-equivalent* (written $P \approx_L Q$) if $P \trianglelefteq Q$ and $Q \trianglelefteq P$. It follows immediately from the definition of $/$ that if P and Q are co-initial reductions in an OERS, then $(P + P')/Q \approx_L P/Q + P'/(Q/P)$ and $P/(Q + Q') \approx_L (P/Q)/Q'$.

The following *strong Church-Rosser (confluence)* property is proved for ERSs in [Kha92]; the same result for other higher-order rewriting formats are obtained, among others, in [Klo80, Nip93, KOR93, OR94, Oos94, KvO95, Raa96].

Theorem 2.1 (Strong Church-Rosser) For any co-initial reductions P and Q in an OERS, $P + Q/P \approx_L Q + P/Q$.

3 Relative Normalization

In this section, we review some notions and results concerning relative normalization from [GlKh94].

Definition 3.1 Let S be a set of terms in an OERS R. We call a redex $u \subseteq t$ S-*needed*, written $NE_S(u, t)$, if at least one residual of it is contracted in any reduction from t to a term in S, and call it S-*unneeded*, written $UN_S(u, t)$, otherwise.

Definition 3.2 (1) We call a set S of terms *stable* iff (a) S is *closed under parallel moves*: for any $t \notin S$, any $P : t \twoheadrightarrow o \in S$, and any $Q : t \twoheadrightarrow e$ which does not contain terms in S, the final term of P/Q is in S; and (b) S is *closed under unneeded expansion*: for any $e \xrightarrow{u} o$ such that $e \notin S$ and $o \in S$, u is S-needed. (2) We call a stable S *regular* iff S-unneeded redexes cannot duplicate S-needed ones.

Below S, resp. $\mathcal{R}$, will denote a stable, resp. regular stable, set of terms in an OERS. $t \downarrow_S$ will denote that t is S-normalizable, i.e., reducible to a term in S, and similarly for $t \downarrow_{\mathcal{R}}$.

Lemma 3.1 (1) Residuals of S-unneeded redexes in a term $t \notin S$ are S-unneeded.
(2) Let $t \notin S$, $t \xrightarrow{u} t'$, $UN_S(u, t)$, and let $u' \subseteq t'$ be a u-new redex. Then $UN_S(u', t')$.
(3) Let $t \downarrow_S$, $t \xrightarrow{u} s$, $NE_S(v, t)$, and $v \neq u$. Then v has an S-needed residual in s.

Theorem 3.1 (Relative Normalization) Let S be a stable set of terms in an OERS R. Then any S-normalizable term t in R not in S-normal form contains an S-needed redex; and any S-needed reduction starting from t eventually terminates at a term in S. If S is moreover regular, then S-needed reductions starting from t eventually reach S even if finite sequences of consecutive S-unneeded steps are also allowed.

4 Minimal Relative Normalization

In this section, we define S-*unabsorbed, persistently S-needed*, and S-*erased* redexes, and show that each class is a strict subset of the next when S is regular. Further, we define S-*minimal* reductions as minimal w.r.t. Lévy-embedding $\trianglelefteq$ among co-initial S-normalizing reductions, and show that, when S is regular, an S-normalizing reduction is S-minimal iff it is S-erased, i.e., contracts only S-erased redexes. But S-erased reductions need not be S-needed, hence need not be S-normalizing, and again for regular S, we show existence of S-unabsorbed S-normalizing reductions, which are S-needed S-minimal reductions. We show that S-minimal reductions need not exist for irregular stable S. Below we always consider reductions in OERSs.

Definition 4.1 (1) We call $u \subseteq t$ *persistently S-needed* if all residuals of u are S-needed. (2) We call $u \subseteq t$ *S-erased* if u doesn't have a residual under any S-normalizing reduction. We call a reduction S-*erased* if it only contracts S-erased redexes.

Note that S-erased redexes need not be S-needed (e.g., when S is the set of normal forms and the OERS has an erasing rule, say $f(x) \rightarrow a$). The following example illustrates the introduced concepts using a simple OTRS.

Example 4.1 Consider an OTRS $R = \{f(x) \rightarrow g(x, h(x)), h(x) \rightarrow c, a \rightarrow b\}$, consider a term (redex) $u = f(a)$, and the following sets of terms in R: the set S_1 of normal forms; the set S_2 of terms not containing a redex on the left-spine (i.e., not containing a redex with the top symbol on the left-spine, when the term is considered as a tree); the set S_3 of terms not containing occurrences of a; and the set S_4 of terms not containing a on the right-spine. Then, for the two redexes u and a in $u = f(a)$, we have the following:

1. u is S_1-needed, persistently S_1-needed, and S_1-erased. $a \subseteq u$ is S_1-needed but not persistently S_1-needed (since the second residual of a in $g(x, h(a))$ is S_1-unneeded); still, a is S_1-erased.
2. u is S_2-needed, persistently S_2-needed, and S_2-erased. $a \subseteq u$ is S_2-needed but not persistently S_2-needed; and a is not S_2-erased – a has a residual along the S_2-normalizing reduction $u \rightarrow g(a, h(a)) \rightarrow g(b, h(a))$.
3. u is neither (persistently) S_3-needed nor S_3-erased. $a \subseteq u$ is S_3-needed but not persistently S_3-needed (since the second residual of a in $g(a, h(a))$ is S_3-unneeded); still, a is S_3-erased.
4. both u and a are neither (persistently) S_4-needed nor S_4-erased.

Note that S_1 and S_2 are regular stable sets; S_3 is stable but not regular, since S_3-unneeded redex u duplicates the S_3-needed redex a; and S_4 is not stable (therefore, u does not contain an S_4-needed redex).

Lemma 4.1 Every persistently S-needed redex is S-erased, but an S-erased redex, even if S-needed, need not be persistently S-needed.

Proof. ($\Rightarrow$) Let $u \subseteq t$ be persistently S-needed, and let $P : t \twoheadrightarrow s$ be S-normalizing. If u/P was not empty, then every $u' \in u/P$ (the set of P-residuals of u) would be S-needed, which is not possible since $s \in S$. ($\Leftarrow$) From Example 4.1 (cases 1 and 3).

Definition 4.2 We call $P : t \twoheadrightarrow s$ S-*minimal* if it is S-normalizing and $P \trianglelefteq Q$ for any S-normalizing $Q : t \twoheadrightarrow o$.[2] When P is S-minimal, we call s an S-*minimal* S-normal form of t.

It follows immediately from Definition 4.2 that if $t\downarrow_S \notin S$ (i.e., $t\downarrow_S$ and $t \notin S$), then t has no more than one S-minimal S-normal form s. For any other S-normal form e of t, it holds that $s \twoheadrightarrow e$. Note that the latter property of S-minimal S-normal forms cannot be taken as the definition, because in that case an S-normalizable term could have many S-minimal S-normal forms, due for example to a cycle in S, and some of them may require more reduction to be reached than others. For example, take $R = \{a \to b, b \to a, f(x) \to x\}$ and $S = \{a, b\}$. Then S is stable and regular, $t = f(a)$ has two S-normal forms from which any other one is accessible – a and b, but any reduction from t to b should contract the S-unneeded redex a in t; therefore, no reduction from t to b can be considered as S-minimal.

Lemma 4.2 Every S-erased S-normalizing reduction is S-minimal.

Proof. Let $P : t_0 \xrightarrow{u_0} t_1 \to \ldots \to t_n$ be an S-erased S-normalizing reduction, let $P_i : t_0 \xrightarrow{u_0} \ldots \to t_i$, and let $Q : t_0 \twoheadrightarrow o \in S$. By stability of S, $Q_i = Q/P_i$ is S-normalizing. Since u_i is S-erased and Q_i is S-normalizing, $u_i/Q_i = \emptyset$. Hence $P/Q = \emptyset$, i.e., P is S-minimal.

Definition 4.3 Let F be a set of redexes in t. We call P an F-*reduction* if it contracts only residuals of redexes from F and created redexes; we call such redexes F-*redexes*. Below $F \subseteq t$ will denote that F is a set of redexes in a term t, and $F(t)$ will denote the set of all redexes of t.

Definition 4.4 (1) Let $F \subseteq t$. We call a redex $u \subseteq t$ F-*unabsorbed* (in t) if $u \in F$ and, for any F-reduction P, none of the residuals of u along P appear in arguments of F-redexes; we call u F-*absorbed in* if $u \in F$ and it is not F-unabsorbed.
(2) We call $u \subseteq t$ S-*(un)absorbed* if it is $F_S(t)$-(un)absorbed, where $F_S(t)$ is the set of S-needed redexes of t. (Thus any S-unabsorbed redex is necessarily S-needed.) We call a reduction P S-*unabsorbed* if each redex contracted in it is.

Example 4.2 Consider an OTRS $R = \{a \to c, b \to b', f(c, x) \to c'\}$, and take a term $t = g(f(a, b), a)$. Then both occurrences of a in t are $F(t)$-unabsorbed in t, while b is $F(t)$-absorbed in t: we have $t \to g(f(c, b), a) = s$, and the residual of b in s is in an argument of the created redex $\dot{f}(c, b)$. If $F \subseteq t$ contains two redexes – the first occurrence of a in t and the redex $b \subseteq t$, then only the first $a \subseteq t$ is F-unabsorbed in t. If the set of terms not having a left-spine redex is taken for S, then the first a is the only S-unabsorbed redex in t (it is the only S-needed redex too).

It is shown in [HuLé91, Kha93, GlKh94] that any term t not in normal form contains an $F(t)$-unabsorbed redex (such redexes are called *external* in [HuLé91]). Now, if one ignores all redexes in t except those in $F \subseteq t$, it follows that, for any $F \neq \emptyset$, F contains an F-unabsorbed redex. And by taking $F_S(t)$ for F ($F_S(t) \neq \emptyset$ by Theorem 3.1), we obtain the following proposition:

---

[2] We prefer to use minimal rather than *least* or *smallest*.

Proposition 4.1 Every term $t \notin S$ contains an (S-needed) S-unabsorbed redex.

Below, in the study of S-minimal reductions, we will restrict ourselves to *regular* stable S. The reason is that, as shown by the following example, an S-normalizable term need not have an S-minimal reduction when S is irregular.

Example 4.3 Consider $R = \{f(x) \to g(x,x), \ a \to b\}$, take for S the set of terms not containing a as the leftmost innermost node, and take $t = f(a)$. Obviously, S is closed under unneeded expansion, because the only S-needed redex in a term $s \notin S$ is the leftmost occurrence of a in it, and S is closed under reduction. S is not regular, because the outermost redex in t is S-unneeded, while the innermost one is S-needed. Further, there are three S-normalizing reductions starting from t : $P : f(a) \to f(b)$; $Q : f(a) \to g(a,a) \to g(b,a)$, and $N : f(a) \to g(a,a) \to g(a,b) \to g(b,b)$. (There are two more reductions that continue Q and P, but we do not need to consider them because they cannot be S-minimal.) We have $P \not\trianglelefteq Q$, $Q \not\trianglelefteq P$, and $N \not\trianglelefteq P$. Hence none of the reductions is S-minimal.

Lemma 4.3 For any $P : t \twoheadrightarrow s$ with $t \notin R$, there is an R-needed Q, containing the same number of steps as that of R-needed steps in P, and an R-unneeded N, such that $P \approx_L Q + N$; and if P is R-normalizing or contains infinitely many R-needed steps, then $N = \emptyset$.

Proof. The lemma was proved in [Kha88, Kha93] for the case of essentiality in place of R-neededness. The same proof applies in this case.

Lemma 4.4 If a redex $u \subseteq t$ is R-unabsorbed, then it need not be unabsorbed in t, but it cannot be replicated and is persistently R-needed.

Proof. Let $P : t \twoheadrightarrow o$, not necessarily an $F_R(t)$-reduction. By Lemma 3.1.(3), it is enough to show that if a residual u' of u can appear inside an R-needed redex $w' \neq u'$, then w' cannot replicate u'; therefore u has at most one residual in any term of P. Suppose, on the contrary, that there is $P : t \twoheadrightarrow s$ such that a residual u' of u is inside an R-needed redex w' such that w' replicates u'; and assume that P is a shortest such a reduction, i.e., u has exactly one residual in every term in P. By Lemma 4.3, there are R-needed P' and R-unneeded P'' such that $P \approx_L P' + P''$. Since u' and w' are R-needed and P'' is R-unneeded, it follows from Lemma 3.1.(2) that there are R-needed u'' and w'' in the final term of P' such that u' and w' are the only residuals of u'' and w'', respectively. Since u is R-unabsorbed, $u'' \not\subseteq w''$. Hence u'' has exactly one w''-residual, say u^*. By Theorem 2.1, $w'' + P''/w''$ replicates u'', since w' replicates u'. Thus P''/w'' replicates u^* – a contradiction, since P''/w'' is R-unneeded by Lemma 3.1.(1), and R is regular.

Note that if S is irregular, then an S-unabsorbed redex $u \subseteq t$ need not be persistently S-needed or S-erased. Indeed, take R, S, and Q as in Example 4.3. Then a in t is S-needed, so is its leftmost residual in $g(a,a)$, but the rightmost residual is S-unneeded, and $a/Q = \emptyset$. Hence $a \subseteq t$ is not persistently S-needed or S-erased. But $a \subseteq t$ is S-unabsorbed, since the only $F_S(t)$-reduction is $N : f(a) \to f(b)$, and a is $F_S(t)$-unabsorbed in N.

Proposition 4.2 An $\mathcal{R}$-normalizing reduction is $\mathcal{R}$-minimal iff it is $\mathcal{R}$-erased.

Proof. ($\Leftarrow$) From Lemma 4.2. ($\Rightarrow$) Let $P : t_0 \overset{u_0}{\to} t_1 \to \ldots \to t_n$ be $\mathcal{R}$-minimal, and let $Q : t_0 \twoheadrightarrow o$ be $\mathcal{R}$-unabsorbed, hence $\mathcal{R}$-erased by Lemmas 4.4 and 4.1, $\mathcal{R}$-normalizing reduction; Q exists by Proposition 4.1. Further, let $P_i : t_0 \overset{u_0}{\to} \ldots \to t_i$ and let $Q_i = Q/P_i$. Since Q is $\mathcal{R}$-erased, so is Q_i, and Q_i is $\mathcal{R}$-normalizing by the closure of $\mathcal{R}$ under parallel moves. Hence Q_i is $\mathcal{R}$-minimal by Lemma 4.2. Since P is $\mathcal{R}$-minimal too, $u_i/Q_i = \emptyset$ for every i. But for every $\mathcal{R}$-normalizing reduction $Q_i' : t_i \twoheadrightarrow o_i$, it holds that $Q_i \trianglelefteq Q_i'$ (since Q_i is $\mathcal{R}$-minimal). Hence $u_i/Q_i' = \emptyset$, i.e., u_i is $\mathcal{R}$-erased, and P is $\mathcal{R}$-erased too.

Remark 4.1 It can be shown that a redex $u \subseteq t \notin \mathcal{R}$ is $\mathcal{R}$-erased iff every residual of u (in particular, u itself) along any reductions starting from t is either $\mathcal{R}$-needed or $\mathcal{R}$-*inessential*. Here a subterm $s \subseteq t$ is S-inessential iff there is no S-normalizing P starting from t such that s has a P-*descendant*. The latter notion is a refinement of that of residual, allowing tracing of contracted redexes – the descendant of a contracted redex is its contractum, while it does not have residuals [Kha92]. One can show also that a redex $u \subseteq t \downarrow_{\mathcal{R}} \notin \mathcal{R}$ is $\mathcal{R}$-inessential iff it is $\mathcal{R}$-unneeded and $\mathcal{R}$-erased. Note that the latter proposition can be taken as the definition of S-(in)essentiality, thus avoiding the use of the descendant concept, and the above characterization of $\mathcal{R}$-erased redexes follows logically. See [GlKh94a] for details.

Now we are ready to prove the main result of the paper.

Theorem 4.1 (Minimal Relative Normalization) Let $\mathcal{R}$ be a regular stable set of terms in an OERS, and let $t \downarrow_{\mathcal{R}} \notin \mathcal{R}$. Then repeated contraction of $\mathcal{R}$-needed $\mathcal{R}$-erased redexes in t yields an $\mathcal{R}$-minimal $\mathcal{R}$-normalizing reduction, even if a finite number of $\mathcal{R}$-unneeded $\mathcal{R}$-erased, and only such, redexes are also contracted. In particular, any $t \downarrow_{\mathcal{R}} \notin \mathcal{R}$ has an $\mathcal{R}$-unabsorbed $\mathcal{R}$-minimal reduction, which is $\mathcal{R}$-needed.

Proof. By Proposition 4.1, any $t \downarrow_{\mathcal{R}} \notin \mathcal{R}$ has an $\mathcal{R}$-unabsorbed redex, which is $\mathcal{R}$-needed and $\mathcal{R}$-erased by Lemma 4.4 and Lemma 4.1. It remains to apply Theorem 3.1 and Proposition 4.2.

Remark 4.2 (Relative Standardization) Note that $\mathcal{R}$-normalizing standard reductions (in the sense of [Bar84, Klo80], or in the sense of [GLM92], where left-to-right order of contracted redexes is not required) need not be $\mathcal{R}$-needed. Indeed, take for example $R = \{f(x) \to g(x, x), a \to b\}$, and take for $\mathcal{R}$ the set of terms not containing a redex on the right-spine; then $\mathcal{R}$ is regular, $f(a) \to g(a, a) \to g(b, a) \to g(b, b)$ is standard and $\mathcal{R}$-normalizing, but the second step is $\mathcal{R}$-unneeded. Therefore, we should take standard $\mathcal{R}$-minimal reductions for the $\mathcal{R}$-*standard* $\mathcal{R}$-*normalizing* reductions. It is not difficult to see that $\mathcal{R}$-unabsorbed $\mathcal{R}$-normalizing reductions are then $\mathcal{R}$-standard in the sense of [GLM92], and the left-to-right order of contraction of $\mathcal{R}$-unabsorbed redexes can also be achieved by Klop's standardization theorem [Klo80], which is valid for OERSs as well.

5 Relative optimal versus minimal reductions

Lévy introduced the notion of *redex family* in the λ-calculus, and showed that any multi-step reduction that in each multi-step contracts all redexes in a needed family (i.e., a family containing a needed redex) is optimal in the sense that it reaches a normal form (when it exists) in a minimal number of family-reduction steps [Lév78, Lév80]. This theory has been generalized to OTRSs, Interaction Systems, and higher-order rewrite systems [Mar91, AsLa93, Oos96], and to the case of relative normalization, to all Deterministic Family Structures [GlKh96]. The latter are abstract rewrite systems with axiomatized residual and family relations, and model family concepts in all orthogonal rewrite systems, OERSs among them. Redex families consist of 'redexes with the same origin', and here we only need to know that, in particular, all residuals of the same redex are in the same family.

It is easy to see that any $\mathcal{R}$-needed family-reduction that in each step contracts all the $\mathcal{R}$-needed redexes of some family, but does not necessarily contract its $\mathcal{R}$-unneeded members, is still optimal. We will call such reductions $\mathcal{R}$-needed *semi-complete* family-reductions. It follows from Proposition 4.2 that such a reduction is $\mathcal{R}$-minimal as well iff every $\mathcal{R}$-needed redex contracted in it is $\mathcal{R}$-erased. For example, $g(a) \to f(a, a) \to f(b, a)$ is both $\mathcal{R}$-minimal and $\mathcal{R}$-optimal semi-complete family-reduction in $R = \{g(x) \to f(x, x), a \to b\}$, where $\mathcal{R}$ is the set of terms not containing left-spine redexes. However, the following examples show that a term either in an OTRS or in the λ-calculus need not possess an $\mathcal{R}$-minimal $\mathcal{R}$-optimal family-reduction.

Example 5.1 Consider the OTRS $R = \{f(x) \to g(x, x), g(b, x) \to h(x, x), a \to b\}$, and take for $\mathcal{R}$ the set of terms not containing left-spine redexes. One can show that $\mathcal{R}$ is regular. Now $P : f(a) \to g(a, a) \to g(b, a) \to h(a, a) \to h(b, a)$ is an $\mathcal{R}$-minimal reduction, but $h(b, a)$ is not reachable by an $\mathcal{R}$-needed semi-complete family reduction. If the first step reduces a then we reach the $\mathcal{R}$-normal form $h(b, b)$ which is not $\mathcal{R}$-minimal. Hence, in order to reduce $f(a)$ to $h(b, a)$, one should delay contraction of the $\mathcal{R}$-needed occurrences of a (which all belong to the same family). So $f(a) \to g(a, a)$ must be the first step. In $g(a, a)$, both occurrences of a are $\mathcal{R}$-needed, but their contraction makes $h(b, a)$ unreachable. Thus there is no $\mathcal{R}$-minimal reduction that is $\mathcal{R}$-optimal at the same time.

Example 5.2 Take for $\mathcal{R}$ the set of λ-terms in head-normal form, which is regular, and take $t = (\lambda x.xx)u$, where $u = (\lambda y.\lambda z.zvz)w$, and y, z, v and w are different variables. Then $P : t \to uu \to (\lambda z.zvz)u \to uvu \to (\lambda z.zvz)vu \to vvvu = e$ is an $\mathcal{R}$-minimal reduction. In order to reach e from t by a semi-complete $\mathcal{R}$-needed family reduction, one should delay contraction of $\mathcal{R}$-needed redexes in the family of u. So the outermost redex in t must be contracted first. In the obtained term $o = uu$, both occurrences of u are $\mathcal{R}$-needed, and their contraction would make e unreachable – there is no occurrence of w in $(\lambda z.zvz)(\lambda z.zvz)$.

6 Conclusions and Future Work

We have studied minimal normalization relative to regular stable sets $\mathcal{R}$ of final terms, and have shown that $\mathcal{R}$-normalizing reductions that are both minimal and optimal need not exist for an $\mathcal{R}$-normalizable term t, despite the fact that t possesses minimal as well as optimal $\mathcal{R}$-normalizing reductions. These results were obtained for orthogonal ERSs, but are valid for Klop's CRSs and for context-sensitive conditional OERSs [KvO95], and therefore apply to numerous typed λ-calculi as well. We expect that the results remain valid for other systems of higher-order rewriting too.

Similar questions arise for infinite reductions. Stability and regularity of sets of finite and infinite reductions must be defined first, and we expect a strong connection between this concept and the concept of stability in interpretations [BeLé79].

As already mentioned in [GlKh94], it would be interesting to investigate strong sequentiality and strictness analyses for arbitrary stable sets of normal forms. Investigation of minimal relative normalization in an abstract setting seems also feasible and is useful.

Acknowledgments We thank J. R. Kennaway, J.-J. Lévy, L. Maranget, V. van Oostrom and F. van Raamsdonk for useful comments.

References

[AbOn93] Abramsky S., Ong C.-H. L. Full abstraction in the lazy lambda calculus. Inf.& Comp., 105:159-267, 1993.

[AEH94] Antoy S., Echahed R., Hanus M. A needed narrowing strategy. In: Proc. of POPL'94, Portland, Oregon, 1994.

[AnMi94] Antoy S. and Middeldorp A. A Sequential Reduction Strategy. In Proc. of ALP'94, Springer LNCS, vol. 850, p. 168-185, 1994.

[AsLa93] Asperti A., Laneve C. Interaction Systems I: the theory of optimal reductions. MSCS, 11:1-48, Cambridge University Press, 1993.

[Bar84] Barendregt H. P. The Lambda Calculus, its Syntax and Semantics. North-Holland, 1984.

[BKKS87] Barendregt H. P., Kennaway J. R., Klop J. W., Sleep M. R. Needed Reduction and spine strategies for the lambda calculus. Inf.& Comp., 75(3):191-231, 1987.

[BeLé79] Berry G., Lévy J.-J. Minimal and optimal computations of recursive programs. JACM 26, 1979, p. 148-175.

[Bou85] Boudol G. Computational semantics of term rewriting systems. In: Algebraic methods in semantics. Nivat M., Reynolds J.C., eds. Cambr. Univ. Press, 1985, p. 169-236.

[CuFe58] Curry H. B., Feys R. Combinatory Logic. vol. 1, North-Holland, 1958.

[Gar94] Gardner P. Discovering needed reductions using type theory. In: Proc. of TACS'94, Springer LNCS, v. 789, M. Hagiya, J. C. Mitchell, eds. Sendai, 1994, p. 555-574.

[GlKh94] Glauert J.R.W., Khasidashvili Z. Relative Normalization in Orthogonal Expression Reduction Systems. In: Proc. of CTRS'94, Springer LNCS, vol. 968, N. Dershowitz, N. Lindenstrauss, eds. Jerusalem, 1994, p. 144-165.

[GlKh94a] Glauert J.R.W., Khasidashvili Z. Minimal and optimal relative normalization in Expression Reduction Systems. Report SYS-C94-06, UEA, Norwich, 1994.

[GlKh96] Glauert J.R.W., Khasidashvili Z. Relative normalization in deterministic residual structures. In: Proc. of CAAP'96, Springer LNCS, vol. 1059, H. Kirchner, ed. 1996, p. 180-195.

[GLM92] Gonthier G., Lévy J.-J., Melliès P.-A. An abstract Standardisation theorem. In: LICS'92, p. 72-81.

[HuLé91] Huet G., Lévy J.-J. Computations in Orthogonal Rewriting Systems. In: Computational Logic, Essays in Honor of Alan Robinson, J.-L. Lassez and G. Plotkin, eds. MIT Press, 1991.

[Ken89] Kennaway J.R. Sequential evaluation strategy for parallel-or and related reduction systems. Annals of Pure and Applied Logic, 43:31-56, 1989.

[KeSl89] Kennaway J. R., Sleep M. R. Neededness is hypernormalizing in regular combinatory reduction systems. Preprint, University of East Anglia, Norwich, 1989.

[KKSV95] Kennaway J. R., Klop J. W., Sleep M. R, de Vries F.-J. Transfinite reductions in orthogonal term rewriting. Information and Computation, 119(1):18-38, 1995.

[Kha88] Khasidashvili Z. β-reductions and β-developments of λ-terms with the least number of steps. In: Proc. of the Int. Conference on Computer Logic COLOG'88, Tallinn 1988, Springer LNCS, v. 417, P. Martin-Löf and G. Mints, eds. 1990, p. 105-111.

[Kha92] Khasidashvili Z. The Church-Rosser theorem in Orthogonal Combinatory Reduction Systems. Report 1825, INRIA Rocquencourt, 1992.

[Kha93] Khasidashvili Z. Optimal normalization in orthogonal term rewriting systems. In: Proc. of RTA'93, Springer LNCS, vol. 690, C. Kirchner, ed. Montreal, 1993, p. 243-258.

[Kha94] Khasidashvili Z. On higher order recursive program schemes. In: Proc. of CAAP'94, Springer LNCS, vol. 787, S. Tison, ed. Edinburgh, 1994, p. 172-186.

[KvO95] Khasidashvili Z., van Oostrom V. Context-sensitive conditional expression reduction systems. Electronic Notes in Theoretical Computer Science, vol. 2, A. Corradini, U. Montanari, eds. Elsevier, 1995, p. 141-150.

[Klo80] Klop J. W. Combinatory Reduction Systems. Mathematical Centre Tracts n. 127, CWI, Amsterdam, 1980.

[KOR93] Klop J. W., van Oostrom V., van Raamsdonk F. Combinatory reduction systems: introduction and survey. In: To Corrado Böhm, TCS 121:279-308, 1993.

[Lév76] Lévy J.-J. An algebraic interpretation of the $\lambda\beta K$-calculus; and an application of a labelled λ-calculus. TCS 2(1):97-114, 1976.

[Lév78] Lévy J.-J. Réductions correctes et optimales dans le lambda-calcul, Thèse de l'Université de Paris VII, 1978.

[Lév80] Lévy J.-J. Optimal reductions in the Lambda-calculus. In: To H. B. Curry: Essays on Combinatory Logic, Lambda-calculus and Formalism, Hindley J. R., Seldin J. P. eds, Academic Press, 1980, p. 159-192.

[Lon83] Longo G. Set theoretic models of lambda calculus: theories, expansions and isomorphisms. Annals of pure and applied logic, 24:153-188, 1983.

[Mar91] Maranget L. Optimal derivations in weak λ-calculi and in orthogonal Term Rewriting Systems. In: Proc. POPL'91, p. 255-269.

[Mar92] Maranget L. La stratégie paresseuse. Thèse de l'Université de Paris VII, 1992.

[Nip93] Nipkow T. Orthogonal higher-order rewrite systems are confluent. In: Proc. of TLCA'93, Springer LNCS, vol. 664, Bazem M., Groote J.F., eds., 1993, p. 306-317.

[Nök94] Nöcker E. Efficient Functional Programming. Compilation and Programming Techniques. Ph. D. Thesis, Katholic University of Nijmegen, 1994.

[Oos94] Van Oostrom V. Confluence for Abstract and Higher-Order Rewriting. Ph.D. Thesis, Free University of Amsterdam, 1994.

[Oos96] Van Oostrom V. Higher order families. In proc. of RTA'96, Springer LNCS, vol. 1103, Ganzinger, H., ed., 1996, p. 392-407.

[OR94] Van Oostrom V., van Raamsdonk F. Weak orthogonality implies confluence: the higher-order case. In: Proc. of LFCS'94, Springer LNCS, vol. 813, Narode A., Matiyasevich Yu. V. eds. St. Petersburg, 1994. p. 379-392.

[Raa96] Van Raamsdonk F. Confluence and normalisation for higher-order rewriting. Ph.D. Thesis, CWI Amsterdam, 1996.

[SeRa93] Sekar R.C., Ramakrishnan I.V. Programming in Equational Logic: Beyond Strong Sequentiality. Information and Computation, 104(1):78-109, 1993.

Trace Consistency and Inevitability

R. Ramanujam [1]

The Institute of Mathematical Sciences
C.I.T. Campus
Madras 600 113.
jam@imsc.ernet.in

Abstract. Two runs of a distributed system can be considered equivalent if they represent different interleavings of the same run. Formulas of the propositional temporal logic of linear time (PTL) are said to be trace consistent when they cannot distinguish between equivalent runs. Determining whether a formula is trace consistent is decidable. In this paper, we consider a closely related notion: a PTL formula is said to be *inevitable*, if for every system run, there is at least one equivalent run (that is, one interleaving of that run) which satisfies the formula. We show that determining whether a formula is inevitable is undecidable. However, for a subclass of formulas termed coherent (propositions in them can be affected by either of a pair of independent operations but not both), inevitability becomes decidable.

1 A synopsis

The Propositional Temporal Logic of Linear Time (PTL) is used to describe the temporal evolution of global states of distributed systems. Reasoning in PTL about safety, liveness and fairness properties of systems is well understood by now. With the development of both automata-theoretic model checking techniques [VW86] and theorem proving techniques [MP91], automatic or semi-automatic verification of temporal properties has seen considerable progress.

A number of researchers ([GW94], [KP92a], [V90]) have noted that there is a natural equivalence relation on runs of systems which equates runs obtained by different interleavings of the same run. For instance, if a_1 and a_2 happen to be causally independent operations and a run δ is of the form $s_0 \xrightarrow{a_1} s_1 \xrightarrow{a_2} s_2$, we would consider another run of the form $s_0 \xrightarrow{a_2} s_1' \xrightarrow{a_1} s_2$ to be equivalent to δ. These constitute two different ways of interleaving the concurrent operations a_1 and a_2. If a_1 and a_2 are actions on distinct variables, the sequence of state changes that each variable is subject to is identical in both runs. Often, a system is defined to be truly distributed (or in some contexts, fair) only when it is closed with respect to this equivalence, that is, given any system run, all other interleavings of concurrent operations along that run are also admitted as runs.

---

[1] Part of this work was done while I was visiting Institut für Informatik und Praktische Mathematik, Christian - Albrechts - Universität Kiel, Germany. I thank Wolfgang Thomas for making the visit possible. I also thank the referees for comments.

The systems typically studied in PTL model checking, namely synchronized products of automata, or other parallel programs, are of this kind: their behaviour consists of all possible interleavings. This fact can be utilized for efficient verification of those properties, which hold for an entire equivalence class of runs whenever they hold for one run in the class. Such properties are said to be *equivalence robust* ([P93]) or *trace consistent* ([T95]). Identifying such properties is important, since partial-order based techniques developed in [GW94], [P93], [V90] and other papers become available for the verification of such properties.

Since PTL formulas are interpreted on system runs, when runs are treated as representatives of their equivalence classes, it becomes necessary to revisit the notions of satisfiability of PTL formulas in this context. The standard notions of satisfiability and model checking in PTL are phrased as follows:

- **Satisfiability**: given a formula, is there a system and a run of that system which satisfies the formula?
- **Model checking**: given a system and a formula, does every run of the system satisfy the formula?

The dual notion to satisfiability is that of **validity**: a valid formula is satisfied in every run of every system. When we begin to consider system behaviour as represented by an equivalence class of runs rather than by a single run, two new notions become interesting:

- **Strong satisfiability**: given a formula, is there a system and a run of that system such that *every* run equivalent to it satisfies the formula?
- **Weak model checking**: given a system and a formula, is it the case that for every run of the system, there is *at least one* equivalent run (some interleaving) which satisfies the formula?

The dual notion to strong satisfiability is that of **weak validity**: a weakly valid formula holds in some interleaving of every run of every system. (Weak validity is closely related to **inevitability**, a notion introduced by [MOP89]. In this paper, we simply refer to weak validity as inevitability.) Seen in this light, we can term the classical notions of satisfiability and model checking listed above respectively as **weak satisfiability** (with strong validity as its dual notion) and **strong model checking**.

In terms of language theory, we can see these notions in the following terms: the classical notion of satisfiability corresponds to the question whether a given ω-regular language is nonempty. Given in addition an equivalence on infinite strings, strong satisfiability asks whether there exists a nonempty equivalence-closed subset. Given two such languages L_S and L_α, classical model checking asks whether $L_S \subseteq L_\alpha$, whereas weak model checking only requires to know whether for every string in L_S there exists an equivalent one (a representative) in L_α. We can see the latter relation as a weaker form of inclusion.

Trace consistent formulas are exactly those for which the notions of strong and weak satisfiability coincide. (Correspondingly, for such formulas weak and strong model checking coincide.)

When we study decidability questions for PTL, we now have several questions to answer. The state-of-the-art can be summarised as follows:

- Satisfiability and model checking are decidable for PTL, and in fact PSPACE-complete. The frames for the logic studied in this context are simply labelled transition systems without explicit concurrency information. On the other hand, runs can be equated only when there is some concurrency specified explicitly. Once such concurrency is introduced, the frames include commuting of independent transitions, and then it is unclear whether the original results still obtain. This is important, particularly in light of the strong negative results shown in [LPRT95] [P92] and other work, which suggest that logics interpreted over global states of systems with commuting transitions tend to be undecidable.
- In [DGP95], it is shown that checking whether an ω-regular language is trace equivalence closed is decidable, and this implies that determining whether a PTL formula is trace consistent is also decidable. (See the recent paper [PWW96] giving an algorithmic proof of this, with lower bound results on deciding closure under trace and other equivalences.) Therefore, once we show that the standard notions of (weak) satisfiability and (strong) model checking are decidable, it follows that for trace consistent formulas, *all* the notions mentioned above are decidable.

In this paper we show that: (a) In the context of concurrent systems, despite the presence of commuting transitions, (weak) satisfiability and (strong) model checking are decidable. (b) Strong satisfiability is undecidable, when there are both local and common propositions in the language, whose truth or falsity can be affected by independent operations.

Once we find that strong satisfiability is undecidable, we ask: can we at least find subclasses of formulas for which strong satisfiability is decidable? (Obviously, this class cannot be pinned down effectively; if it were, we would get a decision procedure for strong satisfiability contradicting our result.) We already know of one subclass, namely the trace consistent ones. (In this context, it would be nice to have a syntactic characterization of trace consistent formulas. [T95] provides a semantic characterization.) We offer here a different subclass of PTL formulas for which strong satisfiability is decidable, and which is obtained by a syntactic restriction. We call such formulas *coherent*, and these closely correspond to the version of PTL studied in [T95]. For coherent formulas, weak model checking is seen to be decidable as well.

Apart from formal interest, is weak model checking relevant in the context of specifying and reasoning about distributed systems? Rather interestingly, the "p causes q" modality discussed by [R95] has the same flavour as asserting reachability in some interleaving. [PP94] studies a logic which is more expressive than PTL where these situations are easily described. However, we have no detailed examples of system verification necessitating weak model checking.

A word about the syntax of logic and the definition of frames for the logic studied here: PTL modalities refer only to successor states and eventuality, whereas state transitions in systems are labelled by actions. When we define equivalence on runs, it is by studying concurrency implicit in the dependency alphabet of actions. Therefore, we must have some way of referring to such dependence in the syntax of formulas as well. (Otherwise formulas can never force concurrency.) We do this by defining a dependence structure on propositions: for each proposition, this specifies which system variables are involved in determining its truth value. This also helps us in defining the class of coherent formulas: a proposition is coherent, if no two independent actions may both affect its truth value; a formula is coherent when every proposition mentioned in it is coherent.

This study could equally well be carried out with different definitions of frames. For instance, we could have action-indexed modalities in the logic. Ensuring that systems generate all possible interleavings can be done with different (and weaker) conditions on the systems than the one given here, with the same technical results as in this paper.

2 Preliminaries

2.1 Programs

A program is given by a tuple $Pr = (Q, \Sigma, \rightarrow)$, where Q is a finite set of states, Σ is a finite nonempty set of operations and $\rightarrow \subseteq (Q \times \Sigma \times Q)$ is the transition relation. An operation a is said to be *enabled* at a state s if there exists s' such that $(s, a, s') \in \rightarrow$, denoted $s \xrightarrow{a} s'$.

Partial order based verification methods involve an *independence relation* on transitions, so that whenever independent transitions occur in sequence, they can be 'commuted', resulting in the same state (they can be 'summed' up in any order). A good deal of effort is required to determine which transitions in a program are independent. Obviously it is impractical to enumerate reachable states and check commutation for all states and pairs of transitions. More messy is the question of when two transitions within a run are independent. (See [KP92b] for details on discovering and refining independence information.)

Below we take the approach of determining independence syntactically. Let us assume that a program operates on n variables, for some fixed $n > 0$. Since states describe values of program variables, we can think of Q as a subset of $Q_1 \times Q_2 \times \ldots \times Q_n$, where Q_i represents possible (finitely many!) values of the ith variable. Further assume that we are given a function $\theta : \Sigma \rightarrow 2^{\{1,\ldots,n\}}$; $\theta(a)$ specifies which variables are affected when an a operation is performed. This automatically gives an irreflexive, symmetric independence relation I_θ on Σ : $(a, b) \in I_\theta$ iff $\theta(a) \cap \theta(b) = \emptyset$. We will refer to (Σ, θ) as a *dependence alphabet*. (An action a can be thought of as a simultaneous assignment of values to variables in $\theta(a)$. In this sense, updates of distinct sets of variables are independent.)

Definition 2.1 *Let $n > 0$. A finite state n-variable program over a dependence alphabet (Σ, θ) is a tuple $Pr = (\widetilde{Q}, \rightarrow)$, where $\widetilde{Q} \subseteq (Q_1 \times \ldots \times Q_n)$, for all i, $1 \leq i \leq n$, Q_i is a finite set of states and $\rightarrow \subseteq (\widetilde{Q} \times \Sigma \times \widetilde{Q})$, such that*

1. *if* $(q_1, \ldots, q_n) \overset{a}{\to} (q_1', \ldots, q_n')$ *then* $\forall i \notin \theta(a), q_i = q_i'$, *and*
2. $\forall x_0, x_1, x_2 \in \widetilde{Q}$, *if* $x_0 \overset{a}{\to} x_1, x_1 \overset{b}{\to} x_2, (a, b) \in I_\theta$, *then* $\exists x_3 \in \widetilde{Q}$ *such that* $x_0 \overset{b}{\to} x_3$ *and* $x_3 \overset{a}{\to} x_2$.

The latter condition is called *the forward diamond condition* and is typical in concurrency theory (for instance, asynchronous automata exhibit this property).

In order to have nontrivial independence relations, we will confine our interest to programs where $n > 1$, and alphabets (Σ, θ) such that I_θ is nonempty. This will be an unstated assumption throughout the discussion in the paper. Further, we fix a dependence alphabet (Σ, θ) and refer to programs (and later formulas too) over this alphabet, unless otherwise stated.

A *run* of a program is a finite or infinite sequence $x_0 \overset{a_0}{\to} x_1 \overset{a_1}{\to} \ldots$ generated by the transition relation of the program. We denote runs by δ, δ' etc. By $\delta \lceil i$, we mean the sequence generated by projecting down to the ith components of states and erasing all a such that $i \notin \theta(a)$. This gives a finite or infinite sequence $q_0 \overset{a_0}{\to} q_1 \overset{a_1}{\to} \ldots$ such that for every $j, q_j \in Q_i, i \in \theta(a_j)$.

We can now define an equivalence relation on runs as follows : $\delta \sim \delta'$ iff $\forall i \in \{1, \ldots, n\}$, $\delta \lceil i = \delta' \lceil i$. It can be checked that the induced equivalence relation on Σ^ω is the same as the infinite trace equivalence (with respect to the concurrency alphabet (Σ, I_θ)) obtained from Mazurkiewicz trace theory and used by [P93] and other work on partial order based verification.

2.2 The logic

The logic we study is standard linear time temporal logic, except that we include some information to reflect the dependency structure of programs in the logic. A *propositional structure* is a pair (P, η), where P is a countable set of atomic propositions, and $\eta : P \to 2^{\{1, \ldots, n\}}$ is a map which, for any $p \in P$ specifies which variables **affect** the truth or falsity of p ([P93]). In a sense, η delimits the vocabulary of the statements denoted by atomic propositions in the logic.

Let $p \in P$ be a proposition. We say that p is **coherent** with respect to (Σ, θ) if and only if the following condition holds:

$$\forall a, b \in \Sigma, \text{ if } (a, b) \in I_\theta, \text{ then } (\eta(p) \cap \theta(a) = \emptyset) \text{ or } (\eta(p) \cap \theta(b) = \emptyset).$$

A formula (defined below) is coherent if and only if every proposition mentioned in it is coherent. (Since we have assumed a fixed dependence alphabet for discussion in the paper, we will simply talk of coherent formulas, where coherence is with respect to the fixed alphabet.) Thus, a coherent formula is distributable in the sense that if X is the set of propositions mentioned in it, then *independent operations affect disjoint subsets of propositions in* X.

It is worth noting what kind of formulas are declared incoherent by this condition. When variables r and s are acted on by independent operations, statements of the form "$r = 1$ or $s = 0$" or "the value of r is updated if and only if that of s is also updated" or "eventually $(r = 1$ and $s = 0)$" can always be expressed in the logic using separate propositions involving r and s, logical connectives and modalities. What we **cannot** express are statements of the form "the values of r and s are the same" when these variables can take on unboundedly many values. Since this needs infinitary expressions not part of the logic, such 'nonlogical' properties require atomic propositions and these are incoherent (in case they involve variables affected by independent operations).

The syntax of formulas is defined below. We assume special propositions which allow us to speak of actions being enabled or not. (These propositions are not important for the decidability results, but merely convenient.)

$$\mathcal{L} ::= p \in P \mid \lambda_a, \, a \in \Sigma \mid \neg\alpha \mid \alpha \vee \beta \mid \bigcirc \alpha \mid \alpha \mathbf{U} \beta$$

The derived connectives and modalities $\wedge$, $\supset$, $\equiv$, $\Diamond$, $\Box$ are all defined as usual. (In particular, $\Diamond\alpha \overset{\text{def}}{=} True\mathbf{U}\beta$ where $True$ is defined to be $p_0 \vee \neg p_0$, for some $p_0 \in P$. $\Box\alpha \overset{\text{def}}{=} \neg\Diamond\neg\alpha$.)

A *system* is a pair $S = (Pr, V)$ where Pr is an n-variable program and $V : \tilde{Q} \to 2^P$ is a partial valuation map on program states such that for all $p \in P$, whenever $x \overset{a}{\to} x'$, $\eta(p) \cap \theta(a) = \emptyset$ and both $V(x)$ and $V(x')$ are defined, $p \in V(x)$ iff $p \in V(x')$. Since the operation a can only update values of variables in $\theta(a)$ and these do not affect the truth of p, the valuation must respect this. Note that even with this condition, we have more general models than those having only 'local' valuations, namely, $V_i : Q_i \to 2^P$. (Having partial valuation maps is a matter of technical convenience: we can choose to ignore the truth or falsity of propositions in program states which are unreachable in the runs of interest.)

Given a system $S = (Pr, V)$, a *model* is a pair $M = (S, \delta)$, where $\delta = x_0 \overset{a_0}{\to} x_1 \overset{a_1}{\to} \ldots$ is an infinite run of Pr such that for all k, $V(x_k)$ is defined. (Excluding finite runs is technically convenient, though not critical.) The notion $S, \delta, k \models \alpha$ denoting that the formula α is satisfied at instant k along run δ of the system S is defined in the usual manner. We leave S and δ implicit below.

- $k \models p$ iff $p \in V(x_k)$.
- $k \models \lambda_a$ iff $\exists x' \in \tilde{Q}$ such that $x_k \overset{a}{\to} x'$ in Pr.
- $k \models \neg\alpha$ iff $k \not\models \alpha$.
- $k \models \alpha \vee \beta$ iff $k \models \alpha$ or $k \models \beta$.
- $k \models \bigcirc\alpha$ iff $k + 1 \models \alpha$.
- $k \models \alpha\mathbf{U}\beta$ iff $\exists m : k \leq m, m \models \beta$ and $\forall l : k \leq l < m : l \models \alpha$.

We say $S, \delta \models \alpha$ if $S, \delta, 0 \models \alpha$.

A formula α is said to be **trace consistent** if and only if for every system $S = (Pr, V)$, for every δ of Pr, if $S, \delta \models \alpha$ then for all runs $\delta' \sim \delta$, we have $S, \delta' \models \alpha$ as well.

We say that a given system $S = (Pr, V)$ *weakly satisfies* a formula α if there exists a run δ of Pr such that $S, \delta \models \alpha$. We say that a given system $S = (Pr, V)$ *strongly satisfies* a formula α if there exists a run δ of Pr such that for every $\delta' \sim \delta$, $S, \delta' \models \alpha$. A formula α is said to be **weakly (strongly) satisfiable** if there exists a system S which weakly (strongly) satisfies it.

It is easily seen that for a trace consistent formula α, any system S weakly satisfies α if and only if it strongly satisfies α. Thus the two notions of satisfiability coincide for trace consistent formulas.

The dual notions are interesting for model checking. Given a system $S = (Pr, V)$, call a formula α *strongly S-valid*, if $S, \delta \models \alpha$, for every run δ of Pr. Similarly, call α *weakly S-valid*, if for every run δ of Pr, there exists $\delta' \sim \delta$ such that $S, \delta' \models \alpha$. A *strongly valid* formula is one which is strongly S-valid for every system S, and a *weakly valid* or **inevitable** formula is one which is weakly S-valid for every system S.

Consider a propositional structure which has propositions p and q such that $\eta(p) = \{1\}$ and $\eta(q) = \{2\}$. Further suppose that there is no action a such that $\{1, 2\} \subseteq \theta(a)$. Then consider the formula $\alpha = p \wedge q \wedge \bigcirc(\neg p \wedge \bigcirc \neg q)$. α is coherent but not trace consistent, and weakly satisfiable but not strongly satisfiable. On the other hand, if $\eta(r) = \{1, 2\}, \theta(a) = \{1\}$ and $\theta(b) = \{2\}$, the formula $r \vee \neg r$ is obviously valid and trace consistent, yet not coherent.

3 Satisfiability

We first show that the standard notions of weak satisfiability and strong model checking remain decidable, despite the presence of diamond conditions on frames. (We will simply call these notions satisfiability and model checking in this section). This problem is nontrivial, since the standard proof for deciding PTL formulas does not yield a commuting frame by itself. That such a commuting frame can be extracted is the central claim in the following argument.

As usual, we need the notion of *subformula closure* of a formula. $CL(\alpha)$ is defined to be the smallest set of formulas containing the formula α and satisfying the following conditions:

- $\neg\beta \in CL(\alpha)$ iff $\beta \in CL(\alpha)$, where $\neg\neg\beta$ is considered as the same as β.
- if $\beta_1 \vee \beta_2 \in CL(\alpha)$ then $\{\beta_1, \beta_2\} \subseteq CL(\alpha)$.
- if $\bigcirc\beta \in CL(\alpha)$ then $\beta \in CL(\alpha)$.
- if $\beta_1 \mathbf{U} \beta_2 \in CL(\alpha)$ then $\{\beta_1, \beta_2, \bigcirc(\beta_1 \mathbf{U} \beta_2)\} \subseteq CL(\alpha)$.

The size of $CL(\alpha)$ is linear in the length of α.

Fix a formula α_0, whose satisfiability is to be decided. For the rest of this section, we will call $CL(\alpha_0)$, simply CL. An *atom* A is a subset of CL which is propositionally consistent, and satisfies the additional condition : $\alpha \mathbf{U} \beta \in A$ iff (either $\beta \in A$ or both α and $\bigcirc(\alpha \mathbf{U} \beta)$ are in A). Let AT denote the set of all atoms. We use A, B, A_1 etc to denote atoms.

We define a *successor* relation $Succ \subseteq AT \times \Sigma \times AT$ as follows: $(A, a, B) \in Succ$ iff $(\forall \bigcirc\alpha \in CL, \bigcirc\alpha \in A$ iff $\alpha \in B)$ and $(\forall p : \eta(p) \cap \theta(a) = \emptyset : p \in A$ iff $p \in B)$. In this case, we say that B is an a-successor of A.

The standard decision procedure for PTL ([VW86]) consists of building a nondeterministic Büchi automaton whose states are atoms and transitions are given by $Succ$ above, with suitable modifications for keeping track of $\mathbf{U}$ requirements. It is then shown that α_0 is satisfiable if and only if the ω-language accepted by the associated automaton is nonempty. The proof below can be presented in terms of such an automaton; we have chosen a different presentation mainly as a preparation for the proof in Section 5.

Consider the finite graph $G = (AT, Succ)$. $H = (W, \Rightarrow)$ is a subgraph of G if $W \subseteq AT$ and $\Rightarrow \subseteq Succ$. H is said to be *good* if and only if it satisfies the following conditions :

- There exists $A_0 \in W$ such that $\alpha_0 \in A_0$.
- $\forall A \in W, \exists a \in \Sigma$ such that A has an a-successor in H.
- $\forall \alpha U \beta \in CL$, if $A \in W$ such that $\alpha U \beta \in A$, then there exists a path $A = A_0 \overset{a_1}{\Rightarrow} A_1 \ldots \overset{a_m}{\Rightarrow} A_m$ in H such that $\beta \in A_m$.

Lemma 3.1 α_0 *is satisfiable if and only if the graph G defined above contains a good subgraph.*

Note that the lemma at once yields the theorem below as a corollary :

Theorem 3.2 *Satisfiability of a formula α_0 is decidable in time $2^{O(m)}$, where m is the length of α_0.*

One direction of the lemma is straightforward to prove. Suppose that the formula α_0 is satisfiable. Let $S = (Pr, V)$ be a system and δ a run of Pr such that $S, \delta, 0 \models \alpha_0$, where $\delta = x_0 \overset{a_1}{\rightarrow} x_1 \overset{a_2}{\rightarrow} \ldots$. Define $A_k \overset{\text{def}}{=} \{\alpha \in CL | M, k \models \alpha\}$, $W \overset{\text{def}}{=} \{A_k | k \geq 0\}$, and $X \overset{a}{\Rightarrow} Y$ iff there exists k such that $X = A_k$, $Y = A_{k+1}$ and $a_{k+1} = a$. It can be easily checked that each member of W is in fact an atom, that $\Rightarrow \subseteq Succ$ and that $H = (W, \Rightarrow)$ is good.

On the other hand, suppose G contains a good subgraph $H = (W, \Rightarrow)$. Building an n-variable program from H is nontrivial. We proceed in two steps: we first unfold H to get an infinite sequence $\sigma = x_0 \overset{a_1}{\Rightarrow} x_1 \overset{a_2}{\Rightarrow} \ldots$ along which all eventuality requirements are met, and then fold σ into an n-variable program. This is done in such a way that σ has the crucial property (*) that whenever for any $k \geq 0$, $\alpha U \beta \in x_k$, there exists $l \geq k$ such that $\beta \in x_l$. Further, by definition of atoms and $Succ$, for every j such that $k \leq j < l$, $\alpha \in x_j$. Also, for all k, when $\bigcirc \alpha \in x_k$, we have that $\alpha \in x_{k+1}$.

Based on σ, we now define another sequence $\rho = \chi_0 \overset{a_1}{\Rightarrow} \chi_1 \overset{a_2}{\Rightarrow} \ldots$ where for all k, χ_k is an n-tuple of the form $(X_1^k, X_2^k, \ldots, X_n^k)$, where for $i \in \{1, \ldots, n\}, X_i^k \in 2^{AT}$, and the action sequence is the same as in σ.

X_i^k is defined to be the set of all atoms in σ after the last i-action before k and before the next i-action (if any) after k. Formally, $X_i^k \overset{\text{def}}{=} \{x_j | (j \leq k$ and $\forall l, j < l \leq k, i \notin \theta(a_l))$ or $(j > k$ and $\forall l, k < l \leq j, i \notin \theta(a_l))\}$. Clearly, for all k we have $X_i^k = X_i^{k+1}$ if $i \notin \theta(a_k)$.

We can now construct the model : let $Pr_i = (Q_i, \rightarrow_i)$ be defined by : $Q_i = \{X_i^k | k \geq 0\}$; for $i \in \theta(a)$, $q \overset{a}{\rightarrow}_i q'$ iff $\exists k: X_i^k = q, X_i^{k+1} = q'$ and $a_{k+1} = a$. Consider $Pr = (Q_1 \times \ldots \times Q_n, \rightarrow)$ be the n-variable program, where $\rightarrow$ is the product transition relation: $(q_1, \ldots, q_n) \overset{a}{\rightarrow} (q_1', \ldots, q_n')$ iff $\forall i \in \theta(a), q_i \overset{a}{\rightarrow}_i q_i'$ and $\forall i \notin \theta(a), q_i = q_i'$. It is easy to check that the frame conditions are satisfied and that ρ constructed above is a run of Pr. The valuation needs to be defined only for χ_k: $V(\chi_k) \stackrel{\text{def}}{=} x_k \cap P$. We now have $M = (Pr, \rho, V)$, it remains to show that M is a model for α_0.

Claim: $\forall \gamma \in CL$, $\forall k \geq 0$, $M, k \models \gamma$ if and only if $\gamma \in x_k$.

The claim is proved by induction on the complexity of γ. The proof is routine and follows from the assertion (*) above.

We can easily adapt the decision procedure for satisfiability to obtain a decision procedure for model checking as well: given a system $S = (Pr, V)$ and α, we need a procedure which checks whether every model based on S satisfies α. For this, it is sufficient to build a procedure which checks whether *there exists* a model based on S which satisfies α (running the latter on $\neg \alpha$ answers the former question). For this, we proceed as above, but instead of working with AT, we work with $\widetilde{Q} \times AT$, where $\widetilde{Q}$ is the state space of the given program Pr and whenever we consider $(\widetilde{q}, A)$, $p \in A$ iff $p \in V(\widetilde{q})$. The rest of the proof is similar. Thus we have the following theorem :

Theorem 3.3 *Model checking for a system S and formula α can be done in time $k.2^{O(m)}$, where k is the size of S and m is the length of α.*

4 Inevitability

We now show that strong satisfiability, and hence inevitability, is undecidable, when there are at least two groups of agents in the system with propositions local to each group as well as common propositions. For this we recursively reduce every instance of the Finite Colouring Problem (FCP) [LPRT95] to the strong satisfiability of a formula. The result then follows from the undecidability of FCP (which is just a variant of standard tiling problems). We merely outline the construction below; the proof follows easily from [LPRT95].

In the finite colouring problem, one is given a finite set of colours, two functions 'right' and 'up', and asked whether there is a finite rectangle that can be coloured at lattice points such that the colouring is consistent with the right and up functions. Formally, an *instance* of FCP is a tuple $\Delta = (C, R, U, c_0, c_1)$, where $C = \{c_0, c_1, \ldots, c_k\}$, $k > 0$ is a finite set of **colours**, and $R, U : C \to 2^C$ are the **right** and **up** functions respectively. A *solution* to Δ is a triple (u, v, Col), where $u \geq 0, v \geq 0$ and $Col : \{0, \ldots, u\} \times \{0, \ldots, v\} \to C$ is a **colouring function** which satisfies the conditions:

- $Col(0,0) = c_0$ and $Col(u, v) = c_1$,
- $\forall i, j : 0 \leq i < u, 0 \leq j \leq v, Col(i+1, j) \in R(Col(i,j))$, and
- $\forall i, j : 0 \leq i \leq u, 0 \leq j < v, Col(i, j+1) \in U(Col(i,j))$.

Given an instance Δ, we construct a formula α_Δ as follows. Firstly, associate a proposition with each colour in C. Without loss of generality we will use these colours themselves as propositions. Secondly, by nontriviality of the alphabet, $I_\theta \neq \emptyset$, and hence there exist actions a and b such that $(a, b) \in I_\theta$. Without loss of generality, let $1 \in \theta(a)$, $2 \in \theta(b)$. Assume that for $c \in C, \eta(c) = \{1, 2\}$. Further let $\{p, q\} \subset P$ such that $\eta(p) = \{1\}$ and $\eta(q) = \{2\}$. Consider now the formula

$$\alpha_\Delta \stackrel{\text{def}}{=} \bigwedge_{i=1}^{5} \alpha_i, \text{ where } (\otimes \text{ denotes exclusive disjunction below}):$$

- $\alpha_1 \stackrel{\text{def}}{=} c_0 \wedge p \wedge q \wedge \Diamond c_1 \wedge ((\bigwedge_{d \in \Sigma - \{a,b\}} \neg \lambda_d) U c_1).$

- $\alpha_2 \stackrel{\text{def}}{=} \bigwedge_{\beta \in \{p, \neg p\}} \bigwedge_{\gamma \in \{q, \neg q\}} \Box((\beta \wedge \gamma) \supset (c_1 \vee (\bigcirc(\neg \beta \wedge \gamma) \otimes \bigcirc(\beta \wedge \neg \gamma)))).$

- $\alpha_3 \stackrel{\text{def}}{=} \Box \bigwedge_{i=0}^{k} (c_i \equiv \bigwedge_{j \neq i} \neg c_j).$

- $\alpha_4 \stackrel{\text{def}}{=} \bigwedge_{\beta \in \{p, \neg p\}} \Box \bigwedge_{i=0}^{k} (c_i \supset ((\beta \wedge \bigcirc \neg \beta) \supset (c_1 \vee \bigcirc \bigvee_{c \in R(c_i)} c))).$

- $\alpha_5 \stackrel{\text{def}}{=} \bigwedge_{\beta \in \{q, \neg q\}} \Box \bigwedge_{i=0}^{k} (c_i \supset ((\beta \wedge \bigcirc \neg \beta) \supset (c_1 \vee \bigcirc \bigvee_{c \in U(c_i)} c))).$

Lemma 4.1 Δ *has a solution if and only if* α_Δ *is strongly satisfiable.*

Theorem 4.2 *Strong satisfiability and hence inevitability is undecidable when* L *contains incoherent propositions.*

This raises the possibility that weak model checking may also be undecidable, but we have not been able to establish either the decidability or undecidability of weak model checking.

The use of the enabling propositions above is mainly a technical convenience. These can be eliminated but the proof becomes more complicated: we need to reduce the strong satisfiability of a formula to that over alphabets whose actions are 'necessitated' by the formula.

5   Coherent formulas

We now turn our attention to showing decidability of strong satisfiability for coherent formulas. Recall that for a coherent formula, independent operations affect disjoint subsets of propositions mentioned in it.

The notion of subformula closure of a formula is as before. Again fix a formula α_0 whose strong satisfiability is to be decided, and let CL denote $CL(\alpha_0)$. The definition of atoms, AT, the graph $G = (AT, Succ)$ and good subgraphs of G are as before.

Let $H = (W, \Rightarrow)$ be a subgraph of G. By $H \lceil Prop$, we mean the graph $(U, \rightarrow)$, where $U = \{A \cap P | A \in W\}$ and $Q_1 \stackrel{a}{\rightarrow} Q_2$ iff $\exists A, B \in W$ such that $A \cap P = Q_1$, $B \cap P = Q_2$ and $A \stackrel{a}{\Rightarrow} B$ in H.

Let $J_1 = (U_1, \rightarrow_1)$ and $J_2 = (U_2, \rightarrow_2)$ be graphs such that $U_1, U_2 \subseteq 2^P$ and $\rightarrow_j \subseteq (U_j \times \Sigma \times U_j)$, $j \in \{1, 2\}$. We say $J_1 \doteq_I J_2$ iff there exist $Q \in U_1, Q' \in U_2$

such that $U_2 = (U_1 - \{Q\}) \cup \{Q'\}$ and there exist $Q_1, Q_2 \in U_1 \cap U_2$ such that for some $(a, b) \in I_\theta$, $Q_1 \xrightarrow{a}_1 Q \xrightarrow{b}_1 Q_2$ and $\rightarrow_2 = (\rightarrow_1 - \{(Q_1, a, Q), (Q, b, Q_2)\}) \cup \{(Q_1, b, Q'), (Q', a, Q_2)\}$. Let $=_I$ denote the reflexive transitive closure of $\doteq_I$.

Call a subgraph $H = (W, \Rightarrow)$ of $G = (AT, Succ)$ *strongly good* iff it contains a good subgraph, and for every good subgraph $H_1 = (W_1, \Rightarrow_1)$ of H, if $J_1 = H_1 \lceil Prop$, and there exists $J_2 =_I J_1$, then there exists $H_2 = (W_2, \Rightarrow_2)$ a good subgraph of H such that $H_2 \lceil Prop = J_2$.

Given any good subgraph $H = (W, \Rightarrow)$ of G, it is easy to see that there is an infinite path δ in H of the form $A_0 \xrightarrow{a_0} A_1 \xrightarrow{a_1} \ldots$, where $\alpha_0 \in A_0$ and for every j, if $\alpha \cup \beta \in A_j$, there exists $k \geq j$ such that $\beta \in A_k$. Call δ a *good path induced by* H, and we say δ is *on* $\rho = a_0 a_1 \ldots \in \Sigma^\omega$.

We can then show the following: suppose that H is strongly good. Then for every good subgraph $H_1 = (W_1, \Rightarrow_1)$ of H and $\rho_1 \in \Sigma^*$, if there exists a good path induced by H_1 on $\rho_1 \rho \in \Sigma^\omega$, and $\rho_1 \sim \rho_2$, then there exists a good subgraph $H_2 = (W_2, \Rightarrow_2)$ of H such that there is a good path induced by H_2 on the string $\rho_2 \rho$.

From this we can prove the following stronger statement, which will be needed later: suppose that H is strongly good. Then for every good subgraph $H_1 = (W_1, \Rightarrow_1)$ of H, if there exists a good path induced by H_1 on $\rho_1 \rho_2 \rho_3 \ldots \in \Sigma^\omega$, where for all $j, \rho_j \in \Sigma^*$, and for all $j, \rho_j \sim \chi_j$, then there exists a good subgraph $H_2 = (W_2, \Rightarrow_2)$ of H such that there is a good path induced by H_2 on the string $\chi_1 \chi_2 \chi_3 \ldots \in \Sigma^\omega$.

Lemma 5.1 α *is strongly satisfiable if and only if* G *above has a strongly good subgraph.*

When α_0 is strongly satisfiable, constructing a strongly good subgraph of G is done as follows. Let (Pr, δ, V) be the given model satisfying α_0, where $\delta = x_0 \xrightarrow{a_1} x_1 \xrightarrow{a_2} \ldots$. For $k \geq 0$ and $\delta' \in [\delta]$, let $\mu(\delta', k)$ denote the set of formulas $\{\phi \in CL | \delta', k \models \phi\}$. It is easily seen that every such set is an atom. Collect all such sets to form W. Transitions between them are induced by the transitions in the model: suppose $A, B \in W$. Define $A \xrightarrow{a} B$ iff there exists $\delta' \in [\delta]$ and $k \geq 0$ such that $A = \mu(\delta', k)$, $B = \mu(\delta', k+1)$ and a is the action in the kth transition in δ'. It can be easily checked that $(W, \Rightarrow)$ is a subgraph of G. To show that it is strongly good, first notice that it contains a good subgraph: simply collect all atoms which are μ-images along δ. Clearly $\alpha_0 \in \mu(\delta, 0)$, and U requirements are met within this subgraph, say H_0. Consider $H_0 \lceil Prop$. Because of the coherence of α_0, and the fact that α_0 is strongly satisfied in the given model, we can observe the following: for all $i \in Loc$, the sequence of sets of i-propositions which hold is the same for every $\delta' \in [\delta]$; with these n sequences, every shuffle of these corresponds to a run in $[\delta]$ which correspondingly generates a good subgraph. Thus, we see that $(W, \Rightarrow)$ is a strongly good subgraph of G.

In the other direction, when we are given a strongly good subgraph, we use the good subgraph in it to first build an infinite sequence σ with the property that every eventuality requirement is met. We then build n transition systems whose i-local states are sets of the form $\{p \mid p \in A_j \cap P \text{ and } i \in \eta(p)\}$, where A_j is the

j^{th} atom in the sequence, and the i-local transitions are defined by transitions in σ in which i participates. When we take the product of these, we get the required n-variable program, which has σ as a run. Now, when we consider any run σ' equivalent to σ, we need to show that eventuality requirements are met along σ' as well. For this it suffices to consider $\sigma' = v_1 v_2 \ldots$ such that $\sigma = u_1 u_2 \ldots$ and $u_1 \sim v_1$, $u_2 \sim v_2 \ldots$, where the u_j and v_j are finite sequences (this follows from [DGP95]). We now use the commuting property above for strongly good subgraphs to show that requirements are met along σ'.

Theorem 5.2 *Strong satisfiability, and hence inevitability, are decidable for coherent formulas α in time $2^{O(m^2)}$, where m is the length of α.*

A similar argument can be used to show the decidability of weak model checking for coherent formulas, where the complexity is again linear in the size of the system being checked.

References

[DGP95] Diekert, V., Gastin, P. and Petit, A., "Rational and recognizable complex trace languages", *Information and Computation*, vol 116, #1, 1995, 134-153.

[GW94] Godefroid, P. and Wolper, P., "A partial approach to model checking", *Information and Computation*, vol 110, 1994, 305-326.

[KP92a] Katz, S. and Peled, D., "Verification of distributed programs using representative interleaving sequences", *Distributed Computing*, vol. 6, 1992, 107-120.

[KP92b] Katz, S. and Peled, D., "Defining conditional independence using collapses", *TCS*, vol. 101, #3, 1992, 337-359.

[LPRT95] Lodaya, K., Parikh, R., Ramanujam, R., Thiagarajan, P.S., "A logical study of distributed transition systems", *Inf & Comp.*, vol. 119, #1, 1995, 91-118.

[MP91] Manna, Z. and Pnueli, A., *The temporal logic of reactive and concurrent systems (Vol. I: Specification; Vol. II: Verification)*, Springer-Verlag, 1991.

[MOP89] Mazurkiewicz, A., Ochmanski, E., and Penczek, W.,"Concurrent systems and inevitability", *TCS*, vol. 64, #3, 1989, 281-304.

[P92] Penczek, W., "On undecidability of propositional temporal logics on trace systems", *Inf. Proc. Letters*, vol. 43, 1992, 147-153.

[P93] Peled, D., "All from one and one from all: on model checking using representatives", *LNCS 697*, 1993, 409-423.

[PP94] Peled, D., and Pnueli, A., "Proving partial order properties", *TCS*, vol. 126, 1994, 143-182.

[PWW96] Peled, D., Wilke, T. and Wolper, P., "An algorithmic approach to proving closure properties of ω-regular languages", Proc. CONCUR, *LNCS*, 1996.

[R95] Reisig, W., "Petri net models of distributed algorithms", *Tech. Rep. 58*, Humboldt Univ., Berlin, 1995 (to appear in *LNCS 1000*).

[T94] Thiagarajan, P.S., "A trace based extension of propositional linear time temporal logic", *Proc LICS*, 1994, 438-447.

[T95] Thiagarajan, P.S., "A trace consistent subset of PTL", *LNCS 962*, 438-452.

[V90] Valmari, A., "A stubborn attack on state explosion", *LNCS 531*, 1990, 156-165.

[VW86] Vardi, M.Y., and Wolper, P., "An automata theoretic approach to program verification", *Proc LICS*, 1986, 332-345.

Finite State Implementations of Knowledge-Based Programs

(Extended Abstract)

Ron van der Meyden

Computing Science
University of Technology, Sydney
PO Box 123, Broadway NSW 2007
Australia
email: ron@socs.uts.edu.au

Abstract. Knowledge-based programs have been proposed as an abstract formalism for the design of distributed systems, based on the idea that an agent's actions are a function of its state of knowledge. We identify two natural cases in which finite state implementations of atemporal knowledge-based programs in finite environments may be automatically constructed. The first concerns an interpretation of knowledge in which agents are aware only of their current observation and the current time. The second concerns the perfect recall interpretation of knowledge, in environments in which all communication is by synchronous broadcast. These results contribute towards a theory of automated synthesis of protocols from knowledge-based specifications.

1 Introduction

Viewing agents as having states of *knowledge* has been found to be a useful abstraction for the design and analysis of distributed systems [HM90, DM90, Had87, HZ92]. Central to this approach is a focus on the relationship between an agent's actions and its state of knowledge. This has lead to the proposal of knowledge-based programming formalisms [FHMV95a], in which agents' actions have as preconditions formulae expressing properties of their knowledge. Knowledge-based programs allow for highly intuitive descriptions of protocols, abstracting both from the agents' data structures and the environment in which they run. Thus, these programs provide a promising approach to the *synthesis* of protocols from high level descriptions.

There is an impediment to this goal, however: knowledge-based programs cannot be directly executed — rather, it is necessary to *implement* a knowledge-based program by translating it to a standard program in which the preconditions for actions are tests on the agents' concrete states. In a knowledge-based

---

* Work begun while the author was with the Information Sciences Laboratory, NTT Basic Research Laboratories, Kanagawa, Japan, and continued at the Department of Applied Math and Computer Science, Weizmann Institute of Science. Thanks to Yoram Moses and Moshe Vardi for helpful discussions.

program an agent's state of knowledge depends on a number of factors, including the behaviour of the environment in which the program runs, and the actions being performed by the agents in this environment. These actions in turn depend on the agents' states of knowledge. This means that the relationship between a knowledge-based program and its implementations is subtle, involving a non-trivial fixpoint definition.

Consequently, a knowledge-based program may, in general, have many behaviourally distinct implementations, or none. In this paper we focus on the class of *atemporal* programs and *synchronous* interpretations of knowledge, for which this problem does not arise, and for which there always exists an implementation, unique up to behavioural equivalence. The main issue then concerns the representation and construction of this implementation. We consider the simplest possible type of representation — *finite state protocols* — and ask "when does a knowledge-based program have a finite state implementation, and how can it be computed?"

In previous work [Mey96], we have shown that with respect to a perfect recall interpretation of knowledge, finite state implementations of atemporal programs do not always exist, even when the environment is finite state. The contribution of the present paper is a general condition sufficient for the existence of finite state implementations. Using this condition, we identify two cases in which such implementations may be automatically constructed. One of these cases involves interpretations of knowledge in which agents are forgetful, being aware only of their current observation and the present time — this assumption on its own suffices for the existence of finite state implementations. The second concerns the perfect recall interpretation of knowledge, but requires a restricted class of finite environments: *broadcast environments*, in which all communication between agents is by synchronous broadcast.

The structure of the paper is as follows. Sections 2 to 4 define knowledge-based programs and their semantic interpretation. Section 5 states the sufficient condition for the existence of finite state implementations. Section 6 applies this condition to an interpretation of knowledge in which agents are aware only of their current observation and the time. The application to perfect recall in broadcast environments is presented in Section 7. Section 8 discusses related work and concludes.

2 Knowledge-Based Programs

To make the paper self-contained, we recall in the next three sections the definitions from [Mey96] of knowledge-based programs, the environments in which they run, and their implementations. These definitions are a variant of the definitions in [FHMV95a], to which the reader is referred for motivation. For a description of how our framework differs from that of [FHMV95a], and motivation for the changes, see [Mey96].

To describe the agents' states of knowledge we work with the propositional multi-modal language for knowledge $\mathcal{L}_n^C$ generated from some set of basic propositions *Prop* by means of the usual boolean operators, the monadic modal operators K_i, where $i = 1 \ldots n$ is an agent, and the monadic operators C_G, where G is a set of two or more agents. Intuitively, $K_i\varphi$ expresses that agent i knows φ, and $C_G\varphi$ expresses that φ is common knowledge amongst the group of agents G.

This language is interpreted in the standard way [FHMV95b] in a class of $S5_n$ Kripke structures of the form $M = \langle W, \sim_1, \ldots, \sim_n, V \rangle$, where W is a set of worlds, for each $i = 1 \ldots n$ the accessibility relation $\sim_i$ is an equivalence relation on W, and $V : W \times Prop \to \{0, 1\}$ is a valuation on W. If G is a group of agents then we may define the equivalence relation $\sim_G$ on W by $u \sim_G v$ if there exists a sequence $u_0, \ldots, u_k$ of worlds such that $u_0 = u$, $u_k = v$ and for each $j = 0 \ldots k - 1$ there exists an agent $i \in G$ with $u_j \sim_i u_{j+1}$. The crucial clauses of the definition of satisfaction of a formula at a world u are given by

1. $(M, u) \models p$, where p is an atomic proposition, if $V(u, p) = 1$.
2. $(M, u) \models K_i\varphi$ if $M, v \models \varphi$ for all worlds v with $u \sim_i v$.
3. $(M, u) \models C_G\varphi$ if $M, v \models \varphi$ for all worlds v with $u \sim_G v$.

We now describe the structure of knowledge-based programs. For each agent $i = 1 \ldots n$ let ACT_i be the set of actions that may be performed by agent i. Similarly, let ACT_e be the set of actions that may be performed by the environment in which the agents operate. If $a_e \in ACT_e$ and $a_i \in ACT_i$ for each $i = 1 \ldots n$, we say that the tuple $\mathbf{a} = \langle a_e, a_1, \ldots, a_n \rangle$ is a *joint action*, and we write ACT for the set of all joint actions.

Call a formula of $\mathcal{L}_n^C$ *i-subjective* if it is a boolean combination of formulae of the form $K_i\varphi$. An *atemporal knowledge-based program* for agent i is a finite statement $\mathbf{Pg}_i$ of the form

case of
> **if** φ_1 **do** a_1
>
> $\vdots$
>
> **if** φ_m **do** a_m

end case

where the φ_j are *i*-subjective formulae of $\mathcal{L}_n^C$ and the $a_j \in ACT_i$ are actions of agent i. Intuitively, a program of this form is executed by repeatedly evaluating the case statement, ad infinitum. At each step of the computation, the agent determines which of the formulae φ_j accurately describe its current state of knowledge. It non-deterministically executes one of the actions a_j for which the formula φ_j is true, updates its state of knowledge according to any new input it receives, and then repeats the process. We will give a more precise semantics below.

To describe the behaviour of the world in which agents operate, we define a *finite interpreted environment* to be a tuple of the form $E = \langle S_e, I_e, P_e, \tau, O, V_e \rangle$ where the components are as follows:

1. S_e is a finite set of *states of the environment*. Intuitively, states of the environment may encode such information as messages in transit, failure of

components, etc. and possibly the values of certain local variables maintained by the agents.

2. I_e is a subset of S_e, representing the possible *initial states* of the environment.

3. $P_e : S_e \rightarrow \mathcal{P}(ACT_e)$ is a function, called the *protocol of the environment*, mapping states to subsets of the set ACT_e of actions performable by the environment. Intuitively, $P_e(s)$ represents the set of actions that may be performed by the environment when the system is in state s.

4. τ is a function mapping joint actions $\mathbf{a} \in ACT$ to state transition functions $\tau(\mathbf{a}) : S_e \rightarrow S_e$. Intuitively, when the joint action $\mathbf{a}$ is performed in the state s, the resulting state of the environment is $\tau(\mathbf{a})(s)$.

5. The component O is a function mapping the set of states S_e to $\mathcal{O}^n$, where $\mathcal{O}$ is some set of *observations*. If s is a global state then the i-th component $O_i(s)$ of $O(s)$ will be called the *observation* of agent i in the state s.

6. $V_e : S_e \times Prop \rightarrow \{0, 1\}$ is a valuation, assigning a truth value $V(s, p)$ in each state s to each atomic proposition $p \in Prop$.

A *trace* of an environment E is a *finite* sequence $s_0 \ldots s_m$ of states such that for all $i = 0 \ldots m - 1$ there exists a joint action $\mathbf{a} = \langle a_e, a_1, \ldots, a_n \rangle$ such that $s_{i+1} = \tau(\mathbf{a})(s_i)$ and $a_e \in P_e(s_i)$. We write $init(r)$ and $fin(r)$ for the initial and final states of a trace r, respectively.

3 Protocols

Next, we introduce the standard protocols which will be used as implementations of knowledge-based programs, and describe the set of traces produced by executing such a protocol. Define a *protocol* for agent i to be a tuple $P_i = \langle S_i, q_i, \alpha_i, \mu_i \rangle$ consisting of (1) a set S_i of *protocol states*, (2) an element $q_i \in S_i$, the protocol's *initial state*, (3) a function $\alpha_i : S_i \times \mathcal{O} \rightarrow \mathcal{P}(ACT_i)$, such that $\alpha_i(s, o)$ is a nonempty set representing the possible next actions that agent i may take when it is in state s and is making observation o, and (4) a function $\mu_i : S_i \times \mathcal{O} \rightarrow S_i$, such that $\mu_i(s, o)$ represents the next protocol state the agent assumes after it has been in state s making observation o. In general, we allow the set of protocol states to be infinite. A *joint protocol* is a tuple $\mathbf{P} = \langle P_1, \ldots, P_n \rangle$ such that each P_i is a protocol of agent i.

Intuitively, protocol states represent the memory that agents maintain about their sequence of observations for the purpose of implementing their knowledge-based programs. For each trace r of an environment E, a protocol P_i determines a protocol state $P_i(r)$ for agent i by means of the following recursive definition. If r is a trace of length one, consisting of an initial state of E, then $P_i(r) = q_i$, the initial state of the protocol. If r is the trace $r's$, where r' is a trace and s is a state of the environment, then $P_i(r) = \mu_i(P_i(r'), O_i(fin(r')))$, where $fin(r')$ is the final state of r'. Thus $P_i(r)$ represents the agent's memory of its *past* observations in the trace r, excluding the current observation.

In executing a protocol, an agent's next action in a given trace is selected from a set determined by its memory of past observations together with its current observation. Define the *set of actions of agent i enabled by the protocol P_i at a trace* r with final state s to be the set $act_i(P_i, r) = \alpha_i(P_i(r), O_i(s))$. Similarly, the set of joint actions $\mathbf{act}(\mathbf{P}, r)$ enabled at r by a joint protocol $\mathbf{P}$ contains precisely the joint actions $\langle a_e, a_1, \ldots, a_n \rangle$ such that $a_e \in P_e(s_e)$ and $a_i \in act_i(P_i, r)$ for each $i = 1 \ldots n$.

We may now describe the set of traces that result when a particular protocol is executed in a given environment. Given a joint protocol $\mathbf{P}$ and an environment E, we define the *set of traces generated by* $\mathbf{P}$ *and* E, to be the smallest set of traces $\mathcal{R}$ such that (1) for each initial state $s \in I_e$ of the environment $\mathcal{R}$ contains the trace of length one composed just of the state s, and (2) if r is a trace in $\mathcal{R}$ with final state s, and if $\mathbf{a} \in \mathbf{act}(\mathbf{P}, r)$ is a joint action enabled by $\mathbf{P}$ at r then the trace $r \cdot \tau(\mathbf{a})(s)$ is in $\mathcal{R}$. Intuitively, this is the set of traces generated when the agents incrementally maintain their memory using the update functions μ_i, and select their next action at each step using the functions α_i.

4   Implementation of Knowledge-Based Programs

Clearly, in order to execute a knowledge-based program according to the informal description above, we need some means to interpret the knowledge formulae it contains. To do so, we introduce a particular class of Kripke structures.

These structures will be obtained from a set of traces by means of *views*, a generalisation of observations. Intuitively, a view captures the information available to the agents in each trace as the result of a sequence of observations. Define a *joint view* of an environment E to be a function $\{\cdot\}$ mapping traces of E to X^n for some set X. We write $\{r\}_i$ for the i-th component of the result of applying $\{\cdot\}$ to the trace r.

We will focus in this paper on two views, the *synchronous perfect recall view* $\{\cdot\}^{pr}$ and the *clock view* $\{\cdot\}^{clock}$. The synchronous perfect recall view provides the agent with a complete record of all the observations it has made in a trace. If r is the trace $s_1 \ldots s_k$ then this view is defined by $\{r\}_i^{pr} = O_i(s_1) \ldots O_i(s_k)$. The clock view provides the agent with information only about its current observation and the current time. This view is defined by $\{r\}_i^{clock} = (|r|, O_i(fin(r)))$, where $|r|$ is the length of the trace r.

We will assume that an agent's view of a trace always includes the agent's current observation. That is, for all traces r and r' and all agents i we have that if $\{r\}_i = \{r'\}_i$ then $O_i(fin(r)) = O_i(fin(r'))$. Secondly, we assume that the observations are the agent's only source of information about a trace. Thus all views $\{\cdot\}$ are required to be a function of the perfect recall view. That is, for each agent i there must exist a function f such that for all traces r we have $\{r\}_i = f(\{r\}_i^{pr})$.

A joint view $\{\cdot\} : S \to X^n$ of an environment E is *incremental* if for each agent i there exists a function $\nu : X \times \mathcal{O} \to X$ such that for all $rs \in traces(E)$ we have $\{rs\}_i = \nu(\{r\}_i, O_i(s))$. A view is *synchronous* when for all agents i, if $\{r\}_i = \{r'\}_i$ then $|r| = |r'|$. Intuitively, this means that the current time can be determined from the view. Both the perfect recall view and the clock view are synchronous and incremental. Given the assumptions above, we may consider the perfect recall view to be the maximal synchronous view, and the clock view to be the minimal synchronous view.

Given a set $\mathcal{R}$ of traces of environment E with valuation V_e, and a joint view $\{\cdot\}$ of E, we may define the Kripke structure $M(\mathcal{R}, \{\cdot\}, E) = (W, \sim_1, \ldots, \sim_n, V)$, where

- the set of worlds $W = \mathcal{R}$, and
- for all $r, r' \in \mathcal{R}$ we have $r \sim_i r'$ iff $\{r\}_i = \{r\}_i$, and
- the valuation $V : \mathcal{R} \times Prop \rightarrow \{0, 1\}$ is defined by $V(r, p) = V_e(fin(r), p)$.

That is, the accessibility relations are derived from the view, and truth of basic propositions at traces is determined from their final states according to the valuation V_e provided by the environment. Intuitively, $r \sim_i r'$ if, based on the information provided by the view $\{\cdot\}_i$, the agent cannot distinguish between the traces r and r'. We will call $M(\mathcal{R}, \{\cdot\}, E)$ the *interpreted system* obtained from $\mathcal{R}$ and $\{\cdot\}$ in E.

We may now define the *set of actions enabled by the program* $\mathbf{Pg}_i$ *at a trace* r *of system* M to be the set $\mathbf{Pg}_i(M, r)$ consisting of all the a_i such that $\mathbf{Pg}_i$ contains a line "**if** φ **do** a_i" where $(M, r) \models \varphi$. Similarly, the set of joint actions $\mathbf{Pg}(M, r)$ enabled by a joint knowledge-based program in a trace r with final state having environment component s_e contains precisely the joint actions $\langle a_e, a_1, \ldots, a_n \rangle$ such that $a_e \in P_e(s_e)$ and $a_i \in \mathbf{Pg}_i(M, r)$ for each $i = 1 \ldots n$.

This definition leaves open the question of what system we are to use when executing a knowledge-based program. The answer to this is that we should use a system that is itself generated by running the program. Say that *a joint protocol* $\mathbf{P}$ *implements a knowledge-based program* $\mathbf{Pg}$ *in an environment* E *with respect to the joint view* $\{\cdot\}$ if for all r in the set of traces $\mathcal{R}(\mathbf{P}, E)$ generated by $\mathbf{P}$ and E, we have $\mathbf{Pg}(M, r) = \text{act}(\mathbf{P}, r)$, where $M = M(\mathcal{R}(\mathbf{P}, E), \{\cdot\}, E)$ is the system obtained from $\mathcal{R}(\mathbf{P}, E)$ and $\{\cdot\}$ in E. That is, the joint actions prescribed by the knowledge-based program, when the tests for knowledge are interpreted according to the system M, are precisely those prescribed by the standard protocol $\mathbf{P}$.

Note that this definition (unlike that of [FHMV95a]) refers only to the behaviour of the protocol, not to its internal states. More precisely, say that two joint protocols $\mathbf{P}$ and $\mathbf{P}'$ are *behaviourally equivalent* with respect to an environment E if they generate precisely the same set of traces by means of the same sets of action at each step. That is, $\mathbf{P}$ and $\mathbf{P}'$ are behaviourally equivalent when $\mathcal{R}(\mathbf{P}, E) = \mathcal{R}(\mathbf{P}', E)$, and for all $r \in \mathcal{R}(\mathbf{P}, E)$ we have $\text{act}(\mathbf{P}, r) = \text{act}(\mathbf{P}', r)$. When this relation holds, $\mathbf{P}$ implements the knowledge-based program $\mathbf{Pg}$ with respect to the view $\{\cdot\}$ if and only if $\mathbf{P}'$ also implements $\mathbf{Pg}$ with respect to the view $\{\cdot\}$.

In the framework of [FHMV95a] knowledge-based programs, even atemporal ones, can have no, exactly one, or many implementations, which may be behaviourally different. Our notion of implementation is more liberal, so this is also the case for our definitions. However, the notion of implementation is better behaved when we consider implementations with respect to synchronous views.

Proposition 1. *For every finite environment E and atemporal joint knowledge-based program* **Pg**, *implementations of* **Pg** *in E with respect to a synchronous view $\{\cdot\}$ always exist. Moreover, all such implementations are behaviourally equivalent.*

Although our formulation is slightly different, this result can be viewed as a special case of Theorem 7.2.4 of [FHMV95b]. If $\mathcal{R}$ is the unique set of all traces generated by any implementation of **Pg** in E with respect to a synchronous view $\{\cdot\}$, we refer to $M(\mathcal{R}, \{\cdot\}, E)$ as the *system generated by* **Pg** *in E with respect to $\{\cdot\}$*, denoted by $M(\mathbf{Pg}, \{\cdot\}, E)$.

The implementation guaranteed to exist by Proposition 1 uses the values of the synchronous perfect recall view $\{\cdot\}_i^{pr}$ as the protocol states for agent i. In case the view $\{\cdot\}$ is incremental, we may use the values of $\{\cdot\}_i$ instead, and update these using the incremental update function ν promised by the incrementality of the view. In general, both these implementations are very inefficient in their usage of space. For example, the values of the synchronous perfect recall view grow as a linear function of the length of the trace; in the case of the clock view the values grow as the log of the length of the trace. However, our notion of implementation does not require that an agent maintain its view of a trace, only that it behave as if it did. This brings us to the central question we study in this paper: under what conditions do there exist *finite state* implementations? We will present some natural conditions under which this is the case.

5   A Sufficient Condition for Finite State Implementations

In this section we present a sufficient condition for the existence of a finite state implementation of a knowledge-based program. We will give two applications of this result in the following sections, where we identify a variety of circumstances where the condition applies.

Define a *simulation* from an $S5_n$ structure $M = \langle W, \mathcal{K}_1, \ldots, \mathcal{K}_n, V \rangle$ to an $S5_n$ structure $M' = \langle W', \mathcal{K}'_1, \ldots, \mathcal{K}'_n, V' \rangle$ to be a function $\kappa : W \to W'$ such that

1. for all worlds $w \in W$ and propositions p, $V(w, p) = V'(\kappa(w), p)$,
2. for all $w, w' \in W$ and agents i, if $w\mathcal{K}_i w'$ then $\kappa(w)\mathcal{K}'_i \kappa(w')$,
3. for all $w \in W$, $w' \in W'$ and agents i, if $\kappa(w)\mathcal{K}'_i w'$ then there exists $v \in W$ with $w\mathcal{K}_i v$ and $\kappa(v) = w'$.

An easy induction on the construction of a formula $\varphi \in \mathcal{L}_n^C$ shows that if κ is a simulation from M to M' then $M, w \models \varphi$ iff $M', \kappa(w) \models \varphi$.

Theorem 2. *Let* **Pg** *be an atemporal knowledge-based program and suppose that the joint view $\{\cdot\}$ of environment E is synchronous and incremental. If there exists a simulation from $M(\mathbf{Pg}, \{\cdot\}, E)$ to a finite $S5_n$ structure M' then there exists a finite state implementation of* **Pg** *in E with respect to $\{\cdot\}$.*

Perhaps somewhat surprisingly, the preconditions of this result refer only to the knowledge relations, and not to the relationship between agents' states of knowledge from one instance to the next. Potentially, this relationship could be highly irregular and non-computable. The proof involves showing that this cannot be the case. The finite state implementation uses the equivalence classes of the relations $\mathcal{K}'_i$ of M' as the states of the protocol for agent i.

6 The Clock View

As a first application of Theorem 2, we show that finite state implementations are guaranteed to exist with respect to the clock view. Intuitively, this view provides the agents with two pieces of information: the current time and the current observation. Since all agents have access to the current time, the information derived from this is common knowledge. As we will show, the additional information an agent derives from its current observation is "orthogonal" to this common knowledge.

To make this precise, define the finite $S5_n$ structure $M' = \langle W', \mathcal{K}_1, \ldots, \mathcal{K}_n, V' \rangle$ as follows. The worlds in W' are the pairs (X, s) where X is a subset of the set of states S of the environment E and the state s of E is an element of X. The accessibility relations $\mathcal{K}_i$ are defined by $(X, s)\mathcal{K}_i(X', s')$ when $X = X'$ and $O_i(s) = O_i(s')$. The valuation V' is defined by $V((X, s), p) = V_e(s, p)$, where V_e is the valuation of the environment E.

Proposition 3. *Suppose $\mathcal{R}$ is any subset of the set of traces of environment E. Define the mapping $\kappa : \mathcal{R} \to W'$ by $\kappa(r) = (X(r), \text{fin}(r))$, where $X(r) = \{\text{fin}(r') \mid r' \in \mathcal{R} \text{ and } |r'| = |r|\}$. Then κ is a simulation from $M(\mathcal{R}, \{\cdot\}^{clock}, E)$ to M'.*

The following is an immediate corollary of Proposition 3 and Theorem 2.

Theorem 4. *Let E be a finite environment and $\mathbf{Pg}$ an atemporal knowledge-based program. Then $\mathbf{Pg}$ has a finite state implementation in E with respect to the clock view.*

7 Perfect Recall in Broadcast Environments

In the previous section we showed that knowledge-based programs always have finite state implementations with respect to the clock view. As is shown in [Mey96], this is not the case for knowledge-based programs interpreted with respect to the perfect recall view. Indeed, the complexity of computing an agent's next action from its sequence of observations may be as high as PSPACE complete. By adapting the proof of this result, we may establish the following.

Theorem 5. *Given an atemporal knowledge-based program $\mathbf{Pg}$ and a finite environment E, the following are undecidable: (i) determining whether $\mathbf{Pg}$ has a finite state implementation in E with respect to $\{\cdot\}^{pr}$, and (ii) determining if there exists a simulation from $M(\mathbf{Pg}, \{\cdot\}^{pr}, E)$ to a finite $S5_n$ structure.*

While Theorem 5 states that determining the existence of finite state implementations is in general undecidable, it does not prevent the existence of classes of environments in which knowledge-based programs *always* have finite state implementations with respect to the perfect recall view. In this section we present a natural class of such environments. This class, called *broadcast environments*, models situations in which agents may maintain private information, but in which the only means this information can be communicated is by synchronous simultaneous broadcast to all agents. This sort of situation arises in systems in which components communicate by means of a shared bus, and protocols that operate in a sequence of synchronised *rounds* with broadcasts between rounds may also be modelled in this way. Broadcast environments are able to represent a variety of games of incomplete information, including Battleships and Bridge.

Formally, a broadcast environment is an environment $E = \langle S_e, I_e, P_e, \tau, O, V_e \rangle$ of a specific structure we now describe. The states of the environment will indicate a private state for each of the agents, a state for the remainder of the system, and a record of the public part of the most recent joint action performed. For each agent $i = 1 \ldots n$, we assume that there exists a set S_i of *instantaneous private states*, intuitively representing the state of the private objects maintained by the agent. The private states S_i will be observable and modifiable by agent i only. We also assume a set of *shared* states S_0, representing the remainder of the system, which is under the shared control of the agents.

The actions performed by agent i in a broadcast environment will be of the form $a_i \| b_i$ where a_i is in a set A_i of *external* actions and b_i is in a set B_i of *internal* actions of agent i. The internal component b_i will affect only the agent's private state, and will be unobservable to the other agents. On the other hand, the external component a_i will be observable to all agents, but it will affect only the shared state. The actions performed by the environment itself (which we treat as agent 0) will similarly be comprised of two components, an internal component unobservable to agents $1 \ldots n$, and an observable external component. However, in this case, both components affect only the shared state.

The set of states S_e of a broadcast environment is composed from the above: these states are tuples of the form $\langle a_0, \ldots, a_n; p_0, \ldots, p_n \rangle$, where for each $i = 0 \ldots n$, the component $p_i \in S_i$ is a private state of agent i and the component $a_i \in A_i$ is an external action of agent i. Intuitively, a tuple $\langle a_0, \ldots, a_n; p_0, \ldots, p_n \rangle$ models a situation in which the shared component of the system is in state p_0, in which agents i's private objects are in state p_i, and in which the most recent set of external actions performed is given by the a_i. To distinguish them from the private and shared states, we refer to the elements of S_e as *global* states. In initial states, there is no most recent external action, so here we require that $a_i = \epsilon$ for all $i = 0 \ldots n$, where ϵ is a special null action. We allow the set I_e of initial states to be any nonempty set of states of this form.

The action interpretation function τ is required to be some function such that the effect of executing a joint action $\langle a_0 \| b_0, a_1 \| b_1, \ldots, a_n \| b_n \rangle$ in a global state $\langle a'_0, \ldots, a'_n; p'_0, \ldots, p'_n \rangle$ is to produce a global state $\langle a_0, \ldots, a_n; p_0, \ldots, p_n \rangle$ in which the action part records the external portion of the joint action, in which the shared state p_0 is computed as a function of p'_0 and the component $\langle a_0, b_0, a_1, a_2, \ldots, a_n \rangle$ affecting the shared state, and in which each private state p_i is computed as a function of p'_i and the private action b_i.

In a broadcast environment, agents are able to observe their own private state, as well as some aspects of the shared state. However, we assume that all agents make the *same* observation of the shared state. Formally, we suppose that there exists a "common" observation function O_c mapping each shared state in S_0 to some observation. Using this, the agent's observation functions are defined by $O_i(\langle a_0, \ldots, a_n; p_0, \ldots, p_n \rangle) = (a_0, \ldots, a_n, O_c(p_0), p_i)$. That is, in each global state, agent i observes the most recent set of external actions performed, the common observation of the shared state, and its own private state. We will comment below on the requirement that the external actions be observable.

Finally, we require that the protocol P_e of the environment depend only upon the shared state and the most recent external action. We allow the finite set of propositions *Prop* to describe any property of the states S_e, captured semantically by the valuation $V_e : S_e \times Prop \to \{0, 1\}$. We now define a *broadcast environment* to be any environment of the form described above.

Suppose we are given a finite broadcast environment E. We will use Theorem 2 to demonstrate that all knowledge-based programs have finite state implementations in E with respect to the perfect recall view. To define the finite Kripke structure required by Theorem 2, we first need a few definitions.

If $s = \langle a_0, \ldots, a_n; p_0, \ldots, p_n \rangle$ is a global state as above then we define the *joint external action at s*, denoted $\text{ext}(s)$, to be the tuple $\langle a_0, \ldots, a_n \rangle$. If $r = s_0 s_1 \ldots s_n$ is a trace of a broadcast environment, we will write $\text{ext}(r)$ for the sequence $\text{ext}(s_0) \ldots \text{ext}(s_n)$. If e is a sequence of joint external actions and $\mathcal{R}$ is a set of traces then we define the function $f_e^{\mathcal{R}} : I_e \to \mathcal{P}(S_e)$, as follows. If $s \in I_e$ is an initial state then $f_e^{\mathcal{R}}(s)$ is the set of states $t \in S_e$ such that there exists a trace $r \in \mathcal{R}$ with $init(r) = s$ and $\text{ext}(r) = e$ and $fin(r) = t$. Intuitively, $f_e^{\mathcal{R}}(s)$ represents the set of states that would be considered possible by an agent who knows the trace to be in $\mathcal{R}$, knows that the initial state is s and observes only the sequence of external actions e.

Of course, the agents in a broadcast environment also have access to their own private states, so they have extra information that enables them to eliminate certain states from the set $f_e^{\mathcal{R}}(s)$. However, we will show that this information is orthogonal to the information derived from the sequence of external actions. Define the finite Kripke structure $M' = \langle W', \mathcal{K}_1, \ldots \mathcal{K}_n, V' \rangle$ to have

1. set of worlds W' equal to the set of triples (s, f, t) where $s \in I_e$, f is a function from I_e to $\mathcal{P}(S_e)$ and $t \in f(s)$;
2. $(s, f, t)\mathcal{K}_i(s', f', t')$ if and only if $O_i(s) = O_i(s')$ and $f = f'$ and $O_i(t) = O_i(t')$;
3. $V'((s, f, t), p) = V_e(t, p)$, where V_e is the valuation on the global states of E.

Given a set of traces $\mathcal{R}$ of the broadcast environment E, define the mapping $\kappa : \mathcal{R} \to W'$ by $\kappa(r) = (init(r), f_{\text{ext}(r)}^{\mathcal{R}}, fin(r))$. Note that whenever r is a trace in $\mathcal{R}$ we have $fin(r) \in f_{\text{ext}(r)}^{\mathcal{R}}(init(r))$, so this mapping is well-defined.

Lemma 6. *If $\mathcal{R}$ is the set of traces of the system M generated in a broadcast environment by a knowledge-based program with respect to the perfect recall view, then κ is a simulation from M to M'.*

Using Theorem 2 this immediately gives the following result.

Theorem 7. *If E is a finite broadcast environment then all knowledge-based programs have finite state implementations in E with respect to the perfect recall view.*

It is possible to slightly generalise this result, by modifying the definition of broadcast environment to allow agents to make distinct observations of the shared state, provided they gain no information from this observation that they would not have been able to derive from their observation of the external actions. This helps to extend the result to cover games like stratego and puzzles like the muddy children puzzle [FHMV95b].

However, we remark that Theorem 7 breaks down under a generalisation in which agents still make the same observation of the shared state, but in which the external actions are unobservable. We will show in the full version of the paper that if we take agent i's observation in state $\langle a_0, \ldots a_n; p_0, \ldots p_n \rangle$ to be $(O_c(p_0), p_i)$, then a finite state implementation may no longer exist.

8 Conclusion

The computational problems involved in the implementation of knowledge-based programs have thus far received only limited attention. Results in [FHMV95a] can be interpreted in our framework as dealing with the complexity of determining the existence and uniqueness of implementations of knowledge-based programs containing temporal operators with respect to the "observational" view defined by $\{r\}_i^{obs} = O_i(fin(r))$, in which an agent is aware only of its current observation. Implementations are not guaranteed to exist with respect to this view, but when they do they can be assumed to be finite state. Vardi [Var96] deals with implementations with respect to $\{\cdot\}^{obs}$ of atemporal programs, and also considers the problem of determining whether a given protocol implements a knowledge-based program.

Because of space limitations, we have suppressed in this extended abstract a number of issues that will be covered in the full version of the paper. We will show there that the results may be generalised to deal with programs in which the tests contain not just operators for knowledge, but also *past-time* temporal operators. We also deal more carefully with the constructive nature of the proofs that finite state implementations exist, showing how to compute these implementations. Finally, we treat there the problem of deciding whether a given finite state protocol implements a knowledge-based program with respect to the views $\{\cdot\}^{clock}$ and $\{\cdot\}^{pr}$.

These results begin to map out the decidable problems concerning the implementation of knowledge-based programs, but the feasibility of this approach for automated protocol synthesis remains to be seen. One issue that will clearly need to be addressed is the state space explosion problem, known from the literature on temporal logic model checking. However, we note that the constructions of the present paper appear to be amenable to the symbolic techniques that have recently been used with some success in this area [BCM+90].

References

[BCM+90] J.R. Burch, E.M. Clarke, K.L. McMillan, D.L. Dill, and L.J. Hwang. Symbolic model checking: 10^{20} states and beyond. In *Proc. Symposium on Logic in Computer Science*, pages 428–439. IEEE, 1990.

[DM90] C. Dwork and Y. Moses. Knowledge and common knowledge in a byzantine environment. *Information and Computation*, 88:156–186, 1990.

[FHMV95a] R. Fagin, J. Halpern, Y. Moses, and M. Vardi. Knowledge-based programs. In *Proc. ACM Symposium on Principles of Distributed Computing*, 1995.

[FHMV95b] R. Fagin, J. Halpern, Y. Moses, and M. Y. Vardi. *Reasoning about Knowledge*. MIT Press, Cambridge, MA, 1995.

[Had87] V. Hadzilacos. A knowledge theoretic analysis of atomic commitment protocols. In *Proc. 6th ACM SIGACT-SIGMOD-SIGART Conf. on Principles of Database Systems*, pages 129–134, 1987.

[HM90] J. Halpern and Y. Moses. Knowledge and common knowledge in a distributed environment. *Journal of the ACM*, 37(3):549–587, 1990.

[HZ92] J. Halpern and L. Zuck. A little knowledge goes a long way: Simple knowledge based derivations and correctness proofs for a family of protocols. *Journal of the ACM*, 39(3):449–478, 1992.

[Mey96] R. van der Meyden. Knowledge-based programs: on the complexity of perfect recall in finite environments. In *Proc. of the Conf. on Theoretical Aspects of Rationality and Knowledge*, pages 31–50. Morgan Kaufmann, 1996.

[Var96] M. Vardi. Implementing knowledge-based programs. In *Proc. of the Conf. on Theoretical Aspects of Rationality and Knowledge*, pages 15–30. Morgan Kaufmann, 1996.

Higher-Order Proof by Consistency

Henrik Linnestad*[1], Christian Prehofer**[2] and Olav Lysne***[1]

[1] Department of Informatics, University of Oslo, PB 1080 Blindern, 0316 Oslo, Norway.
[2] Institut für Informatik, Technische Universität München, 80290 München, Germany.

Abstract. We investigate an integration of the first-order method of proof by consistency (PBC), also known as term rewriting induction, into theorem proving in higher-order specifications. PBC may be seen as well-founded induction over an ordering which contains the rewrite relation, and in this paper we extend this method to the higher-order rewrite relation due to Nipkow. This yields a proof procedure which has several advantages over conventional induction. First, it is less control demanding; second, it is more flexible in the sense that it does not instantiate variables precisely with every constructor, but instantiates according to the rewrite rules. We show how a number of technical problems can be solved in order for this integration to work, and point out some desirable refinements that involve challenging problems.

1 Introduction

The field of term rewriting has attracted much attention over the last twenty-odd years, largely triggered by seminal work of Knuth and Bendix on completion [14]. From the late seventies we have seen an ever increasing body of research on methods for the analysis of first-order rewrite systems. For a survey of this part of the field we refer to [4]. Due to their expressive power, higher-order logics are widely used for specification and verification. For the extension of term rewriting in this direction, there exist several different formalisms which integrate typed lambda calculus and term rewrite systems, including Klop [13], Breazu-Tannen [3] and Nipkow [22]. We follow the approach given in the latter work, where a rewriting relation modulo α-, β- and η-conversion is considered.

In this paper we adapt the first-order proof method called *inductionless induction*, or *proof by consistency*, to the higher-order setting. The rationale behind this method, which was first described in a paper by Musser [21], is that the Knuth and Bendix completion process can be used to prove or disprove properties of a rewrite system. This is roughly done by studying the new equations that emerge in the completion process wrt. a notion of consistency. Since 1980 we have seen a lot of work on this first-order method, removing some of its limitations [6, 8], relaxing its close connection with the full completion process [5, 1], and extending the set of rewrite-based specifications that the method applies to [2, 16, 17]. In [26] it was pointed out

---

* Email: henrikl@ifi.uio.no. Partly supported by the Norwegian Research Council.
** Email: prehofer@informatik.tu-muenchen.de
*** Email: olavly@ifi.uio.no. Supported by Esprit projects OMI-MACRAME and OMI-ARCHES.

that proof by consistency can be seen as induction over a well-founded ordering on the term universe.

The main motivation for this work is to utilize these sophisticated induction techniques for higher-order theorem proving. Assuming that recursive data types are given, we basically exploit the initial structures provided by these types to apply (implicit) induction schemes. This means that in order to prove an equation $s \simeq t$, we instead try to prove $s\sigma \simeq t\sigma$ for every substitution σ that assigns (almost) ground terms to first-order variables of data types. Although our data-types are essentially first-order, they may contain higher-order subterms, e.g. consider induction on lists of functions. For this we need a particular notion of substitutions, since we cannot reason about higher-order terms via ground instances.

Theorem provers like HOL [7] and Isabelle/HOL [23] apply an explicit induction scheme in which variables are instantiated with constructor terms spanning the data type. Our proposed integration of proof by consistency to higher-order equational reasoning can be seen as a generalization of this approach, where an explicit set of constructors for data types is not needed. Since most commonly used interactive theorem provers usually perform induction manually, our techniques are particularly interesting.

The paper is organized as follows. In section 2 we recall basic concepts and notation for term rewriting; our notation is roughly consistent with [22]. The proof procedure itself is given in section 3 followed by a correctness proof in section 4. Some examples are provided in section 5.

2 Preliminaries

From a set of *base types* $\mathcal{B}$, we construct the set of *types* $\mathcal{T}$ with the function space constructor $\rightarrow$ in the obvious way. Assume given a set of typed *variables* $\mathcal{V} = \cup_{\tau \in \mathcal{T}} \mathcal{V}_\tau$ and a set of *constants* (function symbols) $\mathcal{F} = \cup_{\tau \in \mathcal{T}} \mathcal{F}_\tau$, where $\mathcal{V} \cap \mathcal{F} = \emptyset$ and $\mathcal{V}_\tau \cap \mathcal{V}_{\tau'} = \mathcal{F}_\tau \cap \mathcal{F}_{\tau'} = \emptyset$ for all distinct τ, τ' from $\mathcal{T}$. The set of *simply typed λ-terms* (shorter: *terms*) is then defined inductively as follows:

$$\frac{x \in \mathcal{V}_\tau}{x : \tau} \qquad \frac{c \in \mathcal{F}_\tau}{c : \tau} \qquad \frac{s : \tau \to \tau' \quad t : \tau}{(s\,t) : \tau'} \qquad \frac{x : \tau \quad s : \tau'}{(\lambda x.s) : \tau \to \tau'}$$

Usually we shall implicitly assume that all terms, constants and variables are of suitable type, and omit the type specification.

Every occurrence of the variable x in a (sub-)term of the form $\lambda x.s$ is said to be *bound*. An occurrence of a variable which is not bound, is *free*. We use $\lambda \overline{x_n}.t$ as a simpler notation for $\lambda x_1 \ldots \lambda x_n.t$, and we write $s(t_1, \ldots, t_n)$ or $s(\overline{t_n})$ instead of $(\cdots((s\,t_1)\,t_2)\cdots t_n)$. We denote terms by s, t, u, v, constants by f, g, h, bound variables by lowercase w, x, y, z and free variables by uppercase F, G, H, W, X, Y, Z. Variables and constants are called *atoms*. We denote atoms by a, b.

A *position* ω in a term t is a sequence of integers identifying a subterm t/ω of t. In a term of the form $\lambda x.t$, the proper subterms are t and every proper subterm of t. In a term $s(t_1, \ldots, t_n)$, the proper subterms are $s, t_1, \ldots, t_n$ and every proper subterm of these terms. The empty position in a term t is written ϵ, and corresponds to the (non-proper) subterm t. We write $s[t]_\omega$ to indicate the term s, but with s/ω

replaced by the term t. Sometimes we omit the specification of the actual position ω and write $C[t]$ to express a term with t as subterm. Here, the term C is called a *context*.

Two terms s and t are *α-equivalent*, written $=_\alpha$, if each can be obtained from the other by a renaming of bound variables. A *β-reduction* is the transformation of a (sub-)term of the form $((\lambda x.s)\, t)$ into the term that is equal to s except that t is substituted for every occurrence of the variable x that is free in s. A term is in *β-normal form* if it cannot be β-reduced. An *η-reduction* is the transformation of a term $\lambda x.(t\, x)$ into t whenever t has no free occurrences of x. A term $t = \lambda\overline{x_n}.a(\overline{u_m})$ in β-normal form has an *η-long form* defined as $t\!\uparrow = \lambda\overline{x_{n+k}}.a(\overline{u_m\uparrow}, x_{n+1}\uparrow, \ldots, x_{n+k}\uparrow)$, where t is of type $\overline{\tau_{n+k}} \to \tau$ and $x_{n+1}, \ldots, x_{n+k}$ are fresh variables of appropriate types. The β-normal η-long form of a term t is written $t\!\downarrow$ or $\hat{t}$. If two terms s and t can be obtained from each other by α-, β- and η-conversion, we write $s \equiv t$.

To improve syntactical control over terms, we shall from now on assume that they are represented by their β-normal η-long forms. A term with no occurrences of free variables is called a *ground term*. For a term s of the form $\lambda\overline{x_k}.v(\overline{t_n})$, the position of v is called the *root position*. A term t is called a *pattern* if the list of arguments to each occurrence of a free variable is (η-equivalent to) a list of distinct bound variables.

Substitutions are finite and type preserving mappings from variables to terms. We use $\sigma, \gamma, \mu, \rho, \theta$ to denote substitutions. If $\sigma = \{x_1 \mapsto t_1, \ldots, x_n \mapsto t_n\}$ is a substitution and s is a term, we define $s\sigma$ by $s\sigma = (\lambda\overline{x_n}.s)(\overline{t_n})\!\downarrow$. We say that σ is a *ground substitution* if $t\sigma$ is a ground term, for all terms t.

Let $\mathcal{E}$ be a set of equations. By $=_\mathcal{E}$ we denote *equality modulo $\mathcal{E}$*, that is, the relation resulting from taking α-, β- and η-conversion together with all instances of equations from $\mathcal{E}$ as axioms, and closing under reflexivity, symmetry, transitivity and the congruence laws associated with the constructions $\lambda x.s$ (abstraction) and $(s\, t)$ (application). A *rewrite rule* is an ordered pair $s \to t$ of terms of the same base type, both in β-normal η-long form, such that all variables with free occurrences in t have free occurrences in s as well. We additionally require that the left-hand side of all rewrite rules be patterns. A *rewrite system* is a set of rewrite rules, and may also be viewed as a set of (ordered) equations. Symbols not occurring at the root position of any left-hand side of $\mathcal{R}$ will be called a *constructor* of $\mathcal{R}$. Following Nipkow [22], a rewrite system $\mathcal{R}$ induces a relation $\underset{\mathcal{R}}{\to}$ on terms, defined as follows:

$$s \underset{\mathcal{R}}{\to} t \;\Leftrightarrow\; \exists\, (l \to r) \in \mathcal{R}, \omega, \sigma \mid \hat{s}/\omega \equiv l\sigma \wedge t \equiv \hat{s}[r\sigma]_\omega$$

It should be noted that this relation is invariant under $\equiv$, in the sense that $s' \equiv s \underset{\mathcal{R}}{\to} t \equiv t'$ implies $s' \underset{\mathcal{R}}{\to} t'$. Hence, $\underset{\mathcal{R}}{\to}$ may be viewed as a relation on $\equiv$-equivalence classes of terms.

As in the first-order case, *critical pairs* are equations formed by unifying the left-hand side of one rule with a subterm of the left-hand side of another one and executing the corresponding rewrite step. Consult [22] for an exact definition which easily extends to our context. The set of critical pairs formed by superposing rules from a rewrite system $\mathcal{R}$ onto equations from a set $\mathcal{E}$ is denoted by $CP(\mathcal{R}, \mathcal{E})$.

Let $\to$ denote a binary relation on terms. By $\leftarrow$, $\leftrightarrow$, $\overset{+}{\to}$, $\overset{*}{\to}$ and $\overset{*}{\leftrightarrow}$ we denote the inverse of $\to$ and the symmetric, the transitive, the reflexive-transitive and the reflexive-symmetric-transitive closures of $\to$, respectively. We write $s \overset{!}{\to} t$ if $s \overset{*}{\to} t$

and t is *irreducible*, that is, there is no u such that $t \to u$. A substitution $\sigma = \{x_1 \mapsto t_1, \ldots, x_n \mapsto t_n\}$ is said to be irreducible if $t_1, \ldots, t_n$ are irreducible. If there is no infinite sequence $t_1 \to t_2 \to \cdots \to t_i \to \cdots$, we say that $\to$ is *terminating*. We say that $\to$ is *confluent* if $\leftarrow \circ \to \subseteq \to \circ \leftarrow$ and *convergent* if it is confluent and terminating. (The symbol $\circ$ is used for relation composition.) A convergent rewrite system $\mathcal{R}$ defines exactly one normal form (up to $\equiv$-equality) for each term t, which we denote by $t!_{\mathcal{R}}$.

Higher-order rewrite systems are not in general *stable*, in the sense that $s \to_{\mathcal{R}} t$ implies $s\sigma \to_{\mathcal{R}} t\sigma$ for arbitrary substitution σ. However, $\twoheadrightarrow_{\mathcal{R}}$ is stable (see [19]).

3 Higher-order proof by consistency

The goal of this paper is to achieve inductive proof methods for higher-order systems, that is, to prove or disprove inductive theorems. We do this by integrating a first-order method into the higher-order setting. Consequently, our equational reasoning will essentially be first-order, yet some problems pertaining to the higher-order setting must be solved in order for this to work. For the correctness proof of our procedure, we need to identify a subset of provable equations which will be of special interest to us. More precisely, the equations which we aim at proving are contained in the set of *initial consequences*.

Definition 1. A term t is *first-order rigid*, if all subterms of base type in the η-normal form of t are rigid (i.e. have no free variable as the root symbol). A substitution is called *first-order ground (fo-ground)* if it assigns first-order rigid terms to all variables.[3]

For instance, the term $map(\lambda x.F(x), empty)$ is fo-rigid, but $map(\lambda x.F(x), Q)$ and $\lambda x.map(\lambda y.F(y), H(x))$ are not, since neither Q nor $H(x)$ are rigid.

Definition 2 (Initial consequence). We say that a higher-order equation $s \simeq t$ is an *initial consequence* of a higher-order equation set $\mathcal{E}$ if $s\sigma =_{\mathcal{E}} t\sigma$ for all fo-ground substitutions σ.

This definition of initial consequences extends the first-order notion. As a motivation for its design, recall that we are essentially trying to adapt induction over data types to a higher-order setting. The idea is to prove all instances of candidate equations where variables are assigned terms which are as "concrete as possible". This stems from the fact that we must consider any instances, including free variables, for higher-order subterms.

As in the first-order case, we get an operational grip on the initial consequences of $\mathcal{E}$ through a convergent[4] rewrite system $\mathcal{R}$ which represents the same theory as $\mathcal{E}$. In that case, $=_{\mathcal{E}}$ coincides with $\leftrightarrow_{\mathcal{R}}$ ([22]). Since $\mathcal{R}$ is assumed to be convergent, we easily conclude that an equation $s \simeq t$ is an initial consequence of $\mathcal{E}$ iff the $\mathcal{R}$-normal forms of $s\sigma$ and $t\sigma$ are identical, for every fo-ground substitution σ. This last property is given a particular name:

---

[3] This implicitly refers to all variables in the terms of current interest.

[4] Actually, ground convergence suffices in the first-order case. We conjecture that 'fo-ground' convergence is sufficient for our higher-order setting, but we do not pursue this.

Definition 3 (Initial consistency). We say that a higher-order equation $s \simeq t$ is *initially consistent* with a convergent higher-order rewrite system $\mathcal{R}$ if for all fo-ground substitutions σ we have $s\sigma!_{\mathcal{R}} \equiv t\sigma!_{\mathcal{R}}$.

We see it as our main objective to prove equations. However, proof by consistency also has considerable refutational power; the first-order method is complete in this respect. For this reason, we pursue refutational aspects to some extent here. In the first-order setting, an equation is either consistent or inconsistent. We must take more care in our setting, since our concept of initial consistency may not exhaustively contain all provable equations. For the purpose of refuting equations, we develop a dual notion to initial consistency.

Definition 4. A position ω in a term t is *persistent* in t if all symbols in t above ω are either constructors or lambda binders.

Note that the root position in a term is always persistent.

Definition 5 (Initial inconsistency). We say that a higher-order equation $s = t$ is *initially inconsistent* with a convergent higher-order rewrite system $\mathcal{R}$ if for some fo-ground substitution σ there is a persistent position ω in $t\sigma!_{\mathcal{R}}$ and $u\sigma!_{\mathcal{R}}$ such that $t\sigma!_{\mathcal{R}}/\omega$ and $u\sigma!_{\mathcal{R}}/\omega$ have distinct constructors as root symbols.

The carrying idea behind the definition of initial inconsistency is as follows: if a term t has a persistent position ω then all symbols above ω persist whatever rewriting is performed, and whatever values are given to the variables. Thus, from the definition of constructor it is easy to see that if two terms s and t have distinct constructors in a position that is persistent in both of them, then for all interpretations of variables, s and t will rewrite to distinct terms.

A set $\mathcal{E}$ of equations is deemed initially consistent with $\mathcal{R}$ if every equation in $\mathcal{E}$ is initially consistent, and initially inconsistent if some equation in $\mathcal{E}$ is initially inconsistent. In order to conclude that $\mathcal{E}$ is initially consistent, we need to verify that there is no *inconsistency witness* of $\mathcal{E}$ wrt. $\mathcal{R}$, that is, an equation $s \simeq t \in \mathcal{E}$ and fo-ground substitution σ such that $s\sigma \xrightarrow{!}_{\mathcal{R}} s' \not\equiv t' \xleftarrow{!}_{\mathcal{R}} t\sigma$. We write this witness as $W = (s \simeq t, \sigma)$. To conclude that $\mathcal{E}$ is initially *inconsistent* wrt. $\mathcal{R}$, we must find a *strong inconsistency witness* $W = (s \simeq t, \sigma)$ of $\mathcal{E}$ wrt. $\mathcal{R}$, where $s \simeq t \in \mathcal{E}$ is initially inconsistent wrt. $\mathcal{R}$ and σ is a fo-ground substitution playing the part of the substitution in definition 5. Note that every strong witness is a witness.

Typical examples of strong witnesses are clashes between different constructors, e.g. in $0 \simeq s(0)$. For a non-strong witness, suppose that f and g are extensionally equal, e.g. both have identical definitions. Then $\lambda x.f(x) \simeq \lambda x.g(x)$ holds under extensionality, though this equation is not by our definition an initial consequence.[5] Furthermore some witnesses, such as $F(a) \simeq F(b)$, can be reduced to strong witnesses via projections, here $F \mapsto \lambda x.x$. Since such cases seem to appear rarely, we do not consider this further.

In the first-order case, the proof by consistency procedure basically computes critical pairs between a set $\mathcal{E}$ of equational conjectures and the convergent rewrite

---

[5] By extensionality, we have to prove $f(X) \simeq g(X)$ instead of $\lambda x.f(x) \simeq \lambda x.g(x)$, where X is a new free variable. This extension of our framework remains to be investigated.

system $\mathcal{R}$ representing the given theory. This necessitates a unification procedure. However, for higher-order terms, the unification problem is undecidable in general. (Consult [25] for a treatment of higher-order unification.) As an important special case, Miller [20] showed that it is decidable whether two patterns are unifiable, and if they are, a most general unifier can be computed, and the Critical Pair Lemma is retained (Nipkow [22]). As is customary, we assume that the left-hand side of each rewrite rule is a pattern. But even if the equations we want to reason about happen to be patterns, the procedure may generate non-pattern equations, so we have no guarantee that unification will always behave as in the first-order case. For example, we run the risk of being confronted with a situation in which no minimal and complete set of unifiers exists. However, this happens very rarely in practice. In the second-order case with functional (linear) rules, it does not occur at all ([24]).

From now on, let $\mathcal{R}$ be a fixed, convergent rewrite system. To reason about our proposed procedure, we need an ordering on witnesses. For this purpose it is natural to exploit the orderings on higher-order terms proposed by e.g. [27, 18, 11, 10]. Our method can be seen as induction over any such ordering containing $\xrightarrow{*}_{\mathcal{R}}$. In the following, we assume an ordering which is based on the well-founded ordering $\xrightarrow{+}_{\mathcal{R}}$ and a subterm notion. We write $s \trianglerighteq t$ if $s \equiv C[t]$ for some context C which does not bind any free variables in t. We define $\trianglerighteq_{\mathcal{R}}$ as the transitive closure of $\trianglerighteq \cup \xrightarrow{+}_{\mathcal{R}}$. The strict part of $\trianglerighteq_{\mathcal{R}}$, written $\triangleright_{\mathcal{R}}$, is a well-founded ordering (see [25]).

Definition 6. Let $\mathcal{W} = (s \simeq t, \sigma)$ and $\mathcal{W}' = (s' \simeq t', \sigma')$ be witnesses. We write $\mathcal{W} \geq_{W} \mathcal{W}'$ if $s\sigma \trianglerighteq_{\mathcal{R}} s'\sigma$ and $t\sigma \trianglerighteq_{\mathcal{R}} t'\sigma'$. We define $>_{W}$ as the strict part of $\geq_{W}$.

It is easy to see that $>_{W}$ is a well-founded ordering. We are now ready to introduce the important concept of *covering sets*, which is a straight-forward adaptation of the first-order notion, cf. [1].

Definition 7 (Covering set). Let $\mathcal{E}$ and $\mathcal{E}'$ be sets of equations and $\mathcal{R}$ a convergent rewrite system. We say that $\mathcal{E}$ is covered by $\mathcal{E}'$, or that $\mathcal{E}'$ is a *covering set* for $\mathcal{E}$, *with respect to* $\mathcal{R}$ if for every (strong) witness $\mathcal{W} = (s \simeq t, \sigma)$ of an equation $s \simeq t$ in $\mathcal{E}$, there is a (strong) witness $\mathcal{W}' = (s' \simeq t', \sigma')$ of an equation $s' \simeq t'$ in $\mathcal{E}'$ such that $\mathcal{W} >_{W} \mathcal{W}'$.

We shall return to the operational aspects of this concept. For now, we only state the following evident result.

Lemma 1 *Assume that equation set $\mathcal{E}'$ covers equation set $\mathcal{E}$ with respect to $\mathcal{R}$. If $\mathcal{E}$ is initially inconsistent with $\mathcal{R}$ then $\mathcal{E}'$ is initially inconsistent with $\mathcal{R}$. Furthermore, if $\mathcal{E}$ is not initially consistent with $\mathcal{R}$, then $\mathcal{E}'$ is not initially consistent with $\mathcal{R}$.*

Proof by consistency is based on the computation of critical pairs between the given rewrite system $\mathcal{R}$ and the candidate equation $s \simeq t$ to be investigated. In the same fashion as completion can be seen as a proof normalization process, proof by consistency can be seen as witness normalization. Our correctness proof will illustrate this.

We now describe our proof procedure which accepts as input a set $\mathcal{E}_0$ of equations and aims at proving that every equation in $\mathcal{E}_0$ is initially consistent with $\mathcal{R}$, or at detecting an initially inconsistent equation in $\mathcal{E}_0$. The rewrite system $\mathcal{R}$ is left unchanged throughout the process, and the data structure is only a set of (unordered) equations. The procedure is started with input $\mathcal{E}_0$, and each step in a derivation sequence $\mathcal{E}_0 \vdash \mathcal{E}_1 \vdash \cdots$ is governed by the following inference system:

DEDUCE:	$\dfrac{\mathcal{E}}{\mathcal{E} \cup \{s \simeq t\}}$	if $s \simeq t \in CP^*(\mathcal{R}, \mathcal{E})$.
SIMPLIFY:	$\dfrac{\mathcal{E} \cup \{s \simeq t\}}{\mathcal{E} \cup \{s' \simeq t\}}$	if $s \underset{\mathcal{R}}{\rightarrow} s'$.
DECOMPOSE:	$\dfrac{\mathcal{E} \cup \{c(\overline{s_n}) \simeq c(\overline{t_n})\}}{\mathcal{E} \bigcup \{s_i \simeq t_i\}_{i=1}^{n}}$	if c is a constructor symbol.
COVER:	$\dfrac{\mathcal{E} \cup \{s \simeq t\}}{\mathcal{E}}$	if $s \simeq t$ is covered by $\bigcup_i \mathcal{E}_i$.
DELETE:	$\dfrac{\mathcal{E} \cup \{t \simeq t\}}{\mathcal{E}}$	
PROVE:	$\dfrac{\emptyset}{\text{PROOF}}$	
REFUTE:	$\dfrac{\mathcal{E} \cup \{c(\overline{s_m}) \simeq c'(\overline{t_n})\}}{\text{REFUTATION}}$ if c and c' are distinct constructors.	

A higher-order pattern t is a *strong pattern*, if every non-variable subterm of base type in the η-normal form is rigid. (This disallows subterms $F(\overline{y_n})$ of base type.) The set $CP^*(\mathcal{R}, \mathcal{E})$ quoted in the DEDUCE rule is the subset of the critical pairs $CP(\mathcal{R}, \mathcal{E})$ in which the involved unifier maps variables only to strong patterns. In practice, this is not a severe restriction, and it has the following pleasant and useful effect:

Lemma 2 *If σ is a fo-ground substitution and μ is a unifier involved in the computation of a critical pair in $CP^*(\mathcal{R}, \mathcal{E})$, then $\mu\sigma$ is fo-ground.*

4 Correctness of the procedure

We now prove the system to be correct in the sense that each step preserves initial consistency as well as initial inconsistency, and that the conclusions made by the halting inference rules are sound. To complete the first part of the proof, we employ our ordering on witnesses and show that they occur in a "down-hill" manner in the process. The careful reader will see that the ordering machinery is essentially only necessary for the COVER rule, where the absence of cycles in the ordering is crucial.

Proposition 3 *Let $\mathcal{E}_k \vdash \mathcal{E}_{k+1}$ be a derivation step of the above procedure with input $\mathcal{E}_0$. If $\mathcal{W} = (s \simeq t, \sigma)$ is a (strong) witness in $\mathcal{E}_k$, then there is a (strong) witness $\mathcal{W}' = (s' \simeq t', \sigma')$ in $\mathcal{E}_{k+1}$ such that $\mathcal{W} \geq_W \mathcal{W}'$.*

Proof. By inspection of each non-halting inference rule which removes an equation. SIMPLIFY: If $s \underset{\mathcal{R}}{\to} s'$, then stability of $\underset{\mathcal{R}}{\to}$ yields $s\sigma \underset{\mathcal{R}}{\to} s'\sigma$ for all substitutions σ. Since $\mathcal{R}$ is convergent, $s\sigma!_{\mathcal{R}} = s'\sigma!_{\mathcal{R}}$. This implies that if $\mathcal{W} = (s \simeq t, \sigma)$ is a (strong) witness in $\mathcal{E}_k$, then $\mathcal{W}' = (s' \simeq t, \sigma)$ is a (strong) witness in $\mathcal{E}_{k+1}$. Furthermore, $\mathcal{W} \geq_W \mathcal{W}'$.

DECOMPOSE: If there is a witness $\mathcal{W} = (c(\overline{s_n}) \simeq c(\overline{t_n}), \sigma)$ in $\mathcal{E}_k$, then the $\mathcal{R}$-normal forms $c(\overline{s_n\sigma})!_{\mathcal{R}} = c(\overline{u_n})$ and $c(\overline{t_n\sigma})!_{\mathcal{R}} = c(\overline{v_n})$ would be distinct for some fo-ground substitution σ. But then, $s_i\sigma \underset{\mathcal{R}}{\to} u_i \not\equiv v_i \underset{\mathcal{R}}{\leftarrow} t_i\sigma$ for some i, implying that $\mathcal{W}' = (s_i \simeq t_i, \sigma)$ is a witness in $\mathcal{E}_{k+1}$. Furthermore, since $c(\overline{s_n})\sigma \rhd s_i\sigma$ and $c(\overline{t_n})\sigma \rhd t_i\sigma$, we have $\mathcal{W} >_W \mathcal{W}'$. Assume now that $\mathcal{W} = (c(\overline{s_n}) \simeq c(\overline{t_n}), \sigma)$ was a strong witness in $\mathcal{E}_k$, so in addition the terms $c(\overline{s_n\sigma})!_{\mathcal{R}} = c(\overline{u_n})$ and $c(\overline{t_n\sigma})!_{\mathcal{R}} = c(\overline{v_n})$ both have a persistent position ω in which they have occurrences of distinct constructors. Then, the position ω' with $\omega = i.\omega'$ is persistent in u_i and v_i, so $\mathcal{W}' = (s_i \simeq t_i, \sigma)$ is a strong witness as well.

COVER: Assume that $\mathcal{W} = (s \simeq t, \sigma)$ is a $>_W$-minimal (strong) witness of the equation $s \simeq t$ being removed. If $s \simeq t$ is covered by an equation $s' \simeq t' \in \mathcal{E}_j$, where $j \leq k$, then there is a (strong) witness $\mathcal{W}_j$ with $s' \simeq t'$ such that $\mathcal{W} >_W \mathcal{W}_j$, furthermore (by an induction argument over this proposition) there must be a sequence $\mathcal{W}_j \geq_W \mathcal{W}_{j+1} \geq_W \cdots \geq_W \mathcal{W}_k$, where each $\mathcal{W}_i$ is a (strong) witness of an equation in $\mathcal{E}_i$. By well-foundedness of $>_W$, we must have $\mathcal{W} \neq \mathcal{W}_k$. Now recall that $\mathcal{W}$ is assumed to be a $>_W$-minimal witness of $s \simeq t$. This implies that $\mathcal{W}_k$ is a witness of another equation in $\mathcal{E}_k$ than $s \simeq t$.

DELETE: Trivial, since every equation of the form $t \simeq t$ is initially consistent. □

Proposition 4 *If $\mathcal{E}_k \vdash \mathcal{E}_{k+1}$ is a derivation step of the above procedure with input $\mathcal{E}_0$ and there is no (strong) witness in $\mathcal{E}_k$, then there is no (strong) witness in $\mathcal{E}_{k+1}$.*

Proof. By inspection of the inference rules that introduce equations. SIMPLIFY: Note that if $s \underset{\mathcal{R}}{\to} s'$, then $s\sigma!_{\mathcal{R}} \equiv s'\sigma!_{\mathcal{R}}$ for all substitutions σ. Thus, if $\mathcal{W}' = (s' \simeq t, \sigma)$ is a (strong) witness in $\mathcal{E}_{k+1}$, then $\mathcal{W} = (s \simeq t, \sigma)$ is a (strong) witness in $\mathcal{E}_k$.

DEDUCE: Suppose that μ is the mgu involved in the computation of a critical pair (in $CP^*(\mathcal{R}, \mathcal{E})$) for an equation $s \simeq t$, so that the actual critical pair deduced is a simplified version of $s\mu \simeq t\mu$. If the critical pair has a (strong) witness σ, then σ is also a (strong) witness of $s\mu \simeq t\mu$ (cf. the immediately preceding treatment of SIMPLIFY). By lemma 2, $\mu\sigma$ is fo-ground. Consequently, $\mu\sigma$ can be seen to be a (strong) witness of $s \simeq t$.

DECOMPOSE: If $\mathcal{W}' = (s \simeq t, \sigma)$ is a witness in $\mathcal{E}_{k+1}$, then $s\sigma!_{\mathcal{R}} \not\equiv t\sigma!_{\mathcal{R}}$. But then $c(\ldots, s, \ldots)\sigma!_{\mathcal{R}} \not\equiv c(\ldots, t, \ldots)\sigma!_{\mathcal{R}}$, so $\mathcal{W} = (c(\ldots, s, \ldots) \simeq c(\ldots, t, \ldots), \sigma)$ is a witness in $\mathcal{E}_k$. If $\mathcal{W}'$ is a strong witness, then there is a persistent position ω in s and t in which these terms have occurrences of distinct constructors. Assume that i is the position of s and t in $c(\ldots, s, \ldots)$ and $c(\ldots, t, \ldots)$, respectively. Then $\mathcal{W}$ is strong as well, since the position $i.\omega$ is persistent in $c(\ldots, s, \ldots)$ and $c(\ldots, t, \ldots)$. □

Applying Propositions 3 and 4 and inspecting the inference rules PROVE and REFUTE, we obtain the following correctness theorem.

Theorem 5 *Assume $\mathcal{E}_0$ is given as input to the above procedure. If the procedure terminates with* PROOF, *then $\mathcal{E}_0$ is initially consistent with $\mathcal{R}$; if it terminates with* REFUTATION, *then $\mathcal{E}_0$ is initially inconsistent with $\mathcal{R}$.*

For practical application, the COVER rule requires methods for deciding whether an equation is covered by the set $\bigcup_i \mathcal{E}_i$ of all generated equations. We do not address this question in full generality, but point out important tractable cases. (A first-order approach to this is summarized in [1].)

Definition 8 (Complete position). A position ω in a term t is *inductively complete* with respect to a convergent rewrite system $\mathcal{R}$ if ω is not inside a flexible subterm of t and t/ω is not $\equiv$-equivalent to a variable and $(t/\omega)\sigma$ is an instance of the left-hand side of a rule in $\mathcal{R}$ whenever σ is an irreducible fo-ground substitution.

In the first-order case, it is well known that the property of *ground reducibility* is decidable for terms as well as for equations ([12]). As an important tractable case for higher-order systems, suppose that functions, say f, are totally defined by rewrite rules having left-hand sides $f(c_1(\overline{X_{n_1}}), \overline{Y}), \ldots, f(c_m(\overline{X_{n_m}}), \overline{Y})$, where $c_1, \ldots, c_m$ are constructors spanning a recursive data type. Then any (sub-)term of the form $f(X, \overline{s})$ will correspond to a complete position, unless it occurs below a free variable.

Lemma 6 *Let $\mathcal{R}$ be a convergent rewrite system and $s \simeq t$ be an equation in which a position ω is complete wrt. $\mathcal{R}$. Then, the set of critical pairs computed by superposing rules from $\mathcal{R}$ on $s \simeq t$ in position ω yields a covering set for $s \simeq t$.*

This lemma indicates how COVER can remove an equation after its critical pairs in a complete position have been computed. Another application is as follows: Suppose $s \xrightarrow{\rightarrow} s'$, so that some equation $s \simeq t$ may be simplified by $\mathcal{R}$ to some equation $s' \simeq t$ in $\bigcup_i \mathcal{E}_i$ (equal up to variable renaming) by applying a rule from $\mathcal{R}$ in a position in s which is not below a free higher-order variable. Then, we also have $s\sigma \xrightarrow{\rightarrow} s'\sigma$ for all substitutions σ. In this case it is easily seen that $s \simeq t$ is covered by $s' \simeq t$, so the former equation may be discarded. Finally, suppose given some equation $c(\overline{s_n}) \simeq c(\overline{t_n})$ such that for each j, the equation $s_j \simeq t_j$ occurs (up to variable renaming) in $\bigcup_i \mathcal{E}_i$ or is covered by $\bigcup_i \mathcal{E}_i$. Then $c(\overline{s_n}) \simeq c(\overline{t_n})$ is removed by the COVER rule. Note that the use of COVER sketched above will sometimes correspond to the application of an induction hypothesis.

5 Examples

Example 1. Consider the type of binary trees containing node elements of some fixed, possibly higher-order type. The binary trees are generated by the constructors *empty* giving the empty tree, and *root* taking a node of the tree and two (sub-)trees as arguments. Functions *rev* (mirror image of a tree) and *map* (application of a function to every node) are defined as follows:

$$
\begin{aligned}
rev(empty) &\rightarrow empty \\
rev(root(W, X, Y)) &\rightarrow root(W, rev(Y), rev(X)) \\
map(F, empty) &\rightarrow empty \\
map(F, root(W, X, Y)) &\rightarrow root(F(W), map(F, X), map(F, Y))
\end{aligned}
$$

(Note that in order to improve readability we do not write a higher-order variable F in its η-expanded form $\lambda x.F(x)$ here.) We want to prove the equation

$$map(F, rev(Z)) \simeq rev(map(F, Z)) \qquad (1)$$

There is a complete position identifying the subterm $rev(Z)$ in the left-hand side. Computing critical pairs here yields a covering set for equation (1), so we may use DEDUCE and COVER to replace (1) with $map(F, empty) \simeq rev(map(F, empty))$ and $map(F, root(W, rev(Y), rev(X))) \simeq rev(map(F, root(W, X, Y)))$. The former equation is simplified to $empty \simeq empty$ and then deleted; the latter simplifies to

$$\begin{aligned} root(F(W), map(F, rev(Y)), map(F, rev(X))) \simeq \\ root(F(W), rev(map(F, Y)), rev(map(F, X))) \end{aligned} \qquad (2)$$

If we try to decompose equation (2), we get the new equation $F(W) \simeq F(W)$ as well as $map(F, rev(Y)) \simeq rev(map(F, Y))$ and $map(F, rev(X)) \simeq rev(map(F, X))$. The first of these is deleted, and the last two are equal to (1) modulo variable renaming. Hence (2) is covered and we end up with the empty equation set, proving equation (1).

Example 2. Consider again binary trees defined in the previous example. Add to this rewrite system the rule $(F \circ G)(W) \rightarrow F(G(W))$ defining function composition. We now want to prove the equation

$$map(F \circ G, Z) \simeq map(F, map(G, Z)) \qquad (3)$$

The empty position in the left-hand side of this equation is complete, so we may replace this equation with the set of critical pairs deduced in this position. First we obtain $empty \simeq map(F, map(G, empty))$, which simplifies to a trivial equation $empty \simeq empty$. The next critical pair is

$$root((F \circ G)(W), map(F \circ G, X), map(F \circ G, Y)) \simeq map(F, map(G, root(W, X, Y)))$$

which simplifies to

$$\begin{aligned} root(F(G(W)), map(F \circ G, X), map(F \circ G, Y)) \simeq \\ root(F(G(W)), map(F, map(G, X)), map(F, map(G, Y))) \end{aligned} \qquad (4)$$

Decomposing this equation we get the trivial equation $F(G(W)) \simeq F(G(W))$, as well as the equations $map((F \circ G), X) \simeq map(F, map(G, X))$ and $map((F \circ G), Y) \simeq map(F, map(G, Y))$, which are both equal to (3) modulo variable renaming. Hence we can complete the proof by the COVER rule.

6 Conclusion and further work

We have presented a way of integrating the first-order method of *proof by consistency* to theorem proving in higher-order equational specifications and given a correctness proof of our proposed procedure. The main motivation is to expand the scope of this sophisticated induction technique.

There are several advantages of this approach over conventional induction on first-order data types. First, proof by consistency does not demand an explicit choice of variables on which to do induction, and can be viewed as a more general and less control-demanding method for inductive reasoning. Second, the instantiations for the variable can be more specific than just covering all constructors, since they depend on the rewrite rules, not on the data type declarations. In general, there can even be simultaneous induction on several variables. Furthermore, the convergent rewrite rules can be used for optimizations.

For using our technique in a higher-order theorem proving system, the precise relation between our notion of first-order ground terms and recursive data types should be formalized. Furthermore, one either needs to assume (as implicit in the first-order case with initial semantics) that all first-order types are recursive data types, or to restrict our procedure to the set of variables whose types admit induction.

Our approach to higher-order proof by consistency as presented here would benefit from refinements in several directions. First, a facility for applying lemmata would certainly be helpful, just as it is in the first-order case. However, this extension relies heavily on orderings on terms, and it remains to be seen whether existing higher-order orderings are suitable for this problem.

First-order proof by consistency as described in [9] considers the property of *ground reducibility* to give more general criteria for refutation of equations. In full generality, this concept seems to be problematic in a higher-order setting, but might be tractable for interesting special cases.

In his treatment of higher-order narrowing, Loría-Sáenz [15] restricts candidate equations to *quasi-first-order* and rewrite rules to *simple* rewrite rules. We believe that corresponding restrictions for proof by consistency would lead to practically useful improvements in the directions that we have just sketched.

References

1. L. Bachmair. *Canonical Equational Proofs*. Birkhäuser, 1991.
2. E. Bevers and J. Lewi. Proof by consistency in conditional equational theories. In *Proc. 2nd International Workshop on Conditional and Typed Rewriting Systems*, volume 516 of *Lect. Not. in Comp. Sci.*, pages 194–205. Springer-Verlag, 1990.
3. V. Breazu-Tannen. Combining algebra and higher-order types. In *Proc. 3rd IEEE Symposium on Logic in Computer Science, Edinburgh (UK)*, July 1988.
4. N. Dershowitz and J.-P. Jouannaud. Rewrite systems. In J. van Leeuwen, editor, *Handbook of Theoretical Computer Science*, volume B, chapter 6. Elsevier, 1990.
5. L. Fribourg. A strong restriction on the inductive completion procedure. In *Proc. 13th International Colloquium on Automata, Languages and Programming*, volume 226 of *Lect. Not. in Comp. Sci.*, pages 105–115. Springer-Verlag, 1986.
6. J. A. Goguen. How to prove inductive hypotheses without induction. In W. Bibel and R. Kowalski, editors, *Proc. of the 5th Conference on Automated Deduction*, volume 87 of *Lect. Not. in Comp. Sci.*, pages 356–373. Springer-Verlag, 1980.
7. M. J. C. Gordon. HOL: A proof generating system for higher-order logic. In G. Birtwistle et al., editor, *VLSI Specification, Verification and Synthesis*. Kluwer Academic Press, 1988.
8. G. Huet and J.-M. Hullot. Proofs by induction in equational theories with constructors. *Journal of Computer and System Sciences*, 25(2):239–266, 1982.

9. J.-P. Jouannaud and E. Kounalis. Automatic proofs by induction in equational theories without constructors. In *Proc. Logic in Computer Science*, pages 358–366, 1986.

10. J.-P. Jouannaud and A. Rubio. A recursive path ordering for higher-order terms in η-long β-normal form. In H. Ganzinger, editor, *Proc. 7th International Conference on Rewriting Techniques and Applications*, volume 1103 of *Lect. Not. in Comp. Sci.* Springer-Verlag, 1996.

11. S. Kahrs. Towards a domain theory for termination proofs. In *Proc. of the 6th International Conference on Rewriting Techniques and Applications*, volume 914 of *Lect. Not. in Comp. Sci.*, pages 241–255. Springer-Verlag, 1995.

12. D. Kapur, P. Narendran, and H. Zhang. On sufficient-completeness and related properties of term rewriting systems. *Acta Informatica*, 24(4):395–415, 1987.

13. J. W. Klop. *Combinatory Reduction Systems*. Mathematical Centre Tracts 127, Mathematisch Centrum, Amsterdam, 1980.

14. D. Knuth and P. Bendix. Simple word problems in universal algebras. In J. Leech, editor, *Computational Problems in Abstract Algebra*, pages 263–297. Pergamon Press, Oxford, 1970.

15. C. A. Loría-Sáenz. *A Theoretical Framework for Reasoning about Program Construction Based on Extensions of Rewrite Systems*. PhD thesis, Universität Kaiserslautern, 1993.

16. O. Lysne. Proof by consistency in constructive systems with final algebra semantics. In *Proc. 3rd International Conference on Algebraic and Logic Programming, Pisa (Italy)*, volume 632 of *Lect. Not. in Comp. Sci.*, pages 276–290. Springer-Verlag, 1992.

17. O. Lysne. Extending Bachmair's method for proof by consistency to the final algebra. *Information Processing Letters*, 51:303–310, 1994.

18. O. Lysne and J. Piris. A termination ordering for higher order rewrite systems. In *Proc. 6th Conference on Rewriting Techniques and Applications, Kaiserslautern (Germany)*, volume 914 of *Lect. Not. in Comp. Sci.*, pages 26–40. Springer-Verlag, 1995.

19. R. Mayr and T. Nipkow. Higher-order rewrite systems and their confluence. Technical report, Institut für Informatik, Technische Universität München, August 1994. To appear in Theoretical Computer Science.

20. D. Miller. A logic programming language with lambda-abstraction, function variables, and simple unification. In *Extensions of Logic Programming*, volume 475 of *Lect. Not. in Comp. Sci.*, pages 253–281. Springer-Verlag, 1991.

21. D. L. Musser. On proving inductive properties in abstract data types. In *Proceedings of the 7th Annual ACM Symposium on Principles of Programming Languages*, pages 154–162, January 1980.

22. T. Nipkow. Higher-order critical pairs. In *Proc. of the 6th IEEE Symposium on Logic in Computer Science*, pages 342–359, 1991.

23. L. C. Paulson. *Isabelle: A Generic Theorem Prover*, volume 828 of *Lect. Not. in Comp. Sci.* Springer-Verlag, 1994.

24. C. Prehofer. Decidable higher-order unification problems. In *Proc. 12th International Conference on Automated Deduction, Nancy*, volume 814 of *Lect. Not. in Art. Intell.*, pages 635–649. Springer-Verlag, 1994.

25. C. Prehofer. *Solving Higher-Order Equations: From Logic to Programming*. PhD thesis, Technische Universität München, 1995.

26. U. S. Reddy. Term rewriting induction. In *Proc. 10th International Conference on Automated Deduction, Kaiserslautern*, volume 449 of *Lect. Not. in Comp. Sci.*, pages 162–177. Springer-Verlag, 1990.

27. J. van de Pol. Termination proofs for higher-order rewrite systems. In *1st International Workshop on Higher-Order Algebra, Logic and Term Rewriting*, volume 816 of *Lecture Notes in Computer Science*, pages 305–325. Springer-Verlag, 1993.

Advocating Ownership

Henning Fernau, Klaus-Jörn Lange, Klaus Reinhardt

Wilhelm-Schickhard Institut für Informatik, Universität Tübingen
Sand 13, D-72076 Tübingen, Germany
e-mail: {fernau,lange,reinhard}@informatik.uni-tuebingen.de

Abstract. We show the equivalence of deterministic auxiliary push-down automata to owner write PRAMs in a fairly large setting by proving that $DAuxPDA\text{-}TISP(f^{O(1)}, \log g)$ and $CROW\text{-}TIPR(\log f, g^{O(1)})$ coincide. Such, we provide the first circuit characterizations of depth $O(\log f)$ for deterministic sequential automata which are f time-bounded.

1 Introduction

Parallel models provided fruitful extensions to structural complexity theory, a prominent example being the class NC. Ruzzo exhibited the tight connections between alternating Turing machines, auxiliary push-down automata, and boolean circuits [20]. By results of Stockmeyer and Vishkyn [21] and by the intertwining of the NC hierarchy with the polylogtime hierarchy of $EREW$-PRAMs these relations are also valid for the various types of PRAMs defined by the *concurrent* and the *exclusive* read and write feature.

In 1986, Dymond and Ruzzo introduced the concept of *owner write* for PRAMs and showed close connections between owner write PRAMs and deterministic auxiliary push-down automata [6]. Later, by considering unambiguous circuits it was possible to exhibit similarly close relationships between unambiguous auxiliary push-down automata and $CREW$-PRAMs [11,15]. Together, these results show the correspondence between determinism, unambiguity, and nondeterminism on the one hand, and the features of owner write, exclusive write, and concurrent write, on the other hand.

In particular, the unambiguous nature of the concept of exclusive access explains the difficulty of structural analysis of these classes. Neither they seem to possess complete problems nor to be recursively presentable. This is the reason why so many $CREW$- and $EREW$-algorithms only work exclusively if their inputs fulfill certain "promises" which cannot be checked by the machine itself. Furthermore, many CREW-algorithms are actually CROW-algorithms, which underlines the necessity to study this model more thoroughly.

It is one aim of this paper to stress the importance of the owner concept by exhibiting more of its close relations to deterministic sequential machine models. In fact, our results will show that $CROW$-PRAMs may be regarded as parallel versions of deterministic auxiliary push-down automata: we show the equivalence of $f^{O(1)}$ time-bounded deterministic auxiliary push-down automata, which have a work-tape of length $O(\log g)$, to $O(\log f)$ time-bounded $CROW$-PRAMs with $g^{O(1)}$ processors under rather general conditions. This will enable us to interrelate both models more closely into the framework of SC and NC classes. Another consequence will be a very general depth (i.e., stack height) reduction result for deterministic auxiliary push-down automata as it was known before in this generality only in the nondeterministic case. The first main ingredient to prove our results will be a simplified and on the other hand much more general version of the algorithms of Dymond and Ruzzo [6], resp. of Monien, Rytter, and Schäpers [14], which in turn may be seen as related to the algorithm of Cook [4]. Our second main tool is a new circuit-like representation of owner write PRAMs which enables us to simplify the presentation and analysis of the recursive structure behind the sequential simulation of a $CROW$-PRAM. In this way, we get a circuit representation of depth $O(d)$ for owner write PRAMs which are $O(d)$ time-bounded. Characterization like that were known before for exclusive write and concurrent write PRAMs, resp. for nondeterministic or unambiguous auxiliary push-down automata, but are new in case of determinism and owner write.

An enhanced version of this paper containing all proofs in detail can be obtained from the authors.

2 Preliminaries and the owner concept

We assume the reader to be acquainted with the basic notions of complexity theory as they are contained, e.g., in the books [1] or [9]. In particular, we denote in the following by $LOG(\mathcal{X})$ the set of all languages that are logspace many-one reducible to any element of $\mathcal{X}$. Further on, let $DTISP(f, g)$ be the set of all languages accepted by $O(g)$-space bounded Turing machines in time $O(f)$. In addition, we will refer to the numerous classes built upon boolean circuits like NC, SC, NC^k, AC^k, SAC^k, and SC^k (see [2,10]). We use throughout this paper the following function classes: $pol := \bigcup_{k \geq 1} n^k$ as polynomial bounds, $expol := \bigcup_{k \geq 1} 2^{n^k}$ as exponential bounds, $polylog := \bigcup_{k \geq 1} \log^k n$ as polylogarithmic bounds, and $expolylog := \bigcup_{k \geq 1} 2^{\log^k n}$ as pseudopolynomial bounds.

Finally, we explain the notions of a parallel random access machine and that of an auxiliary push-down automaton in more detail.

The concept of a $PRAM$ goes back to [7,8]. Roughly, a PRAM is a set of Random Access Machines, called *Processors*, working synchronously and communicating via a *Global Memory*. Each step takes one time unit regardless whether it performs a local or a global (i.e., remote) operation. We assume the word length to be logarithmically bounded in the number of used processors. Further, all participating processors are active at the first step and need not be activated.

There are several versions of this device concerning the way how the simultaneous memory access is handled. Currently, there are two main versions concerning the write access: a machine with *Concurrent Write* access allows the simultaneous write access of several processors to the same memory cell in one step. A machine with *Exclusive Write* access forbids simultaneous writes and requires that in each step at most one processor may change the contents of a global memory cell. Correspondingly, we get two ways to manage read access to the global memory: *Concurrent Read and Exclusive Read*. In this way, we get four versions of PRAMs, denoted as $XRYW$-PRAMs with $X, Y \in \{E, C\}$, where XR specifies the type of read access and YW that of the write access, the access types being designated by their initials. If we work with a polynomial number of processors, we denote the class of all languages recognizable in time f by $XRYW$-PRAMs by $XRYW$-*TIME(f(n))*. By definition, we know that $XRYW$-*TIME(f)* $\subseteq X'RY'W$-*TIME(f)* for X,X',Y,Y' $\in \{E, C\}$ if X $\leq$ X' and Y $\leq$ Y' where we set $E \leq C$. If we are working with a nonpolynomial number of processors, we let $CRYW$-*TIPR(f, g)* be the class of all languages accepted by $CRYW$-PRAMs in time $O(f(n))$ using $O(g(n))$ processors on inputs of size n.

In 1986, Dymond and Ruzzo came up with a new concept to handle write conflicts in a PRAM [6]. A PRAM obeys the *owner write* restriction if, for every cell of the global memory, there is a designated processor which is the only one which is allowed to write into that cell. This processor is called the owner of that cell. This concept turned out to be invariant under several obvious modifications, like the coexistence of several owners to one cell or the time dependence of the ownership relation. One of the main result of their investigations was the equation $CROW$-*TIME*$(\log n) = DAuxPDA$-*TIME(poly)*.

While the inclusions of *CFL* in $CRCW$-*TIME*$(\log n)$ and that of *UCFL* in $CREW$-*TIME*$(\log n)$ are not difficult to derive, the corresponding algorithm for putting *DCFL* in $CROW$-*TIME*$(\log n)$ turned out to be the difficult part in Dymond and Ruzzo's proof. Later and independently, Monien, Rytter, and Schäpers gave a simplified and more effective version of this algorithm [14]. Although they designed their algorithm only for an exclusive write PRAM, it indeed fulfills the owner write restriction. A drawback of their algorithm is that it is explicitly limited to elements of *DCFL*. It is not clear how to extend their results even to the case of push-down automata with a two-way access to the input word.

Another device of interest in this context is the *Auxiliary Push-Down Automaton* which might be thought of as a push-down automaton augmented with a $S(n)$-space bounded working tape and two-way access to its input. Throughout this paper, we will work mostly with the case $S(n) = \lceil \log n \rceil$. In that case, let $DAuxPDA$-*TIME(f)* be the class of all languages recognizable by deterministic auxiliary push-down automata with logarithmically space bounded working tapes which are time bounded by $O(f(n))$. $NAuxPDA$-*TIME(f)* denotes the corresponding nondeterministic class. By [3,22], we have

$$P = NAuxPDA\text{-}TIME(expol) = DAuxPDA\text{-}TIME(expol),$$
$$LOG(CFL) = NAuxPDA\text{-}TIME(pol), \text{ and}$$
$$LOG(DCFL) = DAuxPDA\text{-}TIME(pol).$$

When we work with auxiliary push-down automata with a tape which is not logarithmically bounded in length, we let $DAuxPDA$-*TISP(f, g)* be the set of all languages accepted by $O(f)$-time bounded deterministic auxiliary push-down automata with a $O(g)$-bounded working tape. If we are only interested in space bounds, we come to the class $DAuxPDA$-*SPACE(g)*.

3 Main theorem

In this section we present our main result and show, as a first half of its proof, how to simulate deterministic auxiliary push-down automata by owner write PRAMs. We will state our main result for the case of constructible resource bounds. As usual it is not hard to extend the results to the general case.

Theorem 1. *Let* $\log(f)$ *and* $\log(g)$ *be constructible functions fulfilling* $f(n) \geq n$, $g(n) \geq n$, $\log(f) \in O(g)$, *and* $\log(g) \in O(f)$. *Then we have*
$$DAuxPDA\text{-}TISP\big(f^{O(1)}, \log g\big) = CROW\text{-}TIPR\big(\log f, g^{O(1)}\big).$$

Proof. We will now sketch the inclusion from left to right. So let A be an f time-bounded push-down automaton augmented by a $\log g$ bounded working tape. Our algorithmical framework follows closely its predecessors by Dymond and Ruzzo ([6]) and by Monien, Rytter, and Schäpers ([14]) by using a doubling technique on the successor function on configurations. The latter algorithm nicely solves the problem of the growing set of possible stack contents by the use of so-called k-intervals of the form $[(i-1)2^k + 1, \ldots, i2^k]$ in the k-th stage, which results in a clear and clean recursive scheme. In order to hit the interval borders exactly, it is required to store the time within a configuration (in case of a one way input, this is the position on the input tape), which is impossible if $g \in o(f)$. The key to break this barrier is to use an algorithm that calculates as far as possible in every step and to show that the progress is at least doubling in every step.

The push-down itself needs not be stored as long as it is not altered. Therefore, instead of "classical" surface configurations (consisting in the position within the input string, the current state of the push-down automaton and the top symbol on the push-down store), we use extended surface configurations (configuration for short) which contain as additional piece of information the height of the current push-down. Let K denote the set of all such configurations. For $x, y \in K$, we call y "positively reachable" from x, iff for every sequence of configurations $x_0, \ldots, x_m$, where x corresponds to x_0, and y corresponds to x_m, and for every $1 \leq i \leq m$, the push-down of x_i is at least as high as the push-down of x. This means, of course, that (besides the unaltered contents of the push-down) the configuration x uniquely determines y. Since, by $g(n) \geq n$, the number of "classical" surface configurations is bounded by $g^{O(1)}$, and since the maximal depth of the push-down store is bounded not only directly by the time f but also indirectly by the states ([24]), in this case by $g^{O(1)}$, the number of "interesting" configurations is bounded by $g^{O(1)}$. For each pair of extended configurations in K, there will be a processor in the simulating CROW-PRAM. Since the height information is contained in configurations, we can define a transitive relation $\leq_h$ on K by $x \leq_h y$ iff the height of x is less than or equal to the height of y. Similarly, an equivalence relation $\equiv_h$ can be defined on K by $x \equiv_h y$ iff height of x equals the height of y. For $x \in K$ and $k \geq 0$, the k-interval is the sequence of configurations reachable in the next 2^k computation steps starting from x. Notation: $x[k]$ for $x \in K$. In this way, the computation time of $f(n)$ is reduced to $\log(f(n))$. There may be a subtle problem concerning the question whether $\log(f(n))$ can be computed with our imposed resource restrictions. This problem can be circumvented by replacing the **for**-loop by a **repeat until**-loop which terminates when a final configuration is reached from the start configuration. Due to the time restriction $f(n)$ imposed on the DAuxPDA, such a configuration is reached after at most $\log(f(n))$ steps of the CROW-PRAM.

In our algorithm we use a function $\mathrm{JUMP}_k(x)$, which calculates a configuration which is positively reachable from x in at least 2^k steps if possible. This function can be compared with the function Δ^k in [6] and with the function $\mathrm{POP}_k(x,\mathrm{next}_k(x))$ in [14]. The functions $\mathrm{pop}_k(x,y)$ and $\mathrm{POP}_k(x,y)$ calculate a configuration which is reachable from y using the push-down contents written in steps following x. They can be compared to the function LOW^k in [6] and with the functions POP_k and DOWN_k in [14]. Furthermore we extend the common scheme of both algorithms by using a function $\mathrm{GO}_k(x)$ which tries to expand a computation as far as possible while leading to a configuration of the same push-down height.

Initializations: In order to define $\mathrm{GO}_0(x)$, $\mathrm{POP}_0(x,y)$ and $\mathrm{JUMP}_0(x)$, let x' and y' denote the successor configurations of x and y, respectively. We basically have to distinguish the cases when the height of the push-down is incremented by the considered step, decremented or left unchanged.

$$\mathrm{GO}_0(x) := \begin{cases} x' , \text{ if } x \equiv_h x', \\ x , \text{ if } x \not\equiv_h x'; \end{cases} \quad \mathrm{Next}_0(x) := \begin{cases} x' , \text{ if } x \leq_h x', \\ x , \text{ if } x >_h x'; \end{cases}$$

$$\mathrm{POP}_0(x,y) := \begin{cases} y' & , \text{ if } y \text{ has popped the symbol that was pushed by } x, \\ \mathrm{GO}_0(y) & , \text{ otherwise.} \end{cases}$$

$$\mathrm{JUMP}_0(x) := \mathrm{POP}_0(x, \mathrm{Next}_0(x))$$

Our algorithm is depicted in Fig. 1. The index k is just a help for the reader, the values of the functions are only stored in a register for the the last k.

For the correctness and fast termination of the simulation we need that certain properties are satisfied by the functions GO_k, JUMP_k and POP_k. They can be shown by induction. In detail, these properties are as follows:

- $\mathrm{GO}_k(x)$: We have $x \equiv_h \mathrm{GO}_k(x)$ and no other configuration y (after $G_k(x)$) in $x[k]$ is positively reachable (starting from x) such that $x \equiv_h y$.
- $\mathrm{JUMP}_k(x)$: The configuration $\mathrm{JUMP}_k(x)$ is (if possible) in a k-interval $z[k]$ which lies behind $x[k]$ and no other configuration y in $z[k]$ is positively reachable (starting from x) such that $\mathrm{JUMP}_k(x) >_h y$ or $\mathrm{JUMP}_k(x) \equiv_h y$ and y is after $\mathrm{JUMP}_k(x)$.
- $\mathrm{POP}_k(x,y)$: For $x \leq_h y \leq_h \mathrm{JUMP}_k(x)$ there is a point of reference z which lies on the computation path from x to $N_k(x)$ with $z \equiv_h y$. If the push-down contents belonging to y and z are the same (this is of course true if y lies on the computation path starting, e.g., with $\mathrm{JUMP}_k(x)$ as long as there is no configuration z' on the path from $\mathrm{JUMP}_k(x)$ to y such that $z <_h y$), then no other configuration $\bar{y}$ in $y[k]$ is reachable (starting from y) such that $\mathrm{POP}_k(x,y) >_h \bar{y}$ or $\mathrm{POP}_k(x,y) \equiv_h \bar{y}$ and $\bar{y}$ is after $\mathrm{POP}_k(x,y)$.

for each $x, y \in K$ **do in parallel**
   begin
        Initialize $\text{GO}_0(x)$, $\text{POP}_0(x)$, $\text{JUMP}_0(x, y)$ [see main text]
   end
for $k := 0$ **to** $\log(f(n))$ **do**
   for each $x, y \in K$ **do in parallel**
      begin
         if $\text{JUMP}_k(x) \equiv_h x$
            then $\text{GO}_{k+1}(x) := \text{JUMP}_k(x)$
            else $\text{GO}_{k+1}(x) := \text{GO}_k(x)$
         if $y \leq_h \text{JUMP}_k(x)$
            then $\text{pop}_k(x, y) := \text{POP}_k(x, y)$
            else $\text{pop}_k(x, y) := \text{POP}_k(\text{JUMP}_k(x), y)$
         $\text{POP}_{k+1}(x, y) := \text{pop}_k(x, \text{GO}_{k+1}(\text{pop}_k(x, \text{GO}_{k+1}(\text{pop}_k(x, y)))))$
         $\text{JUMP}_{k+1}(x) := \text{POP}_{k+1}(x, \text{JUMP}_k(\text{JUMP}_k(x)))$
      end

Fig. 1. CROW-PRAM-Algorithm for DAuxPDA Simulation

The function $\text{GO}_k(x)$ is easily computed by storing the last $\text{JUMP}_k(x)$ having the height of x.

We define the auxiliary function $\text{pop}_k(x, y)$ in order to extend the function $\text{POP}_k(x, y)$ from using the push-down at $\text{JUMP}_k(x)$ to using the push-down at $\text{JUMP}_k(\text{JUMP}_k(x))$. Therefore, we distinguish the cases $y \leq_h \text{JUMP}_k(x)$ (now, the push-down contents built up from x to $\text{JUMP}_k(x)$ is valid) and $y >_h \text{JUMP}_k(x)$ (in this case, the push-down contents constructed starting with the local minimum $\text{JUMP}_k(x)$ is of interest , see the dashed line from $\text{JUMP}_k(x)$ in Fig. 2).

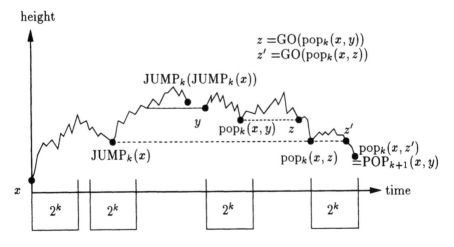

Fig. 2. Clarifying the definition of $\text{POP}_{k+1}(x, y)$.

For the calculation of $POP_{k+1}(x, y)$, we must find a configuration reachable from y so that no other configuration $\bar{y}$ in $y[k+1]$ is reachable (starting from y) such that $POP_k(x, y) >_h \bar{y}$ or $POP_k(x, y) \equiv_h \bar{y}$ and $\bar{y}$ is after $POP_k(x, y)$. This requires two applications of $pop_k(x, .)$: one applications of $pop_k(x, y)$ to get down in $y[k]$, which is the the first half of $y[k+1]$ followed by an application of GO_{k+1} to find appropriate configuration in the second half of $y[k+1]$ (z in Fig. 2) (if the height is not increasing in the entire rest of $y[k+1]$) and one application of $pop_k(x, .)$ to get down in the second half of $y[k+1]$. Since one application of $pop_k(x, .)$ can have a shortcut when it reaches the border from $JUMP_k(x)$, we apply $pop_k(x, .)$ once more. In total this results in three applications of $pop_k(x, .)$ alternating with $GO_{k+1}(.)$. □

We consider the number of processors our algorithm needs. If the working of the simulated automaton A allows for $O(g^c(n))$ different inscriptions, we can bind the stack height either by $O(g^c(n) \cdot n)$ or by $f(n)$ whichever is smaller. This leads either to $O(g^c(n) \cdot n \cdot f(n))$ or $O(g^{2c}(n) \cdot n^2)$ different configurations and hence to $O(g^{2c}(nc) \cdot n^2 \cdot f^2(n))$ or to $O(g^{4c}(n) \cdot n^4)$ processors. In case of an unaugmented push-down automaton, our construction would lead to an algorithm using $O(n^4)$ processors which is clearly worse than the $O(n^3)$ of Monien, Rytter, and Schäpers. On the other hand, our algorithm would tolerate two-way access to the input of the simulated automaton which is excluded for their algorithm.

4 Deterministic Circuits

This section presents the simulation of $CROW$-PRAMs by deterministic auxiliary push-down automata. Although not stated explicitly in [6], this fact has already been shown by Dymond and Ruzzo. The basic idea is to describe the work of the owner write PRAM by a recursion of bounded width and depth $\log f$ which leads to a time bound of $f^{O(1)}$. The space requirement is determined by the word length of the PRAM which is $\log g$. Observe the importance of the boundedness of the recursion width which is made possible by the owner write restriction of the simulated PRAM.

We will now exhibit this relation by investigating *multiplex select* gates which were introduced by Reinhardt [17]. They were inspired by the *select* gates of Niepel and Rossmanith [16,19]. While characterizations by circuits of depth $O(\log f)$ for $f^{O(1)}$ time-bounded nondeterministic auxiliary push-down automata and for $O(\log f)$ time-bounded concurrent write and exclusive write PRAMs are well-known [11,16,20,23], this will lead to the first characterization of this type in the case of determinism and owner write.

A multiplex select gate has two kinds of input signals: one bundle of $O(\log(s))$ steering signals and up to s bundles of $O(\log(s))$ data signals. Here, s is the size of the circuit containing the gate. The multiplex select gate, interpreting the steering bits as the binary encoding of a number j, will switch the data bits of bundle j to its bundle of output signals. We will say that the gate *selected* its jth input. A gate like that might be drawn as sketched in Fig. 3.

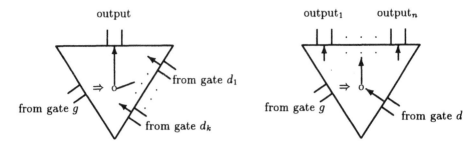

Fig. 3. Select and deselect gates

A multiplex select gate can be described by the encoding of $(g, d_1, ..., d_n)$ where g is the description of the steering input bundle, n is the number of data input bundles and d_j is the description of the j'th data input bundle. A description of an input bundle may start with fixed signals for the bits with higher values and may continue with the number of an output bundle of another gate for the bits with lower value. For example, the description $01100\$i$ says that the first 5 signals of the bundle are 01100 followed by the signals from the output bundle number i (this is the output of gate number i, if we have only this type of gates).

We will not go into further details of defining the uniformity of a family of circuits with multiplex select gates. This is handled as in the boolean case (see, e.g., [20]). Let $MDepthSize(d, s)$ be the class of languages which can be recognized by a uniform family of multiplex select circuits with depth d and size s.

Theorem 2. *Let f and g be constructible functions fulfilling $f(n) \geq n$, $g(n) \geq n$, $\log(f) = O(g)$, and $\log(g) = O(f)$. Then we have*

$$CROW\text{-}TIPR(\log f, g^{O(1)}) \subseteq MDepthSize(\log f, g^{O(1)}).$$

Proof: W.l.o.g. we may assume that every processor has at most c local memory cells and that it always uses the last local cell to store the result of a reading from a global memory cell. Such a configuration of a processor p at time t including its local memory cells can be described by a number m encoding

$$state(p, t)local(p, t, 1)...local(p, t, c)$$

with $O(\log g)$ bits forming a bundle of signals. This bundle is the steering input for a multiplex select gate which has to calculate the following configuration, which is determined by the number m except the contents of the local cell c which is eventually loaded from a global cell i indexed with a local cell. Since i is also determined by m, the description of the m'th data input bundle d_m is $state(p, t + 1)local(p, t + 1, 1)...local(p, t + 1, c - 1)\$i$. The bundle encoding m is also the steering input for a multiplex select gate which has to calculate $global(t + 1, j)$ for all global cells j for which processor p is the write owner.

If processor p writes to cells j in the current step, then the description of the m'th data input bundle d_m contains just the fixed signals encoding the contents being written. Otherwise, d_m contains the number of the gate, whose output is $global(t, j)$. $\square$

Theorem 3. *Let f and g be constructible functions fulfilling $f(n) \geq n$, $g(n) \geq n$, $\log(f) = O(g)$, and $\log(g) = O(f)$. Then we have*
$$M\,DepthSize(\log f, g^{O(1)}) \subseteq DAuxPDA\text{-}TISP(f^{O(1)}, \log g) \,.$$

Proof idea: To evaluate a gate in the circuit, the AuxPDA needs two recursive calls: one call for the steering input and one call for the selected data input. Thus, the evaluation leads to a tree of depth $\log f$ with constant degree having the size $f^{O(1)}$.

Corollary 4. $CROW\text{-}TIPR\left(\log^k n, pol\right) = M\,DepthSize(\log^k n, pol)$, *and*
$CROW\text{-}TIPR\left(\log n, c^{\log^k n}\right) = M\,DepthSize(\log n, c^{\log^k n})$ *for each $k \geq 1$.*

If we want to characterize $OROW$-PRAMs with multiplex select gates, the restriction to allow only one processor to read a specific memory cell corresponds to a bounded fan-out of the gate simulating this memory cell. This seems to contradict the ability of the processors to write to several memory cells. In order to cope with that, we introduce *multiplex deselect* gates, see Fig. 3. A multiplex deselect gate has two kinds of input signals: one bundle of $O(\log(s))$ steering signals and one bundle of $O(\log(s))$ data signals. The number m, which is binary encoded by the steering signals, is the number of the output bundle in the gate to which the data bundle is switched through. All other output signals of the gate are zero. All output bundles in the circuit have a unique number, which is consecutive, meaning if l is the number of the number zero output bundle in a gate, then the output bundle number m in the gate has the number $l + m$ in the circuit. A multiplex deselect gate can be described by the encoding of (g, d, n) where g is the description of the steering input bundle, d is the description of the data input bundle and n is the number of output bundles. Let $MbfDepthSize(d, s)$ be the class of languages which can be recognized by a uniform family of circuits of depth d and size s consisting in multiplex select and multiplex deselect gates of constant fan-out.

Theorem 5. *Let f and g be constructible functions fulfilling $f(n) \geq n$, $g(n) \geq n$, $\log(f) = O(g)$, and $\log(g) = O(f)$. Then we have*
$$OROW\text{-}TIPR(\log f, g^{O(1)}) = MbfDepthSize(\log f, g^{O(1)}) \,.$$

5 Corollaries

We will now demonstrate the universality of our main result by listing some of its consequences. In this way, we get nearly all that was known before on deterministic auxiliary push-down automata and owner write PRAMs with respect to SC and NC classes. (The intertwining of the various NC and SC hierarchies was demonstrated by Ruzzo [20].)

1. $P = DAuxPDA\text{-}TIME(expol)$. (Cook [3])
2. $DCFL \subseteq SC^2$. (Cook [4])
3. $LOG(DCFL) = CROW\text{-}TIPR(\log, pol)$. (Dymond and Ruzzo [6])
4. $P = CROW\text{-}TIPR(\log n, expol)$. (Lange and Rossmanith [13])
5. $CROW\text{-}TIME(\log^k n) \subseteq SAC^k$ for $k \geq 1$.
6. $DAuxPDA\text{-}TISP\left(c^{\log^k n}, \log n\right) = CROW\text{-}TIPR\left(\log^k n, pol\right)$ for $k \geq 1$.
7. $NC = CROW\text{-}TIPR(polylog, pol)$. (By Rossmanith [18], we know $NC^k \subseteq OROW\text{-}TIME(\log^k n)$)
8. $DAuxPDA\text{-}TISP\left(pol, \log^k n\right) = CROW\text{-}TIPR\left(\log n, c^{\log^k n}\right)$ for $k \geq 1$.
9. $CROW\text{-}TIPR(\log f, g) \subseteq DTISP\left(f^{O(1)} \log g, \log g \log f\right)$.
10. $DAuxPDA\text{-}TISP\left(pol, 2^{\log^k}\right) \subseteq SC^{k+1}$ for $k \geq 1$.
11. $SC = CROW\text{-}TIPR(\log, expolylog)$.
12. If we take the assumptions of Theorem 1 on f and g, all sets in the class $DAuxPDA\text{-}TISP(f, \log g)$ can be accepted by deterministic auxiliary pushdown automata in time $f^{O(1)}$ and with a $\log g$ bounded working tape such that the height of the push-down store never exceeds $O(\log g \cdot \log f)$. This depth reduction for deterministic machines was first pointed out by Dymond and Ruzzo who showed it for the case $f = g = n$.

6 Discussion

The owner concept turns out to be an extremely universal feature allowing for the structural classification or characterization of an abundance of complexity classes. Thus, it yields purely quantitative comparisons of different qualities very similar to results of Dymond and Cook [5]. For instance, we can compare time and space: $\qquad PSPACE = CROW\text{-}TIPR(pol, expol)$, and

$$P = CROW\text{-}TIPR(pol, pol) = CROW\text{-}TIPR(\log n, expol),$$

which leads to the question whether we are able to separate logarithmic time from polynomial time in the presence of an exponential number of processors, or to separate a polynomial number of processors from an exponential one in the presence of polynomial time. Similarly, we can see the comparison of SC with NC: $SC = CROW\text{-}TIPR(\log, expolylog)$ and $NC = CROW\text{-}TIPR(polylog, pol)$. Only a part of these equations are known for EW or CW instead of OW.

The closeness of owner write PRAMs to deterministic auxiliary pushdown automata as we demonstrated it let $CROW$-PRAMs appear just as a parallel version of deterministic auxiliary pushdown automata. This gives us a conversion between recursion and dynamic programming for various subclasses of P.

Compared to the concepts of concurrent and exclusive write the owner model occurred rather late. It took some more five years to exhibit the close relationships between unambiguity and exclusiveness [11–13,15,16]. They explain the awkward nature of the concept of exclusiveness, for instance its lack of complete problems. A large number of algorithms designed by their authors for $CREW$- or

EREW-PRAMs in fact are *CROW*- or *OROW*-PRAM algorithms, demonstrating the unfamiliarity of this concept. The very striking example is the algorithm of Monien, Rytter, and Schäpers which is only announced as a *CREW*-PRAM algorithm. Another example is provided by the recent algorithms for undirected graph connectivity in time $o(\log^2 n)$ which are explicitly dedicated by their authors to *CREW*- and *EREW*-PRAMs . Their reason for choosing this model is always the statement that the *EREW*-PRAM would be the weakest of all PRAM models. Often the indication for their algorithms to follow the *EREW* paradigm uses subroutines like pointer jumping, prefix sums, list compression, and sorting or the simulation of a few number of concurrent read or write accesses to the global memory by an *EREW*-PRAM with logarithmic delay. But all this can be done also by an *OROW*-PRAM without loss of time. What seems to be more difficult with *OROW*-PRAMs is to do that without increasing the number of processor by more than a constant factor. In fact, the time preserving constructions are sometimes combined with a polynomial increase of the processors.

Even worse, nearly all algorithms which really use the exclusive access to the global memory are in a strong sense not *CREW*-PRAM algorithms. Indeed, they only follow the exclusive write paradigm if their inputs fulfill certain conditions, for instance that a graph possesses at most one s-t-path or that a context-free grammar admits at most one derivation to a word. In fact, in the area of polynomial size there seems to be at present no single problem to be known which is solvable or computable with the help of unambiguity without having a deterministic algorithm. Examples for this are only known for the case of polynomial time where problems like factoring or primality are contained in unambiguous language and function classes but yet resisted every deterministic attack.

The Exclusive-Write model is (1) *not* the weakest write-access restriction (2) *not* the access restriction that is most useful in practice, and (3) *not* the access restriction that most algorithm designers actually use. Hence, we view most uses of this model as resulting from either historical accident or from insufficient care in algorithm design, and this leads us to advocate the owner-write model.

Acknowledgements: This research was supported by Deutsche Forschungsgemeinschaft, grant La 618/3-1. The authors wish to thank Eric Allender for several very helpful discussions.

References

1. J. Balcázar, J. Díaz, and J. Gabarró. *Structural Complexity Theory I*. Springer, 1988.
2. J. Balcázar, J. Díaz, and J. Gabarró. *Structural Complexity Theory II*. Springer, 1990.
3. S. Cook. Characterizations of pushdown machines in terms of time-bounded computers. *J. Assoc. Comp. Mach.*, 18:4–18, 1971.
4. S. Cook. Deterministic CFL's are accepted simultaneously in polynomial time and log squared space. In *Proc. of the 11th Annual ACM Symp. on Theory of Computing*, pages 338–345, 1979.

5. P. Dymond and S. Cook. Complexity theory of parallel time and hardware. *Inform. and Control*, 80:201–226, 1989.

6. P. Dymond and W. Ruzzo. Parallel RAMs with owned global memory and deterministic context-free language recoginition. In *Proc. of the 13th ICALP*, number 226 in LNCS, pages 95–104. Springer, 1986.

7. S. Fortune and J. Wyllie. Parallelism in random access machines. In *Proc. of the 10th Annual ACM Symposium on Theory of Computing*, pages 114–118, 1978.

8. L. M. Goldschlager. A unified approach to models of synchronous parallel computation. In *Proc. of the 10th Annual ACM Symposium on Theory of Computing*, pages 89–94, 1978.

9. J. Hopcroft and J. Ullman. *Introduction to Automata Theory, Language, and Computation*. Addison-Wesley, Reading Mass., 1979.

10. D. S. Johnson. A catalog of complexity classes. In J. van Leeuwen, editor, *Handbook of Theoretical Computer Science, Vol. A*, pages 67–161. Elsevier, Amsterdam, 1990.

11. K.-J. Lange. Unambiguity of circuits. *Theoret. Comput. Sci.*, 107:77–94, 1993.

12. K.-J. Lange and P. Rossmanith. Characterizing unambiguous augmented pushdown automata by circuits. In *Proc. of the 15th MFCS*, number 452 in LNCS, pages 399–406. Springer, 1990.

13. K.-J. Lange and P. Rossmanith. Unambiguous polynomial hierarchies and exponential size. In *Proc. of the 9th IEEE Structure in Complexity Conference*, pages 106–115, 1994.

14. B. Monien, W. Rytter, and H. Schäpers. Fast recognition of deterministic cfl's with a smaller number of processors. *Theoret. Comput. Sci.*, 116:421–429, 1993. Corrigendum, 123:427,1993.

15. R. Niedermeier and P. Rossmanith. Unambiguous auxiliary pushdown automata and semi-unbounded fan-in circuits. *Inform. and Control*, 118(2):227–245, 1995.

16. I. Niepel and P. Rossmanith. Uniform circuits and exclusive read PRAMs. In *Proc. of the 11th FST&TCS*, number 560 in LNCS, pages 307–318. Springer, 1990.

17. K. Reinhardt. Strict sequential P–completeness. Manuscript, 1996.

18. P. Rossmanith. The owner concept for PRAMs. In *Proc. of the 8th STACS*, number 480 in LNCS, pages 172–183. Springer, 1991.

19. P. Rossmanith. Characterizations of memory access for PRAM's and bounds on the time complexity of boolean functions. Ph.D. thesis, Technische Universität München, 1993.

20. W. Ruzzo. On uniform circuit complexity. *J. Comp. System Sci.*, 22:365–338, 1981.

21. L. Stockmeyer and C. Vishkin. Simulation of random access machines by circuits. *SIAM J. Comp.*, 13:409–422, 1984.

22. I. Sudborough. On the tape complexity of deterministic context-free languages. *J. Assoc. Comp. Mach.*, 25:405–414, 1978.

23. H. Venkateswaran. Properties that characterize LOGCFL. In *Proc. of the 19th Annual ACM Symp. on Theory of Computing*, pages 141–150, 1987.

24. J. Vogel and K. Wagner. Two-way automata with more than one storage medium. *Theoret. Comput. Sci.*, 39:267–280, 1985.

Non-cancellative Boolean Circuits:
A Generalization of Monotone Boolean Circuits*

Rimli Sengupta[1] and H. Venkateswaran[2]

[1] Dept. of Computer Science
Rose-Hulman Institute of Technology
Terre Haute, IN 47803-3999
e-mail: rimli@cs.rose-hulman.edu
[2] College of Computing
Georgia Institute of Technology
Atlanta, GA 30332-0280
e-mail : venkat@cc.gatech.edu

Abstract. Cancellations are known to be helpful in efficient algebraic computation of polynomials over fields. We define a notion of cancellation in Boolean circuits and define Boolean circuits that do not use cancellation to be *non-cancellative*. Non-cancellative Boolean circuits are a natural generalization of monotone Boolean circuits. We show that in the absence of cancellation, Boolean circuits require super-polynomial size to compute the determinant interpreted over $GF(2)$. This non-monotone Boolean function is known to be in $\mathcal{P}$. In the spirit of monotone complexity classes, we define complexity classes based on non-cancellative Boolean circuits. We show that when the Boolean circuit model is restricted by withholding cancellation, $\mathcal{P}$ and popular classes within $\mathcal{P}$ are restricted as well, but classes $\mathcal{NP}$ and above remain unchanged.

1 Introduction

Using the power of cancellation to compute more efficiently has been a recurrent theme in the study of computational complexity. Strassen [15] made elegant usage of cancellation to obtain a surprising $O(n^{2.81})$ algorithm for matrix multiplication, improving the obvious $O(n^3)$ algorithm. Valiant [19] showed that usage of cancellations can lead to an exponential gain in size for counting the number of perfect matchings in triangular grid graphs. Nisan [10] showed that if cancellation is inhibited by withholding commutativity, then computing the determinant is as hard as computing the permanent. This paper investigates the power of cancellation in Boolean computation. We define a Boolean circuit to be *non-cancellative* if the formal polynomial associated with the circuit does not have a monomial that has both a literal and its complement. Non-cancellative circuits are a natural generalization of monotone Boolean circuits which have been

---

* This work was supported by NSF grant CCR-9200878 and was done while the first author was at the College of Computing, Georgia Tech.

studied extensively in the past [1, 4, 5, 11, 12, 16]. An important difference between the two models is that, unlike monotone Boolean circuits, non-cancellative circuits can compute all Boolean functions. This is because the circuit based on the representation of a Boolean function as the disjunction of its prime implicants is non-cancellative. All known lower bounds in the monotone circuit model carry over to the non-cancellative circuit model in a straightforward way. We also show that the lower bounds in the monotone circuit model can be adapted to similar lower bounds for a large class of non-monotone functions in the non-cancellative setting.

In the past, researchers have studied Boolean circuits with limited number of negations [9, 13, 17] to better understand the power of negations in Boolean computation. The study of non-cancellative circuits is of interest for the same reason. But in non-cancellative circuits the restriction is not on the number of negations but rather on the manner in which negations are used, namely, that they are not used for cancellation. This leads to the question as to whether non-trivial usage of negation is at all possible if cancellation is not allowed. The answer is yes. We have already observed that non-cancellative circuits can compute all Boolean functions. Moreover, there are examples of small non-cancellative circuits such as an $\mathcal{NC}^1$ circuit for PARITY.

This paper has three parts. In the first part, we generalize the lower bounds in the monotone Boolean circuit model to an appropriate class of non-monotone functions. We begin by showing that for every non-monotone function f such that $f(0) = 0$ or $f(1) = 0$, there is a monotone function g such that the non-cancellative complexity of f^3 is the same as the monotone complexity of g. We derive two important consequences of this result. First, in the context of computing monotone functions non-cancellative circuits are no more powerful than monotone circuits. This formalizes the intuition that for computing monotone functions, negations can only be used for cancellation. Thus, all lower bounds known for the monotone model apply in the non-cancellative model as well. The second consequence is that, for any monotone f, the non-cancellative complexity of the non-monotone function $\oplus f$ (see Sect. 3.2 for a definition) is at least the monotone complexity of f. This provides, for instance, a super-polynomial size lower bound for non-cancellative circuits that compute the determinant interpreted over $GF(2)$. This function is known to be in $\mathcal{P}$ [18]. This is the first example of a non-monotone Boolean function for which cancellations help.

In the second part of the paper, we quantify the amount of cancellation in a general non-monotone circuit. This quantity is defined to be the number of input variables that appear cancellatively in the formal polynomial associated with the circuit. We then show that non-monotone circuits in which $O(log(n))$ variables appear cancellatively can be converted into an equivalent non-cancellative circuit without blowing up the size by more than a polynomial. This implies a lower bound on the number of variables that appear cancellatively in the formal polynomial of general Boolean circuits that compute certain monotone functions. For

---

[3] The non-cancellative complexity of f is the size of the smallest non-cancellative circuit computing f.

instance, it follows that in the formal polynomial of any sublinear depth circuit for the bipartite perfect matching function at least a $o(n)$ of the input variables must appear cancellatively. Conversely, we have a linear depth lower bound on any circuit that computes the bipartite perfect matching function using $o(n)$ of the input variables cancellatively. This provides new insight into the role of cancellation in efficient computation of the perfect matching function; namely, in the context of depth requirement, allowing cancellations $o(n)$ input variables is as bad as withholding negations all together.

The third part of the paper is motivated by monotone complexity classes [5]. We define non-cancellative analogues of popular classes, such as $\mathcal{NL}$, $\mathcal{SAC}^1$ and $\mathcal{NP}$, using non-cancellative Boolean circuits. In addition to being a natural extension of the study of monotone complexity classes, the study of non-cancellative classes provides insight about the role of cancellation in structural issues, such as closure properties of complexity classes. For instance, while $\mathcal{NL}$ and $\mathcal{SAC}^1$ are known to be closed under complement [8, 3], we show that their non-cancellative analogues are not. As mentioned earlier, non-cancellative circuits can compute all Boolean functions, given enough size. It is therefore meaningful to ask how much size is necessary before cancellation becomes useless. To answer this, we show that the non-cancellative analogue of $\mathcal{NP}$ spans the whole of $\mathcal{NP}$. This implies that for all classes containing $\mathcal{NP}$, non-cancellativeness is not a restriction. However, we show that non-cancellativeness is a strict restriction for $\mathcal{P}$ and all popular classes within it.

Section 2 contains definitions and preliminary results used in the rest of the paper. The three parts of the paper are covered in Sections 3, 4 and 5. Concluding remarks are presented in Section 6.

2 Preliminaries

2.1 Definitions

Definition 2.1 A *Boolean circuit* B_n is a directed acyclic labeled graph in which nodes either have in-degree 0 or 2. Nodes with in-degree 0 are called *inputs* and are labeled from the set $\{x_i, \bar{x}_i, 0, 1 \mid 1 \leq i \leq n\}$. The other nodes (also called *gates*) are labeled from the set $\{\vee, \wedge\}$. The in-degree of a gate will be referred to as its *fanin*. The circuit has exactly one node with 0 out-degree and it is called the *output*. A *formula* is a Boolean circuit in which the gates have out-degree ≤ 1. B_n is *positive monotone* if the inputs are labeled only from $\{x_i, 0, 1 \mid 1 \leq i \leq n\}$. B_n is *negative monotone* if the inputs are labeled only from $\{\bar{x}_i, 0, 1 \mid 1 \leq i \leq n\}$. The *size* of a Boolean circuit is the number of gates in it and its *depth* is the length of the longest path from any input to the output.

Definition 2.2 Each element in the set $\{x_i \mid 1 \leq i \leq n\}$ is a *variable*. A *literal* is a variable x_i in positive form x_i or negative form $\bar{x}_i$. A *term* is a conjunction of literals, both positive and negative, and constants from $\{0, 1\}$. Each term t can be expressed as $c \cdot t_+ \cdot t_-$, where each literal in t_+ is positive and each literal in t_- is negative and $c \in \{0, 1\}$. For any term t, t_+ is the *positive term* of t and

t_- is its *negative term*; $var(t_+)$ denotes the set of variables in t_+ and $var(t_-)$ is the analogous set for t_-.

Each Boolean circuit B_n computes a Boolean function $f : \{0,1\}^n \to \{0,1\}$. We shall use $PI(f)$ to denote the set of prime implicants of a function f (see for instance [14] for a definition of prime implicants).

Definition 2.3 A *parse-graph* G of a Boolean circuit B_n is defined inductively as follows: G includes the output of B_n; for any $\vee$ gate v included in G, exactly one immediate predecessor of v in B_n is included as its only predecessor in G; and for any $\wedge$ gate v included in G, both the immediate predecessors of v in B_n are included as its predecessors in G.

Every gate v of a parse-graph G computes a term which is the conjunction of the labels on the inputs of the sub-graph rooted at v.

Definition 2.4 Let $\mathcal{G}$ denote the set of parse-graphs of B_n and let $t(G)$ be the term computed at the output of parse-graph G. The *formal polynomial* $P(B_n)$ of a circuit B_n is

$$\sum_{G \in \mathcal{G}} t(G).$$

Example 2.1 Consider the circuit B_3 in Fig. 1. The circuit is monotone and has eight parse-graphs. $P(B_3) = abc + a^2b + ac^2 + a^2c + b^2c + ab^2 + bc^2 + abc$. Note that the prime implicants of the function computed by B_3 are ab, bc and ac. Thus, the number of monomials in the formal polynomial of a circuit is in general not the same as the number of prime implicants of the function that it computes.

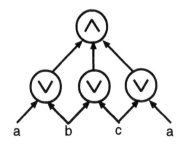

Fig. 1. The circuit B_3.

Definition 2.5 [4] A Boolean function f is said to be *positive monotone* (*negative monotone*) if the terms in $PI(f)$ do not contain negative (positive, resp.) literals.

Definition 2.6 Let $\mathcal{F}$ be the class of Boolean functions such that $f(0) = 0$. For any $f \in \mathcal{F}$, we define the positive monotone function f_m as: $f_m = \bigvee_{t \in PI(f)} t_+$. Similarly, let $\bar{\mathcal{F}}$ be the class of Boolean functions such that $f(1) = 0$. For any $f \in \bar{\mathcal{F}}$, we define the negative monotone function $f_{\bar{m}}$ as: $f_{\bar{m}} = \bigvee_{t \in PI(f)} t_-$.

We shall henceforth say a function or a circuit is "monotone" to mean that it is either positive or negative monotone, in the style of [4]. Thus for a monotone function f, its complement $\bar{f}$ is monotone as well.

Definition 2.7 A term t is said to be *cancelled* if $var(t_+) \cap var(t_-) \neq \emptyset$. A term t is said to be *trivial* if it is cancelled or has 0 as its constant.

Definition 2.8 A Boolean circuit B_n is *non-cancellative* if there are no cancelled terms in its formal polynomial $P(B_n)$.

2.2 The Canonical Formal Polynomial

Given a general Boolean circuit B_n computing a function f such that $f(0) = 0$, we derive a canonical form for $P(B_n)$. A similar canonical form then follows for the dual class of functions for which $f(1) = 0$.

We first establish some relationships between the non-trivial monomials of $P(B_n)$ and the terms of $PI(f_m)$ leading to a canonical form for $P(B_n)$. The proofs of the following lemmas are based on the idea that since B_n computes f, $P(B_n)$ and f must agree on every input assignment.

Lemma 2.1 For each non-trivial monomial ρ of $P(B_n)$, there exists a term $t \in PI(f_m)$ such that $var(t) \subseteq var(\rho_+)$.

Lemma 2.2 For all terms $t \in PI(f_m)$, there exists a non-trivial monomial ρ of $P(B_n)$, such that $var(t) = var(\rho_+)$.

For any B_n computing a function $f \in \mathcal{F}$ the non-trivial monomials of $P(B_n)$ can be partitioned into $|PI(f_m)|$ groups, using lemmas 2.1 and 2.2, such that each group has at least one monomial whose positive variable set coincides with that of the prime-implicant of f_m corresponding to the group and each of the rest of the monomials in the group contains this set as a subset of its positive variable set.

The above results can be adapted for functions f such that $f(1) = 0$. Given a general Boolean circuit B_n computing a function $f \in \bar{\mathcal{F}}$, we have the following analogues of lemmas 2.1 and 2.2 and the canonical form for $P(B_n)$ follows in the manner similar to above.

Lemma 2.3 For each non-trivial monomial ρ of $P(B_n)$, there exists a term $t \in PI(f_{\bar{m}})$ such that $var(t) \subseteq var(\rho_-)$.

Lemma 2.4 For all terms $t \in PI(f_{\bar{m}})$, there exists a non-trivial monomial ρ of $P(B_n)$, such that $var(t) = var(\rho_-)$.

2.3 Functions Used

Here we define the functions used in this paper:

1. The bipartite perfect matching function BPM : $\{0,1\}^{n^2} \to \{0,1\}$, takes as input the standard $n \times n$ adjacency matrix representation of a bipartite graph G and outputs 1 if and only if G has a perfect matching. BPM is a monotone function.

2. The following function was considered by Tardos in [16] as an example for which the gap between the non-monotone and monotone complexity is exponential. TF: $\{0,1\}^{n^2} \to \{0,1\}$, takes as input the standard $n \times n$ adjacency matrix representation of a graph G and outputs 1 if and only if $\Phi(G) \leq f(n)$, where Φ, defined in [16], is a monotone graph property whose value lies between the clique number and chromatic number of G and f is any function such that $3 \leq f(n) \leq ((n/log(n))^{2/3})/4$. For the purpose of this paper, we choose $f(n) = ((n/log(n))^{2/3})/4$. TF is a monotone function.

3. $\oplus$BPM : $\{0,1\}^{n^2} \to \{0,1\}$ takes as input the standard $n \times n$ adjacency matrix representation of a bipartite graph G and outputs a 1 if and only if G has an odd number of perfect matchings. $\oplus$BPM is a non-montone function. It is exactly the determinant function interpreted over $GF(2)$.

4. $\oplus$TF is defined analogously, by interpreting TF over $GF(2)$.

3 Non-cancellative vs. Monotone Complexity

Non-cancellative circuits are a strict generalization of monotone circuits since monotone circuits cannot compute non-monotone functions. In [11], Razborov had shown that monotone Boolean circuits are strictly weaker than general Boolean circuits for computing a monotone function: bipartite perfect matching. One interesting question is whether non-cancellative circuits are as powerful as general Boolean circuits. In Sect. 3.1 we show that non-cancellative circuits for monotone functions are no more powerful than monotone circuits. In Sect. 3.2 we exhibit a natural non-monotone function that is computable by polynomial size Boolean circuits but requires super-polynomial size non-cancellative circuits. To prove these results, we first show that for a large class of functions f, there exist monotone functions whose monotone complexity is similar to the non-cancellative complexity of f.

Based on the lemmas 2.1 and 2.2 and the canonical form presented in section 2.2, we can relate the non-cancellative complexity of any $f \in \mathcal{F}$ to the monotone complexity of f_m.

Theorem 3.1 For any function f such that $f(0) = 0$, if there is a non-cancellative circuit of size s and depth d computing f then there is a monotone circuit of size s and depth d computing f_m.

By the above theorem, any lower bound in the monotone model for a monotone function g applies to non-cancellative circuits that compute any function f such that $f_m = g$.

The non-cancellative complexity of any $f \in \bar{\mathcal{F}}$ can be analogously related to the monotone complexity of $f_{\bar{m}}$, using lemmas 2.3 and 2.4.

Theorem 3.2 For any function f such that $f(1) = 0$, if there is a non-cancellative circuit of size s and depth d computing f then there is a monotone circuit of size s and depth d computing $f_{\bar{m}}$.

3.1 Monotone Functions

Since monotone circuits are trivially non-cancellative, by applying Theorem 3.1 and 3.2 to monotone functions[4], we conclude that the monotone complexity and non-cancellative complexity of monotone functions are identical.

Theorem 3.3 For any monotone function f, there is a non-cancellative circuit of size s and depth d computing f if and only if there is a monotone circuit of size s and depth d computing f.

The above theorem formalizes the intuition that for computing monotone functions, negations can only be used for cancellation. As an immediate consequence of this theorem, known bounds in the monotone model [1, 16, 11, 12] apply for non-cancellative circuits.

Corollary 3.1 Non-cancellative circuits for BPM require size $n^{\Omega(\log n)}$ and depth $\Omega(n)$. Non-cancellative circuits for TF require size $2^{\Omega(n^{\frac{1}{3} - o(1)})}$.

The above corollary implies that the polynomial size circuits for BPM [7] and TF [16] must critically use the power of cancellation to compute these functions efficiently. Cancellations can therefore lead to exponential savings in size for computing monotone functions.

3.2 Non-monotone Functions

Negations are essential to computing non-monotone functions, but cancellations are not. In this section we show that non-cancellative circuits for the non-monotone function $\oplus$BPM can be no smaller than monotone circuits for BPM. The function $\oplus$BPM is exactly the determinant function interpreted over $GF(2)$ and is known to be in $\mathcal{P}$ [18].

We begin with the definition of the parity version of any Boolean function.

Definition 3.1 For any f, the function $\oplus f$ is defined as follows: $\oplus f$ outputs 1 on input x if and only if an odd number of prime implicants of f evaluate to 1 on input x.

---

[4] Except for the constant function $f = 1$, all monotone functions have $f(0) = 0$ or $f(1) = 0$. We say monotone functions to mean non-constant monotone functions.

For any function f, $\oplus f$ is non-monotone. The following facts are worth noting: (a) if $f(0) = 0$, then $\oplus f(0) = 0$; (b) for any monotone f, $(\oplus f)_m = f$, where $(\oplus f)_m$ is the monotone counterpart of $\oplus f$ as defined in Sect. 2.1. Therefore, for the class of functions $\{\oplus f \mid f \text{ is monotone}\}$ we have the following analogue of Theorem 3.3:

Theorem 3.4 For any monotone function f, if there is a non-cancellative circuit of size s and depth d computing $\oplus f$ then there is a monotone circuit of size s and depth d computing f.

As an immediate consequence of the above theorem and the known bounds for BPM in the monotone setting [16, 11, 12] we have,

Corollary 3.2 Non-cancellative circuits for $\oplus$BPM require size $n^{\Omega(\log n)}$ and depth $\Omega(n)$. Non-cancellative circuits for $\oplus$TF require size $2^{\Omega(n^{\frac{1}{3}-o(1)})}$.

Since $\oplus$BPM is known to be in $\mathcal{P}$ [18], this demonstrates that cancellations can lead to super-polynomial savings in size even for computing non-monotone functions.

In summary, any polynomial size circuit for BPM or $\oplus$BPM must necessarily use cancellation. The result for BPM follows in a straightforward fashion from Razborov's lower bound [11]. The result for $\oplus$BPM is new.

4 Quantifying Cancellations

In this section, we quantify the amount of cancellations in a Boolean circuit and show that a circuit with a small amount of cancellations can be efficiently converted into a non-cancellative circuit. Throughout this section and in the next section we will use n to mean the number of input variables.

Definition 4.1 A variable x is said to *occur cancellatively* in B_n if there is a monomial $\rho \in P(B_n)$ such that $x \in var(\rho_+) \cap var(\rho_-)$. A circuit B_n is said to be *k-cancellative* if there are k variables that occur cancellatively in B_n, $0 \le k \le n$.

Theorem 4.1 Let B_n be a k-cancellative circuit of size s and depth d computing f, then there is an equivalent non-cancellative circuit of size $O(s2^k)$ and depth $(d + k)$, $0 \le k \le n$.

Proof: Let $P(B_n)$ have k variables $\{x_1, x_2, \cdots, x_k\}$ occurring cancellatively in B_n. We give a procedure to make the circuit non-cancellative with respect to one variable at a time, such that the circuit size is at most doubled at any step and the depth increases by 1. Thus, the resulting circuit, non-cancellative with respect to all the k variables, has size $O(s2^k)$ and depth $(d + k)$. We give the construction for x_1, the rest is immediate.

Let B_n^1 and B_n^2 be two copies of B_n such that in B_n^1 the leaf labeled $\bar{x}_1$ is relabeled with z and in B_n^2 the leaf labeled x_1 is relabeled with z. Consider the circuit B'_n obtained by $\vee$-ing B^1_n and B^2_n and tying the leaf z to 0. It is easy to verify that B'_n is equivalent to B_n and that x_1 does not occur cancellatively in B'_n. Also, the size of B'_n is $2s + 1$ and its depth is $d + 1$. $\square$

Corollary 4.1 Non-cancellative circuits can compute f within polynomial size if and only if f is computable by $O(\log n)$-cancellative circuits within polynomial size.

4.1 Consequences

The construction in the above proof has interesting consequences in relating the size or depth of a circuit to the number of variables that appear cancellatively within it.

Theorem 4.2 If non-cancellative circuits are known to require size $\Omega(s)$ for a function f, then any circuit computing f within size $s' \leq s$ must be k-cancellative, for $k = \Omega(\log(\frac{s}{s'}))$.

Based on the non-cancellative size lower bounds for BPM and $\oplus$BPM in the previous section we have,

Corollary 4.2 Any polynomial size circuit for BPM or $\oplus$BPM must be k-cancellative for $k = \Omega(\log^2(n))$.

Since $s' \cdot 2^k = \Omega(s)$ (in proof of Theorem 4.2), we also have the converse that any k-cancellative circuit for BPM or $\oplus$BPM with $k = o(\log^2 n)$, must have size $2^{\Omega(\log^2 n)}$. This result generalizes the size lower bounds in corollaries 3.1 and 3.2 and says that even allowing cancellations for $o(\log^2 n)$ variables is not enough to compute bipartite perfect matching within polynomial size.

All of the above results have depth analogues.

Theorem 4.3 If non-cancellative circuits are known to require depth $\Omega(d)$ for a function f, then any circuit computing f within depth $d' = o(d)$ must be k-cancellative, for $k = \Omega(d)$.

Based on the non-cancellative depth lower bounds for BPM and $\oplus$BPM in the previous section we have the following corollary. Note that $\sqrt{n}$ appears in place of n since in this section n refers to the number of input variables.

Corollary 4.3 Any $o(\sqrt{n})$ depth circuit for BPM or $\oplus$BPM, must be k-cancellative for $k = \Omega(\sqrt{n})$.

Conversely, any k-cancellative circuit for BPM or $\oplus$BPM with $k = o(\sqrt{n})$, must have depth $\Omega(\sqrt{n})$. This result generalizes the depth lower bounds in corollaries 3.1 and 3.2 and implies that in the context of depth requirement of circuits computing bipartite perfect matching, allowing cancellations on only $o(\sqrt{n})$ of the variables is as bad as withholding negations all together.

5 Non-cancellative Complexity Classes

Grigni [4] used monotone Boolean circuits to define monotone analogues of standard complexity classes such as $\mathcal{N}C^k$, $\mathcal{N}L$, $\mathcal{P}$ and $\mathcal{N}\mathcal{P}$. In this section we consider non-cancellative analogues of standard complexity classes. In addition to being a natural extension of the study of monotone complexity classes, the study of non-cancellative classes is interesting because it lends insight into the role of cancellation in the context of structural issues, such as closure properties of complexity classes. As has been mentioned earlier, non-cancellative Boolean circuits can compute all functions given enough resources. A natural question is: what is the smallest class for which non-cancellativeness is not a restriction? Our result is that for $\mathcal{P}$ and popular classes within it, non-cancellativeness is a strict restriction, but not so for classes $\mathcal{N}\mathcal{P}$ and above.

To define non-cancellative classes uniformly, we use the uniformity notions defined in [4] for monotone classes. A Boolean circuit is said to be *skew* if any $\wedge$-node has at most one gate as a predecessor. A Boolean circuit is said to have *semi-unbounded* fanin if any $\wedge$-node has fanin 2 but $\vee$-nodes could have unbounded fanin.

Definition 5.1 The following are classes of functions computable by uniform families of non-cancellative circuits within the indicated resources: (i)$\Diamond\mathcal{N}L$: skew polynomial size; (iii) $\Diamond\mathcal{N}C^k$: bounded fanin polynomial size and $O(log^k(n))$ depth; (iv) $\Diamond\mathcal{S}\mathcal{A}C^k$: semi-unbounded fanin polynomial size and $O(log^k(n))$ depth; (v) $\Diamond\mathcal{A}C^k$: unbounded fanin polynomial size and $O(log^k(n))$ depth; (vi) $\Diamond\mathcal{P}$: polynomial size; (vii) $\Diamond\mathcal{N}\mathcal{P}$: skew polynomial depth.

As a direct consequence of theorem 3.3, we get the following separations between non-cancellative and non-monotone classes based on the analogous separations between monotone and non-monotone classes [5, 2, 11, 12] using monotone functions.

Theorem 5.1 $\Diamond\mathcal{A}C^0 \neq \mathcal{A}C^0$, $\Diamond\mathcal{N}C^k \neq \mathcal{N}C^k$, $\Diamond\mathcal{N}L \neq \mathcal{N}L$, $\Diamond\mathcal{S}\mathcal{A}C^k \neq \mathcal{S}\mathcal{A}C^k$, $\Diamond\mathcal{A}C^k \neq \mathcal{A}C^k$, $\Diamond\mathcal{P} \neq \mathcal{P}$.

The results in section 3 have other interesting consequences for complexity classes. For monotone classes that are known not to be closed under complement, we can prove the analogous non-closure results in the non-cancellative setting, using arguments similar to those above. Grigni [5] had shown that $m\mathcal{S}\mathcal{A}C^1$ and $m\mathcal{N}L$ are not closed under complement.

Theorem 5.2 $\Diamond\mathcal{S}\mathcal{A}C^1$ and $\Diamond\mathcal{N}L$ are not closed under complement.

The classes $\mathcal{N}L$ and $\mathcal{S}\mathcal{A}C^1$ are both known to be closed under complement [8, 3]. The above result therefore implies that cancellations are critical to attain closure under complementation of these classes. For monotone classes that are known to be closed under complement, we do not know if the closure result also holds for the analogous non-cancellative class. For example, $m\mathcal{N}C^k$ and $m\mathcal{P}$ [4] are closed under complement by definition, but we cannot say the same about $\Diamond\mathcal{N}C^k$ and $\Diamond\mathcal{P}$.

5.1 $\mathcal{NP}$ Is Non-cancellative

In [5], Grigni had shown that the monotone analogue of $\mathcal{NP}$ is exactly the class of monotone functions in $\mathcal{NP}$. We now show that the non-cancellative analogue of $\mathcal{NP}$ covers the whole of $\mathcal{NP}$. To prove this, we carry through the construction in the proof of Theorem 4.1 for all the variables. The resulting circuit has size $O(s2^n)$ and depth $d + n$, where n is the number of input variables. The construction in the proof of Theorem 4.1 is uniform and has the nice property that if the original circuit is skew, so is the final circuit. Therefore, based on the circuit definition of $\mathcal{NP}$ as the class of functions computable by uniform families of polynomial depth skew circuits [20], we have

Theorem 5.3 $\Diamond\mathcal{NP} = \mathcal{NP}$.

It follows that $\Diamond\mathcal{C} = \mathcal{C}$, for all known classes $\mathcal{C}$ containing $\mathcal{NP}$ that has a circuit definition in terms of size and/or depth.

Since non-cancellative circuits can compute all Boolean functions given enough resources, we had earlier posed the question of how much size is necessary before cancellation becomes useless. The above result shows that $\mathcal{NP}$ circuits are large enough for cancellation to become useless.

6 Summary and Open Questions

Non-cancellative Boolean circuits appear to be an appropriate generalization of monotone Boolean circuits such that all Boolean functions are computable. By defining a notion of cancellation in Boolean circuits, we study the power of negation at a finer granularity than previously considered and clarify the role of negation versus that of cancellation. Previous work with monotone computations shows that cancellations are essential for efficiently computing certain monotone functions. The work presented in this paper extends that to the computation of non-monotone functions and shows that it is the cancellative aspect of negation that allows Boolean circuits to efficiently compute even certain non-monotone functions. We present the first example of a non-monotone Boolean function for which cancellations help. We also show that cancellations are crucial for certain classes to be closed under complement, for example $\mathcal{NL}$. By showing $\mathcal{NP}$ is non-cancellative we identify the boundary at which cancellations are rendered powerless.

This work raises several questions, here are a few: (i) In general, what can be said about the closure under complement of non-cancellative analogues of classes whose monotone versions are known to be closed under complement? (ii) Are there examples of $\mathcal{P}$-complete functions in $\Diamond\mathcal{P}$? (iii) Like $\mathcal{NP}$, does the non-cancellative analogue of $\mathcal{CO} - \mathcal{NP}$ span the whole of $\mathcal{CO} - \mathcal{NP}$? (iv) What is the class of functions f such that the non-cancellative complexity of f is polynomially related to its non-monotone complexity? (v) Theorem 3.4 states that for any monotone f, the non-cancellative complexity of $\oplus f$ is bounded below by the monotone complexity of f. Does the converse hold?

References

1. N. Alon and R.B. Boppana, *The monotone circuit complexity of Boolean functions*, Combinatorica, 7 (1987), 1-22.
2. M. Ajtai and Y. Gurevich, *Monotone versus positive*, J. Assoc. Comput. Mach., 34:4 (1987), 1004-1015.
3. A. Borodin, S. Cook, P. Dymond, W. Ruzzo, M. Tompa, *Two applications of inductive counting for complementation problems*, SIAM J. Comput., 18 (1989), 559-578.
4. M. Grigni, *Structure in monotone complexity*, Ph.D. thesis, M.I.T., 1991.
5. M. Grigni and M. Sipser, *Monotone separation of Logspace from NC^1*, Proc. 6th IEEE Structures (1991), 294-298.
6. M. Grötschel, L. Lovász and A. Schrijver, *The ellipsoid method and its consequences in combinatorial optimization*, Combinatorica, 1 (1981), 169-197.
7. J.E. Hopcroft and R.M. Karp, *A $n^{5/2}$ algorithm for maximum matching in bipartite graphs*, SIAM J. Comput. 2 (1973), 225-231.
8. N. Immerman, *Nondeterministic space is closed under complement*, SIAM J. Comput., 17 (1988), 935-938.
9. A. Markov, *On the inversion complexity of systems of Boolean functions*, Soviet Math. Doklady 4:3 (1963), 694-696.
10. N. Nisan, *Lower bounds for non-commutative computation*, Proc. 23nd annual ACM STOC (1991), 410-418.
11. A.A. Razborov, *A lower bound on the monotone network complexity of the logical permanent*, Mathematischi Zametki 37 (1985), 887-900.
12. R. Raz and A. Wigderson, *Monotone circuits for matching require linear depth*, Proc. 22nd annual ACM STOC (1990), 287-292.
13. M. Santha and C. Wilson *Polynomial size constant depth circuits with a limited number of negations*, Proc. 8th STACS (1991), 228-237.
14. J. E. Savage, *The complexity of computing*, R. E. Kreiger Publishing Co., Malabar, Florida, 1987.
15. V. Strassen, *Gaussian elimination is not optimal*, Numer. Math. 13 (1969) 354-356.
16. É. Tardos, *The gap between monotone and non-monotone circuit complexity is exponential*, Combinatorica 7 (1987), 141-142.
17. K. Tanaka and T. Nishino, *On the complexity of negation-limited Boolean networks*, Proc. 26th ACM Symposium on Theory of Computing (1994), 38-47.
18. L. Valiant, *The complexity of computing the permanent*, Theoretical Computer Science 8 (1979), 189-201.
19. L. Valiant, *Negation can be exponentially powerful*, Theoretical Computer Science 12 (1980), 303-314.
20. H. Venkateswaran, *Circuit definitions of nondeterministic complexity classes*, SIAM J. Comput. 21 (1992) 655-670.

Limitations of the QRQW and EREW PRAM Models[*]

Mirosław Kutyłowski,
Heinz Nixdorf Institute   and   Dept. of Mathematics & Computer Science
University of Paderborn, D-33095 Paderborn, Germany,
mirekk@uni-paderborn.de

Krzysztof Loryś
Institute of Computer Science, University of Wrocław, and Dept. of Computer Science, University of Trier, D-54286 Trier, Germany, lorys@TI.Uni-Trier.DE

Abstract. We consider parallel random access machines (PRAMs) with restricted access to the shared memory resulting from handling congestion of memory requests. We study the (SIMD) QRQW PRAM model where multiple requests are queued and serviced one at a time. We also consider exclusive read exclusive write (EREW) PRAM and its modification obtained by adding a single bus.

For the QRQW PRAMs we investigate the case when the machine can measure the duration of a single step. Even for such a (powerful) QRQW PRAM PARITY of n bits (PARITY$_n$) requires $\Omega(\log n)$ time while OR of n bits can be computed deterministically in a constant time. On randomized QRQW PRAM the function PARITY$_n$ is still difficult. We prove a lower time bound $\Omega(\sqrt{\log n / \log \log n})$ for algorithms that succeed with probability $0.5 + \epsilon$ ($\epsilon > 0$). These bounds show that implementing concurrent writes may degrade runtime of a CRCW PRAM algorithm.

The simple 2-compaction problem is known to be hard for EREW PRAM. The same time bound $\Omega(\sqrt{\log n})$ for this problem has been proved for both deterministic and randomized EREW PRAM. We show that this is not a coincidence since the time complexity of this problem is the same for deterministic and randomized case. The technique which we apply is quite general and may be used to obtain similar results for any problem where the number of input configurations is small.

We also show that improving time bound $\Omega(\sqrt{\log n})$ for 2-compaction on EREW PRAM requires novel and more sophisticated techniques.

1 Introduction

Parallel Random Access Machines (PRAMs) are widely used for designing parallel algorithms (for a detailed definition of PRAMs see for instance [6]). There are many fast and work-efficient parallel PRAM algorithms. However, many of them can be hardly implemented in the real world, due to communication problems. Even if the messages between processors and the shared memory are routed efficiently (say by optical channels), it remains a problem how they are serviced at the memory locations that are claimed by many processors. Processing these read or write requests can significantly decrease time efficiency of the algorithm. For this reason many fancy CRCW PRAM algorithms has no practical relevance.

In order to avoid the situation described exclusive-read exclusive-write (EREW) PRAMs have been proposed as a model for algorithm design. In this model it is prohibited to

---

[*] partially supported by KBN grants 8 S503 002 07, 2 P301 034 07, DFG-Sonderforschungsbereich 376 "Massive Parallelität" and EU ESPRIT Long Term Research Project 20244 (ALCOM-IT)

attempt to write or read from the same location of the shared memory at the same time. This solves the congestion problems, but makes designing efficient algorithms significantly more difficult or sometimes even impossible. A good example of the last phenomenon is the 2-compaction problem: *given an array of size n storing at most 2 nonempty elements, move these elements to the first two positions in the array.* It is known that 2-compaction problem requires $\Omega(\sqrt{\log n})$ steps of the EREW PRAM [7]. This bound holds even for the randomized EREW PRAM [10]. On the other hand, 2-compaction requires a constant time if 2 requests addressed to the same memory location at the same time may be serviced.

Gibbons, Matias and Ramachandran introduced the Queue Read Queue Write (QRQW) PRAM in which capabilities of servicing many requests concerning the same memory location have been taken into account ([8, 9]). The motivation is that the real machines may queue the requests and therefore the EREW model is too restrictive. The QRQW model differs from the CRCW PRAMs, because the time needed to serve the queue is taken into consideration when analyzing the runtime of an algorithm:

Definition 1. A (SIMD) QRQW PRAM is a CRCW PRAM for which the time spent to execute a parallel step equals $1 + \max(r - 1, 0) + \max(w - 1, 0)$ where r is the maximal number of processors reading the same memory location during this step, and w is the maximal number of processors trying to write into the same memory location during this step. The runtime of the algorithm is defined as the total time used to execute all steps. For lower time bounds, we assume that during a concurrent-write operation all messages to be written are combined with the old contents of the cell and stored there. (It might be understood that the cells of QRQW PRAM are in fact memory modules.)

A number of efficient and tricky algorithms has been designed for the QRQW PRAMs, including for instance k-compaction and linear approximate compaction [8, 9]. But QRQW PRAMs have also their limitations, for instance the $\Omega(\log m)$ bound for broadcasting a message to m locations holds as for the EREW model [9].

Typical Boolean functions used to test the strength of different communication modes on the PRAM are PARITY_n (sum modulo 2 of n input bits) and OR_n (the OR of n input bits). These functions require $\Omega(\log n)$ on the CREW PRAM, even in the randomized case [5, 10].

Definition 2. QRQW PRAMs with latency detection is a QRQW PRAM for which every processor can measure the execution time of each write or read phase.

The latency detection seems to be a natural mechanism that may be considered as a hardware option, and could be useful even if the clock is not very precise. For instance OR_n can be computed in $O(1)$ time on QRQW PRAMs with latency detection (Proposition 4). On the other hand we show that PARITY_n requires $\Omega(\log n)$ steps on QRQW PRAMs (and even on CRQW PRAMs, see Theorem 5). Time complexity of PARITY_n on a CREW PRAM, which is a model weaker than CRQW PRAM, is $\Theta(\log n)$ [4, 5] so admitting queues brings no runtime improvements for PARITY_n. The lower bound that has been previously known for PARITY_n was $\Omega(\log n / \log \log n)$ for the CRQW model with no latency detection. It follows from a general bound $\Omega(\frac{\log \deg f}{\log \log \deg f})$, where $\deg(f)$ is the degree of f, derived from the bound on the Few-Write CRCW (see [9, 5]).

We cannot expect that for PARITY_n the situation is much better when we add randomization; for QRQW PRAM with polynomially many resources it follows from a generalization of the theorem of Beame and Håstad on CRCW [2]. For randomized QRQW PRAMs with arbitrary resources, latency detection and with success probability at least $0.5 + \epsilon$ ($\epsilon > 0$) we prove the time bound $\Omega(\sqrt{\log n / \log \log n})$.

In the second part of the paper we turn our attention to complexity of 2-compaction problem on EREW PRAMs. As already mentioned, there is a bound of $\Omega(\sqrt{\log n})$ for the runtime on deterministic and randomized EREW PRAMs. We show that it is no coincidence that these bounds are equal, since the runtime of the best randomized algorithm for 2-compaction is the same (up to a constant) as the deterministic runtime on the EREW PRAM (Corollary 11). This follows from a general observation that if the set of all possible input strings to a problem consists of m elements, then with extra $O(\log \log m)$ steps it is possible to derandomize any PRAM algorithm solving the problem (Theorem 10). Hence very complicated analysis of 2-compaction problem on EREW PRAM that was one of the main contributions of [10] can be avoided.

It seems that time complexity of 2-compaction on EREW is $\Theta(\log n)$. However, we found out why new type of arguments must be designed to prove this conjecture:

Definition 3. EREW$^+$ PRAM is an EREW PRAM for which any processor may halt the computation at any time (many of them may do it simultaneously). After halting the correct output should be stored at fixed locations.

Obviously the EREW$^+$ PRAM may compute OR$_n$ in $O(1)$ time. On the other hand, the proof from [7] establishing the bound $\Omega(\sqrt{\log n})$ for 2-compaction may be applied to the EREW$^+$ PRAM after slight changes. However, we show how to compute 2-compaction within this time on the EREW$^+$ PRAM (Proposition 12).

In order to shed some light light on EREW$^+$ PRAM model let us remark that time complexity of PARITY$_n$ is $\Theta(\log n)$ in deterministic case and $\Omega(\sqrt{\log n})$ in randomized case (Theorem 14).

2 Complexity of PARITY Function on QRQW PRAMs

2.1 Deterministic QRQW PRAMs with Latency Detection

Proposition 4. OR$_n$ *can be computed in a constant time on QRQW with latency detection.*

Proof. We use $2n$ processors. Processor P_i, for $i \leq n$, reads the ith input bit and if it is a 1, P_i writes it to cell C_i during the write phase. At this moment, for every $i \leq n$ processor P_{n+i} writes to C_i, too. The write phase takes 1 time unit if and only if globally no conflict occurs, that is, if the input contains no 1. No write conflict may cost more than 2 time units, since for a cell C_i only processors P_i and P_{n+i} may try to write there. By measuring duration of the write phase every processor may determine the value of OR$_n$. □

Proposition 4 shows that measuring latency is a powerful tool. However, its power is limited to disseminating only a small portion of information from a single source (even if the source is unknown) of the form "there was a write conflict of this size". For some functions it does not help at all, as shown by the following theorem:

Theorem 5. PARITY$_n$ *has time complexity* $\Theta(\log n)$ *on CRQW PRAM with latency detection.*

(CRQW PRAM is a PRAM for which concurrent reads are executed in one time unit, but concurrent writes are executed as for QRQW PRAM.) For the proof of Theorem 5 we have to recall some techniques for describing processor and cell states of a PRAM machine.

2.1.1 Technical Preliminaries

Boolean functions [5]. Each Boolean formula f has a characteristic function that can be represented by a polynomial P_f with integer coefficients. Then obviously

$$P_{\neg f} = 1 - P_f, \qquad P_{f \wedge g} = P_f \cdot P_g, \qquad P_{f \vee g} = P_f + P_g - P_f \cdot P_g.$$

Note that in particular for $P_{f_1 \vee \ldots \vee f_k}$ we get the following inclusion-exclusion formula:

$$\sum_{i \leq k} P_{f_i} - \sum_{\substack{i,j \leq k \\ i \neq j}} P_{f_i} \cdot P_{f_j} + \sum_{\substack{i,j,l \leq k \\ i \neq j \neq l}} P_{f_i} \cdot P_{f_j} \cdot P_{f_l} + \ldots + (-1)^{k+1} \cdot P_{f_1} \cdot \ldots \cdot P_{f_k}. \tag{1}$$

It is known that for every Boolean function f the polynomial P_f is unique provided that we reduce every x^i to x for $i \geq 1$ (simply x and x^i have the same values for arguments $0, 1$). The degree of a Boolean function f, $deg(f)$, is defined as the degree of this unique polynomial P_f. The fundamental properties of degree are:

$$deg(\neg f) = deg(f),$$
$$deg(f_1 \wedge \cdots \wedge f_k) \leq deg(f_1) + \cdots + deg(f_k), \tag{2}$$
$$deg(f_1 \vee \cdots \vee f_k) \leq deg(f_1) + \cdots + deg(f_k), \tag{3}$$
$$\text{and } deg(f_1 \vee \cdots \vee f_k) = \max(deg(f_1), \ldots, deg(f_k))$$
$$\text{if} \quad f_1, \ldots, f_k \text{ are mutually exclusive.} \tag{4}$$

Representing processor and memory states. With each possible state of a processor (or a cell) at a given moment of the computation we associate a Boolean function on the input bits that describes for which inputs this state is reached.

It is also convenient to assume that the processors and cells forget no information: for instance if a processor P in a state described by a function f reads a cell being in a state described by function g, then the state of P after reading is described by $f \wedge g$. So, by (2), the upper bound on the degrees of Boolean functions describing processor states at most double at each reading phase. The growth of degrees while writing may be bounded similarly provided that latency detection brings no information. Initially the processors and cells are described by functions of degree at most 1. On the other hand, PARITY$_n$ has degree n. Therefore the time required to compute PARITY$_n$ may be bounded by the time required to achieve degree n by functions describing states of the cells.

The idea of the proof for the CRQW PRAM is to restrict the possible input strings in a way that every step takes a fixed amount of time but nevertheless the restriction is described by a Boolean function of a small degree. The growth of degrees of the functions describing processor and cell states can be controlled similarly as in the case of the CREW PRAM. Finally, after the last step of the computation for such restricted inputs the output cell is described by a function h of bounded degree. A contradiction is reached if the degree of h is smaller than n:

Fact 6 [5] *If h is not a constant function and $h(x) \leq$ PARITY$_n(x)$ for every x, then $deg(h) = n$. Also $deg(h) = n$, if $h(x) \geq$ PARITY$_n(x)$ for every x.*

2.1.2 Proof of Theorem 5.

Let $PARITY_n$ be computed in time T by a CRQW PRAM M. We define inductively sets $A_0 = \{0,1\}^n \supseteq A_1 \supseteq \ldots \supseteq A_l$, such that

(i)   Let t_i be the size of the longest queue that may be formed during write phase of step i for the inputs in A_i. Then there are a cell Z_i and processors $P_{i,1}, \ldots, P_{i,t_i}$ so that they all write to Z_i at step i for all inputs in A_{i+1}.

(ii)   Degree of f_{A_i}, the characteristic function of A_i, is bounded by $b_i = \prod_{j=1}^{i}(4t_j + 2)$.

(iii) For the inputs in A_i the states of memory cells and processors after step i are described by polynomials of degree at most b_i.

(iv)   We stop the construction if M halts for any input in A_l.

Let us assume that we have determined the sets $A_0, \ldots, A_{i-1}$. In order to define A_i we consider step i executed for the inputs in A_{i-1}. Let t_i be the maximal duration of this write step for the inputs in A_{i-1}. So there are processors $P_{i_1}, \ldots, P_{i_{t_i}}$ that may write simultaneously into a cell Z_i during the write phase of step i. Let $f_j \wedge f_{A_{i-1}}$ be the characteristic function of the state of P_{i_j} causing P_{i_j} to write into Z_i. Let A_i be the set with characteristic function $f_{A_i} = f_1 \wedge \cdots \wedge f_{t_i} \wedge f_{A_{i-1}}$. By property (iii), after read phase the state of each processor is described by a polynomial of degree at most $2 \cdot b_{i-1}$, so by (2), $\deg(f_{A_i}) \le (2t_i + 1) \cdot b_{i-1}$. Note that for inputs from A_i the write phase takes **always** t_i time units. So latency detection provides no additional information.

Now let us describe the state of an arbitrary cell C after the write phase of step i. Consider the situation when C contains a symbol a after writing. Then a is a combination of b, the previous contents of C, and the messages sent to C by processors. Let g be the characteristic function describing inputs for which C stores b immediately before the write phase. Let $P_{j_1}, \ldots, P_{j_k}$ be the list of all processors that for some inputs from A_{i-1} may write into C at this step, and let $S = \{j_1, \ldots, j_k\}$. For $T \subseteq S$ let $\phi_T = \left(\bigwedge_{j \in T} h_j \right) \wedge \left(\bigwedge_{j \in S \setminus T} \neg h_j \right)$, where for $l \le k$ function h_l describes the set of inputs for which P_{j_l} writes into C at this step. Then for input $x \in A_i$ cell C stores a after the write phase of step i if and only if the following function has value 1:

$$s(x) = g(x) \wedge \left(\bigvee_{T \subseteq S} \phi_T(x) \right) \wedge f_{A_i},$$

where the disjunction is taken over all $T = \{j_{i_1}, \ldots, j_{i_T}\}$ such that the messages sent by $P_{j_{i_1}}, \ldots, P_{j_{i_T}}$ combined with b give a.

We show that $\deg(s) \le (4t_j + 2) \cdot b_{i-1}$. Since $\phi_{T'}$ and $\phi_{T''}$ are mutually exclusive for $T' \ne T''$, by (4) it suffices to show that $\deg(g \wedge \phi_T \wedge f_{A_i}) \le (4t_j + 2) \cdot b_{i-1}$ for every ϕ_T appearing in the formula defining s. To show that each such ϕ_T has a proper degree we apply formula (1). Long products occur in this formula, but it is impossible to satisfy more than t_i polynomials $P_{h_\bullet}$ simultaneously. Indeed, it follows from the assumption that t_i is the size of the biggest queue at step i for the inputs in A_i. Therefore we may remove all products of more than t_i polynomials P_{h_i}. It follows that $\deg(g \wedge \phi_T \wedge f_{A_i}) \le \deg(g) + t_i \cdot 2b_{i-1} + \deg(f_{A_i}) \le (4t_i + 2) \cdot b_{i-1}$.

We put $b_i = (4t_i + 2) \cdot b_{i-1}$. Then, as we have just seen, (iii) holds for memory cells. In the same way we can prove claim (iii) for the states of processors.

Since T is the runtime of the algorithm, we have $T \ge t_1 + \cdots + t_l$. On the other hand, since the machine stops after step l, the output cell must store the correct values of $PARITY_n$.

Hence by Fact 6 the degree of a Boolean function describing the output cell at this moment for inputs in A_l must be n. Hence

$$n \leq b_l = \prod_{j=1}^{l} (4t_j + 2) \leq \prod_{j=1}^{l} 6^{t_j} = 6^{t_1 + \cdots + t_l} \leq 6^T.$$

It follows that $T = \Omega(\log n)$. □

A more careful examination shows that CRQW PRAMs cannot compute $PARITY_n$ even by one step faster than CREW PRAMs.

2.2 Time Complexity of PARITY on Randomized QRQW PRAMs

We say that a randomized algorithm A succeeds in time T with probability p if for every input x the probability that A halts within T steps **and** gives the correct answer is at least p.

Theorem 7. *Suppose that a randomized QRQW PRAM M with latency detection computes* $PARITY_n$ *in time T with success probability at least $0.5 + \epsilon$ ($\epsilon > 0$). Then $T = \Omega(\sqrt{\log n / \log \log n})$.*

Proof. The first step is to reduce the problem to a deterministic QRQW PRAM by the following (simple) version of Yao's Theorem [11]:

Lemma 8. *Let a randomized QRQW PRAM N compute a function f and succeed with probability p in time T. Then there is a deterministic QRQW PRAM N' that outputs the value of f within T steps for at least a fraction of p of all input sequences.*

By Lemma 8 there is a deterministic QRQW PRAM A that in T steps yields the value of $PARITY_n$ for at least a fraction of $0.5 + \epsilon$ of all inputs. Our analysis of algorithm A is a kind of *independent set technique*. We first sketch the general idea of the construction and then go into details.

Outline of the independent set technique.

To adhere to the standard conventions let every input position be called an (input) variable. The actual input bits will be called values of the input variables.

At each step of the computation we fix and reveal the values of certain input variables to all processors. With this additional knowledge the machine cannot work slower or provide more false answers. The idea is that through revealing the variables we achieve that the configuration of the machine and the next step can be easily described. Which variables should be revealed and which values should they have is a major concern. If V_t denotes the set of variables that remain unrevealed immediately after step t, then we require that the following properties hold at this time:

1. each processor and cell knows at most one unrevealed variable, that is, either the state of the processor (the cell) is the same for all settings of the variables in V_t, or it depends only on the value of exactly one variable in V_t,
2. for each variable $x_i \in V_t$ the number of processors and memory cells that know x_i is bounded by $\approx (\log n)^t$, the locations of these processors and cells are the same for all settings of unrevealed variables,

3. a minimal size of V_t is, roughly speaking, $n/(\log n)^{t^2}$,

4. for all settings of the unrevealed variables in V_t, the duration of each of the steps $1,\ldots,t$ is fixed and follows from the values of the revealed variables; thereby revealing duration of these steps brings no gain,

5. the fraction of settings of the unrevealed variables for which the algorithm yields correct answers is at least $0.5 + \epsilon - \frac{t \cdot \epsilon}{\sqrt{\log n}}$.

Termination conditions.

The process of revealing can be interrupted at step t if for at least half of the settings of the variables from V_{t-1} the computation time of step t exceeds $\sqrt{\log n}$. Indeed, the process of revealing variables guarantees that after revealing the fraction of inputs for which the algorithm terminates in the stated time T and gives a correct answer is greater than 0.5. So we get $T \geq \sqrt{\log n}$ in this case.

The situation mentioned happens if there is a memory cell C that may be read (written) by $\alpha \geq \log n$ processors. The queue in this case is formed by, say β, processors that always read C and $\alpha - \beta$ processors that may read C depending on the values of the unrevealed variables that they know. The process of reading by the latter group can be described as a Bernoulli trial, where each independent random variable X_i corresponds to an unrevealed variable x_i and the processors that know x_i. The value of X_i is the number of processors depending on x_i that read C for a given value of x_i. It is elementary to show that with probability at least 0.5 the number of processors of the latter group reading C is at least $0.5 \cdot (\alpha - \beta)$. This makes the total length of the queue at least $0.5 \cdot \alpha \geq 0.5 \cdot \log n$ with probability at least 0.5. So $T = \Omega(\log n)$.

If we have got a set V_t with $|V_t| > 1$, then the machine cannot halt immediately after step t. Indeed, no matter which variable from V_t is known to the output cell, for exactly 50% settings of the remaining unrevealed variables the correct output is 1 and for the rest it is 0. Since for majority of settings of the variables in $|V_t|$ the algorithm succeeds, the machine does not halt immediately after step t, and $t < T$.

Analysis of a read phase.

We assume, as an inductive hypothesis, that the conditions claimed hold after step t. We analyze the read phase of step $t + 1$ and show how to reveal the variables.

A processor that does not know any unrevealed variable reads always the same cell or no cell at all. A processor P that knows a variable $x_l \in V_t$ may read one of at most two cells, one for each possible value. Both these cells are called to be *referred* by P at this step. If any cell is referred by at least $\log n$ processors, then the termination condition holds and we are done. So we may assume that every cell is referred by less than $\log n$ processors.

Now we choose the variables to be revealed at the read phase of step $t + 1$. Let k_t denote the bound on the number of processors (cells) knowing a single unrevealed variable immediately after step t. We consider a graph $G_{t+1} = (V_t, E)$ with $(x_i, x_j) \in E$, if during the read phase of step $t + 1$, there exist a processor P that knows x_i and a memory cell C that depends on x_j and P refers C at step $t + 1$, or there are processors P', P'' that know, respectively, x_i and x_j and refer the same memory cell. We estimate the degree of the graph G_{t+1}. Let $x_l \in V_t$ be an arbitrary node of this graph.

- Let x_l be known to a memory cell. There are less than $\log n$ processors referring this cell. Hence together there are no more than $k_t \cdot (\log n - 1)$ edges with the endpoint x_l constructed because reading a cell knowing x_l.

– If a processor P knows x_l and refers C and C', then for this reason at most $2 \cdot (\log n - 2)$ edges are constructed. Indeed, C (C') is referred by less than $\log n$ processors, one of them being P itself. Since x_l is initially known to up to k_t processors, there are together at most $2 \cdot (\log n - 2) \cdot k_t$ edges of this kind with endpoint x_l.

We conclude that the degree of graph G_{t+1} is less than than $u_t = (3 \log n - 5) \cdot k_t + 1$. For such a graph we can choose an independent set of cardinality $|V_t|/(\text{degree}(G_{t+1}) + 1) \geq |V_t|/u_t$ [3, page 284]. We fix such an independent set V_t' and reveal the values of all variables that are not in V_t'. The values of the revealed variables are chosen so that the number of correct answers of the algorithm for the resulting subproblem is maximal over all settings of variables in $V_t \setminus V_t'$. This ensures that after revealing the fraction of errors is not larger than before revealing.

By the above construction the properties (1) and (3) obviously hold after the read phase and revealing. Now let us check how many processors may know the value of an unrevealed variable. A processor may learn a variable $x_l \in V_t$ by reading a cell that knows x_l. There are at most k_t memory cells storing x_l, each cell may be read by less than $\log n$ processors. Hence the number of new processors that may learn x_l is less than $k_t \cdot (\log n - 1)$. Together with k_t processors that has known x_l before, it makes at most $k_{t+1}' = k_t \cdot \log n$ processors knowing x_l at the end of the read phase of step $t + 1$. Obviously, the number of cells knowing x_l remains unchanged.

It is still not guaranteed that the length of the longest queue at the read phase is always the same. We only know that for every cell C there is at most one unrevealed variable x_l such that a processor knowing x_l refers C. Therefore we have to reveal some additional variables to fix the length of the longest queue.

Revealing latency.

Let α be the size of the longest queue that may occur during the read phase of step $t + 1$ for the chosen values of the revealed variables. If for some cell C such a queue is formed by the processors that always write into C, then we are done – the queue size is always α and it does not leak any information on the unrevealed variables. So assume that for every cell C where a queue of size α may be formed, the actual size of the queue depends on an unrevealed variable. Let $Z_1, \ldots, Z_m$ be these cells and $d_1, \ldots, d_m$ be the values of unrevealed variables $x_{s_1}, \ldots, x_{s_m}$ such that for $x_{s_j} = d_j$ a queue of length α is formed at Z_j.

Now we consider two cases. First assume that $m > (\frac{c}{\epsilon})^2 \cdot \log n$. Every string $u \in \{0, 1\}^m$ can be considered as a node of the m-dimensional hypercube. For a node u we consider the inputs with $x_{s_j} := d_j$, if $u_j = 1$, and $x_{s_j} := \neg d_j$ if $u_j = 0$, for $j \leq m$, and arbitrary values of the remaining unrevealed variables. Then we define $l(u)$ as the fraction of these inputs on which the algorithm succeeds. Let b_t' be the fraction of settings of the unrevealed variables of V_t', for which the algorithm gives a correct answer. Then obviously b_t' is the average value of all labels $l(u)$. At this moment we need a combinatorial lemma, proved in Appendix:

Lemma 9. *Suppose that every node u of a k-dimensional hypercube H has a label $l(u) \in [0, 1]$. Let $\sum_{u \in H} l(u) = 2^k \cdot (0.5 + \epsilon)$ for $\epsilon > 0$. Then there is an $i \leq k$ and a constant c such that for $F_i = \{(u_1, \ldots, u_k) \in H : u_i = 1\}$ the following inequality holds:*

$$\sum_{u \in F_i} l(u) \geq 2^{k-1} \cdot (0.5 + \epsilon - \frac{c}{\sqrt{k}}). \tag{5}$$

Since $b'_t > 0.5$ we may apply Lemma 9 and find a number $j \leq m$ such that after fixing $x_{s_j} = d_j$ the algorithm yields the correct answer for a fraction of at least $b'_t - c/\sqrt{\log m} \geq b'_t - \epsilon/\sqrt{\log n}$. We reveal the variable x_{s_j} and set it to d_j. This value of x_{s_j} guarantees also that the maximal queue has length α for all settings of the remaining unrevealed variables.

If $m < (\frac{c}{\epsilon})^2 \cdot \log n$, then applying Lemma 9 decreases the fraction of correct answers of the algorithm too much. Therefore we use another strategy. We choose an $u \in H$ such that $l(u)$ is maximal. Then we reveal all variables $x_{s_1}, \ldots, x_{s_m}$ according to the bits of u (i.e. for each $j \leq m$ we put $x_{s_j} = d_j$, if $u_j = 1$, and $x_{s_j} = \neg d_j$ otherwise). If at least one coordinate of u has been 1, then we are done: the fraction of correct answers is at least b'_t, while a queue of length α is formed. The bad case is when $u = (0, \ldots, 0)$. Then no queue of size α is formed. On the other hand, the fraction of the correct answers has not decreased. It may seem that we are in the starting situation, but now the maximal length of a queue, say α', is less than α and we can repeat the same construction for α'. In this way we may be forced to make up to α iterations, each time decreasing the size of the maximal possible queue. At each iteration we reveal $O(\log n)$ variables. Since $\alpha = O(\log n)$, we reveal only $O(\log^2 n)$ variables. The process described terminates either in the case when $m = m(j) > (\frac{c}{\epsilon})^2 \cdot \log n$ at the jth call, or we decrease the size of the maximal queue to 1 (and then no information is leaked through latency detection).

Let V''_t denote the set of unrevealed variables after revealing some variables of V'_t while dealing with latency of the read phase.

Analysis of a write phase.

Revealing variables at the write phase goes as for the read phase. One can easily derive that afterwards each unrevealed variable is known to at most $k_{t+1} = k_t \cdot (2\log n + 1)$ cells, and that we choose an independent set $V_{t+1} \subseteq V''_t$ of at least $|V''_t|/u'_t - O(\log^2 n)$ elements, where $u'_t = k_t \cdot (4\log n + 3) \cdot (\log n - 1) + 1$.

Achieving the time bound.

Since $k_{t+1} = k_t \cdot (2\log n + 1)$, it follows easily that $k_j \leq (e\log n)^j$ for some constant e. We also get

$$|V_{t+1}| \geq (|V_t|/u_t - O(\log^2 n))/u'_t - O(\log^2 n)$$
$$\geq |V_t|/(d\log^3 n \cdot k_t^2) \geq |V_t|/((d \cdot (e\log n))^{2t+3}).$$

Thereby $|V_t| \geq n/(\log n)^{f \cdot t^2}$ for some constant $f > 0$. It follows that $|V_t| > 1$ for $t \leq \sqrt{\log n/(f \cdot \log\log n)}$. For such t the fraction of good answers has been guaranteed to be at least $0.5 + \epsilon - \frac{\epsilon \cdot t}{\sqrt{\log n}} > 0.5$. So the algorithm may not stop after step t and so $T \geq t$. Hence $T = \Omega(\sqrt{\log n/\log\log n})$. $\qquad\square$

3 2-compaction Problem and EREW$^+$ Model

3.1 Complexity of 2-compaction on the EREW PRAM

Theorem 10. *Suppose that A is a randomized PRAM algorithm that solves a decision problem P in time T. Assume further that the number of possible input configurations for P is m and A succeeds with probability at least $0.5 + \epsilon$. Then there is a **deterministic** PRAM algorithm A' for P (with the same access modes for reading and writing as A) that runs in time $T + O(\log\log m)$.*

First let us apply Theorem 10 to the 2-compaction problem. There are $\binom{n}{2} + n + 1$ possible inputs for the 2-compaction problem on n input variables, so from a randomized EREW algorithm for 2-compaction running in time T we can get a deterministic EREW algorithm running in time $T + O(\log \log n)$. Since $T = \Omega(\sqrt{\log n})$ by [7], we get:

Corollary 11. *The time complexity of 2-compaction is the same (up to a constant factor) on deterministic and randomized EREW PRAMs.*

Proof of Theorem 10. First we show that if the error probability of a randomized algorithm is very small, then a deterministic algorithm running in the same time exists.

Claim A. *Let a randomized PRAM B solve a decision problem R in time L and succeed with probability greater than $1 - \frac{1}{m}$, where m is the number of possible input configurations for R. (We assume that probability distribution on such inputs is uniform.) Then there is a deterministic PRAM B' with the same access mode to the shared memory as B that solves R in time L.*

Indeed, by Lemma 8, there is a deterministic PRAM B' (with the same memory access mode as B) that runs in time L and errs on a fraction of less than $\frac{1}{m}$ of all inputs. But there are only m input configurations, so B' may not err at all.

The second step in the proof is to show that given the randomized algorithm A we may construct an algorithm A' that has the runtime $T + O(\log \log m)$ and errs with probability smaller than $\frac{1}{m}$. PRAM A' works as follows. First we make $k = \alpha \log m$ copies of the input sequence (α is an appropriate constant specified later). Even on the EREW PRAM making the copies can be done in time $O(\log \log m)$. Then we run the algorithm A independently on each copy. After T steps we get k answers, some of them correct, and some of them false. At this moment we and perform a majority vote. This takes $O(\log k) = O(\log \log m)$ time on EREW PRAM. Let X be the random variable denoting the number of right answers given by the machines executing algorithm A. Then $E[X] \geq (0.5 + \epsilon) \cdot k$. Let us recall the following bound on the sum X of m independent Bernoulli trials with success probability p (see [1]):

$$\Pr[X \leq (1 - \beta)mp] \leq e^{-\beta^2 mp/2}.$$

Hence for $\beta = 2\epsilon/(1 + 2\epsilon)$, we get

$$\Pr[X < 0.5k] = \Pr[X < (1 - \beta) \cdot k \cdot (0.5 + \epsilon)] \leq e^{-\beta^2 k(0.5+\epsilon)/2} = e^{-k \cdot \epsilon^2/(1+2\epsilon)}.$$

If $\alpha > \frac{1+2\epsilon}{\epsilon^2 \cdot \log e}$, then the last term is smaller than $1/m$, as required. $\qquad\square$

3.2 Tightness of the Bounds and EREW$^+$ PRAMs

Proposition 12. *2-compaction problem can be solved in time $O(\sqrt{\log n})$ on the EREW$^+$ PRAM.*

Proof. The computation consists of at most $O(\sqrt{\log n})$ rounds. After round i:

(i) The input cells are partitioned into blocks $C_1^i, C_2^i, \ldots$ of size $2^{0.5 \cdot i \cdot (i-1)}$.
(ii) With each block C_j^i we associate auxiliary cells $Z_{j,1}^i, \ldots, Z_{j,2^i}^i$. These cells store the position of a nonempty input cell in C_j^i, if there is any.

The computation is interrupted if 2 nonempty input cells are found. We describe round $i + 1$. Let $C_j^{i+1} = C_{(j-1)\cdot 2^i+1}^i \cup \cdots \cup C_{j\cdot 2^i}^i$. Then the following steps are performed for each j:

Step 1. For $k < l \leq 2^i$, we check if $Z_{(j-1)\cdot 2^i+k,l}^i$ and $Z_{(j-1)\cdot 2^i+l,k}^i$ both point to nonempty input cells. If it is so, then these cells are moved to the output positions (since there is at most one such pair (k, l), no write conflict arises) and the machine halts.

Step 2. If the machine has not halted at Step 1, then there is at most one nonempty cell in C_j^{i+1}. For each $k, l \leq 2^i$ if $Z_{(j-1)\cdot 2^i+k,l}^i$ contains a pointer to a nonempty cell, then it is copied into $Z_{j,2l-1}^{i+1}, Z_{j,2l}^{i+1}$. Obviously, no write conflict may occur since otherwise the machine would stop at Step 1.

If finally all input cells are in a single block and the machine is still active, then there is at most one nonempty input cell. Its address can be found in the first auxiliary cell. There are at most $O(\sqrt{\log n})$ rounds of $O(1)$ steps each, so the algorithm runs in $O(\sqrt{\log n})$ steps. $\quad\square$

Some slight modifications of the result for EREW PRAM in [7] yield the following result showing that the above algorithm is optimal.

Proposition 13. *2-compaction requires $\Omega(\sqrt{\log n})$ steps on EREW$^+$ PRAM.*

3.3 Complexity of PARITY on Randomized EREW$^+$ PRAM

To shed some light on the limitations of the EREW$^+$ PRAM let us mention without a proof the following results concerning time complexity of PARITY$_n$ in this model:

Proposition 14. *Computing PARITY$_n$ on EREW$^+$ PRAM requires $\Omega(\log n)$ time. On the randomized EREW$^+$ PRAM PARITY$_n$ has time complexity $\Omega(\sqrt{\log n})$.*

Acknowledgments. We are deeply grateful to Artur Czumaj and ToMasz Wierzbicki for many fruitful discussions. We also thank Yossi Matias and Vijaya Ramachandran for bringing our attention to the QRQW model.

References

1. D. Angluin, L.G. Valiant, Fast probabilistic algorithms for Hamiltonian circuits and matchings, *J. Comput. System Sci.* **18** (1979) 155–193.
2. P. Beame, J. Håstad, Optimal bounds for decision problems on the CRCW PRAM, *JACM*, **36(3)** (1989) 643–670.
3. C. Berge: *Graphs and Hypergraphs.* North–Holland, Amsterdam, 1976.
4. S. Cook, C. Dwork, R. Reischuk, Upper and lower time bounds for parallel random access machines without simultaneous writes, *SIAM J. Comput.* **15(1)** (1986) 87–97.
5. M. Dietzfelbinger, M. Kutyłowski, R. Reischuk, Exact lower time bounds for computing Boolean functions on CREW PRAMs, *JCSS* **48(2)** (1994) 231–253.
6. F.E. Fich, The complexity of computation on the Parallel Random Access Machine, in *Synthesis of Parallel Algorithms*, J.H. Reif (ed.) (Morgan Kaufmann, San Mateo, 1993) 843–899.
7. F. Fich, M. Kowaluk, M.Kutyłowski, K. Loryś, P. Ragde, Retrieval of scattered information by EREW, CREW and CRCW PRAMs, *Comput. Complexity* **5** (1995) 113–131.
8. P. Gibbons, Y. Matias, V. Ramachandran, Efficient low-contention parallel algorithms, in *Proc. 6th ACM Symp. on Parallel Algorithms and Architectures*, (ACM Press, New York, 1994) 236–247.

9. P. Gibbons, Y. Matias, V. Ramachandran, The QRQW PRAM: accounting for contention in parallel algorithms, in *Proc. 5th ACM Symp. on Discrete Algorithms*, (ACM Press, New York, 1994) 638–648.
10. P. D. MacKenzie, Lower bounds for randomized exclusive write PRAMs, in *Proc. 7th ACM Symp. on Parallel Algorithms and Architectures*, (ACM Press, New York, 1995) 254–263.
11. R. Motwani, P. Raghavan: *Randomized Algorithms*, Cambridge University Press, Cambridge 1995.
12. H. Robbins, A remark on Stirling formula, *American Mathematical Monthly* **62** (1955) 26–29.

Appendix

Here we prove combinatorial Lemma 9. First we check one inequality.

Lemma 15. $\binom{k}{k/2} \cdot 2^{-k} \le c \cdot \frac{1}{\sqrt{k}}$ *for some constant c.*

Proof. The following Stirling formula approximates $h!$ [12]:

$$\sqrt{2\pi} \cdot h^{h+0.5} \cdot \frac{1}{e^{h-1/(12h+1)}} < h! < \sqrt{2\pi} \cdot h^{h+0.5} \cdot \frac{1}{e^{h-1/12h}}.$$

Therefore

$$\binom{n}{n/2} = \frac{n!}{((n/2)!)^2} \le \frac{\sqrt{2\pi} \cdot n^{n+0.5}}{e^{n-\frac{1}{12n}}} \cdot \left(\frac{e^{n/2 - \frac{1}{6n+1}}}{\sqrt{2\pi} \cdot (n/2)^{n/2+0.5}} \right)^2$$

$$= \frac{1}{\sqrt{2\pi}} \cdot \frac{1}{\sqrt{n}} \cdot 2^{n+1} \cdot \frac{1}{e^{2/(6n+1)-1/(12n)}} = \frac{1}{\sqrt{2\pi}} \cdot \frac{1}{\sqrt{n}} \cdot 2^{n+1} \cdot e(n)$$

where $e(n) \approx 1$. Then $\binom{n}{n/2}/2^n \le \sqrt{\frac{2}{\pi}} \cdot e(n) \cdot \frac{1}{\sqrt{n}}$. □

Proof of Lemma 9. Consider a function $l' : H \to [0,1]$ such that $\sum_{u \in H} l'(u) = \sum_{u \in H} l(u)$ and the value $\gamma = \sum_{i \le k} \sum_{u \in F_i} l'(u)$ is minimal. Let $u \in H$ and s be the number of coordinates of u that are ones. Then we say that weight$(u) = s$. If weight$(u) = s$, then the node u belongs to s different sets F_i and thereby $l'(u)$ is counted s times in γ.

Note that it is impossible that weight(u_1) < weight(u_2), $l'(u_1) < 1$ and $l'(u_2) > 0$. Indeed, if it would be so, then we could decrease $l'(u_2)$ and increase $l'(u_1)$ by the same amount, and thereby decrease γ. It follows that for a certain d, we have $l'(u) = 1$ if weight$(u) < d$, and $l'(u) = 0$ if weight$(u) > d$. For the sum $\gamma = \sum_{i \le k} \sum_{u \in F_i} l'(u)$ it is immaterial how we assign the values $l'(u)$ for the nodes of the weight d, as long as they are in $[0,1]$ and their sum does not change. So we assume that all nodes of weight d have the same value of l', say p. Since $\gamma \le \sum_{i \le k} \sum_{u \in F_i} l(u)$, it follows that there is an $i \le k$ such that $\sum_{u \in F_i} l(u) \ge \gamma/k$. Therefore it suffices to estimate γ/k. We have

$$2^k \cdot (0.5 + \epsilon) = \sum_{u \in H} l(u) = \sum_{u \in H} l'(u) = \binom{k}{0} + \ldots + \binom{k}{d-1} + p \cdot \binom{k}{d}.$$

Note that $\gamma/k = \sum_{u \in F_i} l'(u)$. Since F_i contains $\binom{k-1}{j}$ nodes of weight $j + 1$, we get

$$\gamma/k = \binom{k-1}{0} + \ldots + \binom{k-1}{d-2} + p \cdot \binom{k-1}{d-1} = 0.5 \cdot (2\binom{k-1}{0} + \ldots + 2\binom{k-1}{d-2} + 2p \cdot \binom{k-1}{d-1}))$$

$$= 0.5 \cdot (((\binom{k}{0} + \ldots + \binom{k}{d-2}) + \binom{k-1}{d-2} + 2p \cdot \binom{k-1}{d-1}))$$

$$= 0.5 \cdot (2^k \cdot (0.5 + \epsilon) - \binom{k}{d-1} - p \cdot \binom{k}{d} + \binom{k-1}{d-2} + 2p \cdot \binom{k-1}{d-1}))$$

$$\ge 0.5 \cdot (2^k \cdot (0.5 + \epsilon) - 2\binom{k}{d})) \ge 2^{k-1} \cdot (0.5 + \epsilon - \frac{c}{\sqrt{k}})$$

(the last inequality follows from Lemma 15.) □

Pinpointing Computation with Modular Queries in the Boolean Hierarchy

Manindra Agrawal *   Richard Beigel †   Thomas Thierauf ‡

Abstract

A *modular query* consists of asking how many (modulo m) of k strings belong to a fixed NP language. Modular queries provide a form of restricted access to an NP oracle. For each k and m, we consider the class of languages accepted by NP machines that ask a single modular query. Han and Thierauf [HT95] showed that these classes coincide with levels of the Boolean hierarchy when m is even or $k \leq 2m$, and they determined the exact levels. Until now, the remaining case — odd m and large k — looked quite difficult. We pinpoint the level in the Boolean hierarchy for the remaining case; thus, these classes coincide with levels of the Boolean hierarchy for every k and m.

In addition we characterize the classes obtained by using an NP(l) acceptor in place of an NP acceptor (NP(l) is the lth level of the Boolean hierarchy). As before, these all coincide with levels in the Boolean hierarchy.

1   Introduction

A set L is *(polynomial-time) truth-table reducible to* a set A [LLS75], if there exist two polynomial-time bounded Turing machines, the *generator* and the *evaluator*. On a given input string x, the generator first generates a list of strings which are then asked of oracle A. Then the evaluator, getting x and the answers of A to the queries as input, decides the membership of x in L. A truth-table reduction is called *bounded* if the number of queries produced by the generator is bounded by a constant for any x.

In this paper, we consider a more restrictive version of a truth-table reduction. Namely, instead of giving the *full information* about the queries to the evaluator, that is, the characteristic sequence with respect to oracle A, the evaluator gets only some partial information about it. The point is that by comparing various kinds of partial information that can be given to an evaluator, one can study the kind of information an evaluator actually needs to solve a certain problem. This setting has been studied in many papers [Bei91, HT95, KT94, W90, Wec85],

*Department of Computer Science, Indian Institute of Technology, Kanpur 208016, India. Email: manindra@iitk.ernet.in. Work done while visiting Abteilung Theoretische Informatik, Universität Ulm, on an Alexander von Humboldt Fellowship.

†Yale University, Dept. of Computer Science, P.O. Box 208285, New Haven, CT 06520-8285, USA. Email: beigel-richard@cs.yale.edu. On sabbatical leave 1996–97 at the Dept. of Computer Science, University of Maryland, College Park, MD 20742-3251, USA. Email beigel@cs.umd.edu. Supported in part by U.S. National Science Foundation grants CCR-8952528 and CCR-9415410 and by NASA (NAG52895)

‡Abteilung Theoretische Informatik, Universität Ulm, Oberer Eselsberg, 89069 Ulm, Germany. Email: thierauf@informatik.uni-ulm.de.

and some surprising results have been obtained. To describe this more formally, we use a notation introduced by Köbler and Thierauf [KT94].

Definition [KT94] Let $\mathcal{C}$ be a class of languages and let $\mathcal{F}$ be a class of functions from Σ^* to Σ^*. A set L is in the class $\mathcal{C}//\mathcal{F}$ if and only if there are a set $A \in \mathcal{C}$ and a function $f \in \mathcal{F}$ such that for all $x \in \Sigma^*$, it holds that $x \in L \Longleftrightarrow (x, f(x)) \in A$.

We consider the following function classes. Let A be a set, $k \geq 0$, and $m \geq 2$.

$$f \in \chi^{A[k]} \quad \Longleftrightarrow \quad \exists g \in \mathrm{FP}\ \forall x: \quad g(x) = (x_1, \ldots, x_k) \text{ and } f(x) = A(x_1) \cdots A(x_k),$$

$$f \in \#^{A[k]} \quad \Longleftrightarrow \quad \exists g \in \mathrm{FP}\ \forall x: \quad g(x) = (x_1, \ldots, x_k) \text{ and } f(x) = \sum_{i=1}^{k} A(x_i),$$

$$f \in \mathrm{Mod}_m^{A[k]} \quad \Longleftrightarrow \quad \exists h \in \#^{A[k]}\ \forall x: \quad f(x) = h(x) \bmod m,$$

where $A(\cdot)$ denotes the characteristic function of A. For $m = 2$, we also write $\oplus^{A[k]}$ instead of $\mathrm{Mod}_m^{A[k]}$. For a class $\mathcal{C}$ of sets, $\chi^{\mathcal{C}[k]}$ denotes $\bigcup_{A \in \mathcal{C}} \chi^{A[k]}$, and analogously for the other two classes.

In other words, $\chi^{A[k]}$ gives the sequence of answers to the queries to A produced by some generator g, $\#^{A[k]}$ counts the number of queries that are in A, and $\mathrm{Mod}_m^{A[k]}$ gives the later number modulo m. As an example, we have $\mathrm{P}//\chi^{\mathrm{NP}[k]} = \mathrm{P}_{tt}^{\mathrm{NP}[k]}$.

One of the motivations to consider such restricted truth-table reductions is a somewhat surprising result that follows from a paper by Wagner and Wechsung [Wec85], see also in [Bei91].

Theorem 1.1. [Wec85] For all $k \geq 0$,

$$\mathrm{P}//\chi^{\mathrm{NP}[k]} = \mathrm{P}//\#^{\mathrm{NP}[k]} = \mathrm{P}//\oplus^{\mathrm{NP}[k]}.$$

In other words, one can drastically reduce the information a polynomial-time evaluator gets when asking an NP oracle, namely from full information to a single bit information: the parity of the number of queries that are in the oracle, without changing the accepted class of sets, $\mathrm{P}_{tt}^{\mathrm{NP}[k]}$.

It follows from Theorem 1.1 that instead of $\oplus^{\mathrm{NP}[k]}$, one can use $\mathrm{Mod}_m^{\mathrm{NP}[k]}$, for any *even* m, and still get the same class, $\mathrm{P}//\oplus^{\mathrm{NP}[k]}$. This is, however, not clear when m is *odd*. Han and Thierauf [HT95] showed that in this case the evaluator gets in fact less information (unless the Boolean hierarchy collapses).

Theorem 1.2. [HT95] For all $k \geq 0$ and $m > 2$ odd,

$$\mathrm{P}//\mathrm{Mod}_m^{\mathrm{NP}[k]} = \mathrm{P}//\oplus^{\mathrm{NP}[k-\lfloor k/m \rfloor]}.$$

In other words, a parity function can ask $\lfloor k/m \rfloor$ less queries to an NP oracle than a modulo m function, for odd m, and still give the same amount of information to a P evaluator.

Extending the evaluator to a *nondeterministic* machine, we get a nondeterministic version of the truth-table reduction. Köbler and Thierauf [KT94] showed that the counterpart of the first equality of Theorem 1.1 holds, and furthermore, that the resulting class coincides with the $(2k+1)$-th level of the Boolean hierarchy.

Theorem 1.3. [KT94] For all $k \geq 0$,

$$NP//\chi^{NP[k]} = NP//\#^{NP[k]} = NP(2k+1).$$

Note that $NP(k) \subseteq P//\chi^{NP[k]} \subseteq NP(k+1)$ for all $k \geq 1$ [KSW87] (see also [Bei91]). Therefore, switching from a P to an NP evaluator roughly doubles the level of the Boolean hierarchy where the resulting classes are located.

When we have a parity function given to an NP evaluator, Han and Thierauf [HT95] showed that the resulting classes are located much lower in the Boolean hierarchy than with full information.

Theorem 1.4. [HT95] For all $k \geq 0$,

$$NP//\oplus^{NP[2k+1]} = NP//\oplus^{NP[2k+2]} = NP(2k+3).$$

For general modulo functions, again, when m is even, $\text{Mod}_m^{NP[k]}$ gives the same information to an NP evaluator as $\oplus^{NP[k]}$. However, when m is odd, only lower and upper bound are known for the resulting classes, the precise location of $NP//\text{Mod}_m^{NP[k]}$, when m is odd, remained open.

Theorem 1.5. [HT95] For all $k \geq 2m - 2$,

(i) $NP//\text{Mod}_m^{NP[k]} = NP//\oplus^{NP[k]}$, for m even,

(ii) $NP//\oplus^{NP[k-\lfloor k/m \rfloor]} \subseteq NP//\text{Mod}_m^{NP[k]} \subseteq NP//\oplus^{NP[k]}$, for m odd.

In this paper, we solve the open problem. Namely, we show that all classes $NP//\text{Mod}_m^{NP[k]}$ in fact coincide with some level of the Boolean hierarchy, and we determine the level. Based on the mind-change technique developed by Wagner and Wechsung [Wec85], we associate with each class $NP//\text{Mod}_m^{NP[k]}$ a certain game. The game consists of a table where one can make certain moves according to rules, we will specify below. Some of the moves increase the counter for the game. The maximum score the counter can reach by any playing strategy will be the level of the Boolean hierarchy the class $NP//\text{Mod}_m^{NP[k]}$ coincides with.

Therefore, we will develop a playing strategy and then prove that this strategy is optimal. Since we also get again the results mentioned above (with NP evaluators), we have now a uniform way of proving results along these lines. Furthermore, our technique extends to more general classes: the evaluator can be in higher levels of the Boolean hierarchy. That is, we can handle classes $NP(j)//\text{Mod}_m^{NP[k]}$, for $j \geq 1$.

Such classes look very technical. However, we think that our methods of locating such, somehow involved classes, in the, much simpler defined, Boolean Hierarchy are interesting enough in its own and might find further applications in other settings.

2 Preliminaries

We follow standard definitions and notations in computational complexity theory (see, e.g., [HU79] or [BDG88]). Throughout this paper, we use the alphabet $\Sigma = \{0, 1\}$.

P (NP) denote the classes of languages that can be recognized by a polynomial-time deterministic (nondeterministic) Turing machine. FP is the class of polynomial-time computable total functions.

The Boolean hierarchy is the closure of NP under Boolean operations, and is usually defined in levels by allowing successively more Boolean operations. This can be done for example by symmetric differences of NP sets [CGH+88]: a set L is in $NP(k)$ $(k \geq 1)$, the k-th level of the Boolean hierarchy, if there exist $A_1, \ldots, A_k \in NP$ such that $L = A_1 \triangle \cdots \triangle A_k$. A set L is in $coNP(k)$, if $\overline{L} \in NP(k)$. The Boolean hierarchy, BH, is the union of all the levels, $BH = \bigcup_{k \geq 1} NP(k)$.

3 Providing the Game

Wagner and Wechsung [Wec85] have shown that any Boolean expression over NP sets coincides with some level (or its complement) of the Boolean hierarchy.

Let α be a Boolean function with k variables, that is $\alpha : (x_1, \ldots, x_k) \in \{0,1\}^k \mapsto \{0,1\}$. This corresponds naturally to the above setting: for an expression using k NP sets $L_1, \ldots, L_k$, set variable $x_i = 1$ if and only if input $x \in L_i$, for $i = 1, \ldots, k$. Then, x is in the set described by α and $L_1, \ldots, L_k$ if $\alpha(x_1, \ldots, x_k) = 1$. Let $NP(\alpha)$ be the class of sets that can be expressed that way. We have that for any α there is some m such that $NP(\alpha)$ coincides with either $NP(m)$ or $coNP(m)$.

Let $a = (a_1, \ldots, a_m)$ be an increasing chain in $\{0,1\}^k$ with respect to the bitwise order $\prec$. That is, $a_i \in \{0,1\}^k$, for $i = 1, \ldots, k$, and $a_1 \preceq \cdots \preceq a_m$. The number of mind-changes of α in a is the number of positions i such that $\alpha(a_i) \neq \alpha(a_{i+1})$. By $m(\alpha)$ we denote the maximum number of mind-changes of α in any increasing chain in $\{0,1\}^k$. The level of the Boolean hierarchy $NP(\alpha)$ coincides with is determined by $m(\alpha)$.

Theorem 3.1. [Wec85] For any k-ary Boolean function α, we have

$$NP(\alpha) = \begin{cases} NP(m(\alpha)), & \text{if } \alpha(0^k) = 0 \\ coNP(m(\alpha)), & \text{otherwise.} \end{cases}$$

For any k-ary Boolean function α, we have $0 \leq m(\alpha) \leq k$. As a trivial example, we can apply Theorem 3.1 to classes $NP(k)$ themselves. According to the definition, function α associated with $NP(k)$ is the k-ary parity function par_k. Clearly, $m(par_k) = k$. Since $par_k(0^k) = 0$, we get back $NP(k)$ by Theorem 3.1.

As another example, consider classes $NP(l)//\#^{NP[k]}$. The Boolean function α associated with $NP(l)//\#^{NP[k]}$ has $k + l(k + 1)$ variables, namely, k variables $x_1, \ldots, x_k$ for the $\#^{NP[k]}$ function and l variables $y_{i1}, \ldots, y_{il}$, for each potential value $i \in \{0, \ldots, k\}$ of the $\#^{NP[k]}$ function. Then the value α is $par_l(y_{i1}, \ldots, y_{il})$, if i of the x_j variables are one. To evaluate α, we don't need to know the exact assignment to its variables: α is composed out of symmetric functions, it is enough to know the number of ones in $(x_1, \ldots, x_k)$ and each tuple $(y_{i1}, \ldots, y_{il})$, for $i = 0, \ldots, k$.

Definition A *state* is a $k + 2$ tuple of integers $(i, c_0, c_1, \ldots, c_k)$ such that $0 \leq i \leq k$, $0 \leq c_j \leq l$ for $0 \leq j \leq k$. We refer to the first component of s (the number i) as the *index* of s, and the number c_j as the *counters* of s. When i is the index of s, counter c_i is the *active* counter of s.

In a state $s = (i, c_0, \ldots, c_{m-1})$, the index i denotes the possible number of ones in $(x_1, \ldots, x_k)$ and the counter c_j denotes the possible number of ones in $(y_{j1}, \ldots, y_{jl})$. The function α can now be thought of as acting on states: $\alpha(s) = c_i \pmod 2$.

An increasing chain of assignments becomes now an increasing sequence of states where we want to maximize the number of mind-changes. We reformulate the problem in terms of a game played on a table.

Definition The *Table* consists of $k + 1$ columns and $kl + 1$ rows. Entry (C, i) of the Table contains all the states $s = (i, c_0, \ldots, c_k)$ with $\sum_{0 \leq j \leq k} c_j = C$.

For a state $s = (i, c_0, \ldots, c_k)$, the row and column neighbors of s in the table are defined as follows. The *left and right row neighbors* of s are

$$
\begin{aligned}
{}^{\leftarrow}s &= (i - 1, c_0, \ldots, c_k), \quad \text{if } i > 0, \text{ and} \\
s^{\rightarrow} &= (i + 1, c_0, \ldots, c_k), \quad \text{if } i < k,
\end{aligned}
$$

respectively. Similarly, The *upper and lower column neighbors* of s are

$$
\begin{aligned}
s{\uparrow} &= (i, c_0, \ldots, c_{i-1}, c_i - 1, c_{i+1}, \ldots, c_k), \quad \text{if } c_i > 0, \text{ and} \\
s{\downarrow} &= (i, c_0, \ldots, c_{i-1}, c_i + 1, c_{i+1}, \ldots, c_k), \quad \text{if } c_i < l,
\end{aligned}
$$

respectively.

The game is played by a *Player* on the Table. When the game begins, the Player is in the state $s_{init} = (0, 0, \ldots, 0)$ of the Table, and is allowed to make the following two kinds of moves.

Definition Let $s = (i, c_0, \ldots, c_k)$ be a state. A *row move* from s takes the Player to the state $s^{\rightarrow}$. It is defined only when $i < k$. A *column move* from s takes the Player to the state $s{\downarrow}$. It is defined only when $c_i < l$. The game ends when no more move is possible.

The *mind-change* for any move is defined to be 1 if the active counters of the two neighboring states involved in the move are different modulo two, 0 otherwise.

So, for a column move, the mind-change is always one. And for a row move from the state $s = (i, c_0, \ldots, c_k)$, the mind-change equals $(c_i + c_{i+1})(\bmod\ 2)$.

The aim of the Player is to make moves, starting from the state s_{init}, such that the sum of the mind-changes is maximized.

Definition A *playing strategy* S for the Player is a sequence of moves having exactly k row moves and such that when the Player plays according to the strategy S, it remains within the Table, i.e., no counter of any state reached during the game exceeds l. For the strategy S, we define the mind-change of the strategy, $mc(S)$, as the sum of the mind-changes of its moves.

The *optimal* playing strategy for the maximizer is a strategy S such that for all other strategies S', $mc(S) \geq mc(S')$. For a strategy S, we shall use $S(i)$, with $S(0) = s_{init}$, to denote the state the Player is in immediately after making the ith row move according to the strategy.

It is clear that the mind-change of an optimal strategy equals $m(\alpha)$. As a column move has always a mind-change of one, it is the row moves that have to be carefully made to arrive at the optimal playing strategy.

Definition A state $s = (i, c_0, \ldots, c_k)$ is *bad* if $c_i = c_{i+1}(\bmod\ 2)$. A row move from a bad state is a *bad move*. The state s is *good* if $c_i \neq c_{i+1}(\bmod\ 2)$. A row move from a good state is a *good move*.

Coming back to classes $\mathrm{NP}(l)//\#^{\mathrm{NP}[k]}$, the optimal strategy is quite easy to see: we repeat doing l column moves and then a row move until we reach the last column, where we do l column moves. Note that in case that l is odd, all our row moves are good, while they are bad in case that l is even. Hence, we get $k(l + 1) + l$ mind-changes, when l is odd, and $l(k + 1)$, if l is even. When l is odd, the number of mind-changes matches the upper bound, therefore the strategy is optimal in this case. When l is even, observe that no strategy can make more than l mind-changes in any column including the row move to the next column. This generalizes the result in [KT94].

Theorem 3.2. For $k, l \geq 1$,

$$\mathrm{NP}(l)//\#^{\mathrm{NP}[k]} = \begin{cases} \mathrm{NP}(l(k + 1) + k), & \text{if } l \text{ is odd,} \\ \mathrm{NP}(l(k + 1)), & \text{if } l \text{ is even.} \end{cases}$$

The argument here was easy because every counter becomes active exactly once, and therefore, it is obvious that a good strategy makes all possible column moves as soon as a counter becomes active. However, when considering classes $\mathrm{NP}(l)//\mathrm{Mod}_m^{\mathrm{NP}[k]}$, this doesn't hold anymore. To adapt the definitions above, we have now only m counters $c_0, \ldots, c_{m-1}$ in a state, and, for any i, the counter $c_{i \bmod m}$ is the active counter. The Table still has $k + 1$ columns, but now $ml + 1$ rows. Column- and row moves and mind-changes are defined in the same way, just the indices of the counters have to be taken modulo m now. To keep notation clean, we will mostly write c_i instead of $c_{i \bmod m}$.

Hence, after every m row moves the counter c_j becomes active, for every j, $0 \leq j < m$. Therefore, it is no longer obvious that it is a good strategy to make all the column moves whenever a counter becomes active for the first time. In fact, it will turn out that this is indeed not the optimal strategy.

4 Playing the Game: Two Strategies

An optimal strategy should have the minimum number of bad moves as these moves have no mind-change. Also, note that the very first state of the Player, s_{init}, is a bad state. How does the Player avoid making bad moves? Here the column moves come to the help of the Player. Suppose that s is a bad state. If the Player makes a column move from s then the resulting state $s\downarrow$ is a good one since the active counter of this state has a different parity than that of s. Now the row move from $s\downarrow$ would be a good one. Therefore, a naive strategy for the Player would be to make a column move from any bad state it reaches and then make a row move. However, this does not always work (in fact, it works for only small values of k) since the number of column moves available is limited ($= ml$). So, when k is large, a more involved strategy is needed. Let

$$K = (l - 1) \cdot (m - 1) \cdot m.$$

We give below two examples of such strategies, these strategies will be shown to be optimal for m even and odd respectively for $k \geq K + 2m$. The optimality of these strategies are proved in the Section 5. Here, we shall just describe the two strategies and give some intuition as to why are they optimal.

4.1 For m even

The Player plays according to the following strategy $\mathcal{A}$.
For even i and $0 \leq i < m$, make $l - 1 + l \pmod 2$ column moves from the state $\mathcal{A}(i)$ ($\mathcal{A}(0) = s_{init}$) followed by a row move. And for odd i and $0 \leq i < m$, make $l - 1 + (l - 1) \pmod 2$ column moves from the state $\mathcal{A}(i)$ followed by a row move. From the state $\mathcal{A}(m)$ onwards, make row moves until the state $\mathcal{A}(k)$ is reached. Now, if the active counter of the state $\mathcal{A}(k)$ does not equal l, then make a column move from $\mathcal{A}(k)$.

For $0 \leq i < m$, the active counter (c_i) of the state $\ulcorner\!\mathcal{A}(i+1)$ equals 1 modulo two if i is even and 0 modulo two if i is odd. Therefore, for $0 \leq i \leq m-2$, the row move from the state $\ulcorner\!\mathcal{A}(i+1)$ to $\mathcal{A}(i+1)$ is good when i is even, and bad when i is odd. The row move from the state $\ulcorner\!\mathcal{A}(m)$ to $\mathcal{A}(m)$ is good since the active counter of $\mathcal{A}(m)$ is already set to 1 modulo two. Now, any two adjacent counters of the state $\mathcal{A}(m)$ have different value modulo two, and therefore, all the row moves after the state $\mathcal{A}(m)$ made by the Player are good ones. Thus, the Player makes exactly $m/2 - 1$ bad moves in the whole game. As for the number of column moves, for any two adjacent counters of the state $\mathcal{A}(k)$, exactly one of them equals l (and the other to $l-1$). So, the number of column moves made by the Player equals $ml - m/2$ without counting the (possible) move made from the state $\mathcal{A}(k)$.

Therefore, the mind-change of the strategy (without counting the possible column move made from the state $\mathcal{A}(k)$) is

$$k + ml - m/2 - (m/2 - 1) = k + ml - m + 1.$$

It is shown below (see Rule 5 and the associated claim in the next subsection) that the column move from the state $\mathcal{A}(k)$ is made iff the above number and l have different parity. So,

$$mc(\mathcal{A}) = k+ml-m+1+(k+ml-m+1+l)(\text{mod } 2) = k+ml-m+1+(k+l+1)(\text{mod } 2).$$

The above strategy allows the Player to arrive at a state $\mathcal{A}(m)$ such that all the states to the right of $\mathcal{A}(m)$ in the Table are good. And so, all the row moves can be made without any loss of mind-change. However, to arrive at this state, the Player has to make $m/2 - 1$ bad moves, and also make at least $m/2 - 1$ less column moves than maximum possible. When k is small, the Player can, using the naive strategy described in the previous section, avoid making bad moves; however, for large values of k, bad moves cannot be avoided and then this strategy becomes optimal.

4.2 For m odd

When m is odd, the Player cannot arrive at a state—unlike the case when m is even—such that any two adjacent counters of the state have different value modulo two. So, the Player does the next best thing, i.e., arrive at a state such that exactly one pair of adjacent counters have the same value modulo two. However, from this state if only row moves are made then one state out of every m will be a bad state. So, to minimize the bad moves, the Player makes a column move from such bad states as long as possible. Thus, the following is the strategy, $\mathcal{B}$, for the Player:

For $0 \leq i \leq m-3$, from the state $\mathcal{B}(i)$ make a column move followed by a row move if i is even, otherwise just make a row move. From the state $\mathcal{B}(m-2)$ make a column move and then a row move. From any state $\mathcal{B}(i)$, $m-1 \leq i < k$, make a row move if $\mathcal{B}(i)$ is a good state. On the other hand, if $\mathcal{B}(i)$ is a bad state and the active counter of $\mathcal{B}(i)$ is less than l, then make a column move from $\mathcal{B}(i)$ and then a row move. Finally, from the state $\mathcal{B}(k)$, make a column move if its active counter is less than l.

For the above strategy, the state $\mathcal{B}(m) = (m, 1, 0, 1, 0, \ldots, 1, 0, 1, 1, 0)$ and the number of bad moves made so far are $(m-3)/2$. As the Player proceeds after $\mathcal{B}(m)$, the first bad state that it encounters is $\mathcal{B}(2m-3)$. It then makes a column move and proceeds. So, $\mathcal{B}(2m) = (2m, 1, 0, \ldots, 1, 0, 2, 1, 0)$. Similarly, $\mathcal{B}(3m) = (3m, 1, 0, \ldots, 1, 0, 1, 1, 2, 1, 0)$, $\mathcal{B}(4m) = (4m, 1, 0, \ldots, 1, 0, 2, 1, 2, 1, 0)$ etc. Here, the bad state is occurring after every $m-1$ row moves by the Player.

So, after $m(m-1)$ row moves from $\mathcal{B}(m)$ the state of the Player would be $(m^2, 2, 1, \ldots, 2, 1, 2, 2, 1)$, i.e., each counter is one more than that in $\mathcal{B}(m)$. The same pattern of moves will now be repeated. So, after K row moves from $\mathcal{B}(m)$, the state of the Player will be $(m + K, l, l - 1, \ldots, l, l - 1, l, l, l - 1)$. Now, no more column moves are made, except at the end. Also, the Player from now onwards, will encounter a bad state after every m row moves (instead of $m - 1$) and it will have to make a bad move then.

Let $d = \lfloor k/m \rfloor$. Then, the number of times that the Player makes a bad move after the state $\mathcal{B}(m + K)$ is $d - (l - 1) \cdot (m - 1) - 1$ if $k - dm < m - 2$, one more otherwise. Also, note that the number of column moves made is exactly $ml - (m-1)/2$ excluding the (possible) column move from the state $\mathcal{B}(k)$. So, the mind-change of the strategy, without counting the possible last column move, is

$$k + ml - (m-1)/2 - (m-3)/2 - (d - (l-1) \cdot (m-1) - 1 + \lfloor (k+2)/m \rfloor - d)$$
$$= k + 2ml + 4 - 2m - l - \lfloor (k+2)/m \rfloor.$$

Adding the correction for the last column move (as noted above), we have

$$mc(\mathcal{B}) = k + 2ml + 4 - 2m - l - \lfloor (k+2)/m \rfloor + (k + \lfloor (k+2)/m \rfloor)(\bmod\ 2).$$

5 Proving the Strategies Optimal

In this section, we shall obtain an upper bound on the mind-change of any optimal strategy. We shall concern ourselves with values of $k \geq K + 2m$. For this case, in the previous section, two different strategies are given—one for m even and the other for m odd. We shall show that the upper bound that we derive matches with the mind-changes for these strategies, thus proving them optimal.

Fix an optimal strategy $\mathcal{S}'$. To prove the desired upper bound on $mc(\mathcal{S}')$, we proceed in stages.

Stage 1: Normalizing the Strategy

The column moves in $\mathcal{S}'$ can be arbitrarily distributed between the row moves, and this makes the direct counting of the mind-change of $\mathcal{S}'$ a difficult task. So, we shall rearrange the column moves in $\mathcal{S}'$ according to certain rules to obtain a new strategy such that the column moves in the new strategy have certain 'order' and given the mind-change of the new strategy, the mind-change of $\mathcal{S}'$ can be easily calculated. We call this process, the *normalization* of $\mathcal{S}'$.

Some of the rules that can be used to rearrange the column moves of $\mathcal{S}'$ are evident: from a good state, the Player should not make a column move and then a row move as this renders the row move bad. So such column moves, if existing in $\mathcal{S}'$, should be 'shifted'. Also, any two consecutive column moves in the strategy can be deleted causing a loss of exactly two mind-changes, as the counters in the state of the Player after these two moves have the same value modulo two as the counters in the state before the moves. Using these rules, and a few others, we get a strategy that satisfies the following properties. A detailed description of the rules, and proofs of the related technical lemmas would be given in the full version of the paper.

Lemma 5.1. Let $\mathcal{S}$ be the strategy obtained by normalizing $\mathcal{S}'$. Let b be the number of the pairs of consecutive column moves deleted during the normalization. Suppose that the Player plays according to $\mathcal{S}$. Then,

1. $mc(\mathcal{S}') = mc(\mathcal{S}) + 2b + (mc(\mathcal{S}) + l)(\bmod\ 2).$

2. Between any two consecutive row moves, the Player makes at most one column move. Also, it makes no column move after the last row move and exactly one column move before the first row move.

3. If a state is good then the Player makes a row move from the state.

Stage 2: Dividing the Column Moves in Two Types

After normalizing S', we proceed to count the mind-change of the resulting strategy, say S. Let us assume that b is the number of pairs of consecutive column moves deleted from S' during the normalization. It follows that in S, the maximum number of column moves made is $ml - 2b$. By the above lemma, we have that the Player makes column moves only when its state is bad. Therefore, the number of bad states of the Player during the game are crucial since the difference of this number and the number of column moves made by the Player gives the bad moves in the strategy. For this reason, we associate with each state s of the Player, a number that estimates the number of bad states of the Player during the next m row moves.

For any state $s_0 = (i, c_0, \ldots, c_{m-1})$ of the Player, we consider the $m - 1$ states, s_1, s_2, $\ldots$, s_{m-1} to the right of s_0 in the Table, i.e., $s_j = s_{j-1}^{\rightarrow}$ for $1 \leq j < m$. Define $b(s_0)$ to be the number of bad states amongst $s_0, \ldots, s_{m-1}$. The following lemma lists some properties of $b(s_0)$.

Lemma 5.2. Let $s_0 = (i, c_0, \ldots, c_{m-1})$.

1. $b(s_{init}) = m$.

2. If the Player makes a row move from s_0 then $b(s_0^{\rightarrow}) = b(s_0)$ and $b(s_0)$ is the number of bad states of the Player between, and including, s_0 and $S(i + m - 1)$.

3. If the Player makes a column move from s_0 then either (1) $b(s_{0\downarrow}) = b(s_0) - 2$ and the row move to the state s_0 (when $i > 0$) is bad, or (2) $b(s_{0\downarrow}) = b(s_0)$ and the row move to the state s_0 (when $i > 0$) is good. Further, $b(s_0)$ is the number of bad states between, and including, $s_{0\downarrow}$ and $S(i + m - 1)$. Moreover, the Player makes the first kind of moves only if $i < m$.

The above lemma suggests that we can divide the column moves made by the Player into two types.

Reducing column moves. Suppose that the Player, from the state $s_0 = (i, c_0, \ldots, c_{m-1})$, makes a column move and $b(s_{0\downarrow}) = b(s_0) - 2$. This column move reduces the number of bad states the Player encounters during the next m row moves and thus is a very useful move. It is called a *reducing* column move. As $b(s_0) \leq m$ for any state, there cannot be more than $\lfloor m/2 \rfloor$ reducing column moves possible. Also, note that if the column move is reducing, then the row move to the state s_0 must be bad (if it exists, i.e., $i \geq 1$). So, just before making a reducing column move, the Player makes a bad move. The only exception is the first state s_{init} from which a reducing column move is made without making a bad move.

If the aim is to make no bad move, then these column moves, except from s_{init}, should not be made. However, for large k—when bad moves cannot be avoided—these moves serve a very useful purpose as illustrated by the two examples in the previous section. In the strategy A there, $m/2$ reducing column moves are made, so that $b(A(m)) = 0$, which implies that there are no more bad states encountered during the row moves after $A(m)$. In the strategy B,

$(m-1)/2$ reducing column moves are made, so that $b(\mathcal{B}(m)) = 1$. This leaves some bad states to be taken care of, which is done by the second kind of column moves described below.

Non-reducing column moves. Suppose that the Player, from the state $s_0 = (i, c_0, \ldots, c_{m-1})$, makes a column move and $b(s_{0\downarrow}) = b(s_0)$. This column move does not reduce the number of bad states of the Player. However, it allows the Player to 'postpone' making the bad move by $m - 1$ row moves and therefore, still serves a useful purpose. It is called a *non-reducing* column move. There can be as many non-reducing column moves as permitted by the bounds on the counters of the states.

The strategy $\mathcal{B}$ of the previous section uses these moves. As noted above, $b(\mathcal{B}(m)) = 1$, and so, after the state $\mathcal{B}(m)$, whenever the Player encounters a bad state, it uses a non-reducing column move to 'postpone' making the bad move for as long as possible.

Stage 3: Counting the Mind-change of $\mathcal{S}$

Suppose that the Player makes c reducing column moves, while following the strategy $\mathcal{S}$. Since $b(s_{init}) = m$, $b(s) \geq m - 2c$ for any state s of the Player. Also, since the Player makes all the reducing column moves before the first m row moves (Lemma 5.2), $b(\mathcal{S}(m)) = m - 2c$. Since every reducing column move must be preceded by a bad move—except when it is made from state s_{init}—the Player must make $c - 1$ bad moves to 'set up' these column moves.

Let $d = \lfloor k/m \rfloor$. We divide the sequence of the states of the Player during the whole game in four segments, S^1, S^2, S^3 and S^4. The first segment, S^1 has states from $\mathcal{S}(0) = s_{init}$ to $\neg\mathcal{S}(m)$. The second segment is the smallest one—it has states from $\mathcal{S}(m)$ to $\neg\mathcal{S}(m + k - dm)$. The third segment, S^3, has states from $\mathcal{S}(m + k - dm)$ to $\neg\mathcal{S}(k - m)$ and the last segment, S^4, has states from $\mathcal{S}(k - m)$ to $\neg\mathcal{S}(k)$ (we disregard the state $\mathcal{S}(k)$ as no move is made from it). Since $d \geq 2$, we have $k - m \geq m + k - dm$, i.e., the second and the last segments do not overlap. We shall count the bad moves in the four segments separately.

First consider the segment S^4. The Player makes exactly m row moves while it is in the states of S^4. It can be shown that,

Lemma 5.3. For $k \geq K + 2m$, the Player makes no column moves while in segment S^4.

Since the values of k that we are interested in satisfy the above bound, there are no column moves by the Player while in S^4. This implies that the Player makes $m - 2c$ bad moves after the state $\mathcal{S}(k - m)$ since $b(\mathcal{S}(k - m)) = m - 2c$.

We can also calculate now the exact number of column moves made by the Player during the entire game. Take any two adjacent good states in S^4. The active counters of these states must be different modulo two. Now consider the original strategy $\mathcal{S}'$. All the counters of the state $\mathcal{S}'(k)$ must be at least $l - 1$ since it is optimal. Also, since the column moves are deleted only in pairs during normalization, the parity of the counters is the same for $\mathcal{S}'(k)$ and $\mathcal{S}(k)$. Therefore, the number of column moves in $\mathcal{S}$ is exactly $ml - 2b - c$.

For the first three segments, the counting of the bad moves cannot be done directly. This is because we cannot say beforehand when the Player makes a column move from a bad state and when not. So, we count the number of bad states in these segments and subtract the number of column moves made by the Player from it. This would give us the number of bad moves in the these segments.

First take the segment S^1. The Player makes exactly m row moves while it is in the states of S^1. Also, by Lemma 5.1, it makes all the c reducing column transitions in this segment. Since we have already counted the bad moves made just before reducing column moves, to avoid recounting, we mark the $c - 1$ bad states from which the bad moves are made. So, there are exactly $m - c$ unmarked bad states in this segment.

Now take the third segment. All column moves in this, and the second segment must be non-reducing (by Lemma 5.2). If there is a column move from the state $S(m + k - rm)$ for any r, $1 \leq r < d - 1$, then, by Lemma 5.2, the number of bad states between $S(m+k-rm)$ and $S(m+k-rm+m-1)$ is exactly $m - 2c + 1$. On the other hand, if there is none, then this number is exactly $m - 2c$. Therefore, the bad states in the segment are exactly $(d-2) \cdot (m-2c) + a'$ where a' is the number of column moves made from the states $S(m + k - rm)$ for $1 \leq r < d - 1$. The following are the bounds for a':

Lemma 5.4. If $2c = m$ then $a' = 0$, otherwise $l - \lceil 2b/m \rceil - m + 2c \leq a' \leq l - 1$.

Finally, we consider the second segment. The Player makes $k - dm < m$ row moves while it is in the states of this segment. Again, we count the bad states in the segment. To minimize such states, the strategy should have as many good states as possible in the segment. The following is the bound on the bad states in the segment:

Lemma 5.5. S^2 has at least $\max\{0, \min\{m - 2c, k + 2 - dm - 2c\}\}$ bad states.

Therefore, the total number of (unmarked) bad states in the first three segments is at least

$$B = m - c + (d - 2) \cdot (m - 2c) + a' + \max\{0, \min\{m - 2c, k + 2 - dm - 2c\}\}.$$

Since the total number of column moves made by the Player is $ml - 2b - c$, the number of bad moves made in the first three segments is at least $c - 1 + \max\{0, B - lm + 2b + c\}$. The Player also makes $m - 2c$ bad moves in the last segment. So, the total number of bad moves by the Player is at least

$$m - 2c + c - 1 + \max\{0, B - lm + 2b + c\} = m - c - 1 + \max\{0, B - lm + 2b + c\}.$$

And therefore,

$$
\begin{aligned}
mc(S) &\leq k + lm - 2b - c - m + c + 1 - \max\{0, B - lm + 2b + c\} \\
&= k + lm - m - 2b + 1 - \max\{0, B - lm + 2b + c\}.
\end{aligned}
$$

Since $d \geq 2$, this expression is maximized if c is chosen as large as possible. As we have the bound $2c \leq m$, we have two cases: m even ($2c = m$ in this case) and odd ($2c = m - 1$ in this case). Now, it can be seen by simply maximizing the above expression that the strategies $\mathcal{A}$ and $\mathcal{B}$ described in the previous section are respectively optimal for these two cases. Therefore, we have

Theorem 5.6. For $k \geq K + 2m$, $NP(l)//\text{Mod}_m^{NP[k]} = NP(t)$, where

$$
t = \begin{cases} k + lm - m + 1 + (k + 1 + l)(\text{mod } 2) & \text{if } m \text{ is even,} \\ k + 2lm - 2m - l - \lfloor (k + 2)/m \rfloor + 4 + (k + \lfloor (k + 2)/m \rfloor)(\text{mod } 2) & \text{otherwise.} \end{cases}
$$

Corollary 5.7. For $k \geq 2m$, $NP//\text{Mod}_m^{NP[k]} = NP(t)$, where

$$
t = \begin{cases} k + 1 + k(\text{mod } 2) & \text{if } m \text{ is even,} \\ k - \lfloor (k + 2)/m \rfloor + 3 + (k + \lfloor (k + 2)/m \rfloor)(\text{mod } 2) & \text{otherwise.} \end{cases}
$$

For values of k less than $K + 2m$, the mind-change of an optimal strategy can be derived in a similar way. When $l = 1$, this was done in [HT95], and for the general case, we have:

Lemma 5.8. For $2m \leq k \leq K + 2m$, and for any optimal strategy $\mathcal{S}'$,

$$mc(\mathcal{S}') \leq k + 1 + ml - m + a + [k + 1 + ml - m + a + l(\mathrm{mod}\ 2)]$$

where a is the largest number satisfying the following three conditions.

(i) $0 \leq a \leq m - 2$, (ii) $a = m(\mathrm{mod}\ 2)$, and (iii) $a \leq m \cdot (l - 1)/\lfloor k/(m - 1)\rfloor$.

A strategy $\mathcal{C}$ that achieves the above bound is one in which the Player makes $(m - a)/2$ reducing column moves in the first segment (segment as defined in Section 5), and then a reducing column moves for every $m - 1$ row moves after the state $\mathcal{C}(k)$. We omit the calculations.

For $m \leq k \leq 2m$, it can be easily shown that the optimal strategy has a mind-change of $ml + m - 1$ when l is odd, and $ml + 2k - 2m$ when l is even. And for $k < m$, it is derived in Section 3 (in this case, $\mathrm{NP}//\mathrm{Mod}_m^{\mathrm{NP}[k]}$ is the same as $\mathrm{NP}//\#^{\mathrm{NP}[k]}$).

References

[BDG88] J. Balcázar, J. Díaz, and J. Gabarró. *Structural Complexity I*. EATCS Monographs in Theoretical Computer Science. Springer-Verlag, 1988.

[Bei91] R. Beigel. Bounded queries to SAT and the boolean hierarchy. *Theoretical Computer Science*, 84:199–223, 1991.

[CGH+88] J. Cai, T. Gundermann, J. Hartmanis, L. Hemachandra, V. Sewelson, K. Wagner, and G. Wechsung. The boolean hierarchy I: Structural properties. *SIAM Journal on Computing*, 17(6):1232–1252, 1988.

[HT95] T. Han and T. Thierauf. In *Proceedings of the 10th Conference in Structure in Complexity Theory*, pages 206–213, 1995.

[HU79] J. Hopcroft and J. Ullman. *Introduction to Automata Theory, Languages, and Computation*. Addison-Wesley, 1979.

[KSW87] J. Köbler, U. Schöning, and K. Wagner. The difference and truth-table hierarchies of NP. *R.A.I.R.O. Informatique théorique et Applications*, 21(4):419–435, 1987.

[KT94] J. Köbler and T. Thierauf. Complexity-restricted advice functions. *SIAM Journal on Computing*, 23(2):261–275, 1994.

[LLS75] R. Ladner, N. Lynch, and A. Selman. A comparison of polynomial time reducibilities. *Theoretical Computer Science*, 1(2):103–124, 1975.

[W90] K. Wagner. Bounded query classes. *SIAM J. on Computing* 19(5), pages 833-846, 1990.

[Wec85]   G. Wechsung. On the boolean closure of NP. In *Proceedings of the 5th Conference on Fundamentals of Computation Theory*, pages 485–493. Springer-Verlag *Lecture Notes in Computer Science #199*, 1985. (An unpublished precursor of this paper was coauthored by K. Wagner).

Characterization of the principal type of normal forms in an intersection type system

Emilie Sayag, Michel Mauny*

INRIA-Rocquencourt, Projet Cristal, B.P. 105, F-78153 Le Chesnay Cedex, France

Abstract. We introduce a restriction of the intersection type discipline that leads to a principal type property in the classical sense for normal forms. We characterize completely the structure of principal types of normal forms and we give an algorithm that reconstructs normal forms from types.

1 Introduction

In the approach of untyped λ-calculus as a model of programming languages, Curry's type system is the basis of type systems of programming languages like ML [11].

Indeed, Curry's type system has the principal type property, which allows using parametric polymorphism. Furthermore, the problem of typability in this system is decidable. However, this type system has some limitations. For example, the λ-terms $(\lambda x.\lambda y.y)$ and $(\lambda x.\lambda y.\lambda z.x \; z \; (y \; z))(\lambda s.\lambda t.s)$ are β-equivalent, but they have two different principal types in this system and the λ-term $(\lambda x.x \; x)$ is not typable.

To supply a type system that does not have these drawbacks, several extensions of Curry's type system have been proposed, the most studied of which being the intersection type discipline [3, 5, 1]. This extension allows terms and term-variables to have more than one type. Types are formed with the constructors $\rightarrow$ and $\wedge$ for system $\mathcal{D}$ [3], a universal type ω for the system $\mathcal{D}_\omega$ [5], and a partial order on types for the system $\mathcal{D}_{\omega\leq}$ [1].

Studies of intersection type systems led to the following theoretical results: a term is strongly normalizable if and only if it is typable in system $\mathcal{D}$ [13, 8], a term is normalizable if and only if it is typable in system $\mathcal{D}_\omega$ with a type in which ω does not occur [5, 8, 7] and the system $\mathcal{D}_{\omega\leq}$ gives rise to a filter lambda model and is semantically complete [1]. Moreover, types in $\mathcal{D}_\omega$ are invariant under β-conversion of terms [2]. Intersection type systems are therefore very expressive and this expressivity justifies the interest and use of this system by many authors [14, 15, 12, 6].

However the price of this expressiveness is that type assignment is only semi-decidable. Another drawback of this system is the loss of principal type property in the classical sense. As a matter of fact, in order to find all possible types

---

* Email: {Emilie.Sayag,Michel.Mauny}@inria.fr.

of a term from a unique type, we must have more than just substitutions. In [4, 17, 21], a property which is similar to the principal type property is proved by adding two new operations on types: *expansion* and *rise* in [17] or *lifting* in [21]. S. Ronchi della Rocca in [16] proposed a semi-algorithm for type inference in system $\mathcal{D}_\omega$. These results give important theoretical benefits, but unfortunately, they provide a good understanding neither of the structure of principal types nor of their characteristic properties, and the semi-algorithm proposed in [16] is not practical because of its conceptual complexity.

The work presented here introduces a restriction of system $\mathcal{D}$ which allows us to completely characterize the structure of principal types of terms in normal forms: we show in this paper that our notion of principal types and λ-terms in normal form are isomorphic by exhibiting two translations (type inference of normal forms and term reconstruction from principal types).

The primary motivation for this work is to tighten the theories of intersection types and λ-calculus: the coincidence of typability and normalizability let us think that both theories can be made closer than they currently are. This work is a first step in this direction.

Tightening intersection types and λ-calculus should provide a greatly simplified presentation of intersection types and therefore, a better understanding of the runtime behaviour of polymorphic programs, which itself could be used as a basis for improving the current technology of debuggers for polymorphic languages.

The general outline of this paper is as follows: in section 2, we introduce the type system that we study. Section 3 presents an inference algorithm for normal forms and proves the correctness and completeness of this algorithm with respect to the inference rules of section 2. In section 4, we state and prove the characteristic properties of principal types for normal forms. Finally, section 5 introduces an algorithm that reconstructs normal forms from types and characterizes the set of principal types of normal forms.

2 Definitions

We know that in classical intersection type systems, the notion of principal type of a term does not exist in the classical sense [2]. In the same way, in our intersection type system, substitutions are not sufficient to deduce all possible types for a term from a unique type. For example in our system, as in [4], we can type the term $\lambda x.x \ (\lambda y.y)$ with the type $[[[\alpha] \to \alpha] \to \beta] \to \beta$, but also with the type $[[[\alpha] \to \alpha, [\gamma] \to \gamma] \to \beta] \to \beta$ where $[\tau_1, \ldots, \tau_n]$ denotes intersection of $\tau_1, \ldots, \tau_n$. Still there is no substitution relating the former (principal type of the λ-term $(\lambda x.x \ (\lambda y.y))$ in the classical theory) to the latter.

However, in this paper, we will study only terms in normal form and we will prove that for this class of terms, the classical notion of principal type exists with a restriction of the term variable inference rule. Then we shall characterize the set of principal types.

First, we recall that the set of normal forms can be defined by the following grammar:

$$N ::= x \qquad\qquad\qquad \text{variable}$$
$$\mid \lambda x.N \qquad\qquad \text{abstraction}$$
$$\mid x\ N_1\ \ldots\ N_n \quad \text{application}$$

We define next the set T of types of our system:

$$\rho \in T ::= \alpha \qquad\qquad\qquad\qquad \text{type variable}$$
$$\mid [\rho_1,\ldots,\rho_n] \to \rho \quad \text{for } n \geq 0$$

where we suppose to have a countable set TV of type variables.

The notion of *occurrence* has been often used in literature. Different refinements have been defined (see for example [7], page 33 and 34 for *positive, negative* and *final occurrences* and [16] for level of an occurrence of a type) according to the precision of informations that the author wants to obtain with this notion. In our case, we only need to distinguish the sign of occurrences and wether or not a type variable has a final occurrence.

Definition 1. We define the *positive* and *negative occurrences* of a type variable α in a type ρ by induction on the structure of ρ in the following way:

- if ρ is a type variable, then the possible occurrence of α in ρ is positive
- if $\rho = [\rho_1,\ldots,\rho_n] \to \rho'$, then the positive (respectively negative) occurrences of α in ρ are the positive (respectively negative) occurrences of α in ρ' and if $n \geq 1$, the negative occurrences of α in ρ_i for $i = 1,\ldots,n$.

Definition 2. Let ρ be a type in T and α a type variable. We say that α has a *final occurrence* in ρ if one of the following cases is verified:

- $\rho = \alpha$
- $\rho = [\rho_1,\ldots,\rho_n] \to \rho'$ and α has a final occurrence in ρ'.

Remark. If a type variable has a final occurrence in some type then this occurrence is positive.

Afterwards, we will need to distinguish sub-terms of a type which occur in left hand side arrows.

Definition 3. Let $\rho \in T$, the set $L(\rho)$ of *left sub-terms* of ρ is defined by induction on the structure of ρ, in the following way:

- if $\rho = \alpha$, $L(\rho) = \emptyset$
- if $\rho = [\rho_1,\ldots,\rho_n] \to \rho'$, $L(\rho) = \{\rho_1,\ldots,\rho_n\} \cup L(\rho')$.

A *substitution* is a mapping from type variables to types, which can be extended in a natural way to a mapping from types to types. The *domain* of a substitution S is the set of type variables which are modified by S. More formally:

$$Dom(S) = \{\alpha \in TV / S(\alpha) \neq \alpha\}$$

We write $[\alpha/\rho]$ the substitution of domain $\{\alpha\}$ which maps α to ρ and leaves other type variables unchanged.

We define the substitution $S_1 + S_2$ where the two substitutions S_1 and S_2 have disjoint domains in the following way:

$$(S_1 + S_2)(\alpha) = \begin{cases} S_i(\alpha) \text{ if } \alpha \in Dom(S_i), \ i = 1 \text{ or } 2 \\ \alpha \quad \text{ if } \alpha \notin Dom(S_1) \cup Dom(S_2) \end{cases}$$

We also define a mapping *TypeVar* from types to sets of type variables, which returns the set of type variables which occur in a type.

We can now define *constraint environments* and their associated operations. This notion of constraint environment was introduced by Z. Shao & A. Appel in [19] where it was called *assumption environment*. Informally, a constraint environment links the free term variables of a λ-term with their type constraints.

Definition 4. A *constraint environment E*, is a mapping from the set $\mathcal{V}$ of term variables to the multi-sets of types.

We use multi-sets rather than simple sets to keep track of the different occurrences of the same type. The multi-set of types $\rho_1, \ldots, \rho_n$ is written $[\rho_1, \ldots, \rho_n]$ and the empty multi-set is written $[\,]$. These noations allows us to write $E(x) \to \tau$ consistently with the syntax of types in any case.

Definition 5. Let E be a constraint environment. We define the *domain* of E, written $Dom(E)$, in the following way:

$$Dom(E) = \{x \in \mathcal{V}/\, E(x) \neq [\,]\}$$

Let E be a constraint environment, then if $Dom(E) = \{x_1, \ldots, x_n\}$ and for all $i \in \{1, \ldots, n\}, E(x_i) = [\rho_{i1}, \ldots, \rho_{ip_i}]$, we will write E as:

$$\{x_1 : [\rho_{11}, \ldots, \rho_{1n_1}], \ldots, x_n : [\rho_{n1}, \ldots, \rho_{np_n}]\}$$

Now, in order to restrict and extend the domain of a constraint environment, we define two operations in the next definitions.

Definition 6. Let E be a constraint environment and x be a term variable, we define the constraint environment $E \setminus \{x\}$ by:

$$E \setminus \{x\}(y) = \begin{cases} E(y) \text{ if } y \neq x \\ [\,] \quad \text{ otherwise} \end{cases}$$

Definition 7. Let E_1 and E_2 be two constraint environments, the constraint environment $E_1 + E_2$ is defined as:

$$(E_1 + E_2)(x) = E_1(x) \cup E_2(x), \text{ for all } x \in \mathcal{V}$$

where $\cup$ is the union of multi-sets.

We adopt the usual conventions for omitting parentheses in types and terms, and some other syntactic conventions: we use meta-variables $x, y, \ldots$ to denote term variables, $\alpha, \beta, \gamma, \ldots$ for type variables, $E, E', E_1, \ldots$ for constraint environments.

The type assignment relation $\vdash$, relating λ-terms, types and constraint environments, is defined in figure 1.

$$\vdash x : [\rho_1] \to \cdots \to [\tau_n] \to \alpha; \{x : [[\rho_1] \to \cdots \to [\tau_n] \to \alpha]\} \qquad (n \geq 0) \qquad \text{(VAR)}$$

$$\frac{\vdash e_1 : \rho_1; A_1}{\vdash \lambda x.e_1 : A_1(x) \to \rho_1; A_1 \setminus \{x\}} \qquad \text{(ABS)}$$

$$\frac{\vdash e_1 : [\rho_2^1, \ldots, \rho_2^n] \to \rho_1; A_1 \quad \vdash e_2 : \rho_2^1; A_2^1 \quad \ldots \quad \vdash e_2 : \rho_2^n; A_2^n}{\vdash e_1 \, e_2 : \rho_1; A_1 + A_2^1 + \ldots + A_2^n} \qquad (n \geq 0) \qquad \text{(APP)}$$

Fig. 1. Inference rules

$Infer(N) =$
- **Case** $N = x$
  - **let** α be a new type variable
  - **return** $(\alpha, \{x : [\alpha]\})$
- **Case** $N = \lambda x.N_1$
  - **let** $(\tau_1, A_1) = Infer(N_1)$
  - **return** $(A_1(x) \to \tau_1, A_1 \setminus \{x\})$
- **Case** $N = x \, N_1 \, \ldots \, N_n$
  - **let** $(\tau_1, A_1) = Infer(N_1)$
    $$\vdots$$
    $(\tau_n, A_n) = Infer(N_n)$
    α be a new type variable
  - **return** $(\alpha, \{x : [[\tau_1] \to \cdots \to [\tau_n] \to \alpha]\} + A_1 + \cdots + A_n)$

Fig. 2. Type inference algorithm

3 Type assignment

In this section, we present a type assignment algorithm for normal forms and we prove its soundness and completeness with respect to the inference rules given in the previous section. This algorithm is not really original, since we can find similar definitions in [4, 17, 16, 21, 10] where the principal type property in the intersection type discipline is studied. Their authors introduce the notion of *approximant* or *λ-Ω-normal forms*, and define principal typing for these extended normal forms before generalizing to λ-terms using an approximation property, i.e. $B \vdash e : \tau$ if and only if there exists an approximant a of e such that $B \vdash a : \tau$. The novelty in the work presented here, is not the type assignment algorithm itself but the study of the structure of pairs inferred by this algorithm.

The type inference algorithm is presented in figure 2. For clarity, we do not formalize the notion of *new type variable* (see [9] for a precise definition).

This algorithm is defined modulo the name of type variables, since we do not fix the choice of the new type variables. This algorithm is sound and complete, as expressed by the two following theorems. Their proofs can be found in [18][2].

Theorem 8. *Let N be a normal form, if $Infer(N) = (\tau, A)$, then $\vdash N : \tau; A$.*

Theorem 9. *Let N be a normal form such that $\vdash N : \tau; A$, then $Infer(N) = (\tau_p, A_p)$ and there exists a substitution S such that $S(\tau_p) = \tau$ and $S(A_p) = A$.*

As an example, type inference of $\lambda x.\lambda y.x(y\ x)$ produces the type $([\alpha, [\beta] \to \gamma] \to [[\alpha] \to \beta] \to \gamma)$. This type, as well as any other type returned by the algorithm *Infer*, possesses a few peculiarities, the most obvious being that *each type variable has exactly two occurrences: one positive and one negative*. In section 4, we characterize pairs computed by the algorithm. In section 5, we will see that, given such a type (e.g. $[\alpha, [\beta] \to \gamma] \to [[\alpha] \to \beta] \to \gamma$), one can reconstruct a λ-term in normal form, by (roughly speaking):

- following the arrows from left to right: that gives the outermost abstractions of the result ($\lambda u.\lambda v.\_$ in our example)
- following type variables, starting from the rightmost one, in order to built the body of the normal form ($\lambda u.\lambda v.u(v\ u)$ in this case).

In the following, the *principal pair* of a λ-term in normal form is the pair of type and constraint environment given by *Infer*. The previous theorem justifies this name.

4 Characterization of principal pairs

In order to characterize the set of principal pairs of normal forms, we define a set of types $\mathcal{T}_p$ and a set of constraint environments $\mathcal{E}_p$ and we prove that the algorithm *Infer* produces only types and constraint environments belonging to $\mathcal{T}_p$ and $\mathcal{E}_p$ respectively. Then we restrict further this two sets to provide a complete characterization of the set of pairs (τ, A) given by *Infer*.

4.1 Principal pairs belong to $\mathcal{T}_p \times \mathcal{E}_p$

We first define $\mathcal{T}_{E_p}$ and $\mathcal{T}_p$, two sub-sets of $\mathcal{T}$ in a mutually recursive way. In the following, we write $\sigma, \sigma', \sigma_1, \ldots$ for elements of $\mathcal{T}_{E_p}$ and $\tau, \tau', \tau_1, \ldots$ for elements of $\mathcal{T}_p$. $\mathcal{T}_{E_p}$ is the set of types of constraint environments and is defined by:

$$\sigma \in \mathcal{T}_{E_p} ::= \alpha$$
$$| \ [\tau] \to \sigma$$

with $\tau \in \mathcal{T}_p$, $TypeVar(\tau) \cap TypeVar(\sigma) = \emptyset$.
    Then, we define the set $\mathcal{T}_p$ of principal types:

$$\tau \in \mathcal{T}_p ::= \alpha$$
$$| \ [\sigma_1, \ldots, \sigma_n] \to \tau$$

---

[2] The details of all other proofs can also be found in [18].

with $n \geq 0$ and $\forall i \in \{1, \ldots, n\}, \sigma_i \in T_{E_p}$.

When we do not want to specify whether a type belongs to T_{E_p} or to T_p, we write it as $\rho, \rho', \rho_1, \ldots$

Finally, we define the set $\mathcal{E}_p$ of principal constraint environments:

$$
\begin{aligned}
A ::= \ & \{\,\} \\
& | \ \{x : [\sigma]\} \\
& | \ A_1 + A_2
\end{aligned}
$$

We notice here that the only difference with a general constraint environment is that the type constraints only belong to T_{E_p}. The following lemma proves that principal pairs belongs to $T_p \times \mathcal{E}_p$.

Since T_{E_p} and T_p are sub-sets of T, the notions define for types in T or constraint environments in $\mathcal{E}_p$ can be used for elements of T_{E_p}, T_p or $\mathcal{E}_p$.

Lemma 10. *Let N be a normal form, if $Infer(N) = (\tau, A)$, then $\tau \in T_p$ and $A \in \mathcal{E}$.*

Proof. By an easy induction on the structure of N.

If we regard *Infer* as a function from the set of normal forms to the set of pairs (τ, A), we can define $Image(Infer)$ by the set of pairs (τ, A) such that there exists a normal form N which verifies $Infer(N) = (\tau, A)$. So we can restate the previous lemma as:

$$
Image(Infer) \subset T_p \times \mathcal{E}_p
$$

4.2 Restriction of $T_p \times \mathcal{E}_p$

Now we want be more precise about the structure of principal pairs, so we define several easy notions which restrict the set of pairs $T_p \times \mathcal{E}_p$ in order to obtain the set of principal pairs.

A-types To handle consistently types and type constraints, we introduce A-types, using a double arrow in order to write type constraints negatively. Formally, we define the set of A-types by the following grammar:

$$
\begin{aligned}
T ::= \ & [\sigma_1, \ldots, \sigma_n] \Rightarrow \tau \quad \text{with } n \geq 0 \\
& | \ [\sigma_1, \ldots, \sigma_n] \Rightarrow \quad \text{with } n \geq 1
\end{aligned}
$$

where $[\sigma_1, \ldots, \sigma_n]$ is a multi-set of elements of T_{E_p}.

The function *TypeVar*, returning the set of types variables of a type, is naturally extended to A-types.

Since the algorithm *Infer* returns a pair (τ, A), in the following we often want to go from this pair to the correspondent A-type. So we define an operation which simply consists of collecting constraints from a constraint environment in order to obtain a single multi-set of type constraints.

Definition 11. Let A be a constraint environment, we define $\overline{A}$ by induction on the structure of A:

- if $A = \{\ \}$, then $\overline{A} = []$
- if $A = \{x : [\sigma]\}$, then $\overline{A} = [\sigma_1, \ldots, \sigma_n]$
- if $A = A_1 + A_2$, then $\overline{A} = \overline{A_1} \cup \overline{A_2}$

So, for any type τ and any constraint environment A, $\overline{A} \Rightarrow \tau$ is a A-type.

Definition 12. We say that T' is *held* in T, if $T = [\sigma_1, \ldots, \sigma_n] \Rightarrow \tau$ and T' is one of the following forms: $[\sigma_{i_1}, \ldots, \sigma_{i_p}] \Rightarrow \tau$ or $[\sigma_{i_1}, \ldots, \sigma_{i_p}] \Rightarrow$ where $[\sigma_{i_1}, \ldots, \sigma_{i_p}]$ sub-multi-set (non empty in the second case) of $[\sigma_1, \ldots, \sigma_n]$. Moreover, if T' is held in T and distinct of T, we say that T' is *strictly held* in T.

Extending the notion of left sub-terms of a type, we define for each A-type T, the set $L(T)$ of left sub-terms of T by induction on the structure of T:

- if $T = [\sigma_1, \ldots, \sigma_n] \Rightarrow \tau$, $L(T) = \{\sigma_1, \ldots, \sigma_n\} \cup L(\tau)$
- if $T = [\sigma_1, \ldots, \sigma_n] \Rightarrow$, $L(T) = \{\sigma_1, \ldots, \sigma_n\}$.

We also extend to A-types the notion of sign of occurrences. Let T be a A-type and α a type variable. The positive (respectively negative) occurrences of α in T are defined by induction on the structure of T:

- if $T = [\sigma_1, \ldots, \sigma_n] \Rightarrow \tau$, then the positive (respectively negative) occurrences of α in T are the positive (respectively negative) occurrences of α in τ and the negative (respectively positive) occurrences of α in σ_i for $i = 1, \ldots, n$
- if $T = [\sigma_1, \ldots, \sigma_n] \Rightarrow$, then the positive (respectively negative) occurrences of α in T are the negative (respectively positive) occurrences of α in σ_i for $i = 1, \ldots, n$.

In order to characterize the structure of principal pairs, we define three structural properties on pairs. The first of them expresses that the inference algorithm always introduces two occurrences of a new type variable with different signs. The second one is less significant but is used in the reconstruction algorithm. The last one is used to express that the inference algorithm *Infer* produces the minimal constraint environment.

Definition 13. An A-type T is *closed* if each type variable of $TypeVar(T)$ has exactly one positive occurrence and one negative occurrence in T.

Definition 14. Let $T = [\sigma_1, \ldots, \sigma_n] \Rightarrow \tau$ be an A-type. T is *finally closed* if the type variable which has a final occurrence in τ has also a final occurrence in a type of $L(T)$.

Definition 15. Let T be an A-type. T is *minimally closed* if there is no closed A-type strictly held in T.

Example 1. $T = [[\alpha, [[\alpha] \rightarrow \beta] \rightarrow \beta] \rightarrow \gamma, [\delta] \rightarrow \delta] \Rightarrow \gamma$ is closed, finally closed but not minimally closed because the A-type $[[\alpha, [[\alpha] \rightarrow \beta] \rightarrow \beta]\gamma] \Rightarrow \gamma$ is closed and strictly held in T

Properties of principal typing In this paragraph, we define the properties of A-types characterizing principal pairs. The main result is the last theorem of this section.

The following definition gives a short way to talk about the three previous properties simultaneously. We prove in lemma 9 that a principal pair always satisfies these properties.

Definition 16. Let $T = [\sigma_1, \ldots, \sigma_n] \Rightarrow \tau$ be a A-type. T is *complete* if:

- T is closed
- T is finally closed
- T is minimally closed.

Lemma 17. *Let N be a normal form, if $Infer(N) = (\tau, A)$, then $\overline{A} \Rightarrow \tau$ is complete.*

Proof. By structural induction on N.

The next definition specifies the structure of principal pairs. Intuitively, we want to say that for any given normal form, we can find the principal pair of these sub-terms from its principal pair. Since it is easier to study a A-type than a pair (type,constraint environment), we formalize our intuition on A-types.

Definition 18. Let T be a A-type. We say that T is *principal* if it is complete and if it is in one of the following cases:

- $T = [\alpha] \Rightarrow \alpha$.
- $T = [\sigma_1, \ldots, \sigma_n] \Rightarrow \alpha$ and there exists a partition $(E_j)_{j=1,\ldots p}$ of the multi-set $[\sigma_1, \ldots, \sigma_{i-1}, \sigma_{i+1}, \ldots, \sigma_n]$ such that each $E_j \Rightarrow \tau_j$ is principal where i and the τ_j, $j = 1, \ldots, p$ are defined by $i \in \{1, \ldots, n\}$ such that σ_i has the shape of $[\tau_1] \rightarrow \cdots \rightarrow [\tau_p] \rightarrow \alpha$, $p > 0$.
- $T = [\sigma_1, \ldots, \sigma_n] \Rightarrow [\sigma^1, \ldots, \sigma^p] \rightarrow \tau'$ and $[\sigma_1, \ldots, \sigma_n, \sigma^1, \ldots, \sigma^p] \Rightarrow \tau'$ is principal.

Lemma 19. *Let N be a normal form. If $Infer(N) = (\tau, A)$, then $\overline{A} \Rightarrow \tau$ is principal.*

Proof. By structural induction on N.

If we write $\mathcal{P} = \{(\tau, A)/\tau \in \mathcal{T}_p, A \in \mathcal{E}_p \text{ and } \overline{A} \Rightarrow \tau \text{ is principal}\}$, the previous lemma proves the following inclusion:

$$Image(Infer) \subset \mathcal{P}$$

5 Reconstruction of normal forms

In order to characterize the principal pairs of normal forms, we want to prove the opposite inclusion. We give in figure 3 an algorithm $\mathcal{R}$ which, given a type and a constraint environment, constructs a normal form typable with this type and this constraint environment.

$$
\begin{array}{l}
\mathcal{R}\ (\tau, A) = \\
\bullet\ \textbf{Case } (\alpha, \{\ \}) \\
\quad \textbf{fail} \\
\bullet\ \textbf{Case } (\alpha, A) \\
\quad \text{let } \{(\tau^1, x_1), \ldots, (\tau^m, x_m)\} = F(\alpha, A) \\
\quad \textbf{if } m = 1 \text{ and } \tau^1 = [\tau_1] \to \cdots \to [\tau_n] \to \alpha \\
\qquad \textbf{then if } \text{for } i = 1, \ldots, n, \text{ there exists } A_i \subset A \text{ such that } \overline{A_i} {\Rightarrow} \tau_i \text{ is principal} \\
\qquad\qquad \textbf{then let } (N_1, A_1') = \mathcal{R}(\tau_1, A_1) \\
\qquad\qquad\qquad\qquad\qquad \vdots \\
\qquad\qquad\qquad (N_n, A_n') = \mathcal{R}(\tau_n, A_n) \\
\qquad\qquad\qquad A' = \{x : [[\tau_1] \to \cdots \to [\tau_n] \to \alpha]\} + A_1 + \cdots + A_n \\
\qquad\qquad \textbf{return } (x\ N_1\ \ldots\ N_n, (A \setminus Dom(A')) + A_1' + \cdots + A_n') \\
\qquad\qquad \textbf{else fail} \\
\qquad \textbf{else fail} \\
\bullet\ \textbf{Case } ([\sigma^1, \ldots, \sigma^n] \to \tau', A) \\
\quad \text{let } x \text{ be a new term variable} \\
\qquad A' = A + \{x : [\sigma^1, \ldots, \sigma^n]\} \\
\qquad (N, A'') = \mathcal{R}(\tau', A') \\
\quad \textbf{if } A''(x) = [] \\
\quad \textbf{then return } (\lambda x.N, A'') \\
\quad \textbf{else fail}
\end{array}
$$

Fig. 3. Reconstruction algorithm

5.1 Reconstruction algorithm

Let α be a type variable and A be a constraint environment. We write $F(\alpha, A)$ the set of types which belong to A and such that α has a final occurrence. More precisely: $F(\alpha, A) = \{(\tau, x)/\tau \in A(x) \text{ and } \alpha \text{ is the final occurrence of } \tau\}$. We define the reconstruction algorithm $\mathcal{R}$ in figure 3

Remark. We define $\mathcal{R}$ in a general way without any hypothesis on its domain. But in the following, we only use $\mathcal{R}$ with principal pairs and we show that with principal pairs, its result is always well-defined.

5.2 Properties

Lemma 20. *If* $(\tau, A) \in \mathcal{P}$, *then* $\mathcal{R}(\tau, A) = (N, A')$ *is well defined and* $A' = \{\ \}$.

Proof. By recurrence on the number of calls to $\mathcal{R}$.

From now on, for each $(\tau, A) \in \mathcal{P}$, we can consider the result of $\mathcal{R}(\tau, A)$ without verifying its existence. Moreover, in the following, if the pair (τ, A) belongs to $\mathcal{P}$, we write $\mathcal{R}(\tau, A) = N$ instead of $\mathcal{R}(\tau, A) = (N, \{\ \})$.

Lemma 21. *Let* $(\tau, A) \in \mathcal{P}$ *and* $N = \mathcal{R}(\tau, A)$, *then* $Infer(N) = (\tau, A)$.

Proof. By recurrence on the number of calls to $\mathcal{R}$ and using the proof of the previous lemma.

Theorem 22.
$$Image(Infer) = \mathcal{P}$$
in other words : *The types and the constraint environments inferred for normal forms are exactly the pairs (τ, A) such that $\overline{A} \Rightarrow \tau$ is principal.*

Proof. The lemma 10 give $Image(Infer) \subset \mathcal{P}$. Moreover according to lemma 21, for any $(\tau, A) \in \mathcal{P}$, there exists a normal form N such that $Infer(N) = (\tau, A)$. So $\mathcal{P} \subset Image(Infer)$ and we can conclude.

6 Conclusion

In this paper we have introduced a restriction of system $\mathcal{D}$ in the sense that intersections only occur in the left hand side of an arrow and are not types. This restriction corresponds to strict types defined by S. van Bakel in [20, 21]. But in the strict types system, S. van Bakel defines a partial order on types. His system is a restriction of the system defined in [1]. He proves that despite the restriction, his system verifies the same properties as the original system. Moreover his approach to the construction of principal pairs uses the approximate normal forms of a λ-term and he is only interested in the existence of the principal type property, not in the structure of principal pairs.

Furthermore, our system further restricts van Bakel's system because of the specified structure of types which are assigned to term variables. This restriction leads to a principal type property in the classical sense for normal forms.

We then have completely characterized the structure of principal types inferred for normal forms and we have given an algorithm for reconstruction of normal forms from principal types.

Extension of this work for general λ-terms would give us a better comprehension of links between polymorphic typing and β-reduction.

References

1. Henk P. Barendregt, Mario Coppo, and Mariangiola Dezani-Ciancaglini. A filter lambda model and the completeness of type assignment. *Journal of Symbolic Logic,* 48(4):931–940, 1983.
2. Felice Cardone and Mario Coppo. Two extensions of Curry's type inference system. In P. Odifreddi, editor, *Logic in Computer Science,* volume 31, pages 19–75. APIC Studies in Data Processing, Academic Press, 1990.
3. Mario Coppo and Mangiola Dezani-Ciancaglini. An extension of the basic functionality theory for the λ-calculus. *Notre Dame Journal of Formal Logic,* 21(4):685–693, 1980.
4. Mario Coppo, Mariangiola Dezani-Ciancaglini, and Betti Venneri. Principal type schemes and λ-calculus semantics. In J.P. Seldin and J.R. Hindley, editors, *To H.B. Curry: Essays in Combinatory Logic, Lambda-calculus and Formalism,* pages 536–560. Academic Press, London, 1980.

5. Mario Coppo, Mariangiola Dezani-Ciancaglini, and Betti Venneri. Functional characters of solvable terms. *Zeitschrift fur Mathematische Logik und Grundlagen der Mathematik*, 27:45–58, 1981.

6. Philippa Gardner. Discovering needed reductions using type theory. In M. Hagiya and John C. Mitchell, editors, *Proceedings of TACS'94*, volume 789 of *Lecture Notes in Computer Science*. Springer-Verlag, 1994.

7. Jean-Louis Krivine. *Lambda-calcul, types et modèles*. Etudes et Recherches en Informatique. Masson, 1990.

8. Daniel Leivant. Typing and computational properties of lambda-expressions. *Theoretical Computer Science*, 44:51–68, 1986.

9. Xavier Leroy. *Typage polymorphe d'un langage algorithmique*. PhD thesis, University of Paris 7, June 1992.

10. Ines Margaria and Maddalena Zacchi. Principal typing in a ∀∧-discipline. *Journal of Logic Computation*, 5(3):367–381, 1995.

11. Robin Milner. A theory of type polymorphism in programming. *Computer and System Sciences*, 17(3):348–375, 1978.

12. Benjamin Pierce. *Programming with Intersection Types and Bounded Quantification*. PhD thesis, Carnegie Mellon University, 1991.

13. Garel Pottinger. A type assignment for the strongly normalizable λ-terms. In J. R. Hindley and J. P. Seldin, editors, *To H.B. Curry: Essays in Combinatory Logic, λ-Calculus and Formalism*, pages 561–577. Academic Press, 1980.

14. John C. Reynolds. Preliminary design of the programming language Forsythe. Technical Report CMU-CS-88-159, Carnegie Mellon University, June 1988.

15. John C. Reynolds. Syntactic control of interference, part 2. Technical Report CMU-CS-89-130, Carnegie Mellon University, April 1989.

16. Simona Ronchi Della Rocca. Principal type scheme and unification for intersection type discipline. *Theoretical Computer Science*, 59:181–209, 1988.

17. Simona Ronchi Della Rocca and Betti Venneri. Principal type schemes for an extended type theory. *Theoretical Computer Science*, 28:151–169, 1984.

18. Émilie Sayag and Michel Mauny. Characterization of principal types of normal forms in intersection type system. Technical report, INRIA, 1996. To appear.

19. Zhong Shao and Andrew W. Appel. Smartest recompilation. Technical Report CS-TR-395-92, Princeton University, October 1992.

20. Steffen van Bakel. Complete restrictions of the intersection type discipline. *Theoretical Computer Science*, 102:135–163, 1992.

21. Steffen van Bakel. Principal type schemes for strict type assignment system. *Logic and Computation*, 3(6):643–670, 1993.

Correcting Type Errors in the Curry System

Milind Gandhe and G. Venkatesh* and Amitabha Sanyal**

Department of Computer Science and Engineering
Indian Institute of Technology
Bombay 400 076

Abstract. In this paper, we address the problem of suggesting corrections to terms that are ill-typed in the Curry System. For this, we convert the term into a set of constraints over type expressions, and use a method due to Cox [3] to compute the maximal consistent subset of this set. The main result of this paper is an interesting correspondence between the automaton constructed in Cox's method and a graphical representation of the term called *sharing graphs*, which allows us to read back a term from the maximal consistent subset. We also characterise ill-typed terms using paths in the sharing graph.

1 Introduction

Type Systems are a distinctive feature of higher order functional languages such as Standard ML [9] that support *implicit* typing – i.e. types are inferred by the compiler at compile time.

Terms that cannot be typed contain program errors. Thus type inferencing can be used as an aid to debugging. However, as Beaven and Stanisfer [2] put it, "one annoying aspect of strongly typed languages with parametric polymorphism is that it is sometimes unclear why an expression cannot be typed". This means that though we know for certain that the program has an error, we cannot locate its cause.

Let M be an ill-typed λ-term. We define a *correction* to M as a well-typed term M' which is obtained by replacing one or more subterms of M by fresh variables (i.e., variables that do not occur free in M) and is well-typed. In this paper, we address the problem of suggesting corrections to terms that cannot be typed in the Curry type System. Consider, for example, the smallest ill-typed term xx. There are three possible corrections to this term, *viz.* y, xy and yx. Our algorithm will suggest only the *minimal* corrections *viz.* xy and yx.

Our proposed algorithm to compute corrections has three steps:

1. Use a type inferencing algorithm due to Wand [13] to convert the given term into a set of constraints over type variables. Since the given term is ill-typed, the resultant constraint set is unsatisfiable.

---

* The first two authors are with Silicon Automation Systems, 3008, 12B Main, 8 Cross, HAL II Stage, Bangalore 560008 Email: {msg,gv}@sas.soft.net

** as@cse.iitb.ernet.in

2. Use an algorithm due to Cox to compute maximal consistent subsets of the constraint set computed in step 1.

3. For each maximal consistent subset computed in step 2, compute a correction to the original term whose constraint set "corresponds" to the maximal consistent subset.

Steps 1 and 2 are relatively straightforward applications of methods used previously. Our main contribution lies in Step 3 for which we use a graphical representation of λ-calculus known as sharing graphs. Edges in a sharing graph are labeled to indicate the kind of interaction that can take place along that edge. The representation of a λ-term tells us how its subterms *interact* to produce the term. The main result of this paper is an interesting demonstration of a one-to-one correspondence between the constraints created by Wand's Type Inferencing Algorithm and the edges in the sharing graph. Thus, we identify the portion of the sharing graph that corresponds to a maximal consistent subset of the original constraint set, and read off a correction to the original term from this sharing graph. This correspondence also allows us to prove the correctness of our algorithm. We also present a characterisation of ill-typed terms using paths in sharing graphs.

2 Type Inferencing in the Curry System

The Curry type system [10] uses the type expressions $\tau ::= \alpha | \tau_1 \to \tau_2$ where $\alpha, \beta, \ldots$ range over type variables, and $\tau, \tau_1, \ldots$ range over type expressions. A term M is said to have a type τ if $\vdash M : \tau$ can be proved using the system shown below:

$$\frac{}{\Gamma \vdash x : \tau} \quad x : \tau \in \Gamma \quad \frac{\Gamma, x : \tau \vdash M : \tau_1}{\Gamma \vdash \lambda x.M : \tau \to \tau_1} \quad \frac{\Gamma \vdash M : \tau \to \tau_1 \quad \Gamma \vdash N : \tau}{\Gamma \vdash M N : \tau_1}$$

2.1 Wand's Algorithm for Type Inferencing

Wand [13] formulates type inferencing as a special case of the unification problem for terms. Each subterm is labeled by a fresh type variable and constraints of the form $\tau_1 = \tau_2$ are induced. A constraint set is *satisfiable* if there is a unifier that causes all equalities in the set to hold. $\mathcal{C}_\Gamma[M : \alpha]$ denotes the constraint set corresponding to the term $M : \alpha$ under type assumptions Γ and is computed as follows:

$$\mathcal{C}_\Gamma[x : \alpha] = \{\alpha = \beta\} \qquad x : \beta \in \Gamma$$
$$\mathcal{C}_\Gamma[(\lambda x.M) : \alpha] = \{\alpha = \beta \to \alpha_1\} \cup \mathcal{C}_{\Gamma, x:\beta}[M : \alpha_1]$$
$$\mathcal{C}_\Gamma[(M_1 M_2) : \alpha] = \{\alpha_1 = \alpha_2 \to \alpha\} \cup \mathcal{C}_\Gamma[M_1 : \alpha_1] \cup \mathcal{C}_\Gamma[M_2 : \alpha_2]$$

Example 1. The constraint set for the ill-typed term xx would be

$$\mathcal{C}_{x:\beta}[((x : \alpha_1)(x : \alpha_2)) : \alpha] = \{\alpha_1 = \alpha_2 \to \alpha, \alpha_1 = \beta, \alpha_2 = \beta\}$$

It is easy to see that this constraint set is unsatisfiable.

Lemma 1. *[13] A term M cannot be typed in the Curry system iff ∀Γ, the constraint set $C_\Gamma[M : \alpha]$ is unsatisfiable. In particular, a closed term cannot be typed in the Curry system if the constraint set $C_\emptyset[M : \alpha]$ is unsatisfiable*

2.2 Explaining Type Errors

Wand [12] suggests a method to provide some extra information when a type inferencing algorithm fails. When the analysis algorithm discovers an error, it stops and presents to the programmer the list of expression fragments that forces the binding of the relevant type variables. Beaven and Stanisfer [2] improve on Wand's approach by decorating the parse tree of a sub-expression of the program with the deductions made during inferring the type for that sub-expression.

3 Removing Inconsistencies in Constraints

We now use Cox's method [3] to generate maximal consistent subset of an inconsistent constraint set.

Let C be a constraint set. We say that a term t occurs in a constraint $t_1 = t_2$ if t is a subterm of t_1 or t_2. Let T_C be the set of all terms that occur in C. We denote by $F(C)$ the following set:

$$F(C) = \{\{t\} | t \in T_C\}$$

Thus $F(C)$ is the finest partition of T_C. If F is a partition of a set of expressions, and $p \in \cup F$, then we use $[p]_F$ to denote the class of F to which p belongs.

Cox's algorithm involves the following steps:

1. Partition T_C such that two expressions t and t' will be in the same class iff C forces us to unify t and t'. **Classify** takes a set of constraints and outputs such a partition. This algorithm is similar to conventional unification algorithms, except that it does not halt when non-unifiability is first discovered.

2. A set of constraints C is unsatisfiable if some class $[t]$ of **Classify(C)** cannot be unified. This is known as a *resolution conflict* or simply a conflict. However, this simple characterization is not enough to capture non-unifiability due to *sub-expression cycles*[3] (also known as occur-check [7]).
   The unification graph $U(C)$ for a set of constraints C is a labeled directed graph with vertex set **Classify(C)**, which has an arc from X to Y labeled by a function symbol f iff X contains a term $f(q_1, \ldots, q_n)$ where $q_i \in Y$ for some $1 \leq i \leq n$. It is easy to see that cycles in the unification graph correspond to sub-expression cycles.

3. Finally, we identify what constraints must be deleted from C so that each conflict or cycle is removed. To achieve this, Cox introduces yet another graph constructed from the constraint set called the *automaton* of the constraint set. Constraints to be deleted must be the minimal set of transitions that must be deleted to disconnect two states from each other or break a cycle.

---

[3] Which, as we will see later, is what we are really interested in.

3.1 The Automaton of a Constraint Set

Definition 2. [3] The *pushdown automaton* $A(C)$ for a constraint set C has state set C and transitions $q_i \xrightarrow{push(f,i)} f(q_1, \ldots, q_n)$, $f(q_1, \ldots, q_n) \xrightarrow{pop(f,i)} q_i$, $t \xrightarrow{t=t'} t'$ and $t' \xrightarrow{t=t'} t$.

For simplicity, each pair of *push/pop* arcs is represented by a single arc in the push direction, and each pair of constraint arcs is represented by a single undirected arc.

We represent the stack as a string, the left hand end of which is the top of the stack. We use λ to denote the empty string. A *configuration* of $A(C)$ is a triple $\langle q, w, \gamma \rangle$, where q is a state, w is an input string and γ is a stack string. We denote by $\langle t, w, \gamma \rangle \vdash^* \langle t', w', \gamma' \rangle$ a computation that takes the automaton from configuration $\langle t, w, \gamma \rangle$ to configuration $\langle t', w', \gamma' \rangle$. We say that a state t is attached to a state t' by a string w iff $\exists \gamma . \langle t, w, \gamma \rangle \vdash^* \langle t', \lambda, \gamma \rangle$. It is easy to see that if a path attaches t to t', then the reverse of the path attaches t' to t and hence we can simply say that t and t' are attached.

Lemma 3. *[3] Terms occurring in a constraint set C are attached in $A(C)$ iff they are in the same class of* **Classify(C)**.

A conflict between expressions t and t' discovered during unification can be removed by breaking all paths that attach t and t' in $A(C)$ [3]. For this, we first find all strings $w_1, \ldots, w_n$ that attach t and t' and then find a set of constraints $\{c_1, \ldots, c_m\}$, such that for each $1 \leq i \leq n$ there is at least one $1 \leq j \leq m$ such that c_j occurs in w_i. Let $w_i = c_{i1} \ldots c_{in_i}$. To break an attachment due to w_i, we need to remove either c_{i1} or $\ldots$ or c_{in_i} – this can be represented by the Boolean sum $c_{i1} + \ldots + c_{in_i}$. We refer to the Boolean sum corresponding to w_i as its covering expression s_i. Then, to break all attachments given by the strings $w_1, \ldots, w_n$, we take the product of these sums $\Pi_{1 \leq i \leq n} s_i$. We reduce this product of sums to a sum of products. It is enough to remove all constraints in any one of the products in the reduced expression to break all the attachments.

Let us now consider the problem of removing sub-expression cycles.

Definition 4. *[3] A* loop *on state t with value w is a computation of the form* $\langle t, w, \lambda \rangle \vdash^* \langle t, \lambda, \gamma \rangle$ *where $\gamma \neq \lambda$.*

Lemma 5. *[3] The unification graph $U(C)$ of a set of constraints C has a cycle containing an arc e with label f iff there is a term $f(q_1, \ldots, q_n)$ in the source of e on which there is a loop in $A(C)$.*

Thus to remove sub-expression cycles, we find all loops in the automaton, create covering expressions for them as before and choose a product from the sum of products forms of the covering expression.

Example 2. The set C of constraints arising out of the term xx is:

$$c_1 : \alpha_1 = \alpha_2 \rightarrow \alpha \qquad c_2 : \alpha_1 = \beta \qquad c_3 : \alpha_2 = \beta$$

Classify outputs the following partition:

$$\textbf{Classify}(C) = \{A_1, A_2\} \; A_1 = \{\beta, \alpha_1, \alpha_2, \alpha_2 \rightarrow \alpha\} \; A_2 = \{\alpha\}$$

The unification graph $U(C)$ for this set is shown in Figure 1. As can be seen, there is a cycle in this graph on A_1. To remove this cycle, we construct the automaton for this constraint set as shown in Figure 1. We see that this automaton has a loop in A_1 with value $c_1 c_2 c_3$. The sum of products of covering expressions of loops is $c_1 + c_2 + c_3$. This tells us that removing any one of c_1, c_2 or c_3 is sufficient to make the set C consistent.

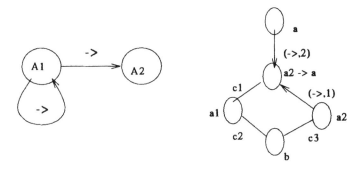

Fig. 1. The Unification Graph and the Automaton for Constraint Set C

4 Sharing Graphs

Definition 6. Let M be an ill-typed λ-term. We say $M' \equiv C[y_1, y_2, \ldots, y_n]$ is a correction to M if $y_1, y_2, \ldots, y_n$ do not occur free in $C[\,]$, M' is well-typed and $\exists M_1, M_2, \ldots, M_n$ such that $M \equiv C[M_1, M_2, \ldots, M_n]$.

We need a formalism that allows us to read back a well-typed λ-term from a maximal consistent constraint set. For this, we use a representation of λ-calculus called *sharing graphs*. Sharing graphs were introduced by Lamping [6] to solve the problem of optimal reductions of λ-calculus. Gonthier, Abadi and Levy [5] showed that Lamping's sharing graphs were a special case of the Interaction Nets of Girard [4]. There are several different translations of λ-calculus into sharing graphs [8] – here we follow the translations adopted in [1].

Definition 7. A sharing graph is a labeled, directed graph. Vertex labels have two components – a kind and an index number. The kind of a vertex is one of following: *context, variable, application, lambda, croissant, fan, bracket* or *weakening*. The index number is a natural number. Edge labels are of the form $!^n(x)$ where n is a natural number and $x \in \{p, q, r, s, t, d\}$. A distinguished vertex of the graph is marked as a root vertex.

In addition to the root vertex, every sharing graph also has some *free* vertices – one corresponding to every free variable.

We present our scheme for translating a λ-term M into a sharing graph $\mathcal{G}(M)$ in Figure 2. Note that only context, variable, application and lambda vertices arise due to the structure of the term. The other four kinds of vertices – the croissant, the fan, the bracket and the weakening represent only control information and hence are also called control vertices.

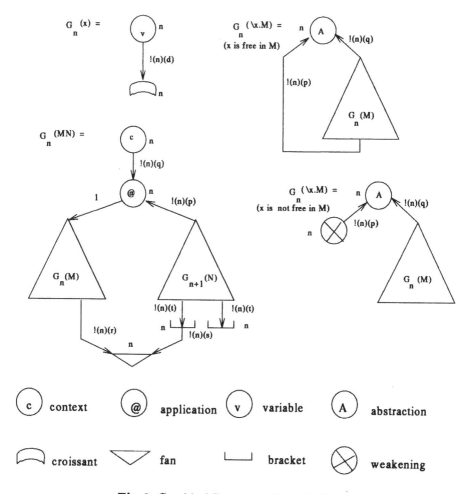

Fig. 2. Graphical Representation of λ-Terms

Definition 8. *Example 3.* The sharing graph $\mathcal{G}$ in Figure 3 is the graph for the term xx.

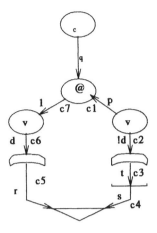

Fig. 3. The sharing graph for xx

The *multiplicative weight* $w_\times(u)$ of an edge u is given as follows:

- If $w(u) = v^*$, then $w_\times(u) = (w_\times(v))^*$.
- If $w(u) = !^n(p)$ (or $!^n(q)$), then $w_\times(u) = p$ (or q respectively).
- In all other cases, $w_\times(u) = 1$.

The multiplicative weight of a path $u_1 \ldots u_n$ is given by $w_\times(u_n) \ldots w_\times(u_1)$.

Example 4. Consider the path $c_1 c_2$ in the sharing graph for xx. Then $w_\times(c_1^* c_2) = 1.p^*$. Also there is a path from the context node to the croissant node with weight $1.p^*.q$.

A *multiplicative dynamic algebra* is a 7-tuple $\langle A, ., *, p, q, 0, 1 \rangle$, where A is a set, $p, q, 0, 1$ are four distinct elements of A, and '.' and '*' are binary and unary functions over A respectively such that

$$\forall x, y \in A.(x.y)^* = y^*.x^* \qquad 0^* = 0 \qquad 1^* = 1$$
$$\forall x \in A.1.x = x.1 = x \qquad p^*.p = q^*.q = 1$$
$$\forall x \in A.0.x = x.0 = 0 \qquad p^*.q = q^*.p = 0$$

A path is *regular* if it has a reduced weight not equal to zero.

Example 5. The reduced weight of the two paths in the previous example is p^* and 0 respectively.

5 Reporting Type Errors

We now apply Cox's algorithm to sharing graphs. This is possible because of a one-to-one correspondence between sharing graphs and constraint automaton, which we will show in the next section. We will attempt to edit the given λ-term so that the offending constraint is removed. Since only the context, application, abstraction and the variable vertices arise due to the structure of the term (the other four kinds of vertices – the croissant, the bracket, the fan and weakening have only control information), we will permit deletion of only those edges which are marked $1, !^n(p)$ or $!^n(q)$ and will not permit the deletion of edges marked $!^n(t), !^n(r), !^n(s)$ or $!^n(d)$.

For each edge to be delete, the suggested correction is:

1. If the edge in question is labeled 1 and arises out of the sub-term $M'M''$ of M, then the suggested correction is $M[yM''/M'M'']$, where y is a variable that does not occur in M.
2. If the edge in question is labeled $!^n(p)$ and arises out of the sub-term $M'M''$ of M, then the suggested correction is $M[M'y/M'M'']$, where y is a variable that does not occur in M.
3. If the edge in question is labeled $!^n(q)$ and arises out of the sub-term $M'M''$ of M, then the suggested correction is $M[y/M'M'']$, where y is a variable that does not occur in M.
4. If the edge in question is labeled $!^n(p)$ and arises out of the sub-term $\lambda x.M'$ of M, then the suggested correction is $M[\lambda x.(M'[y/x])/\lambda x.M']$, where y is a variable that does not occur in M.
5. If the edge in question is labeled $!^n(q)$ and arises out of the sub-term $\lambda x.M'$ of M, then the suggested correction is $M[\lambda x.y/\lambda x.M']$, where y is a variable that does not occur in M.

Example 6. Recall the graph for xx (Figure 3). The covering boolean expression for the offending cycle is $c_1 + c_2 + c_3 + c_4 + c_5 + c_6 + c_7$. However, of these, we can only delete c_1 and c_7, since the remaining are control edges. The suggested correction to delete c_1 is xy and the suggested correction to delete c_7 is yx. Thus, the set of suggested corrections is $\{xy, yx\}$

6 Correspondence between Constraint Automata and Sharing Graphs

Cox's technique works on sharing graphs because of a strange and interesting correlation between sharing graphs and constraint automata. The demonstration of this correspondence is the main result of this paper.

For this, we extend Wand's type inferencing algorithm to sharing graphs. We annotate each vertex n of the sharing graph with a type $\chi(n)$. Initially, all vertices are labeled with fresh type variables (called *initial type variables*). All other type variables are called *place-holders*.

Definition 9. Let u be an edge from a to b. The constraint Φu associated with edge u is defined as:

- If u has a label $!^n(p)$, then $\Phi u = \chi b \equiv \chi a \to \alpha$, where α is a new variable.
- If u has a label $!^n(q)$, then $\Phi u = \chi b \equiv \alpha \to \chi a$, where α is a new variable.
- In all other cases, $\Phi u = \chi a \equiv \chi b$.

The constraint set $\Phi \mathcal{G}$ of graph $\mathcal{G} = \Phi \mathcal{G} = \{\Phi u | u$ is an edge in $\mathcal{G}\}$

Let α_1, α_2 be some initial type variables (labeling vertices n_1 and n_2 respectively) and β be a type variable which is not initial. Let $t' = t'' \in \Phi \mathcal{G}$ be a constraint. Then $t' = t''$ is either of the form $\alpha_1 = \alpha_2$, $\alpha_1 = \alpha_2 \to \beta$ or $\alpha_1 = \beta \to \alpha_2$. From this, we can see that both t' and t'' have exactly one initial variable. Also note that whenever a place-holder variable is needed, we use a new variable. This means that no place-holder variable occurs in more than one constraint.

We now construct the automaton for the constraint set $\Phi \mathcal{G}$. Every initial variable (corresponding a vertex in the sharing graph) will give rise to a vertex in the automaton for the set $\Phi \mathcal{G}$.

We now examine what each edge in the original graph contributes to the automaton of the set. Since edges with weight $1, r, s, t$ or d give rise to a constraint $c_1 \equiv \alpha_1 = \alpha_2$, such edges in the sharing graph give rise to a single transition in the automaton. Now let us consider edges with weight p. These edges give rise

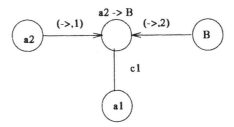

Fig. 4. The automaton due to a p edge

to a constraint of the form $c_1 \equiv \alpha_1 = \alpha_2 \to \beta$. The automaton created by this context is shown in Figure 4. Note that the expression β and $\alpha_2 \to \beta$ do not occur in any other constraint and hence there will not be any other transitions incident on these vertices. Thus, instead of creating the entire automaton corresponding to this constraint, we only create vertices corresponding to the initial variables and add a directed transition labeled $\langle c_1, p \rangle$ from α_2 to α_1. If we traverse this transition in the forward direction, we consume input c_1 and push $\langle \to, 1 \rangle$ onto stack. If we traverse this transition in the reverse direction, we consume input c_1 and pop $\langle \to, 1 \rangle$ from stack. By a similar argument, for a constraint of the form $c_1 \equiv \alpha_1 = \beta \to \alpha_2$, we simply introduce a directed transition from α_2 to α_1 labeled $\langle c_1, q \rangle$. If we traverse this transition in the forward direction, we consume input c_1 and push $\langle \to, 2 \rangle$ onto stack. If we traverse this transition in the reverse direction, we consume input c_1 and pop $\langle \to, 2 \rangle$ from stack. This simplified construction gives us a modified automaton for the constraint set $\Phi \mathcal{G}$ which we denote by $A'(\Phi \mathcal{G})$. As the following result shows, in this process, we do not lose any interesting information.

Lemma 10. *Let* α_1, α_2 *be vertices corresponding to initial variables. Then* $\langle \alpha_1, w_1, \sigma_1 \rangle \vdash^* \langle \alpha_2, w_2, \sigma_2 \rangle$ *is a computation in* $A(\Phi \mathcal{G})$ *iff it is a computation in* $A'(\Phi \mathcal{G})$.

We are now in a position to prove our main result.

Theorem 11 Main Result. *Let* $\mathcal{G}$ *be a sharing graph representation for some* λ*-term* M. *Then* $\mathcal{G}$ *is isomorphic to* $A'(\mathcal{G}_M)$.

Proof. By induction on the structure of the term M. Since our construction of the modified automaton does not create any states corresponding to place-holder variables, the initial labeling function χ is an isomorphism between the vertices of the graph and the states of the automaton . As the base case, consider the case when $M = v$. Recall that the graph $\mathcal{G}_M$ is a two vertex graph. In this case, $\Phi(\mathcal{G}_M) = \{\alpha_1 = \alpha_2\}$. Then it is easy to see that the modified automaton $A'(\Phi(\mathcal{G}_M))$ is isomorphic to $\mathcal{G}_M$.

Now consider the inductive step. Consider the case where $M = \lambda x.M'$. By the inductive assumption, we can assume that $\mathcal{G}'_M$ is isomorphic to $A'(\Phi(\mathcal{G}'_M))$. Now, by our definition of Φ, we can see that

$$\Phi(\mathcal{G}_M) = \Phi(\mathcal{G}'_M) \cup \{\alpha_1 = \alpha_2 \to \beta_1, \alpha_1 = \beta_2 \to \alpha_3\}$$

Then by our construction it follows that $\Phi(\mathcal{G}_M)$ is isomorphic to $A'(\Phi(\mathcal{G}_M))$. The proof is similar if M is of the form $M'M''$. $\square$

Definition 12. The state projection $State(C)$ of a configuration $\langle s, w, t \rangle$ is given as $State(\langle s, w, t \rangle) = s'|\chi s' = s$ The state projection of a computation $C_1 C_2 \dots C_n$ (where $C_1, \dots, C_n$ are configurations) is given as

$$State(C_1 C_2 \dots C_n) = State(C_1)State(C_2) \dots State(C_n)$$

Let $t.t'$ denote the concatenation of two strings t and t'.

Remark. Let t be an arbitrary string. Then $c \equiv \langle s_1, w_1, t_1 \rangle, \langle s_2, w_2, t_2 \rangle \dots \langle s_n, w_n, t_n \rangle$ is a computation in an automaton A' iff $\langle s_1, w_1, t_1.t \rangle, \langle s_2, w_2, t_2.t \rangle \dots \langle s_n, w_n, t_n.t \rangle$ is also a computation in A'.

Proof. Note that the stack in the original computation can never be "less" than λ. The observation follows from the definition of a computation. $\square$

Corollary 13. *Let* $\mathcal{G}$ *be a sharing graph and* $A'(\mathcal{G})$ *be its modified automaton. If* c *be a computation in* $A'(\mathcal{G})$, *then* $State(c)$ *is a regular path in* $\mathcal{G}$.

The following results show that the correspondence between computations and regular paths is two-way. The next lemma tells us that the multiplicative weights of paths give us useful information about how a computation affects the stack.

Lemma 14. *Let $\mathcal{G}$ be a sharing graph and $A'(\mathcal{G})$ be its modified automaton. Let $C = \langle s_0, w_0, t_0 \rangle \vdash^* \langle s_1, \lambda, t_1 \rangle$ and $C' = \langle s_0', w_0', t_0' \rangle \vdash^* \langle s_1', \lambda, t_1' \rangle$ be two computations such that $w_\times(State(C)) = w_\times(State(C'))$. Then $\exists t, t', \gamma, \gamma'$ such that the following equations hold:*

$$t_0 = t.\gamma \; 0.5cm \; t_1 = t'.\gamma \; 0.5cm \; t_0' = t.\gamma' \; 0.5cm \; t_1' = t'.\gamma'$$

Corollary 15. *Let $\mathcal{G}$ be a sharing graph and $A'(\mathcal{G})$ be its modified automaton. Further let ψ be a path in $\mathcal{G}$ such that $w(\psi) \neq 0$. Then, there exists a computation c such that $State(c) = \psi$.*

Corollary 16. *A path ψ is an attachment path iff its multiplicative weight $= 1$.*

Corollary 17. *Let $\mathcal{G}$ be a sharing graph and $A'(\mathcal{G})$ be its modified automaton. Further let C be a loop in $A'(\Phi(\mathcal{G}))$. Then $State(C)$ is a cycle and $w_\times(State(C))$ is neither 0 nor 1.*

Proof. The fact that $State(C)$ is a cycle follows from the definition of a loop. Due to Corollary 13, $w_\times(State(C))$ cannot be 0. Let $C = \langle s_0, w_0, \lambda \rangle \vdash^* \langle s_1, \lambda, t_1 \rangle$. By Lemma 14, if $w_\times(State(C)) = 1$, then $t_1 = \lambda$. However, since C is a loop, $t_1 \neq \lambda$. Hence the result. □

6.1 Characterizing Ill-typed Terms

Definition 18. A cycle c is said to be positive if no rotation of c has weight 0 or 1.

Lemma 19. *Let u be a path from a to b. If $w(u)$ is positive, then u induces a constraint of the form $\chi(b) = t(\chi(a))$, such that $t(x) \neq x$.*

Lemma 20. *A positive cycle cannot be typed.*

We have now shown that the presence of a positive cycle is a sufficient condition for ill-typing. We will now show that it is also a necessary condition. Let G be an ill-typed sharing graph. Let $A \subseteq \Phi(G)$ be a minimal inconsistent subset of $\Phi(G)$. Further, let E_0 be a set of edges in G such that $\Phi(E_0) = A$. Then, as the following two lemmata show, E_0 can neither be a straight line nor can it be disconnected.

Lemma 21. *Suppose that ψ is a straight line path in a sharing graph. Then $\Phi\psi$ is consistent.*

We have thus shown that E_0 must contain a cycle. We now show that E_0 must in fact be a cycle.

Lemma 22. *Let M be an ill-typed term and $\mathcal{G}$ be its sharing graph. Then $\mathcal{G}$ has a positive cycle.*

Theorem 23 Characterisation. *A term is ill-typed iff its sharing graph contains a positive cycle.*

7 Future Work

In this paper, we have demonstrated an interesting relation between maximal consistent subsets of a constraint set used in type inferencing, and paths in a sharing graph. We have shown this for the Curry Type System. However, most functional languages use an extension of the Curry System called the Hindley-Milner system [9]. The question of whether the correspondence holds for polymorphic systems such the Hindley-Milner is still an open issue. Note that both sharing graphs and Wand's algorithm can handle polymorphism.

References

1. Andrea Asperti, Vincent Danos, Cosimo Laneve, and Laurent Regnier. Paths in the lambda calculus – Three years of communications without understanding. In *Proceedings of the Ninth Annual IEEE Symposium on Logic in Computer Science*, Washington, 1994. IEEE Computer Society Press.
2. M. Beaven and R. Stanisfer. Explaining type errors in polymorphic languages. *ACM Letters on Programming Languages and Systems*, 2:17–30, 1993.
3. P. T. Cox. Finding backtrack points for intelligent backtracking. In J. A. Campbell, editor, *Implementations of Prolog*, pages 216–233. Ellis Horwood, Chichester, 1984.
4. J. Y. Girard. Linear logic. *Theoretical Computer Science*, 50, 1987.
5. Georges Gonthier, Martín Abadi, and Jean-Jacques Lévy. The geometry of optimal lambda reductions. In *Conference Record of the Nineteenth Annual ACM SIGPLAN-SIGACT Symposium on Principles of Programming Languages*. Association for Computing Machinery, ACM Press, January 1992.
6. J. Lamping. An algorithm for optimal lambda calculus reductions. In *Conference Record of the Nineteenth Annual ACM SIGPLAN-SIGACT Symposium on Principles of Programming Languages*. Association for Computing Machinery, ACM Press, January 1990.
7. J. W. Lloyd. *Logic Programming*. Springer Verlag, 1984.
8. Ian Craig Mackie. *The Geometry of Implementation (Applications of the Geometry of Interactions to Language Implementation)*. PhD thesis, University of London, September 1994.
9. Robin Milner and Mads Tofte and Robert Harper The Definition of Standard ML. The MIT Press, 1990.
10. J. C. Mitchell. Type systems for programming languages. In Jan van Leeuwen, editor, *Formal Models and Semantics : Handbook of Theoretical Computer Science*, volume B, chapter 8, pages 365–458. Elsevier, Amsterdam, 1990.
11. J. A. Robinson. A machine-oriented logic based on the resolution principle. *Journal of Association of Computing Machinery*, 12:23–41, 1965.
12. M. Wand. Finding sources of type errors. In *Proceedings of the 13th ACM Conference on Principles of Programming Languages*, pages 38–43. ACM Press, Jan 1986.
13. Mitchell Wand. A simple algorithm and proof for type inference. *Fundamenta Informaticae*, 10:115–122, 1987.

Immediate Fixpoints and Their Use in Groundness Analysis

Harald Søndergaard

Dept. of Computer Science, University of Melbourne, Parkville Vic. 3052, Australia

Abstract. A theorem by Schröder says that for a certain natural class of functions $F : B \to B$ defined on a Boolean lattice B, $F(x) = F(F(F(x)))$ for all $x \in B$. An immediate corollary is that if such a function is monotonic then it is also idempotent, that is, $F(x) = F(F(x))$. We show how this corollary can be extended to recognize cases where recursive definitions can immediately be replaced by an equivalent closed form, that is, they can be solved without Kleene iteration. Our result applies more generally to distributive lattices. It has applications for example in the abstract interpretation of declarative programs and deductive databases. We exemplify this by showing how to accelerate simple cases of strictness analysis for first-order functional programs and, perhaps more successfully, groundness analysis for logic programs.

1 Introduction

It is well-known that any monotonic function $F : L \to L$, defined on a complete lattice L, has at least one fixpoint, and in particular a least fixpoint. This follows from the celebrated Knaster-Tarski theorem. A standard way of giving meaning to a recursively defined object

$$x = \ldots x \ldots$$

is to consider the function F defined by

$$F(x) = \ldots x \ldots$$

and to stipulate that the recursively defined object x is exactly the least fixpoint of F (assuming x can be considered an element of some complete lattice, on which F is monotonic). Several special cases are of interest. If L is of finite height then the least fixpoint for F can be reached in finite time using a method sometimes referred to as Kleene iteration: With 0 denoting the least element of L, calculate the elements of the chain $0, F(0), F(F(0)), \ldots$ until the first i is reached for which $F^{i+1}(0) = F^i(0)$. Then $F^i(0)$ is the least fixpoint.

The technique of iterating to a fixpoint is very important, since recursive definitions are abundant in many areas of mathematics and computer science. The particular application that we use for examples in this paper is that of *abstract interpretation*, a theory which has been successful as a unifying framework for dataflow analysis. The key idea is that dataflow analysis is seen as approximating extreme fixpoints of certain semantic functions. The process of doing "approximate fixpointing" is itself a fixpoint computation. This paper contains some examples of this, but for a detailed treatment and references to the literature, the reader is referred to Cousot and Cousot [5].

We consider the case where the abstract domain is a distributive lattice. This is the case in the simple strictness analysis considered in the next section and also the groundness analysis we study in Section 4. The key to avoiding fixpoint iteration in these cases is a theorem which we state and prove in Section 3. The scope of this theorem is extended by the results we give in Section 4.

Our work continues the line of Nielson and Nielson [11], who gave bounds for various classes of functions and identified cases where the number of fixpoint iterations needed is linear. The same authors have also addressed the issue of when a constant bound can be given [9, 10]. Chuang and Goldberg [2] have suggested a syntactic approach to fixpoint computation, using a simply typed lambda calculus augmented with the basic lattice operations. Reduction is β-reduction supplemented with algebraic rules for manipulating expressions involving the lattice operations. As with the Nielsons' work, Chuang and Goldberg's method is firmly in the context of abstract interpretation of (higher-order) functional programs. For example, Nielson and Nielson [9] primarily investigate functionals of the form $F(d) = d_0 \vee G(d)$, where d_0 is a function and G is a functional that uses function composition.

The results given in this paper are tailored for abstract interpretation of logic programs and less useful for functional programs. However, in passing we do show an application to strictness analysis of first-order functional programs. In the case of logic-program analysis, it appears that our theorems cover a sufficiently common class of programs that a groundness analyser should benefit from the associated method for avoiding fixpoint iteration.

2 Outline

If the values of a function $F : B \to B$, defined on a Boolean lattice B, is determined entirely by F's values on the extreme points of B then $F(x) = F(F(F(x)))$. Rudeanu [12] explores this theorem, attributing it to Schröder, and gives the corollary that if such a function is monotonic then it is also idempotent.

Many of the lattices used in abstract interpretation are distributive, but often they are not complemented, or, if they are, the complement is usually not used when we express dataflow information. As an example, the lattice used in classical [8] strictness analysis of first-order functional programs consists of the *monotonic* Boolean functions over {*false, true*}, ordered by logical consequence. This lattice is distributive, but not complemented (although it does have an involutive operation satisfying the De Morgan laws). As another example, the lattice used in classical [6] groundness analysis of (constraint) logic programs consists of all the *positive* Boolean functions over {*false, true*}. This lattice, *Pos*, is Boolean, but the complement operation (explored in [3]) is not utilised in traditional groundness analysis [1, 4].

For this reason we shall weaken Schröder's theorem, obtaining a result applicable more widely to distributive lattices. The resulting "immediate fixpoint" theorem only obtains its full value when supplemented with rules for simplifying expressions of propositional logic. We sketch this idea in the following, but it will not be fully developed until Section 4.

Consider the functional program

```
power(x,n) = if n=0 then 1 else x*power(x,n-1)
```

Following Mycroft [8] we can analyse this program for strictness by translating it to a recursively defined Boolean function:

$$power(x, n) = n \wedge true \wedge (true \vee (x \wedge power(x, n \wedge true))).$$

The idea is to translate termination behaviour into propositional logic, associating *truth* with possible termination and *falsehood* with definite non-termination. Thus a constant such as 0 translates to *true*, while n=0 translates to $n \wedge true$ because '=' is strict in both positions: evaluation of the expression n=0 terminates if and only if evaluation of n does.

We are interested in a closed form for $power(x, n)$, and the standard approach to solving the recursive equation is Kleene iteration. However, the immediate-fixpoint theorem given in the next section allows us to avoid fixpoint iteration entirely. The least solution to the equation can be obtained simply by replacing $power(x, n \wedge true)$ on the right-hand side by the "smallest" Boolean function, *false*. This yields

$$power(x, n) = n.$$

In this case applying the theorem may be overkill, since straightforward simplification of the right-hand side yields the same result anyway. The interpretation, incidentally, is that power is strict in its second position.

What does the immediate-fixpoint theorem say? It states that iteration is unnecessary if the recursive definition is written using only $\wedge$, $\vee$, Boolean functions (such as the constant function *true*), and recursive calls, provided these are similar to the left-hand side. The strictness equation generated for a first-order functional program is *always* written using only $\wedge$, $\vee$, basic functions and recursive calls, so we only need to check recursive calls, no matter how complicated the definition is. In our example, the call $power(x, n \wedge true) = power(x, n)$ is clearly identical to the equation's left-hand side.

3 Immediate Fixpoints

Definition 1. Let $\langle D, \wedge, \vee, 0, 1 \rangle$ be a lattice with least element 0 and greatest element 1. A function $F : D \to D$ is *contracting* iff, for all $d \in D$,

$$F(d) = F(0) \vee (F(1) \wedge d). \quad \blacksquare \tag{1}$$

The term "contracting" is justified by the following proposition. We use $[a, b]$ to denote the segment, or convex closure, $\{d \mid a \leq d \leq b\}$.

Proposition 2. *Let D be a distributive lattice. If $F : D \to D$ is contracting then*

1. *F is monotonic.*
2. *F is idempotent.*
3. *$F(d) = F(1) \wedge (F(0) \vee d)$ for all $d \in D$.*
4. *The range of F is $[F(0), F(1)]$.*
5. *The set of fixpoints for F is $[F(0), F(1)]$.*
6. *F can be written in the form $F(d) = d_0 \vee (d_1 \wedge d)$, and this form determines d_0 uniquely, namely $d_0 = F(0)$.*

Proof. 1. Let $d, d' \in D$ be chosen such that $d \leq d'$. Then $F(1) \wedge d \leq F(1) \wedge d'$, and hence $F(0) \vee (F(1) \wedge d) \leq F(0) \vee (F(1) \wedge d')$. So $F(d) \leq F(d')$, and F is monotonic.

2. $F(F(d)) = F(0) \vee (F(1) \wedge F(d)) = F(d)$ since F is monotonic.

3. We have:

$$\begin{aligned} F(d) &= F(0) \vee (F(1) \wedge d) & \text{(since } F \text{ is contracting)} \\ &= (F(0) \vee F(1)) \wedge (F(0) \vee d) & \text{(by distributivity of } D) \\ &= F(1) \wedge (F(0) \vee d) & \text{(by monotonicity of } F) \end{aligned}$$

4. $F(d) = F(0) \vee (F(1) \wedge d)$, so $F(0) \leq F(d)$ for all $d \in D$. Similarly $F(d) = F(1) \wedge (F(0) \vee d)$, so $F(d) \leq F(1)$ for all $d \in D$.

5. Let d be a fixpoint for F. Since the range of F is $[F(0), F(1)]$, d must be in this range. Conversely, for every $d \in [F(0), F(1)]$ we have $F(d) = F(0) \vee (F(1) \wedge d) = d$.

6. By definition, a contracting F can be written in the given form. To see that d_0 is uniquely determined, substitute 0 for d to get $F(0) = d_0$. ∎

Definition 3. Let D be a distributive lattice. The class $\mathcal{F}_D$ is the smallest class of functions $F : D \to D$ that can be constructed using the following rules a finite number of times:

1. Every constant function $\lambda d \,.\, d_0$ is in $\mathcal{F}_D$.
2. The identity function $\lambda d \,.\, d$ is in $\mathcal{F}_D$.
3. If F_1 and F_2 are in $\mathcal{F}_D$, so are $F_1 \wedge F_2$ and $F_1 \vee F_2$. ∎

Proposition 4. *Every $F \in \mathcal{F}_D$ is contracting.*

Proof. We show (1) by structural induction on the form of F.

1. For $F(d) = d_0$, we get $d_0 = d_0 \vee (d_0 \wedge d)$ which holds, since $d_0 \wedge d \leq d_0$.
2. For $F(d) = d$, we get $d = 0 \vee (1 \wedge d)$ which clearly holds.
3. Assume that (1) holds for F_1 and F_2. That is, $F_1(d) = F_1(0) \vee (F_1(1) \wedge d)$ and similarly for F_2. We then have

$$\begin{aligned} F_1(d) \wedge F_2(d) &= (F_1(0) \vee (F_1(1) \wedge d)) \wedge (F_2(0) \vee (F_2(1) \wedge d)) \\ &= (F_1(0) \wedge F_2(0)) \vee (F_1(1) \wedge F_2(1) \wedge d) \vee \\ &\quad\;\; (F_1(1) \wedge F_2(0) \wedge d) \vee (F_1(0) \wedge F_2(1) \wedge d) \\ &= (F_1(0) \wedge F_2(0)) \vee (F_1(1) \wedge F_2(1) \wedge d) \\ &= (F_1 \wedge F_2)(d). \end{aligned}$$

Here we made use of the distributivity of D and the monotonicity of F_1 and F_2. Furthermore we have

$$
\begin{aligned}
F_1(d) \vee F_2(d) &= F_1(0) \vee (F_1(1) \wedge d) \vee F_2(0) \vee (F_2(1) \wedge d) \\
&= F_1(0) \vee F_2(0) \vee ((F_1(1) \vee F_2(1)) \wedge d) \\
&= (F_1 \vee F_2)(d). \quad \blacksquare
\end{aligned}
$$

From Proposition 2 (1) and (2) we immediately get:

Corollary 5. *Every $F \in \mathcal{F}_D$ is monotonic and idempotent.* $\quad \blacksquare$

If D is a distributive lattice, so is D^n for every $n > 0$. It is straightforward to generalise Propositions 2 and 4 to functions $F : D^n \to D$, allowing in $\mathcal{F}_D$ also functions defined using projection. However, since we are interested in fixpoints, we shall stick to the case $F : D \to D$. The importance of Proposition 4 for fixpoint computation is expressed in the following theorem, which is an immediate consequence of the proposition. The theorem gives a sufficient condition for when a least fixpoint can be found by instantiation rather than iteration.

Theorem 6. (Immediate-Fixpoint Theorem.) *Let D be a distributive lattice. For $F \in \mathcal{F}_D$, the recursive equation $d = F(d)$ is solvable, and the least solution is $F(0)$.* $\quad \blacksquare$

4 Groundness Analysis without Fixpoint Iteration

We now consider a case with considerable scope for "immediate fixpoints", namely groundness analysis for logic programs. Related analyses which may also benefit from the idea include determinedness analysis for constraint logic programs and finiteness analysis for deductive databases [1]. These analyses are all based on "positive logic"—the fragment of (classical) propositional logic that is independent of a concept of negation. The Boolean function F is *positive* if $F(true, \ldots, true) = true$. We let *Pos* denote the set of positive Boolean functions. Ordered by logical consequence, $\models$, *Pos* is a complete Boolean lattice [1] with meet and join being conjunction and disjunction, respectively. Figure 1 shows the case of two variables.

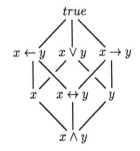

Fig. 1. Positive functions of two variables

As a simple example of a groundness analysis using positive logic, consider the program

```
p(X,Y,Z) :- X = a.
p(X,Y,Z) :- X = Y, p(Z,X,Y).
```

We want in the strongest possible statement about groundness and groundness dependencies in successful calls to the predicate p. The (recursive) equation

$$p(x, y, z) = x \vee ((x \leftrightarrow y) \wedge p(z, x, y))$$

captures the groundness dependencies. For example, $x \leftrightarrow y$ expresses the fact that X is ground if and only if Y is ground, and if neither are ground presently, one will become ground as soon as the other does. All we need to do is to find a closed form for the equation, that is, solve for p. Using Kleene iteration and starting from the least element $x \wedge y \wedge z$,[1] we get the series of approximations:

$$p_1(x, y, z) = x$$
$$p_2(x, y, z) = x \vee ((x \leftrightarrow y) \wedge z) \qquad\qquad = (y \to x) \wedge (x \vee z)$$
$$p_3(x, y, z) = x \vee ((x \leftrightarrow y) \wedge (x \to z) \wedge (y \vee z)) = (y \to x) \wedge (x \vee z)$$

Thus, $p_2 = p_3$ is the least fixpoint.

The example program is rather contrived and not representative of the kind of programs that programmers typically write. We now turn to realistic examples where the immediate-fixpoint theorem can be applied, albeit only after a bit of formula manipulation. First we consider the 'partition' relation used in quicksort:

```
partition(Xs,X,Ys,Zs) :-
    Xs = [], Ys = [], Zs = [].
partition(Xs,X,Ys,Zs) :-
    Xs = [U|Us], U =< X, Ys = [U|Vs], partition(Us,X,Vs,Zs).
partition(Xs,X,Ys,Zs) :-
    Xs = [U|Us], U > X, Zs = [U|Vs], partition(Us,X,Ys,Vs).
```

Abbreviating 'partition' to p, the groundness equation is:

$$p(xs, x, ys, zs) =$$
$$(xs \wedge ys \wedge zs)\vee$$
$$\exists u, us, vs : ((xs \leftrightarrow (u \wedge us)) \wedge u \wedge x \wedge (ys \leftrightarrow (u \wedge vs)) \wedge p(us, x, vs, zs))\vee$$
$$\exists u, us, vs : ((xs \leftrightarrow (u \wedge us)) \wedge u \wedge x \wedge (zs \leftrightarrow (u \wedge vs)) \wedge p(us, x, ys, vs)).$$

For details and justification of this kind of translation see Armstrong et al. [1] or Marriott and Søndergaard [7]. Suffice it to say that the existentially quantified variables are those that are local to a predicate, that is, of no interest outside a given clause. Such variables shall have to be eliminated for the immediate-fixpoint theorem to apply. Recall the elimination principle

$$\exists u : \phi \quad \equiv \quad \phi[u \mapsto \textit{false}] \vee \phi[u \mapsto \textit{true}]$$

and the rules of passage for the existential quantifier:

- $\exists u : \phi \vee \psi \quad \equiv \quad \exists u : \phi \vee \exists u : \psi.$
- $\exists u : \phi \wedge \psi \quad \equiv \quad \phi \wedge \exists u : \psi$, provided u does not occur in ϕ.

[1] *Pos* is often extended with an extra, least element *false* to capture non-termination. This is of no importance here—starting from *false* yields the same sequence.

Elimination of u in the equation for p yields

$$p(xs, x, ys, zs) = (xs \wedge ys \wedge zs) \vee$$
$$\exists us, vs : (x \wedge (xs \leftrightarrow us) \wedge (ys \leftrightarrow vs) \wedge p(us, x, vs, zs)) \vee$$
$$\exists us, vs : (x \wedge (xs \leftrightarrow us) \wedge (zs \leftrightarrow vs) \wedge p(us, x, ys, vs))$$

and subsequent elimination of us and vs then yields

$$p(xs, x, ys, zs) = (xs \wedge ys \wedge zs) \vee (x \wedge p(xs, x, ys, zs)).$$

The immediate-fixpoint theorem applies, and the solution $xs \wedge ys \wedge zs$ can be read off the equation. No fixpoint iteration is necessary.

A few standard patterns of simplification turn out to be recurrent. List-processing programs such as partition are typically defined by pattern matching, which in turn translates to a few typical Boolean expressions. The following propositions capture many of these cases. Notice that the forms of recursive definitions we consider are those that naturally arise from the translation of a (multi-clause) recursive predicate.

In the following, existential quantification may not always be made explicit, as it tends to clutter formulas. Local variables are then understood to be existentially quantified. We let $\exists \phi$ denote the existential closure (with respect to local variables) of ϕ. If X denotes the set of variables in an equation's left-hand side and V denotes the set of other variables used then the variables $u_1, \ldots, u_m$ range over $X \cup V$ and the existential closure is with respect to V.

Proposition 7. *Consider a recursive definition of the form*

$$p(x_1, \ldots, x_m) = \phi_0 \vee \exists (\phi \wedge p(u_1, \ldots, u_m)). \tag{2}$$

If $\phi \models (x_1 \leftrightarrow u_1) \wedge \ldots \wedge (x_m \leftrightarrow u_m)$ then the least solution to (2) is ϕ_0.

Proof. If $\phi \models (x_1 \leftrightarrow u_1) \wedge \ldots \wedge (x_m \leftrightarrow u_m)$ then we can rewrite the right-hand side as follows:

$$p(x_1, \ldots, x_m) = \phi_0 \vee \exists (\phi \wedge p(u_1, \ldots, u_m))$$
$$= \phi_0 \vee \exists (\phi \wedge p(x_1, \ldots, x_m))$$
$$= \phi_0 \vee (\exists \phi \wedge p(x_1, \ldots, x_m))$$

so the proposition follows from the immediate-fixpoint theorem. ∎

Proposition 7 helps in many simple cases. Consider the program

```
sumlist(Xs,K) :- Xs = [], K is 0.
sumlist(Xs,K) :- Xs = [I|Ys], sumlist(Ys,J), K is I+J.
```

We get the groundness equation

$$sumlist(xs, k) = (xs \wedge k) \vee \exists i, j, ys : ((xs \leftrightarrow (i \wedge ys)) \wedge k \wedge i \wedge j \wedge sumlist(ys, j))$$
$$= (xs \wedge k) \vee \exists j, ys : ((xs \leftrightarrow ys) \wedge k \wedge j \wedge sumlist(ys, j))$$

Clearly,

$$(xs \leftrightarrow ys) \wedge k \wedge j \models (xs \leftrightarrow ys) \wedge (k \leftrightarrow j)$$

so by Proposition 7, $sumlist(xs, k) = xs \wedge k$.

For typical list-processing programs we need a more powerful result. In the following proposition we abbreviate $(x_1, \ldots, x_m)$ to $(\overline{x})$ and $(u_1, \ldots, u_m)$ to $(\overline{u})$, and we make explicit the fact that ϕ_0 depends on $\overline{x}$ only.

Proposition 8. *Consider a recursive definition of the form*

$$p(\overline{x}) = \phi_0(\overline{x}) \vee \exists (\phi \wedge p(\overline{u})). \tag{3}$$

If there is an existentially quantified variable u such that

1. $\phi[u \mapsto true] \models (x_1 \leftrightarrow u_1) \wedge \ldots \wedge (x_m \leftrightarrow u_m)$,
2. $\phi[u \mapsto false]$ *contains no existentially quantified variables, and*
3. *either (a) $\models \exists \phi_0(\overline{u})$ or (b) $\phi[u \mapsto false] \models \phi_0(\overline{x})$*

then the least solution to (3) is $\phi_0 \vee \phi[u \mapsto false]$.

Proof. Let us use ϕ^f for $\phi[u \mapsto false]$ and ϕ^t for $\phi[u \mapsto true]$. If $\phi^t \models (x_1 \leftrightarrow u_1) \wedge \ldots \wedge (x_m \leftrightarrow u_m)$ then we can rewrite the right-hand side of (3):

$$p(\overline{x}) = \phi_0(\overline{x}) \vee \exists (\phi \wedge p(\overline{u}))$$
$$= \phi_0(\overline{x}) \vee \exists (\phi^f \wedge p(\overline{u})) \vee \exists (\phi^t \wedge p(\overline{u}))$$
$$= \phi_0(\overline{x}) \vee \exists (\phi^f \wedge p(\overline{u})) \vee \exists (\phi^t \wedge p(\overline{x}))$$
$$= \phi_0(\overline{x}) \vee (\phi^f \wedge \exists p(\overline{u})) \vee (\exists \phi^t \wedge p(\overline{x})).$$

In the last step we utilised the fact (requirement 2) that ϕ^f contains no existentially quantified variables. Any solution p to (3) satisfies $\phi_0 \models p$, so in particular $\exists \phi_0(\overline{u}) \models \exists p(\overline{u})$. In case 3a, then, $\models \exists p(\overline{u})$ and we get the equivalent equation

$$p(\overline{x}) = \phi_0(\overline{x}) \vee \phi^f \vee (\exists \phi^t \wedge p(\overline{x})).$$

In case 3b, $\phi_0(\overline{x})$ is a logical consequence of the disjunct $(\phi^f \wedge \exists p(\overline{u}))$, so

$$p(\overline{x}) \quad = \quad \phi_0(\overline{x}) \vee (\exists \phi^t \wedge p(\overline{x})) \quad = \quad \phi_0(\overline{x}) \vee \phi^f \vee (\exists \phi^t \wedge p(\overline{x})).$$

In either case the immediate fixpoint is $\phi_0(\overline{x}) \vee \phi^f$. ∎

At the end of this section we generalise this result, but first we consider some examples. The purpose is to show that the proposition's requirements are both natural and readily recognisable. First consider the program

```
perm(Xs,Ys) :- Xs = [], Ys = [].
perm(Xs,Ys) :- Xs = [U|Vs], perm(Vs,Ws), select(U,Ys,Ws).
select(X,Ys,Zs) :- Ys = [X|Zs].
select(X,Ys,Zs) :- Ys = [U|Vs], Zs = [U|Ws], select(X,Vs,Ws).
```

This is the standard program for generating permutations of a list. The program is translated into groundness equations in a mechanical fashion:

$$perm(xs, ys) = (xs \land ys) \lor ((xs \leftrightarrow (u \land vs)) \land perm(vs, ws) \land select(u, ys, ws))$$

$$select(x, ys, zs) = (ys \leftrightarrow (x \land zs)) \lor$$
$$((ys \leftrightarrow (u \land vs)) \land (zs \leftrightarrow (u \land ws)) \land select(x, vs, ws)).$$

In the right-hand side for $select$, ϕ is $(ys \leftrightarrow (u \land vs)) \land (zs \leftrightarrow (u \land ws))$ so we pick u for elimination. Indeed

1. $\phi[u \mapsto true] \models (x \leftrightarrow x) \land (ys \leftrightarrow vs) \land (zs \leftrightarrow ws)$,
2. $\phi[u \mapsto false] = \neg ys \land \neg zs$ contains no existentially quantified variable, and
3. We have $\neg ys \land \neg zs \models ys \leftrightarrow (x \land zs)$, satisfying requirement 3b. In fact requirement 3a is also satisfied: $\exists \phi_0(x, vs, ws) = \exists vs, ws : vs \leftrightarrow (x \land ws) = true$.

So Proposition 8 applies, and the solution is

$$select(x, ys, zs) \quad = \quad (ys \leftrightarrow (x \land zs)) \lor (\neg ys \land \neg zs) \quad = \quad ys \leftrightarrow (x \land zs).$$

Replacing $select(u, ys, ws)$ in the definition of $perm(xs, ys)$ with its newly found solution $ys \leftrightarrow (u \land ws)$ yields

$$perm(xs, ys) = (xs \land ys) \lor ((xs \leftrightarrow (u \land vs)) \land (ys \leftrightarrow (u \land ws)) \land perm(vs, ws)).$$

Choosing u for elimination clearly satisfies requirements 1 and 2. Furthermore $\exists \phi_0(vs, ws) = \exists vs, ws : vs \land ws = true$. That covers requirement 3a, so the solution is immediate:

$$perm(xs, ys) \quad = \quad (xs \land ys) \lor (\neg xs \land \neg ys) \quad = \quad xs \leftrightarrow ys.$$

There are even more remarkable cases where Proposition 8 can be of help. Consider the well-known naive reverse program. Because of the intricate dataflow in app this constitutes a challenging analysis task.

```
rev(Xs,Ys) :- Xs = [], Ys = [].
rev(Xs,Ys) :- Xs = [U|Us], rev(Us,Vs), app(Vs,[U],Ys).
app(Xs,Ys,Zs) :- Xs = [], Ys = Zs.
app(Xs,Ys,Zs) :- Xs = [U|Us], Zs = [U|Vs], app(Us,Ys,Vs).
```

The groundness equations are

$$rev(xs, ys) = (xs \land ys) \lor ((xs \leftrightarrow (u \land us)) \land rev(us, vs) \land app(vs, u, ys))$$

$$app(xs, ys, zs) = (xs \land (ys \leftrightarrow zs)) \lor$$
$$((xs \leftrightarrow (u \land us)) \land (zs \leftrightarrow (u \land vs)) \land app(us, ys, vs)).$$

The traditional approach using Kleene iteration solves the equation for *app* in three iterations:[2]

$$app_0(xs, ys, zs) = xs \wedge ys \wedge zs$$
$$app_1(xs, ys, zs) = (xs \wedge (ys \leftrightarrow zs)) \vee (ys \wedge (xs \leftrightarrow zs))$$
$$app_2(xs, ys, zs) = (xs \wedge ys) \leftrightarrow zs$$
$$app_3(xs, ys, zs) = (xs \wedge ys) \leftrightarrow zs.$$

(The last iteration is needed to verify that we have a fixpoint.) However, the definition of *app* is of the form required by Proposition 8, and so the solution can be obtained immediately. The reader is urged to check that the proposition's requirements 1, 2, and 3a all are fulfilled. The solution is

$$app(xs, ys, zs) \quad = \quad (xs \wedge (ys \leftrightarrow zs)) \vee (\neg xs \wedge \neg zs) \quad = \quad (xs \wedge ys) \leftrightarrow zs.$$

This yields the equation for *rev*:

$$rev(xs, ys) = (xs \wedge ys) \vee ((xs \leftrightarrow (u \wedge us)) \wedge (ys \leftrightarrow (u \wedge vs)) \wedge rev(us, vs)).$$

Again Proposition 8 applies, so the solution is immediate:

$$rev(xs, ys) \quad = \quad (xs \wedge ys) \vee (\neg xs \wedge \neg ys) \quad = \quad xs \leftrightarrow ys.$$

As it stands, Proposition 8 does not apply to cases with several recursive calls. However, the generalisation is straightforward:

Proposition 9. *Consider a recursive definition of the form*

$$p(\overline{x}) = \phi_0(\overline{x}) \vee \exists \, (\phi_1 \wedge p(\overline{u_1})) \vee \ldots \vee \exists(\phi_n \wedge p(\overline{u_n})).$$

If, for each $k \in [1, n]$ there is an existentially quantified variable u_k such that

1. *$\phi[u_k \mapsto true] \models (x_1 \leftrightarrow u_{k1}) \wedge \ldots \wedge (x_m \leftrightarrow u_{km})$,*
2. *$\phi[u_k \mapsto false]$ contains no existentially quantified variables, and*
3. *either (a) $\models \exists \, \phi_0(\overline{u_k})$ or (b) $\phi_k[u_k \mapsto false] \models \phi_0(\overline{x})$*

then the least solution to the recursive equation is

$$p(\overline{x}) = \phi_0 \vee \phi_1[u_1 \mapsto false] \vee \ldots \vee \phi_n[u_n \mapsto false]. \quad \blacksquare$$

To see this version in action, consider the original, un-simplified groundness equation from the `partition` example above:

$$p(xs, x, ys, zs) = (xs \wedge ys \wedge zs) \vee$$
$$((xs \leftrightarrow (u \wedge us)) \wedge u \wedge x \wedge (ys \leftrightarrow (u \wedge vs)) \wedge p(us, x, vs, zs)) \vee$$
$$((xs \leftrightarrow (u \wedge us)) \wedge u \wedge x \wedge (zs \leftrightarrow (u \wedge vs)) \wedge p(us, x, ys, vs)).$$

In both of the last two disjuncts, replacing u by *true* clearly has the effect of making the recursive call identical to the left-hand side. And in both cases the result of replacing u by *false* is *false*. Thus the solution is

$$(xs \wedge ys \wedge zs) \vee false \vee false = xs \wedge ys \wedge zs.$$

It is also straightforward to incorporate Proposition 7 into the generalisation.

---

[2] Starting iterations from *false* yields a different sequence but of the same length.

5 Conclusion

We have presented a general theorem for "immediate fixpoints." In the context of distributive lattices the theorem gives sufficient conditions for when fixpoint iteration can be avoided and replaced by a simple instantiation.

To exemplify its use in a simple setting, we have shown how the theorem can sometimes speed up strictness analysis for first-order functional programs. The value of this example is mostly didactic, as the strictness deduced is the most basic (two-valued) kind, and we did not handle higher-order functions. However, much of the recent work on strictness analysis and "strictness logic" indicates that propositional logic may still be a useful tool for the non-flat (see for example Sekar and Ramakrishnan [13]) and/or higher-order cases.

As a more practical contribution we have developed versions of the immediate-fixpoint theorem to recognize cases where groundness analysis (based on positive logic) can be performed without fixpoint iteration. Several examples of this were given. The basic problem in this case is that the recursive definitions describing groundness properties usually contain existentially quantified propositional variables, so that some sophisticated methods are needed to eliminate these variables and/or recognise special cases of recursive definitions that contain such variables and yet lead to immediate fixpoints.

While the general theorem is pleasing, specialized versions such as those in Section 4 are more likely to lead to faster analysis in practice. Many classes of programs, such as the list-processing programs in our examples, share common patterns. If a fast, specialized method works for sufficiently many typical programs, then it may be worth incorporating into a general method.

We are currently experimenting with methods associated with the theorems in Section 4, incorporating them in a groundness analyser [1] to assess their usefulness experimentally. Preliminary results are as follows. For the predicates we use (a standard benchmark suite), the number of Kleene iterations varies from zero to four, with one and two being the most common. (The groundness analyser does not start iterations from a bottom element such as *false* or the conjunction of all variables—it is clever enough to use the information from all non-recursive clauses as its starting point.) So in the groundness case, Kleene sequences are short, and the immediate-fixpoint theorem will typically save just one iteration. It may be argued that the overhead of testing its applicability is likely to outweigh the time saved by avoiding one fixpoint iteration, and we intend to test this hypothesis. However, the overhead usually has a pay-off even if it does not discover an immediate fixpoint, since elimination of existentially quantified variables *always* speeds up fixpoint iteration. More specifically we can check the requirements of Proposition 7 by solving a slightly more general task: finding *every* existentially quantified variable v such that for some other variable u (existentially quantified or not), $u \leftrightarrow v$ is a logical consequence of the current formula ϕ. Whenever this is the case, v can be replaced by u. Even if this simplification does not lead to the discovery of an immediate fixpoint, it still accelerates fixpoint computation, as in this type of analysis, the number of variables in a formula is the single most important cost factor.

Generalizing our results to handle mutual recursion does not seem worthwhile. It makes sense to consider equations $\langle x_1, \ldots, x_n \rangle = \langle \cdots, \ldots, \cdots \rangle$ that define $x_1, \ldots, x_n$ recursively, but not too many mutually recursive programs result in equations that will fit the straight-jacket of the class $\mathcal{F}_{D^n}$. Moreover, at least in logic programs, mutual recursion seems uncommon. For example, in the suite of test programs used by Armstrong et al. [1], the 734 predicates are grouped in 661 strongly connected components, indicating that a strongly connected component with more than one predicate is rare. The test suite includes "real-world" programs, so the ratio of 1.1 predicates per strongly connected component is probably quite typical.

References

1. T. Armstrong, K. Marriott, P. Schachte and H. Søndergaard. Two classes of Boolean functions for dependency analysis. To appear in *Science of Computer Programming*.

2. T.-R. Chuang and B. Goldberg. A syntactic approach to fixed point computation on finite domains. *Proc. 1992 ACM Conf. Lisp and Functional Programming*, pages 109–118. ACM Press, 1992.

3. A. Cortesi, G. Filé and W. Winsborough. *Prop* revisited: Propositional formula as abstract domain for groundness analysis. *Proc. Sixth Ann. IEEE Symp. Logic in Computer Science*, pages 322–327. Amsterdam, The Netherlands, 1991.

4. A. Cortesi, B. Le Charlier and P. Van Hentenryck. Evaluation of the domain Prop. *Journal of Logic Programming* **23** (3): 237–278, 1995.

5. P. Cousot and R. Cousot. Abstract interpretation and application to logic programs. *Journal of Logic Programming* **13** (2&3): 103–179, 1992.

6. K. Marriott and H. Søndergaard. Notes for a tutorial on abstract interpretation of logic programs. North American Conf. Logic Programming, Cleveland, Ohio, 1989.

7. K. Marriott and H. Søndergaard. Precise and efficient groundness analysis for logic programs. *ACM Letters on Programming Languages and Systems* **2** (1–4): 181–196, 1993.

8. A. Mycroft. *Abstract Interpretation and Optimising Transformations for Applicative Programs*. PhD Thesis, University of Edinburgh, Scotland, 1981.

9. F. Nielson and H. R. Nielson. Finiteness conditions for fixed point iteration. *Proc. 1992 ACM Conf. Lisp and Functional Programming*, pages 96–108. ACM Press, 1992.

10. F. Nielson and H. R. Nielson. Finiteness conditions for strictness analysis. In P. Cousot et al., *Static Analysis: Proc. Third Int. Workshop*. Lecture Notes in Computer Science 724, pages 194–205. Springer-Verlag, 1993.

11. H. R. Nielson and F. Nielson. Bounded fixed point iteration. *Proc. Nineteenth Ann. ACM SIGPLAN-SIGACT Symp. Principles of Programming Languages*, pages 71–82. ACM Press, 1992.

12. S. Rudeanu. *Boolean Functions and Equations*. North-Holland, 1974.

13. R. Sekar and I. V. Ramakrishnan. Fast strictness analysis based on demand propagation. *ACM Trans. Programming Languages and Systems* **17** (6): 896–937, 1995.

Graph Types for Monadic Mobile Processes

NOBUKO YOSHIDA

ABSTRACT. While types for name passing calculi have been studied extensively in the context of sorting of polyadic π-calculus [5, 34, 9, 28, 32, 19, 33, 10, 17], the same type abstraction is not possible in the monadic setting, which was left as an open issue by Milner [21]. We solve this problem with an extension of sorting which captures dynamic aspects of process behaviour in a simple way. Equationally this results in the full abstraction of the standard encoding of polyadic π-calculus into the monadic one: the sorted polyadic π-terms are equated by a basic behavioural equality in the polyadic calculus if and only if their encodings are equated in a basic behavioural equality in the typed monadic calculus. This is the first result of this kind we know of in the context of the encoding of polyadic name passing, which is a typical example of translation of high-level communication structures into π-calculus. The construction is general enough to be extendable to encodings of calculi with more complex operational structures.

1. INTRODUCTION

The monadic π-calculus [22, 20] is a powerful formalism in which we can construct complex structures of concurrent computing by combining simple monadic name passing. The construction of significant computational structures in this calculus is done by passing and using private names between interacting parties to control the sharing of interaction points. For example, the following process expresses communication of a sequence of names (below $ax.P$ is input and $\bar{a}v.P$ is output, $(a)P$ denotes scope restriction, and c, z are fresh).

$$az.zx_1.zx_2.zx_3.P \mid (c)\,\bar{a}c.\bar{c}v_1.\bar{c}v_2.\bar{c}v_3.Q \longrightarrow\!\!\!\!\rightarrow P\{v_1v_2v_3/x_1x_2x_3\} \mid Q \qquad (1.1)$$

In this example, coming from [22], the private channel c is used during interaction, so that, after the initial step, the communication of v_1, v_2 and v_3 is done deterministically without interference from the third party. This example also shows that we can represent polyadic (multiple) name passing from monadic name passing. Another example with a more complex communication structure follows.

$$az.zx_1.\bar{z}v_1.zx_2.\bar{z}v_2.P \mid (c)\,\bar{a}c.\bar{c}w_1.cy_1.\bar{c}w_2.cy_2.Q \longrightarrow\!\!\!\!\rightarrow P\{w_1w_2/x_1x_2\} \mid Q\{v_1v_2/y_1y_2\}$$
$$(1.2)$$

Note input and output are mixed together. As in (1.1), once two parties start interaction, a sequence of communications is done following a prescribed protocol using a private channel. The same scheme can be used to realise more complex communication structures, including those with parallelism and intricate information flow.

As a means to study rich computational structures representable in name passing processes, a notion of types called *sorting* was introduced by Milner [21] and has been studied extensively since then [5, 34, 9, 28, 32, 19, 33, 10, 17]. Sorting shows how a name carries another name. For example, if v has a type, say, nat, and we have a term $\bar{a}v.0$, then a should have a type (nat), a type which carries nat. This idea and its ramifications

Department of Computer Science, University of Edinburgh, The King's Buildings, Mayfield Road, Edinburgh, EH9 3JZ, UK. e-mail: ny@dcs.ed.ac.uk. Partially supported by JSPS Fellowship for Japanese Junior Scientists and Ogata-jyosei grant of Keio University.

have been used to analyse significant semantic properties of calculi with polyadic name passing. However, as was already noticed in [21], sorting in monadic π-calculus is not powerful enough to type-abstract known encodings of polyadic name passing. Indeed, (1.1) becomes ill-sorted if v_1, v_2, v_3 have different sorts. As far as we know, the situation remains the same with the refinements of sorting proposed in [28, 17, 10]. This means, among other things, sorting restricted to monadic terms does not give a rich semantic analysis as in the polyadic case, while behaviourally the above encoding does mimic polyadic name passing. In general, this is because sorting does not capture the dynamic structure of interaction, especially those using the transmission of private names as in (1.1) and (1.2), which is omnipresent even in the polyadic setting.

In this paper we develop a syntactic theory of types for monadic π-calculus which extends sorting in a simple way and by which we can extract the abstract operational structures of π-terms including those of (1.1) and (1.2) as well as more complex ones. The key technical idea is to represent a class of dynamic communication behaviours using simple combinatorial expressions, i.e. graphs. In a graph type, nodes denote atomic actions and edges denote the activation ordering between them, representing as a whole a deterministic protocol a process will be engaged in. This departure from the type abstraction of static usage of names to that of dynamic process behaviour makes it possible to type-abstract many non-trivial computational structures representable in π-calculus. Indeed it allows us to solve Milner's open issue mentioned above in a sharper form: We show that not only the encoding of sorted polyadic π-terms into the monadic terms is typable preserving the original type structure, but also it results in *equational full abstraction*: let $=_P$ and $=_\pi$ be suitably defined behavioural equalities over sorted polyadic π-terms and typed monadic π-terms, respectively. Then we get:

$$P =_P Q \iff [P] =_\pi [Q]$$

where $[\cdot]$ is the standard encoding from polyadic π-terms to monadic π-terms. In the untyped setting, we can only get "$\Leftarrow$" (adequacy) direction in terms of usual weak behavioural equivalences. This is due to possible violation of "protocols" by environment processes, and suggests the lack of precise type abstraction of the communication structure of various encodings such as (1.1) and (1.2) in preceding type disciplines, even though the effect of process types on behavioural equalities has been known since the work of Pierce and Sangiorgi [28, 17]. In this context, our result, which seems the first of this kind, shows how precisely our type discipline captures essential behavioural information these protocols carry, while using a simple idea of graph-based types and a small typing system. Moreover the results can be easily extended to calculi with more complex communication structures, cf. 6.2 later. Because polyadic name passing is a typical example of encoding of high-level communication structures into π-calculus, cf. [22, 20, 16], the presented construction and its extensions will hopefully become a basis for using typed equality over π-terms to verify the semantic equality of various target languages and calculi in a uniform framework.

Some preliminaries: throughout the paper, we fix a countable set $\mathcal{N}$ of *names*, ranged over by $a, b, c, ..$ or $x, y, z, ...$ The syntax of monadic π-calculus follows that of [20] (writing $ax.P$ for $a(x).P$ in [20]):

$$P ::= ax.P \mid \bar{a}x.P \mid P|Q \mid (a)P \mid !P \mid 0$$

The definitions for free and bound names in P are standard and denoted by $\mathcal{FN}(P)$ and $\mathcal{BN}(P)$. The structural congruence $\equiv$, the reduction relation $\longrightarrow$ and the early transition relation $\overset{l}{\longrightarrow}$ again follow the standard definitions [22, 20]. For the space sake, detailed definitions, technical lemmas and all proofs of the results in the paper are left to the full version [36].

The structure of the rest of the paper: Section 2 introduces the basic notion of graph types. Section 3 gives the typing system and presents the subject reduction. Section 4 clarifies relationship between types and the behaviour of typed terms. Section 5 proves the full abstraction of the standard encoding of polyadic π-calculus into the monadic one, together with preservation of type structure. Section 6 concludes with comparison with related work and discussions on further issues.

2. Graph Types

2.1. Given a finite poset $\langle X, \leq \rangle$, its *covering relation* $\to$ is defined: $x \to y$ iff (1) $x \lneq y$ and (2) for no z, $x \lneq z \lneq y$ where $x, y, z \in X$ (cf. [3], Chap.1). Then $\langle X, \to \rangle$ gives an acyclic directed simple graph (equivalent to the familiar Hasse diagram), from which $\leq$ is recovered as $\to^*$ (the reflexive transitive closure) and $\lneq$ as $\to^+$ (the transitive closure). In this paper the term "graph" always means this kind of a directed graph, presented by the covering relation denoted $\to$. We write $G, G', \ldots$ for such graphs, $N(G)$ for the sets of nodes of G, and $G_1 \uplus G_2$ for the (disjoint) graph union of G_1 and G_2.

2.2. **Definition.** (graph types) A *graph type* is a graph in the above sense whose nodes are occurrences of the following *atomic types*[1]:

$$\mathbf{n} \quad ::= \quad a \downarrow (b) \mid a \uparrow (b) \mid a \downarrow \mathbf{x} \mid a \uparrow \mathbf{x}$$

where $a, b, c, \ldots$ range over $\mathcal{N}$ (cf. Sec.1) and $\mathbf{x}, \mathbf{x}', \ldots$ range over the set $\mathcal{V}$ of *base types*. In $a \updownarrow (b)$ or $a \updownarrow \mathbf{x}$, a is the *subject* and $b, \mathbf{x}$ are *objects*. Over atomic types we define a self-inverse function $\overline{(\cdot)}$ such that: $\overline{a \downarrow (b)} = a \uparrow (b)$ and $\overline{a \downarrow \mathbf{x}} = a \uparrow \mathbf{x}$, which is extended to graph types so that $\overline{G}$ (the *dual* of G) is the result of replacing all occurrences of atomic types in G by their duals. *Heads* of a graph type are those occurrences of atomic types which are minimal w.r.t. the order $\to^*$. We often use atomic types to denote their occurrences in a graph type, writing, for example, $\mathbf{n}_1 \to \mathbf{n}_2$, if no confusion arises.

Intuitively, nodes in a graph type denote atomic actions of a process (best understood as abstraction of labels in a transition relation), while edges denote their synchronisation ordering. If a graph type represents the structure of interaction from one party's viewpoint, then its dual represents the same interaction from another party's viewpoint.

2.3. **Binding.** In atomic types, the only bound occurrence of a name is b in $a \updownarrow (b)$, others occurring free. $\mathrm{bn}(\mathbf{n})$ and $\mathrm{fn}(\mathbf{n})$ are the sets of a bound/free name in $\mathbf{n}$, respectively. In a graph type, $\mathbf{n}$ binds the set of nodes $\{\mathbf{n}' \mid \mathbf{n} \to^+ \mathbf{n}' \wedge \mathrm{bn}(\mathbf{n}) = \mathrm{fn}(\mathbf{n}')\}$. We write $\mathbf{n} \twoheadrightarrow \mathbf{n}'$, if $\mathbf{n}$ binds $\mathbf{n}'$. A graph type is *normal* if, in any of its bindings, no two binders bind the same name occurrence (see Example 2.4). *Hereafter a "graph type" always means a normal graph type.* For (normal) graph types, the standard idea of the sets of free/bound names and the α-equality applies, which we denote $\mathrm{bn}(G)$, $\mathrm{fn}(G)$ and $\equiv_\alpha$, respectively. We always assume that a graph type obeys the usual *binding condition*, i.e. no two binding occurrences are of the same name and $\mathrm{bn}(G)$ and $\mathrm{fn}(G)$ are disjoint.

---

[1] Equivalently nodes of a graph type are labeled by atomic types. Graph types are considered modulo the graph isomorphism preserving these labels and the direction of edges.

2.4. Example. Some simple graph types can be written syntactically, for example, $b \downarrow x \to a \uparrow x'$ and $b \uparrow(c) \to a \uparrow x$. Further examples are given in Figure 1. Notice (2) and (3) of Figure 1 are normal while (1) is not (so (1) is not considered as a graph type). We can also see (2) and (3) are α-convertible to each other and both obey the binding condition.

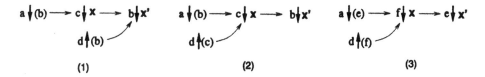

(1)   (2)   (3)

FIGURE 1. Graph Types

The following two kinds of graph types are important for our theory.

2.5. Definition. (safe and pointed graph types)

(i) (safety) A graph type G is *safe*, if, for any distinct $n_1, n_2 \in N(G)$, $fn(n_1) = fn(n_2)$ implies either $n_1 \to^+ n_2$ or $n_2 \to^+ n_1$.

(ii) (pointedness) A graph type G is *pointed*, if: (1) There is a unique head in G. (2) All name occurrences except the subject of the head are bound, and (3) G is safe. We write $G_{(a)}$ if G is pointed with a free.

Notice G is safe (resp. pointed) iff $\overline{G}$ is safe (resp. pointed). In a safe graph type, two nodes with the same subject are strictly ordered so that, while the same subject may be used several times in interaction, at any one time, only one input and one output are active, making interaction deterministic. In Figure 2, (1) is not safe because there is no ordering between $c \uparrow x$ and $c \uparrow(e)$.

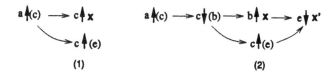

(1)   (2)

FIGURE 2. Unsafe and Safe Types

The pointedness says that an interaction starts at a single interacting point, and that, after the initial interaction, the communications are always done using private channels, so that they are free from the interference of the third party. An example of a pointed (and hence also safe) graph type is shown in (2) of Figure 2.

2.6. Composition Function. We next discuss composition of graph types. Write $dom(\Psi)$ for the domain of a partial function Ψ. Given G and G', assume $n, n_i \in N(G)$ and $n', n'_i \in N(G')$. Then a *composition function* Ψ from G to G' is a partial injection $\Psi : N(G) \rightharpoonup N(G')$ such that:

(duality) If $n \in dom(\Psi)$, then $\Psi(n) = \overline{n}$.

(acyclicity) If $n_1, n_2 \in dom(\Psi)$, both $n_1 \to^+ n_2$ and $\Psi(n_2) \to^+ \Psi(n_1)$ cannot hold.

(covering) (1) if $a \in \text{fn}(G) \cap \text{fn}(G')$, then $a \in \text{fn}(\mathbf{n})$ implies $\mathbf{n} \in \text{dom}(\Psi)$ (resp. $a \in \text{fn}(\mathbf{n}')$ implies $\mathbf{n}' \in \text{dom}(\Psi^{-1})$). (2) if there is any binding chain $\mathbf{n}_1 \twoheadrightarrow \mathbf{n}_2 \twoheadrightarrow \cdots \twoheadrightarrow \mathbf{n}_n$ in G and $\mathbf{n}_i \in \text{dom}(\Psi)$ for some $i \leq n$, then for all $1 \leq j \leq n$, $\mathbf{n}_j \in \text{dom}(\Psi)$, and then $\Psi(\mathbf{n}_1) \twoheadrightarrow \Psi(\mathbf{n}_2) \twoheadrightarrow \cdots \twoheadrightarrow \Psi(\mathbf{n}_n)$. Similarly for any binding chain in G' and Ψ^{-1}.

Observe that, when G and G' are safe, there can be at most one composition function from G to G'. We write $G_1 \asymp G_2$ if, for some $G_1' \equiv_\alpha G_1$ and $G_2' \equiv_\alpha G_2$, there is a composition function from G_1' to G_2'. For convenience we assume, when we write $G_1 \asymp G_2$, they are already suitably α-converted so that the composition function relates their nodes directly. We now introduce two operations on graph types.

2.7. Operations on Graph Types.

(i) (prefix) "$\mathbf{n} \to G$" denotes the result of adding a new node (occurrence) of $\mathbf{n}$ to G together with edges from the new node to all heads of G.

(ii) (parallel composition) Given safe graph types G_1 and G_2 s.t. $G_1 \asymp G_2$ and the corresponding composition function Ψ, the *composition* of G_1 and G_2, denoted by $G_1 \odot G_2$, is a graph type obtained by: first identifying Ψ-related nodes of $G_1 \uplus G_2$, getting a graph, say, G', and then by eliminating every identified node, preserving and reflecting $\to^*$ of G', deleting all redundant edges if any.

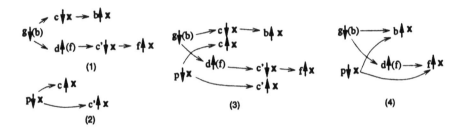

FIGURE 3. Cut Elimination

Figure 3 shows a simple example of parallel composition. Given two safe graphs in (1) and (2), first we identify the same nodes as in $\langle c{\downarrow}x, c{\uparrow}x \rangle$ and $\langle c'{\downarrow}x, c'{\uparrow}x \rangle$ in (3), next eliminate one by one (the order does not matter). Then we have the final graph (4). In this way the original dependency relations are merged to generate a more complex one.

We can easily show if G is safe then $\mathbf{n} \to G$ is also (normal and) safe, similarly if G_1 and G_2 are safe and $G_1 \asymp G_2$, then $G_1 \odot G_2$ is again (normal and) safe. Another notable fact is that any graph type can be constructed from graph types with a unique node by repeatedly applying these two operations.

3. THE TYPING SYSTEM AND ITS BASIC PROPERTIES

3.1. General Idea.
This section introduces a typing system based on graph-types for monadic π-terms and establishes its basic syntactic properties, including the subject reduction property. For simplicity of presentation we do not treat recursive types, whose incorporation is straightforward, cf. 6.2. The typing judgment for a term P has a form:

$$\Gamma \vdash P \triangleright_A G$$

where Γ is an *environment* assigning protocol types introduced in 3.2 to some of free names in P, P is a π-term, A is a *hidden name set*, and G is a graph type. Roughly this judgment tells us: "P has a linear behaviour specified in G, and otherwise obeys the protocols specified in Γ." The separation between linear behaviour and "shared" interaction is essential for tractability of type inference. A is an auxiliary name set to record the linear usage of names. We start from introducing the idea of *protocol types*, which are essentially pairs of pointed types, and which generalise the notion of sorting.

3.2. Protocol Types. Write "$\lambda a.G_{(a)}$" for the *name abstraction* of a in a pointed graph $G_{(a)}$, with the usual notion of binding (We only need this restricted abstraction in this paper[2]). Then a *protocol type* of $\lambda a.G_{(a)}$ is the set $\{\lambda a.G_{(a)}, \lambda a.\overline{G}_{(a)}\}$.

Using this notion, we fix the set of types we shall use in our typing system. Given any base $\mathcal{V}'$, we get the set of atomic types, from which we get the set of graph types, and then that of protocol types. The corresponding set functions are written $\psi_A(\mathcal{V}')$, $\psi_G(\mathcal{V}')$ and $\psi_P(\mathcal{V}')$, respectively. Then we define, given an initial base $\mathcal{V}$ (say $\{nat\}$), $A_\mathcal{V}$, $G_\mathcal{V}$ and $P_\mathcal{V}$ as the smallest sets closed under

$$\mathbf{P}_\mathcal{V} \supseteq \mathcal{V} \cup \psi_P(\mathbf{P}_\mathcal{V}), \quad \mathbf{A}_\mathcal{V} \supseteq \psi_A(\mathbf{P}_\mathcal{V}) \quad \text{and} \quad \mathbf{G}_\mathcal{V} \supseteq \psi_G(\mathbf{P}_\mathcal{V}).$$

$\alpha, \beta, \ldots$ range over $\mathbf{P}_\mathcal{V}$. We shall use these sets for our typing system. Some notations:

- "$\updownarrow(x) \to G$" denotes abstraction $\lambda a.(a\updownarrow(x) \to G)$.
- For $\alpha \in \mathbf{P}_\mathcal{V}$, we write (α) for $\{\lambda a.a\downarrow\alpha, \lambda a.a\uparrow\alpha\}$.

The notation "(α)" comes from the monadic sorting [21], and it indeed functions as such (representing one-time usage of name passing). Protocol types in general, however, carry more dynamic information, by which we can specify refined communication behaviour a process may be engaged in. A protocol type (similar to a pointed graph (2) in Figure 2) is given in Figure 4.

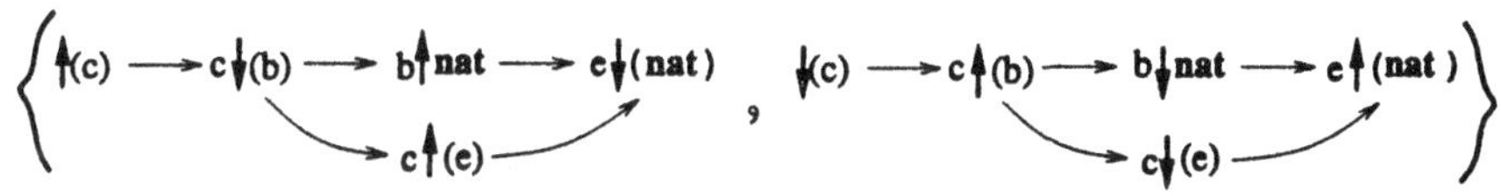

FIGURE 4. Protocol Type

3.3. Typing Function. A *typing function* is a function from a finite subset of $\mathcal{N}$ to a set of protocol types. The set of typing functions are ranged over by $\Gamma, \Delta, \ldots$. We often regard Γ as a finite set of elements of form $a : \alpha$. $\mathsf{fn}(\Gamma)$ denotes $\{a \mid a : \alpha \in \Gamma\}$. Let $A, A', \ldots$ denote a finite subset of $\mathcal{N}$. "$\Gamma \backslash A$" denotes $\{a : \alpha \in \Gamma \mid a \notin A\}$, while "$\Gamma \lceil A$" denotes $\{a : \alpha \in \Gamma \mid a \in A\}$. "$a : \alpha, \Gamma$" means $\Gamma \cup \{a : \alpha\}$ together with the assumption $a \notin \mathsf{fn}(\Gamma)$. "$\Gamma \asymp \Delta$" represents, if $x : \alpha \in \Gamma$ and $x : \beta \in \Delta$, we have $\alpha = \beta$. If we get Γ by α-conversion of some protocol type in Δ, then we write $\Gamma \equiv_\alpha \Delta$.

3.4. Sequent and Typing System. The sequent has a form $\Gamma \vdash P \triangleright_A G$, which we read: "$P$ has a type G under Γ with hidden names A". Γ is called the *basis* of the sequent, P is its *subject*, A is the *hidden name set*, and G is its *type*. We write $\Gamma \vdash P \triangleright G$ if $A = \emptyset$ (read "P has a type G under Γ"), $\Gamma \vdash P \triangleright_A$ if $G = \emptyset$, and $\Gamma \vdash P$ if both are empty. The typing system, denoted π_G, is given in Figure 5, where "$\langle G_1, A_1 \rangle \asymp \langle G_2, A_2 \rangle$" denotes both $G_1 \asymp G_2$ and $(\mathsf{fn}(G_i) \cup A_i) \cap A_j = \emptyset$ for $i \neq j$. We hereafter write $\Gamma \vdash P \triangleright_A G$ if the sequent is derivable in π_G.

---

[2]It is possible to consider extensions such as a general name abstraction of pointed types with two or more heads (cf. [4]), and with a non-dual pairs (cf. [19]), though we do not treat them here.

(I) **Prefix Rules.**

(in_1) $\dfrac{\Gamma \vdash P \triangleright_A G}{\Gamma \vdash ax.P \triangleright_A a{\downarrow}(x) \to G}$ $(1,2)$ (out_1) $\dfrac{\Gamma \vdash P \triangleright_A G}{\Gamma \vdash \bar{a}x.P \triangleright_{A \cup \{x\}} a{\uparrow}(x) \to G}$ $(1,2)$

(in_2) $\dfrac{x:\alpha, \Gamma \vdash P \triangleright_A G}{\Gamma \vdash ax.P \triangleright_A a{\downarrow}\alpha \to G}$ (1) (out_2) $\dfrac{x:\alpha, \Gamma \vdash P \triangleright_A G}{x:\alpha, \Gamma \vdash \bar{a}x.P \triangleright_A a{\uparrow}\alpha \to G}$ (1)

(in_3) $\dfrac{a:\beta, \Gamma \vdash P \triangleright_A G}{a:\beta, \Gamma \vdash ax.P \triangleright_A}$ $(2,3)$ (out_3) $\dfrac{a:\beta, \Gamma \vdash P \triangleright_A \overline{G}}{a:\beta, \Gamma \vdash \bar{a}x.P \triangleright_{A \cup \{x\}}}$ $(2,3)$

(in_4) $\dfrac{a:(\alpha), x:\alpha, \Gamma \vdash P \triangleright_A}{a:(\alpha), \Gamma \vdash ax.P \triangleright_A}$ (out_4) $\dfrac{a:(\alpha), x:\alpha, \Gamma \vdash P \triangleright_A}{a:(\alpha), x:\alpha, \Gamma \vdash \bar{a}x.P \triangleright_A}$

(II) **Other Rules.**

(par) $\dfrac{\Gamma \vdash P \triangleright_{A_1} G_1 \quad \Gamma \vdash Q \triangleright_{A_2} G_2}{\Gamma \vdash P \mid Q \triangleright_{A_1 \cup A_2 \cup A} G_1 \odot G_2}$ (4) (res) $\dfrac{\Gamma \vdash P \triangleright_A G}{\Gamma \backslash a \vdash (a)P \triangleright_{A\backslash\{a\}} G}$ (5)

(alpha) $\dfrac{\Gamma \vdash P \triangleright_A G \quad G \equiv_\alpha G' \quad \Gamma \equiv_\alpha \Gamma'}{\Gamma' \vdash P \triangleright_A G'}$ (weak) $\dfrac{\Gamma \vdash P \triangleright_A G}{a:\alpha, \Gamma \vdash P \triangleright_{A \cup \{b\}} G}$ (6)

(nil) $\vdash \mathbf{0}$ (rep) $\dfrac{\Gamma \vdash P}{\Gamma \vdash !P}$

(1) $a \notin \mathrm{fn}(\Gamma) \cup A$. (2) $x \notin \mathrm{fn}(\Gamma) \cup A$. (3) $\beta = \{{\downarrow}(x) \to G, {\uparrow}(x) \to \overline{G}\}$. (4) $\langle G_1, A_1 \rangle \asymp \langle G_2, A_2 \rangle$, $A = \mathrm{fn}(G_1) \cap \mathrm{fn}(G_2)$. (5) $a \notin \mathrm{fn}(G)$. (6) $a \notin A \cup \mathrm{fn}(G)$, $b \notin \mathrm{fn}(\Gamma) \cup \mathrm{fn}(G)$.

FIGURE 5. Typing System π_G

3.5. Comments on Typing Rules. First notice there are four pairs of (in) and (out) rules corresponding to what kinds of atomic types will be introduced.

- **(in_1, out_1):** In (in_1), "$a{\downarrow}(x) \to G$" represents the behaviour of a process of getting a fresh name x and then acting with behaviour G (corresponding to $ax.P \xrightarrow{a(x)} P$ in the late transition [22]). Similarly (out_1) represents a "bound output" $(x)\bar{a}x.P \xrightarrow{\bar{a}(x)} P$. In the latter x is recorded as a hidden name to be later eliminated by (res) rule.

- **(in_2, out_2):** These rules specify the situation where a process gets/emits a name of a protocol type α, and then acts like G.

- **(in_3, out_3):** If we have successfully constructed a protocol type β by finally putting $a \updownarrow (x)$ to G, then we may remove the whole pointed graph type to the shared environment by these rules. In (out_3), we memorize "x" as a hidden name. Notice that, by using (in_1) and (out_1) instead of (in_3) and (out_3), we can keep $a\updownarrow(x) \to G$ in the linear realm to construct a more complex protocol type. Notice also this shows the usual notion of principal type scheme does not exist in π_G.

- **(in_4, out_4):** These rules correspond to monadic sorting, so that (together with (par) and other rules) this system subsumes monadic sorting. By ($\mathrm{in}_{3,4}$) and ($\mathrm{out}_{3,4}$), we make it possible to infer types of a term which contains a shared name at which multiple agents with consistent protocols may interact.

- **(par):** This is the key rule which allows us to extract versatile forms of interaction structures from π-terms. Notice that, even if G_1 and G_2 are sequential (i.e. $\to^*$ is a total order), we may get a non-sequential graph (but still representing a linear behaviour, see 4.5). In the rule we memorise the set of names lost by cut-elimination: this prevents further connection to these names so that reduction at these points is deterministic (cf. 4.3). Finally it is notable that, if we only allow composition of disjoint graphs, we lose the subject reduction property we establish later: thus the present rule not only extends the typability of terms but also is essential to the fundamental property as a typing system.

(res): The combination of this rule and other rules that manipulate the hidden name set such as (out$_{1,3}$) and (par) enables us to record the linear usage of names during the type inference before the actual occurrence of the scope restriction.

Other rules are standard. By (alpha), we hereafter safely consider graph types and basis modulo their respective α-equality.

3.6. Example. Below we give a simple example of typing. Let $P_1 \overset{\text{def}}{=} z_1 y.cx.\overline{z_1}c$, $P_2 \overset{\text{def}}{=} z_2 x.\overline{c}w$ and $P \overset{\text{def}}{=} az_1.z_1 z_2.(c)(P_1 \mid P_2)$. Then we have:

$$w : \mathsf{nat} \vdash P_1 \triangleright z_1 \downarrow \mathsf{nat} \to c \downarrow \mathsf{nat} \to z_1 \uparrow (\mathsf{nat}) \quad \text{and} \quad w : \mathsf{nat} \vdash P_2 \triangleright z_2 \downarrow \mathsf{nat} \to c \uparrow \mathsf{nat}$$

Note z_1 carries two different types. By (par) rule a proper graph structure arises.

$$w : \mathsf{nat} \vdash (P_1 \mid P_2) \triangleright_{\{c\}} \begin{array}{l} z_1 \downarrow \mathsf{nat} \to z_1 \uparrow (\mathsf{nat}). \\ z_2 \downarrow \mathsf{nat} \nearrow \end{array}$$

After restricting and prefixing, we have the final state.

$$v : \mathsf{nat}, w : \mathsf{nat} \vdash P \triangleright \begin{array}{l} a \downarrow (z_1) \to z_1 \downarrow (z_2) \to z_1 \downarrow \mathsf{nat} \to z_1 \uparrow (\mathsf{nat}). \\ \searrow z_2 \downarrow \mathsf{nat} \nearrow \end{array}$$

Note that the final graph type is a-pointed, so that we could have moved them using (in$_3$) to the l.h.s. as protocol types.

The basic properties of the typing system follow. Notice, by (i,ii) below, we safely assume binding occurrences in types and a term of $\Gamma \vdash P \triangleright_A G$ are all distinct and disjoint from free occurrences.

3.7. Lemma.

(i) (properties of names) *Suppose* $\Gamma \vdash P \triangleright_A G$. *Then:* $\mathsf{fn}(\Gamma) \cap \mathsf{fn}(G) = A \cap \mathsf{fn}(G) = A \cap \mathsf{fn}(\Gamma) = \emptyset$, $\mathsf{fn}(P) \subset \mathsf{fn}(G) \cup A \cup \mathsf{fn}(\Gamma)$, $\mathsf{fn}(G) \subset \mathsf{fn}(P)$, *and* $\Gamma \lceil \mathsf{fn}(P) \vdash P \triangleright_{A \cap \mathsf{fn}(P)} G$.

(ii) (renaming) *Suppose* $\Gamma \vdash P \triangleright_A G$ *and* $b \notin \mathsf{fn}(\Gamma) \cup A \cup \mathsf{fn}(G)$. *Then we have* $\Gamma\{b/a\} \vdash P\{b/a\} \triangleright_{A\{b/a\}} G\{b/a\}$.

(iii) ($\equiv$) *If* $\Gamma \vdash P \triangleright_A G$ *and* $P \equiv Q$, *then* $\Gamma \vdash Q \triangleright_A G$.

(iv) (substitution) *If* $a : \beta, b : \beta, \Gamma \vdash P \triangleright_A G$, *then* $b : \beta, \Gamma \vdash P\{b/a\} \triangleright_A G$.

Using Lemma above, we can establish the subject reduction theorem, the key property of the typing system.

3.8. Theorem. (Subject Reduction).
$$\text{If } \Gamma \vdash P \triangleright_A G \text{ and } P \longrightarrow\!\!\!\!\rightarrow P', \text{ then we have } \Gamma \vdash P' \triangleright_A G.$$

It is notable that not only the environment Γ (which corresponds to sorting) but also the graph type of a term is invariant under reduction. This is because all possible reduction concerning the (names of the) graph type is already consumed when (par) rule is applied: and reduction concerning the (names of the) basis only creates dual graphs which eliminate each other to leave the graph type unchanged.

4. Behavioural Equality over Typed π-terms

This section introduces the basic constructions of typed behavioural equality over monadic π-terms following the untyped construction in [15]. Using this equality we clarify relationship between types and process behaviour they guarantee.

4.1. Typed Terms and Relation. A typed term is a tuple $\langle \Gamma, P, A, G \rangle$ such that $\Gamma \vdash P \triangleright_A G$. We simply write $\Gamma \vdash P \triangleright_A G$ for a typed term $\langle \Gamma, P, A, G \rangle$. A relation over typed terms, ranged over $\mathcal{R}, \mathcal{R}'...$, is called a *typed relation*, if:

(a) $\Gamma \vdash P \triangleright_A G \, \mathcal{R} \, \Delta \vdash Q \triangleright_B G' \;\Rightarrow\; A = B,\, G = G'$, and $\Gamma = \Delta$, and

(b) $\Gamma \vdash P \triangleright_A G \, \mathcal{R} \Gamma \vdash Q \triangleright_A G \;\Rightarrow\; (a{:}\alpha, \Gamma \vdash P \triangleright_{A \cup \{b\}} G) \, \mathcal{R} \, (a{:}\alpha, \Gamma \vdash P \triangleright_{A \cup \{b\}} G)$ with (6) of Fig.5.

We often write $\Gamma \vdash P \mathcal{R} Q \triangleright_A G$ for a tuple of a typed relation, or just $P \mathcal{R} Q$ if the type assignment is obvious from the context.

Notice $\equiv$ and $\longrightarrow$ restricted to typed terms are typed relations (by Lemma 3.7 (iii) and Theorem 3.8 respectively). Several important classes of typed relations are:

(i) A typed relation is *reflexive* if it contains the structural equality over typed π-terms. The *transitive/symmetric relations* are defined in a similar way. If a typed relation is reflexive, transitive and symmetric, then it is an *equivalence*.

(ii) A typed relation $\mathcal{R}$ is a *congruence* if $\mathcal{R}$ is an equivalence and moreover is closed under the following rules, for each inference rule (and in (par) for each selection of one side of the antecedents) of Figure 5: $\Gamma \vdash P_1 \, \mathcal{R} \, P_2 \triangleright_A G \;\Rightarrow\; \Gamma' \vdash C[P_1] \, \mathcal{R} \, C[P_2] \triangleright_{A'} G'$ if, in an instance of the inference rule, $\Gamma' \vdash C[P_i] \triangleright_{A'} G'$ is the conclusion with an antecedent $\Gamma \vdash P_i \triangleright_A G$, for $i = 1, 2$, respectively. We write $\cong, \cong', ...$ for congruence relations.

4.2. Behavioural Equality. For the behavioural equality over typed π-terms, we use the reduction-based semantics which can be equally applicable to both untyped and typed settings. The formulation is extensively studied for untyped systems in [15, 13, 14]. First we set: $a \in \mathcal{AN}_+(P)$ iff $P \equiv (\tilde{c})(\overline{a}v.Q \mid R)$ with $a \notin \{\tilde{c}\}$, and $a \in \mathcal{AN}_-(P)$ iff $P \equiv (\tilde{c})(ax.Q \mid R)$ with $a \notin \{\tilde{c}\}$. With θ ranging over $+$ and $-$, we define a family of *action predicates*: $P \Downarrow_{a\theta} \stackrel{\text{def}}{\iff} \exists P'.\, P \longrightarrow\!\!\!\!\rightarrow P' \wedge a \in \mathcal{AN}_\theta(P')$. Then $\Gamma \vdash P \Downarrow_{a\theta} \triangleright_A G \stackrel{\text{def}}{\iff} (\Gamma \vdash P \triangleright_A G \wedge P \Downarrow_{a\theta} \wedge a \notin A)$. Next we define:

- A typed congruence $\cong$ is *reduction-closed*, i.e., whenever $\Gamma \vdash P \cong Q \triangleright_A G$, $P \longrightarrow\!\!\!\!\rightarrow P'$ implies, for some Q', $Q \longrightarrow\!\!\!\!\rightarrow Q'$ and $\Gamma \vdash P' \cong Q' \triangleright_A G$.

- A typed relation $\mathcal{R}$ *respects the action predicates* iff both $\Gamma \vdash P \mathcal{R} Q \triangleright_A G$ and $\Gamma \vdash P \Downarrow_{a\theta} \triangleright_A G$ implies $\Gamma \vdash Q \Downarrow_{a\theta} \triangleright_A G$.

We say a congruence $\cong$ is $\Downarrow_{a\theta}$-*sound*, or simply *sound*, if it is reduction closed and respects the action predicates. Then, by taking the congruent closure of the whole family of sound congruences, we immediately know there is the maximum sound congruence, denoted by $=_\pi$, within the family of all sound congruences.[3]

We now clarify basic behavioural properties types ensure for typed π-terms. We start from the property of reduction corresponding to cut elimination.

---

[3]We notice that we get the same equality if we use other observability predicates: $P \Downarrow_a \stackrel{\text{def}}{\iff} \exists \theta.\, P \Downarrow_{a\theta}$ [30] and $P \Downarrow \stackrel{\text{def}}{\iff} \exists a.\, P \Downarrow_a$ [23], or even if we use the notion of insensitivity of [15], combined with reduction-closure. Another possible equational framework would be the equality called *barbed congruence*, which does not require reduction-closure at the congruence level. This construction may accompany difficulties when combined with algebraic notions such as quotient, though we believe that the same full abstraction result can be gained with it.

4.3. Definition. *(β-reduction)* The β-reduction, $\rightarrow_\beta$, is the relation generated by:

(β_1) $\Gamma \vdash ax.P \mid \bar{a}v.Q \rightarrow_\beta P\{v/x\} \mid Q \triangleright_A G$ $(a \in A)$

(β_2) $\Gamma \vdash (a)(ax.P \mid \bar{a}v.Q) \rightarrow_\beta (a)(P\{v/x\} \mid Q) \triangleright_A G$

(par) $\Gamma \vdash P \rightarrow_\beta P' \triangleright_{A_1} G_1 \wedge \Gamma \vdash Q \triangleright_{A_2} G_2 \Rightarrow \Gamma \vdash P \mid Q \rightarrow_\beta P' \mid Q \triangleright_{A'} G_1 \odot G_2$

(res) $\Gamma \vdash P \rightarrow_\beta P' \triangleright_A G \Rightarrow \Gamma \backslash a \vdash (a)P \rightarrow_\beta (a)P' \triangleright_{A\backslash\{a\}} G$

(str) $P \equiv P' \quad \Gamma \vdash P' \rightarrow_\beta Q' \triangleright_A G \quad Q \equiv Q' \Rightarrow \Gamma \vdash P \rightarrow_\beta Q \triangleright_A G$

with $A' = A_1 \cup A_2 \cup A$ plus (4) of Fig. 5 in (par), and (5) of Fig. 5 in (res), respectively. $\twoheadrightarrow_\beta$ is reflexive transitive closure of $\rightarrow_\beta$, while $=_\beta$ is the congruent closure of $\rightarrow_\beta$.

We note $\rightarrow_\beta$, which is a subset of $\longrightarrow$, generalises the *linear reduction* studied in [18, 10, 17] in that it allows the case when one name occurs many times in a process but at any one time only one input/output pair occurs actively (cf. Figure 3, see also [13, 14]). The basic properties of $\twoheadrightarrow_\beta$ and $=_\beta$ follow. (ii) is easy from (i-a,b).

4.4. Proposition.

(i) (a) If $P \twoheadrightarrow_\beta Q_1$ and $P \longrightarrow Q_2$, then there exists Q' s.t. $Q_1 \longrightarrow Q'$ and $Q_2 \twoheadrightarrow_\beta Q'$. (b) $P \twoheadrightarrow_\beta Q$ and $P \Downarrow_{a\bullet}$ implies $Q \Downarrow_{a\bullet}$.

(ii) $=_\beta$ is a sound congruence, hence $P =_\beta Q$ implies $P =_\pi Q$.

The above proposition shows $\rightarrow_\beta$ can be semantically neglected. This is essential to the understanding of the following proposition, which clarifies the relationship between types and the behaviour they guarantee. (i–v) give the case for "linear behaviour" corresponding to a graph type: a term does act as its graph type specifies, following the activation ordering in the graph modulo $\rightarrow_\beta$. Combining with the behaviour of "protocol type" shown in (vi), we know that once a term performs an atomic action $a\updownarrow(x)$ in a protocol type $a\updownarrow(x) \rightarrow G$, then it should automatically do the rest of action G (because G is now in the linear space). (vii) corresponds to the behaviour of sorting.

4.5. Proposition. *(behaviour of typed terms)* Write $\mathsf{Hd}(G)$ for the set of heads in G and $G\backslash n$ for the elimination of the head n from G. Then $\Gamma \vdash P \triangleright_A G$ implies:

(i) $a\downarrow(x) \in \mathsf{Hd}(G) \Rightarrow P \twoheadrightarrow_\beta \xrightarrow{ax} P'$ and $\Gamma \vdash P' \triangleright_A G\backslash a\downarrow(x)$ (1)

(ii) $a\uparrow(x) \in \mathsf{Hd}(G) \Rightarrow$
$\begin{cases} P \twoheadrightarrow_\beta \xrightarrow{\bar{a}(x)} P' \text{ and } \Gamma \vdash P' \triangleright_A G\backslash a\uparrow(x) & (1) \\ P \twoheadrightarrow_\beta \xrightarrow{\bar{a}x'} P' \text{ and } \Gamma \vdash P' \triangleright_{A\backslash\{x'\}} (G\backslash a\uparrow(x))\{x'/x\} & (2) \end{cases}$

(iii) $a\downarrow\alpha \in \mathsf{Hd}(G) \Rightarrow P \twoheadrightarrow_\beta \xrightarrow{ax} P'$ and $\{x:\alpha\} \cup \Gamma \vdash P' \triangleright_A G\backslash a\downarrow\alpha$ (3)

(iv) $a\uparrow\alpha \in \mathsf{Hd}(G) \Rightarrow$
$\begin{cases} P \twoheadrightarrow_\beta \xrightarrow{\bar{a}(x)} P' \text{ and } \{x:\alpha\} \cup \Gamma \vdash P' \triangleright_A G\backslash a\uparrow\alpha & (3) \\ P \twoheadrightarrow_\beta \xrightarrow{\bar{a}x} P' \text{ and } \Gamma \vdash P' \triangleright_A G\backslash a\uparrow\alpha & (4) \end{cases}$

(v) $a \in \mathsf{fn}(G) \wedge a \notin \mathsf{fn}(\mathsf{Hd}(G)) \cup A \Rightarrow \neg \exists l.\ P \xrightarrow{l} \text{ with } a \in \mathsf{fn}(l)$.

(vi) Assume $a: \{\downarrow(x) \rightarrow G', \uparrow(x) \rightarrow \overrightarrow{G}\} \in \Gamma$. Then:

    (a) $a \in \mathcal{AN}_-(P) \Rightarrow P \xrightarrow{ax} P'$ and $\Gamma \vdash P' \triangleright_A G \uplus G'$ (1)

    (b) $a \in \mathcal{AN}_+(P) \Rightarrow$
$\begin{cases} P \xrightarrow{\bar{a}(x)} P' \text{ and } \Gamma \vdash P' \triangleright_A G \uplus \overrightarrow{G} & (1) \\ P \xrightarrow{\bar{a}x'} P' \text{ and } \Gamma \vdash P' \triangleright_{A\backslash\{x'\}} (G \uplus \overrightarrow{G}'\{x'/x\}) & (2) \end{cases}$

(vii) Assume $a: (\alpha) \in \Gamma$. Then:

    (a) $a \in \mathcal{AN}_-(P) \Rightarrow P \xrightarrow{ax} P'$ and $\{x:\alpha\} \cup \Gamma \vdash P' \triangleright_A G$ (3)

$$\text{(b)} \quad a \in \mathcal{AN}_+(P) \Rightarrow \begin{cases} P \xrightarrow{\bar{a}(x)} P' \quad \text{and} \quad \{x:\alpha\} \cup \Gamma \vdash P' \rhd_A G \quad (3) \\ P \xrightarrow{\bar{a}x} P' \quad \text{and} \quad \Gamma \vdash P' \rhd_A G \quad (4) \end{cases}$$

where (1) x fresh (2) $x' \in A$ (3) $\{x:\alpha\} \asymp \Gamma$ and $x \notin (\mathsf{fn}(G) \cup A)$ (4) $x:\alpha \in \Gamma$.

5. FULLY ABSTRACT ENCODING OF POLYADIC π-CALCULUS

This section establishes the full abstraction result for the standard encoding of polyadic π-calculus into monadic π-calculus in terms of a basic behavioural equality in each setting, as a non-trivial application of our type discipline. We first give a brief review of polyadic π-calculus and its sorting, including behavioural equality. Then, after introducing the encodings, we make it clear what is the essential problems for such an equational embedding. Then we go into the main technical discussions, establishing the full abstraction result.

5.1. Review of Polyadic π-calculus.
The syntax of the polyadic π-calculus is given below [21, 30].

$$P \quad ::= \quad a(x_1..x_n).P \mid \bar{a}\langle v_1..v_n \rangle.P \mid P \mid Q \mid (a)P \mid !P \mid \mathbf{0}$$

$a(x_1..x_n).P$ and $\bar{a}\langle v_1..v_n \rangle.P$ are input and output processes respectively, with n being the arity of the input (output) prefix. The set of *sortings* ranged over by $S_1, S_2,...,$ is given by the following grammar:

$$S ::= \mathbf{x} \mid (S_1 S_2 ... S_n)$$

with $n \geq 0$ (we omit the recursive sorting for simplicity of presentation, cf. 6.2). $\Gamma, \Gamma', \ldots$ denote typing functions, i.e. functions from a finite subset of $\mathcal{N}$ to the above set. The typing system in [34], essentially equivalent to the system in [21], gives the sequent of form $\vdash P \succ \Gamma$, which we write $\Gamma \vdash P$ here. [34] shows the typing system satisfies the subject reduction property. To avoid ambiguity, we often write $\Gamma_P, \Delta_P, \ldots$ for typing functions, $\rightarrow_P$ for the reduction, and $\xrightarrow{l}_P$ for the early transition relation on polyadic π-calculus. The maximum sound equality over sorted polyadic π-terms is defined as in 4.2, which we denote by $=_P$.

The following mapping of polyadic π-terms into monadic π-terms is standard except we present the mapping at the level of *types* too (which plays the central role for our main result).

5.2. Definition.
(translation from polyadic to monadic π-calculus, [22, 21])

- Mapping for terms (with c, z fresh).

$$[\bar{a}\langle v_1..v_n \rangle.P] \stackrel{\text{def}}{=} \bar{a}(c).\bar{c}v_1...\bar{c}v_n.[P] \qquad [P_1 \mid P_2] \stackrel{\text{def}}{=} [P_1] \mid [P_2] \qquad [\mathbf{0}] \stackrel{\text{def}}{=} \mathbf{0}$$

$$[a(x_1..x_n).P] \stackrel{\text{def}}{=} az.zx_1...zx_n.[P] \qquad [(a)P] \stackrel{\text{def}}{=} (a)[P] \qquad [!P] \stackrel{\text{def}}{=} ![P]$$

- Mapping for types (with x fresh).

$$[\mathbf{x}] \stackrel{\text{def}}{=} \mathbf{x} \qquad [(S_1...S_n)] \stackrel{\text{def}}{=} \{ \downarrow(x) \to x\downarrow[S_1] \cdots \to x\downarrow[S_n], \ \uparrow(x) \to x\uparrow[S_1] \cdots \to x\uparrow[S_n] \}$$

Notice a sorting is mapped to a protocol type which consists only of consecutive inputs or outputs. Indeed we get the following result, addressing the issue Milner raised [21].

5.3. Proposition. $\Gamma_P \vdash P \iff [\Gamma_P] \vdash [P]$.

This shows that, *at least at the syntactic level*, the embedding of types closely reflects the embedding of terms (which by the way seems the first result in this generality with respect to polyadic name passing, cf. [28, 27, 10, 17]). The objective of the present section is to show that this faithfulness extends to the semantic level, i.e. at the level of $=_\pi$ and $=_P$. Before going into technical development, we need some discussions on the background of such equational embeddings.

5.4. The Problem in Equational Embedding. The embedding [ ] (the term part) is a most basic example of embedding the high-level operational structures into π-calculus, cf. [22, 20, 21, 16], and, as such, presents the key issue involved in this kind of embedding in a simple setting. The power of π-calculus in encoding various calculi and programming languages lies in the use of two kinds of name passing, free and bound, to simulate one single action of a high-level operation by *a sequence of interactions which is semantically atomic*. For example, with the above encoding, we get:

$$[a(x_1..x_n).P] \mid [\bar{a}\langle v_1..v_n\rangle.Q] \longrightarrow =_\pi^u [P\{v_1..v_n/x_1..x_n\}] \mid [Q]$$

where $=_\pi^u$ is some weak behavioural equivalence, say the maximum sound equality constructed as $=_\pi$ in the untyped setting. This shows that if two encoded terms interact together, the original interaction structure is preserved in the strongest possible operational sense. Indeed the above property easily leads to the following adequacy result:

$$[P] =_\pi^u [Q] \implies P =_P^u Q$$

where $=_P^u$ is the basic behavioural equality in the polyadic calculus (say $=_P$ itself). Such an embedding result motivates us to study various operational structures through their encodings into π-calculus. However, in many situations including polyadic name passing, the embedding cannot be wholly satisfactory, in the sense that the converse of the above implication does *not* hold: in another word, the translation is not equationally fully abstract. To see this, we take two terms $P \stackrel{\text{def}}{=} \bar{a}\langle v\rangle.\bar{a}\langle v\rangle.0$ and $Q \equiv \bar{a}\langle v\rangle.0 \mid \bar{a}\langle v\rangle.0$ and translate them by $[\cdot]$. Seen as polyadic terms, P and Q are strongly congruent so we safely say $P =_P^u Q$. However $[P] =_\pi^u [Q]$ usually fails: With $C[\,] \stackrel{\text{def}}{=} (a)([\,] \mid ax.ax.\bar{e}.0)$ where e is fresh, $C[[Q]]$ gives an observable at e while $C[[P]]$ does not. There are other examples. This context also explains why the completeness ($\Leftarrow$) in general fails: *if an encoding interacts with a monadic term which is not itself an encoding, the protocol can be violated, leading to the detection of difference of two originally equated terms.*

We now observe that, in the present setting too, where sorted polyadic terms are mapped to typed monadic terms, an encoding of a polyadic term *can indeed be composed to interact* with a term which is *not* the encoding itself. For example, let R be given by:

$$R \equiv (b_1 b_2)(\bar{a}(c).(b)(\bar{b}v \mid \bar{c}v_1.bz.\bar{c}v_2) \mid \bar{e}b_1.\bar{f}b_2)$$

R is clearly not in the form of the encoding, but R is typable in the way $[a : (x_1 x_2)] \vdash R \triangleright e\uparrow(b_1) \to f\uparrow(b_2)$, and therefore can be composed to, say, $[a : (x_1 x_2)] \vdash [a(x_1 x_2).0]$. This shows that the completeness result, if we ever get it, may not be an easy task, since we cannot rely only on the properties of the encodings: at the same time, the above example suggests there is some hope for the completeness, since it does seem that R will interact with any encoded term *as if it were itself an encoded term*, which is explicitly specified as R's protocol types.

In the following, we give the basic technical development to validate this prospect, i.e. to establish the equational full abstraction of the standard encoding. The completeness part crucially relies on two essential roles of the types in the present setting, i.e. as information to control the composition of terms and as the guarantee of terms' behaviour.

We start from the following operational correspondence.

5.5. Proposition. (operational correspondence)

(i) If $\Gamma_P \vdash P \to_P Q$, then $[\Gamma_P] \vdash [P] \longrightarrow \twoheadrightarrow_\beta [Q]$.

(ii) If $[\Gamma_P] \vdash [P] \longrightarrow P'$, then for some Q, $[\Gamma_P] \vdash P' \twoheadrightarrow_\beta [Q]$ with $\Gamma_P \vdash P \to_P Q$.

(iii) $\Gamma_P \vdash P \Downarrow_{a^\bullet} \Leftrightarrow [\Gamma_P] \vdash [P] \Downarrow_{a^\bullet}$.

For finer analysis of behaviour of typed terms, we use the following mapping of labels.

$$[\tau] \stackrel{def}{=} \tau \quad [a\langle x_1...x_n\rangle] \stackrel{def}{=} az \cdot zx_1 \cdots zx_n \quad [(\tilde{b})\bar{a}\langle v_1...v_n\rangle] \stackrel{def}{=} \bar{a}(c) \cdot (\tilde{b}_1)cv_1 \cdots (\tilde{b}_n)cv_n$$

where c, z are fresh, $\tilde{b}_i \stackrel{def}{=} \tilde{b} \backslash v_1..v_{i-1}$ (the result of taking off each $v_1..v_{i-1}$ from $\tilde{b}$), and $(\tilde{b}_i)cv_i \stackrel{def}{=} c(v_i)$ if $v_i \in \{\tilde{b}_i\}$. The decomposition of labeled transition relation becomes:

$$\stackrel{[l]}{\longrightarrow} \stackrel{def}{=} \stackrel{l_1}{\longrightarrow}\stackrel{l_2}{\longrightarrow} \cdots \stackrel{l_n}{\longrightarrow} \qquad \stackrel{[l]}{\Longrightarrow} \stackrel{def}{=} \longrightarrow\twoheadrightarrow\stackrel{l_1}{\longrightarrow}\twoheadrightarrow\stackrel{l_2}{\longrightarrow}\twoheadrightarrow \cdots \longrightarrow\twoheadrightarrow\stackrel{l_n}{\longrightarrow}\twoheadrightarrow$$

where $[l] = l_1 \cdot l_2 \cdots l_n$. In particular, if all $\longrightarrow\twoheadrightarrow$ is $\twoheadrightarrow_\beta$ in the second line, we write $\stackrel{[l]}{\Longrightarrow}_\beta$.

We easily observe: $P \stackrel{l}{\longrightarrow}_P P' \Leftrightarrow [P] \stackrel{[l]}{\longrightarrow} [P']$ for $l \neq \tau$. The following key lemma for our completeness result shows how typed terms which are composable with the encodings never violate protocols the encoded terms are engaged in. For the proof, we use the behavioural properties over typed terms shown in Proposition 4.5.

5.6. Lemma. (Composition Lemma) *First assume $\Gamma_P \vdash P$. Next suppose, with $\Gamma_0 \supset [\Gamma_P]$, we have a derivation:*

$$\frac{\Gamma_0 \vdash [P] \qquad \Gamma_0 \vdash R \triangleright_A G}{\Gamma_0 \vdash [P] \mid R \triangleright_A G} \; (par)$$

Then if $[P] \mid R \longrightarrow P_0$, one of the following is satisfied.

(1) $P_0 \equiv [P] \mid R'$ with $R \longrightarrow R'$. (2) $P_0 \twoheadrightarrow_\beta [P'] \mid R$ with $P \to_P P'$.

(3) $P_0 \twoheadrightarrow_\beta (\tilde{c})([P'] \mid R')$ with $[P] \stackrel{[l]}{\longrightarrow} [P']$ and $P \stackrel{l}{\longrightarrow}_P P'$, such that either:

$l = a\langle v_1...v_n\rangle$ and $R \stackrel{[(\tilde{c})\bar{a}\langle v_1...v_n\rangle]}{\Longrightarrow}_\beta R'$, or $l = (\tilde{c})\bar{a}\langle v_1...v_n\rangle$ and $R \stackrel{[a\langle v_1...v_n\rangle]}{\Longrightarrow}_\beta R'$.

We also use the following technical lemma concerning sound congruences. We say a typed relation $\mathcal{R}$ is *substitution closed* if it is closed under: (1) $\Gamma \vdash P \mathcal{R} Q \triangleright_A G$ and $b \notin fn(\Gamma) \cup A \cup fn(G)$, then $\Gamma\{b/a\} \vdash P\{b/a\} \mathcal{R} Q\{b/a\} \triangleright_{A\{b/a\}} G\{b/a\}$, and (2) $a : \beta, b : \beta, \Gamma \vdash P \mathcal{R} Q \triangleright_A G$, then $b : \beta, \Gamma \vdash P\{b/a\} \mathcal{R} Q\{b/a\} \triangleright_A G$. We need a notation: $C_r[\;]_{\Delta,A_0,G_0}$ denotes a typed reduction context, i.e. a context whose hole is not under prefix nor replication, with the type of the hole specified.

5.7. Lemma. *Suppose $=_s$ is a substitution-closed sound congruence, and $\mathcal{R}$ is substitution-closed and is closed under parallel composition, and satisfies the following property:*

(i) *whenever $\Gamma \vdash P \mathcal{R} Q \triangleright_A G$, $P \longrightarrow P'$ implies, for some Q', $Q \longrightarrow Q'$, $P' =_s C_r[P_0']_{\Delta,A_0,G_0}$, $\Delta \vdash P_0' \mathcal{R} Q_0' \triangleright_{A_0} G_0$, and $C_r[Q_0']_{\Delta,A_0,G_0} =_s Q'$, and the converse.*

(ii) *$\mathcal{R}$ respects the action predicates.*

Then the congruent closure of $=_s \cup \mathcal{R}$ is sound and substitution closed.

For the proof, see Section 6 of [36]. Now we show the main result of this paper.

5.8. Theorem. (Main Theorem, Full Abstraction)

$$\Gamma_P \vdash P =_P Q \;\; \Leftrightarrow \;\; [\Gamma_P] \vdash [P] =_\pi [Q].$$

Proof outline: ($\Leftarrow$) direction is straightforward by Propositions 5.5 and 4.4. For ($\Rightarrow$) direction, we first construct the relation $\cong^-$ as the smallest typed relation including the following base equations and closed under parallel composition.

$$\Gamma_P \vdash P =_P Q \;\; \Rightarrow \;\; [\Gamma_P] \vdash [P] \cong^- [Q]$$

Clearly $\cong^-$ is neither congruent nor reduction-closed. However we can show $\cong^-$ satisfies the conditions of $\mathcal{R}$ in Lemma 5.7, taking $=_\beta$ for $=_s$. Notice $\Gamma_0 \vdash P_1 \cong^- Q_2 \triangleright_A G$ implies $P_1 \equiv [P] \mid R$ and $Q_1 \equiv [Q] \mid R$ with $\Gamma_P \vdash P =_P Q$ and $[\Gamma_P] \subset \Gamma_0$ by induction of the derivations. From this the substitution-closure of $\cong^-$ is easily shown, together with that of $=_\beta$ and $=_P$, so that we only have to show $\cong^-$ satisfies (i,ii) of Lemma 5.7. For the clause (i), it is enough to prove the case when $P_1 \equiv [P] \mid R$ reduces by one step. There are three cases, corresponding to (1,2,3) in Lemma 5.6. The case (1) is trivial. (2) is by Proposition 5.5 (i). In (3), the case for input is direct from an observability property of $=_P$ (cf. 4.13 of [15]). Since values in output can not be observed (cf. [15]), the case of output is non-trivial. But we can easily find a simple context C_r which satisfies Lemma 5.7. For (ii), we again use Lemma 5.6 together with a certain context formation. For detailes, please consult [36]. □

6. Discussion

6.1. Related Works. While there have been many studies on types for mobile processes [21, 5, 28, 9, 34, 32, 19, 17, 10, 33], as far as we know, the present work is the first one which captures the structure of protocol construction as types and establishes the full abstraction results for the basic encoding such as polyadic name passing.

(**types with sequencing**): A study to give a type-abstraction in the monadic asynchronous π-calculus with the same aim had been tried by Honda [8] in 1992, whose idea is reflected to the present construction to some extent. However, his formulation (especially binding construction) was very complex and hard to grasp. Independently, Pierce discovered the way to type-check a class of encodings of polyadic name passing in (a variant of) monadic π-calculus in which two local names are used only for input and output, respectively [27]. The differences are (1) a name can only carry one kind of types so typable terms are restricted, and (2) however the length of sequence can be indefinite. In both studies, the basic results as we established here, such as the subject reduction theorem and the full abstraction, are not presented.

(**linearity in processes**): The notion of linearity is studied by Kobayashi and others [17] in Pict language and by [10] in an algebraic framework, though dynamic communication structures are not captured. In the former, the idea of "linearizability," based on the above mentioned Pierce's work, was proposed as an extension of their linear channel types. However structures of polyadic name passing may not be typable when a name carries different types. Another difference is our explicit treatment of name transmission in a type, which we believe to be important for the kind of results we have obtained here.

(**linear logic**): Some ideas of Linear Logic [7] and Interaction Categories [1] are related (e.g. "multi-cuts" in [6]). Prasad [31] studies a term assignment to a generalisation of linear logic, where the distinction between "linear" and "classical" realms exists, which is also related.

(true concurrency): The causality of communication in process calculi has been studied in the setting of true concurrency, cf. [25, 35]. The order relation in our safe graph is a concise way to encapsulate linear interaction behaviour rather than to describe general dependency among communication events. To capture more complex causality (such as labeled event structure in [35]) may be one possibility, though we may lose a simple combinatorial expression as we have in the present paper.

6.2. Extensions and Further Issues.
There are several possible extensions and further issues of the present typing system, which we outline below.

(recursive type): For simplicity of presentation we do not form recursive protocol types. Its incorporation is standard by introducing the expressions $\mu x.\alpha$ and consider them modulo their tree unfoldings, cf. [34]. Immediately all results in the paper hold with this extension w.r.t. recursive sortings.

(full abstraction): Since Prop. 4.4 and 4.5 about behaviours of typed terms do not depend on the standard encoding [ ], we can easily extend the full abstraction result in the present paper to calculi with more complex communication structures, such as those with mixed input/output and parallel communication. Such examples are discussed in [36]. It is interesting how the present construction and its extensions can be applied to various significant translations into π-calculus, as found in [20, 16, 26, 4].

(ν and its combinators): In this paper we have exclusively dealt with graph types for synchronous monadic π-calculus. It is however possible to extend the present type discipline so that we can type ν-calculus (asynchronous monadic π-calculus) and their combinators [12, 2, 15, 13, 14] (cf. [26, 29]), which are smaller than the present system but as expressive. Because there is no direct sequencing in output, the same notion of "safety condition" cannot be used. However, an extension of the notion of graph types and the safety condition can be done so that we can form a typing system for the asynchronous calculus along the same line as in Section 5. This will be treated in the sequel to present paper.

(other typing constructs): The construction of present types can be combined with various refinements on sorting studied by e.g. in [28, 9, 32, 19, 17, 10, 33] in either monadic or polyadic setting, which will be an interesting subject of study.

(algorithm): The present system does not induce the typing algorithm because a name can be used in several ways in linear space and classical space (cf. [17]). Finding some analogue of the principal type schemes would be an interesting subject of study.

(semantics): Apart from practical viewpoints, one of the most essential issues for further study is to seek the canonical notion of semantics of types in process calculi, like "arrow types" well studied in λ-calculi and combinators [24]. Since our framework suggests one way to build up a significant computational causal chains in the basic π-calculus like functional types, we hope this work becomes a stepping stone in this line of research, cf. [11].

Acknowledgments. The author is indebted to Kohei Honda for his invaluable suggestion and continuous discussions on this work. Naoki Kobayashi provided helpful comments on the full version. She thanks Samson Abramsky, Cliff Jones, Benjamin Pierce, Kenjiro Taura and the members of Interaction Club at Edinburgh for their discussions, and Mario Tokoro for his encouragements.

REFERENCES

[1] Abramsky, S., Gay, S. and Nagarajan, R., Interaction Categories and Foundations of Typed Concurrent Computing. *Deductive Program Design*, Springer-Verlag, 1995.

[2] Boudol, G., *Asynchrony and π-calculus*. INRIA Report 1702, INRIA, Sophia Antipolis, 1992.

[3] Davey, B.A. and Priestley, H.A., *Introduction to Lattices and Order*, CUP, 1990.

[4] Fournet, C. and Gonthier, G., The reflexive CHAM and the join-calculus, *POPL'96*, pp.372–385, ACM Press, 1996.

[5] Gay, S., A Sort Inference Algorithm for the Polyadic π-Calculus. *POPL'93*, ACM Press, 1993.

[6] Gay, S. and Nagarajan, R., A Typed Calculus of Synchronous Processes. *LICS'95*, IEEE, pp.210–220, 1995.

[7] Girard, J.-Y., Linear Logic, *TCS*, Vol. 50, pp.1–102, North-Holland, 1987.

[8] Honda, K., Pre-types in mobile processes, *a manuscript*, 1992.

[9] Honda, K., Types for Dyadic Interaction. *CONCUR'93*, LNCS 715, pp.509–523, Springer, 1993.

[10] Honda, K., Composing Processes, *POPL'96*, pp.344–357, ACM Press, 1996.

[11] Honda, K., Name-Passing Games (I): Semantics of Sortings, *a type-script*, July, 1996.

[12] Honda, K. and Tokoro, M., An Object Calculus for Asynchronous Communication. *ECOOP'91*, LNCS 512, pp.133–147, Springer-Verlag 1991.

[13] Honda, K. and Yoshida, N., Combinatory Representation of Mobile Processes, *POPL'94*, pp.348–360, ACM Press, 1994.

[14] Honda, K. and Yoshida, N., Replication in Concurrent Combinators, *TACS'94*, LNCS 789, pp.786–805, Springer, 1994.

[15] Honda, K. and Yoshida, N., On Reduction-Based Process Semantics. *TCS*, pp.437–486, No.151, North-Holland, December, 1995.

[16] Jones, C.B., *Process-Algebraic Foundations for an Object-Based Design Notation*. UMCS-93-10-1, Manchester University, 1993.

[17] Kobayashi, N., Pierce, B., and Turner, D., Linear Types and π-calculus, *POPL'96*, pp.358–371, ACM Press, 1996.

[18] Lafont, Y., Interaction Nets, *POPL'90*, pp. 95–108, ACM press, 1990.

[19] Liu, X. and Walker, D., A polymorphic type system for the polyadic pi-calculus, *CONCUR'95*, LNCS 962, pp.103–116, Springer, 1995.

[20] Milner, R., Functions as Processes. *MSCS*, 2(2), pp.119–146, 1992.

[21] Milner, R., Polyadic π-Calculus: a tutorial. *Logic and Algebra of Specification*, Springer, 1992.

[22] Milner, R., Parrow, J.G. and Walker, D.J., A Calculus of Mobile Processes, *Information and Computation* 100(1), pp.1–77, 1992.

[23] Milner, R. and Sangiorgi, D., Barbed Bisimulation. *Proc. of ICALP'92*, LNCS 623, pp.685–695, Springer-Verlag, 1992.

[24] Mitchell, J., Type Systems for Programming Languages. *Handbook of Theoretical Computer Science* B, pp.367–458, MIT Press, 1990.

[25] Montanari, U. and Pistore, M., Concurrent Semantics for π-calculus, *MFCS'95* and ENTCS, Vol. 1. Elsevier, 1995.

[26] Odersky, M., Polarized Name Passing. *FSTTCS'15*, LNCS 1026, pp.324–335, Springer, 1995.

[27] Pierce, B.C., Linearized Types for the π-calculus, *a type script*, December, 1994.

[28] Pierce, B.C. and Sangiorgi. D, Typing and subtyping for mobile processes. *LICS'93*, pp.187–215, IEEE, 1993.

[29] Raja, N. and Shyamasundar, R.K., Combinatory Formulations of Concurrent Languages, pp. 156–170, ACSC'95, LNCS 1023, Springer-Verlag, 1995.

[30] Sangiorgi, D., *Expressing Mobility in Process Algebras: First Order and Higher Order Paradigms*. Ph.D. Thesis, University of Edinburgh, 1992.

[31] Prasad, S., *Towards a Formulae-as-Types View of Communicating Applicative Processes*, Technical report ECRC-94-32, ECRC, 1994.

[32] Takeuchi, K., Honda, K. and Kubo, M., An Interaction-based Language and its Typing System. *PARLE'94*, LNCS 817, pp.398–413, Springer-Verlag, 1994.

[33] Turner, D., The π-calculus: Types, polymorphism and implementation, Phd Thesis, University of Edinburgh, 1996.

[34] Vasconcelos, V. and Honda, K., Principal Typing Scheme for Polyadic π-Calculus. *CONCUR'93*, LNCS 715, pp.524–538, Springer-Verlag, 1993.

[35] Winskel, G., An Introduction to Event Structures. *In Linear Time, Branching Time and Partial Order in Logics and Models for Concurrency*, LNCS 354, pp. 364–397,

[36] Yoshida, N., Graph Types for Mobile Process Calculi I. The full version of this paper. CS technical report, Keio University, 1996. Available from ftp.dcs.ed.ac.uk/export/ny/pub/graph1.ps.Z.

Author Index

Springer
and the
environment

At Springer we firmly believe that an international science publisher has a special obligation to the environment, and our corporate policies consistently reflect this conviction.
We also expect our business partners – paper mills, printers, packaging manufacturers, etc. – to commit themselves to using materials and production processes that do not harm the environment. The paper in this book is made from low- or no-chlorine pulp and is acid free, in conformance with international standards for paper permanency.

 Springer

Lecture Notes in Computer Science

For information about Vols. 1–1101

please contact your bookseller or Springer-Verlag